THE
ELVIS
ENCYCLOPEDIA

THE ELVIS ENCYCLOPEDIA

The Complete And Definitive Reference Book On The King Of Rock & Roll

BY DAVID E. STANLEY
(ELVIS' STEPBROTHER)
WITH FRANK COFFEY

Foreword by Lamar Fike

Publisher: W. Quay Hays
Editor: Murray Fisher
Art Director: Kurt Wahlner
Managing Editor: Colby Allerton
Production Director: Nadeen Torio
Copy Editor: Charles Neighbors

Published in Great Britain in 1998 by
Virgin Books Ltd
Thames Wharf Studios
Rainville Road
London W6 9HA

First published in the USA in 1994 by General Publishing Group, Inc.

A catalogue record for this book is available from the British Library

ISBN 0-7535-0293-3

Printed and bound in Spain

CONTENTS

INTRODUCTION
David E. Stanley
9

FOREWORD
Lamar Fike
11

HIS LIFE
A Complete Chronology
16

HIS INNER CIRCLE
The People Around Elvis
152

HIS MOVIES
A Complete Filmography
166

HIS MUSIC
A Complete Discography
202

TRIVIA
All About Elvis
270

TRIVIA QUIZ
How Much Do You Know?
278

INDEX
285

ACKNOWLEDGMENTS
· ·

There are certain people who made the difficult task of putting this encyclopedia together a little easier. I would first like to thank my wife Jennifer for her patience and unconditional love during the difficult times. Thanks also to my managers Lamar Fike and Jim Prator for never losing the faith, and to Mary Fike for loving New York so much. And also my appreciation to my agent Tony Seidl, who kept on keeping on, and his lovely wife Sherry; to John Pynchon Holmes for his great research, writing skills and hard work; to the so-called Memphis Mafia for being such a big part of my life and to Quay Hays, my publisher, for allowing me to set the record straight. And to my collaborator, Frank Coffey: I couldn't have done it without you, buddy, thanks for all your good work. Many thanks to John Dawson, a truly professional photographer and good friend. And a special thanks to George and Jeannette Nicholas for showing me there's more to life than Rock & Roll.

Thanks also to photographers Sean Shavar and Larry Inman, as well as to Jimmy Velvet, Dee Presley, Billy Stanley and Aurelia Yarbrough, for providing photographs which, coupled with my own personal collection, helped make this book come visually to life.

And, finally, thanks to the Elvis Presley fan clubs and fans around the world for their constant love and affection for my brother, Elvis.

INTRODUCTION

BY DAVID E. STANLEY

In 1960, shortly after my mother Dee married Elvis Presley's father Vernon, I moved into Graceland. I was four years old, and I had no idea that my life had changed forever. For the next seventeen years, Elvis was my family, my friend, my brother and later, my employer. I shared his tumultuous public appearances before tens of thousands of fans and his most intimate private moments in his own home. And for the last six years of his life, I was with him virtually 24 hours a day.

I want you to know Elvis Presley as well as I did. You may think you already do, because there have been almost one hundred biographies of the King of Rock & Roll. I've written one myself, and I've contributed to another with my mother and brothers. But a biography is essentially a detached narrative of a person's life; sometimes nothing more than a greatly expanded resumé. By the time I got done filling in all the "who, what and where," I found that I had room to write only a fraction of what I really knew about Elvis Presley. The only way to know Elvis is to have lived his life with him. That's what I did, and that's what I am trying to help you do, too.

That's why I decided to write *The Elvis Encyclopedia.* I got together with Lamar Fike, who first met Elvis way back in 1954, went to work for him in 1957, lived with him during his entire time in the army, and remained a constant companion until the very end. Lamar and I sat down and divided our knowledge of Elvis' life into almost 100 categories, organized alphabetically. Using this outline, I exhaustively interviewed Lamar and dozens of other family members, friends and acquaintances to add to my storehouse of facts and memories.

The result is a unique and comprehensive portrait of the most intimate details of every aspect of the life of Elvis Presley. Most of the public details about his life have been thoroughly catalogued in reference books compiled by obsessive researchers. If you're a record collector, other books will tell you the exact catalogue numbers of the seven different pressings of *Jailhouse Rock.* If you're a movie fanatic, you can find film guides that name the third assistant directors and key grips on all the Elvis films.

What you'll find in *The Elvis Encyclopedia* is the important information about every song the King ever sang and recorded, and about every film he ever made. But you'll also learn which songs were his favorites, which songs he disliked, which co-stars he loved and which he couldn't stand, what actually happened in his recording sessions and on the set of the films... and a lot more.

You'll read about his everyday life in the army, his relationship with Lisa Marie, his favorite television shows and his life-long friendship with his own pets. And you'll find that I don't shy away from controversy. While Elvis was one of the most famous personalities of the Twentieth Century, he was also a man with human weaknesses. I provide what I believe is an unprecedented look at the *facts* of such issues as his drug use and his sex life. While some of these facts are sad, they also shatter many of the even more vicious rumors that have blotted the image of the great man I knew so well. Part of human nature, an unattractive part, seems to involve finding joy in bringing others down. To such people I say read the Gospel according to John, where Jesus says, "He that is without sin among you, let him cast the first stone."

All in all, I hope this book will provide endless hours of fascinating reading for everyone who loved Elvis Presley and the golden age of Rock & Roll he helped create. This is, in effect, a brand new kind of book: a personal, anecdotal encyclopedia full of facts presented in an entertaining, readable format. *The Elvis Encyclopedia* is, more than anything else, a book of stories about Elvis by the people who knew him best. By the time you've finished reading, your new appreciation of his life will make you feel like you're family, too.

FOREWORD

BY LAMAR FIKE

I was on the dizzy, wild, marvelous ride that was Elvis Presley's life. When I met Elvis in the summer of 1954, he was nineteen years old, and I was fourteen months younger. I was his friend/employee/confidant/partner for the next 23 years, until the sad day he died. We were Southerners, born and bred, used to a certain pace and rhythm, something Yankees might call sleepy. But when we left that world, everything accelerated. Elvis started going full bore all the time. It was a life on fast forward. That will age you, and it did him. And wear you out, which it did him.

Elvis was fun to be around, it's as simple as that. He had a quality about him I'd never seen before, and don't expect to ever see again. They call it charisma now, and I guess that describes it as well as anything. People wanted to be around him. People wanted to hear and see him perform. Hell, people wanted to *be* him.

And that effect he had on people, that power he had over them, was something Elvis thought about. It was something that bothered him and ultimately preyed upon him. No joke, being Elvis wasn't easy. Dealing with that weighed on him. And finally it helped bring him down.

I make no excuses for some of the choices Elvis made. They were his choices, and he was a grown man in control of his own destiny, despite what you may have read elsewhere. He acted crazy sometimes, but he wasn't crazy. He acted mean sometimes, but he wasn't a mean man. In fact, the opposite is true. Elvis felt for people. Treated people—most people anyway—very well. I know the image some people have of Elvis in those last, bad years. That wasn't the real Elvis, not in my mind. Not anything like it. It was what he had become, but it wasn't him.

Elvis had a gift. A remarkable gift. He didn't know why the good Lord had picked him, but pick him He certainly did. Elvis once said to me, real early on—1957, I believe—"It feels like this is happening to somebody else. I don't feel like it's me up there." But I told him, "Don't worry, it's you, all right. And don't let anybody tell you different. And don't ever forget that. It's you."

He understood what I was saying, though it took a long time for him to really accept that fact. But maybe he never did accept it. He was the son of dirt poor farmers from Tupelo, Mississippi. His family lived in what we used to call a "shotgun house," that was built by Elvis' father, Vernon, and it was there that he was born. His twin brother, Jesse, was stillborn and buried in an unmarked grave. Dr. William Hunt, who was the attending doctor, had his $15 fee paid by welfare because the family couldn't afford it. When I say the Presleys were poor, I mean *poor*.

How could a boy with so little all of a sudden have so much? What was it like to be him, with the world living and dying on your every breath? How does anyone make sense of that? Elvis couldn't, I don't think. I couldn't have, in his shoes. And that's one of the reasons I don't place myself in judgment of him.

But Elvis Aron Presley from Tupelo did his best. He took care of his family. He took care of his friends, me included. He was generous to a fault. He loved his daughter. He loved his work, his music. He made a lot of people happy—the people around him and millions and millions of people he didn't even know. When all is said and done, how many of us can say that?

Elvis died too soon. But he lived, he really lived. John Kennedy once said something like, "Living fully is using your powers in the pursuit of excellence." By that definition, as far as I'm concerned, Elvis Presley lived to the very fullest. In the end, the bottom line is that I believe Elvis died of apathy. He'd done everything he wanted to do. Fulfilled every fantasy. There was nowhere left to go, at least in his mind. But make no mistake, it was a grand adventure. The last years were not good. Sometimes they were frustrating, and sometimes they were unhappy. But before that, for most of the time, we had a blast.

On the day he died, a little piece of me died too. But mostly, I'll remember the good times. Elvis Presley was my friend. That was a once-in-a-lifetime privilege, and I wouldn't trade a second of it.

For my sons Austin and Tyler:

For seventeen years,
Elvis Presley was my brother
and my friend.

Through the pages of this book,
my sons,
I hope you will grow to love him
and understand him
as I do.

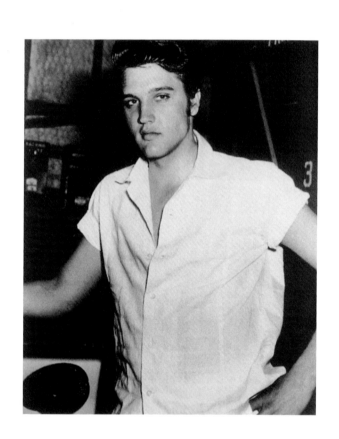

"I'm afraid to wake up each morning.

I can't believe all this has happened to me.

I just hope it lasts."

–ELVIS PRESLEY

Sometime in the Fifties

HIS LIFE

*"I want to entertain people.
That's my whole life—
to my last breath."*

—ELVIS

1935

January 8: Gladys Presley of Tupelo, Mississippi gives birth to twin boys in a two-room "Shotgun" house built by her husband, Vernon, on Old Saltillo Road. The first, Jesse Garon, is stillborn. Elvis Aron Presley arrives 30 minutes later.

January 9: Jesse Garon Presley is buried at Priceville Cemetery in an unmarked grave.

1936 – 1937

November 17, 1937: Vernon Presley, Travis Smith and Luther Gable are indicted on one count of forgery and placed on $500 bond. The three men are charged with changing the amount of a check from Vernon's boss from $3.00 to $8.00 and cashing it at the local bank. Elvis' father pleads guilty and is sentenced to three years at Parchman Farm State Penitentiary. Vernon's boss, Mr. Bass, calls in a note Vernon signed for the money he borrowed to build the house, and Gladys is forced to vacate. Moving in with Vernon's parents, she takes work as a seamstress.

1941 – 1942

January 4, 1941: Vernon is released from Parchman Farm after serving about two and a half years of his three-year sentence. He returns home and finds work in a Tupelo lumberyard.

Elvis' beginnings could not have been more humble. The Presleys of Tupelo, Mississippi—Gladys, Vernon and baby Elvis—were dirt poor. Elvis was born in a shack his father had built himself, and the doctor who delivered him was paid his fee by the welfare office. Elvis' twin brother, Jesse Garon, was stillborn, which may help explain why Elvis was especially cherished by his parents. His middle name was misspelled on his birth certificate (right).

September 15, 1942: At six, Elvis enters first grade at Lawhon School in Tupelo. Vernon finds work in a defense plant in Memphis, returning to Tupelo on weekends. But by the end of 1942, he is again unemployed.

1943 – 1944

Continuing his elementary school education at Lawhon, Elvis is considered a well-mannered and quiet child. Although his parents are forced to change housing on a regular basis because of Vernon's inability to find steady work near home, Elvis' life is similar to that of most children in this rural Mississippi area. The boy is often heard singing the gospel songs he hears in the First Assembly of God Church down the block from his house, and during services he is known to run down the aisle to be nearer the choir.

1945

Entering the fifth grade, Elvis is asked by his teacher, Mrs. J. C. Grimes, to sing in the high school cafeteria and in chapel.

October 3: At the suggestion of Mrs. Grimes, Elvis is entered in the talent contest on "Children's Day" at the Mississippi-Alabama Fair and Dairy Show, and he makes his first public appearance as a singer at the age of ten. Dressed in a cowboy suit and standing on a chair to reach the microphone, he sings *Old Shep* without accompaniment—winning second place, a five-dollar prize and a free ticket to all the rides.

1946

January 8: Elvis is torn between wanting a bicycle or a .22 caliber rifle for his eleventh birthday. He gets a six-string guitar instead. Over the next year, Vernon Presley's brother Vester gives Elvis basic guitar lessons.

1947

September 15: He starts the sixth grade at Milam Junior High School. For his birthday the following year, he finally gets the bicycle. And some 30 years later, rather than that .22 rifle, he purchases more than $19,000 worth of weapons at a California gun shop in a single shopping spree.

1948

September 12: After losing yet another job and almost penniless, Vernon packs the family into their old car and heads for a better life in Memphis. Gladys' brothers get him a job at the Precision Tool Company, and the Presleys move into a tiny apartment at 572 Poplar Avenue. Vernon may have been involved in moonshining and had to leave Tupelo just ahead of the law.

LAMAR FIKE
ON THE SHOTGUN HOUSE:

Was Elvis dirt-poor growing up? You bet he was. The Presleys lived in a little shack. They called it a "Shotgun house" because it was so small that if you opened the front door and fired a shotgun, you'd blow out the back door.

ELVIS
ON POVERTY:

We were broke, man. We just left overnight. Things had to be better.

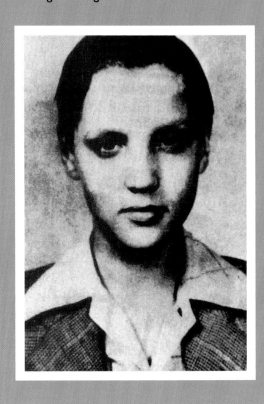

Elvis, at age 12 (above), is already developing his trademark sneer. At 15, Elvis poses with Betty McCann (below), who may possibly be his very first girlfriend.

Elvis' yearbook picture appeared in his senior year at L.C. Humes High School in Memphis. His diploma (below) from Humes High (opposite, top) was later to be displayed along with his trophies at Graceland as one of his most prized possessions.

PRESLEY, ELVIS ARON

Major: Shop, History, English.
Activities: R. O. T. C., Biology Club, English Club, History Club

September 13: Elvis enrolls at L.C. Humes High School in Memphis. Vernon leaves Precision Tool in late November to drive a truck for a wholesale grocer in December, while Gladys finds work as a seamstress.

1949

February 17: After losing his job packing up gallon paint cans for a local paint company, Vernon applies for public assistance to pay the rent. The Memphis Housing Authority finds a two-room apartment in a housing project, Lauderdale Courts, at 185 Winchester Avenue, and the family moves in with Vernon's mother Minnie Mae on May 1.

1950

September: Starting his sophomore year at Humes, Elvis works in the school library and also moonlights as an usher at Loew's State Theater on Main, his first job. Cousin Gene Smith has become his best friend. In November Gladys forces him to quit over the late hours. Elvis begins dating. He is such a success at the annual Christmas high school talent show that he does an encore.

1951

January 8: Elvis gets his driver's license shortly after his sixteenth birthday.

June: After joining the ROTC unit at Humes High, he returns to work at Loew's but is fired after a fistfight with another usher over a female employee.

August: He tries out for the football team but is cut by the coach when he won't trim his ducktail and sideburns. He becomes friends with future Memphis Mafian, Red West, who throws some muscle his way when some local toughs try to cut his hair.

Elvis begins to hang around local blues joints and gospel "sings," listening to the music and talking to the musicians. B.B. King remembers seeing him on Beale Street and J.D. Sumner (who later backed Elvis on concert tours in the '70s) remembers him at the Memphis Auditorium during gospel nights.

1952

September: Beginning his senior year, Elvis has become a somewhat difficult student, failing exams that bring down his

Memphis City Schools

DIPLOMA

This Certifies That *Elvis Aron Presley* *having completed*
the Course of Study prescribed by the Board of Education of the Memphis City Schools in the

L. C. HUMES HIGH SCHOOL

of this City, and having sustained a sound moral deportment is entitled to this

TESTIMONIAL

the highest honor in our power to bestow and is leaving the school with the respect and confidence of the Board and Instructors and with their best wishes for continued success.
In Testimony Whereof, the President and Secretary of the Board of Education, the Superintendent of Schools and the Principal have affixed their signatures at Memphis, Tennessee.
the ____ day of ____

average and often missing school. He is spending more time around the Memphis music scene. His good looks and flashy style of dress gain him notice, not always positive, and Red West intervenes on several occasions. He meets Marty Lacker, a fresh kid from New York.

September: He takes on night work at Marl Metal, a metal fabricator, but his mother forces him to quit two months later because his grades are slipping again. She finds a job as a nurses' aide, but it's discovered that the combined family income disqualifies them from public assistance housing and in November they're told to move.

1953

January: The Presley family rents two rooms of a house.

March: Elvis gets his first car, a 1942 Lincoln Zephyr, from Vernon.

April: After two more moves, the family settles into an apartment at 462 Alabama.

April 3: Elvis sings in the Humes High Band Annual Minstrel show, listed 16th on the bill as a guitarist, and the audience response is terrific.

June 3: Majoring in Shop, History and English, Elvis graduates from Humes High at eighteen. The next day he takes a job at Parker Machinists Shop.

July 18: He goes to Sam Phillips' Memphis Recording Service to make an acetate record. He brings his guitar and accompanies himself singing *My Happiness* and *That's When Your Heartaches Begin*. Marion Keisker makes history by turning on the studio tape machine when she hears him sing and she makes a note of his phone number and address to pass on to Sam.

September: Elvis has moved from Parker's shop to Precision Tool. His uncles Travis and Johnny get him and buddy Gene Smith on the crew. After less than a month on the assembly line at Precision, Elvis finds a job at Crown Electric. A short stint in the stock room ends in a promotion to driver, and he is seen around Memphis in the Crown truck delivering electrical supplies to construction sites. Elvis decides to become an electrician and studies the trade at night when he isn't following the music scene.

Looking uncomfortable, unkempt and older than his years, Elvis poses for his first publicity shot sporting what he considered to be a very stylish look. The young Elvis has a ways to grow before he settles on his image.

1954

THE BEGINNING

Elvis and long-time friend, Jimmy Velvet, relax backstage in Memphis before a show. Velvet started as a singer about the same time as Elvis, recording on the Phillips and ABC Paramount labels. Sincere and pleasant, Velvet was a friend to all and especially to Elvis during the difficult tours of the early years. Later in his life, Jimmy became a collector of Elvis memorabilia, gathering so much material that he eventually opened the Elvis Presley Museum in Nashville and in Branson, Missouri, as well as taking numerous exhibits with him on mobile tours.

January 4: Parking his delivery truck out front, Elvis makes his second appearance at the Memphis Recording Studio. He meets Sam Phillips and they talk. He records *Casual Love Affair* and *I'll Never Stand In Your Way* on acetate, possibly for a girlfriend. Phillips likes what he hears enough to put him in the file but tells Marion Keisker that the boy needs a lot of work.

February: Elvis meets Dixie Locke, age sixteen, possibly at the First Assembly of God church or at the Rainbow Rollerdome. They begin to date, become serious and it's thought that Elvis is considering marriage.

June 26: He gets a call from Phillips to fill in on a demo session because the original singer can't be located. Elvis rushes to Sun Studios and records *Without You*. Phillips doesn't get what he wants, but he and Marion still have a feeling about the young man. He contacts Scotty Moore and asks him to work with Elvis.

June 27: Scotty invites Elvis to his apartment. They work on a few tunes, but the session doesn't go particularly well. After another date, however, Scotty calls Phillips to tell him that Elvis might pull it off. Phillips sets a recording session for the next day.

July 5: Elvis, Scotty Moore and Bill Black meet at Sun Studios in the morning to record several songs. Elvis is nervous and the session stalls without any really satisfactory takes. Scotty feels he's

LAMAR FIKE
ON MEETING ELVIS:

I first met Elvis in 1954. Sam Phillips introduced us. I was learning how to be a disk jockey, Sam was teaching me. Sam was an engineer, and I'd hang around him, trying to pick up whatever crumbs of knowledge he'd share. Then one night, Sam took me over to the label (Sun Studios) and said, "I want you to hear something." He played the demo that Elvis had made and asked me what I thought. Now I was a little green and I was kinda hedging my bets. "I don't know for sure," I said, "but to me it sounds really good". And Sam said I should come over that afternoon and meet him. Which I did. They were working on That's All Right (Mama). It was Elvis' first professional recording session.

I watched all afternoon. And Sam asked me again what I thought. "God almighty, he's different looking," I said. "I like him. He's exciting. He sounds good." Now, I didn't know a lot about the record business at the time, my opinion didn't mean diddley, but I sure liked what I heard. Simple as that.

Sun Records owner and producer, Sam Phillips, shows Elvis a few chord changes at the studio in the early 50's. Although Elvis had a gift for music and a player's ear, he considered himself an average guitarist. The ever-present ax was more of an ornament than a tool, and in later years Elvis discarded it completely. From the beginning he relied on his band, primarily Scotty Moore, to help him create the sound that changed Rock & Roll. Over the years his playing improved steadily to the point that he was able to more than hold his own in jam sessions on tour and at Graceland.

trying too hard to please Phillips instead of relaxing and being himself. During a break, Elvis picks up his guitar and tries to get loose, riffing on a blues tune called *That's All Right (Mama)* by Arthur Crudup. Scotty picks up the beat and Bill joins in. Phillips overhears the jam session and knows in his gut he's found the sound he's looking for. They will later discover that they've cut Elvis' first hit. It will eventually sell 20,000 copies.

July 10: Phillips gives his friend, partner and local DJ, Dewey Phillips (no relation), a disc of *That's All Right (Mama)* and *Blue Moon of Kentucky* to air on his *Red, Hot and Blue* radio show. Response is so strong that he plays the record at least fourteen times. Dewey makes some frantic phone calls, friends locate Elvis at a local movie theater and hustle him over to the station. "Mr. Phillips," Elvis says, "I don't know nothin' about bein' interviewed." "Just don't say nothin' dirty," Dewey tells him. Elvis doesn't.

July 12: Two days later, he signs his first management contract with Scotty Moore.

July 19: Sun Records releases *That's All Right (Mama)*.

July 30: Elvis makes his first billed appearance on *The Slim Whitman Show* at Overton Park Shell. He is listed third.

August: Throughout the month, Elvis appears at local clubs in the Memphis area and then the trio heads for Texas. They play small clubs and do local radio shows, with Red West along for the ride. The single continues to climb the charts.

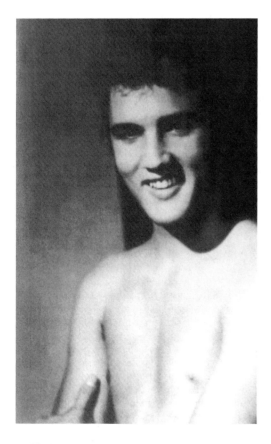

Elvis' big break came when he picked up his guitar after an unsuccessful recording session and tried to relax by playing a blues song called *That's All Right (Mama)*. The other players in the studio joined in, and Sam Phillips recorded the song, which became Elvis' first hit.

September 4: Elvis is booked on the *Grand Ole Opry*. He travels to Nashville with Sam, Marion, Scotty and Bill. They sing on the Hank Snow segment. It's a disaster. The country establishment isn't interested in Memphis' hottest ticket, and some suggest he go back to driving a truck.

September 10: Elvis goes back into the studio. The session is slow and unproductive until late in the evening when he completes a successful take of *Just Because*. Scotty suggests that since they're on a roll they give *Good Rockin' Tonight* another shot. Combined with *I Don't Care If The Sun Don't Shine*, they will be his next hit.

September 25: *Good Rockin' Tonight* is released.

September: Through the month, Elvis continues to gig local clubs in Memphis, primarily the Eagle's Nest, and makes personal appearances at supermarkets and record stores. His picture appears regularly in local newspapers. The kids at Humes High are discovering they went to school with a celebrity.

October 16: Elvis does his first appearance on *Louisiana Hayride*. The show is broadcast live from the Municipal Auditorium on Radio KWKH in Shreveport. He, Scotty and Bill do *That's All Right (Mama)*. But the gig doesn't pay enough to get them out of town. They find a local booker and play some dates at small clubs in Texas to get the money to return to Memphis.

October 22: Elvis does *The Old Barn Dance* radio show in New Orleans.

October 23: *Blue Moon Of Kentucky* is #6 in Nashville and #3 in New Orleans. It's Elvis' first time on a *Billboard* chart outside Memphis.

November 6: *Billboard* says that *Good Rockin' Tonight* could break out. Elvis signs a one-year contract to appear once a week with *Louisiana Hayride*.

November 15: Elvis receives what may have been his first royalty check from Sun Records.

November: Elvis continues to appear on *Louisiana Hayride* and play the Eagle's Nest in Memphis. The boys gig in small towns all over east Texas. The schedule is grinding and the pay is low, but Elvis quits Crown Electric, becomes a full-time singer and buys his first Cadillac: It's pink. The task of playing gigs and running Elvis' career, meanwhile, is becoming more than Scotty wants to handle. He is a musician, not a booker, but he works hard at both jobs.

December 7: Marty Robbins cuts *That's All Right (Mama)* for Columbia Records. It's a huge hit and the first cover of an Elvis song by another artist.

December 20: Elvis records *Milkcow Boogie Blues* and *You're a Heartbreaker* at Sun Studios.

December 25: Christmas is spent with Gladys, Vernon and family at home. It's becoming clear that there is much to celebrate.

December: Elvis becomes a headliner on *Louisiana Hayride* and is clearly the most popular performer on the Saturday night show. He is touring constantly. He's not yet the King, but he's come an amazing distance in one short year.

On the road in the early days, Elvis made his mark with his incredible voice, personality and ability to sell a song. From the beginning he treated each performance as special and his loyalty to his fans soared across the footlights. The early tours were grueling affairs with more time spent getting from gig to gig than actually performing.

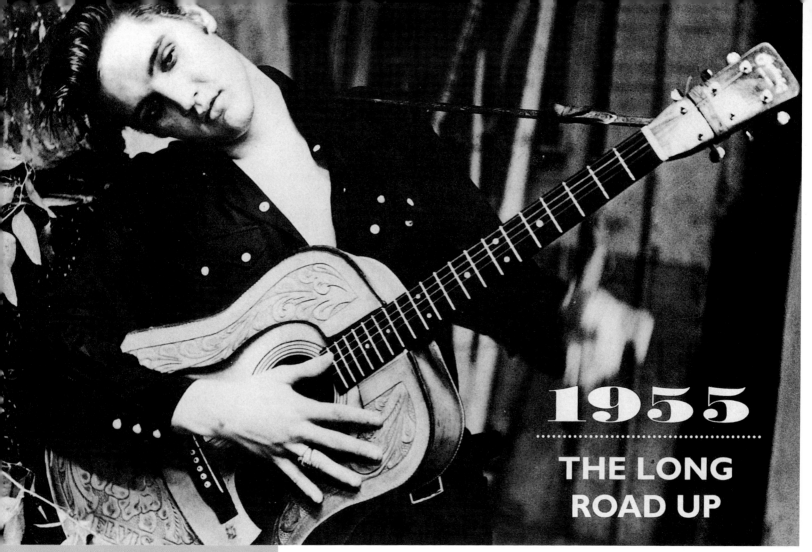

1955
THE LONG ROAD UP

Scotty Moore once said that Elvis seemed to come alive on stage, a switch just turned on and he became a different person. Although polite in private and possessed with a typical Southern sense of manners and decorum, he would become a wild man on stage, moving with a passion that was so clearly sexual, conservative America was aghast. Describing his feelings about the music, he would say, "It's just how it makes me feel."

LAMAR FIKE
ON ELVIS AS AN "OVERNIGHT SUCCESS":

People say Elvis was an overnight success, but that really isn't true. What is true is that he certainly didn't spend years and years working to make it. But he did a lot of one nighters in '54 and '55 through Texas and Louisiana, bars and fairs in little places hardly anyone heard of. It wasn't a glamorous thing, it was lonely and boring and who the hell knew if it was gonna lead anywhere? Elvis sure didn't.

Increasingly in demand, Elvis makes personal appearances and does radio interviews, and his visits on *Louisiana Hayride* continue. Red remarks on how different the reactions of female fans are from the males. He calls it "crazy, the way the women react." Elvis is becoming a headliner in Memphis, selling out local shows. The band is constantly on the road performing as far away as Arkansas. In Houston he sells out a concert sponsored by a local radio station. He's finding a niche in both country and the emerging world of rockabilly.

January 1: At Scotty's urging and with his blessing, Elvis signs with Memphis DJ and manager, Bob Neal. Neal will take full control of Elvis' career for a 15% commission on all gigs. D.J. Fontana, house drummer for *Lousiana Hayride*, joins the band.

January 8: Sun Records releases *Milkcow Boogie Blues/ You're a Heartbreaker.*

February 4: The band, which includes Elvis, Scotty, Bill and D.J., is now called The Blue Moon Boys. They headline a show at an amusement park in New Orleans.

February: Elvis records *Baby Let's Play House* at Sun. And The Blue Moon Boys hit New Mexico, Arkansas, Louisiana and Texas, linking up with Hank Snow and touring with his Jamboree. Elvis finishes February in Cleveland, Ohio.

March: More of the same. The travel schedule is grueling and the dates fall one on top of the other. In this era of one-night stands, the band hits Tennessee, Arkansas, Mississippi, Missouri and Louisiana.

March 5: Elvis makes his first television appearance, a local broadcast of *Louisiana Hayride* seen in Shreveport.

March 14: Elvis does a TV interview with Jimmy Dean at a local station in Washington D.C.

March 15: Elvis buys out his contract on *Louisiana Hayride* so he can have more freedom to expand his touring possibilities, though he continues to make occasional appearances through 1955.

March: Elvis attracts the attention of New York producers and is offered an audition for *Arthur Godfrey's Talent Scouts*. He and the band travel to New York City, but the audition is a failure and they return to more comfortable southern climes.

April: The band is on the road all month, drawing larger and more frantic crowds. Unbeknownst to Elvis, he has begun to attract the attention of a promoter named Colonel Tom Parker.

April 30: *Baby, Let's Play House/ I'm Left, You're Right, She's Gone* is released by Sun. The printing is the largest run to date.

May 1: The Blue Moon Boys sign up to go on the road with Hank Snow's All Star Jamboree. The month-long tour is booked by Snow's manager, Colonel Parker.

May 13: At a show in Jacksonville, fans mob the stage when Elvis ad-libs "Girls, I'll see ya'll backstage." The excited fans rip his clothes and write messages in lipstick on his car.

May 20: The Snow tour ends in Chattanooga, Tennessee.

May: Elvis stays on the road for the remainder of the month. Parker is impressed by Elvis and has begun to "advise" Bob Neal about career directions for "The Hillbilly Cat." Parker is getting him bookings at larger venues in Dallas and Houston, using connections beyond the reach of Neal. Distances between gigs begin to make flying essential.

June: Jamboree goes back on the road, and Elvis is all over the place splitting time between the tour, *Louisiana Hayride* and his one-night stands. The first national magazine article on Elvis appears in the June issue of *Cowboy Songs*. Elvis moves himself, Gladys and Vernon to larger quarters at 1414 Getwell Street in Memphis.

July 5: Elvis vacations at his new home in Memphis, with Parker continuing to be a strong force, booking him heavily for the remainder of the summer and well into the fall.

July 11: Elvis goes into the studio and cuts *I Forgot To Remember To Forget, Mystery Train, Trying To Get To You* and *When It Rains It Pours*.

July 29: In a replay of the May concert, Elvis is mobbed in Jacksonville and spends part of the night in a local hospital, complaining of exhaustion.

August 3: Elvis breaks out of his touring schedule to do a gig in his hometown of Tupelo, Mississippi.

Elvis appeared frequently on the *Louisiana Hayride*, a popular radio show of the time. As his appearances on this show and at other live venues increased, word of mouth quickly spread that the exciting new personality heard on the radio was even stronger in person. Approving fans mob Elvis after a show at the Armory in Memphis (below). The crowds, mostly young women, began to chase Elvis from the very beginning and crowd control became a major issue for local authorities. As time went on, Elvis and the band would have serious problems getting away from the hoards of wild-eyed teenagers with their clothes and equipment intact.

Colonel Tom Parker was a promoter and manager (experienced promoting at carnivals and fairs) who had success with country acts like Eddy Arnold and Hank Snow. Known as a tough negotiator, he saw great potential in Elvis, and eventually took him on as his sole client. Elvis was a tireless performer (below). He once said that touring was hard and that he was only happy twice a day, when he was on stage.

August 6: *Mystery Train/ I Forgot To Remember To Forget* is released.

August 15: Colonel Tom Parker signs Elvis to a one-year contract plus renewals with Hank Snow Enterprises. Bob Neal stays on as advisor and Elvis continues to pay Neal's 15% out of his own pocket.

September 2: Elvis has an automobile accident en route from New Orleans to Texarkana. There is considerable damage to his new Cadillac, but no injuries. He makes the gig and performs on a bill with Johnny Cash.

September 10: *Billboard* notes that *Mystery Train/ I Forgot To Remember To Forget* is creating intense action on the charts. Elvis makes his first appearance without his band on *Louisiana Hayride*.

September 11: Elvis picks up with another Jamboree tour in Norfolk, Virginia.

September 17: Elvis has a big week on the latest *Billboard* charts with *Baby, Let's Play House, Mystery Train* and *I Forgot To Remember To Forget* making big numbers and rising steadily.

September: Closes on the road, continues into October. Elvis continues to do dates on the *Louisiana Hayride* and begins his first tour as a headliner, performing constantly through the month.

October 11: The Elvis Presley Jamboree tour begins in Abilene, Texas. It's Elvis' first tour as a headliner. Also on the bill are Johnny Cash, Floyd Cramer, Porter Wagoner, Jimmy Newman, Jean Shepard, Bobby Lord and Wanda Jackson.

October 15: The Elvis Presley Jamboree stops in Lubbock, Texas. The opening act is a duo called "Buddy and Bob," the Buddy being Buddy Holly, who later said that "without Elvis none of us would have ever made it."

October: Colonel Parker and Sam Phillips work out a deal to sell Elvis' contract to raise cash for Phillips, and a bidding war begins. By the end of the month, three major labels have made offers up to $25,000.

November 4: RCA comes in with a bid of $35,000 plus a $5,000 bonus to Elvis for back royalties owed him by Sun records. Parker is interested.

November 5: *Mystery Train/I Forgot To Remember To Forget* hits the country charts, reaching #7 in sales.

November 10: Elvis and Bob Neal head for Memphis and the Country Music Disc Jockey Convention. The purpose of the trip is to meet with executives of RCA to hammer out a recording contract. Steve Sholes and Bill Bullock represent the label.

November 20: Contract Day. Elvis signs a standard three-year deal with renewal option with RCA Victor. Parker also cuts a deal with Hill and Range Publishing Company to set up a separate entity called Elvis Presley Music, Inc. It will handle all of Elvis' songs and royalties that accrue to them. This arrangement is what the Colonel will use in later years to make songwriters give back some of their royalties and why the better writers ultimately refused to work for Elvis, causing a marked decline in the quality of his music over the years.

November 21: An internal press release from RCA New York notes that Elvis has been signed.

November: Elvis finishes the month on *Louisiana Hayride.*

December: RCA begins heavy promotion of its newest star.

December 2: RCA re-releases *Mystery Train/I Forgot To Remember To Forget.* It becomes Elvis' first single on "His Master's Voice."

December 10: Hill and Range produces Elvis' first songbook.

Elvis with early friend and DJ, Dewey Phillips.

LAMAR FIKE

ON DISC JOCKEYS:

Disc jockeys ruled music back then. And people like Tony Martin and Eddie Fisher were the stars. And here came Elvis, a real young guy, doing something real different. At first, the DJs hated him. Broke his records, couldn't stand his movements, the way he acted on stage. People were scared of Elvis. It was something different. People don't like change. They'd rather stay the way they are. Elvis represented change. Big change.

After a heated bidding war involving three major labels, Elvis signed a deal to transfer his recording contract with Sam Phillips and Sun Records to RCA. Elvis is shown with Steve Sholes (above center), an RCA executive, and Colonel Parker (above right) shortly after signing the contract.

December 17: CBS announces that Elvis will do four guest appearances on *Jackie Gleason's Stage Show* starting in January 1956.

December 20: RCA re-releases the remainder of the songs Elvis recorded at Sun Records: *That's All Right (Mama)/Blue Moon Of Kentucky, Good Rockin' Tonight/I Don't Care If The Sun Don't Shine, Milkcow Boogie Blues/You're a Heartbreaker* and *Baby, Let's Play House/I'm Left, You're Right, She's Gone.*

1956
BLASTOFF

"Nobody knew I sang. I wasn't popular in school, I wasn't dating anybody. In the eleventh grade they entered me in another talent show. I came out and did two songs and heard people kind of rumbling and whispering. I was amazed at how popular I was after that." —Elvis in 1956

January 5: In Nashville, Elvis meets with RCA's Steve Sholes and the A&R man for country, Chet Atkins, to finalize plans for his first recording session.

January 10: Elvis, Scotty, Bill and D.J. meet at RCA Nashville for their first session. Chet Atkins produces and plays guitar and Floyd Cramer is at piano. The session, which starts in the afternoon and goes into the morning of January 11, produces: *I Got A Woman, Heartbreak Hotel, Money Honey, I'm Counting On You* and *I Was The One*.

January 23 – 27: Elvis and the boys rehearse for the Jackie Gleason show on January 28.

January 27: RCA releases *Heartbreak Hotel/ I Was The One* and Elvis returns from a gig in Austin to head for New York with Scotty and Bill.

January 28: Elvis, Bill and Scotty make their national television debut on *Jackie Gleason's Stage Show*. Elvis sings *I Got A Woman, Shake, Rattle and Roll* and *Flip, Flop and Fly*.

January 30: Elvis returns from a gig in Virginia to do his first session at RCA New York. *Blue Suede Shoes, My Baby Left Me, One-Sided Love Affair, So Glad You're Mine, I'm Gonna Sit Right Down and Cry (Over You)* and *Tutti Frutti* are the results.

February 3: Another session at RCA New York produces: *Shake, Rattle and Roll* and *Lawdy Miss Clawdy.*

February 4: Elvis and the boys make their second appearance on the Gleason show. Elvis sings *Baby, Let's Play House* and *Shake, Rattle and Roll.*

February 11: *Heartbreak Hotel* is released by RCA, and the response is strong. Elvis makes his third appearance on the Gleason show, singing *Heartbreak Hotel* and *Blue Suede Shoes.*

February 18: *Heartbreak Hotel* streaks up the charts and Elvis makes his fourth and last contracted appearance on the Gleason show, singing *Tutti Frutti* and *I Was The One.*

February 23: Colonel Parker and his company Hank Snow Enterprises, along with Jamboree Attractions, move into bigger quarters and hire extra staff to handle the volume of business Elvis is generating.

February 25: *I Forgot To Remember To Forget* is Elvis' first national #1. It stays on top of Country Best Sellers for two weeks, beginning an unprecedented string of #1 hit records.

February: Closes with another appearance on *Louisiana Hayride.*

March 3: Elvis has six singles on RCA's list of top 25 best sellers for the company. *Heartbreak Hotel/ I Was The One, Mystery Train/ I Forgot To Remember To Forget, Good Rockin' Tonight, Baby, Let's Play House, That's All Right (Mama)* and *Milkcow Boogie Blues. Heartbreak Hotel* crosses over from the country charts to the pop charts, entering *Billboard*'s Top 100 at 68. It spends 27 weeks on the chart.

March 7: Three weeks after its release, *Heartbreak Hotel* is estimated to have sold 300,000 copies.

March 13: Elvis' first LP, *Elvis Presley,* is released.

March 15: Colonel Parker and Elvis strike a long-term personal management contract, with Parker getting a 25% commission on everything Elvis does in public.

March 17: Elvis returns to New York to do another Gleason show, singing *Heartbreak Hotel* and *Blue Suede Shoes.*

March 24: Elvis makes his final Gleason appearance singing *Heartbreak Hotel* again, along with *Money Honey.*

March 25: Elvis flies to Los Angeles to meet with Hal B. Wallis, a producer for Paramount Pictures.

March: Ends with the LP *Elvis Presley* selling over 100,000 copies. Elvis spends the week in LA preparing for his screen test.

April: Marks the beginning of Elvis' thirteen-year affair with Hollywood.

April 1: Elvis screentests for Paramount. He sings *Blue Suede Shoes* and does a scene from *The Rainmaker.*

ELVIS

ON WHAT HAPPENED:

I just fell into it, really. My daddy and I were laughing about it the other day. He looked at me and said, "What happened, El? The last thing I remember is I was working in a can factory and you were driving a truck." We all feel the same way about it. Still. It just... caught us up.

The famous cover of Elvis' first album, released March 13, 1956. It was the first indication that just his name and face could sell a million.

LAMAR FIKE
ON THE SCREEN TEST:

The screen test for The Rainmaker went great, according to Elvis. He later told me he was sure it was going to be his first movie. And it was a damned serious film, nothing like the stuff he ended up doing. He was so sure he'd gotten the part that he did an interview saying, "I have a movie coming out in June with Katharine Hepburn and Burt Lancaster," and that "it was a dream come true." Make no mistake, Elvis wanted to be a serious actor. When asked whether he'd perform in The Rainmaker, he even said that he "wouldn't care about singing in the movies." Of course, the exact opposite happened. Elvis was never in a movie in which he didn't sing.

D.J. Fontana, Scotty Moore, Bill Black and Elvis take a break beside the pool at the Frontier Hotel in Las Vegas. Even though the boys seem to be having fun, the 1956 show in Vegas bombed. The mainstream casino crowd just wasn't ready for Elvis Presley, and his engagement there closed two weeks early. He wouldn't return to the glitzy city until 1969. Booking Elvis in Las Vegas prematurely was one of the few marketing mistakes Colonel Parker made in handling Elvis' early career.

April 3: Elvis does *The Milton Berle Show* from the deck of the *USS Hancock* in San Diego. He sings several of his recent hits and does a skit with Berle.

April 6: Elvis signs a seven-year deal with Paramount, with Hal B. Wallis producing. He'll do three pictures on a rising pay scale starting at $100,000 and capping at $200,000 each.

April 7: His last appearance on *Louisiana Hayride*.

April 10: Elvis' plane limps into Memphis after losing an engine and almost going down over Texas. He is reluctant to fly for years afterward.

April 11: *Heartbreak Hotel* is Elvis' first million seller and he receives his first gold record at the Nashville studio where he goes to record *I Want You, I Need You, I Love You.*

April 23: Elvis does his first gig in Vegas at the New Frontier Hotel's Venus Room, on the same bill with comedian Shecky Greene. Elvis bombs, and Colonel Parker cuts the engagement from four weeks to two. It will be his last appearance in Vegas for thirteen years.

April: Closes with *Heartbreak Hotel* breaking every kind of record there is and still climbing. *Life* magazine's April 30 issue marks the first story on Elvis in a national magazine.

May: The records are selling like hotcakes and everywhere he goes, the crowds are mammoth and almost uncontrollable. Elvis has become a show business phenomenon unseen since the early days of Frank Sinatra. Shows are ending early because fans mob the stage before he can finish. Ticket prices that started at a quarter the year before have risen to an amazing $2.50 and people are still being turned away. His face is everywhere: Magazines and newspapers are fighting for his photo because it sells copies like no one else. On top of all this, he's about to do a movie.

May 4: RCA releases *I Want You, I Need You, I Love You/ My Baby Left Me.*

May 11: Vernon, Gladys and Elvis move into the first home they have ever owned. It costs $40,000 and Elvis pays cash for it. Gladys is overwhelmed.

Elvis paid cash for 1034 Audubon Drive, Memphis, Tennessee, and he, Gladys and Vernon lived there for almost a year, adding a swimming pool and customizing the interior. Fans were frequently seen gathering on the front lawn, and it was rumored that the neighbors in this upper-class section of Memphis were not unhappy to see the Presleys go when they moved to Graceland in 1957.

May 12: *Heartbreak Hotel* has sold 1,350,000 copies and is moving at a rate of 70,000 per week. The album *Elvis Presley* is RCA's biggest-selling LP ever.

May 15: Elvis performs in the round at Ellis Auditorium in Memphis. So many seats are sold he has to turn around to include all the fans. Elvis' appeal is so strong that Eddie Fisher, performing at the Show Boat, closes his show early.

June: Marks the move to California. Critics continue to be lukewarm to his obvious success, but the fans go wild. To skeptics, he is well on his way to becoming a threat to modern values and personally responsible for the decline of western civilization. To fans, there has never been anyone like him.

June 5: Elvis does his second *Milton Berle Show*, singing *I Want You, I Need You, I Love You*. The hype is so strong that Berle's Neilsen ratings surpass CBS's popular *Sergeant Bilko* for the first time.

June 13: Elvis' sexuality begins causing problems. NBC states that he will not "bump and grind" during his upcoming appearance on *The Steve Allen Show* in July.

June 28: Elvis does a show in Charlotte, North Carolina, then catches a train to New York and his date with Steve Allen.

While waiting to tape his second Milton Berle show, Elvis consults with Colonel Parker. Behind them is Irish McCalla (in leopard skin, star of *Sheena of the Jungle*), who appeared on the show with Elvis.

June 29: After a rehearsal for the Allen show in New York, Elvis catches a train to Virginia for a show in Richmond, then returns immediately to New York.

July 1: Elvis appears on *The Steve Allen Show*, singing *Hound Dog* (to a basset named Sherlock, left) and *I Want You, I Need You, I Love You*. He does a skit with comedienne Imogene Coca and talks with Steve Allen. And Allen beats Ed Sullivan in the ratings.

July 2: Ed Sullivan, who once said, "I wouldn't have Elvis Presley on my show at any time," calls the Colonel to discuss terms. Elvis goes into the studio in New York to record *Hound Dog, Don't Be Cruel* and *Any Way You Want Me*.

July 3: Elvis returns to Memphis by train.

July 4: A benefit concert in Russwood Park in Memphis for the local milk fund draws 15,000 screaming fans. Maybe it's the door prize: a diamond ring with Elvis' initials.

July 13: RCA releases *Hound Dog/Don't Be Cruel* and Ed Sullivan signs Elvis to three appearances for $50,000, making him the highest-paid guest star on a variety show in television history.

July 31: A little more than two weeks after its release, *Hound Dog* has sold a million copies.

August: *Hound Dog* is selling off the racks, and Elvis is on the road in Florida, hitting Tampa, Lakeland, St. Petersburg, Orlando, Daytona Beach and Jacksonville, where a local judge is so incensed by "The Pelvis" that he issues a warrant for Elvis' arrest. The

LAMAR FIKE
ON "HOUND DOG":

Elvis and I were walking through the lounge of the Sahara Hotel in late '56 and Freddie Bell and The Bellhops were up on stage singing Hound Dog. Elvis stopped and said, "I really like that." It was a bluesy version, which Elvis lightened up on a little, but it was at that moment he remembered the Mama Thornton version, which he had a record of, and decided to do Hound Dog himself.

Elvis thought his first movie would be *The Rainmaker*, but instead he starred in *Love Me Tender*. Originally, his character died at the end, but it proved so unpopular with fans that it was re-shot with Elvis living after all.

LAMAR FIKE
ON GLADYS PRESLEY:

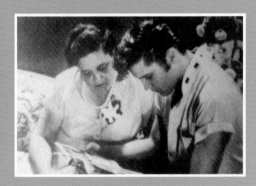

Basically, Elvis' personality was that of Gladys'. There wasn't a dime's worth difference between them. He was just like her: short-tempered. To the point. Up in your face. I first met Gladys in 1955, when the Presleys moved to Audubon Drive. Even then the fans were hanging around outside making Gladys real uncomfortable. The house didn't afford any protection and the fans were standing around on the lawn.

It took me quite a while to understand Gladys. She was a simple person, she didn't require a lot. The Presley family was extremely matriarchal. And Gladys was the leader. A very strong personality. Vernon was the exact opposite: a follower. Gladys made all the decisions.

ON ELVIS AND DESTINY:

If ever there's been proof that God has a plan, Elvis is it. He was such a perfect prototype. Like the Lord stamped him out and everybody from that point on had someone to compare themselves to. He was so unique, so perfectly in tune with what was happening in the country, or rather what the country was ready to have happen. Everything that's changed since Elvis has changed as a result of Elvis. He brought youth into a position of dominance in American culture and it's stayed there ever since. It's like it was meant to be.

Colonel puts out the fire and Elvis tones it down for the remainder of his time in the Citrus State. The stats on record sales continue to mount and after gigs in Louisiana, Elvis heads west to begin his movie career.

August 22: Elvis arrives in Los Angeles and turns the top floor of the Knickerbocker Hotel into his base of operations for the duration of his stay in movieland.

August 23: Principal shooting begins on *Love Me Tender.*

August 24: At Radio Recorders in Hollywood, Elvis records the song *Love Me Tender.*

August 28: Colonel Parker grants RCA the rights to market Elvis charm bracelets.

August 30: Elvis gets his first formal death threat. It comes on a postcard and is turned over to the FBI.

August 31: RCA releases six singles based on the cuts from Elvis' first album.

September: Elvis mixes a busy schedule of shooting and recording and performing. The unprecedented demand for records forces RCA to lease pressing plants from other major labels in order to keep titles in the stores. The company estimates that Elvis will sell almost 10,000,000 records in 1956 alone.

September 1: Elvis, Scotty, Bill and D.J. go into the studio at Radio Recorders and cut *Love Me, How Do You Think I Feel* and *How's The World Treating You?*

September 2: The Radio Recorders session continues with *When My Blue Moon Turns To Gold Again, Paralyzed, Long Tall Sally, Old Shep* and *Too Much.*

September 3: The session continues with *Ready Teddy, Rip It Up, First In Line* and *Anyplace Is Paradise.*

September 4: RCA releases *Elvis Presley* and *The Real Elvis,* both in the extended-play (EP) format.

September 5: Elvis surprises Gladys with a present: a custom pink Cadillac. The car will remain in the family till the end and is now on view at Graceland.

Ed Sullivan's initial resolve to never have the controversial performer on his show dissolved after he realized how much Elvis' appearances helped the ratings of rival shows. Elvis appeared on *The Ed Sullivan Show* three times.

September 9: Elvis is in New York for his first appearance on *The Ed Sullivan Show.* The ratings go through the roof. An estimated 54 million people watch Elvis sing *Don't Be Cruel, Hound Dog, Ready Teddy* and *Love Me Tender.* Not until The Beatles appear in 1964 will a larger audience gather to watch a television show.

September 15: *Don't Be Cruel* hits #1 and Elvis is presented with another gold record.

September 22: Elvis returns to Memphis from Hollywood after completing *Love Me Tender.*

September 26: Accompanied by his new friend, actor Nick Adams, Elvis performs at the Mississippi-Alabama Fair and Dairy Show in his hometown of Tupelo, Mississippi. The governor calls out the National Guard to handle the crowds, and it turns out to be necessary. Elvis is forced to stop the show at one point to allow everyone to calm down. Afterwards he and Adams are seen cruising Memphis on matching black Harleys.

September 28: With orders already at close to one million copies, RCA hustles *Love Me Tender/Anyway You Want Me* to release.

October: The Presley rocket is soaring ever upwards. So is conservative, middle-class America. Elvis is being damned in pulpits and papers all over the country. Radio stations refuse to air his songs, causing DJs to stage their own kinds of protests. In San Francisco, a local DJ named Bruce Vanderhoot plays *Love Me Tender* fourteen times in a row at different speeds and is asked to seek other employment by management. Elvis is so recognizable it's becoming difficult for him to venture out in public without causing near riots.

October 1: Studio tests have shown that the audience is upset over Elvis dying at the end of *Love Me Tender,* so the producers call him back to re-shoot the ending, and this time Elvis lives.

October 18: After a whirlwind tour of major venues in Texas, playing to packed houses, Elvis returns to Memphis, where he gets involved in the now-famous fistfight at Hopper's gas station. Elvis pulls into Hopper's to gas up his brand new Lincoln Continental and a crowd begins to gather. Hopper asks him to leave. Elvis refuses and a shoving match ends with Elvis being forced back into his car, so Elvis slugs him in the eye. The police charge everyone with assault and disorderly conduct.

October 19: Elvis is acquitted in court, but Hopper and his attendant are found guilty and fined.

October 21: Elvis is mobbed at a local movie theater and his Cadillac is severely damaged by adoring teenagers. The police have a difficult time bringing things under control. For the first time, fame is beginning to seem a double-edged sword.

October 24: Elvis gets a letter from his local draft board concerning his draft status.

Elvis appearing at the Mississippi-Alabama Fair and Dairy Show in the summer of 1956 in Tupelo. Billed as a homecoming, the performance was a huge success and remained one of Elvis' personal favorites. It was a classic case of local boy makes good. In the background are The Jordanaires and Scotty Moore. The State Police were on hand to control what almost turned into a riot.

October 28: His second appearance on *The Ed Sullivan Show* draws big numbers again. He sings *Hound Dog, Don't Be Cruel, Love Me Tender* and *Love Me.* Sullivan presents him with gold record #5 for *Love Me Tender* on the show. The hype for *Love Me Tender*'s premiere in New York City begins with the unveiling of a 40-foot Elvis billboard above the Paramount Theater in Times Square.

October 31: Nick Adams and Natalie Wood arrive in Memphis for a visit with Elvis. They all buy Harleys and cruise town. There are rumors that Elvis and Natalie are an item. The press calls it a "Motorcycle Romance."

November: The word from Hollywood is that Elvis has potential as an actor and may surprise some people. He continues to tour and the songs continue to chart. A "no wiggle" injunction is placed on him by Louisville Police Chief Carl Heustis for his concert at the Armory in November. The world waits to see what will happen.

November 3: Elvis does his first radio commercials to promote RCA's new Elvis Presley line of record players.

November 16: *Love Me Tender* premieres at the Paramount in New York City. The show is sold out and crowds are turned away. That night, Elvis is in Las Vegas to see Liberace.

November 21: *Love Me Tender* opens nationally. The reviews are mixed but overall there is grudging admiration for Elvis' debut. The consensus is that maybe there's an actor in there.

Elvis, Natalie Wood and Nick Adams wait outside Bob Neal's studio in Memphis for a live radio interview. Elvis' first trip to Los Angeles resulted in long-standing friendships with the two up-and-coming stars. Natalie and Nick often traveled to Memphis to hang out with Elvis backstage during shows and the gang cruised the city on custom Harleys.

November 23: After a concert in Toledo, a fan, upset that his wife carries Elvis' picture in her wallet, finds Elvis at his hotel and starts a fight. He assaults Scotty Moore and Elvis wades in, impressing the local police with his pugilistic skills.

November 25: Elvis performs in Louisville. The "no wiggle" ban is not enforced. Several hundred fans wait outside the home of Jesse Presley, Presley's grandfather, as Elvis pays his respects.

December 4: Elvis drops by Sun Records with his latest flame, showgirl Marilyn Evans, and finds Carl Perkins in a recording session with Jerry Lee Lewis on piano. Johnny Cash is hanging around as well. The four men begin to riff and wail on standards, blues and gospel, and Sam Phillips has his engineer turn on the tape. Several hours later the result is a lot of songs that will become the basis for the fabled Million Dollar Quartet. The tapes of the session will remain in Phillips' vault for many years until a bootleg recording is finally released in 1977. It takes RCA several more years to resolve legal difficulties and release an authorized version of one of the most famous recording sessions in musical history.

December 16: Elvis does his final, final performance on *Louisiana Hayride*.

December 25: The Presleys spend Christmas at the house on Audubon Drive with a few friends, including a Vegas showgirl named Dottie Harmony and several members of the fledgling Memphis Mafia. Red West, on leave from the Marines, joins the crew in a game of touch football.

December 29: *Billboard* reveals that Elvis has the most songs in the Top 100 since the chart began.

December 31: Elvis' last appearance of 1956 is Wink Martindale's *Holiday Hop* on a local Memphis TV station.

Elvis and Liberace clown around backstage in Vegas in 1956. Colonel Parker was a genius at keeping the publicity machine rolling even in less-than-perfect conditions. By getting Liberace to pose with Elvis during the ill-fated Vegas gig in 1956, he began the slow process of introducing Elvis to mainstream America.

(Below) An impromptu jam session at Sun Studios in 1956 with Jerry Lee Lewis, Carl Perkins and Johnny Cash resulted in what came to be called The Million Dollar Quartet. The four men riffed on blues and gospel tunes for hours. The session was taped by Sam Phillips and released as a bootleg album twenty years later.

1957
THE TOP OF THE MOUNTAIN

January 4: Elvis reports to Kennedy Veteran's Hospital for his pre-induction physical, administered by Dr. Leonard Glick, who becomes the most famous army doctor in military history. Elvis passes and gets his number.

January 6: Elvis makes his final appearance on *The Ed Sullivan Show*. He sings seven songs including a gospel number, *Peace In The Valley*.

January 8: Elvis is classified 1-A by the Memphis draft board.

January 12: RCA releases *Playing For Keeps/Too Much*. At Radio Recorders, Elvis, Scotty, Bill and D.J. cut some gospel tunes with The Jordanaires as backup for a forthcoming gospel album, as well as future hits, *Got A Lot Of Livin' To Do*, *Mean Woman Blues* and *All Shook Up*.

Elvis cuts tunes in the studio for *Jailhouse Rock*. The results were some of his best. Although RCA did its best to keep news of sessions under wraps in order to cut down on crowds of fans at the studios, word always seemed to leak out. One source of information in Nashville was a local hamburger joint. Whenever an order was placed for 100 or so hamburgers and cheeseburgers, the waitresses guessed that Elvis and the boys were in a session. The Hamburger Hotline was usually 100% accurate.

The King was fascinated by anything on wheels, whether it had a motor or not. Even a bicycle could provide both escape and a good publicity shot (far left). A string of beautiful women began to appear at Graceland as soon as Elvis got the keys. Yvonne Lime (above left), an actress, was one of the first to get the grand tour.

Elvis was extremely proud of his new home. It was the single most tangible result of his success and he never tired of showing it off or of saying how important it was to him. Elvis paid a heartfelt tribute to his famous backup singers, The Jordanaires, (above) when he said, "If it hadn't been for you guys, there might not have been a me."

January 19: Back in the studio, Elvis records *Blueberry Hill, Have I Told You Lately That I Love You* and *Is It So Strange*, as well as another song for the gospel album.

January 21: Principal photography begins for *Loving You* at Paramount. It's the first film of a three-picture deal at Paramount. Elvis had been farmed out to Fox for *Love Me Tender* because Hal Wallis couldn't find a suitable project at Paramount.

January 24: Elvis records a short version of *Teddy Bear* and a blues number called *One Night* at Radio Recorders.

February 14: The version of *Teddy Bear* that will ultimately be released is cut at Radio Recorders along with songs from the soundtrack of *Loving You.*

February 23: Elvis interrupts his shooting schedule to have lunch at the Paramount commissary with fans from San Francisco. He also records more tracks for the *Loving You* soundtrack.

March 9: *Billboard* reports that Elvis sold 12.5 million singles and 2.75 million LPs in 1956.

March 19: After completing shooting for *Loving You*, Elvis returns with his family to Memphis, where he purchases Graceland for $100,000. The mansion will be his family home for the rest of his life.

March 22: RCA releases *All Shook Up/ That's When Your Heartaches Begin* and Elvis' first gospel EP, *Peace In The Valley*. Army Private Hershal Nixon brings Elvis up on charges of pulling a gun on him at a Memphis restaurant. The charges are later dropped.

March 27: Elvis makes a swing to the upper midwest through Chicago, St. Louis and Detroit. The fan response is so rowdy and the tour so successful that local preachers have several months of sermon fodder about the end of life as we know it.

April: The road trips continue as usual, but the revenues have multiplied in the last couple of years. A concert in Buffalo grosses a staggering $40,000. But four concerts in the northeast and Canada bring in over $300,000. Elvis is a money machine.

April 2: On a two-city swing through Canada, Elvis wears a suit made with real gold for a concert in Toronto. Community leaders in Ottawa campaign to keep attendance down at his performances.

April 5: Elvis starts a two-night gig in Philadelphia.

April 10: Gladys, Vernon and Elvis move into Graceland, where he spends the rest of the month resting.

May 1: Elvis is in LA for pre-production on *Jailhouse Rock* and to cut the tunes for the soundtrack.

May 2: A recording session at MGM produces *Young and Beautiful, I Want to be Free,*

Dolores Hart, above, on the set of *Loving You*, also went on to play opposite Elvis in *King Creole*. She said, "Elvis is a young man with an enormous capacity of love... but I don't think he has found his happiness yet." (far left) Nudie, the famous Hollywood fashion designer, was the creator of Elvis' Gold Lamé suit. The costume was conceived by the Colonel as a publicity stunt and cost $10,000. But it was so heavy, hot and uncomfortable that Elvis hated to wear it. He eventually gave it away.

LAMAR FIKE

ON JOINING ELVIS:

In 1957 I called him up in California where he'd just started Jailhouse Rock. He asked what I was up to. I said I was bored to tears, doing nothing, back home in Waco, Texas. I had just quit my job as a DJ at KED in Jacksonville, Texas. Matter of fact, I put an LP on the turntable, walked out the door and locked it. By the time they figured I wasn't there, I was out of town. Never looked back. Elvis loved that.

So he said to me, "Why don't you get in your car and come on out here?" I got in my '56 Chevy and drove straight from Waco to the Wilshire Hotel in Los Angeles. Suite 850. And from that point on, I was with Elvis until the day he died. I became the first non-family member living at Graceland, so I guess that makes me the first true member of the so-called Memphis Mafia. The originals also included Red West and Gene Smith, plus, on and off, there was Junior Smith, Gene's brother, and George Klein. But in '57 Elvis only had me to harass, probably 'cause he enjoyed me harassing him back. I remember when I got there, he asked me why I liked him. And I said, "Because you're a hit singer and a pretty neat person. Other than that, I can't think of anything."

The combo of satin jacket, black shirt and black pants was Elvis' standard stage costume for most of 1957 and 1958. He checks out the crowd from the stage in Seattle.

(You're So Square) Baby, I Don't Care and *Treat Me Nice*. The band is the usual combo of Scotty, Bill and D.J. plus composer Mike Stoller on piano.

May 13: Principal photography begins on *Jailhouse Rock* and continues throughout the month. In the midst of production, rumors of marriage with various public figures surface, but they're denied.

May 14: Elvis swallows a cap from one of his front teeth on the set and is rushed to the hospital, where it's removed the following day.

June 11: RCA releases *Loving You/ Teddy Bear*. In the following week, it will sell over a million copies making it his eighth million seller.

July 8: Elvis has his first date with Anita Wood, to whom he was introduced by Cliff Gleaves at Elvis' request.

July 9: *Loving You* premieres in Memphis at the Strand Theater. Fearing for his personal safety, Elvis does not attend.

July 10: Vernon, Gladys, Elvis and Anita double date at a special midnight screening of *Loving You*.

July 13: Anita has dinner with Elvis and his folks at Graceland.

July 30: *Loving You* opens nationally to sold-out houses.

August: The month is spent mostly at Graceland, where Elvis continues to see Anita, with the relationship growing steadily closer. Gladys and Vernon seem to like the pretty and ambitious young woman, and the rumor mill is churning out possible wedding bells. Everyone seems excited except Colonel Parker, who sees dollar signs in his client remaining single. Elvis prepares to tour the Northwest: Spokane, Vancouver, Seattle and Portland.

August 27: Anita waves goodbye at the railroad station as Elvis and the gang take off for Spokane. She wears a sapphire and diamond ring, a token of affection from the "Hillbilly Cat."

August 30: Elvis sings 18 songs at the concert in Spokane.

September 3: The fans riot in Portland, and Elvis is forced to leave the stage after only fifteen minutes so that security can restore order.

September 4: Elvis trains to LA, meeting Anita at the station. She

Elvis would find a steady companion and friend in Anita Wood (above), an aspiring actress introduced at Elvis' request by Cliff Gleaves. (Below left) Elvis warms up for a performance in 1957. Candid shots of Elvis backstage before shows were common in the early years. As time went on and his fame grew, so did his need for more privacy. Consequently, fewer people were allowed backstage before concerts. The members of the Memphis Mafia were responsible for keeping the area clear of all except invited guests.

LAMAR FIKE

ON ELVIS' EXPECTATIONS FOR HIMSELF:

Early on, Elvis' expectations about his career were extremely conservative. He thought he'd last two or three years. Maybe five tops. Never thought he was gonna be a monster. You see, Elvis first wanted to be a gospel singer. Then a country singer, like when he did Blue Moon of Kentucky, which was an old Bill Monroe song. He never thought he'd be what he turned out to be. God, when we started touring in '57, the mobs of people were just huge. It was scary to him. Very, very scary.

LAMAR FIKE
ON ELVIS AND THE DRAFT:

Everybody was telling Elvis how important it was to get the picture done and how he should write the draft board for a deferment. But Elvis didn't want any special favors. He was afraid people would think he got something because he was Elvis Presley. Well, some people did and some would've no matter what the truth was. Anyway, you have to remember, this was peace time. Nobody was shooting at us. Lots of men got deferments at that time and nobody said a word. So finally Elvis and Vernon and I drove over to the draft board in Memphis—in Elvis' '57 Cadillac Eldorado—and asked in person if he could have a deferment until after he finished the picture. "Sure," they said, "'long as you go in as soon as you finish."

The Los Angeles Police Department was so afraid of the potential mayhem caused by Elvis rockin' the house at the Pan Pacific Auditorium in California in October of 1957 that they instituted a no-wiggle rule for his second show, but no problems arose. (Below left) Elvis and the inevitable fans take the sun on the deck of the cruise ship *Matsonia* en route to Hawaii, 1957. It was Elvis' first trip to the islands. He would fall in love with Hawaii and return many times both to perform and vacation.

has good news: She's a winner in the "Hollywood Star Hunt" held in New Orleans.

September 5 – 7: Elvis goes into the studio to re-cut *Treat Me Nice*. He also does *My Wish Came True, Don't* and songs for his Christmas album including: *Blue Christmas, White Christmas, Silent Night, Oh Little Town of Bethlehem, Santa Bring My Baby Back To Me, Santa Claus Is Back In Town* and *I'll Be Home For Christmas.*

September 21: Scotty Moore and Bill Black resign as full-time members of the band. Money is the issue: Elvis has made a fortune, but they're still working for peanuts. They will continue to record with Elvis on and off over the years (Bill until 1958 and Scotty until 1969), but will never be full-time band members again. Drummer D.J. Fontana stays on board.

September 24: *Jailhouse Rock/ Treat Me Nice* is released by RCA.

September 27: Elvis does another benefit performance at the Mississippi-Alabama Dairy Show and Fair stadium in Tupelo.

October 10: Press preview of *Jailhouse Rock*. Elvis doesn't attend.

October 17: *Jailhouse Rock* premieres in Memphis. Elvis doesn't attend.

October 28: Elvis does a concert in Los Angeles. After the show, the LAPD apply their own "no wiggle" rule to the next night's concert.

October 29: The LAPD films the entire concert in search of a reason to bust Elvis. But the show goes on as usual and the matter is not pursued.

October 30: The EP *Jailhouse Rock* is released by RCA.

November 4: The *Jailhouse Rock* album is selling like hotcakes, and RCA predicts another million seller. They will be proven right.

November 5: Elvis sails for Hawaii.

November 6: The movie *Jailhouse Rock* opens nationally.

November 10: Elvis performs in Honolulu at the Honolulu Stadium. It's business as usual: sold out.

November 11: Elvis performs for the men in uniform at Schofield Barracks and sails back to Los Angeles two days later.

November 19: RCA releases *The Elvis Christmas Album.* His rendition of *White Christmas* starts another conservative backlash and DJs around the country are fired for playing it.

November: Elvis returns to Graceland for the holidays near the end of the month.

December 19: Elvis receives a formal notification of induction into the United States Army and is ordered to report to the induction center in downtown Memphis on January 20, 1958 at 7:45 A.M. He wants to do his duty, but the timing is terrible. He's scheduled to begin shooting *King Creole* on January 13 in New Orleans. Shutting down the picture will cost the studio several hundred thousand dollars and put a lot of people out of work.

December 25: The Presley family spends a quiet Christmas with gifts, dinner and a display of fireworks in the backyard.

December 27: The draft board grants Elvis a 60-day extension so he can do the picture. He will report for duty on March 20, 1958.

December 31: Elvis gives a concert in St. Louis.

Backstage at the Opry in Nashville, Elvis is joined by Ferlin Husky, Faron Young, Hawkshaw Hawkins and an unidentified producer (left). Christmas was a special time to Elvis and he arranged his touring schedule to make sure he was at Graceland for the holidays. The house was elaborately decorated top to bottom for family and friends. No expense was spared and Elvis lavished extravagant gifts on his loved ones. He often said that these were some of the best times of his life.

1958
"KING CREOLE" AND ARMY DAYS

January: 1958 starts with a blaze of activity. There's a lot to do and not much time to do it in. The Colonel wants some songs in the can before Elvis leaves for the service because his "boy" won't be singing in the army. No USO, no entertaining the troops for free. Elvis will be just another dogface, doing his stint like a patriot, no special treatment, no special favors. Elvis goes into the studio and cuts tunes for *King Creole*. The grueling session produces: *As Long As I Have You, Crawfish, Dixieland Rock, Don't Ask Me Why, Hard Headed Woman, King Creole, Lover Doll, New Orleans, Steadfast, Loyal and True, Trouble* and *Young Dreams*.

January 7: RCA releases *Don't/I Beg Of You*.

January 13: Elvis catches the train to Hollywood.

January 20: Shooting begins on *King Creole* at Paramount, a week later than hoped, so the schedule is tight and there's not much room for error.

January 27: Both sides of *Don't/I Beg Of You* enter *Billboard*'s Top 100.

February 1: At Radio Recorders, Elvis cuts: *Doncha' Think It's Time, Your Cheating Heart* and *Wear Your Ring Around My Neck*.

February 6: Elvis and the *King Creole* cast and crew head to New Orleans for location shooting. Nick Adams and several members of the Memphis Mafia are along for the ride.

March 10: Elvis finishes shooting and has to go to Los Angeles to be formally released by Paramount, then turns around and heads for Memphis and induction.

March 14: In Memphis with ten days to go, Elvis rents the Rainbow Rollerdome for parties every night until he leaves.

March 15: Elvis does his last concert date before induction at Russwood Park in Memphis—and tosses a diamond ring into the packed audience.

March 23: The last fling in Memphis starts at Graceland and ends in the wee hours at the Rainbow Rollerdome for a last round of power skating.

March 24: At 6:30 A.M., accompanied by Anita Wood, Judy Spreckles, Lamar Fike, Vernon, Gladys, Vester, several other family members and Colonel Parker, Elvis reports to the office of the local draft board. A little after 7:00, he boards a bus with other recruits to Kennedy Veteran's Hospital for his final physical and processing. The entourage follows in various Cadillacs and Continentals. At 4:00 P.M. he's returned to the draft board for swearing in, and Private Elvis Aron Presley (#55310761) is put in charge of the other fourteen recruits. At 5:00 P.M. he boards an olive drab army bus for the ride to Fort Chaffee, Arkansas and basic training, arriving shortly after 11:00. He's in the army now.

March 25: On Elvis' first day as a soldier, he is awakened at 5:30 A.M. and met by Colonel Parker and a horde of media who will follow this simple soldier as he makes the transition into army life. They watch as he receives his first military paycheck: $7.00. They wait as he takes an aptitude test. There is a frenzy of flashbulbs as James

Even with an unflattering military haircut and fatigues, the Elvis magic is clearly present (opposite). Elvis' roots were in rural America where doing your time in the military was considered an honor and he was proud to serve his country. Elvis signed up even though it would not have been difficult for him to get out of the draft. It was also smart business on the part of Colonel Parker, who saw that a stint in the army would only add to the All-American image he was creating for Elvis. Director Michael Curtiz, who directed *Casablanca* among other classics, producer Hal Wallis and Elvis confer on the set of *King Creole* at Paramount (above). It will be Elvis' last film before serving in the army.

LAMAR FIKE

ON ELVIS GOING INTO THE ARMY:

People today ask why Elvis went into the army. Couldn't he have gotten out of it? And the answer is, of course, he could've. But why take the chance? Eddie Fisher wiggled out of it and it damned near wrecked his career. This was the Cold War, remember. Doing your duty was a given, part of the country's commitment to fighting communism. And Elvis genuinely felt he ought to do his part. His number came up, it was simple as that. So he went.

B. Peterson, now the most famous barber in America, trims off that famous ducktail.

March 26: Members of the press watch as Elvis is issued his uniform. They report that he will be going through the required eight weeks of basic at Fort Hood, Texas, and receiving advanced tank training with the 2nd Armored Division.

March 27: Elvis gets his shots.

March 28: Private Presley heads for Fort Hood, with crowds lining the roads in the little towns they pass by on their way to Texas. On arrival he is assigned to Company A, 2nd Medium Tank Battalion, 37th Armor, 2nd Armored Division. During basic training he will live on base in recruit barracks. The army leaves the press corps stranded at the gate, and Elvis Presley is just another guy being yelled at by drill instructors.

March 31: In basic training, Elvis discovers a fascination with the martial arts that will remain with him for the rest of his life. During the time he's learning the ropes, away from the crowds, the army is dodging thousands of letters a week and fielding hundreds of phone calls from desperate fans.

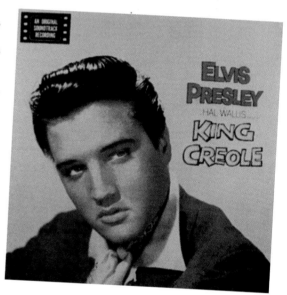

April 1: RCA releases *Wear My Ring Around Your Neck/Doncha' Think It's Time*. It will enter the charts at #7 and reach as high as #3.

June 1: Elvis completes basic training and is granted the traditional two weeks' leave before beginning school in tanks and armor. Anita meets him at Fort Hood and drives with him to Memphis, where he'll spend his leave.

June 4: Vernon, Gladys and Elvis attend a private screening of *King Creole*.

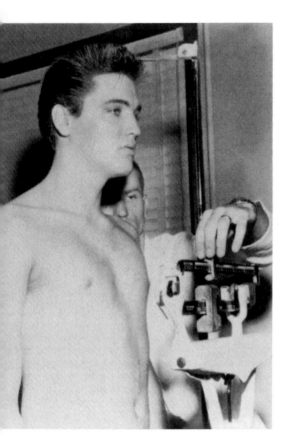

Elvis asked for and received no special treatment from the army even though many of his most routine requirements such as receiving his physical garnered worldwide media coverage. Private Presley could look forward to visits from his current girlfriend, Anita Wood, and friends like Eddie Fadal and his wife on his time off at Fort Hood.

June 10: RCA releases *Hard Headed Woman/Don't Ask Me Why*, the last RCA release of simultaneous 78 and 45 rpm disks. Elvis is in the studio at RCA Nashville recording *A Fool Such As I, I Need Your Love Tonight, A Big Hunk O' Love, Ain't That Lovin' You Baby* and *I Got Stung*.

June 13: Colonel Parker gets a call from Ed Sullivan, who wants to book Elvis the instant he's discharged.

June 14: After another raucous all-night skating party in Memphis with the gang, Elvis reports back for duty at Fort Hood.

June 16: Elvis begins eight weeks of armor crewman school.

June 18: Now that he's out of basic training, Elvis is free

LAMAR FIKE
ON GLADYS' DEATH:

Gladys had a weight problem, partly caused by a very fatty diet, partly from a tendency to compulsive eating. Then she started in on diet pills to control the weight, probably because she didn't want to embarrass Elvis. And eventually she became a heavy drinker. Gladys just didn't take care of herself at all. So though she was young, her dying wasn't really a surprise. I think Elvis thought about his life like his mother did. She died at 46, but she lived a full life. I think that's the way he thought about it. It's a fatalism, an acceptance of things as they are, that they shared. He always used to say that she was more than a mother to him.

to seek housing off base. He finds a large house in Killeen, Texas, and is joined there by Gladys and Vernon, Lamar and Grandmother Presley. Anita Wood is a frequent visitor.

July 2: *King Creole* opens nationally. The fans eat it up, and even the critics feel it's his best work to date.

August: Starts on a somber note as Gladys becomes ill and must be taken to a local doctor who recommends that she be taken to a specialist in Memphis.

August 9: Gladys is taken to Methodist Hospital and diagnosed with acute hepatitis.

August 11: Gladys is failing, and the doctors contact the army to request emergency leave for Elvis so he can be with her. The initial request is denied, but the doctors are persistent. Elvis arrives in Memphis the next day, spending the evening by her side.

August 13: The family keeps a vigil as Gladys' condition continues to deteriorate. Elvis, who has been with her since early morning, returns to Graceland around midnight. But Vernon stays with his wife.

August 14: With Vernon beside her, Gladys Presley passes on at 3:15 A.M. from a heart attack directly attributable to her acute hepatitis. Vernon calls Graceland to break the news to his son, and Elvis rushes to the hospital. Late in the afternoon, her body lies in state at Graceland.

August 15: The funeral for Gladys Presley is held at 1:00 P.M. in the Memphis

LAMAR FIKE
ON RED WEST AND ELVIS:

Red's daddy died on the same day as Elvis' mama did. Red and Elvis kind of looked at one another like they couldn't believe the turn life had taken. Everybody was really impressed by the way Elvis reached out to Red. It didn't take a genius to see how hard Elvis was taking Gladys' death, and for him to find the time to mourn for Red and his family, well, Red would never forget it, and I've never seen a thing like it before or since. If anybody ever wanted to know why we stayed with him, that's one of the reasons for sure.

Lamar Fike, who went along to Europe with Elvis, enjoys a trip to Paris with his boss during a lull in the action in Germany.

LAMAR FIKE
ON ELVIS ON GUARD DUTY:

One night some military genius decided to post Elvis on guard duty. That was completely fair, of course, but also seriously dumb. Because Elvis was huge in Europe and the fans must have had some kind of highly developed radar, because whenever Elvis was exposed where the public could get to him, they appeared in droves. And this night a huge crowd gathered, with Elvis doing guard duty at some gate. There he was standing like he was supposed to, but surrounded, absolutely surrounded by hundreds and hundreds of fans. It took platoons to rescue him. That was the last guard duty Elvis pulled.

Funeral Home. Fans by the thousands show up to mourn, many traveling great distances to pay their respects. Anita Wood and Nick Adams are with Elvis constantly. Vernon contacts The Blackwood Brothers, one of Gladys' favorite gospel groups, and they fly to Memphis on a chartered plane to sing at the funeral. She is laid to rest in Forest Lawn Cemetery.

August 16: Elvis, Lamar, Gene and Alan go to the funeral home to pay respects to Red West's father.

August 25: Elvis reports back to Fort Hood and tank school.

September 12: Elvis completes his training and receives his orders: He's assigned to the 3rd Armored Division in West Germany as a tank gunner.

September 19: Anita, Lamar, Red, Vernon and Grandma bid Elvis goodbye at the station in Memphis as he and his unit ship out, traveling by train to the Military Ocean Terminal in Brooklyn. Charlie Hodge, a musician Elvis has known for years, is on the train as well.

September 22: The troop train arrives in Brooklyn, with hundreds of fans waiting to catch a glimpse, but the army won't allow anyone close enough to see. Elvis holds a final press conference on the *USS General Randall*, and these interviews will become the basis of an EP. About mid-morning, the ship leaves port and heads east, bound for Bremerhaven, West Germany. Charlie Hodge is assigned as his roommate for the crossing. Placed in special quarters, Elvis keeps to himself, singing and jamming with Charlie. But he does agree to perform with Charlie in an impromptu variety show on board.

October 1: When the *Randall* arrives at Bremerhaven, the dock is mobbed with screaming fans, but once again they're denied an Elvis sighting. The 1700 soldiers board troop trains for the journey to Ray Caserne, Freidberg and the U.S. 7th Army headquarters. When they arrive after midnight, several female fans break through security and find Elvis, but they are summarily removed from the base.

October 2: Elvis is assigned to Company D, 1st Battalion, 32nd Armor, 3rd Armored Division of the 7th Army. His first assignment is to drive a jeep for Lieutenant Colonel Henry Grimm.

October 5: Vernon, Minnie, Red and Lamar arrive. They will live with Elvis during his tour. Starting out in an apartment at the Hotel Gruenwald—which turns out to be more of a rest home than a hotel—the family soon moves to larger quarters at 14 Goethestrasse. Elvis makes frequent calls to Anita Wood back in Memphis.

October 21: RCA releases *One Night/I Got Stung*. It's Elvis' first record to be released only as a 45.

October 29: German fans pack a concert by Bill Haley and His Comets in Stuttgart. It is likely they came to see Elvis watch the show.

November 3: Elvis goes on his first maneuvers with the 32nd Tank Regiment near the Czech border.

November 27: Elvis is promoted to Private First Class.

December 15: *Billboard* notes a drop in sales of Elvis' records since he joined the army.

December 20: The 32nd finishes maneuvers and returns to base. Elvis is rewarded for his work with a three-day pass. He buys a BMW sports car.

December 25: The family spends a low-key Christmas, probably because the death of his mother stills rests heavily on Elvis' heart.

LAMAR FIKE
ON THE APARTMENT IN GERMANY:

You could say that things livened up a little when we got there. These Germans were kind of quiet and reserved, and we were all young and full of it. The old folks just didn't understand what was going on. We jumped around a lot on the floor, wrestling and what-not, and the old woman downstairs would get scared to death. We joked about whether or not the noise would kill her, but we didn't stop and she was still grouching around when we left. There were squirt-gun fights and, God almighty, one time I believe Red and Elvis even set the place on fire. I think they were glad to see us go.

ON ELVIS AS A GUNNER:

Elvis' army MOS was tank gunner. Which I guess, looking back, was a pretty appropriate assignment. Elvis loved guns, and these were big guns. But there was a problem, because those guns were loud. And one day Elvis came home and I asked him how it went that day and he walked right on past me. Pissed me off royal. And I followed him into the bedroom and said, "Hey, didn't you hear me?"

"What are you talking about?" Elvis answered, and I realized he hadn't heard a word I'd said.

I asked him if he was all right and he said, "My ears are ringing so loud I can't even hear." I immediately got Colonel Parker on the phone in the States and told him we had a problem. A big problem. Colonel Tom knew a guy at the Pentagon, and he just wore this man's butt out until they reassigned Elvis out of that damned tank.

With the exception of an impromptu jam session with Charlie Hodge on the troop ship to Europe, Elvis did no public performances while he was in the army. At home, in his apartment in Gruenwald, West Germany, however, music was a big part of his life and over the years several tapes of sessions in his apartment have surfaced and been released as bootlegs.

1959
PRISCILLA

Elvis became fascinated with martial arts when he was introduced to hand to hand combat in basic training. The love of karate would remain with him for the rest of his life and he would eventually introduce elements of it into his nightclub act. He even had a karate instructor in Paris, France, in 1959.

January 1: Returning from Frankfurt, Vernon and Elizabeth Stefaniak, Elvis's personal secretary, are injured in an automobile accident on the autobahn, and the BMW is destroyed. Rumors began to surface that Elvis has been killed, forcing a public appearance at a charity event.

January 7: *Love Me Tender* has grossed $4.5 million to date.

January 8: Dick Clark interviews Elvis over a transatlantic hookup on *American Bandstand*. It's Elvis' 24th birthday.

March 10: *(Now And Then) There's a Fool Such As I/I Need Your Love Tonight* is released by RCA, with advance orders of over one million copies. Elvis has another gold record before the records hit the stands.

April 13: Elvis receives a Salk vaccination to publicize the anti-polio campaign in the United States.

May 23: The hype to set up Elvis' return to civilian life is beginning. ABC announces plans for a major TV special, but Colonel Parker says Elvis won't do any network shows. Instead he'll do a concert on closed-circuit television.

Elvis and some friends at a nightclub in Paris on leave from the army: (above, left to right) Charlie Hodge, Rex Hodge, Lamar Fike, Ben Star and Elvis.

June 1: Elvis is promoted to Specialist 4th Class with a ten-dollar-per-month increase in salary.

June 3: Tonsillitis forces Elvis into the 97th General Hospital in Frankfurt. He's released on June 9.

June 17: On a two-week leave, Elvis travels to Munich with Red, Cliff and Lamar along for the ride. In Munich he hooks up with Vera Tschechowa, a German actress.

June 20: The crowd heads for Paris, and they spend the next several days nightclubbing and painting the town red.

June 26: Elvis reports back for duty in West Germany.

July 6: Back in the states, *A Big Hunk O' Love* hits the charts. It will reach #1 during its fourteen-week stay. A week later *My Wish Came True* hits and reaches #12.

August 3: *A Big Hunk O' Love* goes gold. That's fourteen in a row.

August 15: Paramount announces *G.I. Blues* as Elvis' first film project when he leaves the Army.

September 14: *A Date With Elvis* (LP) enters the charts.

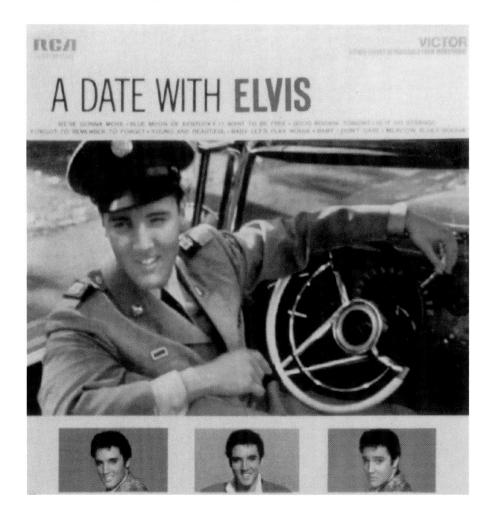

October: Elvis travels with the 32nd near the Swiss border to participate in war games, code named "Winter Shield."

October 24: Trouble again with the tonsils. Elvis is moved back to Frankfurt, where he undergoes tests and stays in the hospital almost a week.

November: The first time since 1954 that Elvis isn't somewhere on the charts. But he couldn't care less, because this month friend Grant Curry introduces Elvis to fourteen-year-old Priscilla Ann Beaulieu, step-daughter of recently transferred Air Force Captain Joseph Beaulieu. Elvis is smitten and pursues her with vigor. Anita Wood goes on the back burner.

November 2: Politics and Rock & Roll are a bad mix in East Germany, where more than a dozen fans are sentenced to long prison terms for demonstrating against the repressive music scene in East Germany. They carry banners and chant "Long Live Elvis."

November 19: An RCA exec creates a furor when he announces that everything about Elvis will be different when he returns, including his singing style. The fans don't want to hear it. The phones begin to ring off the hook back in Memphis with angry protests. Colonel Parker reassures them it isn't so.

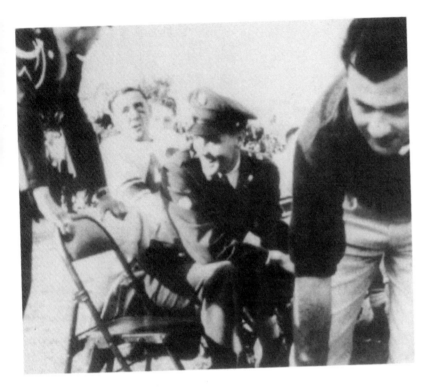

Elvis enjoys watching a football game between fellow servicemen (above). Taking care of business: Elvis enjoyed the challenge of the army, here shown as the forward guard of his battalion, and was promoted several times during his service (right).

December: Elvis is ranked as the 12th "Most Played Artist" in a poll by *Billboard* magazine. And Colonel Parker proves why he earns his money by planting rumors that Elvis will re-up at the end of his hitch.

December 25: Elvis throws a lavish party and Vernon and the regulars attend, along with Priscilla, who is the center of attention. Elvis gives her a watch made of solid gold and studded with diamonds. Army Sergeant Bill Stanley (a veteran of World War II and the Korean War) and Dee Stanley are also present. Vernon has become good friends with the Stanleys, particularily Dee, and spends a great deal of time with them.

DEE STANLEY
ON MEETING VERNON:

I was completely aghast at how handsome he was! I just didn't expect him to look like that. I felt very vulnerable, and I was afraid of saying something foolish, but I must say, it was an immediate physical attraction.

As a capable and respected soldier who did his job, Elvis rose through the ranks to Sergeant during his time in Germany (left, wearing his winter field uniform in Graffeweir, West Germany, 1960). Privately, he was proud of his promotions and took his leadership role seriously. Fourteen-year-old Priscilla Beaulieu waves goodbye to Elvis as he departs for the United States. She will see him very soon back in America.

1960

GETTING BACK ON TRACK

Elvis speaks to reporters at his final press conference in West Germany. The question and answer session focusing on his life in the army took place in a barracks on base. He returned to the United States the next day for mustering out and the return to civilian life. "The army changed me," he said. "I'm just not sure how." The Presley publicity machine, headed by Colonel Parker, was gearing up for his return to public life. The spotlight that had been off for two years had been switched on with a vengeance.

January 20: Elvis makes Sergeant and is given command of a reconnaissance unit for 3rd Armor. His officers feel that Elvis is a good soldier and has conducted himself well in the field.

February: The army starts the paperwork necessary for Elvis' discharge.

February: 17: More teenagers riot in East Germany as the government bans Elvis' films and records.

February 29: *Billboard* says that Elvis' records have sold in excess of $50,000,000.

March 1: The Armed Forces Radio Network broadcasts portions of a press conference at the base where Elvis recaps his time in the service and what Germany has meant to him.

March 2: Elvis and 79 other G.I.s board a military plane and head for McGuire AFB in New Jersey for mustering out. Vernon and Lamar follow on a commercial flight.

March 3: Elvis lands at McGuire. After clearing customs, he goes to Fort Dix for a press conference. At his side are Nancy Sinatra and Colonel Parker.

March 5: The United States Army grants Elvis an honorable discharge and gives him a final paycheck: after taxes, $9.81. Within minutes he's aboard a train to Memphis. Fans fight a blinding snowstorm to line the tracks and welcome him back.

March 7: Elvis arrives in Memphis, steps off the train in full dress uniform, and thousands of fans go wild. He returns to Graceland and civilian life.

March 9: *Jailhouse Rock* is re-released by MGM.

March 20: In the studios at RCA Nashville, Elvis gets back to work. The session produces: *Stuck On You, Fame and Fortune, Make Me Know It, Soldier Boy, It Feels So Right* and *A Mess Of Blues.*

March 21: Elvis passes the necessary tests and gets his first-degree black belt in karate.

March 22: The Colonel arranges a whirlwind publicity tour of the South by train so that adoring fans can welcome Elvis back in person.

At Graceland, Elvis had the endurance to play touch football for hours at a time. He was an enthusiastic quarterback who, according to Lamar Fike, had a pretty good arm if given the protection. The competition in these games was fierce, and the action hot and heavy. During one session, Elvis broke his finger and had to be rushed to the hospital. Although he wasn't seriously injured, the fracture required a cast and Elvis wore it as a badge of honor. The Colonel objected to the games saying that his boy was far too valuable to play games where he could get hurt. Elvis and Anita Wood take a spin on the bumper cars at the Memphis Fairgrounds in 1960 (left).

March 26: At the Fontainebleau Hotel in Miami, Elvis tapes a segment on *The Frank Sinatra Timex Show.* He sings *Fame and Fortune* and *Stuck On You.* The segment closes with the now famous Sinatra/Presley duet. They sing *Witchcraft* and *Love Me Tender.* Nancy Sinatra is on the show as well.

Frank Sinatra's *Timex Special* welcoming Elvis back to show business was Elvis' first public appearance in two years, and he joked with reporters that any leg movements came from fear and trembling. He was paid $125,000 for his six-minute segment and sang a duet of *Witchcraft* with Sinatra which later appeared on bootlegs.

March 29: Elvis returns to Memphis.

April 3: In a grueling session at RCA Nashville, Elvis records: *Fever, Like A Baby, Girl Of My Best Friend, Dirty, Dirty Feeling, Thrill Of Your Love, Such A Night, Girl Next Door Went A-Walking, I Will Be Home Again* (with Charlie Hodge), *It's Now Or Never* and *Are You Lonesome Tonight?*

April 18: Elvis, Lamar and the rest of the gang head for Hollywood in a private railroad car to begin production on *G.I. Blues* at Paramount.

April 20: Elvis arrives in Los Angeles, greeted by Colonel Parker and the usual screaming mob. He travels by limo to the Beverly Wilshire Hotel, which will be his headquarters during the shoot.

April 25: *Stuck On You* reaches #1.

April 26: Elvis begins preproduction work: costume fittings, makeup tests and scheduling.

April 27: At RCA Hollywood, Elvis records: *Didja' Ever, Doin' The Best I Can, G.I. Blues, Tonight Is So Right For Love, What's She Really Like?, Blue Suede Shoes* and *Wooden Heart.* While he recorded a total of fifteen tunes, these were the only ones to be released. Several tunes were started but left to be finished at another session.

May 2: Principal photography begins on *G.I. Blues.*

May 6: Back in the studio, Elvis and the boys pick up where they left off, finishing material from the last session, including: *Big Boots, Shoppin' Around, Pocketful Of Rainbows, Frankfurt Special* and *Tonight's All Right For Love.*

May 8: *The Frank Sinatra Timex Show* airs.

May 12: Anita Wood is back in the picture, and Elvis gives her a diamond necklace.

June: Elvis' face seems to be plastered on every magazine in the country. He has become one of the best-known entertainers in the world. Elvis and his leading lady, Juliet Prowse, have a short but intense fling, and Frank Sinatra isn't happy about it. After shooting is completed, Elvis and the boys kick back in Las Vegas.

Vernon Presley and the soon-to-be Dee Stanley Presley (right) met in Germany while Vernon lived there with Elvis during his stay in the army. After Dee divorced her husband, Bill (below right with their three sons), she married the senior Presley and moved into Graceland with her boys.

Marriage Certificate

Name of Groom __VERNON Elvis Presley__ Age of Groom __44__

Residence of Groom __Memphis, TENNESSEE__

Birthplace of Groom __Mississippi__ Date of Birth __4-10-16__

Name of Bride __DAVADA MAE Elliott__ Age of Bride __32__

Residence of Bride __Huntsville, ALABAMA__

Birthplace of Bride __NAshville, TENNESSEE__ Date of Birth __6-16-28__

Date of License __July 3, 1960__ Date of Marriage __July 3, 1960__

By Whom Solemnized __HARRY L. PENNINGTON, JUDGE__

STATE OF ALABAMA
Madison County

I, __Frank H Riddick__ as Judge of the Court of Probate of Madison County, Alabama, do hereby certify that the above record is taken from Volume __107__, Page __118__, of the Marriage Records in this office.

I further certify that this attestation and certificate is in due form, that I am Judge of said Court of Probate, and as such the proper officer to make this certificate and attestation, that said court is a court of record, and that the Judge thereof is ex-officio its clerk.

Given under my hand and seal of office this __10__ day of __JANUARY__ A.D., 19__85__

__Frank H Riddick__
Judge of Probate

July 3: After a close friendship with Vernon that became much more and results in her divorce from husband Bill, Dee Stanley marries Vernon. She and her three sons Billy, Ricky and David will live at Graceland. Elvis is rumored to be less than excited about the wedding and does not attend.

July 10: Having become enamored of waterskiing, Elvis buys a boat, names it *Karate* and takes lessons.

July 18: *It's Now Or Never* hits the charts. It reaches #1 and remains for twenty weeks.

August 6: After yet another riot in the East German town of Chemnitz, the government declares Elvis an "enemy of the people," and it is recommended that he not show his face in the Republic.

August 12: At Radio Recorders in Hollywood, Elvis records: *Flaming Star, Summer Kisses, Winter Tears, A Cane And A High Starched Collar* and *Britches* (never released).

August 16: Photography on *Flaming Star* begins at 20th Century-Fox. The shooting schedule is tight, a little over a month.

August 18 *G.I. Blues* "sneaks" at a theater in Dallas. The reaction is very strong.

September: Elvis rents the first of several Hollywood homes he and the Memphis Mafia will occupy while shooting in LA. 565 Perugia Way becomes the scene of many parties and high times. *Flaming Star* completes principal photography around the 20th, but Elvis and the boys hang out in LA for the rest of the month before returning to Memphis.

October 16: During a game of touch football at Graceland, Elvis breaks his finger and spends a night in the hospital.

October 30: Elvis heads for Nashville and the RCA Studios where, in a marathon recording session, he cuts most of the tracks for his forthcoming gospel album, *His Hand In Mine*. Gospel has always been an important part of his life, and this first album is extremely important to him. Recorded are: *Milky White Sky, His Hand In Mine, I Believe In The Man In The Sky, He Knows Just What I Need, Mansion Over The Hilltop, In My Father's House, Joshua Fit The Battle, Swing Down, Sweet Chariot, I'm Gonna Walk Dem Golden Stairs, If We Never Meet Again, Known Only To Him* and *Working On The Building*. Non-gospel tunes cut during this amazing session are *Crying In The Chapel* and *Surrender*.

October 31: *G.I. Blues* enters the charts. The album will spend six weeks at #1 and remain there for a staggering 111 weeks, the longest stay Elvis will ever have.

November 5: Another skating party at the Rollerdome. These all-night events are becoming rituals that precede major trips.

November 6: Elvis flies to Los Angeles to begin work on *Wild In The Country*. It's his most serious film role to date. With a screenplay by Clifford Odets and a strong cast, he's hoping to be taken more seriously as an actor.

November 7: At Radio Recorders, Elvis cuts tracks for *Wild In The Country*: *Lonely Man, I Slipped I Stumbled I Fell, Wild In The Country* and *Husky Dusky Day* (never released).

November 10: Elvis and the rest of the cast assemble on location in Napa,

California. Shooting for *Wild In The Country* will begin the next morning.

November 11: As principal photography begins, Elvis is seeing a wardrobe girl named Nancy Sharp.

November 12: Shooting stops for a day while Elvis is treated for "a minor infection."

November 14: *Are You Lonesome Tonight?* and *I Gotta Know* chart.

November 19: Elvis gets a couple of days' break after completion of location photography and heads for San Francisco with Red and Nancy.

November 21: Interior shooting begins at the studio in Los Angeles. The picture will be completed on schedule near the end of the month.

November 23: *G.I. Blues* opens nationally. The audience response is strong and the picture has a successful opening week.

December 2: Elvis has become convinced that he and Priscilla are meant for each other and begins a campaign to get her over to Graceland for the holidays. Returning to Graceland, he waits to hear of Captain Beaulieu's decision concerning his daughter. Elvis brings in the big guns, asking Vernon and Dee to contact the captain and talk him into allowing Priscilla to spend the holidays in Memphis.

December 8: Vernon and Dee succeed, and Priscilla arrives from Germany to visit the King. The visit will be carefully controlled and low key.

December 22: *Flaming Star* opens nationally to decent, even good, reviews. Critics say that Elvis is beginning to get the hang of this acting business.

December 25: During this quiet Christmas at Graceland, Elvis is clearly falling for Priscilla. He keeps asking the boys if she's OK, and they say she is: charming, mature for her age and fun to have around. Her original two-week stay turns into almost a month and she will reluctantly return to Germany in January.

Elvis strikes a beefcake pose for a studio publicity shot for *Flaming Star*. Elvis was said to be uncomfortable appearing in films without his shirt but did it when necessary.

1961
....
WILD ABOUT THE GIRL

Elvis' love of country cooking guaranteed that weight would be a problem throughout his life. He had to work hard to stay trim but rather than exercise regularly, he relied on crash diets to get himself in shape for film roles such as *Blue Hawaii* (above). Although he later learned to water ski and loved it, he wasn't a big fan of water.

January 9: *His Hand In Mine* hits the charts, where it will remain for twenty weeks.

January 18: Elvis signs a five-year contract with Hal B. Wallis and Paramount to do a picture a year.

February 5: RCA releases *Surrender/ Lonely Man*, and *Surrender* hits the charts on the 20th.

February 25: The state of Tennessee and Governor Buford Ellington declare this "Elvis Presley Day." The King is celebrated and honored as a true man of the South and a cultural resource to the state. Elvis uses the opportunity to raise money for charity.

March 8: Elvis goes to Nashville with Lamar and Red to be honored at a joint session of the Tennessee legislature, and the Tennessee Volunteers make him an honorary Colonel.

March 12: At RCA Nashville, Elvis goes into the studio and records cuts for *Something For Everybody*: *Gently, Give Me The Right, I Feel So Bad, I Want You With Me, I'm Comin' Home, In Your Arms, It's A Sin, Judy, Put The Blame On Me, Sentimental Me, Starting Today* and *There's Always Me*.

March 18: Elvis adds a Rolls Royce to his collection and decides to drive it to Los Angeles.

March 21: Arriving in LA, he goes straight to the studio at Radio Recorders to cut tunes for *Blue Hawaii*, which will shoot on location in the Pineapple State. The movie will showcase fourteen songs and even at three days, the recording schedule is tight. Day one: *Aloha Oe, Hawaiian Sunsets, Ku-U-I-Po, No More* and *Slicin' Sand*.

March 22: Day two: *Almost Always True, Blue Hawaii, Hawaiian Wedding Song, Island Of Love, Ito Eats, Moonlight Swim* and *Steppin' Out Of Line*.

March 23: Day three: *Beach Boy Blues, Can't Help Falling In Love* and *Rock-a-Hula-Baby*.

March 25: Elvis and the gang arrive at Honolulu International Airport. After a press conference, he heads to Bloch Arena to perform in a benefit to help build the memorial to the *USS Arizona* at Pearl Harbor.

March 27: Principal shooting begins on *Blue Hawaii*. The film will showcase not only Elvis but the state, and almost every square inch of the islands are to be used as locations.

April 17: The company completes location shooting for *Blue Hawaii*. Interiors will be shot at Paramount in Hollywood.

May 1: The picture wraps in Hollywood, and Elvis spends the rest of the month relaxing in California and back in Memphis.

June 22: *Wild In The Country* opens nationally, but the news isn't good: Reviews are bad to horrible.

June 25: At RCA Nashville, Elvis records: *(Marie's The Name) His Latest Flame, I'm Yours, Kiss Me Quick, Little Sister* and *That's Someone You Never Forget.*

July 1: Red West marries Pat Boyd, one of Elvis' secretaries, in Memphis. Elvis brings Anita.

July 5: At another session in Nashville, Elvis records cuts for his next movie, *Follow That Dream: Angel, Follow That Dream, I'm Not The Marrying Kind, Sound Advice* and *What A Wonderful Life.*

July 13: Elvis goes to Hollywood to begin filming *Follow That Dream* for United Artists. They will shoot interiors until the end of the month, when the company will go on location in Florida through the month of August.

August 21: *Little Sister* hits the charts.

August 22: *His Latest Flame* hits the charts.

October 15: At RCA Nashville, Elvis records: *Anything That's Part Of You, For The Millionth And Last Time, Good Luck Charm* and *I Met Her Today.*

October 23: *Blue Hawaii* enters the charts. The album will get to #1, stay there for twenty weeks and remain on the charts for a total of 79 weeks.

October 26: Elvis arrives in Los Angeles for preproduction on *Kid Galahad* and goes right to Radio Recorders to cut tunes for the soundtrack: *A Whistling Tune, Home Is Where The Heart Is, I Got Lucky, King Of The Whole Wide World, Riding The Rainbow* and *This Is Living.*

November 6: Principal shooting begins for *Kid Galahad* on location in Idyllwild, California. The cast and crew will be in the San Jacinto Mountains for almost a month, but foul weather will shut it down on the 26th and the picture will finish filming in the studio.

November 22: *Blue Hawaii* opens nationally.

November 29: *Blue Hawaii* is knocking 'em dead around the country. Fans and critics seem to like Elvis better in a less serious mode.

December 15: Elvis is forced to return to LA to re-shoot portions of *Kid Galahad*, which finally wraps in January.

December 18: The trades announce that four Elvis singles topped the chart in 1961: *Are You Lonesome Tonight?, Flaming Star, Little Sister* and *Surrender.*

December 25: Elvis has to spend Christmas in LA. With the exception of his hitch in Germany, it's the only time he hasn't been in Memphis for the holidays. It will not happen again.

Elvis is caught in a very rare moment smoking a cigarette with Marty Lacker (below). Although he would enjoy an occasional pipe or cigar, Elvis' good friends attest to the fact that, true to his image, he was neither a smoker nor a drinker.

1962
GOING HOLLYWOOD

Elvis strikes a seaworthy pose on the fore-deck of an ocean liner docked in Los Angeles in 1962. Elvis loved costumes all his life so it would follow that if he was on a boat, he would appear in appropriate sailing gear.

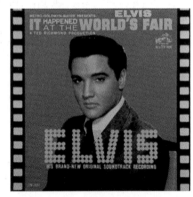

LAMAR FIKE
ON ELVIS AND FLYING:

He was uncomfortable flying. I don't want to say scared, because Elvis didn't scare much, but from the time in the spring of 1957 when his plane lost an engine and almost went down in Texas, he never liked flying. He also got tired of taking the train, which was too public for him. So he bought what's called now a motorhome. It was really a bus. And he'd drive that sucker to LA, often doing most of the driving himself. So I can say Elvis Presley was my bus driver.

January 8: Back home in Memphis for the rest of this month and February, Elvis gets a car from Colonel Parker for his birthday, which is spent at Graceland with his family and members of the Memphis Mafia.

January 27: *Can't Help Falling In Love* becomes Elvis' gold record # 29.

March 10: *Good Luck Charm* hits the charts for a thirteen-week stay. It will reach #1.

March 18: Elvis goes to Nashville to cut the songs for *Pot Luck*: *(Such An) Easy Question, Fountain Of Love, Gonna Get Back Home Somehow, I Feel That I've Known You Forever, Just For Old Times Sake, Just Tell Her Jim Said Hello, Night Rider, She's Not You, You'll Be Gone, Something Blue* and *Suspicion*.

March 20: Back to LA and Paramount Studios for the filming of *Girls! Girls! Girls!*

March 26: The soundtrack for *Girls! Girls! Girls!* is cut at Radio Recorders: *A Boy Like Me, A Girl Like You, Because Of Love, Earth Boy, Girls! Girls! Girls!, I Don't Wanna Be Tied, I Don't Want To, Song Of The Shrimp, Thanks To The Rolling Sea, The Walls Have Ears, We'll Be Together* and *We're Comin' In Loaded*.

April 7: Elvis flies to Oahu on location on *Girls! Girls! Girls!* The company will continue shooting through the middle of the month and return to LA for interiors, wrapping in early May.

April 21: *Good Luck Charm* briefly hits the top of the chart, but it won't be until 1969 that Elvis has another #1 single.

May 17: Trade papers report that Elvis is the biggest box-office draw in the movies.

May 23: *Follow That Dream* opens nationally to the usual lukewarm response from critics—who want him to tackle meatier roles—but the fans love him the way he is. The fact is that Colonel Parker won't allow Elvis to do a film in which he can't sing.

Elvis wants to be a good actor, and many close to him feel his frustration at being stuck in mediocre films, as he says, "singing to girls, dogs and walls."

May 30: The single of *Blue Hawaii* is Elvis' 30th gold record.

June – July: Elvis returns to Graceland, is seen around Memphis on his motorcycle and in various cars. He frequently rents local movie theaters after the midnight showing and watches his favorite films over and over. He also rents the Fairgrounds for late nights of private time on the grounds, riding the rides and walking up and down the midway. He has established a pattern of staying up all night and sleeping all day. The Memphis Mafia has to adjust to his schedule and balance their personal lives as well, but it isn't easy.

August 6: Anita Wood announces that she's breaking up with Elvis for good. "It's all or nothing with me," she says. But they will continue to see each other until Priscilla forces him to break it off for good.

August 20: Elvis buys a Greyhound bus and has it customized to make the trip back and forth between Memphis and LA. A small apartment on wheels, with all the comforts of home and plenty of room for him and the boys, it's the latest addition to Elvis' bulging garage.

August 27: Principal photography begins on *It Happened At The World's Fair* for MGM. After doing some interiors in Los Angeles, cast and crew will move to Seattle on September 4 for location shooting on site at the Fair.

August 29: *Kid Galahad* opens nationally to generally favorable reviews.

September: Elvis records the soundtrack for *It Happened At The World's Fair* at MGM Studios in Culver City: *A World Of Our Own, Beyond The Bend, Cotton Candy Land, Happy Ending, How Would You Like To Be, I'm Falling In Love Tonight, One Broken Heart For Sale, Relax, Take Me To The Fair* and *They Remind Me Too Much Of You.*

September 13: Elvis muffs his role as goodwill ambassador from Memphis when he gives the wrong Tennessee smoked ham to the governor of Washington.

September 17: The movie company returns to Hollywood to complete shooting *It Happened At The World's Fair*, and the film wraps near the end of the month.

October: A milestone month in Elvis' life. After intense negotiations with her father, Priscilla joins the King at Graceland and finishes high school at Immaculate Conception High School in Memphis, with Elvis responsible for her education and her well-being. She will live with Vernon and Dee in their house on Hermitage, which is just off the Graceland property. Elvis is ecstatic, and Graceland will never be the same.

November 21: *Girls! Girls! Girls!* opens nationally.

December 8: The *Girls! Girls! Girls!* LP hits the charts, where it will remain for 37 weeks, reaching as high as #3.

December 25: Elvis and Priscilla celebrate her first real Christmas at Graceland. The King assembles family and friends in the dining room and presents her with a diamond ring. His intentions are clear, but it will be four years before wedding bells chime.

Elvis and a friend share terror on the ferris wheel at an amusement park in Memphis. Elvis loved going out in his hometown, it was the crowds he didn't like. He solved the problem by renting the entire grounds after closing and inviting a few friends for some free rides. He did the same with roller rinks and movie theaters, skating or watching favorite films over and over until dawn sent everyone home.

DAVID STANLEY
ON PRISCILLA AS BIG SISTER:

By the time Priscilla came to Memphis from Germany, Vernon and Dee had moved our family out of Graceland to a nearby house. And the stipulation was that Priscilla, who was seventeen, would live with us. Which she did. So Priscilla was like a big sister to me. I remember on one birthday she came and picked me up in the little Corvair that Elvis had given her, and took me out. She bought me a toy helicopter, a parrot and a skateboard.

I have great memories of Priscilla. Lots of them. I remember that when Priscilla moved into Graceland, before they were married, we'd go over there a lot, especially when Elvis was filming. Without him, it was kind of a lonely house. And she used to dress up as a vampire. With that black hair and dark eyes she made a very convincing vampire. Then she'd turn off all the lights and chase us around the dark house. Those were good times.

1963
YEAR OF CHANGE

In the recording studio, Elvis was heavily involved in the entire process of cutting a record. Although not a trained musician, he had excellent instincts and when paired with quality engineers produced excellent results. In the early days he was dedicated and hard working and would not be satisfied until a take was exactly what he wanted it to be. Although he began to lose interest in the recording process as the quality of his material declined, he still created music that sent his fans to the record stores in large numbers.

January: Priscilla is solidly ensconced in the Presley stronghold. Even at her tender age, she exerts a lot of influence on Elvis, and around the house he is even more polite and protective than usual. It's during this period that he stops seeing Anita Wood for good. Anita has been a major figure in his life for many years, surviving a great many flings and other girlfriends, but this one is serious, and it's all over between them.

January 22: Elvis is back in the studio at Radio Recorders to do the sound track for *Fun In Acapulco. Bossa Nova Baby, I Think I'm Gonna Like It Here, Marguerita, Mexico, The Bullfighter Was A Lady* and *Vino, Dinero Y Amor* were cut in a single session.

January 23: The session continues with: *El Toro, Fun In Acapulco, Guadalajara, No Room To Rhumba In A Sports Car* and *You Can't Say No In Acapulco.*

January 28: Principal photography begins on *Fun In Acapulco* for Paramount. Unlike Elvis' last several films, all footage will be shot in the studio with a second unit doing coverage in Mexico.

February – March: While shooting continues, rumors fly about Elvis and his co-star Ursula Andress. Meanwhile, the party in LA never ends: The lights are always on and the house on Perugia rocks all night long. When the movie wraps Elvis hangs around in LA through the end of March into early April.

April: RCA announces that Elvis has sold in excess of 100 million records.

April 5: The Elvismobile arrives back in Memphis.

April 10: *It Happened At The World's Fair* opens nationally to mixed reviews.

April: Elvis spends the month in recording sessions in Nashville and fooling around in Memphis, with Priscilla as his constant companion.

May 26: In Nashville, Elvis records *(You're The) Devil In Disguise, Echoes Of Love, Finders Keepers, Losers Weepers, Love Me Tonight, Never Ending, Please Don't Drag That String Around, What Now, What Next, Where To?* and *Witchcraft.*

May 27: The session continues with: *Blue River, Long Lonely Highway, Slowly But Surely* and *Western Union.*

June 14: Priscilla graduates from Immaculate Heart. In the best Southern tradition, she will attend Memphis' Patricia Stevens Finishing School, a proving ground for generations of Southern belles.

June 29: *Devil In Disguise* hits the charts.

July 7: Elvis arrives in Hollywood and goes into the Radio Recorders studio to cut the soundtrack for his new movie, *Viva Las Vegas: C'mon Everybody, Do*

Elvis and Ann-Margret became close friends during the making of *Viva Las Vegas* and would remain in touch throughout Elvis' life. She and her husband, Roger Smith, were among the small number of celebrity friends who came to Graceland to pay their respects after Elvis died.

The Vega, I Need Someone To Lean On, If You Think I Don't Need You, Night Life, Santa Lucia, Tomorrow And Forever, Viva Las Vegas, What'd I Say?, Today and *Yellow Rose Of Texas.*

July 11: Elvis' co-star in *Viva Las Vegas,* Ann-Margret, joins Elvis at Radio Recorders to cut a duet called *The Lady Loves Me.* It will be unreleased for many years. But she is soon to become another woman of his dreams, one who will remain part of his life to the very end. She's talented, beautiful—and already knows how to ride a motorcycle.

July 15: The cast and crew head to Las Vegas—staying at the Sahara—for two weeks on location. The gambling capital of

An active Elvis enjoyed karate (above with Red West) and is caught between touchdowns in an Elvis Presley Enterprises team picture (right). Elvis never did anything halfway. If he wanted to play football he did it in no less than full uniform. The games were played at local high schools and at Graceland by teams of friends, guests and the occasional ringer. EPE also had a west coast branch during movie shoots, consisting of Elvis, the Memphis Mafia, and any celebrities who wanted to join in.

America will play a major role in this film with shooting taking place all over the city. It is a coup for the tourist office.

July 27: The company returns from Las Vegas to LA for completion of the film, with the rumor mill churning out stories of romance and intrigue between Elvis and Ann-Margret. When the gossip filters back to Memphis, Elvis denies everything.

August: Elvis returns home to rest and recuperate. There are rumors that Priscilla is less than pleased at what she's been hearing, but according to Red West, Elvis is a silver-tongued devil and Graceland becomes once again a haven of peace and contentment.

August 14: *Elvis' Gold Records–Volume 3* hits the charts, where it will remain for 40 weeks, peaking at #3.

September: Elvis has a little time on his hands, so he starts a football team. Called Elvis Presley Enterprises, it's made up of locals, members of the inner circle, Elvis and anyone else who happens to be visiting, including a long list of celebrities. They have uniforms and play a tough and demanding contact version of touch, complete with refs.

October 3: The soundtrack for *Kissin' Cousins* is recorded at RCA Nashville: *Anyone, Barefoot Ballad, Catchin' On Fast, Once Is Enough, One Boy, Two Little Girls* and *Smokey Mountain Boy*.

October: Shooting *Kissin' Cousins* in LA. Close to the bottom of the barrel in terms of songs and script, it's a throwaway for the studio and for Elvis, with a two-week shooting schedule and budgeted at a fraction of the last several pictures. It seems ironic that while Elvis continues to improve as an actor, the quality of the material continues to decline. But that decline is a direct consequence of Colonel Parker's unwillingness to compromise record sales by allowing Elvis to do more challenging work. According to Lamar Fike, "The Colonel would always say 'Elvis makes his living as a singer and you don't kill the chicken that lays the golden egg.'" One critic calls *Kissin' Cousins* "dreary and lifeless," and the strain is starting to take its toll on Elvis.

November: Elvis' songs are charting modestly (for him) when he returns to Memphis to hang out with Priscilla and the guys. He rides his golf carts on the grounds of Graceland and his Harleys around Memphis. He buys another Rolls. He makes donations to local charities, as is his custom around the holidays

December: Elvis spends a quiet Christmas at Graceland with family and friends, and the year ends with a bash at a local nightspot called the Manhattan Club on New Year's Eve. But there's a different feeling in the air as 1963 rolls to a close. A President has just been assassinated, and the world of Rock & Roll is about to change forever: The British are coming.

The grounds at Graceland were a great excuse to indulge in Elvis' love of wheels and motors. Almost every form of transportation was available in the garage or under the carport. Motorcycles, go-karts, cars, limos, trucks, even a bus and eventually a stable of horses were ready 24 hours a day to satisfy the King's thirst for speed and action. All the toys were one way of dealing with the increasing discontent at being trapped in a cycle of boring movie roles and equally boring records. But Elvis was locked in by lucrative film and recording contracts and had little or no choice in the selection of his material. The hours at Graceland were his own to do with as he pleased. Graceland was one of the few places Elvis was free.

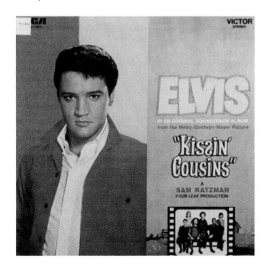

A pensive look on his face, Elvis, dressed in full leathers for his role in 1964's *Roustabout*, waits between takes for his next shot. Although he publicly denied it, Elvis was becoming concerned about his career and the impact of the Beatles on American Rock & Roll. His connection to the audience and his love of performing were strong elements in his life and he was beginning to miss the concert tours.

1964

INVASION!

January 8: Elvis celebrates his 29th birthday at Graceland, and *Elvis' Christmas Album* receives a gold record.

January 12: At RCA Nashville, Elvis records: *Ask Me, It Hurts Me* and *Memphis, Tennessee.*

January 25: Two Canadians, one disguised as a priest and the other described by police as along for the ride, are arrested in Memphis after they tried to knock on Elvis' door at Graceland. Elvis is in Los Angeles at the time, but they are questioned concerning the theft of some cowboy boots and a watch from the home of Hank Snow by a man also dressed as a priest.

January 30: In an attempt to do a good deed for the March of Dimes, Elvis purchases the former presidential yacht, *Potomac,* at an auction for $55,000, but the charity turns it down because the vessel, built in 1934, is considered unsafe. Next he tries the Coast Guard, which also turns it down. So he gives it to Danny Thomas in Long Beach, California at a special ceremony for the St. Jude's Children's Hospital in Memphis. The yacht finally sinks in 1981.

February 9: Making their first appearance on a major variety show, The Beatles sing *I Want To Hold Your Hand* on *The Ed Sullivan Show,* and proceed to take the country by storm. Turning the music business on its collective ear, they are the first real threat to Elvis' unchallenged position as the King Of Rock & Roll.

February 15: *Kissin' Cousins/It Hurts Me* hits the charts.

February 24: While the country is reeling from the impact of The Beatles, Elvis heads for Hollywood and the beginning of *Roustabout.* He checks in at Radio Recorders and cuts the soundtrack over a period of several days. The sessions include: *Big Love, Big Heartache, Carny Town, Hard Knocks, I Never Had It So Good, It's A Wonderful Life, It's Carnival Time, Little Egypt, One Track Heart, Poison Ivy League, Roustabout, There's A Brand New Day On The Horizon* and *Wheels On My Heels.*

March 6: *Kissin' Cousins* opens nationally, and *Viva Las Vegas* is released as a single in Great Britain before it's released in the states, probably to compete with the increasing frenzy over The Beatles. In an attempt to stem The Beatles tide, Colonel Parker promotes a series of awards and medals for Elvis that show him as a true American and worthy patriot. Buy American seems to be the message.

March 9: Principal photography begins for *Roustabout* at Paramount in Los Angeles.

March 31: Elvis isn't present for a ceremony in Memphis when the Elks give him the "First Americanism Award," an honor promoted by Colonel Parker to decrease the Beatles' surge from Britain. The boy from Tupelo, Mississippi has come a long way from the early Fifties, when he was branded responsible for the moral decline of the country from pulpits and seats of government across the country.

Elvis, the consummate animal lover, jokingly gets his pet chimpanzee, Scatter, to help him with his lines at the Goldwyn Studios in Los Angeles. "All I do anymore is sing to horses, chimps or dogs," Elvis remarked about his movie career.

April 9: Beatles records are selling like hotcakes, but the president of the Official

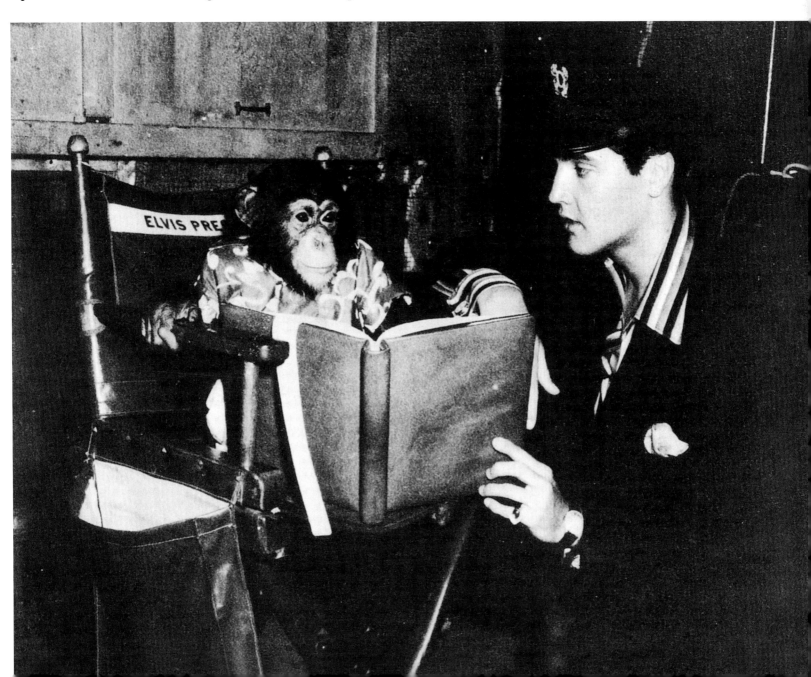

Shelley Fabares appeared in three of Elvis' films and Elvis considered her one of his favorite actresses. He felt that she liked him as a person and wasn't awed by his celebrity. They dated for a while, became and remained close friends. Her spark, sense of humor and enthusiasm helped Elvis through some difficult times. One of the films in which they appeared together is *Girl Happy* (right).

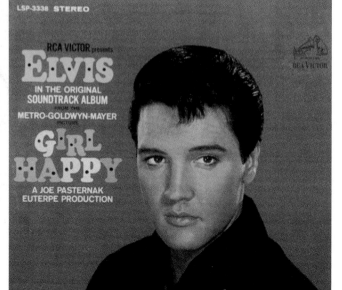

Elvis Presley Fan Club of Great Britain comes to Los Angeles to meet with the King, and the AP names Elvis "Performer of the Year."

June 5: Elvis begins filming *Girl Happy* for MGM in Culver City.

June 16: At Radio Recorders, Elvis lays down the vocals on previously recorded tracks for the *Girl Happy* soundtrack: *Cross My Heart And Hope To Die, Do Not Disturb, Do The Clam, Fort Lauderdale Chamber Of Commerce, Girl Happy, I've Got To Find My Baby, Puppet On A String, Spring Fever, Startin' Tonight, The Meanest Girl In Town* and *Wolf Call.*

June 17: *Viva Las Vegas* opens nationally to mixed reviews, as usual.

July: *Girl Happy* moves on location to Fort Lauderdale. When the movie wraps and he returns to Memphis at the end of August, Elvis has been gone from home for over eight months.

September 21: Elvis captures another childhood dream when he's made an honorary sheriff of Shelby County, Tennessee by childhood friend Sheriff Bill Morris. After high school, Elvis had considered joining the Memphis police but at nineteen was too young to apply. He is given all the "rights and privileges" of a peace officer, including the right to make arrests and carry a sidearm. Elvis and the boys celebrate at an all-night movie fest at the Memphian Theater.

September 22: In a newspaper interview, Elvis says that he and Ann-Margret are just friends and that according to the terms of the contract for his next film, *Tickle Me*, he has to give up riding a motorcycle.

October 12: Principal photography begins on *Tickle Me*, with Allied Artists producing. *Tickle Me* is the first of Elvis' films to use no original material; songs already in the can are remixed to keep costs down.

November 11: *Roustabout* opens nationally, with Elvis receiving good to excellent notices for his performance.

November 14: The LP of *Roustabout* enters the charts, where it will stay for 27 weeks, reaching #1.

December 3: *Tickle Me* wraps and Elvis returns to Memphis for Christmas.

December 5: RCA announces that *Elvis' Christmas Album* has sold over 800,000 copies since its release in 1957.

December 25: Elvis celebrates Christmas at Graceland, with the King tapped as "Best Male Singer" by *American Bandstand* for the eighth year in a row, having withstood the British invasion of The Beatles.

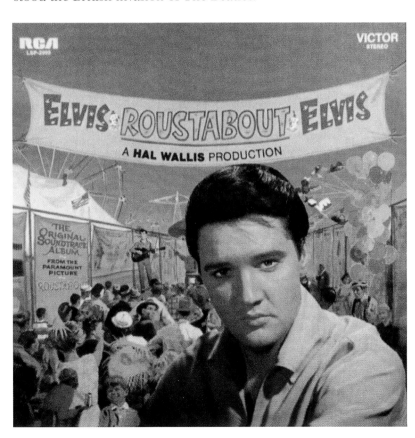

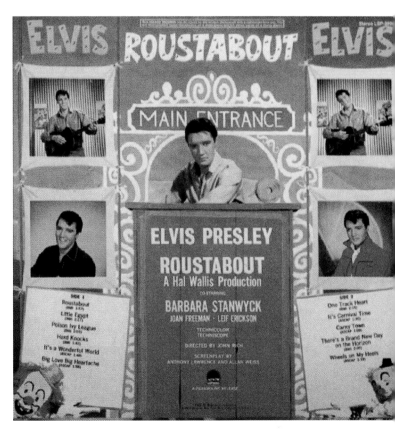

1965
THE BEAT GOES ON

January 2: The LP of *Roustabout* reaches #1, but will be Elvis' last album to hit the top until 1973.

January 8: With no discernible neurotic reactions, Elvis turns 30.

February 24: At RCA Nashville, Elvis records the tracks for his next movie, *Harum Scarum: Animal Instinct, Go East Young Man, Golden Coins, Harem Holiday, Hey Little Girl, Kismet, Mirage, My Desert Serenade, Shake That Tambourine, So Close, Yet So Far* and *Wisdom Of The Ages.*

March 15: Principal shooting begins on *Harum Scarum* for MGM. Another quickie, *Harum Scarum* will be shot entirely in the studio at Culver City and will be completed in less than three weeks.

April: A month of leisure that Elvis spends in LA.

April 7: *Girl Happy* opens nationally to strong box office and positive reviews.

April 17: The single *Girl Happy* hits the charts, where it will remain for 31 weeks.

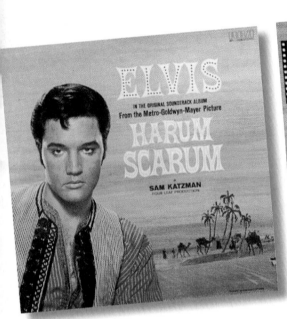

April 24: The single of *Crying In The Chapel* begins a fourteen-week run on the charts, selling almost two million copies by December.

May 13 – 15: At Radio Recorders, Elvis records the soundtrack for *Frankie And Johnny: Beginner's Luck, Chesay, Come Along, Down By The Riverside/When The Saints Go Marching In, Everybody Come Aboard, Frankie And Johnny, Hard Luck, Look Out Broadway, Petunia The Gardener's Daughter, Please Don't Stop Loving Me, Shout It Out* and *What Every Woman Lives For.*

May 23: Principal photography begins on *Frankie And Johnny* at MGM studios in Culver City, wrapping in less than three weeks.

June: *Crying In The Chapel* tops the Beatles in England, and Elvis takes a break in his schedule before heading off to Hawaii for *Paradise, Hawaiian Style* in August.

July: Elvis spends the month lounging and laughing in Los Angeles, especially after *Variety* reports that *Tickle Me* will save the financially troubled Allied Artists by grossing an expected three million plus.

July 30: Freed from the no-motorcycle clause in his contract that hog-tied him during the making of *Tickle Me*, Elvis and nine members of the Memphis Mafia roar out of a Harley dealership in LA with brand new bikes. Lamar Fike says the King called them "El's Angels."

August 2: At Radio Recorders in LA, Elvis lays down vocals for the *Paradise* soundtrack: *A Dog's Life, A House Of Sand, Datin', Drums Of The Islands, Paradise, Hawaiian Style, Queenie Wahine's Papaya, Sand Castles, Scratch My Back, Stop Where You Are* and *This Is My Heaven.*

August 5: Elvis touches down in Honolulu to make his third picture in paradise. It's another heavy location shoot, with lots of stunt work in the two helicopters featured in the film. Even with his fear of flying, Elvis is fascinated by the choppers and tours the island in his off-time.

August 7: Principal photography begins on *Paradise, Hawaiian Style.*

August 14: The LP of *Elvis For Everyone* enters the charts for a 27-week stay.

August 15: Elvis and the Colonel visit the *USS Arizona* at Pearl Harbor. The navy gives the group a personal tour and Elvis places wreaths at the base of the memorial. Elvis is presented an award to thank him for his work with the navy to preserve the *Arizona.*

August 17: *Paradise, Hawaiian Style* finishes its location shooting in Hawaii, and on his return to the mainland, Elvis signs another long-term deal with Hal B. Wallis.

August 24: Elvis begins shooting interiors for *Paradise* at Paramount Studios.

August 27: Elvis meets The Beatles when the Fab Four drop in at his LA home on Perugia Way, where they hang out for several hours singing and shooting the bull.

September: Elvis' contract with RCA is extended by Colonel Parker for another ten years. He also moves to a new LA address: 10550 Rocca Place in Bel Air. When *Paradise, Hawaiian Style* wraps, Elvis drives back to Memphis.

October 7: The caravan of Cadillacs and the Elvismobile wind their way up the drive at Graceland. The King is home.

October 9: Go-karts become the designated new toy at Graceland. Elvis can be seen by onlookers racing about the grounds.

October 13: Rumor has it that Elvis drove his go-kart off the grounds of Graceland wearing a burnoose and took a midnight ride down Highway 51.

November 3: Products with Elvis' name attached have sold more than $30,000,000 so far in 1965, though he's received only $60,000 in royalties.

November 13: The LP of *Harum Scarum* hits the charts, where it will remain for 23 weeks, peaking at #8.

November 24: *Harum Scarum* opens nationally to the usual mixed reviews.

December: Aside from his usual donations to local charities, Elvis gives an elderly woman a motorized wheelchair after he reads in the paper that hers had finally given out.

Whatever happened to be the current rage seemed to appear almost instantly at Graceland. When America was gripped by go-kart fever, Elvis outfitted the boys with souped-up, state-of-the-art machines. Without benefit of safety gear they tore up and down the grounds and driveways creating mini-Indy 500s. The noise was intense—as were the fumes—and it's not unlikely that once again many of the neighbors in this exclusive community were wondering if they should consider another part of town.

December 3: RCA releases *Blue Christmas/Santa Claus Is Back In Town*.

December 24: Elvis opens presents with his family at Graceland. The volume is huge and the event lasts most of the evening. The family also opens the hundreds of gifts Elvis gets annually from fans. Most items of value are donated to charity.

December 25: A quiet Christmas day at home.

December 29: It becomes clear that Elvis' favorite Christmas present is a miniature racing set from Priscilla. He and members of the Mafia spend hours racing the tiny cars in the den at Graceland. His fascination will grow along with the size of the track until the racing complex fills most of the room, and eventually a Trophy Room will be added to house the expanded track.

December 31: One of the Memphis papers gives a recap of Elvis' earnings for the year: *Harum Sacrum* – $1,000,000; *Frankie And Johnny* – $650,000; *Paradise, Hawaiian Style* – $350,000; *Tickle Me* – $850,000; RCA record royalties – $1,125,000; music publishing royalties – $400,000; merchandising royalties – $60,000. A Presley spokesman says the figure of $5.5 million in total income is close to accurate. A pretty good year, even for Elvis.

January 1: The first of many "fireworks fights" is held on the lawn at Graceland. The game is a strange one: Elvis and the boys dress up in football helmets and pads, then line up facing each other and fire away with Roman candles. The competition can go on for hours.

January 3: RCA announces that Elvis' total record sales jumped from 49.3 million in 1963 to 78 million by 1966.

1966
WILL YOU BE MINE?

January 8: Happy Birthday to Elvis. A day of celebration ends with a night of movie viewing at the Memphian Theater. More and more addicted to movies, Elvis watches constantly, sometimes until dawn, and the boys are expected to hang in with him. He'll watch certain films, like *Rebel Without A Cause*, so many times he knows the film line for line and will repeat dialogue along with the actors.

January 25: A local fan, Gary Pepper, collects several thousand names on a petition calling for the Memphis Coliseum to be renamed the Elvis Presley Coliseum.

January 30: A small gathering outside Graceland watches the Elvis-mobile and the caravan of Cadillacs pass through the gates and head west for Hollywood. Elvis will be starring in *Spinout*, his 22nd film.

February 21: Elvis is at MGM to cut his vocal tracks for *Spinout: Adam And Evil, All That I Am, Am I Ready, Beach Shack, I'll Be Back, Never Say Yes, Smorgasbord* and *Stop, Look, And Listen.*

February 23: Principal photography begins on *Spinout*. Crowd control for the racing scenes is difficult. Several young women narrowly escape injury when they rush the pit to get to Elvis as race cars approach at high speed. But no one is injured and the shoot continues.

March 13: Colonel Parker confirms a bulletin on the UPI wire that Elvis is the highest-paid entertainer in the world. And also the highest single taxpayer in the country.

March 30: *Frankie and Johnny* opens nationally.

April 23: The motorhome has been replaced by a converted Greyhound bus in which Elvis returns to Memphis after a nonstop drive from the coast. He is at the wheel the whole way.

April: Elvis spends several nights at the Fair Grounds Amusement Park, renting the place after closing and playing with his friends all night long.

May 25: At RCA Nashville, Felton Jarvis comes in to help produce, working with

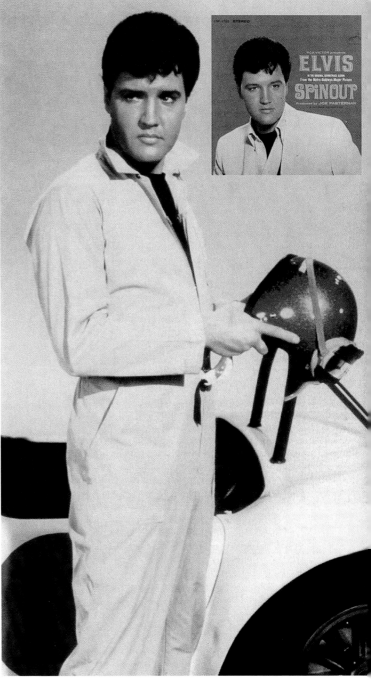

Spinout was Elvis' twenty-second film. His co-star was once again close friend Shelley Fabares. The racing shots were filmed on location and crowd control was difficult. A lapse in security almost caused a tragedy when fans broke through the barriers and rushed Elvis during a racing sequence. They were almost hit by fast cars turning a corner at high speed. Luckily no one was injured, Elvis signed a few autographs and shooting continued without incident.

Vernon's stepsons, David and Billy, visit the Circle G Ranch in Mississippi. When the horses started to overrun Graceland, Elvis bought a ranch near Tupelo to stable them. The Memphis Mafia and their families would join Elvis at the ranch to ride and hold rodeos. They spent so much time at the place that Elvis began buying pickup trucks and installing mobile homes on the grounds so everybody could stay overnight. Eventually, interest in the ranch waned and it was sold. Some of the horses were returned to Graceland. The new owners defaulted on payments, however, and the Circle G eventually came back to Elvis and Vernon. Vernon and Dee (below) loved to vacation at the house in Palm Springs.

Elvis to record stronger, better-written tunes. The sessions, which run through May 28th, produce: *Come What May, Down In The Alley, Fools Fall In Love, Love Letters* and *Tomorrow Is A Long Time.* And for the album *How Great Thou Art*: *By And By, Further Along, How Great Thou Art, If The Lord Wasn't Walking By My Side, In The Garden, Run On, So High, Somebody Bigger Than You And I, Stand By Me, Where Could I Go But To The Lord, Where No One Stands Alone* and *Without Him.*

June 9: *Paradise, Hawaiian Style* opens nationally to decent reviews. Elvis is improving as a comic actor, and even the critics are beginning to see it.

June 10: At RCA Nashville, Elvis cuts: *I'll Remember You, If Every Day Was Like Christmas* (written By Red West) and *Indescribably Blue.*

June 12: In a wagon train of Cadillacs and Lincolns, the Memphis Mafia heads out to Los Angeles to prepare the way for the King and the forthcoming shoot of *Double Trouble* for MGM. They're by themselves because Elvis, concerned for the health of his grandmother and his uncle Travis (a security guard at the main entrance to Graceland), will stay on in Memphis until the last minute.

June 26: Elvis flies to LA and goes directly to the recording studio in Culver City, spending the night laying tracks for *Double Trouble*: *Baby, If You'll Give Me All Your Love, City By Night, Could I Fall In Love, Double Trouble, I Love Only One Girl, It Won't Be Long, Long Legged Girl, Old MacDonald* and *There Is So Much World To See.*

June 29: Uncle Travis dies, but Elvis is unable to return for the funeral because of his shooting schedule.

July 11: Principal shooting begins on *Double Trouble* on the MGM lot in Culver City.

July 16: The LP of *Paradise, Hawaiian Style* hits the charts, where it will remain for nineteen weeks.

September 6: *Double Trouble* wraps.

September 12: Six days later, amazingly, Elvis begins principal photography on *Easy Come, Easy Go* at Paramount.

September 16: Vernon and Dee Stanley join Elvis in Los Angeles for several weeks and include some time at Elvis' place in Palm Springs.

September 28: Elvis is in the studio at Radio Recorders to tape the soundtrack for *Easy Come, Easy Go*: *Easy Come, Easy Go, I'll Take Love, Leave My Woman Alone, She's A Machine, Sing You Children, The Love Machine, Yoga Is As Yoga Does* and *You Gotta Stop.*

October 17: *Spinout* premieres at the Loew's State in Memphis—the same theater Elvis worked when he was in high school, and the same place where he slugged another usher who picked a fight with him.

October 31: In a typical Presley move, Elvis places a birthday call to seven-year-old Gina Williams, suffering from a malignant tumor at St.

Jude's Children's Hospital. That same day, *Easy Come, Easy Go* wraps and he goes to Palm Springs to spend some time with Vernon and Dee.

November 23: *Spinout* opens nationally to decidedly mixed reviews.

November 25: RCA ships *If Every Day Was Like Christmas/How Would You Like To Be.*

November 29: On their way back to Memphis from Los Angeles, Elvis and the gang stop out of town to wait for dark so the Christmas display and lighting at Graceland can be seen as they drive up.

December 12: Elvis makes his usual Christmas donation to local charities, but the amount is somewhat larger than usual: over $100,000.

December 14: Elvis takes a trip to the home of Gary Pepper and gives one of his biggest fans a brand new 1966 Chevrolet convertible.

December 17: George Klein of WHBQ-TV receives a visit from Elvis and the keys to a 1967 yellow Cadillac convertible.

December 24: Christmas Eve in Graceland.

December 25: Elvis announces his engagement to Priscilla in front of family and friends, presenting her with a large diamond engagement ring.

December 31: Celebrity gets in the way of a good time once again. The crowds are so huge at the gates of Graceland that you can hear them from the house, and Elvis is unable to attend his own New Year's party at the Manhattan Club in Memphis because the press has leaked the news and the place is so jammed that he can't find a parking place.

In Hollywood, Elvis (in his costume as a navy officer) and the Colonel accept an arthritis telethon award (above). Every Christmas, the front of Graceland was loaded with decorations and blazing with light. The sight drew thousands of onlookers every season. One year Elvis planned a return to Memphis from Los Angeles especially to arrive at the house after dark so he could see it with all the lights on. They reached the outskirts of Memphis earlier than expected and Elvis pulled the caravan into a rest stop where they waited several hours until the sun finally set.

1967
....
WEDDING BELLS RING

January: Elvis decides everyone should have a horse. He buys seventeen, one for Priscilla, one for each member of his family and one for each member of the inner circle. They are kept in the stables at Graceland and everybody rides the grounds, much to the delight of the fans who constantly surround his home.

January 2: Negotiations between Colonel Parker and Elvis result in a revised agreement between them, and for the next ten years—until December 31, 1976—they will split everything 50–50. It sounds bad for the King and too good to be true for the Colonel, but Parker says Elvis is his only client and he's got to make a living.

January 6: RCA releases *Indescribably Blue/Fools Fall In Love.*

January 8: This year there are 32 candles on Elvis' birthday cake.

February 9: With all the cars, tractors, go-karts, golf carts, motorcycles and the like, Graceland is becoming a little crowded, so Elvis decides to expand. He drives across the border into Mississippi, finds a 163-acre ranch near the town of Walls, and for about $300,000 becomes a gentleman rancher. He calls the place the Circle G, buys some prime stock and goes into the cattle business.

February 21: Elvis takes his brand-new Lear jet to Nashville to record songs for his next movie, *Clambake: A House That Has Everything, The Girl I Never Loved, Clambake, Confidence, Hey, Hey, Hey, How Can You Lose What You Never Had, Who Needs Money?* and *You Don't Know Me.*

February 22: Elvis buys another horse and names her Mare Ingram after the mayor of Memphis.

March 5: Elvis heads for Hollywood to begin *Clambake* for United Artists.

March 8: RCA releases the gospel album, *How Great Thou Art.*

March 10: Principal photography begins on *Clambake.* The set is closed down, however, when Elvis trips on an extension cord in his bathroom and hits his head on the bathtub. He suffers a minor concussion but is ordered by the studio to rest. The film is delayed for almost three weeks. He goes to Memphis.

In 1967, Elvis' dream finally came true. He and Priscilla were married in a private ceremony in Las Vegas on May 1, 1967. Family in the traditional Southern sense was very important to Elvis, and in Priscilla he was convinced he was marrying the girl of his dreams. After winning the approval of her family and waiting years for her to come of age, the moment had finally arrived. In typical Elvis fashion, the occasion involved a lot of complicated travel arrangements both for the fun of it and to keep the crowds of reporters and fans at bay.

DAVID STANLEY
ON ELVIS THE RANCHER:

When Elvis did something, it was all the way. If he had a ranch, we were all going to be ranchers. He set everybody up with cowboy outfits, horses, pickup trucks and all the western stuff you could imagine. The house on the property was too small for everybody to stay in, so Elvis went out and bought some pretty nice trailer houses for the fellas to live in with their wives or whatever. Pretty soon there was a line of trailer houses along one edge of the property. He bought horse trailers and cattle trailers. All of it, including the best prime beef cattle he could find. Of course, nobody knew how to take care of them, so he hired a man to do it. Elvis would rope and ranch until he got bored and then everybody would go back to Memphis. I don't know what happened to all those trailer houses in the end.

But he really and truly loved horses—from the time he was a kid in Mississippi—and when he was able to keep them they became a fixture at both Graceland and the Circle G. He would spend hours touring the grounds at Graceland. He bought enough stock that anyone who happened to be at Graceland would be able to mount up. I think he never felt better than the times he was riding. It must have given him some kind of peace. Riding those horses was one of the things he could do by himself and be happy. He later gave Mare Ingram to me.

March 22: *Easy Come, Easy Go* opens nationally. The reviews are actually pretty good.

March 25: *How Great Thou Art* hits the charts, where it will remain for 29 weeks.

March 27: Elvis returns to Hollywood and the *Clambake* shoot resumes.

April 1: The Beaulieus, along with Priscilla, visit LA to watch the filming.

April 5: *Double Trouble* opens nationally, and the reviews aren't so bad, especially for Elvis.

April 27: *Clambake* wraps.

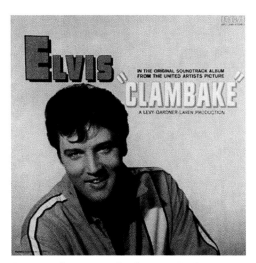

April 29: Elvis and Priscilla, along with Joe Esposito, others and their wives, fly to Palm Springs. There to meet them are Marty Lacker, Jerry Schilling and his wife, who have driven down earlier. Vernon and Dee have taken a plane from Memphis and joined them.

April 30: Priscilla's family arrives in Palm Springs and goes to the house. In Las Vegas, Colonel Parker calls a press conference for May 1 at 1:00 P.M. Rumors are rampant. Although everyone knows or at least guesses what it's about, none can be sure.

May 1: Elvis, Priscilla, and a small group fly out of Palm Springs in a rented jet for Las Vegas, arriving around 3:20 A.M., and the rest of the gang arrives later. Elvis, Priscilla and Joe go to the County Clerk's office by limo and get a marriage license, then pile back into the waiting limo and drive to the Aladdin Hotel, where they are married in a civil ceremony at 9:41 A.M. by a justice of the Nevada Supreme Court, David Zenoff. In attendance are best men, Joe Esposito and Marty Lacker, and the

LAMAR FIKE
ON ELVIS NOT LISTENING TO OTHER MUSIC:

Once Elvis really got going, he didn't listen to much other music. He definitely wasn't up on what was going on. That was odd to some folks, and Elvis knew that reaction, but he once told me, "If I listen to everybody else, it'll take the edge off of me."

The King and his Queen celebrate their wedding in a swirl of confetti. After flying to Palm Springs from Memphis in a chartered plane full of family and selected friends, Elvis and Priscilla went on to the Aladdin Hotel in Las Vegas where they were married by a Nevada Supreme Court Justice at 9:41 A.M. A breakfast followed immediately and the happy couple was off on a honeymoon in Palm Springs.

Marriage Certificate

405254

No. A 175632

that the undersigned JUSTICE DAVID ZENOFF

day of May A.D. 1967 join in lawful

ON PRESLEY

State of TENNESSEE

BEAULIEU

State of TENNESSEE

, in the presence of Joe Esposito

acker who were witnesses.

Zenoff

JUSTICE, SUPREME COURT OF NEVADA
(Sign this in official capacity.)

TO BE GIVEN TO THE RECORDER

The Stanley boys—Billy, Ricky and David—attend a special second wedding reception at Graceland (above) that Elvis held for family and friends who were unable to attend the wedding. For reasons that are not fully understood, Elvis failed to invite several members of the Memphis Mafia, including Red West, to the wedding itself. This oversight created strong tensions within the inner circle and a rift between two old friends that may have never been fully resolved.

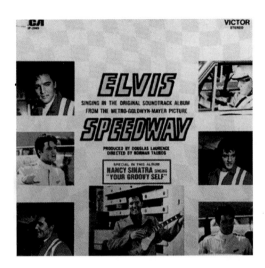

Elvis and Nancy Sinatra co-starred together in *Speedway*. Although cordial but never close to Frank Sinatra, Elvis struck up a friendship with Nancy that lasted throughout most of the rest of his life. Nancy frequently came to Vegas to catch her father's shows and Elvis' as well. She would join the King backstage to hang out and gossip. Elvis enjoyed the company of people who understood the demands of celebrity.

maid and matron of honor, Michelle Beaulieu and Joan Esposito. After the press conference is a lavish reception with a limited guest list. Along with the Beaulieus and Vernon and Dee, Priscilla and Elvis return to Palm Springs that afternoon to begin their honeymoon.

It's ironic that a moment Elvis considered one of the most important in his life is marred because some of his closest friends were not invited. Other members of the Memphis Mafia arrive after the ceremony is over. Red West, for one, is hurt and furious. The trust that existed between Elvis and this small group of loyal supporters is shattered. No satisfactory explanation is given, and it causes a rift that will take a long time to heal.

May 2: United Artists interrupts Elvis' honeymoon. Because of technical problems, he is forced to report to the studio and do some extra dubbing on *Clambake*.

May 4: Elvis, Priscilla and the various families return to Memphis.

May 5: Elvis and Priscilla take a motor tour around the countryside, stopping off at the Circle G.

May 7: The Presleys buy their first home in LA. Until this point Elvis has only rented. The imposing home, in Trousdale Estates, costs a reported $400,000.

May 24: Seven-year-old Kim Sparks of Hernando, Mississippi, is given a horse by the King because he's heard she watches them all ride at the ranch and it looks like such fun. Elvis personally delivers the pony to her door on her birthday.

May 29: Another wedding reception is held at Graceland mostly for the benefit of Grannie Minnie Presley, who was unable to come to Las Vegas, and other members of the family.

June 8: The staff at Graceland throws Priscilla a shower.

June 17: Elvis and Priscilla fly to Palm Springs.

June 19: At MGM, Elvis cuts the tracks for *Speedway: Five Sleepy Heads, He's Not Your Uncle He's Your Dad, Let Yourself Go, Speedway, Suppose, There Ain't Nothing Like A Song, Who Are You* and *Your Time Hasn't Come Yet Baby*.

June 24: The soundtrack album for *Double Trouble* hits the charts, where it will remain for 19 weeks.

June 26: Principal photography begins on *Speedway*.

July 13: The Presley family announces that Priscilla is expecting. The blessed event is scheduled for sometime in February 1968.

August 15: *Speedway* finishes shooting.

August 26: Elvis and Priscilla leave Vegas for Memphis, where they spend the next few weeks buying cars, motorcycles, bicycles and jewelry, riding horses, playing in the yard and relaxing at Graceland with the Memphis Mafia and the family.

September 10: Elvis jets to Nashville with Joe Esposito to cut some singles: *Big Boss Man, Guitar Man, High Heel Sneakers, Just Call Me Lonesome, Mine, Singing Tree, We Call On Him, You Don't Know Me* and *You'll Never Walk Alone*.

September 18: Vandals set fire to a Jeep parked in the rear at Graceland. Joe Esposito puts out the blaze.

September 19: Elvis has a fistfight with one of the yardmen at Graceland, Troy Ivy. Elvis says the man was drunk and loud. Ivy says Elvis is crazy and accuses him of trying to kill Vernon. No charges are filed.

September 29: Governor Buford proclaims September 29 Elvis Presley Day in the great state of Tennessee.

October 2: Elvis goes into the studio in Nashville to record the soundtrack for *Stay Away, Joe*: *All I Needed Was The Rain, Dominic* (unreleased), *Goin' Home, Stay Away* and *Stay Away, Joe.*

October 4: Elvis goes to LA for the filming of *Stay Away, Joe.*

October 9: Principal photography begins on *Stay Away, Joe* at MGM.

October 18: The cast and crew of *Stay Away, Joe* move to location in Arizona.

November 5: An auction of Elvis' personal effects is held at the Circle G Ranch. 2,000 people attend.

November 7: Vernon reports that someone has stolen a yellow go-kart from the grounds. Security will be beefed up.

There was always a wide variety of vehicles in the shed at Graceland. At any given time 30 or 40 cars, motorcycles, trucks, three wheelers and the like could be found on the grounds. Elvis continued during this time to crank out films such as *Stay Away, Joe,* in which he appeared with Joan Blondell (below).

November 18: *Stay Away, Joe* wraps in Arizona, and Elvis returns to LA.

November 19: RCA releases the LP of *Clambake.*

November 22: *Clambake* opens nationally to dismal reviews. It's becoming clear that the quality of scripts and songs is getting lower and lower. It's also clear that Elvis is becoming frustrated with doing mediocre films. No matter, the films continue to pay off at the boxoffice.

December 3: Elvis and the Colonel take to the airwaves, buying 30 minutes of time on 3,000 radio stations to say Merry Christmas.

December 7: They return from LA to Memphis for Christmas.

December 10: Priscilla gets a Cadillac Fleetwood limo from her husband.

December 25: The Presleys are in a stay-at-home mood, and Christmas is a quiet affair. No fireworks or hot-rodding around town.

December 31: New Year's Eve at Graceland. Priscilla is eight months pregnant, and the year ends on what would seem to be a peaceful and contented note. Although not as strong a year as 1965 or 1966, 1967 is important because it marks the last phase of Elvis' career in Hollywood. The fact is that Elvis is itchy to get back on the road: He wants to be in front of his fans instead of the camera. He's beginning to fear it's all slipping away. More and more dissatisfied, he needs the edge to keep that fire going. If he can't find it in his work, he'll find it somewhere else.

1968

THE KING IN TRANSITION

Elvis, looking fit and happy, is ready to say goodbye to the west coast. By 1968 he had made a personal decision to get back to doing what he liked: live performing. All that remained was to convince the Colonel and finish up his movie commitments. After almost 30 films, Elvis' dream of being an actor in the mold of James Dean had faded and died. He was sick and tired of Hollywood and looking for a change.

January: This is a quiet month, spent with Priscilla and the family at Graceland. The Presleys are expecting and Elvis wants to be there for the blessed event.

January 15: Elvis goes to Nashville, where he cuts *Too Much Monkey Business*. He will return on the 17th to do *U.S. Male*.

February 1: Priscilla goes into labor in the early morning hours, and Charlie Hodge drives her and Elvis to Baptist Memorial, arriving around 10:30 A.M. At 5:01 P.M. Priscilla gives birth to a baby girl, Lisa Marie Presley. She weighs six pounds, fourteen ounces and measures fifteen inches. Mother and daughter are both healthy and happy.

February 5: Priscilla and Lisa Marie are taken back to Graceland by the proud father in a stretch limo.

February 6: Nick Adams, one of Elvis' first friends in Hollywood, dies of an overdose in Los Angeles at age 37.

February 25: Elvis goes west to prepare for *Live a Little, Love a Little* at MGM.

February 28: Mother and daughter follow, with Joe Esposito at their side.

March 2: Despite the fact that *Elvis' Gold Records–Volume 4* is an almost total rehash of re-released recordings, it hits the charts and remains there for 22 weeks, reaching #33.

March 8: *Stay Away, Joe* opens nationally to, once again, dismal reviews—but once again the fans don't care.

March 11: Principal photography begins on *Live A Little, Love A Little*, and Elvis goes into the studio that same evening to cut the soundtrack at the Goldwyn Studios: *A Little Less Conversation, Almost In Love, Edge of Reality* and *Wonderful World*.

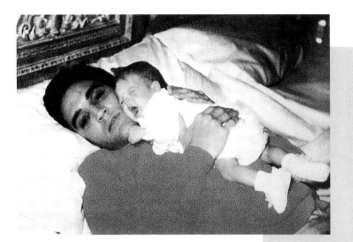

DAVID STANLEY

ON ELVIS' ENTOURAGE:

Elvis could never go anywhere alone, and he didn't want to. When Elvis went anywhere, the entourage always included at least a handful of people—bodyguards, valets and friends—very much like a Presidential motorcade.

ON ELVIS' SHOW BUSINESS FRIENDS:

Elvis didn't know a lot of stars, but a lot of stars knew him. That sounds weird, but it's true. Elvis and Tom Jones were friends. Tom would come over and they'd sing. Elvis loved the way he sang, he thought he was the best of the best. And vice versa. That was the basis of the relationship. They both had a healthy respect for each other.

He was also friends with Ann-Margret. Their friendship developed during the filming of Viva Las Vegas and lasted up until Elvis' untimely death. Ann and Roger Smith came to Elvis' funeral. But as far as hanging out with his peers, it just didn't happen. You know why he didn't associate with others in the business? He was intimidated by his inability to make conversation. He wasn't one to sit around and just talk to anybody. He had to know you, trust you. So he isolated himself. Hell, there were times Elvis made Howard Hughes look like a public person.

Lisa Marie Presley (above) brought a lot of love into Elvis' life. After the birth of their daughter, Elvis and Priscilla experienced some of the best times of their life together. Elvis was a doting father and life at Graceland centered around the new arrival. Elvis co-starred with Michele Carey (left) in *Live a Little, Love a Little*. The one constant in all of Elvis' movies was the parade of beautiful co-stars who played opposite him.

March 27: *How Great Thou Art* is gold record #42.

April 6: Elvis and Priscilla catch Tom Jones' act at the Flamingo in Vegas, and hang out in Jones' suite after the show. They head back to Los Angeles and Elvis returns to the studio to continue shooting the next day.

May 24: *Live A Little, Love A Little* wraps. Priscilla, Elvis and inner circle jet to Hawaii for some R&R.

May 25: Elvis shows up at the Karate Tournament of Champions in Honolulu. It's his first meeting with Mike Stone.

June: Elvis and Priscilla return to Los Angeles, where plans are under way for his first TV special, *Elvis*, on NBC. Although the show will be taped, it will be performed in front of a live audience and as such will be Elvis' first public appearance as a singer in over ten years.

June 12: *Speedway* premieres in Charlotte, North Carolina and opens nationally.

June 21: Final dress rehearsals for the special.

June 27: Taping begins. Elvis does two one-hour sessions in front of a live audience. He's extremely nervous, but the response is strong.

June 30: The special finishes taping in Burbank. It has been a grueling and difficult experience, but one that will prove so satisfying that there'll be no turning back. Elvis has rediscovered something he really loves: live performance.

July 1: Elvis and his group take a break in Palm Springs.

July 4: Elvis' 1964 Rolls Royce is put up for auction in Los Angeles. The proceeds will go to SHARE to benefit retarded children.

July 7: There is some confusion about the actual dates of the Goldwyn Studios recording session that produced *Charro*, the theme for the movie of the same name. It's possible that the instrumental tracks were laid down on this date and Elvis did the vocals on October 15. But it's also possible that the instrumentals were done earlier and that Elvis did the vocals on this date.

July 10: Elvis returns from Palm Springs to Los Angeles to prepare for the filming of *Charro*.

July 22: Elvis and members of the cast travel to Arizona to begin shooting *Charro* on location.

Looking cool and collected but in reality nervous about his first public concert in almost ten years (opposite), Elvis performs in his 1968 comeback TV special. His fears were unfounded. The magic was still there, the show was a smash and the King was back. He was clearly in his element during the live taping, doing what he did best, alone at the mike in front of adoring fans. The 1968 special marked the beginning of almost continuous touring for the next ten years. There were still commitments in Hollywood, but the die was cast and the next phase of Elvis' life was about to begin.

August 27: Location shooting completed in Arizona, the production moves back to Los Angeles for interiors, and will wrap for good in early September.

September: Elvis is beginning to have trouble with his throat. The tonsillitis that bothered him in Germany is coming back and, after the movie wraps, he goes immediately to Palm Springs for a rest.

September 6: A crank places two phone calls to Presley family members in Memphis saying that he has died in a plane crash in Kentucky.

September 15: RCA releases the single *Almost In Love/A Little Less Conversation*.

September 25: Elvis returns to Graceland after an eight-month absence. Laying back with Lisa and Priscilla and the guys, he does the usual things: movie watching, golf cart riding, target shooting, playing touch football in the yard and generally fooling around.

Lisa Marie Presley at age 10 months amuses herself with a close friend. Although Elvis was not one to change the diapers and deal with the day-to-day issues of raising a child, he was a devoted father and spent a lot time with Lisa Marie. Children liked Elvis, maybe because there was so much of the child in him.

September 28: Dewey Phillips, the DJ in Memphis who gave Elvis his first radio interview in 1954, dies. He was a close friend and business partner of Sam Phillips.

October 6: Johnny Smith, the uncle who got Elvis a job at Precision Tools in 1953 and is a security guard at Graceland, dies.

October 13: Elvis goes back to Los Angeles to shoot *The Trouble With Girls* at MGM.

October 14: The usual studio session at MGM to cut the soundtrack for *The Trouble With Girls: Almost, Aura Lee, Clean Up Your Own Back Yard, Signs Of The Zodiac* (duet With Marilyn Mason) and *Swing Down, Sweet Chariot*.

October 15: RCA releases *If I Can Dream/Edge of Reality*.

October 23: *Live A Little, Love A Little* opens nationally. The reviews are predictable, mostly bad.

October 28: *The Trouble With Girls* begins principal photography, shooting through November.

November 30: *If I Can Dream* rises higher on the charts, at #12, than any Elvis single since 1965.

December 3: *Elvis* is aired on NBC, with big ratings and favorable reviews. Elvis is euphoric and seems to feel the burden of nine years of bad films lifting from his shoulders. He's contracted for film work through the end of 1969, but at least there's light at the end of the tunnel.

December 16: *The Trouble With Girls* wraps.

December 19: The annual pilgrimage from LA to Memphis begins. Elvis, Priscilla and Lisa arrive at Graceland for the holidays.

December 21: The *Elvis* LP hits the charts, where it will remain for 32 weeks, reaching #8. It will be Elvis' first top-ten album in almost three years.

December 24: Christmas Eve at Graceland is especially lavish since it's little Lisa's first.

December 25: Vernon dons a Santa suit and entertains his granddaughter.

December 31: Elvis and Priscilla throw a New Year's bash at the Thunderbird Lounge, with 250 people invited. This year Elvis finds a place to park and the Presleys party hearty until very late.

DAVID STANLEY

ON CHRISTMAS AT GRACELAND:

When Elvis released his first Christmas album in 1957, some critics called it crass commercialization. They couldn't have been more wrong. When it came to Christmas, Elvis never grew up. The holiday season made him unabashedly sentimental, and no eight year old looked forward to December 25 with more excitement and anticipation than the King of Rock & Roll.

Purchasing Graceland gave him the opportunity to celebrate the holiday in style. The driveways and the main house were lined with blue lights, and in front were six 8-foot Christmas trees decorated in multicolored lights.

Inside, the mansion was also completely decked out for the season, with the focus on a huge Christmas tree in the dining room. After dinner, everyone would gather around the piano to sing Christmas carols.

Although Elvis loved to receive gifts, his favorite Christmas activity was giving. His friends normally got cash bonuses. The presents for family members ranged from jewelry to new cars. Elvis loved their reactions to his extravagances.

After most of the guests went to bed or went home, Elvis and a few of the guys would bring out Lisa Marie's presents and put them under the tree. The early morning hours of Christmas Day were very often the best times at Graceland. Elvis would talk about his mother and about the Christmases of his boyhood. He would often say something like, "I wonder what all the poor folks are doing tonight. I wish I could feed all the poor kids and give them presents." He would reflect on how grateful he was for his success. Then he would wait with the eagerness of a child for Lisa to awaken and find her presents under the tree.

Vernon is at Graceland to share her first Christmas with his only grandchild, Lisa Marie.

DAVID STANLEY

ON ELVIS GETTING READY FOR HIS VEGAS COMEBACK:

One thing that Elvis always did before doing a concert and major show was lie in the sun to get some color. I can remember many a time when he and Priscilla would go to the pool. Oftentimes, knowing how much I liked being around them, they would call me after school and say, "We're going swimming, get your suit on and come on over." This was always a thrill when I was a kid. After all, I was a hormone with feet and I thought Priscilla looked great in a bikini.

ON ELVIS AND BARBRA STREISAND:

That summer of '69 I was fourteen and deeply committed to Led Zeppelin. And now, all of a sudden, we're in Las Vegas, not exactly counter-culture territory, getting ready for Elvis' big comeback and about to face what I thought would be the ultimate bore, Barbra Streisand. This is something I would have never done on my own at that time in my life. Elvis made me go. He said I needed to be cultured. Two songs into her performance, I was star-struck. She was wonderful. I thank Elvis for exposing me to that beautiful voice.

ON ELVIS SINGING "HEY JUDE":

I was a big Beatles fan, but Elvis wasn't. He felt their music tried to promote an anti-establishment generation, and as we all know, it did. So when he sang Hey Jude, that was a complete surprise to me. I guess he was feeling a little mistreated by The Beatles' massive success and thought if Hey Jude worked for them, then maybe it would work for him. In this case, he was wrong. I've never heard a worse rendition of a Paul McCartney song. Hey, nobody's perfect.

January 8: Elvis celebrates his birthday at Graceland.

January 13: At American Studios, Elvis does his first recording session in Memphis since his work at Sun with Sam Phillips in 1955. The hours are long, the pace relentless, and Elvis comes down with a fever, then goes through another bout of tonsillitis. He will be forced to postpone the rest of the session for several days. But the four all-night sessions produce: *A Little Bit Of Green, Come Out, Come Out* (unreleased), *Don't Cry Daddy, Gentle On My Mind, I'm Movin' On, Inherit The Wind, Long Black Limousine, Mama Liked The Roses, My Little Friend, Poor Man's Gold* (unreleased), *This Is The Story, Wearin' That Loved On Look* and *You'll Think Of Me.*

January 20: Elvis returns to the studio to finish the scheduled songs: *From A Jack To A King, Hey Jude, I'll Be There, I'll Hold You In My Heart, In The Ghetto, Memory Revival, Rubberneckin', Suspicious Minds* and *Without Love.*

January 25: Elvis, Priscilla, Vernon, Dee and members of the Memphis Mafia fly to Aspen to hit the slopes.

February 1: Lisa Marie celebrates her first birthday in Aspen.

February 15: The family returns to Memphis so that Elvis can fulfill another recording commitment, and on the 17th he's back at American Studios for six more nights to cut: *After Loving You, And The Grass Won't Pay No Mind, Any Day Now, Do You Know Who I Am, If I'm A Fool, It Keeps Right On A-Hurtin', Kentucky Rain, Memory Revival* (unreleased), *Only The Strong Survive, Power Of My Love, Stranger In My Own Home Town, The Fair's Movin' On, True Love Travels On A Gravel Road* and *Who Am I?*

This amazing series of sessions in January and February of 1969 will produce three singles that will sell over a million copies each and two gold albums. Elvis is involved in every aspect of the recording process and is almost as much of a producer in these sessions as Felton Jarvis. By all accounts, he's all business in the studio, the glue that holds it all together and keeps things moving. His stamina is probably unmatched in recording history.

February 26: Elvis and Priscilla and friends return to Aspen. Meanwhile, in Las Vegas, history is being made by Colonel Parker and the manager of the as yet unfinished International Hotel. They sign an agreement that will bring Elvis back to Vegas for month-long engagements starting in July of 1969. It marks the beginning of a series of record-setting tours and concerts that will run from now until Elvis' death in 1977.

March 5: Elvis returns to Hollywood and goes into the studio at Universal to cut the soundtrack for *Change Of Habit: Change Of Habit, Have A Happy, Let Us Pray, Let's Be Friends* and *Let's Forget About The Stars.*

On July 26, 1969, Elvis opened big at the International Hotel in Las Vegas. He was in the best shape of his life, looking great and having a ball. The fan response was terrific and it was clear that the King was back in his element. The seven-week engagement broke house records, drawing over 100,000 people and grossing a cool 1.5 million dollars.

DAVID STANLEY

ON WATCHING ELVIS' OPENING SHOW:

I never considered Elvis a Rock & Roll star. He was my big brother. Man, I didn't even care too much for his movies. To me they were so hokey. So I go to his opening concert that night with less than high expectations and less than an open mind. It was the second time I'd ever seen him perform. The first didn't count because I was five years old. It was 1961 at Ellis Auditorium in Memphis. Elvis started singing and the fans rushed the stage, and I thought they were trying to kill him. I cried my eyes out, and my mother had to take me out of there. But this second performance was the second time in two nights that I was totally laid out. First by the mellow voice of Streisand and then the power of the boy who dared to rock. When he came out onto that stage, man, he was <u>dangerous</u>. Lord, what a performance he gave. The people just went nuts. And afterwards I went backstage, my eyes as big as pizza platters, and said, "God, almighty, Elvis, that was unbelievable." And he looked at me and said, "David, that's why they call me the King of Rock & Roll."

ON ELVIS AS NUMBER ONE:

The Beatles, The Stones, Led Zeppelin, Crosby, Stills, Nash and Young were all dominating the American music scene. I remember Elvis telling me that night he found out that his own "Suspicious Minds" had gone number one. He said "David, I been wrong for so long, but I'm right tonight."

ON THE MANSON SCARE:

About a week or so after Elvis' historic opening at the International, Priscilla, my mother and my two older brothers Billy and Ricky and I flew back to L.A. to spend some time. Priscilla stayed at her and Elvis' home in Beverly Hills while my mother and two brothers and I stayed at the Beverly Wilshire Hotel.

On the morning of August 9, Billy, Ricky and I were watching the news and it came out that Charles Manson had massacred all those people up in the hills the night before. And a second later, the phone rang. It was Vernon, saying, "Security's on their way up. Elvis says to pack your things now. We're leaving."

We rushed out of that hotel and were driven under armed guard to the airport. There we were met by Priscilla and Lisa, and we all boarded the Christina, a DH 125 jet owned by Frank Sinatra, and flew to Las Vegas.

We were all surprised at Elvis' reaction: I mean, what did Charles Manson have to do with us? Then we found out later that Elvis was on Manson's hit list, and we realized he was right.

March 7: Principal photography begins for *Change Of Habit* at Universal Pictures.

March 13: *Charro* opens nationally to dismal reviews.

April 15: RCA releases *In The Ghetto/Any Day Now.*

May 2: *Change Of Habit* wraps. It's Elvis' 29th picture—and his last feature.

May 3: *In The Ghetto* cracks the top ten, his first single since *Crying In The Chapel* in 1965.

May 4: Elvis, Priscilla and the inner circle go to Hawaii without Lisa Marie.

May 13: The Presleys catch Tom Jones' show at the Ilikai Hotel.

May 18: Elvis and Priscilla return to Los Angeles.

May 21: Elvis sells the Circle G to a gun club. The horses will move back to the stables at Graceland.

June 10: Elvis goes to Las Vegas to inspect the work on the International Hotel and then flies on to Los Angeles for costume fittings.

June 14: His *Elvis In Memphis* album hits the charts, where it will remain for 34 weeks and peak at #13.

June 21: Costumes for his opening in Vegas are satisfactory and Elvis returns to Memphis, where he will relax and prepare to go into rehearsal for the July opening.

July 5: Elvis flies to Los Angeles to begin rehearsals, also hitting the gym for daily physical workouts. He hires the band and backup singers, selects the music and goes to work.

July 12: Elvis makes the cover of *Rolling Stone*. It's all part of the hype for his upcoming Vegas engagement.

July 25: Elvis, family and friends attend Barbra Streisand's closing night at the International in Vegas.

July 26: Elvis opens at the International Hotel. After two dress rehearsals in the afternoon, he does a special show at 10 P.M. for an invited audience of celebs and press. With the house full of friends, the show goes nervously but well. Elvis is ready. He's come a long way since his disastrous gig at the Frontier in 1956. The shows are great. The King is back.

August 1: The public shows begin, and Elvis gets into the swing of daily performance. He'll do two shows a night, seven nights a week, the first at 8:15 (a dinner show), the second at midnight for drinks only. As always, the first two shows are sold out.

August 17: NBC-TV reruns *Elvis.*

August 22: RCA sets up shop in the International Hotel ballroom, and a mobile recording studio is put into place to tape the proceedings. They will tape each show, each night, for the remainder of the engagement, pick the best takes and put them together to create new LP releases. The first album will be called *From Memphis To Vegas/From Vegas To Memphis.*

August 27: The album from the *Elvis* TV special goes gold.

August 28: The first gig in Vegas ends. The show has broken records, the total attendance is estimated at 101,509 and the gross is $1,530,000. Elvis is back in a big way.

August 29: Elvis, Priscilla, Vernon and Dee stay over to catch Nancy Sinatra's opening in Vegas. They go to a party given by Old Blue Eyes himself to celebrate his daughter's debut.

August 30: Elvis and Priscilla return to Palm Springs.

September 3: *The Trouble With Girls* opens nationally.

September 13: The single of *Suspicious Minds* hits the charts, reaches #1 and remains there for 13 weeks.

September 23: The Presleys return to Memphis, where they will give instructions to the decorators about giving Graceland a makeover during their vacation.

October 5: It's off to Honolulu: Elvis and Priscilla, along with Patsy and Gee Gee Gamble and others, share a private house on Oahu for three weeks.

October 11: Elvis and Priscilla meet Vernon and Dee and catch a show at the Surf Lanai Lounge in the Queen's Surf Hotel.

October 12: Trading sunsets, Elvis and Priscilla fly to an estate on Nassau in the Bahamas.

October 29: Mr. and Mrs. Presley return to Los Angeles.

November 1: *Suspicious Minds* hits #1. It will be Elvis' last Hot 100 #1 single.

November 10: *Change Of Habit* opens nationally. It's one of the straightest roles Elvis has played, and he's given credit for his ease and grace in the part. Maybe the critics are sensing the relief he feels, knowing he's finally getting off the movie treadmill.

November 16: RCA releases *From Memphis To Vegas/From Vegas To Memphis* to great prerelease reviews.

November 29: *From Memphis To Vegas/From Vegas To Memphis* hits the charts, where it will remain for 24 weeks, reaching #12.

December 10: *Suspicious Minds* goes gold, making it #48.

December 18: The Presleys return to Memphis.

December 25: Christmas at Graceland. Lisa Marie is the center of attention and Vernon does a reprise as Santa.

December 31: Elvis hosts his annual New Year's bash at T.J.'s, a local hangout.

The Colonel had a knack for turning any occasion into a publicity stunt, even Christmas. The traditional Presley/Parker Christmas card was Parker in a Santa suit posing with an elfish Elvis.

LAMAR FIKE
ON BOBBY DARIN:

Bobby Darin, who wrote I'll Be There, had a talent for imitating Elvis' singing style. He was so damn good at it that RCA would get him into the studio before Elvis had a session and have him cut sides so Elvis could listen and get some ideas as to how to sing a particular song. You could close your eyes when you listened to the tracks and almost think that Bobby was Elvis.

1970
MOVIN' ON

Elvis helped design an expensive series of white jumpsuits to wear during his second gig in Vegas for a variety of reasons. Based on 19th century Victorian fashions that he had seen in a book, they were unique, comfortable and, for the most part, flattering. Fluctuations in his weight were easier to conceal and he didn't have to think about what he was going to wear. They were a big hit with his fans and soon became as much his trademark in the 1970s as his satin jackets were in the 1950s. There were usually at least two of each of the different styles in case one ripped or got damaged. Whether people liked them or not, and most of his fans did, they never forgot them. The image of Elvis in his heavily jeweled and decorated costumes was and is what showmanship is all about.

January 13: Elvis flies from Memphis to Los Angeles to begin rehearsal for his second gig at the International Hotel in Las Vegas.

January 19: Elvis and the crew head for Vegas.

January 26: The month-long engagement opens to another star-studded audience. As will become the norm, there is one show on opening night followed by a reception. The show goes well and the crowd is enthusiastic.

January 27: Elvis goes back into his routine of two appearances a night—a dinner show and a midnight one. But he's not feeling well and throughout the month he won't be able to shake a sore throat and congestion problems.

February 16: RCA moves in recording equipment and begins to tape the shows. The engineers feel the best work will come after the show has settled in. They will record through the 23rd, and the best takes will appear in *On Stage – February 1970*.

February 23: Elvis closes in Vegas, with the final performance highlighted by Priscilla's appearance on stage at the end.

February 24: Colonel Parker and the advance men arrive in Houston to prepare for Elvis' concerts at the Astrodome.

February 25: Elvis arrives in Houston late in the evening and after a press conference retires to his hotel.

February 27: Elvis does two shows at the Astrodome, but the band has equipment problems and the sound is faulty, creating some tension during the performances.

February 28: Elvis does two more shows, both without a hitch. The attendance breaks records and so does the gate.

March 1: The final two shows at the Astrodome. Total attendance: almost 210,000. The promoters are in heaven. Elvis gets several more gold records from RCA and a gold watch from the promoters at a party after the final show.

DAVID STANLEY
ON THE ASTRODOME CONCERTS:

Mom, Vernon, my two brothers Billy and Rick and myself spent the weekend in Houston and attended all the concerts at the Astrodome. It was one thing to see Elvis perform in a 2000-seat showroom in Vegas, but now here he was in front of 44,000 screaming fans. It was during this weekend that I actually realized that my big brother Elvis Presley was the biggest entertainer in the world.

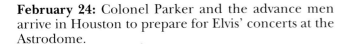

Even by Elvis' standards, this six-door Mercedes limo (now on display at Graceland) was pretty special. If there was an option lacking in this most fantastic of automobiles, even Elvis didn't need it. (Below) Of all of Elvis' passions, Lisa Marie was his singular pride and joy. He'd call her "Buttonhead" and "Yisa," and would name his jet airplane after her. She would later become the sole heir in Elvis' will.

March 2: Elvis, Priscilla and friends return to Palm Springs.

March – April: Elvis splits his time between LA, Palm Springs and Las Vegas. And he purchases a Mercedes limo with six doors.

May: Elvis makes frequent trips to Vegas, sometimes with Priscilla, to catch lounge acts and visit with friends like Tom Jones.

May 24: Elvis gives Priscilla a surprise party for her 25th birthday. It's a real down-home affair with homemade ice cream and good clean fun.

May 26: The Presleys leave Palm Springs and return to Memphis.

June 4: At RCA Nashville, Elvis enters the studio for a five-day, 34-song marathon: *Bridge Over Troubled Water, Cindy Cindy, Faded Love, Funny How Time Slips Away, Got My Mojo Working, Heart Of Rome, How The Web Was Woven, I Really Don't Want To Know, I Was Born About 10,000 Years Ago, I Washed My Hands In Muddy Water, I'll Never Know, I've Lost You, If I Were You, It Ain't No Big Thing, It's Your Baby, You Rock It, Just Pretend, Life, Little Cabin On The Hill, Love, Love Letters, Make The World Go Away, Mary In The Morning, Only Believe, Patch It Up, Stranger In The Crowd, Sylvia, The Fool, The Next Step Is, The Sound Of Your Cry, There Goes My Everything, This Is Our Dance, Tomorrow Never Comes, Twenty Days And Twenty Nights, When I'm Over You* and *You Don't Have To Say You Love Me.*

June 20: *On Stage – February 1970* hits the charts, reaching #13 and remaining for 20 weeks.

July 5: Elvis heads for LA and rehearsal for his August engagement at the International Hotel. Film crews from MGM shoot the rehearsals to use in his next movie, a performance film called *Elvis – That's The Way It Is.*

August 10: Elvis opens at the International. It's his third year in Vegas, and the gig is now hyped as the Elvis Summer Festival. The pattern is the same: The opening is a single show followed by a reception, and the remainder of the run is two shows a night. Elvis introduces his trademark one-piece jumpsuits in white or black with gold trim. MGM catches it all on camera and RCA tapes every show looking for material to use in future albums.

August 14: Far from the glitz of Las Vegas, a paternity suit is filed in Los Angeles Superior Court by Patricia Parker, claiming Elvis is the father of her child.

August 22: *Elvis: Worldwide 50 Gold Hits – Volume 1* hits the charts, where it will remain for 22 weeks.

August 26: Elvis is threatened with kidnapping at the International, and the next day Colonel Parker's office takes a call saying that Elvis will be abducted sometime during the weekend.

August 28: In Los Angeles, Joe Esposito's wife receives a call saying that unless they come up with $50,000 cash Elvis will be killed by a crazy man. The next night, security is beefed up for both shows, but nothing happens.

August 31: Lisa Marie and Priscilla fly to Vegas and spend the last week of the gig with Elvis.

September 7: Elvis closes out in Vegas. For the last night, a third show is added around 3:00 A.M. because of the hundreds who have been turned away.

September 9: Elvis embarks on his first concert tour since 1958. It starts in Phoenix with a full-house performance at Veteran's Memorial Coliseum. He is so tired that he lies down on the stage during the show—but the crowd loves it.

September 10: Keil Auditorium, St. Louis—13,000 paid admissions.

September 11: Olympia Arena, Detroit—16,000 jammed to the rafters.

September 12: Miami Beach Convention Center—two shows at 12,000 fans each.

September 13: Curtis Hixon Hall, Tampa—15,000 over two shows. Elvis jumbles the lyrics of *In The Ghetto* and gets a case of the giggles that he cannot overcome, and the show has to stop until he composes himself.

September 14: Municipal Auditorium, Mobile—11,000 packed in for the last gig.

A 1970 family portrait shows the Presley family shortly after Elvis completed another extremely successful concert series. Elvis looks rested and happy as do Lisa Marie and Priscilla. Looks are slightly deceiving, however. Tensions between Priscilla and Elvis are beginning to surface. A happy extended family: the Memphis Mafia displaying law enforcement badges various local authorities would bestow upon Elvis and friends. (Back row, l to r) Billy Smith, Bill Morris, Lamar Fike, Jerry Schilling, Roy Nixon, Vernon Presley, Charlie Hodge, Sonny West, George Klein, Marty Lacker; (Front row, l to r) Dr. Nichopoulos, Elvis, Red West.

DAVID STANLEY
ON ELVIS AS A NARC:

The day Elvis went to see Nixon was the first day I ever got high on pot. I was sixteen, riding around with my brothers Ricky and Billy, and we got really buzzed. Ricky left to go somewhere else, and Billy and I went back to Graceland.

Riding up the driveway, we were wondering whether Elvis was home yet. He'd gone to Washington, D.C. to meet with the President. We were really curious about what went down at the meeting. "This ought to be really neat," I remember saying to Billy. "Let's see what Nixon had to say." So we go up to the house, but the closer I got the more self-conscious I felt about being stoned. By the time I hit the door, I was hoping Elvis wasn't home. I didn't want him to see me that way. I was over-amped.

Inside the house, there's Lamar, so I know Elvis is back. And the intercom system rings, it's Elvis: "Billy, David, upstairs. Now!" I'm thinking, Oh, no. My eyes look like Jersey roadmaps. I'm wasted out of my mind. We go upstairs and Elvis calls us into his office.

He's sitting behind his desk. "What are you boys doin'?"

"Nothing," I say, scared to death. I don't know where this is going.

Elvis stands up and he's wearing this long, black leather coat, a cane, the whole outfit he was wearing when he met Nixon—and he pulls out this badge. "You know what this is, don't you?"

I thought I was gonna die. I thought we were busted. The first time I smoke pot—and I get busted by Elvis Presley. Half of me is freaked and half of me wants to laugh. So I said, "What is that, Elvis?"

"It's a United States federal narcotics badge."

"Where'd you get it?"

"President Nixon."

I couldn't help myself, I just had to mess with him, so I said, "Did you buy it from him?"

"That's not funny, David. Damn it, no! He gave it to me. And I want to tell you, we're gonna stop this drug trafficking in this country. I'm tired of John Lennon talking about drugs. I'm tired of this free-spirited crap. I'm tired of all these drugs. They're destroying our youth. They're demoralizing our country. Young people are going straight to hell because of these Rock & Roll stars."

And I'm thinking, well, hell, you started Rock & Roll. And you may not smoke pot, but you sure as hell eat amphetamines and sleeping pills like they were candy. But I didn't say that, that would have been a classic bad call.

So he went on talking: "We've all got to band together to stop this. I'm a duly deputized U.S. federal narcotics officer directly linked to the President of the United States. And you two guys are my ears and my eyes at Hillcrest High School." And believe me, Elvis was as serious as a heart attack. He was not fooling around.

"Excuse me," I said. "I'm your eyes and ears?" I mean picture this, it's 1970, I'm a teenager with hair halfway down my back. And Elvis stares at me and says, "Nixon told me to tell you that you will report directly to me."

Now I'm starting to get worried. Me, an undercover narc at Hillcrest. I'd last a day before getting the crap beaten out of me. "Elvis," I said, "this is impossible. They'll kill me."

"You'll be put under the Federal Witness Protection Program."

"But..."

"Just do it!"

So he gave us all these instructions: When you see something, call me on this line and I'll call the President directly... blah, blah. "We'll stop this mess in the U.S. and we'll start in Memphis."

Billy and I finally get out of there, go out of the house and get about halfway down the steps and we just sit down and start crying, we're laughing so hard. We are rolling on the ground, like to die laughing.

But the next day, Elvis is in the backyard with every kinda gun made: Thompson submachine guns, .45s, .357s, Pythons, fully automatic M-16s, M-14s. I mean, this guy is a walking arsenal. And he sets up a gun range. Silhouettes. Big wooden cross ties put up. And just to the right of this wonderful homemade range

was a three-hundred gallon fuel tank. It's a miracle that a stray didn't hit that sucker and just blow us all to Cleveland. Not to mention the fact that this is a residential neighborhood. So we've got a war goin' on here, and the phones were ringing off the wall. You know, the cops tend to come around when you go into your backyard with a .45 caliber-type Thompson submachine gun thundering away.

So Elvis is out there with his guns, and his full costume—complete with wraparound sunglasses and the cape—and he's just blasting away, you know, killing imaginary bad guys. Like hippie dopers.

I turn to Billy and say, "I think he's serious about this narc shit."

It was a while before we began to realize he was even more serious than we thought. Because all of a sudden John O'Grady, Elvis' personal private investigator and crime expert, flies into town. And Elvis tells him, "John, I want you to make sure that Billy and Ricky and David are covered, I don't want anything to happen to them." And we realize O'Grady is supposed to be our protection while we're ferreting out drug villains at Hillcrest High.

I told John, "This ain't gonna happen. We ain't doing it." And John kinda just nodded his head, and we all played along in front of Elvis. But he stayed serious about our undercover work for a good, long time. Every day we'd come home from school and over the intercom would come: "To the house. Report to me." So we'd troop into his office. "You see anything?" he'd ask.

"Not today, Elvis," we'd say.

"Well, keep at it."

Elvis was serious.

September 15: Elvis returns to Memphis and goes into seclusion at Graceland. The word is exhaustion.

September 22: At RCA Nashville, Elvis goes into the studio and records: *Rags To Riches, Snowbird, Where Did They Go Lord* and *Whole Lotta Shakin' Goin' On.*

September 24: Elvis, Priscilla and the entourage go to Las Vegas to hang out and see some shows.

October 11: Elvis is sworn in as a Special Deputy Sheriff of Bel Air, California. He has made a hobby of talking local police chiefs into swearing him in and giving him a shield and ID. He carries the badges around in a briefcase.

October 13: Elvis returns to Memphis.

October 18: Elvis returns to Los Angeles to prepare for another tour.

November 10: Oakland Coliseum, Oakland—14,000 screaming fans.

November 11: *Elvis – That's The Way It Is* opens nationally. And at his live show in Portland's Memorial Coliseum, 11,800 rush the gates.

November 12: The Coliseum, Seattle—15,000 adoring fans.

November 13: Cow Palace, San Francisco—14,300 contented fans.

November 14: The Forum, Los Angeles—37,398 for two shows. That same day, Elvis is served with papers in the paternity suit filed by Patricia Parker.

November 15: International Sports Arena, San Diego—14,659 crowd the gates.

November 16: State Fair Grounds, Oklahoma City—11,000 Sooners in attendance.

November 17: Denver Coliseum—12,000 rowdy fans bring the tour to a rollicking conclusion.

November 18: Elvis flies back to Los Angeles.

December 3: Elvis meets with LAPD Chief Edward M. Davis and presents him with a custom-made Colt .45 and a check for $7,000 earmarked for the community relations fund to buy clothes and toys for needy children. He insists that the donation be made without publicity.

December 12: The album of *Elvis – That's The Way It Is* hits the charts, where it will remain for 23 weeks.

December 16: Elvis goes on the offensive in paternity suit with Particia Parker. His lawyers file a cross complaint alleging that the suit is an attempt to extort money from Presley. He denies paternity and he denies that he slept with her. He requests $1,000 in damages and $1 in court costs.

December 19: Beginning a few of the strangest days in his life, Elvis buys a ticket at Memphis International Airport—using the name John Burroughs—boards a commercial airliner and goes to Washington, D.C., checks into the Washington Hotel, but then returns almost immediately to the airport and boards the next plane for Los Angeles.

Going back to his eleventh birthday when the country boy wanted a .22 caliber rifle to his days in the army, Elvis always had a bond with law enforcement and guns. His collection of police badges was very impressive—some were honorary, some were real. By 1970 Elvis had become obsessed with law enforcement and what he saw as the decline of American morals and values. Even though his own drug use was increasing steadily, he felt it was his duty to come out against the corruption of modern youth. Elvis was so flamboyant in his dress and lifestyle it is easy to forget that his values were those of the conservative rural south.

DAVID STANLEY

ON ELVIS ON STAGE:

I think Elvis might have been happiest when he was on stage. He was in his element. He knew he was good, knew he could control an audience. He loved to make people happy. Elvis was very genuine about his love for people. That must sound strange, because he was practically a recluse. Maybe because he had such trouble forming close relationships with individuals, he transferred his natural affection for people to groups of people, where he knew he could communicate, knew he could connect.

President Richard Nixon and Elvis Presley shaking hands in the Oval Office after the King had been sworn in as a federal narcotics officer is the culmination of one of the strangest and most ironic events in modern American history.

DAVID STANLEY
ON ELVIS' POLITICS:

One of the few things that has not been discussed about Elvis Presley was his political agenda. When Elvis met President Nixon in 1970, he had a genuine concern for America and its youth. He was a true conservative who loved his country. He didn't care too much for the Jane Fondas, the Angela Davises and the John Lennon types. He was wholeheartedly concerned about the influence these kinds of people had on the American public. Elvis was a former army sergeant himself, and he loved and respected all veterans and was always thankful for their sacrifice. Any music that degraded our country, he disliked immensely. He never tried to project in his music or his films anything that would be a disgrace to the country or its fundamental moral standards. As controversal as Elvis was, his beliefs were simple and traditional.

As the father now of two sons myself, I respect the fact that Elvis cared enough to go to the President personally and offer his services as a federal narcotics agent. Even though his own personal battle with prescription drugs shortened his life, Elvis never took illegal drugs himself. Today at 38 years of age and finally drug-free myself, I look back at that historic meeting between Elvis and Nixon and I'm thankful that the President encouraged him to influence many to make the right choices for themselves. If you're still wondering where Elvis stood on the political scale, I believe he would have said mega-dittos to Rush Limbaugh.

December 20: Elvis arrives early in the morning and goes directly to his house, where he grabs Jerry Schilling and Sonny West, heads back to the airport, boarding a flight back to D.C. with Schilling and George Murphy, a California senator, in tow. This time he's traveling under the name of his character in *Change of Habit*, Dr. John Carpenter. En route, he takes a pad and paper and begins to write.

December 21: Arriving in Washington at 6:30 A.M., Elvis rents a limo and goes to the White House, where he delivers the letter he has written on the plane requesting a meeting with the President. The guard takes the letter, and Elvis heads back to the hotel with Jerry and Sonny. Senator Murphy phones the FBI and uses his connections to get Elvis an appointment to visit the Bureau of Narcotics and Dangerous Drugs. A deputy director named John Finlator calls the hotel and makes an appointment with Elvis. Dressed in a purple velvet suit with a gold belt, Elvis arrives in a limo and asks Finlator for a federal narcotics badge. When Finlator refuses, Elvis returns to the hotel with Schilling. Sonny West, fresh from Memphis, is waiting at the hotel. Nixon's office calls and says Nixon will see him. The three men hop back in the limo and head for the White House. Elvis is ushered into the Oval Office and after a little chitchat says that he wants to help in the war on drugs and asks Nixon for a federal narcotics agent badge and ID. Nixon picks up the phone and tells someone to get them from Finlator. Elvis is sworn in and returns to Memphis on a chartered jet.

December 25: A quiet Christmas at Graceland.

December 28: Sonny West marries Judy Morgan, with Elvis as best man and Priscilla the matron of honor.

December 30: Elvis goes back to Washington to visit FBI headquarters. He and former Shelby County Sheriff William Morris are given an extended tour, but they don't get to meet J. Edgar Hoover.

December 31: The gang returns to Memphis and a party at T.J.'s.

Dear Mr. President:

First I would like to introduce myself. I am Elvis Presley and admire you and Have Great Respect for your office. I talked to Vice President Agnew in Palm Springs 3 weeks ago and expressed my concern for our country. The Drug Culture, The Hippie Elements, The SDS, Black Panthers, etc do not consider me as their enemy or as they call it The Establishment. I call it America and I Love it. Sir I can and will be of any Service that I can to help the country out. I have no concern or Motives other than helping the country out. So I wish not to be given a title or an appointed position. I can and will do more good if I were made a Federal Agent at Large, and I will help best by doing it my way through my communication with people of all ages. First and Foremost I am an

entertainer but all I need is the Federal Credentials. I am on this Plane with Sen. George Murphy and We have been discussing the problems that our Country is faced with. So I am Staying at the Washington Hotel Room 505-506-507 - 2 have 2 men who work with me by the name of Jerry Schilling and Sonny West. I am registered under the Name of Jon Burrows. I will be here for as long as it takes to get the credentials of a Federal agent. I have done an in depth study of Drug Abuse and Communist Brainwashing Techniques and I am right in the middle of the whole thing, where I can and will do the most good. I am Glad to help just so long as it is kept very Private. You can have your staff or whomever call me anytime today tonight or Tomorrow. I was nominated this coming year one of America's Ten most outstanding young men. That will be in January 18 in my Home Town of Memphis Tenn. I am sending you the short autobiography about myself so you can better understand this

approach. I would Love to meet you just to say hello if you're not to Busy.

Respectfully
Elvis Presley

P.S. I believe that you Sir were one of the Top Ten outstanding Men of America also.

I have a personal gift for you also which I would like to present to you and you can accept it or I will keep it for you until you can take it

WASHINGTON HOTEL) PHONE ME 85900
RM 505-506-
UNDER THE NAME
OF JON BURROWS

PRIVATE AND CONFIDENTIAL

Atten. President Nixon
Via Sen George Murphy
from
Elvis Presley

The motives and outcome of Elvis' famed meeting with President Nixon are only now becoming more clear. It seems Elvis had a genuine concern for the state and direction of America (see his own reference, "The Drug Culture, The Hippie Elements, The SDS, Black Panthers, etc. do not consider me as their enemy or as they call it The Establishment. I call it America and I love it."). America had been good to Elvis, and despite his increasing dependence on prescription drugs, Elvis saw illegal drugs and the related drug culture, among other factions, to be a threat to the America he loved. The lack of a unified "Say No to Drugs" program led Elvis to an individual notion—getting a federal narcotics agent badge and starting to get the word out "through my communications with people of all ages."

Backstage after the late show was where the King received his court. Invited guests and celebrities would gather and say hello or wait for the invitation to come up to Elvis' suite. A typical gathering included Elvis, Red West and good friend, Glen Campbell.

1971
·····················
STRAINING THE TIES THAT BIND

January 2: Elvis wins a court order that requires Patricia Parker to submit to a blood test and lie detector test before pursuing her paternity suit further.

January 8: Another year older, but the pile of money keeps getting bigger.

January 9: Elvis is on the national list of the Jaycees' "Top Ten Young Men Of The Year," and on the 16th he accepts the Jaycee award in person, the first time he has actually attended an awards ceremony in his honor.

January 23: The *Elvis Country* album hits the charts, where it will remain for 21 weeks.

January 24: Elvis heads for Las Vegas to rehearse his winter engagement at the International Hotel.

January 26: The show opens, but Elvis is ill for most of the one-month engagement.

February 1: Priscilla and Lisa Marie come to visit daddy, attending the dinner show and visiting in Elvis' suite.

February 24: After his show closes, Elvis and Priscilla catch Ann-Margret's opening at the International, hanging out backstage and talking with her and husband Roger Smith till the wee hours.

February 28: The Presleys head for Palm Springs, and a few days later to Bel Air. It seems Elvis is in constant motion.

March 10: Elvis and Priscilla return to Graceland.

March 15: At RCA Nashville, Elvis comes to cut some tunes. But he's suffering from an eye infection and the four-day session has to be cut short. Only four songs are recorded: *Amazing Grace, Early Morning Rain, For Lovin' Me* and *The First Time Ever I Saw Your Face.*

March 16: At the hospital, Elvis learns that he's suffering from secondary glaucoma. He is treated and released after a few days, but will have to wear an eyepatch for a few weeks.

March 20: Elvis and Priscilla fly to Hawaii and spend the rest of the month playing on the sand with several friends, returning to Graceland in early April.

April 21: The Presleys fly to Mt. Holly, New Jersey to pay a surprise call on Priscilla's brother Donald, an army chopper pilot on leave.

April 23: From Mt. Holly, Elvis and Priscilla go to Vegas, where they spend the rest of April catching shows and visiting friends. They spend time with Tom Jones and Sammy Davis, Jr., and they meet Bobbie Gentry. In Vegas Elvis gets the idea for "Takin' Care of Business" necklaces and medals, draws up a design and orders several from a jeweler in Los Angeles.

May 1: Mr. and Mrs. Presley celebrate their fourth wedding anniversary at the International in Vegas.

May 15: At RCA Nashville, Elvis presides over another recording-session endurance contest, producing 30 songs by the 21st: *A Thing Called Love, An Evening Prayer, Don't Think Twice, It's All Right, Fools Rush In, He Touched Me, Help Me Make It Through The Night, Holly Leaves And Christmas Trees* (Red West), *I Will Be True, I'll Be Home For Christmas, I'll Take You Home Again, Kathleen, I'm Leavin', I've Got Confidence, If I Get Home On Christmas Day, It Won't Seem Like Christmas, It's Only Love, It's Still There, Lead Me, Guide Me, Love Me, Love The Life I Lead, Merry Christmas Baby, Miracle Of The Rosary, O Come All Ye Faithful, On A Snowy Christmas Night, Padre, Seeing Is Believing, Silver Bells, The First Noel, The Wonderful World Of Christmas, Until It's Time For You To Go, We Can Make It In The Morning* and *Winter Wonderland.*

May 23: Elvis receives the "Founder's Award" at the Memphis Music Awards banquet, with Vernon accepting for him.

June 1: The East Heights Garden Club of Tupelo, Mississippi has finished the restoration of Elvis' birthplace on Old Saltillo Road and opened it to the public.

June 8: At RCA Nashville, Elvis goes back in the studio to cut some more songs, this

"Takin' Care of Business" was the official motto of Elvis and the Memphis Mafia. The TCB necklace, designed by Elvis and created by a jeweler in Los Angeles, was worn by insiders and other lucky individuals. Elvis carried several with him at all times and passed them out to friends.

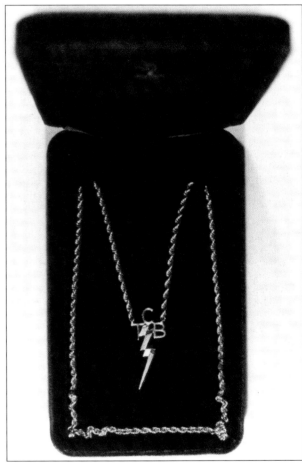

Fans who came to the dinner shows during the 1971 engagement at the Hilton in Las Vegas received a souvenir menu (right).

SOUVENIR MENU
1971
COMPLIMENTARY COPY

time for *He Touched Me*: *Bosom Of Abraham, He Is My Everything, I John, Put Your Hand In The Hand, Reach Out To Jesus* and *There Is No God But God*. But Elvis' temper is beginning to show, and at one point he becomes angry with one of the backup singers and leaves the studio. After the session, he leaves Nashville and goes to Los Angeles.

June 10: After months of debate, the city of Memphis finally finds something to name after Elvis: The stretch of Highway 51 from the Memphis city limits to the Mississippi border will be called Elvis Presley Boulevard.

July 14: A caravan leaves Bel Air for Lake Tahoe, where Elvis will do a gig at the Sahara Tahoe. He begins rehearsals.

July 20: Elvis opens in Tahoe, doing two shows a night, at 8 and 12. The King is on a roll: The shows are strong and the response is amazing. This is live performance at its best and the gig breaks all previous attendance records.

August 2: The Tahoe engagement ends in triumph.

August 3: Elvis leaves Tahoe for Vegas to prepare for his Summer Festival.

August 9: Elvis opens at the Las Vegas Hilton International. The demand for tickets is so high that the 3:00 A.M. show is added on a regular basis to satisfy demand. Elvis tosses stuffed bears into the audience while singing *Teddy Bear* and the crowd goes wild.

DAVID STANLEY

ON ELVIS' BODYGUARDS:

Many people over the years have asked me why Elvis needed so many bodyguards. The answer is simple. When he performed in concert, more often than not 500 young ladies would rush the stage during a show. Two minutes later, 500 old ladies would rush the stage. What I'm trying to say is when you have that many fans trying to touch you at the same time, it can get scary. It wasn't that the fans were trying to hurt him. It was because they all wanted a piece of the same thing at the same time. Sure, you had the jealous boyfriend or husband, and occasional death threats, but we were mostly there for crowd control—to make sure that not only Elvis remained unhurt, but to protect the fans as well.

August 25: As the midnight show draws to a close, a gang of women rush the stage and grab the King, but the ever-present bodyguards leap into action and Elvis is rescued before serious damage is done.

August 28: Between shows, Elvis is presented with "The Bing Crosby Award," recognizing excellence in music and contribution to the culture. In the past, it's gone to Crosby, Frank Sinatra, Duke Ellington, Ella Fitzgerald and Irving Berlin.

September 3: More and more, Elvis is singing songs the band isn't prepared for or forgetting material that has been rehearsed. During one show the band stopped playing because they weren't sure what number Elvis was singing.

September 6: The gig at the Hilton closes. Elvis breaks his own attendance records that will stand forever because fire codes were violated in order to get more people into the room for the final shows.

September 10: Elvis treats himself to a Stutz Blackhawk Coupe. It's the first one made and costs $35,000.

October 8: Back in Memphis, Elvis treats himself again, buying a customized Mercedes Benz for $90,000.

November 5: Elvis hits the road. It will be his first tour with J.D. Sumner and The Stamps Quartet. They start in Minneapolis at the Metropolitan Sports Center and draw 17,600 paying customers.

November 6: Public Hall Auditorium, Cleveland—20,000 SRO.

$35,000 worth of Stutz Blackhawk Coupe sits in the front drive at Graceland. The car was reportedly the first one made. J.D. Sumner (center, left) was a long-time friend of Elvis' and the leader of The Stamps Quartet. The group toured and recorded with Elvis from 1972 until his death in 1977. Sumner had been part of the Memphis gospel scene for many years and would help the young Elvis sneak into local gospel concerts. Elvis was extremely generous with J.D., giving him a steady gig, several cars and a lot of expensive jewelry over the years.

November 7: Freedom Hall, Louisville—18,500, a Louisville record.

November 8: Spectrum, Philadelphia—16,601 paid.

November 9: Civic Center, Baltimore—a full house of 12,228.

November 10: The Garden, Boston—15,509 screaming fans.

November 11: The Gardens, Cincinnati—SRO at 13,272.

November 12: Hofheinz Pavilion, Houston—12,000 sold out.

November 13: Memorial Auditorium, Dallas—20,000 for two shows.

November 14: University of Alabama Field House, Tuscaloosa—12,000 show up.

DAVID STANLEY
ON ELVIS' STAMINA:

If you've never been on the road, you don't know how hard it is, day after day. The farther down the road you get, the more tired you are, and there's no way to catch up, so you just keep going. To be fresh and up in every town you play takes a lot out of you. I swear Elvis was a machine. He was like that battery in the bunny: He'd just keep going.

By the end of 1971, Elvis was balancing a heavy touring schedule booked by the relentless Colonel Parker and a home life that was becoming increasingly strained. Priscilla was extremely unhappy about spending so much time alone at Graceland, and Elvis, for reasons of his own, refused to allow her on tour with him. Things reached a breaking point during the Christmas holidays and at the beginning of the new year Priscilla moved into her own place with Lisa Marie. While everybody tried to put the best face on the situation, it was clear to most insiders that the marriage was heading for the rocks. Vernon (shown here with Elvis in 1969) always loyal and supportive of his son, was a source of comfort. After the death of Gladys the two men became very close and Elvis often relied heavily on Vernon simply because he was family. Although his judgment was often questionable, Vernon was convinced it was his job to protect Elvis from the world and he did his best to do just that.

November 15: Municipal Auditorium, Kansas City—10,400 fans got an extra portion of Elvis because he didn't want to leave the stage. The show ran over 90 minutes.

November 16: Salt Palace, Salt Lake City—13,000 fill the hall on this last night of the tour. After the show, Elvis boards his plane and flies back to Bel Air.

November 17: Elvis flies to Memphis with Vernon to, among other things, congratulate Billy Stanley on his engagement.

November 19: Elvis returns to Los Angeles.

November 21: Billy Stanley marries Angela Payne, but Elvis does not attend.

November 24: The judge examines the results of the blood tests in the paternity suit against Elvis. The results are kept confidential, but insiders say the child is not Elvis'. The case is continued until January 26, 1972, when the court confirms that judgment. After two years, it's finally over.

November 26: Elvis' eye is bothering him again, and he visits a doctor in Los Angeles for treatment. The eyepatch is back on.

December: Elvis returns to Memphis and spends time doing the usual things—movies, roller-skating, horseback riding—but there's strain between him and Priscilla. The touring and performing in Vegas are taking a toll. Live performance is harder than making movies and Elvis is finding that he's constantly in motion even when he's trying to relax. By mid-December, things are tense at Graceland.

December 25: Christmas at Graceland isn't what it used to be. Priscilla gets $10,000 in cash because she didn't want a car.

December 31: Elvis has a bash at Graceland on New Year's Eve. It's a wild party complete with fireworks.

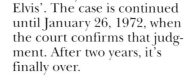

Elvis was becoming increasingly restless and found himself unable to wind down from the grueling concert schedule during vacations. With time on his hands and little to do, Elvis would take to the road on one of his Harleys and cruise aimlessly around the city for hours. He seemed to be searching for a kind of peace and freedom that was just out of reach.

DAVID STANLEY

ON ELVIS AND FIREWORKS:

Elvis loved to go out on New Year's Eve or the Fourth of July and buy fireworks. He would spend thousands of dollars buying them by the truckload. His idea of having fun was to split up into teams and have a fireworks war. I mean we would don flight suits, helmets and goggles and shoot bottle rockets, aerial displays and Roman candles at each other. I know this sounds dangerous, but nothing could have been more fun.

1972
ALONE AGAIN

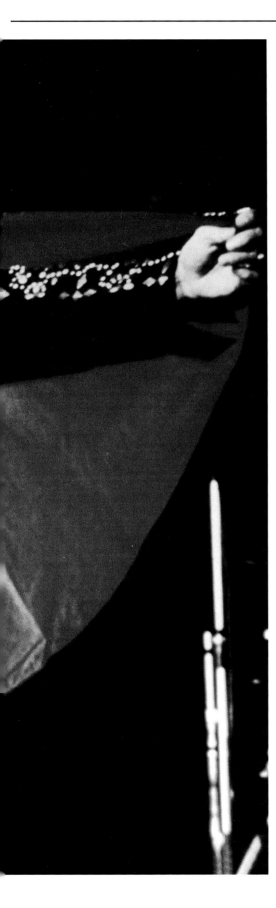

January 8: Elvis celebrates his birthday by announcing that Priscilla has decided to move into her own place in Los Angeles. Lisa Marie is with her. It's clear to everyone that things don't look good.

January 26: Elvis opens at the Las Vegas Hilton International with Jackie Kahane as his warm-up comic and J.D. Sumner and The Stamps Quartet as backup. The show is in a groove. Sometimes it seems as if it's in too much of one. At a tight 45 minutes, there's little room for banter or improvisation.

February 8: Colonel Parker's office denies any rumors of a proposed European tour, but it would seem a natural, considering his incredible popularity over there.

February 14: RCA starts taping shows for the album *Standing Room Only* (which will never be released).

February 23: Before Elvis closes in Vegas on this date, Priscilla has informed him that she intends to file for divorce, and he goes immediately to California, where he discovers that she and Lisa Marie have already moved out of the house there.

March 27: At RCA Hollywood, Elvis goes into the studio for two days of sessions: *Always On My Mind, Burning Love, Fool, For The Good Times, It's A Matter Of Time, Separate Ways* and *Where Do I Go From Here.*

April 5: Elvis begins another concert tour at Memorial Auditorium in Buffalo, arriving in his private jet. A film crew from MGM is on hand to shoot sequences for another documentary feature, *Elvis On Tour.* But organizing the tour is a task complicated by his increasingly unusual lifestyle, which is facilitated by a large retinue of personal friends and retainers who occupy the entire floors at or near the top of the hotel. The group consists of: Vernon

LAMAR FIKE
ON THE COLONEL:

Elvis badly wanted to do a concert tour in Europe. He saw the success of The Stones and The Beatles, and that got his competitive juices flowing. Can you imagine how big Elvis would have been in Europe? But the Colonel always had a reason for not going. Security problems. Tax problems. Technical and production details. God knows what else. Elvis would blow up at the Colonel about it, say he was damn well going—but he'd always end up backing down.

Elvis never had a clue what the real reason was that the Colonel didn't want to go to Europe, and we didn't find out until years later: He was, and is, an illegal alien in the United States. He jumped off a boat to get into this country. In fact, he jumped off twice. The first time they caught him and sent him back to his native country, the Netherlands. The second time, he stayed and never got caught.

The Colonel was afraid that if he left the U.S, he'd never be able to get back in, and that's why he prevented Elvis from taking a Europe tour. He just flat out lied to Elvis. And he really wanted to go. He'd had a wonderful time there when he was in the army. I know, because I was with him the entire time. And he would have been huge in Europe. Huge. But the Colonel denied him that pleasure. Denied him the money and the satisfaction. That's the kind of thing that can really make you bitter.

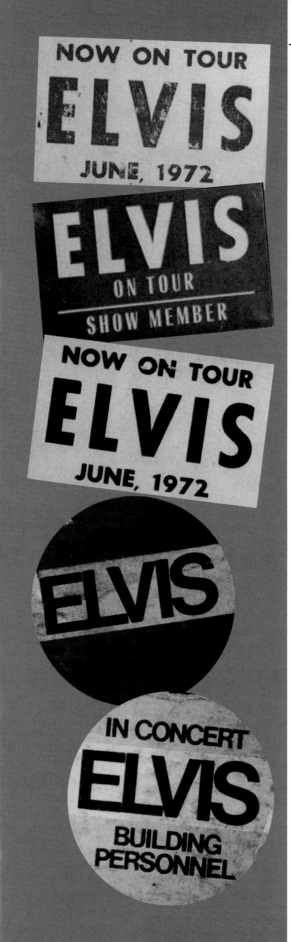

Elvis would always find comfort in his closeness with the "Memphis Mafia," made up entirely of his friends and employees, (left to right) Sonny West, Red West, Elvis, Jerry Schilling, Lamar Fike and Joe Esposito.

Presley, Joe Esposito, Lamar Fike, Charlie Hodge, Red West, Sonny West, Dick Grob, Ricky Stanley, Jerry Schilling, Richard Davis and/or Gee Gee Gamble.

April 6: At Olympia Stadium, Detroit—16,216 fans, the largest audience ever in Olympia.

April 7: University of Dayton Arena, Dayton—13,788 fill it up.

April 8: Stokely Athletics Center, Knoxville—23,800 total for two shows.

April 9: The Coliseum, Hampton Roads, Virginia—21,650 for two shows, filmed by MGM for *Elvis On Tour.*

April 10: The Coliseum, Richmond—11,500 attend. Elvis has to stop singing while some fans calm down after becoming hysterical while being filmed for the documentary.

April 11: Roanoke Civic Center, Roanoke—10,436 fans sell out. The facility is evacuated because of a bomb threat, but the concert goes on after a search reveals nothing. There is another small riot when several women rush the stage, try to get to Elvis and settle for a backup musician.

April 12: Fair Grounds Coliseum, Indianapolis—11,000 brave a tremendous thunderstorm to catch the King.

April 13: Coliseum, Charlotte—12,000 pay and watch.

April 14: The Coliseum, Greensboro—16,300 see the concert and watch the MGM crew film sequences for *Elvis On Tour.*

April 15: The Coliseum, Macon, Georgia—23,000 for two shows.

April 16: Veteran's Memorial Coliseum, Jacksonville, Florida—two shows bring in 18,758 paid attendance.

April 17: T.H. Barton Coliseum, Little Rock—10,000 Razorbacks show up.

April 18: Convention Center Arena, San Antonio—10,500 in attendance, filmed by MGM for *Elvis On Tour.*

April 19: Tingley Coliseum, Albuquerque—the final date on the tour, with 11,847 packing the hall. Elvis visits backstage with a child who is dying of cancer before the show and dedicates *You Gave Me A Mountain* to her during the show.

April 20: After the tour wraps, Elvis flies straight to Hawaii to meet Priscilla and Lisa Marie, along with other friends and family members. He will spend most of May at the Rainbow Towers in Hawaiian Village. While much of the time is spent in seclusion, he does go to Honolulu to watch a karate exhibition.

May 8: Tickets for his four upcoming concerts at Madison Square Garden in New York go on sale and are gone within 24 hours.

May 28: Elvis and several others fly to Las Vegas, where he attends a show by Glen Campbell, but the crowd reaction to his presence forces him to leave so Campbell can finish his act.

June: The gun club interests that had purchased the Circle G Ranch default on mortgage payments and Vernon outbids the competition at the foreclosure auction, so the Circle G is back in Presley hands.

June 7: Against his mother's better judgment, David Stanley, the youngest of Elvis' three stepbrothers, joins the upcoming tour, traveling with the guys throughout the summer and returning to school in the fall. But rather than return to school, Stanley allows Elvis to persuade him to stay on and become a full-time member of the Memphis Mafia, working as an advance man and bodyguard. He will be with Elvis to the end.

June 9: All four concerts at Madison Square Garden are sellouts, with 80,000 paid admissions. Elvis is the first act to sell out the Garden four times in a row. The take reported by Colonel Parker is almost $750,000. RCA tapes the shows to use on a live album, *Elvis Live At Madison Square Garden.*

DAVID STANLEY
ON ELVIS AND GEORGE HARRISON:

The first time I was working for Elvis, we went to New York City. He and I arrived at Madison Square Garden and got out of the limo and off in the distance I spotted this thin guy leaning against a beam. And as we got closer I realized it was George Harrison. Elvis wasn't real impressed and just kept going to his dressing room, but I was bowled over. He was one of my heroes, so I went right over to him and said, "Mr. Harrison, I'm Elvis' stepbrother, David Stanley." He was totally humble, nice as could be, and I asked what he was doing. "Well, I'm here to see the King." I went back to the dressing room and told Elvis that George Harrison would love to come in and say hi. Now, Elvis knew who George Harrison was, so there wasn't any of the usual, "Who's that?" stuff. But all the other guys—Red and Sonny, Joe Esposito—they all jumped my butt, saying, "David, you don't come in here running your mouth and inviting folks in." I mean these guys were used to this. But Elvis came to my defense. He said, "No, wait a minute. This is an exception". And he said to bring Harrison in. And they exchanged some pleasantries. Now this was after Bangladesh, to give you an idea of time frame, but that didn't stop Elvis from saying, "I understand you boys broke up." And George didn't bat an eyelash, said, yes, the boys had indeed broken up. "Well," Elvis said, "I know you'll do well. You're definitely one of the most talented, you and Paul." Never mentioned John. When it came to John Lennon, Elvis just couldn't help himself. Elvis patted George on the back, escorted him to the door and told him he hoped he'd enjoy the show. Harrison smiled. "You don't have to hope. I know I'll enjoy the show."

Rick Stanley, Elvis and David Stanley, the youngest of Elvis' three stepbrothers. David joined Elvis on tour the summer of 1972 and was asked by Elvis to stay on and become a full-time member of the Memphis Mafia, which he did. David would work as an advance man and bodyguard, and would be with Elvis until the end.

June 12: Memorial Coliseum, Fort Wayne—sold out.

June 13: Roberts Memorial Coliseum, Evansville—11,500 in attendance.

June 14: Milwaukee Auditorium, Milwaukee—10,500 show up.

June 15: Milwaukee Auditorium, Milwaukee—11,000 fill it up.

June 16: Chicago Stadium, Chicago—65,000 paid in two days, three shows.

June 18: Tarrant County Convention Center, Ft. Worth—a record 14,122 fans.

June 19: Henry Levitt Arena, Wichita—10,000 pack the house. That same day, RCA releases *Elvis Live At Madison Square Garden*.

June 20: Civic Assembly Center, Tulsa—9,500 in attendance for the last show of the tour.

June 21: Elvis returns to Memphis and rumors of a divorce.

July: Elvis devotes himself to rest and relaxation in Memphis: movies, motorcycles, midnight madness and beefing up his karate skills.

July 5: At a late-night movie marathon in the Memphian Theater, Elvis is introduced to Linda Thompson by George Klein, a mutual friend. She's a stunning woman and Elvis is blown away.

July 6: Elvis rebooks the Memphian, as he often did, and invites the same crowd. He sits next to Thompson the whole evening. It's the beginning of one of the most significant relationships in Elvis' life. He and Linda will be together almost until the end, and she will prove to be a true friend.

July 8: Plans are in the works for another TV special to be broadcast from Hawaii. That same day, *Elvis Live At Madison Square Garden* goes gold in almost 60 days, remaining on the charts for 34 weeks.

July 27: In California, Priscilla files for a formal separation from Elvis. She will have custody of Lisa Marie, but he will have unlimited visitation rights.

July 28: Elvis heads to Vegas and his summer gig at the Las Vegas Hilton.

August 4: *Elvis Live At Madison Square Garden* has gone gold. Elvis opens in Vegas, but he's distracted and in a foul mood.

August 5: Elvis meets Linda Thompson in Vegas, where she spends several days before returning to Memphis. After Linda leaves, Elvis is joined by Cybill Shepherd and then by a woman named Sandra Zancan. Meanwhile, he's gaining noticeable weight and is beginning to show the effects of his increasing drug abuse.

August 18: Elvis files for divorce in Los Angeles. The cause is listed as "irreconcilable differences." Priscilla does not contest.

August 21: When the seam of Elvis' pants splits during the late show, he steps behind a curtain and continues singing while he changes pants. From this point on, he'll perform only in his custom-made jumpsuits.

DAVID STANLEY

ON ELVIS' RELATIONSHIP WITH PRISCILLA:

It's not surprising that the marriage didn't last. For Elvis, the word commitment did not exist. In fact, Elvis married Priscilla because of the Colonel, who told him, "Look, you're the all-American kid here, and you've got this young babe. You've got to make a choice. You either marry her or get her out of here." So in a sense Elvis was forced into marrying her.

He was certainly never faithful to her. He went out with Nancy Sinatra during the making of Speedway in 1967. And God knows there were countless others. And Priscilla was on to it. She would mark the spots where her clothes were in the bureaus when she left. Then she'd leave and a new girl would come in, and Priscilla's clothes would be removed. But Elvis caught on about the marks, so he foiled Priscilla's trap by making sure that her clothes were all lined up when she came back.

Elvis was hard on Priscilla. There was never a quiet moment between the two because Elvis always had the guys around him. It was by no means a traditional marriage, and that's all Priscilla wanted. Lord knows, she had it tough—she must have felt she was married to the whole Memphis Mafia. Because of this, I have had no bitterness myself toward Priscilla.

ON SEEING PRISCILLA:

In 1972, after she and Elvis had broken up, I was in Los Angeles with Elvis and Priscilla called me up. Invited me over to Marina del Rey where she was living. I was a little nervous about it, so I went over there with a girlfriend. Of course I hid the visit from Elvis. No way I could tell him about this. And Mike Stone, her boyfriend, was over there, and he was a badass. A lethal weapon. Now Elvis was bad, but Mike Stone was lethal. Elvis did not want to mess with Mike Stone, who was a karate champion. It was one thing to break boards. It was a whole other thing to be a competitor.

And I looked at Priscilla and said, "I know I'm young and you probably don't think I'm capable of understanding, but I know there have been a lot of lonely nights for you."

"Well, David," she said, "Can I ask you a question? I just want to ask you about what it was like on the road."

I told her that I couldn't tell her anything about that, and if that was the reason she'd asked me over there, I gotta go. Because if Elvis had found out about it, that would have been the end for me.

Many of Elvis' 1972 shows were filmed for *Elvis On Tour*, a documentary the producers called, "a tour of Elvis' life, a close-up of the birth and life of an American phenomenon." Lisa Marie returned to Graceland for the 1972 Christmas holidays, Priscilla stayed in Los Angeles. Many close to him sensed Elvis was hoping Priscilla would fly in at the last minute. That, however, would have been complicated by the fact that Linda Thompson, the woman who would share Elvis' life for the next several years, was all but living at Graceland. Though the mood was subdued, everyone put up a good front for Lisa Marie.

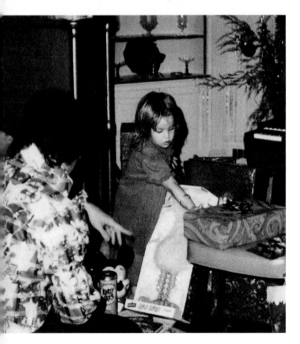

August 27: Priscilla travels with Lisa Marie to Vegas to see Elvis' show. They remain through the last week of the run.

September 4: The summer gig closes, but Elvis will remain in Vegas to see friends and catch other acts.

September 5: The deal to broadcast a special from Hawaii is closed by Colonel Parker and NBC.

September 30: Elvis returns to Memphis and then goes to Los Angeles to record dialogue for *Elvis On Tour*.

October: Elvis returns to Las Vegas and remains there for the rest of the month.

November 1: *Elvis On Tour* opens nationally. The reviews are mixed. But, as usual, the fans love it.

November: In constant motion back and forth from Los Angeles to Memphis and Vegas, Elvis is becoming more reclusive than ever, spending hours on karate—and seething about Priscilla's affair with karate expert Mike Stone.

November 8: The tour begins at the Municipal Auditorium in Lubbock, Texas—10,000 fans sell it out.

November 9: Community Center Arena, Tucson—9,700 attend.

November 10: The Coliseum, El Paso—9,000 tickets sold.

November 11: *Burning Love And Hits From His Movies* hits the charts, where it will remain for 25 weeks. That same day, Elvis sells 14,000 tickets for a live performance at Oakland Coliseum.

November 12 – 13: Swing Auditorium, San Bernardino—7,200 seats sell out each night.

November 14 – 15: Long Beach Arena, Long Beach—14,000 tickets sold each night. Priscilla and Lisa Marie watch the last show.

November 16: The tour flies to Honolulu for the final leg, performing four shows at the International Center—drawing over 27,900 people.

November 20: At a press conference at Hawaiian Village, plans for an upcoming television benefit concert in Honolulu are revealed.

November 30: Elvis returns to Los Angeles.

December 10: He travels to Vegas for a few days, then on to Memphis for the holidays.

December 22: Lisa Marie arrives in Memphis. Priscilla will remain in Los Angeles.

December 25: The family gathers for the usual festivities. Linda Thompson, who is all but living at Graceland, is there as well, and Elvis gives her a mink coat.

December 31: Elvis throws a New Year's party at Graceland. The event is reported to be a little subdued and that he's not in a good mood, but he does his best to keep up a good front for his daughter. Of course, there are the annual fireworks wars.

January 7: Elvis flies from Memphis to Los Angeles in preparation for the trip to Honolulu and the benefit.

January 8: Elvis spends his 38th birthday in Los Angeles.

January 9: Elvis and the boys fly to Honolulu for rehearsal. Cameras follow him everywhere, and the footage will be used during the concert.

January 10: Rehearsals begin at the International Convention Center.

January 12: An invited audience of over 6,000 jams the center to watch the final dress rehearsal.

January 13: Another dress rehearsal, after which several extra songs are recorded. The mayor of Honolulu reads a proclamation declaring this Elvis Presley Day.

January 14: The concert, beginning at 12:30 A.M., is sent by satellite around the world. Elvis is once again at the center of a moment in history. With one billion people estimated to be watching, the show is a smash and its benefit—for a local cancer fund—exceeds its expected goal by $50,000. But the grueling pace is taking its toll: Elvis goes to his room after the show and sleeps for 24 hours straight.

January 26: Elvis opens at the Hilton in Vegas. Linda Thompson is with him.

January 31: Elvis cancels both shows because of throat problems.

February 1: Elvis does the early show but is too ill for the late one. Lisa Marie is on hand celebrating her fifth birthday.

1973
LONELY MAN

February 13: Elvis continues to suffer from throat problems. He is so ill that management considers canceling another show. But after they make the announcement, Elvis decides to perform. He receives a standing ovation from his grateful fans.

February 14: The laryngitis is so severe that Elvis is forced to perform only one show.

February 15: Elvis leaves the stage in the middle of the early show. He is gone for over twenty minutes but returns and picks up where he left off.

February 18: Four men jump on stage during the late show, and in the melee that follows, the Memphis Mafia have their hands full. Even Elvis joins the fray, sending one man flying into the audience. After it's over, he is reported to have offered to "shake the guy's hand or whup his ass." The crowd goes wild and there are several minutes of sustained applause before the show continues.

For Elvis, going back to live performance after ten stifling years in Hollywood was like being reborn. There was such a sense of joy in his early concerts that it was almost impossible not to be moved and a new generation of fans was able to discover for themselves what made Elvis Presley the King of Rock & Roll.

DAVID STANLEY
ON ELVIS' BIGGEST CONCERT EVER:

In all the years that I was with Elvis, I never saw him get nervous. But when you're about to step out to a combined TV audience of over a billion people, as Elvis would say, "This has a tendency to get your attention." Elvis had come a long way from the Louisiana Hayrides of the South. He was about to take another step into history.

Guns were a part of life for kids growing up in the rural south. From the time he was a child in Mississippi, Elvis was fascinated by them and spent most of his life collecting and shooting. The Presley arsenal consisted of almost forty weapons of various kinds, including M-16s, automatic pistols, derringers, rifles and even a Thompson submachine gun. The boys put together a jerry-rigged shooting gallery in the back of Graceland and when the spirit moved him, Elvis would step out back and pop off a few rounds. He was famous for shooting out the lights in hotel rooms and blowing away television sets, but it was always done in fun. As he became more and more controlled by drugs it was the job of Red West and the boys to keep the weapons out of sight or at least unloaded.

DAVID STANLEY
ON ELVIS' RAGE OVER MIKE STONE:

Elvis' rage was just actions of hurt—he would never have tried to kill anyone. And this hurt required heavy sedation over the next several days before his rage passed. But he loved what his bodyguards could do to people. He didn't like it when they went too far, though. And you can't have it both ways. Hell, when Elvis got mad, he'd want people blown away. He watched too many Dirty Harry movies. He was having trouble distinguishing reality from fantasy. When Elvis watched a movie, that movie became his reality. He believed it. Or acted like he did. I always say, Thank God he was gone by the time Scarface came out, because that would have been a rough year.

February 19: Irrational and enraged by Priscilla's refusal to allow a visit from Lisa Marie, Elvis tries to put out a contract on Mike Stone, Priscilla's lover, even asking Red and Sonny West to kill the s.o.b. They don't take him seriously, but he requires heavy sedation over the next several days before he calms down.

February 23: The Vegas gig closes, but Elvis will remain in town through early March.

February 24: *Elvis: Aloha From Hawaii Via Satellite* hits the charts, where it will remain for 35 weeks, peaking at #1. It will be his last album at the top of the charts.

March 1: Elvis signs a new seven-year deal with RCA. Though he makes out well, the Colonel reportedly makes out even better. But Elvis is still the highest single taxpayer in the country.

April 4: *Elvis: Aloha From Hawaii Via Satellite* is broadcast by NBC, then rebroadcast on November 14.

April 7: The crew flies to San Francisco to watch a karate championship. Elvis is supposed to participate, and it's advertised that he will, but the Colonel points out that his contract with the Sahara in Tahoe prevents him from public appearances within a 300-mile radius within 30 days of his concert. So Elvis watches from the stands with Linda and members of the Memphis Mafia.

April 22: Elvis begins his new tour at Veteran's Memorial Coliseum in Phoenix, where 15,000 tickets are sold.

April 23: Anaheim Convention Center, Anaheim—8,500 paid in full.

April 24: Anaheim Convention Center, Anaheim—8,500 again.

April 25: Selland Arena, Fresno—15,000 for two shows.

April 26: International Sports Arena, San Diego—15,000 paid.

April 27: Portland Coliseum, Portland—14,000 tickets sold.

April 28: Spokane Coliseum, Spokane—13,000 in attendance. Technical problems and bad weather made for weak shows.

April 29: Center Arena, Seattle—16,000 paid tickets.

April 30: Denver Coliseum, Denver—13,000 for the final show of the tour.

DAVID STANLEY
ON ELVIS' DRUG ABUSE:

Elvis' drug use wasn't always abusive. In the time I was there, it went from casual use to massive abuse. But in those days, nobody knew the dangers involved. These were still the "feel good" years, with doctors prescribing drugs far less discriminatingly than they do now. Remember President Kennedy used to get shots, and years later those turned out to be full of amphetamine. And it was also before the Betty Ford Clinic, before it was acceptable for celebrities, even the President's wife, to admit they had a problem and to deal with it—and eventually to be praised for taking action. Elvis was living in an earlier era. He was ashamed and embarrassed about what he was doing, and he felt that if it ever came out, he'd be ruined.

It was almost impossible for Elvis to appear anywhere in public, especially after he went back on tour full time. His fans seemed to have some kind of radar, and crowds appeared as if by magic the moment he stepped out of his car. Although the possibility of attack was real and always a potential threat, the biggest job of Memphis Mafia members like bodyguard David Stanely (above left) was to keep Elvis and his fans from getting crushed in the sea of humanity.

DAVID STANLEY
ON ELVIS' CHOICE OF MUSIC:

I can't help but believe that Elvis barely scratched the surface of his potential. If he'd tried harder, worked harder on the music, got into writing, he would have been massive. And I think part of why he didn't was that he didn't have to. And wasn't asked to. As Colonel Parker always used to say, "If it ain't broke, don't fix it." So there weren't a lot of influences around Elvis telling him to go for it. To try new things. Quite the contrary. And Elvis needed to be pushed. And it's a damned shame he wasn't. Some of us tried to point him toward good songs. Lamar did, and Elvis would listen. And I tried to push him to some of the new music that was happening at the time. I remember we gave him Steamroller Blues and Bridge Over Troubled Water.

I think if Elvis could have, he would've sung strictly gospel music. I mean, Elvis wouldn't sit around the house and sing Hound Dog—he was always humming gospel. But he didn't record that much gospel. In fact, he only did two gospel albums—but they both won Grammys, two of the only three he ever won. From an evangelical point of view, Elvis was "called" to sing gospel music. Everybody can remember his gospel music. I mean it would just cut right through you. It just did something to you. I truly believe that Elvis had a God-given anointing on his life when he sang gospel music. Even if you weren't a believer, that music would affect you. And I think there was a struggle in his life between what the "world" wanted to hear and the gospel music he loved. A classic struggle: God's calling, but the world's pulling him the other way.

May 4: Elvis opens in Lake Tahoe. According to Colonel Parker, the hotel had overbooked the engagement and angry fans come close to a riot as they are turned away. But the gig goes on. Elvis is in bad shape, overweight and groggy, distracted and unable to focus, having trouble remembering the show order and even song lyrics. After the late show on the 16th, complaining of illness, he cancels the rest of the engagement and returns to Los Angeles. Elvis rests in seclusion there for the remainder of the month. The inner circle is becoming concerned because they know the real reason for Elvis' problems on stage and off: dependence on prescription drugs. They're too close to see it, but the downhill slide is beginning.

May 29: Priscilla contests the original terms of the divorce settlement.

June 19: Elvis et al fly to Mobile, Alabama for the first leg of a Southern tour.

June 20: The tour begins at the Mobile Municipal Auditorium in Mobile—with 11,000 fans attending.

June 21: Omni, Atlanta—17,200 paid admissions.

June 22: Nassau Coliseum, Uniondale, Long Island—66,000 attend four shows over the next three days. The gross is over $600,000.

June 25: Civic Arena, Pittsburgh—28,000 attend two shows over two days.

June 27: The Gardens, Cincinnati—13,060 paid in full.

June 28: Keil Auditorium, St. Louis—12,000 show up to cheer.

June 30: Omni, Atlanta—34,400 pack the arena for two shows.

July 1: Municipal Auditorium, Nashville—20,000 fans for two shows.

July 2: Myriad Center Arena, Oklahoma City—15,400 sold out.

July 3: Omni, Atlanta—over 17,000 attend the final concert of the Southern tour. Then Elvis flies immediately back to Memphis to prepare for Lisa Marie's impending visit. She will spend the month at Graceland and see her daddy receive his seventh degree black belt in karate.

July 21: At Stax Studios, Memphis, Elvis comes in to cut some tunes for future albums. The studio is booked for three days. New musicians were to be brought on for the third session, but Elvis wasn't happy about the change, there were conflicts, and the session fell apart. Elvis didn't show for the last session, and the group, under the guidance of Felton Jarvis, cut instrumental tracks that Elvis could dub later. The results: *Find Out What's Happening, For Ol' Times Sake, I've Got A Thing About You Baby, If You Don't Come Back, Raised On Rock, Take Good Care Of Her* and *Three Corn Patches.*

July 29: Elvis heads for Los Angeles to get ready for the Vegas gig.

August 6: Elvis opens in Vegas. But he's touchy and difficult, fighting with everybody.

August 19: During a wild and wooly party in the penthouse suite, a playful wrestling match between Elvis and a young woman gets out of hand and he accidentally breaks her ankle. She will later file charges but will also drop them when Elvis apologizes and pays her hospital bills.

September 2: Elvis adds a late show to the schedule, but he's almost unable to complete it when he begins to burst into uncontrollable fits of laughter.

September 3: Elvis closes in Vegas, staying on for at least a week seeing friends and watching the competition around town.

September 11: While breaking boards with karate chops in his Vegas hotel room, Elvis hurts his wrist. After a trip to the hospital, he returns to Memphis with Linda and some of the remaining Memphis Mafia. After a shopping spree there, they all board the plane for Los Angeles.

September 13: Elvis lands in Palm Springs with Linda, but he remains in seclusion, rarely coming out of his room. His dependency on prescription drugs is increasing.

September 30: The Hilton announces that a new contract keeping Elvis in the International Room has been completed. The King will be there until at least 1975, but will perform separate two-week chunks rather than the usual four in a row.

October 9: The settlement for Priscilla is ironed out and the divorce is finalized in Los Angeles. Elvis is present at the hearing and they exit the courtroom together. The agreement is generous and they will share custody of Lisa Marie.

October 12: Elvis returns to Memphis, upset and angry but trying to hide it.

November 9: The King flies to Palm Springs to continue resting.

November 14: Elvis and some of the boys drive to Los Angeles to see Lisa Marie and Priscilla.

November 19: The terms of his contract with RCA require a certain number of new singles and albums a year, and the pressure is on to produce. Elvis returns to Memphis to get ready for a recording session. Rested and in much better health, he is looking forward to going into the studio.

December 10: At Stax Studios, Memphis, Elvis books the studio for a week. The sessions go well and yield: *Good Time Charlie's Got The Blues, Help Me, I Got A Feeling In My Body, If That Isn't Love, If You Talk In Your Sleep, It's Midnight, Love Song Of The Year, Loving Arms, Mr. Songman, My Boy, Promised Land, She Wears My Ring, Spanish Eyes, Talk About The Good Times, There's A Honky Tonk Angel, Thinking Of You, You Asked Me To* and *Your Love's Been A Long Time Coming.* This will be Elvis' last recording session in a studio for almost a year and a half.

December 16: Lisa Marie arrives in Memphis to spend part of her holiday with Elvis.

December 20: Elvis makes his usual donations to local charities, including a children's home and the milk fund.

December 25: Christmas at Graceland is a dreary affair this year. The day passes almost unnoticed and presents sit unopened. Elvis is depressed and spends days in his bedroom.

December 31: There's a New Year's Eve party at Graceland, but after a brief appearance, Elvis and Linda return to their room.

Vernon and Dee celebrated their 13th wedding anniversary on July 3, 1973. Although Elvis welcomed her three sons into the family and treated them like brothers, he was never quite so fond of Dee. Many closest to him felt that Elvis never got over the death of Gladys and he resented someone trying to take her place. Consequently, Dee and Elvis couldn't share space in Graceland. Eventually, she and Vernon packed up the kids and moved into a big house that butted up to the rear of the grounds.

LAMAR FIKE
ON ELVIS AND DRUGS:

Elvis was the kind of guy who would dodge reality. He didn't like to face things. He wasn't a confrontational person. He was always hoping that if he ignored something, it would go away.

DAVID STANLEY
ON ELVIS LOCKING HIMSELF UP:

It wasn't unusual for Elvis to lock himself up in his room and abuse his medication for several weeks. But it never got public until late 1974 – 75. Looking back on that time now, it's like he was acting as if his life was over. Every day of his life at this point was misery. I'd say, "Good morning, Elvis."
And he'd say, "What's so good about it?"

1974
....

GOOD TIME CHARLIE'S GOT THE BLUES

David escorts Elvis through a crowd of fans between shows. Elvis was presented with outfits and uniforms from police departments all over the country. He was especially proud of his regulation Drug Enforcement Administration windbreaker and wore it often to and from hotels and performance venues. Elvis said on several occasions that he would have liked to have been a cop and that maybe he would have done it if all this hadn't happened. The truth was that Elvis was never entirely comfortable with his success and it is interesting to wonder about what his life's work would have been if some of those early talent contests had picked another winner.

January 8: Elvis' 39th birthday is celebrated all over the South. Elvis makes an appearance on his porch, waving to the fans who have gathered around the gates.

January 12: Elvis flies to Los Angeles and prepares for his winter gig in Las Vegas.

January 26: Elvis opens in Vegas for a two-week run. The actual start date was to have been the 25th, but Sinatra is closing at Caesar's Palace that night, so the Hilton pushes the date back. Elvis does two shows.

While he is clearly in better health, the King isn't looking his best, and Elvis watchers wonder if the jumpsuit is his best costume choice. But the fans don't seem to care, and he's tossing his trademark sweat-stained scarves into the audience at a furious rate, seemingly happy only on stage.

February 9: Elvis closes at the Hilton but hangs out for a few more weeks at the hotel before returning to prep in Memphis for his spring tour.

March 1 – 2: The spring tour begins in Tulsa at Oral Roberts University, where 11,000 fans fill the auditorium for two nights.

March 3: It's "Elvis Presley Week" in Alabama, but Elvis is in Houston playing the Astrodome, where his two shows draw an astounding 88,149 paying customers.

March 4: Civic Center, Monroe, Louisiana—8,000 fans attend.

March 5: Auburn University Memorial Coliseum—13,239 fans roar with approval as Elvis salutes the Tigers.

March 6: Garrett Coliseum, Montgomery, Alabama—11,328 tickets sold.

March 7: Civic Center, Monroe—8,000 purchase tickets.

March 9: Charlotte Coliseum, Charlotte, North Carolina—24,900 watch two shows.

March 10: Roanoke Civic Center, Roanoke—10,640 cheer the King.

March 11: Hampton Roads Coliseum, Hampton Roads—10,957 ticket stubs.

March 12: Richmond Coliseum, Richmond, Virginia—11,791 paid.

March 13: The Coliseum, Greensboro—16,200 pack the place.

March 14: Murphy Athletic Center, Murfreesboro—12,500 attend.

March 15: Stokely Athletic Center, Knoxville—26,610 for two shows.

March 16: Mid-South Coliseum, Memphis—49,200 line up to see four shows in two days.

March 18: Coliseum, Richmond—11,791 tickets paid.

March 19: Murphy Athletic Center, Murfreesboro—12,500 in attendance.

March 20: Mid-South Coliseum, Memphis—12,300 pay to see the last stop on the tour. RCA is there to record the show and will release an album called *Elvis Recorded Live On Stage In Memphis*. For once Elvis is home when a tour ends, and he goes to Graceland that night, remaining there through the month of April.

April: There are more rumors of offers to play overseas—including a cool million to play Australia—but the Colonel continues to squash them. Insiders speculate about why.

May 10: Another western swing begins at Swing Auditorium, San Bernardino—with 7,200 in attendance.

May 11: The Forum, Los Angeles—37,000 for two shows. The heavy-metal band Led Zeppelin was sitting in the front row.

May 12: Selland Arena, Fresno—7,500 for a single show.

May 13: Swing Auditorium, San Bernardino—7,200 again.

May 14: Off to Tahoe for ten days at the Sahara Tahoe, starting on the 16th.

May 20: In the hallway outside Elvis' suite, a brutal fight erupts between the guys and a man who claims he has been invited to a party that's going on inside. Elvis,

DAVID STANLEY

ON ELVIS MEETING LED ZEPPELIN:

Being a huge Zeppelin fan, I told Elvis before the show that the entire band was in the audience. He didn't say much, but he did the best show I've seen him do. Later he told me, "I guess I showed those boys how to rock." I simply said, "I guess you did." After the concert, all the members of Zeppelin come over to the hotel to meet Elvis, and from the time they walked in the door to the time they left, they were star-struck. I mean they were like little kids. You could definitely classify them as super fans. I escorted them to the door when it was time to leave and on the way out, Robert Plant turned and in his best Elvis-impersonation voice, began singing "Treat Me Like a Fool," and Elvis finished the line singing, "Treat me mean and cruel." The scary thing was that Plant sounded exactly like Elvis. The band loved it.

LAMAR FIKE

ON ELVIS' GENEROSITY:

Elvis never forgot where he came from and what it was like to be poor. He was always looking in the papers, wherever he was, and when he would see there was someone in trouble with no way out, nine times out of ten he would send them something to help out. He just was like that. It was his upbringing.

DAVID STANLEY
ON THE TAHOE FIGHT:

We were sitting in Elvis' suite, four or five of us, and suddenly the lights started going off and on. And this was during the Symbionese Liberation Army/Patty Hearst kidnapping. Elvis was fascinated with the SLA thing. Fascinated and a little worried about it at the same time. He was afraid for Lisa, who was there for that engagement. And while the lights are going off and on, we're watching the SLA house burning on television. And Elvis is saying, "What's going on?" We were all a little skittish. So I went out to check if everything was okay. I came through the double doors and into the hall and I passed a locked emergency exit. And somebody is banging on it from the other side. So I opened the door, and there was this guy there, a real big guy, dressed to the nines in Vegas style, lots of chains and jewelry, polyester to the max. With a couple of babes. The power circuits are right there on the wall, and he's obviously been switching them on and off. "What are you doing?" I said to him. "That's not necessary." I see hotel security, assigned to Elvis, way down at the end of the hall, starting toward us. I'm telling this guy he's got to leave, but he starts blowing off steam, and I realize he's drunk as a rat. And he's ranting about how rich he is, and how there's a party he wants to go to, and he can't be treated this way, blah, blah, blah.

Then all of a sudden he lurches through the door and slams me back against the wall. Now I'm pretty big, but this guy is huge. So I'm getting ready to lay into him, or at least try. And suddenly Sonny West is there, takes three quick steps and nails this guy with the heaviest shot I've ever seen anybody take. A massive hit. And the guy crashes into the wall, blood everywhere, and slithers to the floor.

Now security is there by this time, and they stop Sonny from going after this guy some more. I went back into the suite to tell Elvis everything's under control. But Elvis has a .45 in one hand, a Thompson submachine gun in the other, and he's got Lisa behind him. "Where's the s.o.b.?" he snarls. He thinks somebody's coming after his daughter. I tell him everything was under control, but that isn't enough for Elvis. He's in his super-hero mode. And he comes into the hall, sees this guy handcuffed and taken down the hall to a suite. So we follow, and Elvis is still snarling.

But after they put the guy on the bed, Elvis took one look at him and said, "Oh, my God." This guy's lip was hanging loose, he was wrecked. So Elvis sat down on the bed next to him, asking him, why did you do this, what were you doing? But the guy is still very upset, and all of a sudden he kicks out at Sonny and nails him. At which point Red drops a fist onto the guy's jaw. Pow! It was like a gun going off. The jaw just shattered. And he falls back, blood gushing. So Elvis grabbed one side of him and me the other and pulled him forward so the blood wouldn't choke him.

Elvis was mad at Red. I mean, this guy was still hand-cuffed when Red hit him. But Elvis' anger turned instantly to pity. He helps the guy out of there, talking to him, trying to settle him down. The guy eventually sued, of course. About a year later, it was settled. But it cost Elvis money. He was mad at Red about the incident and eventually that played a part, I believe, in Red and Sonny being fired. At least, that's what Elvis said.

Sonny, Dick Grob and David Stanley will be named as the attackers and charged with assault. A lawsuit is filed.

May 23: Linda Thompson turns 23 and there's a small party, but Elvis is feeling ill and goes to bed early.

Linda Thompson, the former beauty queen, moved into Graceland in 1972. She stayed for almost five years, during which she was Elvis' constant companion, friend, lover and confidant. When Elvis' drug abuse worsened and his condition deteriorated it became more and more difficult to live with him, and Linda finally left in 1976.

May 26: Elvis officially closes at the Sahara. The demand is so strong, however, that he will add a show on the 27th for the fans who have been turned away.

June 15: After a very short break, Elvis starts a swing of the southland starting in Fort Worth. 56,000 people see four shows at the Tarrant County Convention Center over two days.

June 17: Assembly Center, Louisiana State University—30,000 students attend two shows over two days.

June 19: Civic Center, Amarillo, Texas—14,000 show up.

June 20: Veteran's Memorial Auditorium, Des Moines—11,000 fans watch as over 70 women storm the stage near the end of the concert to get scarves or kisses, which happens as often as not. Since it's Iowa, they are moderately orderly and Elvis sticks it out on stage, laughing and talking, until order is restored.

June 21: Public Hall, Cleveland—10,000 paid attendance.

June 22: Civic Center, Providence, Rhode Island—26,226 for two shows.

June 23: Spectrum, Philadelphia—40,000 total for two shows.

June 24: International Convention Center, Niagara Falls—18,000 watch two shows.

June 25: St. John's Arena, Columbus—14,000 catch the show.

June 26: Freedom Hall, Louisville—20,000 for an evening show.

June 27: Assembly Hall, Indiana University—16,000 paid admissions.

June 28: Milwaukee Arena, Milwaukee—11,800 fill the house.

June 29: Municipal Auditorium, Kansas City, Missouri—20,800 for two shows.

June 30: Civic Auditorium Arena, Omaha—20,557 see two shows.

July 1: Civic Auditorium Arena, Omaha—10,440 turn out.

July 2: Salt Palace, Salt Lake City—13,000 fans show up for the final show of the tour, after which Elvis returns to Memphis.

July 4: Elvis puts his seventh-degree black-belt skills to use in a lengthy demonstration of karate with Ed Parker and Red West at West's Tennessee Karate Institute.

July 10: Elvis creates a bigger stir than the team, receiving a standing ovation when he attends the opening game of the newly formed World Football League in Memphis, pitting the Memphis Grizzlies against the Portland Storm. It isn't important who wins, only that Elvis is there.

July 15: Elvis leaves Memphis for Hawaii, possibly under an assumed name, and almost nothing, except that he has gone, will be known about the trip. But he's back in Memphis by August 10 because on that night he rents a local movie house for a midnight show.

August 12: Off to Los Angeles to rehearse for the next show in Vegas. It will have a new look and some new material, and Elvis is excited about the chance to do something different.

August 19: Elvis opens in Vegas, looking trimmer and more fit. He has also changed the act, with a new opening and more new songs—but it's not what his audience expects and the response is not strong. So much for trying something new. He realizes that they want the Elvis they're comfortable with.

LAMAR FIKE
ON ELVIS' IRON CONSTITUTION:

With all the controversy about Elvis' drug-taking and his physical condition toward the end of his life, people often forget what a tank he was. Nobody did what Elvis did in Las Vegas. Four weeks, seven days a week, two, sometimes three shows a night. An awesome schedule. But he did it. Those of us who were there now understand that the man was working himself to death. Literally.

DAVID STANLEY
ON ELVIS' IRON CONSTITUTION:

Elvis had the stomach of a goat or some damn thing. He could eat and drink anything at all and never feel it. So when he got sick, like the flu, he really got sick and he hated it. It was hard to keep him quiet and in bed. Now that's different than the pills; he took the pills to shut himself off. He was in control of that, so it was OK to him. But he really couldn't stand missing shows and would go a long ways not to have that happen. People just don't realize how tough he was, what a trooper he was.

ON ELVIS' RESTLESSNESS:

He was like a caged animal at that time, always pacing, always moving. We would just get in a car and go, it didn't matter much where, except it was never anywhere new and he was never alone. We would just go back and forth to places he was familiar with, like he was looking for something he'd lost, and if he could find it, he'd be happy. I think he really missed Priscilla and Lisa Marie and couldn't figure out how it had all gone wrong.

August 20: The show returns to a tried-and-true format, and the audience is happy. It's doubtful that Elvis is as happy about it as they are, but he's too much of a professional to do anything but what will please his fans.

August 26: Elvis cancels the day's shows because of illness.

August 27: After a day's rest, he's back on stage and although not 100%, he does a good show.

Elvis was a karate enthusiast ever since he learned the basic moves of martial arts defense during his army years. He received his first black belt in 1960, and would display his skills in a number of movies shortly thereafter, including *G.I. Blues* and *Blue Hawaii*. He eventually would earn an eighth-degree black belt—"master of the art"—and enjoyed incorporating these moves in his stage routine.

August 29: In a presentation on stage during the early show, Elvis is awarded his eighth-degree black belt. He is dressed in full karate garb and demonstrates his skills during the performance.

September 2: Elvis closes in Vegas. By all accounts, the last show in this engagement is one of the great ones. Elvis takes the stage and doesn't leave for almost two hours. He is in good humor, bantering and joking with the audience, and they love it as much as he does. Sheila Ryan, one of Elvis' new girlfriends, is in the audience.

September 3: Still in high spirits, Elvis catches Tom Jones' show and comes up on stage during the final number, whipping through a karate routine while Jones sings. They get a standing ovation.

September 5: Off to Los Angeles.

September 23: Back in Memphis after a few more days in LA, Elvis goes on a buying spree to end all buying sprees, going down to the lot of Schilling Lincoln-Mercury in Memphis and buying every Continental in stock. The six cars are distributed among friends, and he then buys five Cadillacs and passes them out as well. The tab is over $100,000. As always, he pays cash and takes care of all the licensing fees and gift taxes. "Just give Daddy the bill," he always says. Vernon always pays.

September 27: Before the cars are in people's driveways, Elvis is off on an eastern swing. His fourth tour of 1974 will begin in Baltimore at College Park Field House with 15,000 fans attending.

September 29: Olympia Stadium, Detroit—17,105 come to see the King. Elvis is ill with a high fever. He sings for thirty minutes before almost collapsing off stage.

September 30: Notre Dame Convention Center, South Bend—12,301 screaming fans get what they came for, with Elvis in top form after recovering from the flu.

October 1: Notre Dame Convention Center, South Bend—12,301 once again.

October 2: Civic Center, St. Paul—17,163 paid in full.

October 3: Civic Center, St. Paul—17,163 once again.

October 4: Olympia Stadium, Detroit—17,105 in attendance.

October 5: Expo Convention Center, Indianapolis—28,000 for two shows.

October 6: University of Dayton Arena—27,000 for two shows.

October 7: Levitt Arena, Kansas City—10.000 attend.

October 8: Convention Center, San Antonio—10,500 tickets sold.

October 9: Expo Center, Abilene—8,604 fans attend. Linda Thompson and Lisa Marie come along with Vernon.

October 11 – 14: Elvis appears at the Sahara in Tahoe. The eight performances are makeups for the canceled shows from last spring.

October 15 – November 10: Elvis and a couple of the boys head out on a road trip, seemingly unable to stay in one place for long before the urge hits him to move on. He's seen in Palm Springs, Los Angeles, Las Vegas and Memphis.

December 15: Elvis is in Memphis getting ready for the holidays. He gives his usual donations to local charities, the number of which is growing every year.

December 25: A very quiet Christmas at Graceland. It's rumored that Elvis tried unsuccessfully to talk Priscilla into spending it with him and the rest of the family.

December 31: An equally quiet New Year's Eve, despite the news that Elvis earned close to $7,250,000 in 1974.

1975

....

MY WAY

DAVID STANLEY

ON A SURPRISE PRESENT FOR ELVIS:

We were up in the house one night when Vester called from the gate and said there was this big box for Elvis. We asked him what it was and he told us the delivery man said it was some dogs, Russian wolfhounds or something. Elvis said we didn't need no more dogs and to send them back. So Vester tells the truck to go away and it does. Turns out that in the box were these two girls from Mississippi who had decided they would be a birthday present for Elvis and packed themselves inside. I guess they started banging on the box or something and the driver let them out. They never did see Elvis.

January: Elvis is turning 40 and his problems are mounting with his weight. He has become so heavy that the regular January gig in Vegas is canceled so he can focus on dropping some pounds. It isn't as easy as it used to be when he was a kid, and he hasn't lost his taste for that heavy country cookin'. So the battle with the scale is constant, and it makes him edgy and difficult to be around. His close friends are also concerned about the pills that are his constant companions. Elvis has become a master chemist and mixer of potions, he knows as much about the medicines he takes as Dr. Nick, who seems more than willing to keep him in prescription slips. The shy young man who became an animal on stage is in the process of becoming one in real life. It will be a long year.

January 8: Elvis celebrates his 40th birthday at a very small and very private dinner party at Graceland. Linda Thompson, who is with him almost every minute of the day, and David Stanley are the only guests. Fans crowd the main gate to wish him well, unaware of the somber atmosphere inside.

January 17: It's a banner sales day for the local Caddie dealerships. Elvis buys eleven cars and gives them to his friends.

January 21: Elvis has his eye on a Boeing 707. The plane, built for Robert Vesco, has been converted into a luxury suite in the air. He bids $1.5 million and puts down a $75,000 deposit.

January 29: Elvis is admitted to Baptist Memorial Hospital for "tests." The hospital says Elvis is in for a general physical and treatment for a liver problem. According to David Stanley, Elvis is in for detox.

February 5: While Elvis is in the hospital, Vernon suffers a major heart attack, and he's taken to Baptist where Elvis is staying.

When Elvis purchased and converted a Convair 880—which he dubbed the *Lisa Marie*—for his personal use, he had succeeded in creating an almost totally enclosed world. With the heavily customized jet at his disposal, he could literally move from behind the high walls of Graceland to the stage of his next concert and not encounter an unfamiliar face. Elvis' master bedroom on the *Lisa Marie* boasted a queen-size bed and a bathroom with golden fixtures. Like his private bedroom suite at Graceland, the area was off limits to anyone except certain members of the Mafia and then by invitation only. The *Lisa Marie* was on call 24 hours a day and stood ready to depart at a moment's notice.

February 13: The deal on the 707 goes sour when it is discovered that Vesco's people will seize the plane if it ever lands outside U.S. soil. Elvis' lawyers attempt to get his money back.

February 14: Elvis is released from the hospital and returns to Graceland.

February 17: Elvis buys several more horses and cars.

February 20: Feeling and looking better, a relaxed Elvis rents the Memphian movie theater.

February 24: Linda, Red, Joe, Elvis and all the guys are back out for a night at the movies.

Elvis' relationship with the Memphis Mafia had its ups and downs over the years, but by 1975 real strain was developing between some old, old friends. Feeling underpaid, underappreciated and given the challenging job of dealing with an increasingly difficult Elvis, Red (above right with Elvis and Linda), Sonny and the rest of the boys were going through some hard times that would soon become harder.

DAVID STANLEY
ON ELVIS IN THE HOSPITAL:

He would go into the hospital every once in a while to dry out and then it would be fine for a time. If you think about it, you wonder where Elvis would have been if there had been rehabilitation clinics back then. Now it's like if you haven't been through rehab, you aren't in the music business. But then, well, there was so much at stake and it was all a secret that just got harder and harder to keep.

ON ELVIS AND ERIC CLAPTON:

We rented the theater basically every night of the week to watch movies. And one night Jerry Schilling, a really neat guy who worked with Elvis for years, brought over Eric Clapton, who was in town doing a concert. When Clapton came into the theater, Elvis got up and shook his hand.

Clapton said, "I'm Eric Clapton."
And Elvis said, "What do you do?"
"I'm a musician."
"What do you play?"
I honestly think Elvis didn't know. Elvis simply was not plugged into current American music. He never, ever listened to the radio.
"Guitar," Clapton answered.
"Well, if you'd like some lessons, my guitarist James Burton could give you some."
Now, my brother Rick and I are looking for a rock to hide under. Oh, Elvis, you're not offering guitar lessons to Eric Clapton. But Clapton was pure class, not a bit offended.
"I'd give anything to sit in on a session with Elvis Presley and play guitar with James Burton."
Clapton and Elvis and Burton never did have that session. It was Elvis' loss, he just didn't know who Clapton was. And that's a shame, because if he'd heard him play, he would've loved him.

Elvis' favorite animal was his chow chow Getlo. Despite the breed's aggressive reputation, this dog was so laid-back Elvis named him Getlo and the dog would often sleep on the end of his master's bed. The King loved to just hang out with him. After an unsuccessful operation in August of 1975, the dog died, and Elvis took it particularly hard, even spurning replacement pets from friends.

March 1: Elvis wins only his third Grammy for *How Great Thou Art.*

Another disappointment comes when discussions break down between the Colonel and Barbra Streisand concerning Elvis playing opposite her in *A Star Is Born.* Money is the issue, and the Colonel drives too hard a bargain. Elvis had been thrilled about the possibility of doing a meatier role in a classy feature. But Parker's motives are as elusive as ever. Does he really think it's not a good deal for his boy, or does he want to keep Elvis on the road and the money rolling in?

March 10 – 11: At RCA Hollywood, Elvis does his first recording session in many months: *And I Love You So, Bringing It Back, Fairytale, Green Green Grass Of Home, I Can Help, Pieces Of My Life, Shake A Hand, Susan When She Tried, T-R-O-U-B-L-E* and *Woman Without Love.*

March 18: Elvis opens at the newly refurbished and enlarged Hilton in Las Vegas for a two-week engagement to make up for the one that was canceled in January.

April 1: Elvis closes in Vegas. The early show is a special occasion to celebrate the opening of the new wing of the hotel. The midnight show is, by all accounts, insane and chaotic, but lots of fun. Elvis is in good spirits, playing jokes on the audience and the band. His dog, Getlo, even makes it on stage.

April 2: Elvis and the crew return to Memphis, where they'll rest and ready themselves for the spring concert tours. The two tours are almost back to back. It will be a long and tough 60 days for everybody— especially Elvis.

April 24: The first stop on the tour is Macon, Georgia at the Coliseum, where 10,242 fans show up to watch. Elvis seems tired, overweight and pale, but he works hard and the crowd loves him. It feels as if they're family.

April 25: Veteran's Memorial Coliseum, Jacksonville—10,532 pack the stands.

April 26: Curtis-Hixon Auditorium, Tampa—15,000 for two shows.

April 27: Lakeland Civic Center, Lakeland, Florida—8,200 fans crowd the hall.

April 28: Lakeland Civic Center, Lakeland, Florida—another full house of 8,200.

April 29: Murphy Athletic Center, Murfreesboro—12,000 tickets sold.

April 30: Omni, Atlanta—51,684 paid for three concerts in three days.

May 3: Civic Center, Monroe, Louisiana—16,000 file in.

May 4: Civic Center, Lake Charles, Louisiana—20,000 for two shows.

May 5: State Fair Coliseum, Jackson, Mississippi—10,242 pop for a benefit that nets over $100,000 to help tornado victims.

May 6 – 7: Murphy Athletic Center, Murfreesboro—12,000 attend two shows, with the final night as the last show of the tour. Elvis returns to Memphis and will hang out there for the rest of the month.

May 30: The second leg of the tour begins in Huntsville, Alabama at the Von Braun Civic Center, where 40,000 attend five shows in three days.

June 2: Mobile Municipal Auditorium, Mobile, Alabama—11,240 attend.

June 3: Memorial Auditorium, Tuscaloosa—15,400 tickets sold.

June 4: Hofheinz Pavilion, Houston—24,000 at two shows in two days.

June 6: Memorial Auditorium, Dallas—10,000 buy tickets.

June 7: Hirsch Coliseum, Shreveport—22,000 tickets sold.

June 8: State Fair Coliseum, Jackson, Mississippi—22,000 at two concerts in two days.

June 10: Mid-South Coliseum, Memphis—12,367 screaming fans bring Elvis to the end of the tour.

June 11: Elvis finally gets his own plane. It's a Convair 880 jet on which he spends $750,000 remodeling and calls the *Lisa Marie.*

June 16: Elvis goes into the hospital complaining of eye problems relating to his tendency toward glaucoma.

June 17: Elvis is released from the hospital.

July 4: Lisa Marie arrives at Graceland for the 4th of July.

DAVID STANLEY
ON "THE LIFERS":

At the end there were five "Lifers" sharing the job. Me, my brother Ricky Stanley, Al Strada, Dean Nichopoulos and Steve Smith. But the core lifers were Ricky, Al and me because we'd been with Elvis so long. Basically the job of "The Lifers" in the last couple of years of his life was to give Elvis the drugs he demanded. And to watch him—literally watch him. And at the end it got to the point where somebody had to be there 24 hours a day because he was taking so many drugs. Elvis would go to bed with 33 pills and wake up with amphetamines and liquid cocaine. And this was the last sixteen months. Almost everything he took was prescription. We'd have to go to Baptist Hospital to pick up the stuff. And it would be in everybody's name but Elvis'.

The irony is that even now, with his own life almost totally out of control, Elvis would come into my room two or three times a week, catch me smoking a joint and fire me on the spot. And while he was firing me, he'd be rant-ing about druggies and how they're destroying the moral fiber of this great country and they should all be locked up. I guess you could say he was in what they now call denial. Big time.

David Stanley and Joe Esposito help Elvis to his room before a concert in Pine Bluff, Arkansas.

A TYPICAL TOUR DAY FOR ELVIS:

4:00 P.M.: Elvis is awakened by one of his personal aides in the bedroom of his hotel suite. Breakfast is waiting for him when he wakes: 2 cheese omelets, 1 pound of bacon burned almost black, cantaloupe, black coffee. Elvis watches TV while he eats—quiz shows. His favorite is *The Match Game*.

8:00 P.M.: Elvis goes into his bedroom with the "wrecking crew," five aides (led by Al Strada, his wardrobe manager) who have the job of getting him dressed for the show.

8:30 P.M.: Elvis leaves his hotel suite, protected by his personal bodyguards as well as twelve to fifteen local police officers. Three limousines are waiting for him and his entourage. He gets into the first one, which takes off escorted by police cars.

8:48 – 8:55 P.M.: Elvis arrives in his dressing room just before he goes on stage, waiting while J.D. Sumner and The Stamps finish their set.

9:00 P.M.: Elvis takes the stage to wild applause and popping flash bulbs, breaking into *See See Rider*, and the crowd goes wild for the next 58 minutes.

9:58 P.M.: As Elvis starts his final song, *I Can't Help Falling in Love With You*, his bodyguards (David Stanley, Ricky Stanley, Ed Parker, Jerry Schilling, Red West, Sonny West) move onto the front of the stage. The moment he ends the song, thousands of fans crush forward. This is when it's dangerous. The height of the stage determines how easily Elvis will be spirited away to the limo. Eight to ten feet means a piece of cake, while a three-foot stage means potential trouble. Elvis' bodyguards expect the unexpected.

10:00 P.M.: Elvis jumps into the first of three waiting limousines, which head directly for the airport. When Elvis boards the *Lisa Marie*, his customized Convair 880 jet, he heads straight to his bedroom in the rear, which features a $14,000 queen-size bed. Before he does anything else, he spends a few minutes with Dr. George Nichopoulos (Dr. Nick), who gives him Quaaludes, Percodan and Dilaudid to bring him "down" from the concert. When Dr. Nick leaves, the wrecking crew enters to take Elvis out of his costume and put him into a pair of pajamas and a robe. Food is waiting in the bedroom, and Elvis begins to eat almost immediately.

11:30 P.M. — 12:00 A.M.: Landing in the next city, the planes are met by three limousines and a police escort. Before he leaves the plane, Elvis slips on a loose-fitting D.E.A. (Drug Enforcement Administration) jumpsuit over his pajamas. At the hotel, he and his entourage are met by Colonel Parker and by the advance men, who have spent the day making sure everything is ready for Elvis. The windows have been blacked-out, food is waiting, keys are in the doors of all the rooms. When Elvis arrives, the advance men immediately go to the airport and move on to the next city.

12:30 A.M.: The first thing Elvis does when he walks into his suite is to have another visit with Dr. Nick. Then he eats a lot of cheeseburgers or ribs, calls the girlfriend who's traveling with him and goes into the bedroom.

1:30 – 5:00 A.M.: During these last few years of his life, Elvis is obsessed by the spiritual and the occult. He carries a trunk of books and spends hours reading the *Bible*, Cheiro's *Book of Numbers*, *The Prophet* by Kahlil Gibran or *The Impersonal Life* by Joseph Berner.

5:00 – 7:00 A.M.: After taking a few more pills, Elvis eventually slides into a deep, almost catatonic sleep.

4:00 P.M.: Take it from the top.

Course IV	THE NUMBER EIGHT	Lesson 8

path to be narrowly circumscribed in consciousness or environment. The vast spaces are always calling. The inner voice of 8 is ever speaking unutterable things. On the outstretched wings of the Caduceus he must be out and away breathing a rarefied air if he is to do his best work and realize the high idealism of which his soul is ever conscious. He must be free and untrammeled to follow Moses to the heights of Mt Nebo, the peak of Wisdom, there to meet God face to face and to know the glory of a divine transfiguration. Eight in its highest expression elevates man from the realms of mortality to his true position within the radiance of spiritual being.

Sea green is the color of 8, and the Caduceus its symbol. The eighth zodiacal sign, Scorpio, is the emblem of death and also of immortality; it is for the native to choose which of the two it shall be, , the path of the beast or the way of the eagle. The casket is encircled with the rainbow.

The Dragon, or the Serpent, is symbolically related to the number 8. The serpentine or cyclic ebb and flow of all life currents have been shown to be the origin of the cosmic 8. It was the misuse of this serpentine life current within the body of man which caused him to become an exile from the Edenic Garden. When this is understood and the currents corrected through regeneration the gates will open on the New Jerusalem. "That which ascends is the same as that which descends."

A symbolic picture of the New Age depicts a stormy sea typifying the travail of overcoming the turbulence of earthly life. Above the waters shine 8 clear, brilliant stars. A young girl stands with one foot on land, one on sea. In her hands she holds two cups from which flow Charity or Love and Equality or Universal Brotherhood. Above her head shines an eight-pointed star, and near her is an open flower above which is poised a butterfly with wide-stretched wings. This figure represents Truth. The picture as a whole represents symbolically the illumined 8.

Key words of this number are freedom, expansion,

70

This page from the *Sacred Science of Numbers* book was a special gift from Elvis to Aurelia Yarbrough, a good friend who toured with the entourage as a hairdresser. In addition to his traditional Biblical beliefs, Elvis spent hours reading about other facets of spirituality, and these passages that he underlined mirrored his private thoughts.

July 8: Elvis begins the third tour of 1975. First stop: Myriad Convention Center in Oklahoma City, with 15,291 attending.

July 9: Hulman Civic Center, Terra Haute, Indiana—10,244 screaming fans attend.

July 10: Cleveland Coliseum, Richfield, Ohio—21,000 paid admissions.

July 11: Civic Center, Charleston, West Virginia—24,800 fans fill the house for three shows in two days.

July 13: International Convention Center, Niagara Falls—23,000 for two shows.

July 14: Civic Center Hockey Arena, Springfield, Massachusetts—36,000 for two shows.

July 16: Veteran's Memorial Coliseum, New Haven—20,000 tickets sold for two shows in two days.

July 18: Cleveland Coliseum, Richfield, Ohio—21,000 paid in full.

July 19: Nassau Coliseum, Uniondale, Long Island—33,000 watch two shows.

July 20: Norfolk, Virginia—22,600 cheer for two strong performances. In this concert Elvis offends his backup singers by saying that he smells catfish on their breath, and they walk off the stage.

July 21: Greensboro Coliseum, Greensboro—16,300 watch as Elvis apologizes to The Sweet Inspirations during the show. That same day he visits the dentist to deal with a tooth problem, which is generally an excuse to get more drugs.

July 22: Civic Center, Asheville, North Carolina—14,847 at two shows in two nights look on as Elvis does knockout shows. He is presented with personalized underwear during the first show and gives J.D. Sumner a $40,000 ring. Just to keep the good times rolling, he later shoots the screen out of the television set.

There were times when it seemed the only person who mattered to Elvis was his little girl. Lisa Marie was devoted to Elvis and he did his best to make her stays at Graceland memorable occasions.

DAVID STANLEY
ON TWO DEATH THREATS:

The show at the Silverdome was a massive show. And a wild one. In the middle of it, suddenly this guy is running toward the stage from the football field, carrying a gun. And it's my job to stop this sort of thing. Which I did. Took him out, nice and clean, and the cops carted him off. Incidents like this didn't scare Elvis; he wasn't a fearful guy at all. They just pissed him off.

About a week or so later, Elvis calls me in and says he wants to telephone the guy who came after him. "John O'Grady gave me the guy's number in Detroit. He's already out on bail." Now my first reaction was, Oh, no, here's trouble, because Elvis is all 'luded up. And he says, "Get him on the phone!" So I did. And Elvis gets on the phone. "Hey, buddy. You know who this is? This is Elvis. I'm your worst nightmare. I'm gonna blow your brains out." He's stoned as a moose, and just going on and on about it. And the volume is going up and up, he's yelling into the phone. That's when I grabbed it and hung up. "Elvis,' I said, "you're getting yourself in a heap of trouble."

He stared at me hard and said, "Call the plane. We're going to Detroit."

"Elvis," I said, "there's a snowstorm outside and we're not flying out of here tonight to go kill this guy in Detroit."

"Oh, yes we are, damn it!"

Of course we didn't go anywhere, but I bet there was a guy in Detroit who didn't get much sleep that night.

July 24: Civic Center, Asheville, North Carolina—7,437 stare in awe as Elvis gives away his guitar and two diamond rings. It's the last concert of the tour. These three shows are some of the best Elvis has done or will ever do. Right after the show, Elvis returns to Memphis. Although Linda is still in the picture, he continues to see other women on a regular basis.

July 27: Elvis goes car shopping again, buying fourteen Cadillacs for friends plus one for a bank teller he didn't even know, Minnie Person, who had been admiring his car. When she blurts out that her birthday is on the 29th, Elvis writes a check so she can get one for herself. It pays to hang around car lots in Memphis when Elvis is in town.

August 7: Ricky Stanley is arrested at Methodist Hospital while trying to pass a forged prescription for Demerol. Elvis bails him out. It's likely that the prescription is for Elvis.

August 12: Getlo, Elvis' chow chow, comes down with a kidney problem. When he discovers that the best vet is in Boston, Elvis flies the animal on his private jet to the clinic, where the dog will stay until late in November.

August 16: In flight from Memphis to Las Vegas, Elvis has trouble breathing, and the plane is forced to land in Dallas, where he's checked into a motel. In a few hours he is able to continue the trip west.

August 18: Elvis opens in Las Vegas for a two-week run. He seems distracted during the opening show, has trouble with the lyrics and several times during the concert, sweating profusely, he sits down while the backup singers take over.

August 20: Elvis' midnight show is disrupted when two water pistols are thrown on stage. He begins to play with them, and the show disintegrates into giggles and laughter. The audience is confused and the band doesn't seem to know whether

When Elvis worked out at the Tennessee Karate Institute, Linda often came along to watch. Elvis' life-long love of the martial arts gave him a focus in his life and was a continuing source of comfort. In 1975, Elvis received an award from RCA for world record sales in Las Vegas (right). Some say that it is impossible to know the exact figure of records actually sold, but the number is in the hundreds of millions. For over twenty years, Elvis Presley *was* Rock & Roll.

to continue or not. Elvis has gone over the edge, and has to be taken back to his room by members of the Memphis Mafia.

August 21: Elvis is escorted quickly out of the hotel around 6:00 A.M. with Dr. Nick, taken to the airport and flown directly to Memphis, where he's admitted to

Baptist Memorial Hospital suffering from what the doctor calls "extreme fatigue." In fact, he has come close to overdosing on uppers. Back in Vegas, a sign goes up in the lobby saying that the rest of the engagement has been canceled due to illness.

August 26: Though no one will admit it, Elvis is a mess, totally strung out. Years of abuse have weakened his system and his physical shape is appalling. Everyone in his court knows the truth: He's in serious trouble and in need of help, a fact that Elvis continues to deny.

September 5: Elvis is released from the hospital in the evening—accompanied by two nurses—to Graceland, where they will remain on duty for several weeks. One of them, Marion Cocke, will stay with him until January 1976.

October – November: While Elvis is recuperating, he buys some three-wheel motorcycles and speeds around Memphis with Linda Thompson. He's also having a sauna and a racquetball court installed at Graceland, and he spends time watching the work. With the help of the nurses, he is soon in good spirits and regaining his health, playing racquetball regularly and working on his karate.

November 27: Elvis returns to Las Vegas on his recently finished private plane, the *Lisa Marie*. With the cost of interior renovations ending up almost $1,000,000, the plane is either unbelievably beautiful or in extremely bad taste, depending on the point of view—but it's a flying palace.

December 2 – 15: Elvis opens in Vegas at the Hilton, making up the dates that were canceled in August. The rest has clearly done him good, because the shows are tight and Elvis is having fun. He is clearheaded, and his banter between the songs is funny. The engagement is a big success both for him and for the hotel. He packed in 32,000 people for a box-office take of over $800,000.

December 25: A quiet and relaxed Christmas is spent at Graceland with Linda and friends.

December 31: The crew leaves with Elvis and Linda for Pontiac. He hits the stage around 11:00 P.M. and stays on till after midnight. He's in top form and the fans are wild and crazy. The show sells 62,500 tickets and earns $816,000, believed to be the all-time record at the time for a single performer on a single night. Not all goes well, however: Elvis splits his pants, but gracefully does a quick change.

DAVID STANLEY
ON THE OTHER DOCTORS AROUND ELVIS:

It's important to note Dr. Nick wasn't the only one overprescribing drugs to Elvis. Dr. Elias Ghanem also prescribed massive amounts of drugs. Others who prescribed were Dr. Max Shapiro of Los Angeles and Dr. Thomas Newman from Las Vegas. So it wasn't just Nick. What would happen was that one doctor would say, "No way, not anymore," and another one would go ahead and give the prescription. Until right at the end, Dr. Nick would say no a fair amount of the time. But finally he just caved in and basically gave Elvis whatever he wanted.

I believe, and this is just my opinion, that Dr. Nick was just taking advantage of Elvis. I mean, Elvis had bought him a $750,000 home. Had invested in something called Center Court Racketball, which Dr. Nick and Joe Esposito were involved with and which collapsed and was a total disaster. Nick was way into Elvis, so at the end Elvis had him right were he wanted him. Of course, if it hadn't been Dr. Nick, it would have been somebody else. There's no question about that. This is Elvis Presley we're talking about, and if he wanted something, he got it. It was that simple.

DAVID STANLEY
ON ELVIS, DRUGS AND GUNS:

When Elvis didn't get what he wanted, he was a dangerous man. I remember one time we were in Los Angeles at Linda's apartment and Elvis asked me, "Do you have my drugs?" I told him no, but that I was trying to find Doctor Elias Ghanem, his doctor in Las Vegas.

Just then Ghanem calls me up and says, "Look, I'm on Khashoggi's yacht right now. What do you want?"

And I said, "Elvis needs his drugs."

And Ghanem says, "No, David."

I'm practically begging him, 'cause I know how mad Elvis is. But Ghanem says no and hangs up. So I turned to Elvis and said, "Ghanem says no."

Well, Elvis just snapped. He jumped onto a table with two .45s in his hands and just started blasting the ceiling. "I'll buy a goddamn drugstore if I have to!"

And this wasn't a one-time deal. The exact same incident happened at least four times just with me. I remember another time in Denver when I went into his room when he was really zonked out and said, "I'm gonna take your drugs, Elvis, this is crazy."

And he said very evenly, very calmly, "No, you're not." But I did, or tried. I walked across the room and picked up the kit of drugs. And the next thing I felt was a cold barrel pressing against my forehead. I looked at him and said, "You don't have the balls." I knew he wasn't gonna kill me. But I gave him his drugs back.

1976

REMEMBER THE GOOD TIMES

All of Elvis' jumpsuits were custom made and hand tailored at great expense. Although the basic design was the same; high collar, low-cut "V" buttonless front, bell-bottomed pants with high waist and no pockets, the decoration and stitching made each unique. There were over 20 different designs including: American Eagle, Blue Prehistoric Bird, Burning Love, Flame, Indian, Sundial, King Of Spades, Mad Tiger, Red Lion, Tiffany, Inca Gold Leaf, White Eagle and White Prehistoric Bird. Each outfit had a cape and was worn with a long silk scarf. Elvis traveled to each concert with several options. Shown is one of the Prehistoric Bird designs.

January 1: Elvis and Linda return to Memphis.

January 5: Elvis, Linda and the gang fly to Denver, where they caravan to Vail, Colorado, where Elvis has rented three lavish condos to house everyone for a vacation. He also rents snowmobiles for some terrifying midnight rides down the slopes. During this time, Elvis' drug use once again increases.

Pat West, Linda Thompson, and David Leech enjoy the mountain air in Vail, Colorado. In January of 1976, Elvis was looking for a place to hang out and prepare for the next round of touring. He decided on Vail and flew everyone out to start house hunting. A suitable house was never found, so he rented lavish condos for himself and his friends. Elvis loved the area so much that he considered looking for a place to buy.

January 8: Elvis goes house hunting in Vail. Since he doesn't want anyone to know who he is, he wears a ski mask and a jumpsuit. But he looks a little like a terrorist and doesn't have much luck. He also develops a rash that has to be treated with antibiotics.

January 14: After making an appointment, Elvis and company arrive at Kumpf Lincoln-Mercury in Denver. Several of the men with Elvis are local police officers, and he tells them to pick out cars. When they hesitate, he does it for them, buying $70,000 worth of automobiles in about twenty minutes. He also gives a Cadillac to a local DJ.

January 17: The word about Elvis is getting out. He receives a warning from Denver narcs to get out of town before he gets busted.

January 19: RCA releases *Elvis – A Legendary Performer*. That same day, Elvis and Linda leave Vail abruptly and fly to Los Angeles, where she will audition for television roles. They return to Memphis on the 23rd.

February 2: RCA brings mobile recording equipment to Graceland and sets up a studio in the den. Elvis will spend the next six days recording in all night sessions: *Bitter They Are Harder They Fall, Blue Eyes Cryin' In The Rain, Danny Boy, For The Heart, Hurt, I'll Never Fall In Love Again, Love Comin' Down, Moody Blue, Never Again, She Still Thinks I Care, Solitare* and *The Last Farewell*.

February 16: Elvis tries hypnotism to help him relax.

February 20: Elvis returns to Denver to attend a funeral for a friend. The gang stays until it's time to resume touring in mid-March.

March 17: The first tour of the year starts in Johnson City, Tennessee where 21,000 fans fill Freedom Hall to see the King do three shows in three days.

March 20: The Coliseum, Charlotte, North Carolina—24,000 paid for two shows. In the afternoon a young woman broke through security and got on stage, where she bit Elvis' lip in an attempt to kiss him. He's so flustered he forgets the sequence of songs.

March 21: Riverfront Coliseum, Cincinnati—35,000 for two shows.

Joe Esposito stands on the porch of one of the Vail condos. Elvis would pick up the tab for all the Memphis Mafia and their wives to join him on these vacations. No expense was spared and no one would want for anything. Favorite destinations included Palm Springs, Denver and Hawaii. When relaxing at home, Elvis preferred the Jungle Room at Graceland (right).

DAVID STANLEY
ON AN ABORTED "INTERVENTION":

John O'Grady took his family to one of the Sahara concerts, and Elvis was having a bad night, forgetting lyrics and stumbling around the stage. O'Grady said later that he "cried" after seeing Elvis in that condition, and that he "thought he was going to die that night." So he went to Elvis' attorney, Ed Hookstratten, and they cooked up a plan to confront Elvis about his problems—what's now called an intervention.

They told him that since he was the first to do everything, why not be the first to check into rehab? Can you imagine what Elvis would have been like coming out of rehab clean? He could have accomplished anything. He'd have become even bigger than he'd ever been. Imagine how his fans would have responded. "Elvis has a problem and we can help." Lord, they would have loved that.

But it wasn't to be. According to O'Grady, Elvis told them all to "drop dead." He was busy avoiding reality. And like he was with so many things he did, he was world class at it.

Elvis splits another jumpsuit and has to go off stage to change. The supply is dwindling.

March 22: Keil Auditorium, St. Louis—10,564 for the single performance.

March 26: Back in Memphis, Elvis spots a traffic accident at an intersection, pulls over, gets out of his car, walks to the scene of the accident, pulls out one of his many badges and offers the stunned participants any help they need.

April: Elvis relaxes at Graceland, going to movies, playing racquetball and tooling around town in his various vehicles.

April 12: Construction begins on Elvis Presley Center Courts, Inc. The brainchild of Dr. George Nichopoulos and Joe Esposito, it's an attempt to cash in on the racquetball craze and the Elvis myth. The problem is that the public doesn't connect the two diverse concepts and, even though Elvis will pump in a lot of money, the project is doomed from the start. Dr. Nick will go heavily into Elvis' debt trying to keep the business afloat and, along with Esposito, will eventually sue Elvis to try to keep him from dropping out of the failing business.

April 21: The second tour begins in Kansas City at the Kemper Arena—with attendance over 17,600.

April 22: City Auditorium, Omaha—10,564 paid.

April 23: McNichols Arena, Denver—19,000 tickets sold.

April 24: Sports Arena, San Diego—17,500 attend.

April 25: Long Beach Arena, Long Beach, California—28,000 attend two shows.

April 26: Seattle Coliseum, Seattle—14,687 fans show up.

April 27: Final stop on the tour is the Coliseum in Spokane, Washington. Attendance is a sold-out 7,500.

April 30: Elvis opens in Lake Tahoe at the Sahara. He will perform one show a night except on weekends through May 9th.

May 19: Linda Thompson, who has received clothing, jewelry and cash from Elvis, is given a car: He presents her with a brand new Cadillac.

May 27: The show goes out on the road again. First stop is the Assembly Hall in Bloomington, Indiana—with 16,000 fans jammed to the rafters.

May 28: James W. Hilton Coliseum, Ames, Iowa—14,750 paid attendance.

May 29: Myriad Center, Oklahoma City—15,300 capacity crowd.

May 30: Ector Coliseum, Odessa, Texas—16,000 attend two shows.

May 31: Municipal Coliseum, Lubbock—9,600 tickets sold.

June 1: Community Center Arena, Tucson—20,000 are on hand.

June 2: Civic Center, El Paso—7,050 fill the Grand Hall.

June 3: Tarrant County Convention Center, Fort Worth—14,000 fans show up for the King.

June 4: Omni, Atlanta—68,800 fans attend four shows in three days.

June 5: *From Elvis Presley Boulevard* hits the charts, where it will remain for seventeen weeks.

June 6: After the final show at the Omni, Elvis returns to Memphis, where he will rest a couple of weeks before starting the next leg. The King is tired.

June 25: The fourth tour starts in Buffalo at the Memorial Auditorium, where 17,500 flock to see him.

June 26: Civic Center, Providence, Rhode Island—27,000 attend two shows.

June 27: Capitol Center, Largo, Maryland—40,000 paid admissions for two shows. Backstage, Elvis meets Elton John, who is one of Lisa Marie's favorites. John would like to offer Elvis a song, but nothing comes of it.

June 28: Spectrum, Philadelphia—19,000 tickets sold for one show.

June 29: Coliseum, Richmond, Virginia—11,900 tickets sold.

June 30: Coliseum, Greensboro, North Carolina—16,000 fans attend.

July 1: Hirsch Coliseum, Shreveport, Louisiana—11,000 attend.

July 2: Assembly Center, Baton Rouge—16,000 tickets sold.

July 3: Tarrant County Convention Center, Fort Worth—14,000 in attendance.

July 4: Mabee Center, Oral Roberts University, Tulsa—11,974 watch as Elvis debuts his Bicentennial jumpsuit, a wild mix of patriotic themes such as the Liberty bell in studs and colored stones. The costume is awesome, but it's a workout just to wear it.

July 5: Mid-South Coliseum, Memphis—11,999 hometown fans welcome the King home on this final stop of the tour.

July 7: Elvis, Linda and entourage fly to Palm Springs.

July 13: With no warning whatsoever, Vernon fires Red West, Sonny West and David Hebler as bodyguards. The three men are taken by surprise, especially Red and Sonny, who have been with Elvis since the beginning. Elvis is conveniently out of

Tossing scarves to the audience at the end of a concert became an Elvis tradition. The crew carried boxes of them and Charlie Hodge would follow Elvis around the stage supplying them for Elvis to throw. The ritual became so much a part of the show that audience members would begin to move forward near the end of concerts in hopes of getting the ultimate token. The risk of moving forward was worth the effort. When the spirit moved him, Elvis removed rings and jewelry and sent them flying into the house as well, making some lucky fans richer by a few thousand dollars.

DAVID STANLEY
ON THE FIRING OF RED AND SONNY:

Red was getting frustrated with Elvis. There were canceled shows, there'd been a couple of incidents of passing out. So he would confront Elvis. He'd say, "You're doing too much dope, pal." And when that wouldn't work, he'd say, "You son of a bitch. Get a grip." Nobody talked to Elvis that way. Nobody ever.

I tried, but he wouldn't listen. I was just a kid. But Red and Sonny were his contemporaries, his equals, and Elvis couldn't blow them off, couldn't ignore them the way he could me. I think Elvis' last bit of conscience lay in Red West. Red was the last link between what Elvis ought to be and what he was becoming. And I think Elvis may have been unconsciously thinking, I've got to get rid of my conscience. And since Sonny would join in with his cousin Red, he had to go too. These guys were his last connection with reality. With them gone, Elvis didn't have to confront what he was doing to himself.

Elvis and David Stanley boarding the *Lisa Marie* after a concert in Houston, Texas.

touch in Palm Springs when it happens. The reasons are many. Vernon has never liked any of the Memphis Mafia; he thinks they're unnecessary and too expensive—especially after the millions Elvis has had to pay out for people who'd sued him after getting punched out by Sonny and Red. But the deeper reason for their dismissal, at least for Elvis, is probably the fact that Sonny, Red and David are becoming more and more outspoken in their confrontations with Elvis about his continued use of drugs.

July 23: Elvis starts the fifth leg of the '76 tour in Louisville, Kentucky, where 19,400 show up to see the King.

July 24: Civic Center, Charleston, West Virginia—17,000 attend two shows.

July 25: Onondaga War Memorial Auditorium, Syracuse—8,550 in attendance.

July 26: Community War Memorial Auditorium, Rochester—10,000 paid admissions.

July 27: Back to Onondaga War Memorial Auditorium, Syracuse—8,500 attend.

July 28: Civic Center, Hartford—12,314 watch the King.

July 29: Civic Center, Springfield, Massachusetts—10,000 in attendance. The strain is showing. Elvis develops a sore throat that will be with him for months.

July 30: Veteran's Memorial Coliseum, Hartford—9,600 for one show.

July 31: Hampton Roads Coliseum, Hampton Roads, Virginia—22,000 pay tribute at two shows in two days.

August 2: Civic Center, Roanoke—10,598 watch a very tired Elvis get through the show.

August 3: Cumberland County Memorial Auditorium, Fayetteville—21,000 attend three shows in three days. It's the final stop on this leg. Elvis and Linda return to Memphis after the show.

August 21: RCA announces that Elvis has sold more than 400 million records.

August 27: The sixth leg begins at the Convention Center in San Antonio. 11,000 fans gather for the big event.

August 28: Hofheinz Pavilion, Houston—12,000 paid admissions.

August 29: Municipal Auditorium, Mobile, Alabama—10,720 tickets sold. It's in Mobile, before the show, that Elvis finds out Red and Sonny West and David Hebler have written a book about him.

August 30: Memorial Coliseum, Tuscaloosa—12,000 admitted.

August 31: The Coliseum, Macon, Georgia—10,200 in admissions.

September 1: Jacksonville Coliseum, Jacksonville—9,500 attend.

September 2: Curtis Hixon Hall, Tampa—7,500 capacity crowd.

DAVID STANLEY
ON RED AND SONNY'S BOOK:

Elvis called me in my room. He was crying, really crying, and he said, "David, I need to see you now." I walked into his room and he was sitting in the middle of the bed, and I'll never forget it, it was the loneliest thing I ever saw. He was sitting with his legs crossed, face in his hands, and he was surrounded by all the guys and nobody was saying a word. It was a cold scene, and I just thought, Lord, what's going on here?

I said, "Does someone want to fill me in? What the hell's going on here?" And Elvis just held up a manuscript and said, "My life is over. I'm a dead man." And the manuscript was a book called Elvis: What Happened? *It was by Red and Sonny and David. John O'Grady had gotten an advance copy from the publisher.*

"What the hell is this about?" I asked. And Elvis just started blurting out what Red and Sonny had said in the book. That he was taking drugs. That he had tried to have Mike Stone, Priscilla's boyfriend, killed. On and on.

One second he'd be crying, saying, "How could Red and Sonny do this to me, we were in school together, we were friends. I love those guys." And the next second he'd be cursing them, saying, "Those mothers, those dirty bastards, I want to kill 'em." These were guys he thought were as close to him as anybody, and they had turned on him. Now, in some ways this was typical Elvis—seeing things from his own perspective only, because he was conveniently forgetting that he had fired them.

But they didn't have to write a book about him. They called it a plea to Elvis to get his act together, and I'm sure it was, but they had been not only fired but dumped on—dropped like a bad habit—after twenty years of loyalty and dedication, and they felt betrayed, and this was their chance to vindicate themselves. And I think they exaggerated the situation he was in. In my opinion, up until this time, Elvis was not in a life-threatening situation with his drug use. They would affect his personality and his performance, and they'd make him mean sometimes. They'd certainly make him eat too much. But I don't think they were killing him.

Even if they were wrong about Elvis, though, you can never convince me that Red West didn't love him. You can never convince me that Sonny didn't care about him. Now, Dave Hebler was a newcomer—and he didn't really know Elvis very well—so his motivation might have been purely money. But not Red or Sonny. They'd known Elvis for years. They wanted him to get better. I don't have any doubt of that, and I never will.

But their book was completely devastating to Elvis, and I don't think they had any idea what effect it would have on him. This was in the days before celebrities were praised for dealing with their drug problems, and middle America considered most rock musicians a bunch of dope-smoking degenerates. Elvis was held to a higher standard. As far as his fans were concerned, he could do no wrong: He didn't cuss, smoke, drink, chew, lie or lust. It was this all-American image that separated him from stars like Mick Jagger or John Lennon, all those "druggies" who had embraced the hippie culture. Elvis never did; he was a patriotic American with traditional Southern values. And here was this book calling him a junkie. It was the beginning of the end for Elvis. After Red and Sonny wrote their book, his life just was never the same. With them gone and all his secrets out, it was like a wing came off a 747. Elvis just went straight down.

Elvis gives a benefit performance in Mississippi after a tornado wreaked havoc in the state in 1976. Growing up poor in the south made him painfully aware of what it was like to never have quite enough and he felt a real obligation to give something back to those in need. From the very beginning of his career, Elvis involved himself in good works. It has been estimated that he donated more than $20 million to various charities during his lifetime.

September 3: Bay Front Center, St. Petersburg—8,000 paid admissions.

September 4: Civic Center, Lakeland, Florida—16,000 attend two shows.

September 5: State Fair Civic Center, Jackson, Mississippi—12,000 paid admissions.

September 6: Von Braun Civic Center, Huntsville, Alabama—16,000 for two shows.

September 7: Convention Center, Pine Bluff, Arkansas—15,000 fill the house for two shows in this final stop on the tour. Elvis is exhausted and returns to Memphis to rest. After a few days he and some of the guys go to Palm Springs, where he spends time with Priscilla and Lisa Marie.

October 4: Elvis is back at Graceland. He is spotted on one of his Harleys at a local gas station. The usual crowd gathers and he spends some time with his fans.

October 14: Elvis begins yet another leg of the '76 tour. At Chicago Stadium in the Windy City, 38,000 attend two shows over two nights.

October 17: Metropolitan Sports Center, Minneapolis—15,800 watch an inspired performance. For tonight, the fire is back.

DAVID STANLEY
ON LINDA'S LEAVING:

Linda Thompson loved Elvis, she really did. Of all the women around him, I think she was the only one he really allowed to love him. But toward the end it was rough, when you love a guy and you have to drag him from room to room unconscious, Linda couldn't live with that anymore. She'd had enough of the craziness.

ON ELVIS THE SEEKER:

Elvis was really at sea after Linda left. He'd accomplished everything any man could want, but he was missing the simplicity of a relationship. The simplicity of spending time with someone, of being able to communicate. He was still looking for love. Even now, at the end, he was still searching. That's when Ginger Alden came in. But she couldn't help him. Those last two years were all downhill. He kept taking drug after drug after drug. And canceling shows.

And he could never talk about what was happening to him. He just had no ability to do that. In some ways he was even boring to be with because of his inability to talk. Sitting in a room with people talking, Elvis was like a prostitute in church, he'd be that uncomfortable. Communicating was so hard for him that eventually he just gave up. That was a big part of his demise.

October 19: Dane County Coliseum, Madison, Wisconsin—10,211 tickets sold.

October 20: Notre Dame Athletic and Convention Center, South Bend, Indiana—12,000 attend.

October 21: Wings Stadium, Kalamazoo—7,500 attend.

October 22: Assembly Hall, Champaign, Illinois—17,000 tickets sold.

October 23: Cleveland Coliseum, Richmond, Ohio—20,000 tickets sold.

October 24: Roberts Stadium, Evansville, Indiana—13,500 in attendance.

October 25: Memorial Coliseum, Fort Wayne, Indiana—8,500 tickets sold.

October 26: Ohio University, Dayton—13,000 attend.

October 27: Southern Illinois University Arena is sold out for the final stop on this leg of the tour. Afterward Elvis returns to Memphis.

October 29: RCA once again sets up shop in the den at Graceland, this time for a two-night session. The results: *He'll Have To Go, It's Easy For You, Pledging My Love* and *There's A Fire Down Below.*

October 30: Elvis gives one of his Lincolns to J.D. Sumner for his work in the recording session, then splits for Aspen without Linda, who has become increasingly tired of taking care of him and, like many others, is very worried about the scale of his drug abuse. In his absence, she leaves and ends the relationship.

November 10: Elvis returns to Memphis and buys Lamar Fike a Corvette.

November 23: In a bizarre incident, Jerry Lee Lewis is arrested at the gates of Graceland for being drunk and disorderly and for carrying a concealed .38 caliber revolver.

November 24: Elvis begins another tour, starting out at the Centennial Coliseum in Reno.

November 25: McArthur Court, Eugene, Oregon.

November 26: Memorial Coliseum, Portland, Oregon—11,000 gate.

November 27: Back to McArthur Court, Eugene, Oregon for one more show.

November 28 – 29: Cow Palace, San Francisco—two sold-out shows with 14,300 in attendance both nights.

November 30: The six-day tour ends at the Anaheim Convention Center before a huge crowd of 55,000 fans. Then Elvis flies to Las Vegas to open at the Hilton.

December 2: Elvis opens in Vegas, where he'll do one show a night except on Friday and Saturday. People notice that his weight is back down and he seems rested, even though the touring in 1976 has been demanding beyond belief. During this engagement, Elvis meets the next woman in his life. Young and beautiful, Ginger Alden is another Southern belle who reminds many of Priscilla. Her father was in the army and in the draft office when Elvis was sworn in.

December 5: Lisa Marie appears on stage, much to the delight of the fans. Elvis does much of his performance seated in a chair. He says he sprained his ankle falling on a step to the bathroom.

December 6: Elvis does a short version of the show because of his ankle.

December 10: Elvis calls a friend in Los Angeles, Gerald Peters, who owns a car service, and asks him to find a white Lincoln Continental and deliver it to Vegas. A speedy and hectic search discovers the proper car and Peters rushes it to Vegas himself. The King gives it to Ginger after the midnight show. Peters hangs around to drive the car to Memphis so she can have it on her return from Vegas. By the time he arrives at Graceland, he learns that Elvis has bought her a Cadillac in the meantime.

December 12: Elvis closes at the Hilton and returns to Memphis with Ginger.

December 23: Vernon is late with the charitable donations, but he has a good excuse. He's been in the hospital with chest pains.

December 25: Christmas at Graceland. Elvis gives Lisa Marie a golf cart of her own to tool around the grounds.

December 27: The last tour of 1976 begins in Witchita Falls, Texas at the Henry Levitt Arena, with 10,000 attending.

December 28: Memorial Auditorium, Dallas—9,800 paid tickets.

December 29: Civic Center, Birmingham—18,056 in attendance.

December 30: Omni, Atlanta—17,000 cheering fans show up.

December 31: Civic Center Arena, Pittsburgh—16,049 welcome 1977 with the King of Rock & Roll. Ginger, Vernon and Lisa Marie are there to share in the New Year's Eve celebration. It will be his last.

Soon after the breakup with Linda there was another woman in Elvis' life. Ginger Alden, charming and beautiful, was a local girl who reminded members of the Memphis Mafia of Priscilla. Ginger came into Elvis' life at a difficult time, his health was failing and he was susceptible to severe mood swings. But according to many, she was a trooper and hung in as best she could. Elvis convinced her that they would marry and that in her he had found true love at last. Ironically, Ginger's father was in the army and was present at the draft office in Memphis when Elvis was sworn in so many years ago. Vernon Presley (below) loved his son deeply, and was one of many close to Elvis unable to see the damage being done by the drugs and the brutal touring schedule.

1977

THE FINAL BOW

LAMAR FIKE
ON ELVIS THE GUNSLINGER:

Elvis was one of the first gun-slingers. And gunslingers do get slower, but they can still draw. And that's what Elvis did, he kept drawing.

Escorted by his bodyguards, Elvis leaves the stage after what was to be one of his last concerts. None of the fans that night could have known that by coming to see the King they would become part of Rock & Roll history.

January 3: Elvis attends the funeral of Ginger's grandfather in Harrison, Arkansas.

January 5: Elvis and Ginger and members of the Memphis Mafia go to Palm Springs for vacation. Dr. Max Shapiro, Elvis' dentist and reputed West Coast connection for "medication," is married while Elvis is there.

January 8: Elvis' 42nd birthday.

January 12: The inner circle returns to Memphis on the *Lisa Marie*.

January 20: The prescription blitz that will end in Elvis' death begins. From now until August, Dr. Nick will prescribe over 5,000 narcotic and amphetamine pills for Elvis.

January 22: Scheduled for a recording session, Elvis flies to Nashville with Ginger. He meets with Felton Jarvis but doesn't show up at the studio.

January 23: Elvis doesn't come to the scheduled session.

January 24: He returns to Memphis without entering the studio. The musicians are furious and RCA is upset.

January 26: Elvis gives Ginger a huge diamond engagement ring. He wants to marry her at Graceland over the Christmas holidays.

February: In an attempt to get Elvis to record, RCA comes to Graceland and sets up a studio in the racquetball court. The musicians wait at their motels for the call that never comes. Elvis won't leave the bedroom, complaining that he's too ill to sing. It will be RCA's last attempt to get Elvis into a studio.

February 12: Elvis starts his first tour of the year at the Sportatorium in Hollywood, Florida, with 15,500 filling the seats.

February 13: West Palm Beach Auditorium—5,981 attend.

February 14: Bay Front Center, St. Petersburg—8,355 tickets sold.

February 15: Sports Stadium, Orlando.

February 16: Garrett Coliseum, Montgomery, Alabama.

February 17: Georgia Civic Center, Savannah.

February 18: During a concert at the Carolina Coliseum in Columbia, South Carolina, Elvis has another fit of the giggles while introducing *Release Me*. It's a bad sign.

February 19: Freedom Hall, Johnson City, Tennessee—7,000 attend.

February 20: Coliseum, Charlotte, North Carolina—12,000 watch as Elvis introduces Miss Tennessee, Ginger's sister Terry.

February 21: Another show in Charlotte, with 12,000 fans attending. It's a dynamite concert, and Elvis is in a great mood. But behind the scenes, his relationship with the Colonel is on the rocks. It's not surprising, with Elvis' life falling apart and rumors of the impending book by Red and Sonny West beginning to surface in the media.

DAVID STANLEY
ON GRACELAND'S "DRUGSTORE":

At the end, Elvis had a trailer in the back of Graceland where a full-time nurse lived, Tish Hinsley. And in that trailer was a drugstore. Every night about 12 or 1, we'd give Elvis what we called Attack 1. It was a package of eleven drugs, including three shots of Demerol. And then Elvis would eat. And you had to stay with him for that, because sometimes he was so stoned that he'd choke on his food. Then, after he fell asleep, you'd have to sit there and watch him. And about three or four hours later, he'd wake up and take another package of drugs which we called Attack 2. After several more hours of sleep, Elvis would wake once again and take Attack 3.

If Ginger wasn't there, one of us would have to be with him 24 hours a day. It was bad craziness and no one knew how to break the cycle.

ON GINGER ALDEN:

Toward the end of Elvis' life, Ginger just couldn't handle it anymore. Here she was 22 years old having a relationship with the King of Rock & Roll, and all of a sudden he's a junkie. I mean it was like a fantasy that turned into a living nightmare. She didn't stay with him that much anymore. It was all too much for her. She didn't know what she could do to help. And no one could blame her. She was in over her head. I guess we all were.

DAVID STANLEY

ON ELVIS CANCELING THE LAST SHOW OF THE TOUR:

I woke Elvis that day around 4:00 P.M. He didn't look good at all. I knew this was going to be a rough day. I went into the living room and ordered his breakfast and came back to make sure he was up. He wasn't. I told him he had to get it together, we had to go to work, and he said "David, I can't go on tonight. Go get Dr. Nick." About that time Dr. Nichopoulos entered the room, and as I walked out the door, I said, "You're killing him, Nick. I hope you're happy."

ON ELVIS AND DRUGS:

Drugs were Elvis' escape from reality. He didn't take them to get happy. He took them to get unconscious. In fact toward the end, he often said, "I'd rather be unconscious than be miserable." Whether he was dealing with himself or other people, if he didn't want to face something or someone, he'd just go inward. He wouldn't read books or magazines or newspapers—other than mystical-type books, stuff on numerology and scientology, and books on death. But I think his favorite book was the Physicians Desk Reference. He knew that book as well as he knew the Bible. Elvis was like a pharmacist, with himself as the only patient. He'd go through the PDR and pick out combinations, like a drug cocktail, that he felt would be just right for him.

March 3: Elvis makes out his will and signs it in front of Ginger and Charlie Hodge.

March 4: Traveling with over 30 people and several planes, Elvis heads to Honolulu for some rest and relaxation. But with his mob of hangers-on, it's like moving a small army as they tour the island.

March 12: The trip is cut short and Elvis returns to Memphis when he learns that Vernon has suffered a heart attack.

March 20: The local drugstore is working overtime to fill prescriptions for Elvis' upcoming tour, and Ginger is beside herself with worry about him.

March 23: The year's second tour opens in Phoenix, with 14,047 fans turning out. Elvis looks tired and worn.

March 24: Texas Civic Center, Amarillo—7,389 attend.

March 25: Lloyd Noble Center, Norman, Oklahoma—23,000 in attendance for two shows in two nights.

March 27: Taylor County Coliseum, Abilene—7,500 tickets sold.

March 28: Municipal Auditorium, Austin—6,000 see the show.

March 29: Rapides Parish Coliseum, Alexandria, Louisiana—30,000 fans attend two shows in two nights.

March 31: The last show of the tour in Baton Rouge is canceled because Elvis is ill. The fact is, he never showed up at the hall and was already on the plane to Memphis with Dr. Nick.

April 1: Elvis is admitted to Baptist Hospital, and the remainder of the tour is canceled.

April 5: Priscilla and Lisa Marie arrive for a visit as Elvis is released from Baptist Memorial, and he'll spend two weeks recuperating before going back on tour.

April 21: Rested and seemingly ready, Elvis starts his third tour at the Coliseum in Greensboro, North Carolina.

April 22: At Olympia Stadium in Detroit, Elvis is late getting on stage for the show, and when he does, the sellout crowd of 15,600 watches as he gets a case of the giggles that turns to hysterical laughter. He has difficulty bringing himself under control but finally finishes the show.

April 23: Centennial Hall, Toledo, Ohio—9,322 tickets sold.

April 24: Crisler Arena, Ann Arbor—12,000 in attendance.

April 25: Civic Center, Saginaw, Michigan—7,197 watch as RCA records the show for potential future albums.

April 26: Wings Stadium, Kalamazoo, Michigan—7,500 attend.

April 27: Milwaukee Arena, Milwaukee—11,854 tickets sold.

April 28: Brown County Veterans' Memorial Stadium, Green Bay—not a sellout.

April 29: The Arena, Duluth—again not sold out.

April 30: Amidst rumors of an impending split between Elvis and the Colonel, Elvis performs at St. Paul's Civic Center to a sellout crowd of 17,000 fans.

May 1: Chicago Stadium, Chicago—39,600 in attendance for two shows on two nights.

May 3: Saginaw Center, Saginaw, Michigan—7,197 attend the last stop on the tour. Elvis returns to Memphis.

May 5: Vernon files for divorce from Dee.

May: For the remainder of the month, Elvis is seen at Graceland and also touring his old haunts on his Harley.

May 20: The fourth tour of the year begins in Knoxville at Stokely Athletics Center, with 13,000 fans showing up for a concert in sweltering heat.

May 21: Freedom Hall, Louisville, Kentucky—18,000 attend.

May 22: Capitol Center, Landover, Maryland—19,000 fans show up.

May 23: Civic Center, Providence, Rhode Island—13,500 in attendance.

May 24: Augusta, Maine.

May 25: Rochester War Memorial, Rochester, New York.

May 26: Binghamton, New York.

May 29: In front of a full house at the Baltimore Civic Center, obviously very high or very ill, Elvis falls on stage during the concert, and the incident is mentioned in the press.

May 30: Coliseum, Jacksonville, Florida—15,000 attend a makeup concert.

May 31: Another makeup concert, this time for 15,000 fans in Baton Rouge.

June 1: During a makeup concert in Macon, Georgia, Elvis develops a throat problem and doesn't finish.

June 2: The last performance on the tour is another makeup concert in Mobile, Alabama. Afterward, tired and restless, Elvis returns to Memphis.

June 17: The fifth swing of the year begins at the Hammons Center at Southwestern Missouri State.

Many fans think that life on the road with a band would be a dream come true. The realities of touring are something else—it's some of the hardest work there is. The pressure is intense and the hours are long. Each audience expects the best and Elvis, even near the end, felt a responsibility to give them their money's worth.

At the end of what was to be his final concert, Elvis did something unusual: He called his father up on stage to share a bow. The two men who had come so far together stood for a long and touching moment as the fans wildly cheered.

June 18: Kemper Arena, Kansas City—17,000 fans attend.

June 19: Civic Auditorium, Omaha, Nebraska—RCA and CBS-TV record the show as 10,604 fans watch. CBS is filming a special to be called *Elvis In Concert*.

June 20: The concert in Lincoln, Nebraska is also recorded by RCA and CBS. 7,500 attend.

June 21: The concert in Rapid City, South Dakota is recorded by RCA and CBS. 10,000 attend.

June 23: Veteran's Memorial Coliseum, Des Moines, Iowa—11,000 are there.

June 24: On his way from the airport into Madison, Wisconsin, Elvis notices a problem in a gas station. Two guys seem to be assaulting the attendant on duty. Elvis orders the limo to pull over, jumps out of the car, does a few karate moves and says that if there's going to be a fight it'll be with him. After a couple of moments of glaring back and forth, the group is posing for pictures with the King. That night he performs for a crowd of 10,000 fans at Cane County Coliseum.

June 25: The show at Riverfront Stadium in Cincinnati is plagued with difficulties on and off the stage. Elvis has a problem with his hotel and storms out on foot to check into another one down the street. There are technical problems during the show and Elvis is late getting on stage, telling the audience he had to have some dental work.

June 26: Elvis flies from Memphis to Indianapolis, followed by film crews from CBS. He's wired but in a good mood, turning in a strong performance at the Market Square Arena for 18,000 adoring fans. The tour ends on an up note, and after the show he returns to Memphis. No one knows that the 8:30 performance at Market Square Arena is the last time the King of Rock & Roll will ever be seen on stage.

July: Spent in seclusion at Graceland. Elvis sees close friends and spends time with Lisa Marie, who is out for her regular summer visit. But he stays in his room for days at a time with instructions not to be disturbed.

August: Begins ominously with the publication of the dreaded book, *Elvis: What Happened?* by Red West, Sonny West and David Hebler. According to David Stanley, waiting for the publication of that book was like torture for Elvis. He was totally desperate about it, and he tried everything he could to stop it. He even sent John O'Grady to offer the publisher a pile of money to call the whole thing off. But they refused.

August 8: To celebrate Lisa Marie's arrival, Elvis rents the Libertyland Amusement Park for a party. The event is on and off all day long until, at the urging of Ginger and Lisa, he decides to go ahead with it. The group arrives at around 1:30 A.M. and stays until dawn.

August 10: The same group leaves Graceland about 11:30 P.M. and goes to a local movie theater for an all-night movie session. Elvis, Ginger and Lisa Marie sit together, returning to Graceland after 6:00 A.M.

August 13: Back to the moviehouse for another all-night session. Ginger reports that Elvis is in good spirits and the group has a good time.

August 14: With three days left before another tour, Elvis begins his blitzkreig weight-loss diet, cutting his intake of food, eating large quantities of fruit and drinking lots of water. He has put it off much longer than usual, however, and is depressed about not being able to lose the necessary amount in the time left. Since July, his weight has jumped to about 260 pounds and his performance weight is somewhere in the neighborhood of 200 to 220. Elvis is frustrated and angry.

August 15: Elvis is seen on his Harley with Ginger cruising through Memphis, with several friends along for the ride. But he develops another toothache and around 10:30 P.M. drives over to his dentist and gets a tooth filled.

August 16: Wired and edgy, Elvis returns to Graceland in the early morning hours. Around 4:30 A.M. he and Billy Smith begin a game of racquetball that will last until 6:30 that morning. Still unable to sleep, he calls for another dose of medication and tries to read. Ginger stays up with him until around 9:00 A.M. As she's dozing off, Elvis takes a copy of *The Face of Jesus* by Frank Adams and goes into his dressing/bathroom, saying good night to Ginger. She tells him not to fall asleep in the bathroom. Elvis says, "OK, I won't," and shuts the door.

Shortly after 2:00 P.M., Ginger awakes and when she sees that Elvis isn't in bed, goes to the bathroom and knocks on the door. He doesn't answer, so she looks in and sees him curled up in a fetal position on the floor by the toilet. Ginger calls downstairs and Al Strada and Joe Esposito rush in to find Elvis, without color and no apparent signs of breathing. The fire department is called and ambulances rush to the scene. Vernon enters, followed by David Stanley. Elvis is given rudimentary first aid and rushed to Baptist Hospital, where he is pronounced dead at 3:30 P.M. Although the initial cause of death is listed as a heart attack, it will become clear that he had ingested huge quantities of narcotics and probably died of an overdose.

August 17: For the last time, Elvis Presley returns to Graceland, where he will lie in state for one day. At 3:00 P.M., Vernon opens the gates to the 75,000 people waiting outside to pay homage to the King. By the time the gates are closed again at 6:30, only 20,000 had actually viewed the body—leaving more than 3,000 floral arrangements behind—but the rest leave quietly in their grief and disappointment. That evening, a soft, warm rain begins to fall.

Picture of Elvis and Lisa Marie four days before his death.

DAVID STANLEY
ON FINDING ELVIS' BODY:

The minute I walked in there, I knew. "You son of a bitch," I yelled. Elvis was lying there, with pills and empty syringes all around, and I had no doubt what had happened. None. And it just pissed me off. It hurt, but it made me mad, too. Damn it, Elvis! But I didn't spend a lot of time hurting right away, because it was so instilled in me to take care of business. And that's what I did, picking up syringes, picking up the pills. And I've gotten a lot of heat for that. Geraldo Rivera said that's obstruction of justice. But I didn't care. All I knew was there was an ambulance crew fixing to walk through that door and there's stuff lying all over the place, and I had to clean this place up now. So I grabbed everything I could and stuffed it in my pocket and then moved over to Elvis. He was lying face down, kind of all curled up. We turned him over and his eyes were rolled back in his head. His face was blue, bloated, and his tongue was sticking out of his mouth, black, and half bitten off. He was gone.

An autopsy on the body of Elvis Presley was performed on the night of August 16, 1977. It was supervised by the chief medical examiner of the state of Tennessee, Dr. Jerry T. Francisco. The next day, Dr. Francisco held a press conference where he listed three possible causes of Elvis' death: high blood pressure, clogged coronary arteries and an enlarged heart. The official cause of death was listed as cardiac arrhythmia (irregular heartbeat). There was no mention of the presence of drugs in the bloodstream or the vast amount of prescriptions for drugs written for Elvis. In fact, eight prescriptions for dangerous and addictive substances were filled at a local pharmacy on the day Elvis died. It was later revealed under relentless pressure from the media and local authorities that as many as ten highly addictive substances were present in quantity in Elvis' bloodstream when he died and that death was likely caused by overdose.

DAVID STANLEY
ON THE VIGIL AT BAPTIST HOSPITAL:

Joe Esposito, Al Strada, Billy Smith, Charlie Hodge and I were standing in a waiting room while all the efforts were being made to revive Elvis. A doctor came in and Joe asked, "How long has Elvis been without oxygen?" The doctor's response was too long in coming. Joe said, "I guess we should hope he's gone, otherwise he would just be a living vegetable." Moments later Dr. Nick walked in the room and just lowered his head. We already knew, but Elvis was officially pronounced dead. At that moment time stood still. My mind flashed back to that November 22nd day when President John F. Kennedy died. Family and friends much like us were the first to hear the news that would forever be inscribed in the minds of the whole world.

August 18: Elvis' funeral at Graceland is at 2:00 P.M. on a hot, blue-sky day in Memphis. "I remember the organist played *Danny Boy*," David Stanley recalls, "and I don't think I've ever heard anything so sad in my life." The first speaker is evangelist Rex Humbard, representing the Assembly of God Church in which Elvis had grown up. The main eulogy is delivered by C.W. Bradley of the Whitehaven Church of Christ. The last to speak, comedian Jackie Kahane, with whom Elvis had often worked, says simply, "Ladies and gentleman, Elvis has left the building for the last time." And among those who sing are Elvis' favorites, J.D. Sumner and The Stamps.

After the service, the casket is carried by the pallbearers—Lamar Fike, Joe Esposito, Jerry Schilling and others—to a white hearse for transport to Forest Hill Cemetery. Sixteen white Cadillacs follow the hearse down Elvis Presley Boulevard on its three-mile trip to the cemetery. Fans, flowers, National Guard troops and policemen in full-dress uniform line the entire route.

In the cemetery, a few brief prayers are offered, and Elvis' casket is placed in a mausoleum not far from his mother's grave.

And so the long road from Tupelo, Mississippi to the top of the world finally ends. The King is dead. But long live the King, in the hearts and memories of millions around the world. There will never be another.

DAVID STANLEY

ON A STRANGE ACCUSATION:

After Elvis died I went and talked to my stepfather, Vernon. And he looked at me and said, "David I got to ask you a question. Did you kill my son?"

I couldn't believe my ears, so I said, "Excuse me?"

And Vernon repeated his question: "Did you kill my son?"

"What the hell are you talking about, Vernon?"

He said, "The last conversation I had with Elvis, he told me about you and Ginger. He said you and Ginger were having an affair."

Now Ginger and I were about the same age, we shared a lot of interests. Like music. I mean we'd discuss McCartney's tour or a new album from Bad Company, or something like that. Elvis couldn't have cared less about that kind of thing—hell, he might not even ever have heard of Bad Company. But I never touched her. Never.

"Vernon," I said, "think about what you're saying. I loved Elvis, you know that."

And he did. He saw how I felt when Elvis died. I was devastated. God, I was 21 years old, half drugged out myself, with my whole life pulled out from underneath me. It was hard to even get the words out when Vernon and I were speaking. But I managed, and he believed me. But it was sad that he even had to ask. I guess it just shows how bizarre everyone and everything had gotten by the end of Elvis' life.

ON SEEING ELVIS FOR THE LAST TIME:

My brothers Billy and Ricky and I walked up to the open casket, and I put my hand on his, and it hit me so fundamentally that Elvis was truly gone. We were all choked up. There was a feeling of disbelief and unreality, but also a sense of acceptance and even relief. And a tremendous feeling of peace. If anybody ever deserved a rest, it was Elvis. For those of us who had seen him in so much pain through the last months of his life, we were thankful that his suffering was over.

ON THE DAY THE MUSIC DIED:

After the funeral, I remember coming out of Graceland and looking down the hill at this enormous sea of people. All kinds of people, some crying, some screaming, others just solemn and sad. It was like a Presidential funeral, a universally shared grief. When we got into the limousines, I remembered one of Elvis' favorite songs called Long Black Limousine. It was a song about life's last long trip, and here Elvis was doing just that at last. The show was finally over.

HIS INNER CIRCLE

"This is my corporation which travels with me all the time. More than that, all these members of my corporation are my friends."

—ELVIS

There were hundreds of people important to Elvis Presley, but this list of the top 50 represent those who were closest to him—in the inner circle—at the various stages of his life. Many who didn't make the list know who they are, and, more importantly, so did Elvis.

ALDEN, GINGER

Local beauty queen (Miss Traffic Safety, Miss Mid-South and runner-up Miss Tennessee University), she has the distinction of being Elvis' last girlfriend and the last person to see him alive on the night he died. Although it's difficult to document, Alden claims that Elvis proposed marriage in January of 1977. What we do know is that he showered her with gifts, including cars and expensive jewelry. She went on to a brief recording career in the early Eighties and has made many TV commercials. She has also acted in a number of films about Elvis and has sold stories to various newspapers about her life with him.

DAVIS, RICHARD

Elvis' personal valet, he was an active member of the Memphis Mafia for almost eight years. Davis played a tough game of touch football and was a close friend and confidant to Elvis. He left in 1969 and was replaced by the King's stepbrother Rick Stanley. Davis remained a close friend to Elvis to the end.

ESPOSITO, JOE

A high-ranking member of the Memphis Mafia, he met Elvis while they were stationed in West Germany, and their friendship lasted until the end. Over the years he took on a wide range of chores for the Elvis machine—tour manager, bodyguard and part-time bookkeeper, among others. "Diamond Joe," as Elvis called him, was the man Elvis relied on to "meet" female fans. Considered family, he and Marty Lacker stood up for Elvis when he married Priscilla, and Joe's wife Joan was matron of honor. Elvis' loyalty never faltered even after he was sued by Joe and his partner Dr. Nick when their racquetball business, Presley Center Courts, went down after huge financial losses. For his part, Esposito protected Elvis before and after his death, going so far in a postmortem newspaper interview to say that Elvis used no drugs "whatsoever." Esposito did bits in several of Elvis' films, including *Clambake*, *Stay Away, Joe* and *This Is Elvis*. Today he lives and does business in Los Angeles.

FIKE, LAMAR

Born and raised in Memphis, Lamar was interested in the music scene from the time he was a teenager and used to hang out at the various recording studios around town listening to the music and meeting the musicians. One day in 1955, he was in the studio of Sun Records talking with owner Sam Phillips when Elvis Presley walked in wearing one of his wildly colored outfits. "He liked his clothes to be different from everybody else's," says Fike. "He used them to attract attention and make himself different from the other young guys who were around at the time. I wouldn't have dressed like that, but I knew right away what he was doing and I liked it." Fike saw something in Elvis, and the unlikely duo became friends. By 1957 he was a charter member of the Memphis Mafia and firmly on the team. Fike was Elvis' right-hand man, taking care of travel and supervising the technical aspects of mounting the shows on the road. At 300 or so pounds, Fike—who has a "black belt in eating," according to David Stanley—is blessed with a strong sense of humor and a willingness to take, as well as dish out, a joke.

Elvis enjoyed poking fun at him, calling him "Buddha" or "The Great Speckled Bird," but his loyalty was unquestioned, and he was always there whenever Elvis needed him. When Elvis was drafted, Fike tried to enlist, but was turned down because of his weight. He did, however, go to Germany and live with Elvis and his family during his tour of duty. Fike discovered several hits for Elvis, including *Kentucky Rain*, *It's Midnight* and *T-R-O-U-B-L-E*, and over the years with him, devel-

Joe Esposito

oped a vast network of contacts in the music business. One of the pallbearers at Elvis' funeral, Fike went on to a career in music publishing. Today he is also a personal manager, producer and talent scout, living in Nashville, Tennessee with his wife Mary.

FORTAS, ALAN

An all-star Memphis football player, he was a long-timer in the Memphis Mafia, on the team as a bodyguard and assistant from 1958 to about 1969. One of Elvis' closest comrades and confidants, a trusted and loyal employee, Fortas made sure that travel between concerts was smooth and seamless. He would occasionally join Elvis on stage playing the tambourine during concerts and was seen in the 1968 NBC special.

GELLER, LARRY

He left his job at a hair salon in Beverly Hills and became Elvis' personal hairstylist after giving him a particularly good haircut in April of 1964. His fascination with religion and the occult intrigued the King and soon Geller, nicknamed "Guru" by Elvis, was stalking the Beverly Hills library for books on all aspects of the weird and strange. The two friends would talk for hours about religion, parapsychology, the supernatural and the mystical world. To show his appreciation, Elvis gave Geller the usual white Cadillac. Colonel Parker was threatened by the increasing influence of Geller and often tried to get rid of him, but Geller's aura, and Geller, remained. For the rest of his life Elvis continued to dabble in the occult and read about the supernatural aspects of religion, developing a special fascination for contacting his brother Jesse, who died at birth. Geller has written or participated in several personal accounts of his life with Elvis.

Larry Geller and wife, Celeste

GLEAVES, CLIFF

This rockabilly singer was an old friend who introduced Elvis to girlfriend Anita Wood. An early member of the crew that began to accompany Elvis in the Fifties, he went to Hollywood with Elvis for the filming of *Love Me Tender* and was in the studio for the Million Dollar Quartet recording session with Jerry Lee Lewis, Johnny Cash and Carl Perkins in 1956. He also took Elvis in for his draft physical in 1957 and was in Europe during the army days. He remained an insider for several years.

GRANT, CURRIE

A clerk for Air Force Intelligence and married to the sister of Tony Bennett, Currie was stationed near Wiesbaden during Elvis' tour of duty. In November 1959 he made Rock & Roll history by introducing Elvis to Priscilla Beaulieu. At the time, Elvis was 24 and Priscilla was 14. In Currie's version of the story, Priscilla had found him at a club, introduced herself and said she wanted to meet Elvis. She says Currie approached her. Whichever version is true, Currie set some large wheels in motion when he and his wife Carole escorted Priscilla to Elvis' rented house on that fateful day at 15 Goethestrasse in Bad Neuheim, West Germany.

GROB, DICK

A graduate of the Air Force Academy and a fighter pilot, Grob joined the Memphis Mafia in 1969 and quickly became the head of security both at Graceland and on the road. Grob met Elvis when he served as a member of the Palm Springs police department. The two men hit it off and Elvis trusted him literally with his life.

HODGE, CHARLIE

"Slewfoot" Charlie Hodge, a guitarist and singer, was with Elvis from the beginning and was with him at the end, riding in the ambulance that took the King on his last journey to Baptist Hospital in Memphis. For more than seventeen years, he lived at Graceland and took care of personal business for Elvis. On the road he was always there to hand him the trademark scarves he tossed out to the audience during a show. The butt of many jokes because of his height (5' 3"), Hodge met Presley during a television show in 1956 and the two singers hit it off from the start. They joined the army at the same time, did basic training together at Fort Hood, shared the same troop steamer to Europe and were stationed together in Germany. With Elvis and Red West, Hodge wrote *You'll Be Gone*, which Elvis recorded in 1965.

JARVIS, FELTON

He came on as Elvis' producer at RCA in 1966, taking over for Chet Atkins, who had begun to neglect Elvis' career as he moved up the corporate ladder. Aggressive, talented and somewhat eccentric—he liked snakes—Jarvis was the man Elvis needed to pump up a declining career, and in 1970 he left RCA to go to work for Elvis full time. Jarvis produced his recording sessions and supervised his concert performances. He fought with Colonel Parker and the management at Hill and Range to bring back some of Elvis' most successful composers at fair royalty rates and succeeded, allowing Elvis access to material in the Seventies that created another batch of hit records. After Elvis' death, Jarvis went back into the studio and re-recorded several of Elvis' tunes with additional instrumental tracks added.

JENKINS, MARY

The cook at Graceland for fourteen years, Jenkins was on call each day to fix meals for Elvis and whoever else might be around. She was a great Southern cook who supplied Elvis with all his down-home favorites—including peanut butter and mashed banana sandwiches and his standard meal of mashed potatoes, sauerkraut, a couple of pounds of burned bacon and her homemade soup. Elvis took good care of Jenkins over the years, buying her a house and several cars. She was in *This Is Elvis* and wrote a book about her life with the King called *Elvis, The Way I Knew Him.*

THE JORDANAIRES

The Jordanaires backed Elvis on many of his biggest hits. The members of the group were: Gordon Stoker, Neal Matthews, Hoyt Hawkins and Hugh Jarrett. Elvis had seen them perform, and when he was ready to start recording, he sought them out. The first session in 1956 produced: *Hound Dog, Don't Be Cruel* and *Any Way You Want Me.* Over the years, members of the group continued to record with Elvis and appeared in several movies with him, including *King Creole* and *G.I. Blues.* For his part, Elvis felt that his early success was due to the Jordanaires. True or not, it was a debt he never forgot.

KEISKER, MARION

Marion is the person who actually discovered Elvis and should have gotten the credit for it. As studio manager for the Memphis Recording Service, she was in the office the day Elvis came in to record *My Happiness* and *That's When Your Heartaches Begin* in 1953. Seeing something in the young man, she switched on the tape recorder and after the session got his phone number and address. She passed the tape on to Sam Phillips, and the rest is history. Following is the famous exchange between Marion and Elvis that fateful day:

"What kind of singer are you?"
"I sing all kinds."
"Who do you sound like?"
"I don't sound like nobody."
"Hillbilly?"
"Yeah, I sing hillbilly."
"Who do you sound like in hillbilly?"
"I don't sound like nobody."

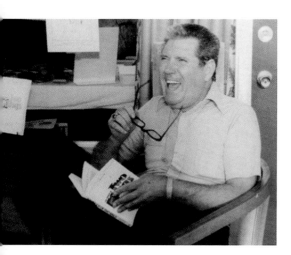

Charlie Hodge

KLEIN, GEORGE

Klein met Elvis at Humes High School, and they formed a lifelong bond. When Klein persuaded Elvis to appear on a local radio show early in his career, the response was enthusiastic, and it put him on the map. As a DJ and program director for WHBQ, he was a strong advocate of Elvis and the "new Rock & Roll." Elvis never forgot his support, including him in several of his films, even appealing to President Carter for aid in his defense when Klein was on trial for mail fraud in 1977. Klein introduced Ginger Alden to Elvis, and was also responsible for connecting Elvis and Dr. "Nick" Nichopoulos.

LACKER, MARTY

A friend of Elvis' ever since high school at Humes, Lacker joined the Memphis Mafia around 1960 and worked for Elvis until 1967. As was the case with other members of the crew, Lacker was many things to Elvis, including personal secretary and bookkeeper. Elvis gave him several automobiles and quite a bit of jewelry over the years, but his wife Patsy feels that Elvis also introduced him to drug abuse. Along with Joe Esposito, he was best man at Elvis' wedding shortly before he was fired in 1967.

LOCKE, DIXIE

Dixie was Elvis' steady date during high school and beyond. They met at a roller rink in 1953 and were an item until 1955. They went to football games, double dated and attended her prom in 1954. Elvis has said that he wanted to marry Dixie, but she turned him down because he was beginning to spend too much time on the road with his band. The pair broke up but remained close, and Dixie was active in Elvis' first fan club.

MARGRET, ANN

Born in Sweden, Ann-Margret made her way to Vegas and was discovered by George Burns while appearing with a small band at the Dunes Hotel. She went on to TV appearances and broke into the movies in the 1961 film, *Pocket Full Of Miracles*. Her first starring role was *Bye, Bye Birdie* (1963). She met Elvis while starring opposite him in *Viva Las Vegas* (1964), and the two struck up a relationship that was to last throughout Elvis' life. In her autobiography, she circumspectly describes what is obviously a powerful connection between her and Elvis; clearly, they were more than merely friends. She and husband Roger Smith attended Elvis' funeral and spent time at Graceland with the family.

THE MEMPHIS MAFIA

Like royalty of ancient times, the King of Rock & Roll needed a court: trusted and loyal companions who could be counted on to provide not only essential services but simple friendship as well. The men who made up what came to be called the Memphis Mafia were all those things and more. The circle that surrounded Elvis was a buffer, a wall of protection from the realities of celebrity and the pressures of fame. They served the King for reasons that went far beyond a job. Bodyguards, road companions, valets, bookkeepers, drivers, pranksters, protectors and playmates, Elvis' boys were always up for a little touch football, a late-night trip to the movies or the roller rink, a couple of games of pool or a ride around the grounds on the golf carts. They were on constant call; whenever Elvis was ready to roll, they were ready too. They also carried guns and studied the martial arts just in case the unthinkable happened. They certainly didn't do it for the money—$250 a week in the Sixties, and by the late Seventies, the top rate was only around $425. Colonel Parker hated them and Vernon Presley felt they cost too much and got in the way. They were hired and fired and fired and hired, but somehow they were always around. It was hard on their families and friends, but there were perks. There was the lifestyle, the travel, the limelight. He gave them money, jewelry, cars

Rick Stanley, Mary Jenkins and David Stanley

and clothes and a sense of belonging to something big. For 25 years, most were loyal and some were not. But all in all, the Memphis Mafia—Charlie Hodge, Billy Smith, Bitsy Mott, Alan Fortas, Cliff Gleaves, David, Ricky and Billy Stanley, Gene Smith, George Klein, Jerry Schilling, Sonny and Red West, Jimmy Kingsley, Joe Esposito, Lamar Fike, Larry Geller, Louis Harris, Marty Lacker, Marvin (Gee Gee) Gambill, Ray Sitton, Richard Davis, Al Strada, Pat Perry, Ed Parker, Dick Grob, Dave Hebler and a lucky few others—went for a wild ride on the Elvis highball express, and for the most part had a hell of a good time.

MOORE, SCOTTY

Moore isn't given much credit for his part in guiding and shaping the style of the young Elvis Presley, but the truth is that Scotty Moore deserves a lot. He was an innovative young guitarist with a driving style gigging around Memphis in the early Fifties. He was playing with Doug Poindexter's Starlight Wranglers when Sam Phillips called and asked him to work with a new kid who had some talent but a lot of rough edges. Elvis met with Scotty at his house, along with another musician named Bill Black, and went over some tunes. The following week they had a session at Sun Studios and cut a track called *That's All Right (Mama)*. Phillips was impressed and Elvis was on his way. Elvis signed Scotty shortly after as his manager, but being an agent and a musician was more than Scotty wanted to handle and the contract was dissolved without hard feelings. Elvis, Scotty and Bill toured the South as the Blue Moon Boys for another two years until they split with him over salary disputes. Both musicians, however, continued to record with Elvis until he went into the army. Black went off on his own in 1960, but Moore continued to work with Elvis until personal differences forced him away for good in 1968. It was Moore's strong lead guitar and his gutsy, driving riffs that were a big part of the early "Elvis Presley sound."

NEAL, BOB

Neal signed on as Elvis' manager after Scotty Moore released him from their contract. A Memphis DJ who had his own radio program, *The Bob Neal Farm Show*, Bob became a manager fulltime in 1952, working with Elvis for three years until Colonel Tom Parker elbowed his way in and stole Elvis away. Parker signed the young singer for 25% of his earnings. Elvis, who felt badly about leaving Neal, continued to pay his 15% out of his own pocket for several years. Neal went on to manage a number of country and rock stars, including Johnny Cash and Jerry Lee Lewis, but never another Elvis.

NICHOPOULOS, DR. GEORGE CONSTANTINE

"Doctor Nick" was Elvis' close friend, personal physician and conduit for medication. Over the years he wrote prescription slips for thousands of highly addictive narcotics, and many consider him at least partially responsible for Elvis' drug abuse. In 1977 alone he prescribed an average of 25 narcotic and amphetamine pills per day for Elvis and wrote eight separate prescriptions on the day that Elvis died. The total number of pills over a seven-month period exceeded 5,000, amounts that can only be described as staggering. Nichopoulos was also involved in several failing business ventures with Elvis and Marty Lacker, including Presley Center Courts, over which he and Joe Esposito sued Elvis for abandoning them in 1976, and he was heavily in debt to Elvis at the time of the King's death. In 1980 he was suspended for a period of months by the Tennessee Board of Medical Examiners for overprescribing drugs in ten cases including Elvis, Jerry Lee Lewis and Marty Lacker, but in the trial stemming from the charges, he was acquitted of malpractice. Many fans consider him partly responsible for Elvis' death, and there has been at least one reported attempt on his life.

NIXON, RICHARD

Elvis showed up at the White House one day and asked to see the President. H.R. Haldeman approved the meeting and shortly after noon on December 17, 1970, Elvis walked into the Oval Office carrying a gift-boxed Colt .45 through security as a gift for Richard Nixon. During what may have been one of the strangest meetings in modern political history, Elvis persuaded the President to make him an agent of the Federal Narcotics Bureau and waited while Nixon authorized the appointment and got him an ID and badge. He then asked Nixon if he would meet two members of the Memphis Mafia who had accompanied him to Washington. Nixon agreed and Jerry Schilling and Sonny West were ushered in to meet him. After handshakes all around, Elvis asked Nixon if the boys could have a couple of souvenirs of the visit. The President, who appreciated Elvis' support in the Vietnam war and felt he could be a positive force in the war on drugs, complied. Elvis left the building a full-fledged narc and over the years took great pleasure in displaying the badge as the gemstone in his collection of law-enforcement badges and IDs. Five years later, Nixon asked Elvis to perform at the White House, but the deal was squashed by Colonel Parker because Elvis wouldn't be paid his standard $25,000 fee for the gig. It didn't matter to Parker that nobody got paid to perform at the White House; his boy didn't sing anywhere for free.

PARKER, ED

Elvis met Ed Parker when the Hawaiian-born karate instructor was recommended to him during a trip to California. In 1972, Elvis went to Parker's studio in Santa Monica and began to study at his school of karate in earnest. It was Parker's style of hand jabs and blows that Elvis used on stage when he demonstrated his karate moves to adoring fans. Parker tried to use Elvis' name to promote a karate championship, but the Colonel refused to let Elvis participate and the incident created friction between Ed and the King for a period of time.

PARKER, COLONEL THOMAS

After success as a dog catcher in Florida, as founder of The Great Parker Pony Circus and as star of Colonel Tom Parker and His Dancing Chickens, it wasn't surprising that 300-pound Tom Parker would become a music promoter. A Dutch citizen, Parker immigrated to the U. S. in 1929, settled in West Virginia and served in the army from 1929 to 1932. During the carny days that followed, he decided that a military title in front of his name added a little class and chose the rank of Colonel because he liked the sound of it. His career as a promoter and manager began in the early Fifties with the signing of Gene Austin, Eddy Arnold, Hank Snow and Tommy Sands. Recognizing Elvis' potential immediately, he signed him away from Bob Neal on March 15, 1956. Elvis agreed to give him a 25% cut and the Colonel managed the King as his only client from then on. Parker proceeded to cut tough and aggressive deals for his new client that ensured a healthy income for both of them and absolute control over every aspect of Elvis' career. From the time he signed with Parker until the day he died, Elvis never did anything for free. While he made his client an enormous amount of money, Parker was also at least in part responsible for the decline of Elvis' career by supplying him with second-rate songs from second-rate writers so that he could take a cut of the royalties. The Colonel also induced Elvis to perform—and sing—in a string of mediocre motion picture vehicles designed to crossplug his money-making record sales. Elvis wanted to be a great actor, and might have turned into one with proper training. But Parker put the kibosh on any and all non-singing roles.

In 1967 Parker renegotiated his contract with Elvis, boosting his cut—incredibly—to 50%. Elvis wanted to fire Parker on several occasions, but the Colonel, who kept meticulous records, presented Vernon with reimbursement vouchers for millions of dollars. Confused and intimidated, the financially unsophisticated Vernon always backed off and Parker remained on board as the keeper of the King. While

Elvis and Colonel Tom Parker

there's no doubt that Parker's genius as a showman and promoter pushed Elvis into the superstar stratosphere, he was also responsible for keeping him in the creatively stultifying—but financially rewarding—status quo. Many people believe that Parker, in his efforts to milk every dollar out of the Elvis machine, kept him from reaching the transcendent level of greatness that seemed to be his due; and by driving him for years beyond physical endurance, contributed to cutting Elvis' life short.

PERKINS, CARL

Considered by many to be the father of Rock & Roll, Perkins' recording of *Blue Suede Shoes* was on the way to the top when he was seriously injured in an automobile accident on his way to New York and a 1956 appearance on *The Ed Sullivan Show.* His brother was killed and Perkins lost the chance to hit the national scene in a big way. But Sam Phillips had such faith in Perkins' potential that in 1955 he sold Elvis' contract to RCA to get the cash to promote Perkins' career. Elvis and Perkins were close friends and had great respect for each other's musical ability. Perkins booked Sun Studios one day in 1956 to record *Matchbox* and when Elvis showed up, along with Johnny Cash and Jerry Lee Lewis, the session resulted in the famous Million Dollar Quartet.

PERRY, PATTI

One of Elvis' dearest friends, Patti met him in 1960 when she and a girlfriend were driving down Santa Monica Boulevard in Los Angeles. While stopped at a red light, Patti simply rolled down the window and introduced herself. Elvis was impressed. He asked her over to his house in Bel Air. The two later became like brother and sister.

PHILLIPS, DEWEY MILLS

Phillips, a Memphis DJ at WHBQ (no relation to Sam), was the first jockey to put Elvis on the air: a country show called *Red, Hot and Blue,* on July 7, 1954. Dewey would get new releases from Sam Phillips to play on his show. When he heard *That's All Right (Mama),* he was so excited that he played it fourteen times in a row. The response was so strong that Phillips brought Elvis in for his first live radio interview.

PHILLIPS, SAM

This legendary record producer, whose genius at recognizing and developing talent makes him one of music's greats, began his career recording rhythm-and-blues demos that he would sell to independent record companies. Sensing that there was big money to be made introducing "Race" records into the mainstream, he started Sun Records in 1952 so he could produce both country/western and R&B. Phillips had always felt that if he could find a white singer who could sing in a black style, he would make a fortune, and when his secretary Marion Keisker told him she had heard a young man who could do just that, he brought him in for a session. Initially he was less than impressed with Elvis, but he sensed that the young man had talent and asked Scotty Moore to work with him. The result was *That's All Right (Mama)* and the beginning of Rock & Roll. If there had been no Sam Phillips and his "Sun Sound"—and the wealth of talented musicians such as B.B. King, Ike Turner, Jerry Lee Lewis, Carl Perkins, Johnny Cash, Roy Orbison, Conway Twitty and Charlie Rich that he brought into the music game—popular music in the United States might have taken an entirely different direction.

PRESLEY, GLADYS LOVE SMITH

Born in Pontotoc County, Mississippi into a family of sharecroppers and migrant workers on April 25, 1912, Gladys Love Smith grew up in the rural poverty that was common to many of her generation. With the exception of her father, her family was a hard-drinking and somewhat troubled mix, but Gladys was known as a cheerful and wisecracking young woman who always seemed to have a good time.

Carl Perkins

She was 22 when she married nineteen-year-old Vernon Elvis Presley on June 17, 1933. The Depression made life difficult for the young couple, and they were struggling to keep their heads above water when Gladys gave birth to twins on January 8, 1935. One of the boys, Jesse Garon, was stillborn—but the other, Elvis Aron, was strong and healthy.

The loss of Jesse turned Gladys' focus entirely on Elvis, and mother and son developed a bond, almost an obsession, that kept them extremely close until her death. Elvis lavished cars, homes, money, jewelry and clothes on his mother and insisted that she and Vernon live with him at Graceland. But "Sattnin," as Elvis called her, was never really comfortable with her son's success, always feeling like an unworthy outsider. As Elvis began to spend more time on the road, she became increasingly sad and lonely, turning to vodka and pills to deal with the deep depressions that seemed to become more and more a part of her life. She contracted an acute case of hepatitis and died of a heart attack on August 14, 1958 at the age of 46. Elvis was devastated and probably never truly recovered from her death.

PRESLEY, JESSE GARON

The stillborn twin brother of Elvis Aron Presley, Jesse was delivered first, and the doctor was uncertain whether the second child would be alive either. But Elvis was delivered some 30 minutes later, alive and healthy. Jesse was buried the next day in an unmarked grave in the Priceville Cemetery near East Tupelo, Mississippi. Gladys never got over his death, and worked actively to keep him a member of the family, talking about him almost as if he were alive and creating fantasies about what Jesse would have been able to do if he had lived. The loss of Jesse made Gladys extremely protective of Elvis and fearful that he too would be taken from her. It's possible that Elvis' drive to succeed grew out of a need to prove his own worth to his mother. At any rate, Elvis grew up in his dead brother's shadow, and Gladys made Jesse so real that in later years Elvis was certain he could speak with Jesse and that Jesse was with him on tour and at Graceland.

PRESLEY, LISA MARIE

Elvis' pride and joy, Lisa Marie was born on February 1, 1968, and lived at Graceland until Priscilla and Elvis split up in 1972. Over the next several years—until shortly before his death—she would visit Elvis on a regular basis. Lisa Marie is the sole heir to Elvis' estate. Priscilla has always been insistent that Lisa Marie be protected from the glare of celebrity, and to this day Lisa avoids the limelight. She is currently divorced and living quietly with her two children in California.

PRESLEY, PRISCILLA ANN

The one and only wife of Elvis Presley, Priscilla Beaulieu was introduced to Elvis while he was stationed in West Germany and she was a fourteen-year-old army brat. Taken with her from the beginning, he invited her to Graceland for the Christmas holidays in 1961, and persuaded her parents to allow her to move to Memphis in 1962, where she attended high school and went on to a finishing school. Over the next several years, Elvis bought her cars and jewelry and it was no secret that they were in love. Finally in 1967 they were married in a very private ceremony in Las Vegas—so private that several of the Memphis Mafia weren't invited, causing friction. On February 1, 1968, Priscilla gave birth to daughter Lisa Marie. The marriage lasted until 1972, when she became involved with Elvis' karate instructor, Mike Stone. Elvis sued for divorce in August of that year, and it was granted in 1973. Though there was constant tension in the relationship, Elvis and Priscilla remained in contact to the end to protect the interests of Lisa Marie. She went on to a successful film and TV career and has become a celebrity in her own right, appearing as a regular on the television show *Dallas* and in the *Naked Gun* films. As executor of the Presley estate, she has a controlling interest in the business of running Graceland.

PRESLEY, VERNON ELVIS

Vernon was born in Fulton, Mississippi on April 19, 1916. The Presleys had lived in Mississippi for generations, and the woods around Tupelo and Fulton were full of them. He met Gladys in the early Thirties, and the pair were married on June 7, 1933. They struggled to survive, money was tight and they relied on family and friends to get through the Depression. When Elvis was born in 1935, Vernon worked hard at the odd jobs available to an eighth-grade dropout, but times were tough. In 1938 he was convicted of forgery and spent two years in the infamous Parchman Farm Penitentiary. After his release, the family remained in Tupelo until 1948, then moved to Memphis seeking greener pastures.

The family fortunes improved as Elvis began to make money singing, and by the mid-Fifties Vernon had essentially retired. By the time of his wife's death in 1958, he was dedicating himself exclusively to his son's exploding career. When Elvis was drafted, Vernon and Lamar Fike accompanied him to Germany and lived there during Elvis' tour of duty. In 1960 he married Dee Stanley and brought her and her three sons—Ricky, David and Billy—to live at Graceland. Eventually the family moved to a house just outside the grounds because of friction between Dee and Elvis. The house on Hermitage street was where Priscilla first stayed when she came to Memphis to go to school and, of course, to be with Elvis.

Elvis was devoted to his "Daddy" and kept him occupied as his business manager, a job for which Vernon was highly unqualified. He did his best, however, and his heart was always in the right place. Unfortunately, Vernon's limitations as a businessman made him easy pickings for the shrewd Colonel Parker. Parker and Vernon were like oil and water, but the Colonel was well aware that a more qualified representative would be a threat to his empire and worked to keep Vernon in charge of Elvis' affairs. It was because of Vernon's country boy fear of government that so much of Elvis' vast earnings were lost unnecessarily to taxes—not invested in ways that could have maintained the estate. Vernon died of heart failure on June 26, 1979.

Billy Stanley, Lamar Fike and David Stanley

SCHILLING, JERRY

In 1964, Schilling became a full-time member of the Memphis Mafia. He remained with Elvis as his personal aide until 1976. Jerry was one of the crew that studied martial arts with Elvis, who called him "Cougar." He left Graceland to become a film editor at Paramount until he went into personal management handling a client list that included Billy Joel, the Beach Boys and The Sweet Inspirations. He dumped Jerry Lee Lewis when "The Killer" started badmouthing Elvis in the late Eighties.

SCRIVENER, MILDRED

Elvis' history teacher at Humes High in Memphis, Mildred had great affection for Elvis as a boy and put him on the bill of the annual spring show. Elvis sang *Keep Them Cold Icy Fingers Off Of Me* and the response was so enthusiastic that she pushed him back for an encore. It was she who gave the young Elvis one of the little boosts of confidence that moved him toward a singing career.

SMITH, BILLY

Billy and Elvis were family, cousins who grew up together and never grew apart. Elvis was closer to Billy than almost anyone else in the Memphis Mafia, and went to great lengths to include him in his world. Billy was never very far away, living in a trailer house on the grounds at Graceland with his wife, Jo. He took care of Elvis' costumes on the road and was his valet at home. Billy and his wife played racquetball with Elvis on the night he died.

SMITH, GENE

One of the earliest members of the Memphis Mafia, he and Elvis were cousins and childhood friends, working odd jobs together, double dating and remaining extremely close. Like his cousin Billy Smith, Gene lived at Graceland and was responsible for Elvis' wardrobe. He and several others left in 1969 over a payroll disagreement with Vernon.

Gil Gilliland and Billy Smith

SPRECKLES, JUDY POWELL

A sugar heiress after her brief marriage to magnate Adolph Spreckles in 1964, Judy dated Elvis in 1958 and rode along to see him inducted into the army.

STANLEY, DAVADA (DEE)

Tennessee-born Dee Elliot met Vernon in West Germany in 1958, and they married in Tennessee in 1960 after her divorce from Army Sergeant William Stanley was final. She and her three sons moved into Graceland in 1960, but she and Elvis didn't get along, and his resentment toward her culminated in a move to a house just off the Graceland compound. She remained with Vernon in the house on Hermitage until her divorce in 1977.

STANLEY, DAVID EDWARD

Born in 1955, David moved along with his brothers into Graceland when his mother Dee married Vernon in 1960. On June 8, 1972, against his mother's wishes, David, just a teenager, started working for Elvis as personal aide and later as personal bodyguard. The yougest member of the Memphis Mafia, he was with his stepbrother to the end and was one of the men on duty at Graceland the day Elvis died. Today, as president of David Stanley Communications and Impello Media Group, he is a nationally known speaker, author/writer and producer. He and his wife Jennifer live in Dayton, Ohio.

STANLEY, RICHARD EARL

Born in 1953, "Restless Rick," one of Dee's three sons and Elvis' stepbrothers, was on the payroll as an aide and personal bodyguard. During his time with Elvis, he developed a drug problem and was arrested in 1975 for trying to pass a forged prescription for amphetamines at a local hospital. It has been said that he was a source of drugs for Elvis. He was fired after an argument with Linda Thompson but came back after Linda and Elvis broke up. Rick underwent treatment for drug abuse and entered the ministry in the late Seventies.

STANLEY, WILLIAM (BILLY)

The oldest of the Stanley boys, Billy was born in January of 1953. Elvis called him "Charlie Manson" because of his sinister look, and used him as a personal aide. In the years since Elvis died, he has been part of several books, including *Elvis: We Love You Tender* with his mother and his brothers David and Rick, and *Elvis: My Brother, An Intimate Family Memoir.*

TAUROG, NORMAN

This well known filmmaker directed ten Elvis films: *Blue Hawaii, Double Trouble, G. I. Blues, Girls! Girls! Girls!, It Happened At The World's Fair, Live A Little, Love A Little, Speedway, Spinout* and *Tickle Me.* He and Elvis worked well together and were good friends. Taurog said consistently that if Elvis had had access to better scripts, he would have proven himself to be a talented actor and possibly a great one.

Sonny West and David Stanley

THOMPSON, LINDA

A former beauty queen, Linda began to date Elvis and moved into Graceland with him in 1972. She stayed for almost five years and during that time she was his constant companion, friend, lover and confidant. Unlike his former girlfriends and even his former wife, Linda accompanied him on tour and stayed with him in Vegas. Elvis spent hundreds of thousands of dollars over the years on clothes and jewelry for her and took care of all her financial needs. As his drug abuse worsened and his condition deteriorated, it became more and more difficult to live with him, and Linda finally left in 1976. The reports on her are mixed—some say she robbed Elvis blind and took advantage of him towards the end—but David Stanley is convinced that she loved Elvis and that he loved her. "She was good for him, she did the best she could and hung in there as long as possible," says Stanley. "It just got real hard near the end." After Elvis died, Linda went on to work in television, appearing on *Hee Haw* and doing commercials. She married and divorced Olympian Bruce Jenner, and eventually married music producer David Foster.

THOMPSON, SAM

At the suggestion of his younger sister, Linda Thompson, Sam was hired to serve as a bodyguard for Elvis on and off in the mid-Seventies. Though he wasn't close to Elvis, Thompson was considered a friend of the family and a trusted member of the Memphis Mafia. A Shelby County deputy sheriff for four years, he went on to serve as a judge in Memphis juvenile court.

WEST, DELBERT (SONNY)

"Mr. Eagle" was introduced to Elvis by his cousin Red. As a member of the Memphis Mafia, he was a tough and determined bodyguard. Living with his wife Judy on the grounds at Graceland, he was also responsible for the care and maintenance of Elvis' fleet of automobiles, motorcycles, snowmobiles, golf carts, vans and anything else that was motorized. His love of cars coincided with Elvis' taste in gifts, and over the years Sonny received numerous Cadillacs, Harleys and pickup trucks from his boss. He also did bits in several films and toured with Elvis until 1976, when he was fired after a fight with Vernon. Along with his cousin and Dave Hebler, he was a co-author of *Elvis: What Happened?,* a book that brought the King's drug problems out in the open and ended their relationship with Elvis forever. The Wests claim that the purpose of the book was to get Elvis to seek help, not to destroy him, but within two weeks after it was published, he was dead.

WEST, ROBERT (RED)

Born in 1936 and bred in Memphis, Red West knew Elvis longer than anyone else in the Memphis Mafia, with the possible exception of Elvis' cousin Gene Smith. They met at Humes High, where Red was a gifted boxer and football player. West liked Elvis and stuck up for him in several schoolyard battles. The two became fast friends, and when Elvis started hitting the road with the Blue Moon Boys in 1955, Red went along as the driver. He joined the Marines in 1956 and hooked up with his old friend in 1960 after Elvis returned from his hitch in the army. Red was a tough guy, aggressive and strong, perfectly capable of taking care of business and not afraid of a fight. The combo of Sonny and Red would never have been noted for their light touch, but they could certainly keep trouble away from the King. As his bodyguard, Red accompanied Elvis to Hollywood and began a film, television and commercial career of his own, appearing in almost all of Elvis' films and doing bits in many other films and TV series as an actor and stuntman. Red was also a singer-songwriter and composed or co-wrote at least eight songs recorded by Elvis, including: *You'll Be Gone, Separate Ways* and *Holly Leaves And Christmas Trees.* According to West, he was becoming increasingly troubled by Elvis' use of drugs and when he, his cousin Sonny and Dave Helber were fired by Vernon in 1976, they decided to collaborate on a book to bring the problem to light. With the publication of *Elvis: What Happened?*, their stated intention was to get a man they loved to "take care of business" of his own.

WOOD, ANITA

This talented and beautiful blonde was a nineteen-year-old Memphis disc jockey and host of the TV show, *Top Ten Dance Party*, when she attracted the attention of Elvis in July of 1957. He called on his friend Cliff Gleaves to introduce him, and five days after their first date, he took her home to Graceland to meet his parents. Independent, intelligent and patient, Wood was one of Elvis' first serious romances, and many family members and friends thought he should marry her. Some intimates have reported that the couple talked about it before Elvis went into the army, but that the idea was quickly squashed by Colonel Parker, who didn't want his boy tied up with any one woman. When Elvis met Priscilla in Germany, however, Wood's relationship with him quickly ended. A beauty pageant winner, she went on to record several songs and eventually married former Cleveland Browns star Johnny Brewer. In the late Seventies, she sued and won a considerable settlement from a local newspaper that claimed she had continued to see Elvis on the side even after marrying Brewer.

WOOD, NATALIE

Natalie and Elvis were introduced in Hollywood by mutual friend Nick Adams and were an item for a short time in 1956. She shared his passion for motorcycles and created a national stir by cruising around Memphis with Elvis on his Harley. They had a real affection for each other, but for reasons that had more to do with career than love, things just didn't seem to work out. Over the years, they remained in touch and continued to speak highly of each other. Natalie died in a drowning accident in 1981.

HIS MOVIES

*"I have a lot that I'd like to accomplish in time.
I'd like to improve in a lot of ways. For one
thing, the acting thing, but it'll take time.
You can't overstep your bounds."*

—ELVIS

THE COMPLETE FILMOGRAPHY

For Elvis, the rise from stage to screen was almost as meteoric as his rise from obscurity in Memphis to world-wide fame as the hottest Rock & Roller on earth. The marketers in Hollywood sensed immediately that Elvis would be a box-office sensation in the right vehicles, and after two screen tests in April of 1956, he was signed to a three-picture deal with Paramount worth almost $500,000. Knowing where the market was, Colonel Parker decreed that Elvis wouldn't do a film in which he couldn't sing. The race was on for appropriate first projects and the winner was a Civil War tale called *Love Me Tender*. The rest is history. In 33 films from 1956 to 1969, the Elvis magic drew millions of adoring fans to the movie houses and sold more millions of albums.

The early films are drawn from the early parts of Elvis' life, his lowly upbringing and early struggles for success told and retold through different characters in different situations. Elevated to myth, the boy from Mississippi became a movie star.

LOVE ME TENDER
(1956)

20th Century-Fox, a David Weisbart Production
  Director: Robert D. Webb
  Screenwriter: Robert Buckner
  Director of Photography: Leo Tover
  Technical Advisor: Colonel Tom Parker
  Running Time: 89 minutes
  Opened: November 15, 1956
  Stats: 23rd top-grossing film of the year
  Budget: $950,000
  Elvis' Salary: $100,000

SYNOPSIS:

During the last days of the Civil War, Confederate Lt. Vance Reno and his platoon—including brothers Brett and Ray—hijack a Union payroll. Splitting up what they consider to be the spoils of war, they all head back to civilian life. But Vance learns that his girl has married his youngest brother Clint (Elvis), after they got word that Vance was killed in action. A man of compassion and high principles, Vance decides the best thing to do is move on, and plans to make his peace with Cathy and Clint and say his goodbyes at a family picnic.

But in the midst of the outing, Major Kincaid and a Pinkerton detective show up with warrants for Vance and his brothers. They are arrested and taken to jail to await trial. Unaware that Vance has agreed to return the payroll and get on with his life, Clint and Vance's old platoon raid the jail and break them out.

Vance tries to convince the others to give up the payroll, but they refuse and Vance takes it from them by force, intending to return it to Major Kincaid. But he is now a fugitive and barely misses capture by the sheriff and a posse. He gives the money to Cathy, but she realizes she still loves him and begs him to stay. So he rides back to town to return the money and face the music.

Meanwhile Clint, at the urging of Vance's old platoon sergeant, is hunting Vance looking for revenge, and when he sees Vance, who has returned to explain everything, he shoots him. As the sergeant moves in for the kill, Clint realizes what he has done and defends his brother at the cost of his own life. Feeling that enough tragedy has already touched their lives, the Major decides drop the charges against Vance and the Civil War is finally over for the Reno family.

CAST:

Vance Reno	Richard Egan
Cathy Reno	Debra Paget
Clint Reno	Elvis Presley
Mr. Siringo	Robert Middleton
Brett Reno	William Campblell
Mike Gavin	Neville Brand
Martha Reno	Mildred Dunnock
Major Kincaid	Bruce Bennett
Ray Reno	James Drury

SONGS:
We're Gonna Move, Love Me Tender, Let Me, Poor Boy

L VI G Y U

(1957)

Paramount Pictures, a Hal B. Wallis production
    Director: Hal Kanter
    Screenwriter: Herbert Baker
    Director of Photography: Charles Lang, Jr.
    Costumes: Edith Head
    Technical Advisor: Colonel Tom Parker
    Running Time: 101 minutes
    Opened: July 9, 1957
    Stats: Elvis' first color film
    Reached #7 on *Variety*'s Weekly List

SYNOPSIS:

At an outdoor rally where he has been sent to deliver a few kegs of beer, Deke Rivers (Elvis) sings a rock number with the band and the crowd goes wild. Glenda, a press agent, and band leader Tex hire him on the spot. Since the band includes Susan, a pretty young singer, Deke signs up. With him on board, things start to go really well and soon the band's left its small-town engagements far behind. They still aren't making a lot of money, but the future is bright.

They finally book Deke for a breakthrough broadcast concert gig just outside Dallas, and for publicity they buy him a fancy new convertible to cruise through town to the concert. Everyone knows money is tight, so Glenda and Tex pretend it's a gift from a rich old lady. The truth is that to pay for the car they have to cut back on employees, and the first is Susan, because Glenda is jealous of her effect on Deke.

Deke wants to go to Susan's farm and bring her back, but Glenda persuades him to stick it out, and makes it clear that she's very attracted to him. Then Deke finds out she is Tex's former wife and that Tex lives in hope that they can work it out and get back together. Driving off in a rage, Deke gets into an accident. Glenda finds the wreck and, realizing his feelings for Susan, tells him he's free to do whatever he wants. Moved by her honesty, Deke goes ahead and does the broadcast. It's a big success—especially since Susan joins them at the studio just in time for the show.

CAST:

Deke Rivers	Elvis Presley
Glenda Markle	Lizabeth Scott
Walter (Tex) Warner	Wendell Corey
Susan Jessup	Delores Hart
Carl Meade	James Gleason
Extras in Audience at Theater	Vernon Presley, Gladys Presley
The Jordanaires	Themselves

SONGS:

You Got a Lot o' Livin' to Do, (Let's Have a) Party, (Let Me Be Your) Teddy Bear, Hot Dog, Lonesome Cowboy, Mean Woman Blues, Loving You

JAILHOUSE ROCK

(1957)

Metro Goldwyn Mayer, An Avon Production
  Producer: Pandro S. Berman
  Director: Richard Thorpe
  Screenplay: Guy Tropser
  Director of Photography: Robert Bonner
  Technical Advisor: Colonel Tom Parker
  Running Time: 96 minutes
  Opened: October 17, 1957
  Rereleased: March 9, 1960 (after Elvis' discharge from the Army)
  Stats: #3 in *Variety*'s Weekly List
  Total Gross: $14 Million
  Ranked #14 for 1957
  Budget: $400,000
  Elvis' Salary: $250,000 plus 50% profits

SYNOPSIS:

Vince (Elvis) is a truck driver who stops in for a quick beer at a local club, gets into a fight over a woman and accidentally kills one of the guys. He is convicted of manslaughter and sent to prison. His cellmate is a former country-western singer, Hunk, who lets the kid play a little on his guitar and sees a lot of raw talent. Vince uses the time in jail well, and pretty soon he's playing and singing like a pro.

Some television producers get the idea to broadcast a live talent show from prison and choose Vince as one of the inmates who will perform. The response is incredible, and the prison is flooded with mail for him. But Hunk has his own plans for Vince and uses his connections with the prison post office to keep the mail away from him. He convinces Vince that he needs some work on his music and that he can help him. He then gets Vince to sign a contract, based on a 50-50 split of whatever Vince makes after he gets out of prison.

Vince gets out of jail before Hunk and is shocked when he is given all the mail that has accumulated since the show. In his lonely room he reads them over and over. Later at a bar, he meets Peggy, an up and coming talent scout for a major label. To impress her he hits the stage and sings, but nobody is impressed except Peggy, who sees real potential in him. She talks him into making a demo, which they pitch to her boss. After first saying no, the man buys it, but Vince is on pins and needles until his song is released and he discovers that the record exec has stolen the tune and given it to a singer who's already on the payroll. Peggy quits and she and Vince start their own label.

Things are going great and just when Vince's career is about to go over the top, Hunk shows up—released from prison—with the contract in hand. When Vince's TV people won't honor it, Vince puts him on his payroll anyway and offers him 10% of the action.

But Hunk is trouble and one drunken night, he picks a fight with Vince and hits him hard in the throat. The doctors say he may never sing again unless he's willing to undergo surgery. It's a difficult operation—and Vince is at great risk—but he comes through with flying colors.

CAST:

Vince Everett ....Elvis Presley
Peggy Van Alden ....Judy Tyler
Hunk Houghton ....Mickey Shaughnessy
Mr. Shores ....Vaughn Taylor
Sherry Wilson ....Jennifer Holden
Teddy Talbot ....Dean Jones
Laury Jackson..Anne Neyland
Warden ....Hugh Sanders

SONGS:

Young And Beautiful, I Want To Be Free, Don't Leave Me Now, Treat Me Nice, Jailhouse Rock, (You're So Square) Baby I Don't Care

KING CREOLE
(1958)

Paramount Pictures, a Hal B. Wallis production
  Director: Michael Curtiz
  Screenwriter: Herbert Baker
  Based on a Novel by: Harold Robbins
  Director of Photography: Russell Harlan
  Makeup: Wally Westmore
  Costumes: Edith Head
  Vocal Accompaniment: The Jordanaires
  Technical Advisor: Colonel Tom Parker
  Running Time: 116 minutes
  Filmed: January 20 to March 10, 1958
  (Elvis was granted a 60-day deferment by the Memphis Draft Board to finish the film)
  Opened: July 2, 1958

SYNOPSIS:

Danny Fisher (Elvis) supports himself and his unemployed father by doing odd jobs at the cheap clubs and sleazy nightspots in the French Quarter of New Orleans. One morning he heads over to the Blue Shade to mop up, and he finds a wild party still going on. He knows some of the guys, and one of them, a man who is really drunk, starts to put the make on Ronnie, the girlfriend of Maxie, who runs the Bourbon Street underworld. Danny gets her away from the drunk and Ronnie is so thankful that she gives him a big hug and kiss and he runs off late for his last day at school.

Some of the guys in his class have seen Danny get kissed by this beautiful woman, and they razz him until he gets into a fight that results in his suspension and the bad news that he won't be graduating from high school. Things get worse when he leaves, and cuts through an alley on the way home: The brother of one of the guys Danny fought in the yard, a tough named Shark, jumps Danny along with a couple of buddies. But Danny more than holds his own and Shark shows him some respect by asking him to join the gang. Danny's first impulse is to turn him down, but when he looks at his life, he can't think of a reason not to. His first job is to distract a counterman at the 5 & 10 while they rob the place. Danny charms Nellie, the girl who works the soda fountain, and gets a date.

Later at the Blue Shade, Ronnie walks in with Maxie, who knows something is up when Danny says hello but Ronnie plays like she doesn't know him. She covers by saying that she's just heard him sing a couple of times. Maxie says: OK, sing. Danny does, and to Maxie's chagrin is offered a full-time spot by Charlie LeGrand at a loser joint down the street called the King Creole. LeGrand is the only guy on the street who isn't afraid of Maxie.

With no prospects ahead of him, Danny takes the job, and it's a surprise to nobody but him when the King Creole starts packing them in. Good things start to happen for him, but there are a few complications: Nellie is his girlfriend, but Ronnie is a hot number and though she's interested in Danny, she's smart enough to know what Maxie would do if he ever found out. But Maxie knows what's going on and he forces Ronnie to use her wiles on Danny to get him to quit the King Creole and work at Maxie's joint. But Ronnie doesn't want Danny under Maxie's thumb, the way she is, so she tells him to say no, which he does. Maxie is furious and calls in Shark and the boys to set Danny up. Danny's part in the 5 & 10 holdup goes without a hitch, but when his dad finds out, he has a breakdown and lands in the hospital.

Danny finds Maxie and beats the tar out of him. In retaliation Maxie sends his boys after him. Shark finds him first and Danny, beaten badly, is left for dead. Ronnie finds him and sneaks him to a secret place where she can nurse him back to health. But Maxie finds them and kills Ronnie—and kills himself in the process. Danny recovers and starts packing them in again at the King Creole.

CAST:

Danny Fisher...Elvis Presley
Ronnie ....Carolyn Jones
Maxie Fields..Walter Matthau
Nellie ....Delores Hart
Mr. Fisher...Dean Jagger
Forty Nina ....Liliane Montevecchi

SONGS:

Crawfish, Steadfast, Loyal and True, Lover Doll, Trouble, Dixieland, Rock Young Dream, New Orleans, King Creole, Don't Ask Me Why, As Long As I Have You

G.I. BLUES
(1960)

Paramount Pictures, a Hal B. Wallis production
   Director: Norman Taurog
   Screenwriters: Edmund Beloin, Henry Carson
   Director of Photography: Loyal Griggs
   Makeup: Wally Westmore
   Costumes: Edith Head
   Vocal Accompaniment: The Jordanaires
   Technical Advisor: Colonel Tom Parker
   Running Time: 104 minutes
   Opened: November 15, 1960
   Stats: #2 on *Variety*'s Weekly List,
         #14 for 1960
   Grossed $4.3 million

SYNOPSIS:

Three army buddies, Tulsa (Elvis), Cooky and Rick, put together a Rock & Roll band to pass the time during their hitch in West Germany. Calling themselves The Three Blazes, they play whatever dates they can get and save their money to open their own club when they get back to the States. They get a big break when they're asked to perform in an Armed Forces show that's coming up.

Tulsa is a good-looking guy, and part of the reason The Blazes are popular is his effect on the local women. So he's the natural choice to take over when the platoon's Casanova is suddenly transferred to Alaska. Seems the guy made a $300 dollar bet for himself and his buddies that he could spend the night with a local cabaret singer who's known for not giving G.I.s the time of day. Seeing the prospect of more money for his stateside nightclub, Tulsa agrees to replace him. He makes a date with Lili and as she shows him the town, he begins to fall for her and begins to forget the task at hand. Lili is falling for him too, totally unaware that Tulsa's buddies are tailing them to keep track of the bet.

Tulsa has agreed to baby-sit for a buddy and his fiancée while they sneak off to tie the knot and give their child a name. Tulsa, however, is a terrible baby-sitter and calls Lili for help, so she invites him over and tells him to bring the baby. He spends the night. On the street below, the guys watch Lili's window and mentally spend their winnings as they wait for dawn.

Rehearsals start the next day for the Armed Forces show. Lili is supposed to sing, as well as Tulsa and The Three Blazes. But things go sour when she overhears Tulsa's sergeant laughing about Tulsa winning his bet. Lili is crushed, and when Tulsa's commanding officer learns about it, he's enraged. Demanding an apology to Lili, he prepares to ship Tulsa off to another base before the show.

Tulsa's buddy and his new wife return to base to reclaim their child, and explain to Lili what a great guy Tulsa was for taking the baby and giving them a chance for happiness. Realizing the whole thing was a big misunderstanding, Lili and Tulsa admit they're in love, decide to get married—and the Armed Forces show goes on as scheduled.

CAST:

Tulsa McLean	Elvis Presley
Lili	Juliet Prowse
Cooky	Robert Ivers
Tina	Letitia Roman
Rick	James Douglas
Maria	Sigrid Maier

SONGS:

What's She Really Like, G. I. Blues, Doin' The Best I Can, Blue Suede Shoes, Frankfort Special, Shoppin' Around, Tonight Is So Right For Love, Wooden Heart, Pocketful of Rainbows, Big Boots, Didja Ever

FLAMING STAR

(1960)

20th Century-Fox, a David Weisbart production
  Director: Don Siegel
  Screenwriters: Clair Huffaker, Nunnally Johnson
  Based on a Novel by: Clair Huffaker
  Director of Photography: Charles G. Clarke
  Music Conducted by: Lionel Newman
  Technical Advisor: Colonel Tom Parker
  Vocal Accompaniment: The Jordanaires
  Running Time: 101 minutes
  Opened: December 20, 1960
  Stats: #12 on *Variety*'s Weekly List of Top-Grossing Films

SYNOPSIS:

Pacer Burton, a half-breed Kiowa (Elvis), and his half brother Clint arrive at the family ranch to discover that their folks, Neddy, a full-blooded Kiowa, and Sam, have prepared a surprise birthday party for Clint. The guest list includes Clint's fiancee Roz, her brother Angus and the Howards: Tom, Will and sister Dorothy. It's a great party, but it breaks up early, since the Howards have a long ride home and Roz and Angus an even longer ride into town. The Howards ride off into the night not knowing that a renegade named Buffalo Horn is waiting for them at their ranch with a full Kiowa war party. In the massacre that follows, everyone is killed and the ranch is burned to the ground.

The Burton family has just learned about the Howards when a band of men from the town storm into the yard. The leader, Dred Pierce, demands a guarantee that Burton, his Indian wife and that half-breed kid, Pacer, side with them, and they make their point by shooting some of the Burton cattle and scattering the rest of the herd. Sam and Clint ride out in the morning to collect their cattle, leaving Pacer to guard his mother. Buffalo Horn rides up and asks Pacer to side with him in the coming fight against the white man. Pacer refuses but he and Neddy go along to Buffalo Horn's camp hoping to stop the bloodshed. Though Neddy is treated badly by her people, they are allowed to return home, but Pacer must make a decision about whose side he will fight on.

On the way back to the ranch, a crazed Will Howard, who has survived the massacre of his family, storms out of the night, kills Pacer's friend Two Moons and badly wounds Neddy in the process. Pacer brings her home to Sam, but she is clearly close to death. When they leave her for a moment, Neddy wanders off into the hills in search of what she calls her "flaming star." Sam and Pacer find her just before she dies.

Out of respect, Pacer takes the body of his friend Two Moons back to the Kiowa camp, where he learns of a raid being planned on the town. He agrees to go along if his family ranch is spared. But Sam is ambushed and killed and Clint is badly wounded during the attack, and in an attempt to lead the war party away from his brother, Pacer is mortally wounded as well. He has saved Clint's life at the cost of his own and just as his mother did, he heads off into the mountains to follow his own "flaming star."

CAST:

Pacer Burton	Elvis Presley
Clint Burton	Steve Forrest
Roslyn Pierce	Barbara Eden
Neddy Burton	Dolores Del Rio
Sam Burton	John McIntire
Buffalo Horn	Rudolph Acosta
Dred Pierce	Karl Swenson
Doc Phillips	Ford Rainey
Angus Pierce	Richard Jaeckel
Dorothy Howard	Anne Benton
Tom Howard	L.Q. Jones

SONGS:

Flaming Star, A Cane and a High Starched Collar

WILD IN THE COUNTRY
(1961)

20th Century-Fox, a Company of Artists, Inc., production
   Producer: Jerry Wald
   Director: Philip Dunne
   Screenwriter: Clifford Odets
   Director of Photography: William C. Mellor
   Running Time: 114 minutes
   Opened: June 22, 1961
   Stats: First Speaking Role for Red West, member of Elvis' "Memphis Mafia"

SYNOPSIS:

Glenn Tyler (Elvis) is bright and talented but has always been in trouble. The best thing in his life is his girl, Betty Lee. His relationship with his family is difficult: During a drunken argument, he fights with his brother and runs away, thinking he has killed him. When he's caught and brought to court, his father won't have anything to do with him and after his conviction, he's placed in the custody of his uncle Phil Macy. Glenn goes to work in Phil's plant and moves into his house, where his sexy cousin Noreen and her baby also live.

As part of his probation, Glenn is required to see Irene Sperry, a court-appointed psychiatrist. Although he is initially against the idea, he comes to see that Irene is perceptive and insightful and that she wants to help him. He finds himself opening up to her and even reveals a strong need to write. Irene encourages him, but the problems with his family and friends make it tough for him to make progress. In the midst of all his turmoil, Glenn is still able to write a short story that Irene thinks is good enough to get him into college. She pulls some strings and Glenn is accepted.

Betty Lee loves him and agrees to wait for him to graduate. But Glenn is unable to control his attraction to cousin Noreen and they start an affair. Glenn begins a long downhill slide during which Betty Lee tries to get him back into counseling with Irene. Finally, he agrees, and she gets him back on track, taking him to look at the college.

On their return to town, Irene and Glenn are forced by bad weather to stop at a motel. Phil Macy's son Cliff sees them at the motel and rumors spread like wildfire. Glenn is furious, finds Cliff, and during the inevitable fight that ensues, Cliff dies. Glenn is to be charged with murder, but Phil gets him off the hook when he reveals that Cliff had a weak heart made worse by boozing. Glenn will get another chance. As the train taking him to away to college pulls out of the station, he opens an envelope and discovers that his first story has been published. He is on his way in more ways than one.

CAST:

Glenn Tyler	Elvis Presley
Irene Sperry	Hope Lange
Noreen	Tuesday Weld
Betty Lee Parsons	Millie Perkins
Davis	Rafer Johnson
Phil Macy	John Ireland
Cliff Macy	Gary Lockwood
Judge Parker	Jason Robards, Sr.
Hank Tyler	Red West
Mr. Longstreet	Pat Buttram

SONGS:
Wild In The Country, I Slipped, I Stumbled, I Fell, In My Way, Husky Dusky Day

BLUE HAWAII

(1961)

Paramount Pictures
  Producer: Hal B. Wallis
  Director: Norman Taurog
  Screenplay: Hal Kanter
  Costumes: Edith Head
  Makeup: Wally Westmore
  Technical Advisor: Colonel Tom Parker
  Running Time: 101 minutes
  Opened: November 22, 1961
  Stats: #2 *Variety*'s Weekly List of Top Grossing Films, #14 Top Grossing Film of 1962
  Total Gross: $14 Million

SYNOPSIS:

Chad Gates (Elvis) is back in Honolulu after his discharge from the army trying to figure out what to do with his life. One thing he knows for sure is that it won't be joining the family pineapple business and settling down with any girl his mother approves of. His girlfriend, Maile, tells him about a job at her travel agency as a tour guide, and with nothing better on the horizon, he takes it. His first assignment is a group of four teenage girls and their teacher, Abigail.

Chad starts the tour with a drive around the island, discovering that three of the girls are well mannered and friendly, but Ellie, the fourth, is a nasty and difficult young woman. When, after a day of being rude to him, Ellie kisses him at a party, Chad understands that she's got a crush on him and tells her to act her age. In revenge, Ellie plays up to a drunken tourist who starts a fight when Chad steps in. Arrested and jailed, Chad is bailed out by his father—but loses his job. His parents think Maile is a bad influence on him, so he leaves home.

Abigail hires him to take her group to Kauai anyway. After a tough day of sightseeing, Ellie knocks on his door, forces her way into the room and is pretty clear about what she wants. The phone rings just in the nick of time—but it's Maile, downstairs with their friend Jack. Chad says he'll meet them in the lobby, but as he's leaving, Ellie's young friends show up looking for her. Just as the girls enter the room, there's still another knock: It's Abigail. Chad hides the teenagers and lets her in. Bubbling, she tells Chad she's fallen in love. Ellie overhears, assuming she's talking about Chad, and runs screaming into the night. Maile, meanwhile, tired of waiting in the lobby, comes upstairs to Chad's room, sees him with Abigail and runs off in tears. Just then the girls rush in saying that Ellie has taken a jeep and driven off, so Chad follows and finds her on the side of the road where the jeep has tangled with a tree.

The next morning is tough. Maile is avoiding Chad like the plague. Abigail finally makes it clear that she's in love with Jack, not Chad, and after a lot of effort he gets Maile to believe him. They decide to use his father's pineapple connections to start their own travel agency.

CAST:

Chad Gates	Elvis Presley
Maile Duval	Joan Blackman
Sarah Lee Gates	Angela Lansbury
Abigail	Nancy Walters
Fred Gates	Roland Winters
Jack Kelman	John Archer
Mr. Chapman	Howard McNear
Tucker Garvey	Steve Brodie
Wihila	Hilo Hattie
Party Guest	Red West

SONGS:

Blue Hawaii, Almost Always True, Aloha Oe, No More, Can't Help Falling In Love, Rock-a-Hula Baby, Moonlight Swim, Ku-u-i-Po, Ito Eats, Slicin' Sand, Hawaiian Sunset, Beach Boy Blues, Island Of Love (Kauai), Hawaiian Wedding Song

F★LL★★ THAT DREAM

(1962)

United Artists, a Mirisch Company production
    Producer: David Weisbart
    Director: Gordon Douglas
    Screenplay: Charles Lederer
    Based on a Novel by: Richard Powell
    Technical Advisor: Colonel Tom Parker
    Running Time: 110 minutes
    Opened: May 23, 1962

SYNOPSIS:

Heading down south in a battered jalopy with all their worldly goods, Pop Kwimper, his son Toby (Elvis) and four stray kids—Ariadne; twins Eddy and Teddy and nineteen-year-old Holly—run out of gas on a deserted stretch of brand new but unopened highway. After sleeping overnight on the beach, they discover that, much to the chagrin of the government, their little campout has made them homesteaders and they can legally stay on the land. After the highway officially opens, they start a little business renting fishing equipment and selling bait. Other people hear about the place and come to settle. When a couple of high rollers figure out that none of the authorities can decide who's responsible for policing Kwimper's little village, they move in a floating crap game. Heavy hitters flock to Nick and Carmine's trailer-home casino, causing disruption and lowering community standards.

In a landslide, the reluctant Toby is elected sheriff and goes about his duty to keep things peaceful and quiet. Nick and Carmine, however, are serious about protecting their investment and will do anything to keep the dice rolling—including putting Toby six feet under. But when he is attacked by some of Nick and Carmine's thugs, they learn that he isn't without skill in the art of self-defense, having learned some martial arts in the army. Toby makes short work not only of the leg breakers but the big boys as well, and they all head up north with their tails between their legs, trailer home and all.

Just when things have returned to normal, a state welfare agent starts investigating the Kwimper family trying to find out about the kids. When Toby doesn't take a shine to her, she gets mad, and to get even she files a court order allowing her to take the kids because Pop is an unfit parent and is raising them in an unsatisfactory moral climate because of Toby's "romantic relationship" with Holly. It's not, but that doesn't stop the welfare agent.

When Toby and Pop are brought to court to defend themselves, they do it so well that the judge not only dismisses the case but singles them out as true examples of the spirit that made America great. Secure at last in their little community, Toby sees Holly for the first time and not only gets interested in her but discovers that she is the girl of his dreams.

CAST:

Toby Kwimper	Elvis Presley
Pop Kwimper	Arthur O'Connell
Holly Jones	Anne Helm
Alicia Claypoole	Joanna Moore
H. Arthur King	Alan Hewitt
Nick	Simon Oakland
Carmine	Jack Kruschen
Teddy Bascombe	Robin Koon
Eddy Bascombe	Gavin Koon
Ariadne Pennington	Pam Ogles
Bank Guard	Red West

SONGS:

What A Wonderful Life, I'm Not The Marrying Kind, Sound Advice, On Top Of Old Smokey, Follow That Dream, Angel

KID GALAHAD

(1962)

United Artists, a Mirisch Company production
 Producer: Davis Weisbart
 Director: Phil Karlson
 Screenplay: William Fay
 Based on a Story by: Francis Wallace
 Technical Advisor: Colonel Tom Parker
 Running Time: 95 Minutes
 Opened: August 29, 1962
 Stats: #9 on *Variety*'s List of Top-Grossing Films
 Total Gross: $1.75 Million

SYNOPSIS:

Out of the service and looking for work, Walter Gulick (Elvis) gets a job sparring in Willy Grogan's training camp. Walter's raw but he can take a punch and has a solid right hand. One day he KOs a strong fighter named Joie Shakes, and Willy sees that with the proper guidance the kid could make some money in the ring. Willy needs a payoff fighter because he's into Otto Danzig for a lot of money. Otto is really bad news, and has guys at the camp keeping tabs on new fighters and to make sure that Willy doesn't welch.

Willy's sister Rose visits the camp, and she and Walter fall in love. Walter just wants to make enough money in the ring to marry Rose and go into the car business, but Willy is against his sister getting involved with a fighter because it's no life for a lady. Walter is coming along fine but not quite ready for the big time when Danzig forces Willy to put him in the ring against a guy who really outclasses him so Danzig can fix the fight.

Danzig offers Walter's trainer a lot of money to quit so he can put his own guy in the corner and make sure his bet is covered. The trainer refuses and Danzig's boys start to break him up. Willy comes into the locker room before the guys are finished and with Walter's help cleans up the floor with them. With Danzig out of the picture, Walter KOs his opponent in the big fight, and Willy blesses his marriage to Rose.

CAST:

Walter Gulick	Elvis Presley
Willy Grogan	Gig Young
Dolly Fletcher	Lola Albright
Rose Grogan	Joan Blackman
Lew Nyack	Charles Bronson
Mr. Lieberman	Robert Emhardt
Mr. Maynard	David Lewis
Joie Shakes	Michael Dante
Frank Gerson	Ed Asner

SONGS:

King Of The Whole Wide World, This Is Living, Riding The Rainbow, Home Is Where The Heart Is, I Got Lucky, A Whistling Tune

GIRLS! GIRLS! GIRLS!

(1962)

Paramount Pictures
   Producer: Hal B. Wallis
   Director: Norman Taurog
   Screenplay: Edward Anhalt
   Story: Allen Weiss
   Costumes: Edith Head
   Makeup: Wally Westmore
   Technical Advisor: Colonel Tom Parker
   Running Time: 106 minutes
   Opened: November 21, 1962
   Stats: #6 on *Variety*'s List of Top-Grossing Films
   Total Gross: $2.7 Million

SYNOPSIS:

Ross Carpenter (Elvis) and his father build a sailboat called the *West Wind* and finish it just before the father's death. But Ross was forced to sell it to Stavros, the Greek who owns the charter fishing boat Ross captains. Stavros is a decent man and has allowed Ross to continue living on the *West Wind* and will sell it back to him whenever he's saved enough to buy it. The arrangement works well until Stavros becomes ill and must move to Arizona, forcing him to sell everything including Ross' beloved *West Wind*.

Upset about the prospect of losing the boat, Ross goes to his girlfriend Robin's club to take his mind off his problems. She has some trouble with a drunk and Ross escorts him outside. In the process he meets the drunk's date, Laurel Dodge, and asks her to join him the following day for lunch. He arrives late, finding Laurel in deep conversation with an older man. For reasons he doesn't fully understand, he leaves in a huff and feels silly when Laurel tells him the gentleman was her father. They go sailing the next day and he tells her his fantasy of finding the money to make the *West Wind* his again. They are falling in love, but she tells Ross she's been burned too many times and is afraid to let herself go.

On their return, Ross finds to his dismay that Stavros has sold the boat to a broker who is jacking up the price and selling it off to the highest bidder. Without a boat to make a living on, Ross goes back to singing in Robin's club. In the meantime Laurel gets some money from her family and buys the *West Wind*, warning the broker not to tell Ross who bought it. But Ross is proud and becomes angry when he discovers who it was and how she did it. When he disappears, Robin takes pity on Laurel and tells her where he might have gone.

Laurel asks the broker if he would sail the *West Wind* to Ross' hiding place. As they set off, a friend of Ross' recognizes them and signals Ross on the radio. Thinking that Laurel is in trouble, he rushes to her rescue. Boarding in an angry mood, he discovers she is coming to find him and swallows his pride, becoming the proud owner of a fine sailboat and the fiancé of a lovely young woman.

CAST:

Ross Carpenter ....Elvis Presley
Robin Gatner ....Stella Stevens
Wesley Johnson ....Jeremy Slate
Laurel Dodge ....Laurel Goodwin
Sam...Robert Strauss
Chen Yung..Guy Lee
Papa Stavros ....Frank Puglia
Mama Stavros ....Lili Valenty
Bongo-Playing Crewman On Tuna Boat...Red West

SONGS:

Girls! Girls! Girls!, I Don't Wanna Be Tied, We'll Be Together, A Boy Like Me, A Girl Like You, Earth Boy, Return To Sender, Because Of Love, Thanks To The Rolling Sea, Song Of The Shrimp, The Walls Have Ears, We're Coming Loaded, Dainty Little Moonbeams

IT HAPPENED AT THE WORLD'S FAIR

(1963)

Metro Goldwyn Mayer
  Producer: Ted Richmond
  Director: Norman Taurog
  Screenplay: Si Rose, Seaman Jacobs
  Technical Advisor: Colonel Tom Parker
  Hairstyles: Sydney Guilaroff
  Running Time: 105 minutes
  Opened: April 10, 1963
  Stats: #55 Top Grossing Film for 1963
  Total Gross: $2.25 Million

SYNOPSIS:

Bush pilots Mike (Elvis) and Danny are usually broke. The jobs are few and far between, but they hang on because they love it. At the moment they're barely hanging on by dusting endless potato fields in Washington State. But it's too little, too late, and the local sheriff serves papers attaching their plane for a big stack of overdue bills. Without the plane there's no point in staying, so they thumb a ride from a Chinese farmer and his niece Sue-Lin, and head to the Seattle World's Fair.

Since her dad is going to be busy, Mike volunteers to take Sue-Lin to the fair while Danny looks for a buddy who might be able to help them out of the jam. After a long day of riding and eating, Sue-Lin gets an upset stomach and Mike has to find the dispensary. The nurse, Diane, is so pretty that Mike tries to be sick as well.

Danny reports in to say that he has found a house trailer for them to stay in. Mike goes back to the fair to see Diane and persuades her to have dinner with him, but they have a huge fight and when Sue-Lin tells them that her uncle has disappeared, it's a good excuse for Mike to leave. Not knowing what else to do, he takes her back to the trailer at the fair to see Diane, but when they arrive an agent from the welfare office shows papers to pick up Sue-Lin. It turns out that Diane was so angry she has called the child welfare agency and told them Sue-Lin should be put under foster care. Mike is furious, but there's nothing he can do.

Danny's buddy has arranged to put up the money to get the plane back if he and Mike will fly some cargo up to Canada. Mike agrees, but when he learns that Sue-Lin has escaped from the welfare board, he rushes to the fair to find her and brings her to the airport with him to meet Danny and head north. But Mike smells a rat and opens one of the containers. Mike's instinct is correct: The boxes are full of illegal furs. Danny's sleazy friend is a smuggler, and Mike gets him arrested. When Sue-Lin's uncle returns, Diane and Mike are free to admit that they love each other—and they decide to become astronauts!

CAST:

Mike Edwards ....Elvis Presley
Diane Warren ....Joan O'Brien
Danny Burke ....Gary Lockwood
Sue-Lin ....Vicky Tiu
Fred ....Red West
Boy Who Kicks Elvis ....Kurt Russell

SONGS:

Beyond The Bend, Relax, Take Me To The Fair, One Broken Heart For Sale, I'm Falling In Love Tonight, Cotton Candy Land, A World Of Our Own, How Would You Like To Be, Happy Ending

FUN IN ACAPULCO

(1963)

Paramount Pictures
    Producer: Hal B. Wallis
    Director: Richard Thorpe
    Screenplay: Allan Weiss
    Costumes: Edith Head
    Makeup: Wally Westmore
    Technical Advisor: Colonel Tom Parker
    Running Time: 97 minutes
    Opened: November 27, 1963
    Stats: #5 *Variety*'s Weekly List of Top-Grossing Films, #33 for 1963
    Total Gross: $1.5 Million

SYNOPSIS:

Sailor Mike Windgren (Elvis), an ex-trapeze artist, arrives in Acapulco, escaping from his past and an accident on the swing in which his partner was badly injured. While in port, a shoeshine boy named Raoul overhears Mike sing and offers to become his manager. At first Mike scoffs, but he becomes a believer when the kid succeeds in getting Mike hired as a singer in a resort hotel. During his engagement, he meets and becomes involved with Dolores Gomez, a lady bullfighter.

In addition to singing gigs at night, Mike works as a part-time lifeguard at the hotel swimming pool, where he meets Marguerita, the hotel's social director. The regular lifeguard, Moreno, has a crush on her and is very jealous of Mike. Moreno is famous in Acapulco for his cliff diving and brags about his skill. In a mood to show off, Mike climbs the pool's high board and tries to dive, but panics when he remembers how his partner was injured in a fall. He's humiliated, and Moreno thinks he can win back Marguerita by using Mike's fear of heights. So one evening Moreno fabricates an argument with Mike that escalates into a fistfight that ends with Moreno pretending to be too hurt to do his nightly high dive off the cliff at La Quebrada. Mike is obliged to make the leap himself, and with Marguerita cheering for him, he confronts his fear and makes the dive, regaining his confidence and his future.

CAST:

Mike Windgren..Elvis Presley
Marguerita Dauphin..Ursula Andress
Dolores Gomez..Elsa Cardenas
Maximillian Dauphin..Paul Lukas
Raoul Almeido..Larry Domasin
Moreno..Alejandro Rey
Poolside Guest..Red West

SONGS:

Fun In Acapulco, Vino, Dinero y Amore, I Think I'm Gonna Like It Here, Mexico, El Toro, Marguerita, The Bullfighter Was A Lady, (There's) No Room To Rhumba In A Sports Car, Bossa Nova Baby, You Can't Say No In Acapulco, Guadalajara

KISSIN' COUSINS

(1964)

Metro Goldwyn Mayer, a Four Leaf production
    Producer: Sam Katzman
    Director: Gene Nelson
    Screenplay: Gerald Drayson Adams, Gene Nelson
    Hairstyles: Sydney Guilaroff
    Technical Advisor: Colonel Tom Parker
    Running Time: 96 minutes
    Opened: March 6, 1963
    Stats: #11 *Variety*'s Weekly List, #26 for 1963
    Total Gross: $2.8 Million

SYNOPSIS:

The U.S. Air Force wants to build a missile base atop a Tennessee mountain owned by a moonshiner named Pappy Tatum. He thinks anyone from the government is Internal Revenue and that they want to bust up his still and therefore his source of both recreation and income. With the help of his family, especially his son Jodie, no one sets foot on Big Smokey.

Stuck, Washington decides to send a local boy, 2nd Lieutenant Josh Morgan (Elvis), who they think will be able to get through to this mule-headed hillbilly. Josh is assigned to work with Captain Salbo, and their orders are to get Pappy's signature for the lease of his property or spend the rest of their tour polishing somebody else's shoes.

But the moment they arrive at Big Smokey mountain with lease in hand, they are immediately ambushed and taken prisoner by the Tatums. When the dust settles, there is a shocked silence because to everyone's utter amazement, Josh and Jodie are the spitting image of each other, the only difference being that Jodie is blond and Josh has a full head of shiny black hair. Everyone sets to pondering this miracle when Josh remembers his great-aunt had married a Tatum, so darned if they're not kissin' cousins!

Since Josh is family, the fun begins in earnest, but it takes a while to distract Pappy long enough to get him to sign the lease. As a condition of his agreement, Pappy insists that he get protection of his privacy, so the Air Force agrees to keep a special patrol at the base of Big Smokey to keep all trespassers off the mountain. This will also stop the Revenuers from busting up his still, which was all Pappy wanted in the first place.

CAST:

Josh Morgan	Elvis Presley
Jodie Tatum	Elvis Presley
Pappy Tatum	Arthur O'Conell
Ma Tatum	Glenda Farrell
Capt. Robert Jason Salbo	Jack Albertson
Selena Tatum	Pam Austin
Azalea Tatum	Yvonne Craig

SONGS:

Kissin' Cousins, Smokey Mountain Boy, One Boy, Two Little Girls, Catchin' On Fast, Tender Feeling, Barefoot Ballad, Once Is Enough, Kissin' Cousins (Duet, Josh and Jodie)

VIVA LAS VEGAS

(1964)

Metro Goldwyn Mayer
    Producers: Jack Cummings, George Sidney
    Director: George Sidney
    Screenplay: Sally Benson
    Costumes: Don Feld
    Hairstyles: Sydney Guilaroff
    Running Time: 86 minutes
    Opened: April 20, 1964
    Stats: #14 on *Variety*'s Weekly List,
        #11 for 1964
    Total Gross: $4.7 Million

SYNOPSIS:

Formula racer Lucky Jackson (Elvis) lives to drive. He also loves to gamble, and winning a good-sized bet is what allows him and his mechanic, Shorty, to head for Las Vegas to enter their car in the Grand Prix. Shortly after hitting town, Lucky meets Italian racing champion, Count Elmo Mancini, who is tuning up his Ferrari for the race. A man who likes to win, Mancini asks Lucky to drive other cars out of the race for Mancini to insure a victory for himself and put some serious money in Lucky's pocket. Lucky feels that knowing who's going to win would take the fun out of it, so he says no.

Meanwhile, a beautiful young woman pulls up and asks them to fix her car. Lucky sees right away that nothing is really wrong, but loosens a wire to get her to stay around long enough to find out who she is. Missing the point, Mancini fixes the car and the girl is on her way before Lucky can learn her name. Guessing that she's a showgirl, the two men begin a casino-by-casino search, but it's no luck for Lucky, and he heads back to the hotel a defeated man. The next morning, he discovers that she's Rusty Martin, the swimming instructor at the very hotel where he's staying. Lucky is so excited to find her he falls into the pool, and the money he had saved to beef up his engine is literally sucked down the drain. Hotel management allows Lucky and Shorty the option of becoming waiters to pay off their hotel bill. To Lucky's surprise this makes them eligible to compete for $2,500 in prizes at the annual employees' talent competition.

He wins first prize, edging out Rusty, but instead of much needed cash, Lucky gets a gold-plated cup and an all-expenses-paid honeymoon in Monaco. Hours before the big race, the money turns up for Lucky's engine—secretly financed by Rusty's father—and he wins the Las Vegas Grand Prix, heading off on his European honeymoon with Rusty.

CAST:

Lucky Johnson...Elvis Presley
Rusty Martin...Ann-Margret
Count Elmo Mancini..Cesare Danova
Mr. Martin...William Demarest
Shorty Farnsworth...Nicky Blair
Jack Carter..Himself
Showgirl...Teri Garr

SONGS:

Viva Las Vegas, The Yellow Rose Of Texas, The Lady Loves Me, C'mon Everybody, Today, Tomorrow And Forever, What'd I Say, Santa Lucia, If You Think I Don't Love You, I Need Somebody To Lean On

ROUSTABOUT
(1964)

Paramount Pictures
    Producer: Hal B. Wallis
    Director: John Rich
    Screenplay: Anthony Lawrence, Allan Weiss
    Makeup: Wally Westmore
    Technical Advisor: Colonel Tom Parker
    Running Time: 101 minutes
    Opened: November 11, 1964
    Stats: #8 *Variety*'s Weekly #28 for 1965
    Total Gross: $3 Million

SYNOPSIS:

After blowing yet another singing job because of his attitude toward the customers—coupled with his temper and his skill at karate—Charlie Rogers (Elvis) straps his guitar on his back and heads for parts unknown on his motorcycle. He gets a job as a roustabout at a carnival run by Maggie Morgan.

At the carnival, Charlie meets Cathy Lean, whose father Joe is less than excited about the budding romance. Business at the carnival isn't exactly booming, so in between odd jobs, Charlie sings a song or two on the midway. Word gets around and suddenly crowds of screaming teenagers flock to the carnival grounds. But as usual, Charlie's attitude gets in the way and things fall apart again.

He gets into a fight with one of the customers and decides to leave again, accepting an offer from a rival carnival. With Charlie gone, Maggie's carnival again takes a nosedive and they're in real danger of shutting down. As a last resort, Cathy goes to find Charlie, who for the first time in his life turns bad into good and returns to save Maggie's carnival.

CAST:

Charlie Rogers	Elvis Presley
Maggie Morgan	Barbara Stanwyck
Cathy Lean	Joan Freeman
Joe Lean	Leif Erickson
Madame Mijanou	Sue Ann Langdon
Harry Carver	Pat Buttram
Marge	Joan Staley
Arthur Neilson	Dabbs Greer
Freddie	Steve Brodie
Lou	Jack Albertson
Billy, The Midget	Billy Barty
Strong Man	Richard Kiel
Carnival Worker	Red West
College Student	Raquel Welch

SONGS:

Roustabout, Poison Ivy, Wheels On My Heels, It's A Wonderful World, It's Carnival Time, Carny Town, One Track Heart, Hard Knocks, Little Egypt, Big Love, Big Heartache, There's A Brand New Day On The Horizon

GIRL HAPPY
(1965)

Metro Goldwyn Mayer, a Euterpe production
    Producer: Joe Pasternak
    Director: Boris Sagal
    Screenplay: Harvey Bullock, R.S. Allen
    Hairstyles: Sydney Guilaroff
    Technical Advisor: Colonel Tom Parker
    Running Time: 96 minutes
    Opened: April 14, 1965
    Stats: #25 for 1965
    Total Gross: $3.1 Million

SYNOPSIS:

Rusty Wells (Elvis) and his band are preparing to split the Windy City, leave winter far behind and head down to Fort Lauderdale for spring break. But they've earned a lot of money for Big Frank and made his nightspot a very popular place, so he decides to hold the band over for a while. It's hard to say no to Big Frank, but Rusty's got Florida on his mind and when he finds out that Big Frank's daughter Valerie is spending her Easter vacation in Fort Lauderdale, he moves into action. Playing on Frank's paranoia about his daughter, Rusty cons her father into sending him and the band to Florida, all expenses paid, to make sure she gets through it OK.

Rusty and the boys hit town, check into the hotel, find Valerie and see that there's no need to watch her, since she appears to be interested only in reading. Rusty gets right to work: He meets Deena and persuades her to visit him at the club where he's playing.

During a set, he spots Valerie in the audience with her date, who turns out to be a rich kid named Brentwood Von Durgenfeld. Rusty leaves Deena to rescue Big Frank's daughter from this creep, but it's not as easy as it seems. She keeps getting herself into trouble, and the whole thing is turning into a pain in the neck until he realizes that he's falling for the little bookworm himself.

But when Valerie discovers that Rusty has been hired to tail her, she is furious and proceeds to get drunk and take her clothes off in a bar. Rusty gets involved and a fight breaks out. When the air clears, Valerie is in the Lauderdale jug. Rusty tunnels into Valerie's cell to break her out, but by the time he arrives, she's not there: Big Frank has already sprung her.

Fearing for his life, Rusty talks to Big Frank, who's mighty angry at first, but finally decides he's got to like a guy who'll dig his way into jail to save his daughter. He takes a "what-the- hell" kind of attitude and gives Rusty and Valerie his blessing.

CAST:

Rusty Wells	Elvis Presley
Valerie Frank	Shelley Fabares
Mr. Frank	Harold J. Stone
Andy	Gary Crosby
Wilbur	Joby Baker
Sunny Daze	Nina Talbot
Deena Shepherd	Mary Ann Mobley
Romano	Fabrizio Mioni
Sergeant Benson	Jackie Coogan
Doc	Jimmy Hawkins
Brentwood Von Durgenfeld	Peter Brooks
Charlie	Dan Haggerty
Extra In Kit Kat Club	Red West

SONGS:

Girl Happy, Spring Fever, Fort Lauderdale Chamber Of Commerce, Startin' Tonight, Wolf Call, Do Not Disturb, Cross My Heart And Hope To Die, The Meanest Girl In Town, Do The Clam, Puppet On A String, I've Got To Find My Baby

TICKLE ME

(1965)

Allied Artists, A Ben Schwalb production.
   Producer: Ben Schwalb
   Director: Norman Taurog
   Screenplay: Elwood Ullman, Edward Bernds
   Makeup: Wally Westmore
   Technical Advisor: Colonel Tom Parker
   Running Time: 90 minutes
   Opened: May 28, 1965
   Stats: Budget: $1.5 Million
   For Elvis: $750,000 + 50%

SYNOPSIS:

   Lonnie Beale (Elvis) is hired by Vera Radford, who owns a high-priced dude ranch/health spa. A rodeo cowboy and a singer, he's a popular romantic figure to all but Pam Merritt, the spa's physical instructor, who sees him as just another gigolo until the night when she discovers someone in her quarters and Lonnie rushes to her aid. By the time he gets there, the man is gone, and when the police arrive, Deputy Sheriff Sturdivant takes her aside and warns that she has been talking too freely about her grandfather's "letter" and how it will help her find his stash of gold. He goes on to say that there will be more of these guys around if she isn't careful and doesn't keep her mouth shut.

   Shortly afterwards, two men in masks attempt to kidnap Pam. Again Lonnie is Johnny-on-the-spot and rescues Pam, but the thugs escape. Out in the desert, the two men wait for their boss—who turns out to be Sturdivant. The deputy is behind the whole thing, and he's furious with them for not getting the job done.

   Pam shows Lonnie her grandfather's letter, and the two are getting along great until he gets in a little trouble with one of the patrons and Pam breaks it off. Upset, Lonnie leaves to pick up the rodeo circuit, but a friend comes to bring him back to find Pam in the ghost town of Silverado, where the gold is hidden.

   A freak storm rises out of the mountains and everyone is stuck there for the night. During the storm, the bad guys try a hundred different ways to get the gold, but they're foiled by Lonnie and Pam. Once again, he was there for her, and this time for keeps: They get married at the ranch and head off for a well deserved honeymoon.

CAST:

Lonnie Beale	Elvis Presley
Vera Radford	Julie Adams
Pam Merritt	Jocelyn Lane
Stanley Potter	Jack Mullaney
Estelle Penfield	Merry Anders
Deputy Sheriff John Sturdivant	Bill Williams
Bully In Bar	Red West

SONGS:

Long, Lonely Highway, It Feels So Right, (Such An) Easy Question, Dirty, Dirty Feeling, I'm Yours, Night Rider, I Feel That I've Known You Forever, Slowly But Surely

HAREM SCARUM
(1965)

Metro Goldwyn Mayer, a Four Leaf production
    Producer: Sam Katzman
    Director: Gene Nelson
    Screenplay: Gerald Drayson Adams
    Technical Advisor: Colonel Tom Parker
    Hairstyles: Sydney Guilaroff
    Running Time: 95 minutes
    Opened: November 24, 1965

SYNOPSIS:

While touring the Middle East, Johnny Tyronne (Elvis), a singer and movie star, is kidnapped and taken into the desert to a large palace. The court clowns and jesters help him jump over the palace wall to what he thinks is freedom, but he ends up instead in the quarters of Princess Shalimar. Excitement and adventure are not a big part of Shalimar's life, so she tells him she's just a simple slave girl and would be honored to help him escape. She asks Johnny why he was imprisoned, and he tells her that all he knows is that they were going to involve him in a plot to kill someone very important. The princess realizes that it has to be the king, her father.

She helps Johnny escape, but he is soon recaptured and told that he must kill the king, or his captors will kill the court clowns and jugglers who risked their lives to help him escape. Johnny has no choice but to agree. The deed will be done at the king's palace while the troupe of entertainers perform. The show starts and Johnny goes through the motions of proceeding with the planned assassination. In the nick of time, Shalimar warns her father and the coup is no more, but Johnny and the clowns and jugglers are locked in the deepest, darkest, dampest dungeon in the palace.

He escapes once again and finds Shalimar's room. She's with the king, so he tells them both the whole story, and together they uncover the plot by the king's brother to murder him and inherit the throne. Now that the king knows who the real culprit is, justice is swift and Johnny is well rewarded for his service to the throne with the hand of Princess Shalimar.

CAST:

Johnny Tyronne	Elvis Presley
Princess Shalimar	Mary Ann Mobley
Aishah	Fran Jeffries
Prince Dragna	Michael Ansara
Zacha	Jay Novello
King Toranshah	Philip Reed
Sinan, Lord Of The Assassins	Theo Marcuse
Baba	Billy Barty
Assassin	Red West

SONGS:

Harem Holiday, My Desert Serenade, Go East, Young Man, Mirage, Kismet, Shake That Tambourine, Hey, Little Girl, Golden Coins, So Close, Yet So Far

FRANKIE AND JOHNNY

(1966)

United Artists
    Producer: Edward Smal
    Director: Frederick de Cordova
    Screenplay: Alex Gottlieb
    Running Time: 87 minutes
    Opened: March 31, 1966
    Stats: Budget – $4.5 Million

SYNOPSIS:

Frankie and Johnny (Elvis) are lovers, but as much as she loves him, she won't walk down the aisle until he gives up his card playing and gambling. That's a difficult task for Johnny, since he's a riverboat gambler and they make their living floating up and down the Mississippi working as a singing act on a riverboat owned by Clint Braden.

Johnny gets his cards read by a fortune teller and learns that his losing streak will be over for good when a new redhead appears on the scene. Sure enough, a redhead appears. Her name is Nellie Bly and she used to know the owner of the riverboat pretty well. These are all jealous people, and Frankie doesn't like Nellie and Nellie doesn't like Frankie, and Braden doesn't like the way Nellie is looking at Johnny. Johnny, of course, is interested in Nellie strictly as a good-luck charm. Johnny's buddy Cully, who plays piano on the boat, watches all this going on and writes a song called "Frankie and Johnny," which causes an immediate sensation and could be the tune that sends Frankie and Johnny to the big time.

Meanwhile, the fortune teller was right on target; with Nellie at his side, Johnny is raking in the chips. He's on a streak that could make history. Then Braden's bodyguard, Blackie, trying to help Braden get Johnny out of Nellie's life, puts a real bullet in the gun that Frankie uses to "kill" Johnny in the finish of the song.

The gun goes off, the bullet flies to its target, but miraculously, Johnny isn't killed. After coming so close to losing him, Frankie realizes that she loves Johnny no matter how much he gambles.

CAST:

Johnny	Elvis Presley
Frankie	Donna Douglas
Cully	Harry Morgan
Mitzi	Sue Ann Langdon
Nellie Bly	Nancy Kovack
Peg	Audrey Christie
Blackie	Robert Strauss
Clint Braden	Anthony Eisley
Abigail	Joyce Jameson
Joe Wilbur	Jerome Cowan

SONGS:

Come Along, Petunia The Gardener's Daughter, Chesay, What Every Woman Lives For, Frankie And Johnny, Look Out Broadway, Beginner's Luck, Down By The Riverside, Shout It Out, Hard Luck, Please Don't Stop Loving Me, Everybody Come Aboard

PARADISE, HAWAIIAN STYLE

(1966)

Paramount Pictures
    Producer: Hal B. Wallis
    Director: D. Michael Moore
    Screenplay: Allan Weiss, Anthony Lawrence
    Set Decoration: Robert Benton, Ray Moyer
    Makeup: Wally Westmore
    Costumes: Edith Head
    Technical Advisor: Colonel Tom Parker
    Running Time: 91 minutes
    Opened: July 6, 1966
    Stats: #40 Top-Grossing Film of 1966
    Total Gross: $2.5 Million

SYNOPSIS:

Pilot Rick Richards (Elvis), down on his luck and out of resources, returns home to Hawaii. At the airport he hitches a ride with an old friend, Danny, who's flying an executive to a convention at the Maui Sheraton. Trying to land on his feet, Rick suggests that they start a helicopter charter service together. Danny doesn't think there's enough potential business, so Rick goes to work and persuades a Sheraton hostess, Lehua, to refer customers. Rick's enthusiasm—and his growing customer list—changes Danny's mind, and Danrick Airways is up and flying.

On a mission to find passengers, Rick locates a girl, Pua, at the Polynesian Cultural Center, who's willing to help—but Rick's got to do something for her. He joins her on stage to sing "Drums of the Islands." His next contact is Joanna at the Kahala Hilton, but she needs a little more convincing, so Rick takes her for a spin. During the ride, Rick has a problem with the chopper, and while regaining control, he forces a car below him into a ditch. Big trouble: The driver of the car was Donald Belden of the FAA.

Rick agrees to take Danny's daughter Jan for a helicopter ride, but she buries the ignition key in the sand and they end up stuck on a remote beach until daylight. Nothing happened, but Danny is furious and dissolves the partnership. Danny and Jan take off, but when they don't return as scheduled, Rick goes on a tense air search and finds them slightly injured but OK. Danny and Rick apologize to each other and become buddies again, but both fear they may lose their licenses and Danrick will go down the tubes.

No one knows quite what to do. Then they hear that Belden of the FAA is to be guest of honor at a local festival. Rick decides to see him in person and find out what can be done. He finds Belden and gives his side of the story. Belden assures him that because of the skill he showed rescuing Danny and Jan, he will continue to fly—and Danrick is saved.

CAST:

Rick Richards	Elvis Presley
Judy Hudson (Friday)	Suzanna Leigh
Danny Kohana	James Shigeta
Jan Kohana	Donna Butterworth
Lani Kaimana	Marianna Hill
Pua	Irene Tsu
Lehua Kawena	Lind Wong
Joanna	Julie Parrish
Betty Kohana	Jan Shepard
Donald Belden	John Doucette
Dancer	Edy Williams
Lehua's Escort	Robert Ito
Rusty	Red West

SONGS:

Paradise, Hawaiian Style, Queenie Wahini's Papaya, Scratch My Back (Then I'll Scratch Yours), Drums Of The Islands, A Dog's Life, Datin', House Of Sand, Stop Where You Are, This Is My Heaven

SPINOUT

(1966)

Metro Goldwyn Mayer
> Producer: Joe Pasternak
> Director: Norman Taurog
> Screenplay: Theodore J. Flicker, George Kirgo
> Hairstyles: Sydney Guilaroff
> Technical Advisor: Colonel Tom Parker
> Running Time: 90 minutes
> Opened: November 23, 1966
> Stats: Elvis' 10th Anniversary in the Movie Business

SYNOPSIS

Mike McCoy loves being single almost as much as he loves racing formula cars. He's made a living as a singer to support his love of speed. But it's a life on the edge, racing is an expensive habit. On the other hand, Mike loves women almost as much as he loves racing. So it's a problem when he dumps his Cobra into a stream because he can't help but race a beautiful young woman out on a deserted California road.

Mike pulls his car out of the mud and heads into Santa Barbara for a gig at a local club. He's got to make some money if he is going to fix his car in time for the big race in Santa Fe. After the last show a man asks Mike and the band to perform at his daughter's birthday party and says he's willing to pay them a lot of money. The problem is that Mike is a man of principles and the date conflicts with gigs already booked. Mike is a man of his word and says no. The man leaves and Mike notices a beautiful woman who is watching him in the club.

The band, including a female drummer named Les, who is secretly in love with him, camps along the roadside and is settling in for the night when Mike notices the mystery woman in the bushes. He confronts her and finds out that she's a famous writer, Diane St.Clair, who's doing a book on the perfect American male. She has decided it's him. Now there are two women in love with the freedom-loving Mike.

During a rehearsal the band gets some bad news. The rest of the tour has been canceled by the man who wanted Mike to sing at his daughter's birthday. If they agree to do the party the tour is back on, if not... Mike shrugs his shoulders and says ok. When the band arrives at the rich guy's house they discover that the birthday girl is none other than the woman who drove Mike off the road and that her father is Howard Foxhugh, the famous designer of formula racing cars. This was all a plan so Mike would drive for him in the upcoming race. Mike sings and splits, even though he is attracted to the beautiful and spoiled young woman. Nobody buys Mike McCoy. The band thinks he's in love and that's bad for their future so they try to distract him... with more women and fast cars. Of course the drummer is hoping he'll see the light and fall in love with her. There are now three women in love with Mike McCoy.

At a wild party, thrown to get Mike's mind off his problems, all three of the women in his life show up and Mike is forced to choose. He panics and says he'll decide after the big race which he will run in the old Dusenberg car in which the band travels. The race is wild and crazy and Mike ends up winning in a car he doesn't even own.

Success is great but Mike's got a problem. Who will he choose? The drummer, the writer, or the heiress? He chooses to marry them all... to other people. They find happiness and he gets to keep his beloved freedom.

CAST:

Mike McCoy	Elvis Presley
Cynthia Foxhugh	Shelley Fabares
Diana St. Clair	Diane McBain
Les	Deborah Walley
Susan	Dodie Marshall
Curly	Jack Mullaney
Lt. Tracy Richards	Will Hutchins
Philip Short	Warren Berlinger
Larry	Jimmy Hawkins
Howard Foxhugh	Carl Betz
Bernard Ranley	Cecil Kellaway
Violet Ranley	Una Merkel
Member Of Pit Crew	Red West

SONGS:

Spinout, Stop, Look And Listen, Adam And Evil, All That I Am, Never Say Yes, Am I Ready, Beach Shack, Smorgasbord, I'll Be Back

EASY COME, EASY GO

(1967)

Paramount Pictures
    Producer: Hal B. Wallis
    Director: John Rich
    Screenplay: Allan Weiss, Anthony Lawrence
    Set Decoration: Robert Benton, Arthur Krams
    Makeup: Wally Westmore
    Costumes: Edith Head
    Technical Advisor: Colonel Tom Parker
    Running Time: 95 minutes
    Opened: March 22, 1967
    Stats: #50 in *Variety*'s List Of Top-Grossing Films
    Total Gross: $1.95 Million

SYNOPSIS:

While on duty off the Pacific coast, navy frogman Ted Jackson (Elvis) discovers a treasure chest in the hull of an old ship. At the local marina, Captain Jack tells him that Joe Symington, as the only descendant of the ship's original owner, can tell him all about the vessel, which he believes to be the *Port of Call*.

At the Symington place, Ted finds a group of scraggly hippie types doing yoga, transcendental meditation and generally tuning in and dropping out. After sorting through the crowd, he finds that Joe is really Jo. She's very much a woman—a beautiful one—and her mission in life is to take care of all the town's artistic types. She confirms that the ship was carrying a cargo of coffee and a chest of gold coins when it went down.

Time passes. Discharged from the navy, Ted cons Judd into helping him go for the gold. But as they prepare to cast off, Captain Jack gets seasick and is replaced by Jo. She makes it clear that he's just money hungry like the rest of the world, but she agrees to help if the money goes toward an art center for all her friends. They head out to sea.

Meanwhile, Dina Bishop's yacht shows up at the dive site. Dina and her friend Gil Carey were there when Ted made the original dives to the ship, and they have the pictures to prove it. Gil takes a closer look at the photos he shot and spots the treasure chest. Determined to get to it first, he fakes a dead battery cable and insists that Ted tow them to shore.

Gil then proceeds to turn Captain Jack against Ted. Indignantly, Jack goes to Ted's boat to reclaim his diving equipment. After protesting in vain, Ted gives it to him, but then tracks down Jo in hopes that she can persuade Captain Jack that he's OK and should get his gear back.

Captain Jack is kidnapped by Dina and Gil and learns that his diving equipment has been stolen by them. They head for the treasure site, and by the time Ted gets there, they've already gone diving. Ted heads them off underwater and retrieves the chest—only to learn that the coins are copper. Value: $4,000. He and Jo decide that would make a perfect down payment on her art center, since it was her grandfather's ship in the first place.

CAST:

Ted Jackson	Elvis Presley
Jo Symington	Dodie Marshall
Dina Bishop	Pat Priest
Judd Whitman	Pat Harrington, Jr.
Gil Carey	Skip Ward
Madame Neherina	Elsa Lanchester
Captain Jack	Frank McHugh

SONGS:

Easy Come, Easy Go, The Love Machine, Yoga Is As Yoga Does, You Gotta Stop, Sing, You Children, I'll Take Love

DOUBLE TROUBLE

(1967)

Metro Goldwyn Mayer, a B.C.W. production
    Producers: Judd Bernard, Irwin Winkler
    Director: Norman Taurog
    Screenplay: Jo Heims
    Costumes: Don Feld
    Technical Advisor: Colonel Tom Parker
    Running Time: 90 minutes
    Opened: April 5, 1967
    Stats: #58 on *Variety*'s List of Top-Grossing Films
    Total Gross: $1.6 Million

SYNOPSIS:

Society entertainer Guy Lambert (Elvis) is having a ball playing the club scene in Europe. Working in London, he's causing quite a stir on stage and off. When he isn't working hard, he's playing hard, choosing between two very beautiful but very different women, worldly and sophisticated Claire and sheltered but eager Jill. Claire is a woman who can clearly take care of herself. Jill, however, is another story, and her guardian, Uncle Gerald, decides to keep her out of Guy's way by sending her away to school in Belgium. What he doesn't know is that Guy's band has a gig in Brussels and is heading there as well.

While crossing the Channel, Jill moves from deck to deck looking for Guy, whom she's met on the ship. To her delight, she finds him, but she also meets some bizarre passengers—an evil-looking guy named Morley, a couple of creeps named Arthur Babcock and Archie Brown, and someone who calls himself "The Iceman" and seems to do nothing but sneak around. When a steamer trunk falls and barely misses Jill, and Guy almost drowns, they get the message that someone is after them. They stay alert and hope things will ease up in Brussels.

It doesn't work out that way, and danger dogs their every step. From the moment they get off the boat, they're hounded, harassed and followed. Babcock and Brown keep turning up, and seedy characters lurk everywhere. Guy is set up by Uncle Gerald and arrested for kidnapping Jill. Worried that she'll be in trouble with him off in jail, Guy gets a message to a buddy and asks for his help. The friend tries his best, but he's not a bodyguard and Jill nearly dies from asphyxiation. Guy has no choice but to break out of jail and hope he's in time to save her. He is, grabbing Jill and hopping on a boat back to England. As usual nothing is easy, and we last see them floating on a raft in the English Channel, safe and sound—with a bag of expensive jewels, which must have been what all the fuss was about.

CAST:

Guy Lambert	Elvis Presley
Jill Conway	Annette Day
Gerald Waverly	John Williams
Claire Dunham	Yvonne Romain
Archie Brown	Chips Rafferty
Arthur Babcock	Norman Rossington
Mr. Morley	Michael Murphy
Iceman	John Alderson

SONGS:

Double Trouble, Baby, If You'll Give Me All Your Love, Could I Fall In Love, Long Legged Girl (With The Short Dress On), City By Night, Old MacDonald, I Love Only One Girl, There Is So Much World To See

CLAMBAKE
(1967)

United Artists
Producers: Arnold Laven, Arthur Gardner, Jules Levy
Director: Arthur H. Nadel
Screenplay: Arthur Browne Jr.
Technical Advisor: Colonel Tom Parker
Running Time: 97 minutes
Opened: November 22, 1967

SYNOPSIS:

Rich and bored, Scott Hayward (Elvis) heads off to see the world, and also to see if he can do something that doesn't require the family fortune. Heading south, he lands in Miami Beach where, on a lark, he trades places with Tom Wilson, a water-ski instructor at a local hotel. It's a total role reversal, with the humble Wilson moving into the fancy suite reserved for Scott while Scott bunks down in the employees' housing.

Quickly he starts to see life from the other side. His very first water skier is a woman by the name of Dianne Carter, who is in Miami Beach for one reason only: Hunting season is open and she wants to bag a rich husband. She's already decided on super-rich James Jamison, who's in town for the season and the races. Despite her gold-digger facade, however, Dianne is really a nice person and Scott is drawn to her. Unwilling to fall back on his personal fortune to impress Dianne, he decides to win her the hard way.

He meets a fellow named Sam Burton, who has designed a power boat with blazing speed—a sure winner if he can stop it from tearing itself apart at high revs—and they go into business together. The protective coating on the boat doesn't seem to withstand high speeds, but Scott remembers a hardening agent he once developed in his father's R & D facility when he was fooling around. He couldn't figure out what to do with it then, but maybe it would work.

When he contacts the lab and asks for the chemical, the family finds out where he is and his father, Duster Hayward, flies to Florida and discovers that his son has some gumption after all. The formula arrives late and the race is scheduled to start before the required hardening time; there's no time to test it under racing conditions. Scott enters the race anyway. It's a huge risk, but after a real nail-cruncher, he wins the race, the respect of his family and the love of a good woman.

CAST:

Scott Hayward	Elvis Presley
Dianne Carter	Shelley Fabares
Tom Wilson	Will Hutchins
James J. Jamison	Bill Bixby
Duster Hayward	James Gregory
Sam Burton	Gary Merrill
Ice Cream Vendor	Red West

SONGS:

Clambake, Who Needs Money, A Mouse That Has Everything, Confidence, You Don't Know Me, Hey, Hey, Hey, The Girl I Never Loved, How Can You Lose What You Never Had

STAY AWAY, JOE
(1968)

Metro Goldwyn Mayer
   Producer: Douglas Laurence
   Director: Peter Tewksbury
   Screenplay: Michael A. Hoey
   Running Time: 102 minutes
   Opened Nationally: March 8, 1968
   Stats: #68 *Variety*'s list of top grossing films

SYNOPSIS:

Joe Lightcloud (Elvis), a hard-drinking, hard-playing but not especially hard-working young man, cons a local politico into giving him twenty cows and a bull so he can become a cattle baron thanks to a new Indian management project for the U.S. government. Joe gets the livestock but instead of learning to become a rancher, spends most of his time riding the bull and his motorbike, starting fights he doesn't finish and generally trying to get ahead without putting out any effort.

Nothing Joe does seems to work out, and disaster follows him everywhere. He finally gets in over his head when he throws a little spur-of-the-moment party for some boozing buddies. It ends with his only bull being used for target practice and later for ribs. Without the bull, Joe's career as a cattle baron is in jeopardy, and he begins selling the cows that the government gave him in an attempt to raise money to buy another bull. When a congressman finds out, the family is threatened with prison for selling government property.

But Joe finally does something right by winning a bull-riding contest. Using his winnings to buy a new bull, he gets the government off his back—but folks are still probably going to be saying, "Stay away, Joe!"

CAST:

Joe Lightcloud..Elvis Presley
Charlie Lightcloud...Burgess Meredith
Glenda Callahan...Joan Blondell
Annie Lightcloud...Katy Jurado
Grandpa (Chief Lightcloud)..Thomas Gomez
Hy Slager ....Henry Jones
Bronc Hoverty..L.Q. Jones

SONGS:

Stay Away, Stay Away, Joe, Lovely Mamie, Dominick, All I Needed Was the Rain

SPEEDWAY

(1968)

Metro Goldwyn Mayer
  Producer: Douglas Laurence
  Director: Norman Taurog
  Screenplay: Phillip Shuken
  Running Time: 94 minutes
  Premiered: June 12, 1968, Charlotte, North Carolina
  Stats: #40 in *Variety*'s list of top-grossing films
  Total gross: $3 Million

SYNOPSIS:

Life is one good time after another for Steve Grayson (Elvis) and his partner Kenny Donford. They travel with their racecar from track to track like modern Robin Hoods winning races, doing good for people and having fun. Until one day the Internal Revenue Service sends Steve a bill for $100,000. Thanks to their good Samaritan tendencies—and Kenny's inability to read a 1040 form—Steve is in a lot of trouble. So he hires a business management firm to help, and Susan Jacks is assigned to travel along with them, keep track of the winnings and make sure the government gets its piece. Steve and Susan are oil and water, but they negotiate a truce and things go pretty smoothly until Kenny gambles away their stash at the track. A lot of people were counting on that money, and Steve feels he's got to do something for his buddy and pay the IRS as well. But $100 per week for living expenses isn't nearly enough, and he asks Susan for more, but she has no choice except to refuse.

Steve decides to sell his car to come up with the cash. When word gets out, people rush to make an offer, and just as his chief competition is about to snap it up—guaranteeing that Steve would be out of the racing game for good—Susan bursts in with the news that the government has granted a temporary reprieve so he can race. Steve gets into the "Charlotte 600," wins it, pays his debts—and decides that Susan isn't so bad after all.

CAST:

Steve Grayson...Elvis Presley
Susan Jacks ....Nancy Sinatra
Kenny Donford ....Bill Bixby
R.W. Hepworth ....Gale Gordon
Stock-Car Racers..................................Richard Petty, Buddy Baker, Cale Yarborough,
          Dick Hutcherson, Tiny Lund, G.C. Spencer, Roy Mayne

SONGS:

Speedway, Let Yourself Go, Your Time Hasn't Come Yet, Baby, He's Your Uncle, Not Your Dad, Who Are You? (Who Am I?), There Ain't Nothing Like a Song

LIVE A LITTLE, LOVE A LITTLE

(1968)

Metro Goldwyn Mayer
   Producer: Douglas Laurence
   Director: Norman Taurog
   Screenplay: Michael A. Hoey, Dan Greenburg
   Running Time: 90 minutes
   Opened: October 23, 1968

SYNOPSIS:

Greg Nolan (Elvis) is a photographer who's got a great job shooting for an LA paper. All he wants is to do his work and be left alone to sing and sit on the beach, but Bernice and her Great Dane, Albert, have something else in mind. She lets the dog chase Greg into the water and keeps him there until the sun sets in the Pacific. By the time he crawls ashore, Greg is too weak to say no when Bernice takes him home, medicates him and tucks him into bed. Recovering several days later, he finds that he's been canned from his job.

Greg then discovers that Bernice moved him out of his apartment while he was recovering at her house, and he's living with her now. He's convinced that he's losing his mind, if it isn't gone already. Bernice is very strange and life around her house is even stranger: People like her ex-boyfriend Harry show up and hang around for no reason at all. And Bernice keeps changing her name. Greg finds it difficult enough to understand her without having to remember who she is today. His only way out is to get a job.

Greg lands work as a commercial photographer for two opposing firms located in the same building. One of his bosses, Mike Lansdown, is cool and very down to earth while the other, Penlow, is conservative and uptight. One thing they have in common is that they expect Greg to act like they do, and he has to adjust his behavior and even his clothing to humor them. It not easy, but it's a living.

To celebrate his new jobs, Bernice finds Greg a new house, then comes over with Harry to have dinner with him. But Harry and Greg hate each other, so the dinner is a tense mess and ends in a hurry. Bernice leaves with Harry. But a few days later, she returns to tell Greg she's decided to leave Harry and the beach house for good. So she has nowhere to go and wants to move in with Greg. At this point, Bernice is almost as confused as Greg and ends up running away. Realizing that this wacky woman and her wacky life are actually a lot of fun, Greg follows Bernice—and finds her down at the beach where it all began.

CAST:

Greg Nolan	Elvis Presley
Bernice	Michele Carey
Mike Lansdown	Don Porter
Louis Penlow	Rudy Vallee
Harry	Dick Sargent
Milkman	Sterling Holloway
Newspaper Worker	Red West

SONGS

Wonderful World, Edge Of Reality, A Little Less Conversation, Almost In Love

CHARRO!
(1968)

National General Pictures
    Executive Producer: Harry Caplan
    Producer: Charles Marquis Warren
    Director: Charles Marquis Warren
    Screenplay: Charles Marquis Warren
    Running Time: 98 minutes
    Opened: March 13, 1968
    Stats: Only film in which Elvis wore a beard

SYNOPSIS:

Mexico 1870. Going to visit a friend, Jess Wade (Elvis Presley) rides into a border town and finds himself taken prisoner by Vince, the leader of his former gang, and by his crazy brother, Billy Roy. Jess is taken to their mountain hideout, where they've hidden the weapon that fired the last shot against Maximilian and freed Mexico from Spain. The outlaws intend to sell it to the highest bidder, but Jess tells them that soldiers on both sides of the border will hunt them down. Vince produces a fake "Wanted" poster naming Jess as the man responsible for stealing the cannon and offering a reward for him "dead or alive."

Jess manages to escape to the village of Rio Seco on the U.S. side of the border, where Sheriff Ramsey, a good friend, believes him to be innocent. Then Billy Roy arrives in Rio Seco to raise hell and seriously wounds the sheriff in a gunfight. After Jess throws him in jail, he's deputized by Ramsey, and his first official act—knowing Vince will try to free his brother—is to arm the townspeople. When Vince demands that Jess free Billy Roy, Jess demands that Vince turn the cannon over to him so that it can be returned to Mexico. But Vince gives Jess until sundown to free Billy Roy or he'll destroy Rio Seco with the cannon.

Jess refuses to release him, and a shot topples the church bell; another kills the sheriff and destroys his house. The townspeople urge Jess to free Billy Roy, and Jess rides out of town with him. They approach Vince's gang and Jess demands that they surrender. If they shoot, he tells them, he'll kill Billy Roy. Several members of the gang are shot in the ensuing gunplay, and Billy Roy dies when the wagon with the cannon breaks loose and crushes him.

Vince is a beaten man. Jess takes him prisoner and drives the wagon back into town. The townspeople ask him to stay on as sheriff, but Jess heads off into the sunset with his prisoner and the cannon in tow.

CAST:

    Jess Wade ....Elvis Presley
    Tracy Winters ....Ina Balin
    Vince Hackett ....Victor French
    Marcie ....Lynn Kellogg
    Sara Ramsey ....Barbara Werle
    Billy Roy Hackett ....Solomon Sturges
    Opie Keetch ....Paul Brinegar
    Gunner ....James Sikking

SONG:

Charro

THE TROUBLE WITH GIRLS

(1969)

Metro Goldwyn Mayer
   Producer: Lester Welch
   Director: Peter Tewksbury
   Screenplay: Arnold Peyser, Lois Peyser
   Running Time: 97 minutes
   Opened: September 3, 1969

SYNOPSIS:

The Chautauqua Tent Show rumbles into Radford Center for a long-anticipated engagement. The excitement and enthusiasm of the public is shared by the new manager of the traveling show, Walter Hale (Elvis), who grew up in the business, first as a singer and then as a manager. He loves his work, but faces problems within the company, especially with Charlene, a beautiful woman and a good performer, but who is committed to unionizing the show. Though they battle about social issues, it's clear that they like each other.

All the high spirits disappear when a local druggist is found floating in the town lake. A member of the Chautauqua troupe, Clarence, is arrested for the murder. It remains for Walter to determine the identity of the real killer, but when he decides to put his detective work on stage to solve the crime—and earn some money doing it—Charlene is furious.

Walter puts on a slam-bang show that leads to the unmasking of the murderer, and by the time the final curtain falls, everything but his relationship with Charlene has been resolved. Hope, however, springs eternal.

CAST:

Walter Hale	Elvis Presley
Charlene	Marilyn Mason
Betty	Nicole Jaffe
Nita Bix	Sheree North
Johnny	Edward Andrews
Mr. Drewcolt	John Carradine
Mr. Jonson	Vincent Price
Carol Bix	Anissa Jones
Maude	Joyce Van Patten
Harrison Wilby	Dabney Coleman

SONGS:

Swing Down, Sweet Chariot, The Whiffenpoof Song, Violet (Flower of NYU), Clean Up Your Own Backyard, Sign of the Zodiac, Almost

CHANGE OF HABIT

(1969)

Universal Pictures and NBC
    Producer: Joe Connelly
    Director: William Graham
    Screenplay: James Lee, S.S. Schweitzer, Eric Bercovici
    Makeup: Bud Westmore
    Running Time: 93 minutes
    Opened: November 10, 1969
    Stats: #17 *Variety*'s list of top-grossing films

SYNOPSIS:

Dr. John Carpenter (Elvis), a physician working in an urban ghetto, comes into contact with three nuns, Sister Michelle, Sister Irene and Sister Barbara, who have moved into the neighborhood to gain experience in the real world before taking their final vows. They move into the roughest part of town and keep their true identities secret. They do, however, report to the old-fashioned priest, Father Gibbons, who is upset by their unconventional dress, informal manners and uninhibited fun.

Dr. Carpenter finds himself attracted to Sister Michelle and, unaware of her commitment to the church, is confused by her seeming lack of interest in him. Through the course of the story, we follow the three sisters as they learn to cope with the outside world.

After a time, they are ordered by the Mother Superior to return to the convent. Sisters Michelle and Irene choose to return, but Sister Barbara doesn't. Dr. Carpenter confronts Michelle and asks her why she won't return his love. She tells him the truth, and the Doctor is left to deal with his pain.

CAST:

Dr. John Carpenter .... Elvis Presley
Sister Michelle Gallagher .... Mary Tyler Moore
Sister Irene Hawkins .... Barbara McNair
Sister Barbara Bennett .... Jane Elliot
Mother Joseph .... Leora Dana
Lieutenant Moretti .... Edward Asner
The Banker .... Robert Emhardt
Father Gibbons .... Regis Toomey
Bishop Finley .... Richard Carlson
Young Man .... A. Martinez

SONGS:

Change of Habit, Rubberneckin', Have a Happy, Let Us Pray

ELVIS:THAT'S THE WAY IT IS
(1970)

Metro Goldwyn Mayer
>   Producer: Herbert F. Soklow
>   Director: Denis Sanders
>   Director of Photography: Lucien Ballard
>   Elvis' Wardrobe Designer: Bill Belew
>   Technical Advisor: Colonel Tom Parker
>   Technical Assistants: Richard Davis, Tom Diskin, Joe Esposito, Lamar Fike, Felton Jarvis, Jim O'Brien, Al Pachuki, Bill Porter, Sonny West
>   Coordinator for RCA Records: George L. Parkhill
>   Running Time: 97 minutes
>   Opened: November 11, 1970
>   Stats: #22 on *Variety*'s weekly list of top-grossing films

SYNOPSIS:

Says Academy Award-winning director Denis Sanders: "The subject of this film is Elvis, and the core is Elvis on stage in Las Vegas performing his incredible, record-breaking act. However, we went much further with the cameras. We attempted to capture the ups and downs he experiences putting his show together, showing the man as a musician. We filmed both sides of the lights, exploring what he feels and the emotions he creates in others." Using documentary techniques, the film follows the King on a public and private journey from rehearsals at MGM studios and in Las Vegas, then onstage in the Showroom Internationale of the International Hilton Hotel, and finally on September 9, 1970, in Phoenix, Arizona, for the opening of the star's first concert tour in thirteen years.

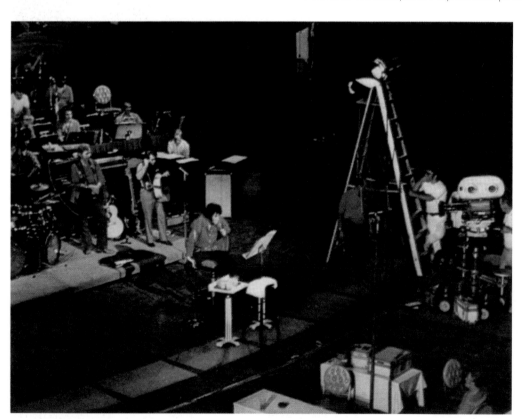

CAST:

Musicians with Elvis..............James Burton, Glen Hardin, Charlie Hodge, Jerry Scheff, Ronnie Tutt, John Wilkinson, Millie Kirkham
Conductor....................................Joe Guercio
Background Vocalists.................The Sweet Inspirations, The Imperials

SONGS:

(Opening Credits): **Mystery Train/Tiger Man**, (Rehearsal at MGM): **Words, The Next Step Is Love, Polk Salad Annie, Crying Time, That's All Right (Mama), Little Sister, What'd I Say, Stranger In The Crowd, How The Web Was Woven** (Elvis on piano), **I Just Can't Help Believin', You Don't Have To Say You Love Me** (Rehearsal with Vocal Groups): **You Don't Have To Say You Love Me, Bridge Over Troubled Water, Words,** (Rehearsal at the Hilton) **You've Lost That Lovin' Feelin', Mary In The Morning, Polk Salad Annie** (Performed at the Hilton:) **That's All Right (Mama), I've Lost You, Patch It Up, Love Me Tender, You've Lost That Lovin' Feelin', Sweet Caroline, I Just Can't Help Believin', Little Sister/Get Back, Bridge Over Troubled Water, Heartbreak Hotel, One Night, Blue Suede Shoes, All Shook Up, Polk Salad Annie, Suspicious Minds, Can't Help Falling In Love**

ELVIS ON TOUR

(1972)

Metro Goldwyn Mayer, a Cinema Associates production
    Producers: Pierre Adidge, Robert Abel
    Directors: Pierre Adidge, Robert Abel
    Director of Photography: Robert Thomas
    Elvis' Wardrobe Designer: Bill Belew
    Technical Advisor: Colonel Tom Parker
    Montage Supervisor: Martin Scorsese
    Assistants to Elvis: Vernon Presley, Joe Esposito, Jerry Schilling, Sonny West, Red
       West, James Caughley, Lamar Fike, Martin Gambill
    Running Time: 93 minutes
    Opened: November 1, 1972
    Stats: #13 on *Variety*'s List of top-grossing films

SYNOPSIS:

The film opens with a voiceover: "My daddy had seen a lot of people who played guitars and stuff and didn't work, so he said, 'You should make up your mind either about being an electrician or playing a guitar. I never saw a guitar player that was worth a damn.' "

The producers' candid interviews with Elvis are used as the narrative thread throughout this documentary, with Elvis' voice heard over footage of his concerts and family stills. Also included is footage from his early career, such as his debut on *The Ed Sullivan Show*. He discusses his reaction to the impact of his first public appearance and, much earlier, the first time he remembers singing. Almost 100 million single records and approximately 26 million-selling albums later, *Elvis on Tour* is an up-close and personal look at an American musical legend.

CAST:

    Musicians with Elvis ....James Burton, Charlie Hodge,
                            Ronnie Tutt, Glen Hardin,
                            Jerry Scheff, John Wilkinson
    Orchestra Conducted by ....Joe Guercio
    Background Vocalists.....................................Cathy Westmoreland,
                            The Sweet Inspirations,
                          J.D. Sumner and The Stamps Quartet
    Onstage Comedian ....Jackie Kahane

SONGS:

Johnny B. Goode (sung over opening credits), See See Rider, Polk Salad Annie, Separate Ways, Proud Mary, Never Been To Spain, Burning Love, Don't Be Cruel (clip from *The Ed Sullivan Show*), Ready Teddy (clip from *The Ed Sullivan Show*), That's All Right (Mama), Lead Me, Guide Me, Bosom Of Abraham, Love Me Tender, Until It's Time For You To Go, Suspicious Minds, I, John, Bridge Over Troubled Waters, Funny How Time Slips Away, An American Trilogy, Mystery Train, I Got A Woman/Amen, A Big Hunk O' Love, You Gave Me A Mountain, Lawdy Miss Clawdy, Can't Help Falling In Love, Memories (sung over closing credits)

HIS
MUSIC

"It's hard to explain Rock & Roll music.
If you feel it, you can't help but move to it.
That's what happens to me, I can't help it."

—ELVIS

THE
COMPLETE
DISCOGRAPHY

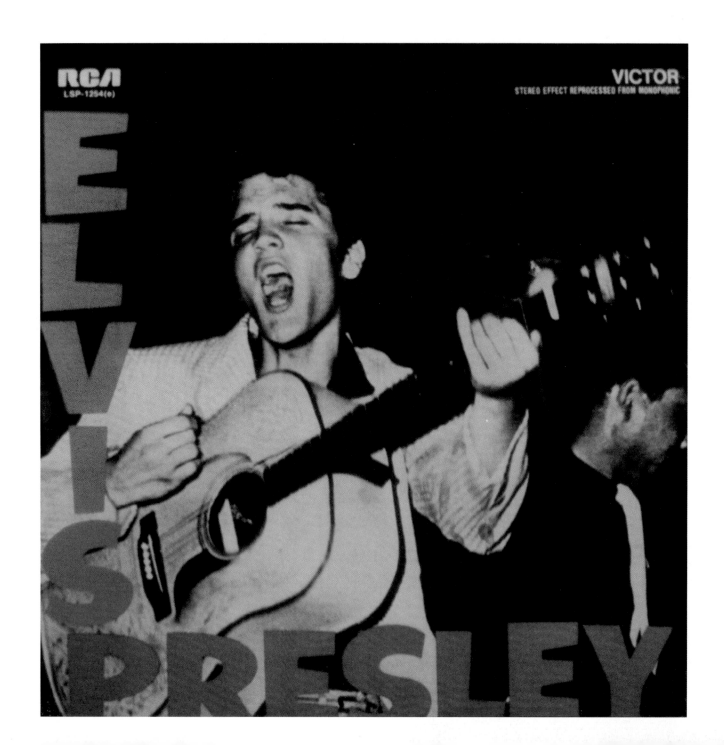

A TUNE-BY-TUNE ANTHOLOGY

This anthology contains only records released commercially—no bootlegs or unauthorized material. After his contract was sold by Sun to RCA, Elvis remained with "His Master's Voice" throughout the remainder of his career. Unless otherwise noted, all the following recordings were made under the RCA label.

● ●

A BIG HUNK O' LOVE
Written By: Aaron Schroeder, Sid Wyche
Recorded: June 1958
Released: July 1959
Flip Side: My Wish Came True
On The Charts: *Billboard*'s Hot 100 (14 weeks–peaked at #1)
Sales: One million plus
Singles: A BIG HUNK O' LOVE/My Wish Came True, July 1959, Standard release, February 1962, Gold Standard Series reissue, December 1986, Collectibles
LPs: Aloha from Hawaii via Satellite, The Alternate Aloha, Elvis, Elvis in Nashville, Elvis: Worldwide 50 Gold Award Hits–Vol. 1, 50,000,000 Elvis Fans Can't Be Wrong—Elvis' Gold Records–Vol. 2, Greatest Hits–Vol. 1, The Number One Hits, The Top Ten Hits

A FOOL SUCH AS I
Written By: Bill Trader
Previous Versions: Hank Snow (1952), Jo Stafford (1953)
Recorded: June 1958
Flip Side: I Need Your Love Tonight
On The Charts: 15 weeks, beginning March 23, 1959
Sales: Went Gold with one million shipped one day after release
LPs: Elvis: A Legendary Performer, Elvis Aron Presley, Elvis: Worldwide 50 Gold Award Hits–Vol. 1, 50,000,000 Elvis Fans Can't Be Wrong, Elvis' Gold Records–Vol. 2, The Top 10 Hits

A LITTLE LESS CONVERSATION
Written By: Billy Strange, Mac Davis
Recorded: March 1968–RCA Nashville
Released: September 15, 1968
Flip Side: Almost in Love
On The Charts: *Billboard*'s Hot 100 (4 weeks–peaked at #69)
LP: Almost in Love

ADAM AND EVIL
Written By: Fred Wise, Randy Starr
Elvis Recorded: February 1966–Radio Recorders
Recorded For Film: *SPINOUT* (1966)
LP: Spinout

AFTER LOVING YOU
Written By: Eddie Miller, Johnny Lantz
Previously Recorded By: Joe Henderson (1962)
Recorded: February 18, 1969–American Sound Studios
LPs: From Elvis in Memphis, Guitar Man, The Memphis Record

AIN'T THAT LOVING YOU BABY
Written By: Clyde Otis, Joe Hunter
Previously Recorded By: Eddie Riff
Elvis Recorded: June 1958
Flip Side: Ask Me
On The Charts: *Billboard*'s Hot 100 (10 weeks–peaked at #16)
Sales: One million plus
Singles: Ain't That Loving You Baby/Ask Me July 1958, Standard Release
LPs: Elvis' Gold Records–Vol. 4, Elvis: Worldwide 50 Gold Award Hits–Vol. 1, Reconsider Baby

ALL I NEEDED WAS THE RAIN
Written By: Sid Wayne, Ben Weisman
Recorded: October 1967–RCA Nashville
Recorded For Film: *STAY AWAY, JOE* (1968)
LPs: Elvis Sings Flaming Star, Singer Presents Elvis Singing Flaming Star and Others

ALL MY TRIALS (See **An American Trilogy**)

ALL SHOOK UP
Written By: Otis Blackwell
Previously Recorded By: David Hill, Vicki Young
Recorded: January 1957

Flip Side: Teddy Bear
On The Charts: *Billboard*'s Top 100 (30 weeks—longest–running Presley single), Top ranking: #1 *Billboard* (8 weeks), *Country Juke Box* (1 week), *Rhythm and Blues* chart (4 weeks), British charts (7 weeks), #3 Country Best Seller
Sales: Over 2 million copies
Hit The Charts: 30 weeks beginning April 6, 1957, Top ranking: #1–8 weeks,
Sales: Went Gold with more than 2 million
Singles: All Shook Up/That's When Your Heartaches Begin March 1957, 78 RPM Standard, March 1957, 45 RPM Standard, March 1959, Gold Standard Series reissue, October 1977, Boxed set: 15 Golden Records, 30 Golden Hits, All Shook Up/Teddy Bear, October 1984, Elvis' Greatest Hits: Golden Singles, Volume 1
EPs: A Touch of Gold–Vol. 3, Tupperware's Hit Parade
LPs: Elvis, Elvis Aron Presley, Elvis as Recorded at Madison Square Garden, Elvis' Golden Records, Elvis in Person, Elvis—TV Special, Elvis: Worldwide 50 Gold Award Hits–Vol. 1, From Memphis to Vegas/From Vegas to Memphis, The Number One Hits, Pure Gold, Top Ten Hits, Essential Elvis

ALL THAT I AM
Written By: Sid Tepper, Roy C. Bennett
Recorded: February 1966–Radio Recorders
Recorded For Film: *SPINOUT* (1966)
Flip Side: Spinout
On The Charts: *Billboard*'s Hot 100 (8 weeks–peaked at #41), Easy-Listening (peaked at #9)
Sales: One million plus
Singles: Spinout/All That I Am September 1966 Standard Release, February 1968 Gold Standard Series reissue
LP: Spinout

ALMOST
Written By: Buddy Kaye, Ben Weisman

Recorded: October 1968–United Recorders
Recorded For Film: *THE TROUBLE WITH GIRLS*
LP: **Let's Be Friends**

ALMOST ALWAYS TRUE
Written By: Fred Wise, Ben Weisman
Recorded: March 22, 1961–Radio Recorders
Recorded For Film: *BLUE HAWAII* (1961)
LP: **Blue Hawaii**

ALMOST IN LOVE
Written By: Rick Bonfa, Randy Starr
Recorded: March 1968–Western Recorders,
Hollywood
Recorded For Film: *LIVE A LITTLE, LOVE A LITTLE*
(1968)
Flip Side: **A Little Less Conversation**
On The Charts: *Billboard's* Hot 100
(2 weeks–peaked at #95)
Singles: **A Little Less Conversation/Almost in
Love** September 1968, Standard release,
December 1970 Gold Standard Series reissue
LP: **Almost in Love**

ALOHA OE (Farewell to Thee)
Written By: Queen Liliuokalani of Hawaii (1878)
Recorded: March 1961–Radio Recorders
Previously Recorded By: Bing Crosby
Recorded For Film: *BLUE HAWAII* (1961)
LP: **Blue Hawaii**

ALWAYS ON MY MIND
Written By: Mark James, Wayne Carson, Johnny Christopher
Recorded: March 1972–RCA Hollywood
Flip Side: **Separate Ways**
On The Charts: Country (13 weeks–peaked at #16)
Singles: **Separate Ways/Always on My Mind**, November 1972 Standard release, February 1976 Gold Standard Series reissue, **The Elvis Medley/Always on My Mind** November 1982, new release, December 1986, Collectibles, **Always on My Mind/My Boy** July 1985, new release, **Always on My Mind** July 1985 Special DJ promo
LPs: **Always on My Mind, The Elvis Medley, Separate Ways, This Is Elvis**

AM I READY
Written By: Sid Tepper, Roy C. Bennett
Recorded: February 1966–Radio Recorders
Film Recorded For: *SPINOUT* (1966)
LPs: **Burning Love and Hits from His Movies–Volume 2, Spinout**

AMAZING GRACE
Written By: Reverend John Newton (1779)
Recorded: March 1971–RCA Nashville
Previously Recorded By: Singin' Billy Walker, Judy Collins, et al.
LP: **He Touched Me**

AMEN
Written By: Anonymous
Recorded: Live in concert (1970–1972)
Previously Recorded By: Pate and Mayfield (The Impressions, 1964), Otis Redding (1968)
LPs: **Elvis Aron Presley, Elvis in Concert, Elvis Recorded Live on Stage in Memphis**

AMERICA (See America the Beautiful)

AMERICA THE BEAUTIFUL
Written By: Katharine Lee Bates (1933) Poem, Samuel Augustus Ward (1888) Music
Recorded: Live in Concert (December 1975–Las Vegas)
Previously Recorded By: Frank Sinatra (1945), Ray Charles, et al.
Singles: **My Way/America the Beautiful**, November 1977, Standard Release, **My Way/America** (Incorrect label), November 1977, DJ promo
LP: **Elvis Aron Presley**

AN AMERICAN TRILOGY
Written By: **Dixie** (Dan Emmett, 1859); **Battle Hymn of the Republic** (Julia Ward Howe, 1861); **All My Trials** (Unknown), Medley arranged by: Mickey Newbury (1971)
Recorded: Live in concert (February 1972–Las Vegas)
Flip Side: **It's Time For You To Go**
On The Charts: *Billboard's* Hot 100 (6 weeks–peaked at #66), Easy–Listening (peaked at #31)
Singles: **An American Trilogy/The First Time Ever I Saw Your Face**, April 1972, Standard release, **An American Trilogy/Until It's Time for You to Go**, May 1973, Gold Standard Series, **The Impossible Dream/An American Trilogy**, August 1982, Promotional giveaway, Tupelo, Mississippi, **An American Trilogy/Poor Boy**, December 1986, Collectibles
LPs: **Aloha from Hawaii via Satellite, Elvis Aron Presley, Elvis as Recorded at Madison Square Garden, Elvis Recorded Live on Stage in Memphis, This Is Elvis**

AN EVENING PRAYER
Written By: C. M. Battersby, Charles H. Gabriel
Recorded: May 1971–RCA Nashville
LPs: **He Touched Me, He Walks Beside Me**

AND I LOVE YOU SO
Written By: Don McLean (1970)
Recorded: March 11, 1975–RCA Hollywood
Previously Recorded By: Don McLean (1970), Bobby Goldsboro, Perry Como (1971)
LPs: **Elvis Aron Presley—Forever, Elvis in Concert, Elvis Today**

AND THE GRASS WON'T PAY NO MIND
Written By: Neil Diamond (1969)
Recorded: February 1969–American Sound Studios
LPs: **Back in Memphis, From Memphis to Vegas/From Vegas to Memphis**

ANGEL
Written By: Sid Tepper, Roy C. Bennett
Recorded: July 5, 1961–RCA Nashville
Recorded For Film: *FOLLOW THAT DREAM* (1962)
EP: **Follow That Dream**
LPs: **C'mon Everybody, Elvis Sings for Children and Grownups Too!**

ANIMAL INSTINCT
Written By: Bill Giant, Bernie Baum, Florence Kaye
Recorded: February 1965–RCA Nashville
Recorded For Film: *HARUM SCARUM* (1965)
LP: **Harum Scarum**

ANY DAY NOW
Written By: Bob Hilliard, Burt Bacharach
Recorded: February 21, 1969–American Sound Studios
Previously Recorded By: Chuck Jackson (1962), Percy Sledge (1969), Ronnie Milsap (1982)
Singles: **In the Ghetto/Any Day Now**, April 1969, Standard release, December 1970, Gold Standard Series reissue, **In the Ghetto/Any Day Now**, October 1977, 15 Golden Records–30 Golden Hits
LPs: **Elvis: The Other Sides—Worldwide Gold Award Hits–Vol. 2, From Elvis in Memphis, The Memphis Record**

ANY WAY YOU WANT ME (That's How I Will Be)
Written By: Aaron Schroeder, Cliff Owens
Recorded: July 1956–RCA New York City
Flip Side: **Love Me Tender**
On The Charts: *Billboard's* Top 100 (10 weeks at #27)
Sales: One million plus
Singles: **Love Me Tender/Any Way You Want Me**, October 1956, Standard 78 RPM release, October 1956, Standard 45 RPM release, March 1959, Gold Standard Series reissue, October 1977, 15 Golden Records–30 Golden Hits
EP: **Any Way You Want Me**
LPs: **Elvis' Golden Records, Elvis: Worldwide 50 Gold Award Hits–Vol.1**

ANYONE (Could Fall In Love With You)
Written By: Bennie Benjamin, Sol Marcus, Louis A. DeJesu
Recorded: October 3, 1963–Radio Recorders
Recorded For Film: *KISSIN' COUSINS* (1963)
LP: **Kissin' Cousins**

ANYPLACE IS PARADISE
Written By: Joe Thomas
Recorded: September 1956–Radio Recorders
EP: Elvis–Volume 2
LP: Elvis

ANYTHING THAT'S PART OF YOU
Written By: Don Robertson (1961)
Recorded: October 15, 1961–RCA Nashville
Flip Side: Good Luck Charm
On The Charts: *Billboard*'s Hot 100 (8 weeks–peaked at #31), Easy-Listening (peaked at #6)
Sales: One million plus
Singles: Good Luck Charm/Anthing That's Part of You, March 1962, Standard release, March 1962, Compact 33 Single release, November 1962, Gold Standard Series reissue
LPs: Elvis' Golden Records–Volume 3, Elvis in Nashville, Elvis: Worldwide 50 Gold Award Hits–Vol. I

ARE YOU LONESOME TONIGHT?
Written By: Roy Turk, Lou Handman (1926)
Recorded: April 1960–RCA Nashville
Previously Recorded By: Al Jolson (1927), Jaye P. Morgan (1959)
Flip Side: I Gotta Know
On The Charts: *Billboard*'s Hot 100 (16 weeks–peaked at #1), Country (peaked at #22), Rhythm & Blues (peaked at #3)
Singles: Are You Lonesome Tonight?/I Gotta Know, November 1960, Standard release, November 1960, Living Stereo release, February 1962, Gold Standard Series reissue, October 1977, 15 Golden Records–30 Golden Hits, Are You Lonesome Tonight?/Can't Help Falling in Love, October 1984, Elvis' Greatest Hits—Golden Singles–Vol. 2
EP: Elvis by Request
LPs: Elvis—A Legendary Performer–Vol. II, Elvis—A Legendary Performer–Vol. 4, Elvis Aron Presley, Elvis' Golden Records–Vol. 3, Elvis in Concert, Elvis in Person, Elvis: Worldwide 50 Gold Award Hits–Vol. I, From Memphis to Vegas/From Vegas to Memphis, A Golden Celebration, The Number One Hits, This Is Elvis, The Top Ten Hits, A Valentine Gift for You

ARE YOU SINCERE
Written By: Wayne P. Walker (1957)
Recorded: September 1973–Palm Springs, California
Previously Recorded By: Andy Williams (1958)
Later Recorded By: Trini Lopez (1965)
Flip Side: Solitaire
On The Charts: Country (12 weeks–peaked at #10)
Singles: Are You Sincere/Solitaire, May 1979, Standard Release, May 1979, DJ promo Are You Sincere/Unchained Melody, May 1980, Gold Standard Series original
LPs: Our Memories of Elvis, Vol. 1, Raised on Rock/For Ol' Times Sake

AS LONG AS I HAVE YOU
Written By: Fred Wise, Ben Weisman
Recorded: January 16, 1958–Radio Recorders
Recorded For Film: *KING CREOLE* (1958)
EPs: King Creole–Vol. I
LPs: Elvis: The Other Sides—Worldwide Gold Award Hits–Vol. 2, King Creole

ASK ME
Written By: Bill Giant, Bernie Baum, Florence Kaye
Recorded: January 1964–RCA Nashville
Flip Side: Ain't That Loving You, Baby
On The Charts: *Billboard*'s Hot 100 (12 weeks–peaked at #12)
Singles: Ain't That Loving You, Baby/Ask Me, September 1964, Standard release, November 1965, Gold Standard Series reissue
LPs: Elvis' Gold Records–Vol. 4, Elvis: The Other Sides—Worldwide Gold Award Hits–Vol. 2

BABY, I DON'T CARE (You're So Square Baby, I Don't Care)
Written By: Jerry Leiber, Mike Stoller, Elvis
Recorded: May 1957
Recorded For Film: *JAILHOUSE ROCK* (1957)
EP: Jailhouse Rock
LPs: A Date with Elvis, Elvis: The Other Sides—Worldwide Gold Award Hits–Vol. 2, Essential Elvis—The First Movies

BABY, IF YOU'LL GIVE ME ALL OF YOUR LOVE
Written By: Joy Byers
Recorded: June 1966–Radio Recorders
Recorded For Film: *DOUBLE TROUBLE* (1967)
LPs: Double Trouble, Mahalo from Elvis

BABY, LET'S PLAY HOUSE
Written By: Arthur Gunter (1954)
Recorded: February 1955–Sun Studios
Previously Recorded By: Arthur Gunter (1954)
On The Charts: *Billboard*'s Country Best-Seller (peaked at #10), Country Disc Jockey (15 weeks–peaked at #5)
Singles: Baby, Let's Play House/I'm Left, You're Right, She's Gone April 1955, Sun 78 RPM & 45 RPM release, November 1955, Standard RCA 78 & 45 RPM reissues, March 1959, Gold Standard Series reissue, December 1986, Collectibles Baby, Let's Play House/Hound Dog, August 1984, recorded in September 1956 at the Mississippi/Alabama Fair and Dairy Show in Tupelo, Mississippi
LPs: The Complete Sun Sessions, A Date with Elvis, Elvis: The First Live Recordings, A Golden Celebration, I Was the One, The Sun Sessions

BABY WHAT YOU WANT ME TO DO
Written By: Jimmy Reed (1960)
Recorded (taped for TV special): June 1968
Previously Recorded By: Jimmy Reed (1960)
LPs: Elvis—A Legendary Performer–Vol. 2, Elvis Aron Presley, Elvis—TV Special, A Golden Celebration

BAREFOOT BALLAD
Written By: Dolores Fuller, Lee Morris
Recorded: October 1963–RCA Nashville
Recorded For Film: *KISSIN' COUSINS* (1964)
LP: Kissin' Cousins

THE BATTLE HYMN OF THE REPUBLIC (See **An American Trilogy**)

BEACH BOY BLUES
Written By: Sid Tepper, Roy C. Bennett
Recorded: March 23, 1961–Radio Recorders
Recorded For Film: *BLUE HAWAII* (1961)
LP: Blue Hawaii

BEACH SHACK
Written By: Bill Giant, Bernie Baum, Florence Kaye
Recorded: February 1966–Radio Recorders
Recorded For Film: *SPINOUT* (1966)
LP: Spinout

BECAUSE OF LOVE
Written By: Ruth Batchelor, Bob Robert, Elvis
Recorded: March 1962–Radio Recorders
Recorded For Film: *GIRLS! GIRLS! GIRLS!* (1962)
LP: Girls! Girls! Girls!

BEGINNER'S LUCK
Written By: Sid Tepper, Roy C. Bennett
Recorded: May 1965–RCA Nashville
Recorded For Film: *FRANKIE AND JOHNNIE* (1966)
LP: Frankie and Johnny

BEYOND THE BEND
Written By: Fred Wise, Ben Weisman, Dolores Fuller
Recorded: September 1962–Radio Recorders
Recorded For Film: *IT HAPPENED AT THE WORLD'S FAIR* (1962)
LP: It Happened at the World's Fair

BEYOND THE REEF
Written By: Jack Pittman
Recorded: May 27, 1966–RCA Nashville

Previously Recorded By: Jimmy Wakely and Margaret Whiting (1950), The Blue Barrons
LP: Elvis Aron Presley

BIG BOOTS
Written By: Sid Wayne, Sherman Edwards
Elvis Recorded: April 28, 1960–RCA Hollywood (1st Version; May 6, 1960–Radio Recorders (2nd Version)
Recorded For Film: G. I. BLUES (1960)
LPs: Elvis Sings for Children and Grownups Too! G. I. Blues

BIG BOSS MAN
Written By: Al Smith, Luther Dixon
Previously Recorded By: Jimmy Reed (1961), Gene Chandler (1964)
Elvis Recorded: September 10, 1967–RCA Nashville, June 20 or 21, 1968, Western Recorders Hollywood, (Elvis TV Special)
On The Charts : Hot 100–6 Weeks (peaked At #38)
Singles: BIG BOSS MAN/You Don't Know Me
September 1967. Standard release, BIG BOSS MAN/You Don't Know Me, 1970. Gold Standard Series reissue, Paralyzed/BIG BOSS MAN, December 1986. Collectibles
EP: Stay Away
LPs: Clambake, Double Dynamite, Elvis Sings Hits from His Movies–Vol. 1, Elvis—TV Special

BIG LOVE, BIG HEARTACHE
Written By: Dolores Fuller, Lee Morris, Sonny Hendrix
Elvis Recorded: March 1964–Radio Recorders
Recorded For Film: ROUSTABOUT (1964)
LP: Roustabout

BITTER THEY ARE, HARDER THEY FALL
Written By: Larry Gatlin (1974)
Elvis Recorded: February 2, 1976–Graceland
LPs: From Elvis Presley Boulevard, Memphis, Tennessee; Always on My Mind

BLESSED JESUS HOLD MY HAND (See **Jesus Hold My Hand**)

BLUE CHRISTMAS
Written By: Billy Hayes, Jay Johnson
Previously Recorded By: Russ Morgan, Hugo Winterhalter, Ernest Tubb (1949); Billy Eckstine (1950)
Elvis Recorded: September 1957– Radio Recorders
Released: 1964 (as Single)
Flip Side: Wooden Heart
On The Charts: Billboard's Special Christmas Singles (peaked at #1)
Singles: BLUE CHRISTMAS/BLUE CHRIST-MAS, November 1957. Disc jockey promo, BLUE CHRISTMAS/ Wooden Heart, November 1964. Gold Standard Series original, BLUE CHRISTMAS/Santa Claus Is Back in Town, November 1965. Gold Standard Series original
EP: Elvis Sings Christmas Songs
LPs: Elvis—A Legendary Performer–Vol. 2, Elvis Aron Presley, Elvis' Christmas Album, Elvis—TV Special, A Golden Celebration, Memories of Christmas

BLUE EYES CRYING IN THE RAIN
Written By: Leon Rose
Recorded: February 1976–Graceland
Previously Recorded By: Roy Acuff (1947), Willie Nelson (1975)
LP: From Elvis Presley Boulevard, Memphis, Tennessee

BLUE HAWAII
Written By: Leo Robin, Ralph Rainger (1937)
Recorded: March 22, 1961–Radio Recorders
Previously Recorded By: Bing Crosby (1937), Billy Vaughn (1959)

Recorded For Film: BLUE HAWAII (1961)
LPs: The Alternate Aloha, Blue Hawaii, Elvis—A Legendary Performer–Vol. 2, Elvis in Hollywood, Mahalo from Elvis

BLUE MOON
Written By: Richard Rodgers, Lorenz Hart (1933)
Elvis Recorded: July 1954–Sun Records
Flip Side: Just Because
On The Charts: Billboard's Top 100 (17 weeks–peaked at #55)
Singles: Blue Moon/Just Because
September 1956. Standard 78 & 45 RPM releases, March 1959, Gold Standard Series reissue
EPs: Elvis Presley, Elvis Presley—The Most Talked About New Personality in the Past Ten Years of Recorded Music
LPs: The Complete Sun Sessions (master), Elvis Presley, The Sun Sessions

BLUE MOON OF KENTUCKY
Written By: Bill Monroe (1947)
Recorded: July 1954–Sun Studios
Previously Recorded By: The Stanley Brothers (1954), Flip Side: That's All Right (Mama)
Singles: That's All Right (Mama)/Blue Moon of Kentucky, July 1954, Sun 78 RPM and 45 RPM releases, November 1955, Standard RCA 78 & 45 RPM reissues, March 1959, Gold Standard Series reissue, October 1984, Elvis' Greatest Hits—Golden Singles–Vol. 2
EPs: Good Rockin' Tonight, Great Country/Western Hits, See the USA, the Elvis Way, A Touch of Gold–Vol. 3
LPs: The Complete Sun Sessions, A Date with Elvis, Elvis: The Hillbilly Cat, A Golden Celebration, The Sun Sessions

BLUE RIVER
Written By: Paul Evans, Fred Tobias
Recorded: May 1963–RCA Nashville
Flip Side: Tell Me Why
On The Charts: Billboard's Hot 100–1 Week (peaked At #95)
Singles: Tell Me Why/BLUE RIVER, December 1965. Standard release. Tell Me Why/BLUE RIVER, February 1968. Gold Standard Series reissue
LPs: Double Trouble

BLUE SUEDE SHOES
Written By: Carl Perkins (1955)
Previously Recorded By: Carl Perkins, Boyd Bennett
Elvis Recorded: January 30, 1956–RCA New York City
Flip Side: Tutti Frutti
On The Charts: Billboard's Top 100–12 Weeks (peaked At #24) EP
Singles: BLUE SUEDE SHOES/ Tutti Frutti, September, 1956. Standard 78 RPM release, BLUE SUEDE SHOES/Tutti Frutti, September 1956. Standard 45 RPM release, BLUE SUEDE SHOES/I'm Counting on You, September 1956. Disc jockey Record Prevue, BLUE SUEDE SHOES/Tutti Frutti, March 1959. Gold Standard Series reissue, BLUE SUEDE SHOES/Tutti Frutti, October 1977. 15 Golden Records–30 Golden Hits, BLUE SUEDE SHOES/Tutti Frutti, October 1984. Elvis' Greatest Hits-–Golden Singles–Vol. 1, BLUE SUEDE SHOES/Promised Land, October 1984, BLUE SUEDE SHOES/BLUE SUEDE SHOES, October 1984. Disc jockey promo, BLUE SUEDE SHOES/Fools Fall in Love, December 1986. Collectibles
EPs: Elvis Presley (RCA EPA–747), Elvis Presley (RCA EPB–1254), Elvis Presley (RCA SPD–22), Elvis Presley (RCA SPD–23), Elvis Presley–The Most Talked About New Personality in the Last Ten Years of Recorded Music
LPs: Aloha from Hawaii via Satellite, The Alternate Aloha, Elvis—A Legendary

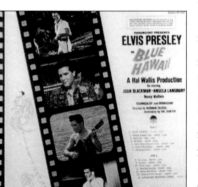

Performer–Vol.2, Elvis Aron Presley, Elvis in Person, Elvis Presley, From Memphis to Vegas/From Vegas to Memphis, G. I. Blues, A Golden Celebration, This Is Elvis

BLUEBERRY HILL
Written By: Al Lewis, Larry Stock, Vincent Rose (1940)
Previously Recorded By: Glenn Miller (vocal by Ray Eberle), Gene Autry, Fats Domino
Elvis Recorded: January 19, 1957–Radio Recorders
EPs: Just for You
LPs: Elvis Aron Presley—Forever, Elvis Recorded Live on Stage in Memphis, Essential Elvis–Vol. 2, Loving You

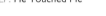

A BLUES JAM (See Reconsider Baby)

BOSOM OF ABRAHAM
Written By: William Johnson George McFaddan, Ted Brooks
Previously Recorded By: The Trumpeteers, The Jordanaires
Elvis Recorded: June 9 or 10 1971–RCA Nashville
Flip Side: He Touched Me
Singles: He Touched Me/BOSOM OF ABRAHAM, March 1972. Standard release.
LP: He Touched Me

BOSSA NOVA BABY
Written By: Jerry Leiber, Mike Stoller (1962)
Previously Recorded By: Tippy and the Clovers
Elvis Recorded: January 22, 1963–Radio Recorders
Recorded For Film: FUN IN ACAPULCO (1963)
Flip Side: Witchcraft
On The Charts: Billboard's Hot 100 (10 weeks–peaked At #8), Rhythm & Blues chart (peaked At #20)
Singles: BOSSA NOVA BABY/Witchcraft, October 1963. Standard release. BOSSA NOVA BABY/Witchcraft, August 1964. Gold Standard Series reissue, BOSSA NOVA BABY/Such a Night, December 1986. Collectibles
LPs: Elvis in Hollywood, Elvis: Worldwide 50 Gold Award Hits–Vol. 1, Fun in Acapulco, The Top Ten Hits

A BOY LIKE ME, A GIRL LIKE YOU
Written By: Sid Tepper, Roy C. Bennett
Elvis Recorded: March 1962–Radio Recorders
Recorded For Film: GIRLS! GIRLS! GIRLS! (1962)
LP: Girls! Girls! Girls!

BRIDGE OVER TROUBLED WATER
Written By: Paul Simon (1970)
Previously Recorded By: Simon & Garfunkel, Aretha Franklin, Buck Owens
Elvis Recorded: June 5, 1970–RCA Nashville
LP: That's the Way It Is

BRINGING IT BACK
Written By: Greg Gordon
Previously Recorded By: Fred Wise, Randy Starr
Elvis Recorded: March 12, 1975–RCA Hollywood
Flip Side: Pieces of My Life
On The Charts: Billboard's Hot 100–5 Weeks (peaked At #65)
Singles: BRINGING IT BACK/Pieces of My Life, October, 1975. Standard release. BRINGING IT BACK/Pieces of My Life, October, 1975. Disc jockey promo
LPs: Elvis Aron Presley—Forever, Elvis Today

BRITCHES
Written By: Sid Wayne, Sherman Edwards
Elvis Recorded: August 8, 1960–Radio Recorders
Recorded For Film: FLAMING STAR (Not used)
Released: 1978

LP: Elvis—A Legendary Performer–Vol. 3

THE BULLFIGHTER WAS A LADY
Written By: Sid Tepper, Roy C. Bennett
Elvis Recorded: January 22,1963–Radio Recorders
Recorded For Film: FUN IN ACAPULCO (1963)
LP: Fun in Acapulco

BURNING LOVE
Written By: Dennis Linde
Elvis Recorded: March 28, 1972–RCA Hollywood
Flip Side: It's a Matter of Time
On The Charts: Billboard's Hot 100 (15 weeks–peaked at #2), Easy-Listening (peaked at #9)
Sales: One million
Singles: BURNING LOVE/It's a Matter of Time, August 1972. Standard release, BURNING LOVE/Steamroller Blues, March 1975. Gold Standard Series original, THE ELVIS MEDLEY/Always on My Mind, November 1982, THE ELVIS MEDLEY/THE ELVIS MEDLEY, November 1982. Disc jockey promo, Suspicious Minds/BURNING LOVE, October 1984. Elvis' Greatest Hits—Golden Singles–Vol.2
LPs: Aloha from Hawaii via Satellite, The Alternate Aloha, Buming Love and Hits from His Movies–Vol. 2, Double Dynamite, Elvis Aron Presley, Elvis' Gold Records–Vol. 5, The Elvis Medley, Greatest Hits–Vol. 1, The Top Ten Hits

BY AND BY
Traditional Gospel Song
Elvis Recorded: May 27, 1966–RCA Nashville
LPs: How Great Thou Art, C. C. RIDER (See See See Rider)

CANE AND A HIGH STARCHED COLLAR
Written By: Sid Tepper, Roy C. Bennett
Elvis Recorded: August 1960–Radio Recorders
Recorded For Film: FLAMING STAR (1960)
Released: Unreleased until January 1976
LP: Elvis—A Legendary Perfomer–Vol. 2

CAN'T HELP FALLING IN LOVE
Written By: George Weiss, Hugo Peretti, Luigi Creatore
Elvis Recorded: March 23, 1961–Radio Recorders
Recorded For Film: BLUE HAWAII (1961)
Flip Side: Rock-a-Hula-Baby
On The Charts: Billboard's Hot 100 (14 weeks–peaked at #2), Easy-Listening (6 weeks–peaked at #1)
Singles: CAN'T HELP FALLING IN LOVE/Rock–a–Hula Baby, December 1961 Standard release, CAN'T HELP FALLING IN LOVE/Rock–a–Hula Baby, December 1961. Compact 33 single release. CAN'T HELP FALLING IN LOVE/Rock–a–Hula Baby, November 1962. Gold Standard Series reissue, CAN'T HELP FALLING IN LOVE/Rock–a–Hula Baby, October 1977. 15 Golden Records–30 Golden Hits, Are You Lonesome Tonight?/CAN'T HELP FALLING IN LOVE, October 1984. Elvis' Greatest Hits—Golden Singles–Vol. 2
LPs: Aloha from Hawaii via Satellite, The Alternate Aloha, Blue Hawaii, Elvis, Elvis—A Legendary Performer–Vol. 1, Elvis Aron Presley, Elvis as Recorded at Madison Square Garden, Elvis in Concert, Elvis in Person, Elvis Recorded Live on Stage in Memphis, Elvis—TV Special, Elvis: Worldwide 50 Gold Award Hits–Vol. 1, From Memphis to Vegas/From Vegas to Memphis, The Top Ten Hits, A Valentine Gift for You

CARNY TOWN
Written By: Fred Wise, Randy Starr
Elvis Recorded: March, 1964–Radio Recorders
Recorded For Film: ROUSTABOUT (1964)
LP: Roustabout

CASUAL LOVE AFFAIR
Elvis Recorded: January 4, 1954–Memphis Recording Service (His second recording session. Elvis paid $4, kept the acetate disk and met Sam Phillips)

CATCHIN' ON FAST
Written By: Bill Giant, Bernie Baum, Florence Kaye
Elvis Recorded: October 1963–RCA Nashville

Recorded For Film: *KISSIN' COUSINS* (1964)
LP: **Kissin' Cousins**

CHANGE OF HABIT
Written By: Ben Weisman, Buddy Kaye
Elvis Recorded: March 1969–Decca Recording Studios, Universal City
Recorded For Film: *CHANGE OF HABIT* (1969)
LP: **Let's Be Friends**

CHARRO
Written By: Billy Strange, Mac Davis
Elvis Recorded: October 15, 1968–Samuel Goldwyn Studios
Recorded For Film: *CHARRO* (1969)
Singles: **Memories/CHARRO**, March 1969. Standard release, **Memories/CHARRO**, December 1970. Gold Standard Series reissue.
LPs: **Almost in Love, Elvis in Hollywood**

CHESAY
Written By: Fred Karger, Sid Wayne, Ben Weisman
Elvis Recorded: May, 1965–Radio Recorders
Recorded For Film: *FRANKIE AND JOHNNY* (1966)
LP: **Frankie and Johnny**

CINDY, CINDY (Adapted from Traditional)
Written By: Buddy Kaye, Ben Weisman, Dolores Fuller
Previously Recorded By: Ricky Nelson, Teddy Vann
Elvis Recorded: June 4, 1970–RCA Nashville
LP: **Love Letters from Elvis**

CITY BY NIGHT
Written By: Bill Giant, Bernie Baum, Florence Kaye
Elvis Recorded: June 1966–Radio Recorders
Recorded For Film: *DOUBLE TROUBLE* (1967)
LP: **Double Trouble**

CLAMBAKE
Written By: Sid Wayne, Ben Weisman
Elvis Recorded: February 21, 1967–RCA Nashville
Recorded For Film: *CLAMBAKE* (1967)
EP: **Clambake**
LP: **Clambake**

CLEAN UP YOUR OWN BACK YARD
Written By: Billy Strange, Mac Davis
Elvis Recorded: August 23, 1968–United
Recorders, Los Angeles
Recorded For Film: *THE TROUBLE WITH GIRLS* (1969)
Flip Side: **The Fair is Moving On**
On The Charts: *Billboard*'s Hot 100 (8 weeks–peaked at #35), Country Chart (peaked at #74), Easy-Listening (peaked at #37)
Singles: **CLEAN UP YOUR OWN BACK YARD/The Fair Is Moving On**, June 1969. Standard release, **CLEAN UP YOUR OWN BACK YARD/The Fair Is Moving On**. December 1970. Gold Standard Series reissue
LPs: **Almost in Love, Elvis' Gold Records–Vol. 5, Guitar Man**

C'MON EVERYBODY
Written By: Joy Beyers
Elvis Recorded: July 7, 1964–Radio Recorders
Recorded For Film: *VIVA LAS VEGAS* (1964)
EP: **Viva Las Vegas**
LP: **C'mon Everybody**

COLD, COLD ICY FINGERS
(See Keep Them Cold Icy Fingers Off of Me)

COME ALONG
Written By: David Hess
Elvis Recorded: May 1965–Radio Recorders
Recorded For Film: *FRANKIE AND JOHNNY* (1966)

LP: **Frankie and Johnny**

COME WHAT MAY
Written By: Franklin Tableporter (1958)
Previously Recorded By: Clyde McPhatter, Elvis Recorded: May 28, 1966–RCA Nashville
Singles: **Love Letters/COME WHAT MAY**, June 1966. Standard release, **Love Letters/COME WHAT MAY**, February 1968. Gold Standard Series reissue.

CONFIDENCE
Written By: Sid Tepper, Roy C. Bennett
Elvis Recorded: February 22, 1967–RCA Nashville
Recorded For Film: *CLAMBAKE* (1967)
LPs: **Clambake, Elvis Sings Hits from His Movies–Vol. 1**

COTTON CANDY LAND
Written By: Ruth Batchelor, Bob Roberts
Elvis Recorded: September 1962–Radio Recorders
Recorded For Film: *IT HAPPENED AT THE WORLD'S FAIR* (1963)
LPs: **Elvis Sings for Children and Grownups Too!, It Happened at the World's Fair**

COULD I FALL IN LOVE
Written By: Randy Starr
Elvis Recorded: June 1966–Radio Recorders
Recorded For Film: *DOUBLE TROUBLE* (1967)
LP: **Double Trouble**

CRAWFISH
Written By: Fred Wise, Ben Weisman
Elvis Recorded: January 15, 1958–Radio Recorders, (Duet with Kitty White),
Recorded For Film: *KING CREOLE* (1958)
EP: **King Creole–Vol. 2**
LPs: **Elvis: The Other Sides—Worldwide Gold Award Hits–Vol. 2, King Creole**

CROSS MY HEART AND HOPE TO DIE
Written By: Sid Wayne, Ben Weisman
Elvis Recorded: June/July, 1964–Radio Recorders
Recorded For Film: *GIRL HAPPY* (1965)
LP: **Girl Happy**

CRYING IN THE CHAPEL
Written By: Artie Glenn (1953)
Previously Recorded By: Darrell Glenn (1953), Rex Allen, Sonny Til and The Orioles, June Valli, Anita Wood
Elvis Recorded: October 31, 1960–RCA Nashville
Flip Side: **I Believe in the Man in the Sky**
On The Charts: *Billboard*'s Hot 100–(14 weeks–peaked at #3), Easy-Listening–(7 weeks–peaked at #1)
Sales: Over one million worldwide
Singles: **CRYING IN THE CHAPEL/I Believe in the Man in the Sky**, April 1965. Gold Standard Series original release, **CRYING IN THE CHAPEL/I Believe in the Man in the Sky**, October 1977. 15 Golden Records–30 Golden Hits.
LPs: **Elvis—A Legendary Performer–Vol. 3, Elvis: Worldwide 50 Gold Award Hits–Vol. 1, How Great Thou Art, The Top Ten Hits**

DANNY
Written By: Fred Wise, Ben Weisman
Elvis Recorded: January 23, 1958–Radio Recorders
Recorded For Film: *KING CREOLE* (1958)
Released: 1978
LP: **Elvis—A Legendary Performer–Vol. 3**

DANNY BOY
Written By: Frederic Edward Weatherly 1913 (from **Londonderry Air**)
Elvis Recorded: February 5–6, 1976–Graceland
LPs: **From Elvis Presley Boulevard, Memphis, Tennessee; A Golden Celebration (West Germany, 1958–1960)**

DARK MOON
Written By: Ned Miller (1957)

Elvis Recorded: Mid 60s–Graceland
LP: **A Golden Celebration** (Graceland, 1960s)

DATIN'
Written By: Fred Wise, Randy Starr
Elvis Recorded: July 26, 1965–Radio Recorders (duet with Donna Butterworth), August 4, 1965 (Vocals)
Recorded For Film: *PARADISE, HAWAIIAN STYLE* (1966)
LPs: **Elvis Aron Presley, Paradise, Hawaiian Style**

DEVIL IN DISGUISE, (YOU'RE THE)
Written By: Bill Giant, Bernie Baum, Florence Kaye
Elvis Recorded: May 26, 1963–RCA Nashville
Flip Side: **Please Don't Drag That String Around**
On The Charts: *Billboard*'s Hot 100 (11 weeks–peaked at #3), Rhythm & Blues (peaked at #9), British–(1 week–peaked at #1)
Sales: Over one million worldwide
Singles: **(YOU'RE THE) DEVIL IN DISGUISE/Please Don't Drag That String Around**, June 1963. Standard release, **(YOU'RE THE) DEVIL IN DISGUISE/Please Don't Drag That String Around**, August 1964. Gold Standard Series reissue, **One Broken Heart for Sale/(YOU'RE THE) DEVIL IN DISGUISE**, December 1986. Collectibles
LPs: **Elvis' Gold Records–Vol. 4, Elvis: Worldwide 50 Gold Award Hits–Vol. 1, The Top Ten Hits**

DIDJA EVER
Written By: Sid Wayne, Sherman Edwards
Elvis Recorded: April 27, 1960–RCA Hollywood
Recorded For Film: *G.I. BLUES* (1960)
LP: **G. I. Blues**

DIRTY, DIRTY FEELING
Written By: Jerry Leiber, Mike Stoller
Elvis Recorded: April 4, 1960–RCA Nashville
Film Used In: *TICKLE ME* (1965)
EP: **Tickle Me**
LP: **Elvis Is Back**

DIXIE (See **An American Trilogy**)

DIXIELAND ROCK
Written By: Aaron Schroeder, Rachel Frank
Elvis Recorded: January 16, 1958–Radio Recorders
Recorded For Film: *KING CREOLE* (1958)
EP: **King Creole–Vol. 2**
LPs: **Elvis: The Other Sides—Worldwide Gold Award Hits–Vol. 2, King Creole**

DO NOT DISTURB
Written By: Bill Giant, Bernie Baum, Florence Kaye
Elvis Recorded: July 1964–Radio Recorders
Recorded For Film: *GIRL HAPPY* (1965)
LP: **Girl Happy**

DO THE CLAM
Written By: Sid Wayne, Ben Weisman, Dolores Fuller
Elvis Recorded: July 1964–Radio Recorders
Recorded For Film: *GIRL HAPPY* (1965)
Flip Side: **You'll Be Gone**
On The Charts: *Billboard*'s Hot 100 (8 weeks–peaked at #21)
Singles: **DO THE CLAM/You'll Be Gone**, February 1965. Standard release. **DO THE CLAM/You'll Be Gone**, November 1965. Gold Standard Series reissue.
LP: **Girl Happy**

DO THE VEGA
Written By: Bill Giant, Bernie Baum, Florence Kaye
Elvis Recorded: July 1963–Radio Recorders
Recorded For Film: *VIVA LAS VEGAS* (1964)
LPs: **Elvis Sings Flaming Star, Singer Presents Elvis Singing Flaming Star and Others**

DO YOU KNOW WHO I AM
Written By: Bobby Russell

Elvis Recorded: February 19, 1969–American Sound Studios, Memphis
LPs: **From Memphis to Vegas/From Vegas to Memphis, Back in Memphis**

A DOG'S LIFE
Written By: Sid Wayne, Ben Weisman
Elvis Recorded: August 4, 1965–Radio Recorders
Recorded For Film: *PARADISE, HAWAIIAN STYLE* (1966)
LPs: **Elvis Aron Presley, Paradise, Hawaiian Style**

DOIN' THE BEST I CAN
Written By: Doc Pomus, Mort Shuman
Elvis Recorded: April 27, 1960–RCA Hollywood
Recorded For Film: *G.I. BLUES* (1960)
EP: **The EP Collection–Vol. 2**
LP: **G.I. Blues**

DONCHA' THINK IT'S TIME
Written By: Clyde Otis, Willie Dixon
Elvis Recorded: February 1, 1958–Radio Recorders
Flip Side: **Wear My Ring Around Your Neck**
On The Charts: *Billboard*'s Top 100 (6 weeks–peaked at #40)
Singles: **Wear My Ring Around Your Neck/DONCHA' THINK IT'S TIME**, April 1958. Standard 78 RPM release, **Wear My Ring Around Your Neck/DONCHA' THINK IT'S TIME**, April 1958. Standard 45 RPM release, **Wear My Ring Around Your Neck/DONCHA' THINK IT'S TIME**, 1961. Gold Standard Series reissue.
LPs: **Elvis: The Other Sides—Worldwide Gold Award Hits–Vol. 2, 50,000,000 Elvis Fans Can't Be Wrong—Elvis' Gold Records–Vol. 2**

DON'T
Written By: Jerry Leiber, Mike Stoller
Elvis Recorded: September 6, 1957–Radio Recorders
Flip Side: **I Beg Of You**
On The Charts: *Billboard*'s Top 100 (20 weeks–peaked at #1), Country Best-Seller (peaked at #2), Rhythm & Blues (peaked at #4)
Sales: Over one million advance
Singles: **DON'T/I Beg of You**, January 1958. Standard 78 RPM release., **DON'T/I Beg of You**, January 1958. Standard 45 RPM release, **Wear My Ring Around Your Neck/DON'T**, January 1960. Disc jockey promotional release, **DON'T/I Beg of You**, August 1961. Gold Standard Series reissue.
EP: **A Touch of Gold–Vol. 1**
LPs: **Elvis: Worldwide 50 Gold Award Hits–Vol. 1, 50,000,000 Elvis Fans Can't Be Wrong—Elvis' Gold Records–Vol. 2, I Was the One, The Number One Hits, The Top Ten Hits**

DON'T ASK ME WHY
Written By: Fred Wise, Ben Weisman
Elvis Recorded: January 16, 1958–Radio Recorders
Flip Side: **Hard Headed Woman**
On The Charts: *Billboard*'s Top 100 (9 weeks–peaked at #28), Rhythm & Blues (peaked at #2)
Singles: **Hard Headed Woman/DON'T ASK ME WHY**, June 1958. Standard 78 RPM release, **Hard Headed Woman/DON'T ASK ME WHY**, June 1958. Standard 45 RPM release, **Hard Headed Woman/DON'T ASK ME WHY**, 1961. Gold Standard Series reissue.
EP: **Touch of Gold–Vol. 3**
LPs: **Elvis: The Other Sides—Worldwide Gold Award Hits–Vol. 2, King Creole**

DON'T BE CRUEL
Written By: Otis Blackwell, Elvis Presley (1955)
Elvis Recorded: July 2, 1956–RCA New York City
Flip Side: **Hound Dog**
On The Charts: *Billboard*'s Top 100 (27 weeks–peaked at #1), Country Juke Box (peaked at #1)
Country Best Seller (peaked at #1), Rhythm & Blues (peaked at #1)
Sales: Over nine million
Singles: **Hound Dog/DON'T BE CRUEL**, July 1956. Standard 78 RPM release, **Hound Dog/DON'T BE CRUEL**, July 1956. Standard 45 RPM release, **Hound Dog/DON'T BE CRUEL**, March 1959. Gold Standard Series reissue, **Hound Dog/DON'T BE CRUEL**, October 1977. 15 Golden Records–30 Golden Hits, **Hound Dog/DON'T BE CRUEL**, October 1984. **Elvis' Greatest Hits—Golden Singles–Vol. 1**
EPs: **Elvis Presley, The Real Elvis**

LPs: Elvis, Elvis—A Legendary Performer–Vol. 1, Elvis Aron Presley, Elvis as Recorded at Madison Square Garden, Elvis' Golden Records, Elvis in Concert , The Elvis Medley, Elvis: Worldwide 50 Gold Award Hits–Vol. 1, A Golden Celebration, The Number One Hits, Pure Gold, This Is Elvis, The Top Ten Hits

DON'T CRY, DADDY
Written By: Mac Davis
Elvis Recorded: January 15, 1969–American Sound Studios, Memphis
Flip Side: Rubberneckin'
On The Charts: *Billboard*'s Hot 100 (13 weeks–peaked at #6), Country (peaked at #13)
Sales: Went gold January 21, 1970
Singles: DON'T CRY DADDY/ Rubberneckin', November 1969. Standard release. DON'T CRY, DADDY/ Rubberneckin', December 1970. Gold Standard Series reissue.

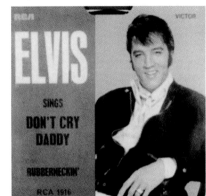

LPs: Always on My Mind, Elvis: Worldwide 50 Gold Award Hits–Vol. Greatest Hits–Vol. 1, The Memphis Record, The Top Ten Hits

DON'T LEAVE ME NOW
Written By: Aaron Schroeder, Ben Weisman.
Elvis Recorded: February 23, 1957–Radio Recorders (LP)
April 30, 1957–Radio Recorders (EP)
Recorded For Film: *JAILHOUSE ROCK* (1958)
EP: Jailhouse Rock
LPs: Essential Elvis—The First Movies, Loving You

DON'T THINK TWICE, IT'S ALL RIGHT
Written By: Bob Dylan
Previously Recorded By: Bob Dylan, Peter, Paul and Mary
Elvis Recorded: May 16, 1971–RCA Nashville
LPs: Elvis, Our Memories of Elvis–Vol. 2

DOUBLE TROUBLE
Written By: Doc Pomus, Mort Shuman
Elvis Recorded: June 1966–Radio Recorders.
Recorded For Film: *DOUBLE TROUBLE* (1966)
LPs: Double Trouble, Elvis in Hollywood

DOWN BY THE RIVERSIDE/ WHEN THE SAINTS GO MARCHING IN
Written By: (Adapted by Bill Giant, Bernie Baum, Florence Kaye)
Elvis Recorded: May 1965–Radio Recorders
Recorded For Film: *FRANKIE AND JOHNNY* (1966)
LPs: Elvis Sings Hits from His Movies–Vol. 1, Frankie and Johnny

DOWN IN THE ALLEY
Written By: Jesse Stone
Previously Recorded By: The Clovers (1957)
Elvis Recorded: May 26, 1966–RCA Nashville
LPs: Reconsider Baby, Spinout (bonus track)

DRUMS OF THE ISLANDS
Written By: Sid Tepper, Roy C. Bennett (based on Tongan chant)
Elvis Recorded: July 26, 1965–Radio Recorders
Recorded For Film: *PARADISE, HAWAIIAN STYLE* (1966)
LP: Paradise, Hawaiian Style

EARLY MORNING RAIN
Written By: Gordon Lightfoot
Previously Recorded By: Peter, Paul and Mary
Elvis Recorded: March 15, 1971–RCA Nashville
LPs: Elvis—A Canadian Tribute, Elvis in Concert, Elvis in Nashville, Elvis Now, Elvis

Aron Presley—Forever, Mahalo from Elvis

EARTH ANGEL
Written By: Jesse Belvin
Elvis Recorded: Private session in West Germany '58 to '60
LP: A Golden Celebration (West Germany: 1958–1960)

EARTH BOY
Written By: Sid Tepper, Roy C. Bennett
Elvis Recorded: March 1962–Radio Recorders (with The Tui Sisters)
Recorded For Film: *GIRLS! GIRLS! GIRLS!* (1962)
LP: Girls! Girls! Girls!

EASY COME, EASY GO
Written By: Sid Wayne, Ben Weisman
Elvis Recorded: After September 28, 1966–Radio Recorders
Recorded For Film: *EASY COME, EASY GO* (1967)
EP: Easy Come, Easy Go
LPs: C'mon Everybody, Double Dynamite

(SUCH AN) EASY QUESTION
Written By: Otis Blackwell, Winfield Scott (1962)
Elvis Recorded: March 18, 1962–RCA Nashville
Recorded For Film: *TICKLE ME* (1965)
Flip Side: It Feels So Right
On The Charts: *Billboard*'s Hot 100 (8 weeks–peaked at #11)
Easy-Listening (7 weeks–peaked at #1)
Singles: (SUCH AN) EASY QUESTION/It Feels So Right, May 1965. Standard release. (SUCH AN) EASY QUESTION/It Feels So Right, November 1966. Gold Standard Series reissue.
LP: Pot Luck

ECHOES OF LOVE
Written By: Bob Roberts, Paddy McMains
Elvis Recorded: May 26,1963–RCA Nashville
LP: Kissin' Cousins

EDGE OF REALITY
Written By: Bill Giant, Bernie Baum, Florence Kaye
Elvis Recorded: March 7, 1968–Western Recorders, Hollywood
Flip Side: If I Can Dream
Singles: If I Can Dream/EDGE OF REALITY, November 1968. Standard release, If I Can Dream/EDGE OF REALITY, December 1970. Gold Standard Series reissue.
LP: Almost in Love

EL TORO
Written By: Bill Giant, Bernie Baum, Florence Kaye
Elvis Recorded: January 23, 1963–Radio Recorders
Recorded For Film: *FUN IN ACAPULCO* (1963)
LP: Fun In Acapulco

THE ELVIS MEDLEY
Medley consisting of selections from Jailhouse Rock, Teddy Bear, Hound Dog, Don't Be Cruel, Burning Love and Suspicious Minds.
On the Charts: *Billboard*'s Hot 100–(7 weeks–peaked at #71), Country (peaked at #31)
Flip Side: Always on My Mind
Singles: THE ELVIS MEDLEY/Always on My Mind, November 1982. Standard release.THE ELVIS MEDLEY/THE ELVIS MEDLEY (short version), November 1982. Disc jockey promotional release, THE ELVIS MEDLEY/Always on My Mind, December 1986. Collectibles
LP: The Elvis Medley

EVERYBODY COME ABOARD
Written By: Bill Giant, Bernie Baum, Florence Kaye
Elvis Recorded: May 1965–Radio Recorders
Recorded For Film: *FRANKIE AND JOHNNY* (1966)
LP: Frankie and Johnny

THE EYES OF TEXAS
(See The Yellow Rose of Texas / The Eyes of Texas)

FADED LOVE
Written By: Bob, John Wills (1950)
Previously Recorded By: Bob Wills and The Texas Playboys, Patsy Cline
Elvis Recorded: June 7, 1970–RCA Nashville
Singles: Guitar Man/FADED LOVE, January 1981 Standard release, Guitar Man/FADED LOVE, January 1981, Disc jockey promo
LPs: Elvis Country, Guitar Man

THE FAIR IS MOVING ON
Written By: Doug Flett, Guy Fletcher
Elvis Recorded: February 21, 1969–American Sound Studios
Singles: Clean Up Your Own Back Yard/THE FAIR IS MOVING ON, June 1969. Standard release, Clean Up Your Own Back Yard/THE FAIR IS MOVING ON, December 1970. Gold Standard Series reissue.
LPs: Back in Memphis, From Memphis to Vegas/ From Vegas to Memphis, The Memphis Record

FAIRYTALE
Written by: Anita, Bonnie Pointer
Previously Recorded By: The Pointer Sisters
Elvis Recorded: March 10, 1975–RCA Hollywood
LPs: Elvis in Concert, Elvis Today

FAME AND FORTUNE
Written By: Fred Wise, Ben Weisman
Elvis Recorded: March 21, 1960–RCA Nashville
Flip Side: Stuck On You
On The Charts: *Billboard*'s Hot 100–10 Weeks (peaked at #17)
Advance Sales: 1,275,077
Singles: Stuck on You/FAME AND FORTUNE, April 1960 Standard release, Stuck on You/FAME AND FORTUNE, April 1960. Living Stereo release, Stuck on You/FAME AND FORTUNE, February 1962. Gold Standard Series reissue. Stuck on You/FAME AND FORTUNE, December 1986. Collectibles
LPs: Elvis—A Legendary Performer–Vol. 3, Elvis' Golden Records–Vol. 3, Elvis: The Other Sides—Worldwide Gold Award Hits–Vol. 2, A Valentine Gift for You

FARTHER ALONG
Written By: Reverend W. B. Stone (1937)
Elvis Recorded: May 27,1966–RCA Nashville
LP: How Great Thou Art

FEVER
Written By: John Davenport (Otis Blackwell), Eddie Cooley (1956)
Recorded: April 4, 1960–RCA Nashville
LPs: Aloha from Hawaii via Satellite, The Alternate Aloha, Elvis Is Back, Pure Gold, A Valentine Gift for You

FIND OUT WHAT'S HAPPENING
Written By: Jerry Crutchfield
Previously Recorded By: Bobby Bare, Barbara Fairchild
Elvis Recorded: July 22, 1973–Stax Studios, Memphis.
LPs: Our Memories of Elvis–Vol. 2, Raised on Rock/For Ol' Times Sake

FINDERS KEEPERS, LOSERS WEEPERS
Written by: Dory and Ollie Jones
Elvis Recorded: May 26, 1963–RCA Nashville
LP: Elvis for Everyone

FIRST IN LINE
Written By: Ben Weisman, Aaron Schroeder
Elvis Recorded: September 3, 1956–Radio Recorders
EP: Strictly Elvis

LP: Elvis

THE FIRST NOEL
Written By: Unknown
Elvis Recorded: May 16, 1971–RCA Nashville
LP: Elvis Sings the Wonderful World of Christmas

THE FIRST TIME EVER I SAW YOUR FACE
Written By: Ewan McColl
Previously Recorded By: Peter, Paul and Mary, Roberta Flack
Elvis Recorded: March 15, 1971–RCA Nashville (duet with Temple Riser)
Singles: An American Trilogy/THE FIRST TIME EVER I SAW YOUR FACE, April 1972. Standard release.
LP: Elvis Aron Presley

FIVE SLEEPY HEADS
Written By: Sid Tepper, Roy C. Bennett
Elvis Recorded: June 1967–MGM Culver City, CA
LPs: Elvis Sings for Children and Grownups Too!, Speedway

FLAMING STAR
Written By: Sid Wayne, Sherman Edwards
Elvis Recorded: August 1960–Radio Recorders
Recorded For Film: *FLAMING STAR* (1960)
On The Charts: *Billboard*'s Hot 100 (7 weeks–peaked at #14)
Singles: FLAMING STAR/Love Me, December 1986 Collectibles
EP: Elvis by Request
LPs: Double Dynamite, Elvis in Hollywood, Elvis Sings Flaming Star, Singer Presents Elvis Singing Flaming Star and Others

FLIP, FLOP AND FLY
Written By: Charles Calhoun, Lou Willie Turner (1955)
Previously Recorded By: Johnny Ray, Bill Haley and The Comets
Elvis Recorded Live: *Stage Show*–Janurary 28, 1956
LPs: Elvis Recorded Live on Stage in Memphis, A Golden Celebration, This Is Elvis

FOLLOW THAT DREAM
Written By: Fred Wise, Ben Weisman
Elvis Recorded: July 5, 1961–RCA Nashville
Singles: When My Blue Moon Turns to Gold Again/FOLLOW THAT DREAM, December 1986. Collectibles
EP: Follow That Dream
LPs: C'mon Everybody, Double Dynamite, Elvis Aron Presley, Elvis in Hollywood, Return of the Rocker

FOOL
Written By: Carl Sigman, James Last
Elvis Recorded: March 28, 1972–RCA Hollywood
On The Charts: *Billboard*'s Hot 100–(12 weeks–peaked at #17), Country (peaked at #31), Easy-Listening (peaked at #12)
Singles: Steamroller Blues/FOOL, April 1973. Standard release.
LPs: Elvis, Elvis Aron Presley

THE FOOL
Written By: Lee Hazelwood (1955); Credited to Naomi Ford
Elvis Recorded: Home tape recorder in West Germany June 4, 1970–RCA Nashville
LP: Elvis Country: A Golden Celebration (West Germany: 1958–1960)

(NOW AND THEN THERE'S) A FOOL SUCH AS I
Written By: Bill Trader (1952)
Previously Recorded By: Hank Snow, Jo Stafford, Tommy Edward, The Robins
Elvis Recorded: June 10,1958–RCA Nashville
On The Charts: *Billboard*'s Hot 100–(15 weeks–peaked At #2), Rhythm & Blues (peaked

at #16), British Charts (peaked at #1–5 Weeks)
Flip Side: I Need Your Love Tonight
Sold: Over one million copies
Singles: (NOW AND THEN THERE'S) A FOOL SUCH AS I/I Need Your Love
Tonight, March 1959. Standard release, (NOW AND THEN THERE'S) A FOOL SUCH
AS I/I Need Your Love, Tonight, 1961. Gold Standard Series reissue.
LPs: Elvis—A Legendary Performer—Vol. 1, Elvis Aron Presley, Elvis: Worldwide 50
Gold Award Hits—Vol. 1, 50,000,000 Elvis Fans Can't Be Wrong—Elvis' Gold
Records—Vol. 2, The Top Ten Hits

FOOLS FALL IN LOVE
Written By: Jerry Leiber, Mike Stoller
Previously Recorded By: The Drifters (1957)
Elvis Recorded: May 28, 1966–RCA Nashville
Flip Side: Indescribably Blue
Singles: Indescribably Blue/FOOLS FALL IN LOVE, January 6,1967. Standard release,
Indescribably Blue/FOOLS FALL IN LOVE, 1970. Gold Standard Series reissue, Blue
Suede Shoes/FOOLS FALL IN LOVE, December 1986. Collectibles
LPs: Double Dynamite, I Got Lucky

FOOLS RUSH IN
Written By: Johnny Mercer, Rube Bloom (1940)
Previously Recorded By: Glenn Miller, Frank Sinatra, Brook Benton, Ricky Nelson
Elvis Recorded: May 18, 1971–RCA Nashville
LP: Elvis Now

FOR LOVIN' ME
Written By: Gordon Lightfoot (1964)
Previously Recorded By: Peter, Paul and Mary, Waylon Jennings
Elvis Recorded: March 15, 1971–RCA Nashville
LPs: Elvis, Elvis—A Canadian Tribute

FOR OL' TIMES SAKE
Written By: Tony Joe White
Elvis Recorded: July 23, 1973–Stax Studios
On The Charts: Hot 100 (9 weeks–peaked at #41), Country (peaked at #42)
Singles: Raised on Rock/FOR OL' TIMES SAKE, September 1973. Standard release.
Raised on Rock/FOR OL' TIMES SAKE, September 1973. Disc jockey promotional
release.
LP: Raised on Rock/For Ol' Times Sake

FOR THE GOOD TIMES
Written By: Kris Kristofferson (1970)
Previously Recorded By: Ray Price
Elvis Recorded: March 27,1972–RCA Hollywood
Version Released: June 10, 1972–Madison Square Garden
LPs: Elvis as Recorded at Madison Square Garden, Welcome to My World

FOR THE HEART
Written By: Dennis Linde
Elvis Recorded: February 5–6, 1976–Graceland
On The Charts: Billboard's Hot 100 (11 weeks–peaked at #28), Country (peaked
at #6)
Flip Side: Hurt
Singles: Hurt/FOR THE HEART, March 1976. Standard release, Hurt/FOR THE GOOD
TIMES, March 1976. Disc jockey promotional release, Moody Blue/FOR THE HEART,
August 1978. Gold Standard Series original release
LPs: Elvis' Gold Records—Vol. 5, From Elvis Presley Boulevard, Memphis, Tennessee,
Our Memories of Elvis—Vol. 2

FOR THE MILLIONTH AND LAST TIME
Written By: Sid Tepper, Roy C. Bennett
Elvis Recorded: October 15, 1961–RCA Nashville
LP: Elvis for Everyone

FORGET ME NEVER
Written By: Fred Wise, Ben Weisman
Elvis Recorded: November 7, 1960–Radio Recorders
Recorded For Film: WILD IN THE COUNTRY (1961)

LPs: Elvis for Everyone, Separate Ways

FORT LAUDERDALE CHAMBER OF COMMERCE
Written by: Sid Tepper, Roy C. Bennett
Elvis Recorded: June or July 1964–Radio Recorders
Recorded For Film: GIRL HAPPY (1965)
LP: Girl Happy

FOUNTAIN OF LOVE
Written By: Bill Giant, Jeff Lewis
Elvis Recorded: March 18, 1962–Radio Recorders
LP: Pot Luck

FRANKFORT SPECIAL
Written By: Sid Wayne, Sherman Edwards
Elvis Recorded: May 6, 1960–Radio
Recorders
Recorded For Film: G. I. BLUES (1960)
LP: Elvis—A Legendary
Performer—Vol. 3, G. I. Blues

FRANKIE AND JOHNNY
Written By: Hughie Cannon (1904)
Previously Recorded By: Ted Lewis,
Johnny Cash, Brook Benton, Sam
Cooke
Elvis Recorded: May 1965–Radio
Recorders
Recorded For Film: FRANKIE AND JOHN-
NY (1966)
On the Charts: Billboard's Hot 100
(8 weeks–peaked at #25)
Flip Side: Please Don't Stop Loving Me
Singles: FRANKIE AND JOHNNY/Please Don't Stop Loving Me, March 1966. Standard
release, FRANKIE AND JOHNNY/Please Don't Stop Loving Me, February 1968. Gold
Standard Series reissue, FRANKIE AND JOHNNY/Love Letters, December 1986.
Collectibles
LPs: Double Dynamite, Elvis in Hollywood, Elvis Sings Hits from His Movies—Vol. 1,
Frankie and Johnny

FROM A JACK TO A KING
Written By: Ned Miller (1957)
Previously Recorded By: Ned Miller, Jim Lowe
Elvis Recorded: January 21, 1969–American Sound Studios, Memphis
LPs: Back in Memphis, From Memphis to Vegas/From Vegas to Memphis

FUN IN ACAPULCO
Written By: Sid Wayne, Ben Weisman
Elvis Recorded: January 23, 1963–Radio Recorders
Recorded For Film: FUN IN ACAPULCO (1963)
LPs: Elvis in Hollywood, Fun in Acapulco

FUNNY HOW TIME SLIPS AWAY
Written By: Willie Nelson (1961)
Previously Recorded By: Billy Walker, Jimmy Elledge
Elvis Recorded: June 7, 1970–RCA Nashville
LPs: Elvis Aron Presley, Elvis as Recorded at
Madison Square Garden, Elvis Country

GENTLE ON MY MIND
Written By: John Hartford (1967)
Previously Recorded By: Glen Campbell, Patti Page, Aretha Franklin
Elvis Recorded: January 15, 1969–American Sound Studios, Memphis
LPs: From Elvis in Memphis, The Memphis Record

GENTLY
Written By: Murray Wizell, Edward Lisbona
Elvis Recorded: March 12, 1961–RCA Nashville
LP: Something for Everybody

GET BACK
Written By: Paul McCartney
Previously Recorded By: The Beatles with Billy Preston
Elvis Recorded: August 13, 1970—International Hotel in Las Vegas (Live)
LP: Elvis Aron Presley

G. I. BLUES
Written By: Sid Tepper, Roy C. Bennett
Elvis Recorded: April 27, 1960–RCA Hollywood
Recorded For Film: G. I. BLUES (1960)
EP: The EP Collection–Vol. 2
Lps: Elvis in Hollywood, G. 1. Blues, This Is Elvis

GIRL HAPPY
Written By: Doc Pomus, Norman Meade
Elvis Recorded: June 1964–Radio Recorder
Recorded For Film: GIRL HAPPY (1965)
LPs: Elvis in Hollywood, Girl Happy

THE GIRL I NEVER LOVED
Written By: Randy Starr
Elvis Recorded: February 22, 1967–RCA Hollywood
Recorded For Film: CLAMBAKE (1967)
LP: Clambake

GIRL OF MINE
Written By: Barry Mason, Les Reed
Elvis Recorded: July 24, 1973–Stax Studios, Memphis
LPs: Raised On Rock/For Ol' Times Sake, Our Memories Of Elvis–Vol. 1

THE GIRL OF MY BEST FRIEND
Written By: Beverly Ross, Sam Bobrick
Elvis Recorded: April 4, 1960–RCA Nashville
LP: Elvis is Back

GIRLS! GIRLS! GIRLS!
Written by: Jerry Leiber, Mike Stoller
Previously Recorded By: The Coasters
Elvis Recorded: March 1962–Radio Recorders
Recorded For Film: GIRLS! GIRLS! GIRLS! (1962)
LP: Elvis in Hollywood, Girls! Girls! Girls!

GIVE ME THE RIGHT
Written By: Fred Wise, Norman Blagman
Elvis Recorded: March 12, 1961–RCA Nashville
LPs: Something For Everybody, A Valentine Gift For You

GO EAST YOUNG MAN
Written By: Bill Giant, Bernie Baum, Florence Kaye
Elvis Recorded: February 24, 1965–RCA Nashville
Film recorded For: HARUM SCARUM (1965)
LP: Harum Scarum

GOIN' HOME
Written By: Joy Byers
Elvis Recorded: October 2, 1967–RCA Nashville
Recorded For Film: STAY AWAY, JOE (1968 not used)
LP: Speedway

GOLDEN COINS
Written By: Bill Giant, Bernie Baum, Florence Kaye
Elvis Recorded: February 24, 1965–RCA Nashville
Recorded For Film: HARUM SCARUM (1965)
LP: Harum Scarum

GONNA GET BACK HOME SOMEHOW
Written By: Doc Pomus, Mort Shuman

Elvis Recorded: March 18, 1962–RCA Nashville
LP: Pot Luck

GOOD LUCK CHARM
Written By: Aaron Schroeder, Wally Gold
Elvis Recorded: October 15, 1961–RCA Nashville
On The Charts: Billboard's Hot 100 (13 weeks–peaked at #1) British–5 weeks (peaked at #1)
Sales: One million plus
Flip Side: Anything That's Part of You
Singles: GOOD LUCK CHARM/Anything That's Part of You, March 1962. Standard release, GOOD LUCK CHARM Anything That's Part of You, March 1962. Compact 33 Single release, GOOD LUCK CHARM/Anything That's Part of You, November 1962. Gold Standard Series reissue.
EPs: The EP Collection–Vol. 2, RCA Family Record Center
LPs: Elvis, Elvis' Golden Records–Vol. 3, Elvis: Worldwide 50 Gold Award Hits–Vol. 1, The Number One Hits, The Top Ten Hits

GOOD ROCKIN' TONIGHT
Written By: Roy Brown (1947)
Previously Recorded By: Roy Brown
Elvis Recorded: September 10, 1954–Sun Records
Flip Side: I Don't Care If the Sun Don't Shine
Singles: GOOD ROCKIN' TONIGHT/I Don't Care If the Sun Don't Shine, September 25,1954. Standard Sun release 78 & 45 RPM, GOOD ROCKIN' TONIGHT/I Don't Care If the Sun Don't Shine, November 1955. 78 RPM RCA reissue of Sun session, GOOD ROCKIN' TONIGHT/I Don't Care If the Sun Don't Shine, November 1955. 45 RPM RCA reissue of Sun original, GOOD ROCKIN' TONIGHT/I Don't Care If the Sun Don't Shine, March 1959. Gold Standard Series reissue, GOOD ROCKIN' TONIGHT/I Don't Care If the Sun Don't Shine, December 1986. Collectibles
EPs: Good Rockin' Tonight, A Touch of Gold–Vol. 1
LPs: The Complete Sun Sessions, A Date with Elvis, Elvis: The Hillbilly Cat, The Sun Sessions

GOOD TIME CHARLIE'S GOT THE BLUES
Written By: Danny O'Keefe (1972)
Elvis Recorded: December 13, 1973–Stax Studios, Memphis
On The Charts: Billboard's Hot 100 (peaked at #9), Easy-Listening (peaked at #5)
LP: Good Times

GOT A LOT O' LIVIN' TO DO
Written By: Aaron Schroeder, Ben Weisman
Elvis Recorded: January 12, 1957–Radio Recorders (record version), February 1957–Radio Recorders (film version)
Recorded For Film: LOVING YOU (1957)
EP: Loving You–Vol. 2
LPs: Elvis: The Other Sides—Worldwide Gold Award Hits–Vol. 2, Essential Elvis—The First Movies, Elvis Aron Presley—Forever, Essential Elvis–Vol. 2 (compact disc), Loving You

GOT MY MOJO WORKING
Written by: Muddy Waters (1957)
Previously Recorded By: Muddy Waters, Jimmy Smith (instrumental)
Elvis Recorded: June 5, 1970–RCA Nashville
LP: Love Letters from Elvis

GREEN, GREEN GRASS OF HOME
Written By: Claude (Curly) Putnam Jr. (1965)
Previously Recorded By: Porter Wagoner, Tom Jones, Skitch Henderson, Jerry Lee Lewis
Elvis Recorded: March 11, 1975–RCA Hollywood
LPs: Elvis Aron Presley—Forever, Elvis Today, Our Memories of Elvis–Vol. 2

GUADALAJARA
Written By: Pepe Guizar
Previously Recorded By: Xavier Cugat (1944)
Elvis Recorded: February 27, 1963–Radio Recorders
Recorded For Film: FUN IN ACAPULCO (1963)
LPs: Burning Love and Hits from His Movies–Vol. 2, Fun in Acapulco, Elvis—A Legendary Performer–Vol. 3

GUITAR MAN
Written By: Jerry Reed (1967)

Previously Recorded By: Jerry Reed
Elvis Recorded: September 10, 1967–RCA Nashville
On The Charts: *Billboard*'s Hot 100–(6 weeks–peaked at #43)
Flip Side: **High Heel Sneakers**
Singles: **GUITAR MAN/High Heel Sneakers**, January 1968. Standard release, **GUITAR MAN/High Heel Sneakers**, 1970. Gold Standard Series reissue, **GUITAR MAN/Faded Love**, January 1981. Disc jockey promotional release, **GUITAR MAN/Faded Love**, January 1981. New remixed version
EP: **Stay Away**
LPs: Clambake, Elvis in Nashville, Elvis Sings Hits from His Movies–Vol. 1, Elvis—TV Special, Guitar Man

HAPPY ENDING
Written By: Ben Weisman, Sid Wayne
Elvis Recorded: September 1962–Radio Recorders (film duet with Joan O'Brien)
Recorded For Film: *IT HAPPENED AT THE WORLD'S FAIR* (1963)
LPs: It Happened at the World's Fair, Mahalo from Elvis

HARBOR LIGHTS
Written By: Jimmy Kennedy, Hugh Williams (Will Grosz) 1937
Previously Recorded By: Frances Langford, Claude Thornhill and His Orchestra, Jimmy Farrell, Sammy Kaye, Guy Lombardo, Bing Crosby, Ray Anthony, Ralph Flanagan, Ken Griffin and The Platters
Elvis Recorded: July 5, 1954–Sun Records (Elvis' first commercial recording session, unreleased until 1976)
LPs: The Complete Sun Sessions, Elvis—A Legendary Performer–Vol. 2, A Golden Celebration

HARD HEADED WOMAN
Written By: Claude DeMetrius.
Elvis Recorded: January 15, 1958–Radio Recorders
Recorded For Film: *KING CREOLE* (1958)
Flip Side: **Don't Ask Me Why**
On The Charts: *Billboard*'s Top 100 (13 weeks–peaked at #2), Country Best–Seller (peaked at #2), Rhythm & Blues (peaked at #2)
Sales: Went Gold August 11, 1958
Singles: **HARD HEADED WOMAN/Don't Ask Me Why**, June 1958. Standard 78 RPM release, **HARD HEADED WOMAN/Don't Ask Me Why**, June 1958. Standard 45 RPM release, **HARD HEADED WOMAN/Don't Ask Me Why**, 1961. Gold Standard Series reissue.
EP: **A Touch of Gold–Vol. 1**
LPs: Elvis, The Elvis Medley, Elvis: Worldwide Gold Award Hits–Vol. 1, King Creole, The Number One Hits, The Top Ten Hits

HARD KNOCKS
Written By: Joy Byers
Elvis Recorded: February 1964–Radio Recorders
Recorded For Film: *ROUSTABOUT* (1964)
LP: Roustabout

HARD LUCK
Written By: Sid Wayne, Ben Weisman
Elvis Recorded: May 1965–Radio Recorders
Recorded For Film: *FRANKIE AND JOHNNY* (1964)
LP: Frankie and Johnny

HAREM HOLIDAY
Written By: Peter Andreoli, Vince Poncia Jr.
Elvis Recorded: February 1965–RCA Nashville
Recorded For Film: *HARUM SCARUM* (1965)
LP: Harum Scarum

HAVE A HAPPY
Written By: Ben Weisman, Buddy Kaye, Dolores Fuller
Elvis Recorded: March 5, 1969–Decca Recording Studios, Universal City, California
Recorded For Film: *CHANGE OF HABIT* (1969)
LPs: Elvis Sings for Children and Grownups Too!, Let's Be Friends

HAVE I TOLD YOU LATELY THAT I LOVE YOU
Written By: Scott Wiseman (1944), Tex Ritter
Previously Recorded By: Gene Autry, Foy Willing and The Riders of the Purple Sage, Bing Crosby, The Andrews Sisters
Elvis Recorded: January 19, 1957–Radio Recorders
Since Recorded By: Ricky Nelson, Kitty Wells, Red Foley
Flip Side: **Mean Woman Blues**
Singles: **HAVE I TOLD YOU LATELY THAT I LOVE YOU/Mean Woman Blues** October 1957. Disc jockey Record Prevue
EP: **Just for You**
LPs: Essential Elvis–Vol. 2, Loving You

HAWAII USA (See **Paradise, Hawaiian Style**)

HAWAIIAN SUNSET
Written By: Sid Tepper, Roy C. Bennett
Elvis Recorded: March 21, 1961–Radio Recorders
Recorded For Film: *BLUE HAWAII* (1961)
LP: Blue Hawaii

HAWAIIAN WEDDING SONG (Ke Kali Nei Au)
Written By: Charles E. King (1926)
English Lyrics By: Al Hoffman and Dick Manning (1958)
Previously Recorded By: Andy Williams
Elvis Recorded: March 22, 1961–Radio Recorders
Recorded For Film: *BLUE HAWAII*
LPs: Blue Hawaii, Elvis Aron Presley—Forever, Elvis in Concert, Mahalo from Elvis

HE IS MY EVERYTHING
Written By: Dallas Frazier
Elvis Recorded: June 9, 1971–RCA Nashville
LPs: He Touched Me, He Walks Beside Me

HE KNOWS JUST WHAT I NEED (Jesus Knows What I Need)
Written By: Mosie Lister (1955)
Elvis Recorded: October 30,1960–RCA Nashville studios
LP: His Hand in Mine

HE TOUCHED ME
Written By: William J. Gaither
Elvis Recorded: May 18, 1971–RCA Nashville
Singles: **HE TOUCHED ME/Bosom of Abraham** March 1972. Standard release.
LP: He Touched Me

HE'LL HAVE TO GO
Written By: Audrey, Joe Allison
Previously Recorded By: Jim Reeves. Elvis Recorded: November 1, 1976–Graceland.
LP: Moody Blue

HE'S ONLY A PRAYER AWAY (I Asked the Lord)
Written By: Johnny Lange, Jimmy Duncan (1955)
Elvis Recorded: Home tape recorder–West Germany (1958–1960)
Released: 1984
LP: A Golden Celebration (West Germany: 1958–1960)

HE'S YOUR UNCLE, NOT YOUR DAD
Written By: Sid Wayne, Ben Weisman
Elvis Recorded: June 1967–MGM Culver City, California
Recorded For Film: *SPEEDWAY* (1968)
LP: Speedway

HEART OF ROME
Written by: Geoff Stephens, Alan Blaikley, Ken Howard
Elvis Recorded: June 6, 1970,–RCA Nashville
Flip Side: **I'm Leavin'**
Singles: **I'm Leavin' /HEART OF ROME**, July 1971. Standard release, May 1972. Gold Standard Series reissue.
LP: Love Letters from Elvis

HEARTBREAK HOTEL
Written By: Tommy Durden, Mae Axton (1955)
Elvis Recorded: January 10, 1956–RCA Nashville
Since Recorded By: The Cadets (1956), Stan Freberg, Roger Miller, Frijid Pink, Willie Nelson, Leon Russell
Flip Side: I Was the One
On The Charts: *Billboard's* Top 100 (27 weeks–peaked at #1), Country Best Seller (17 weeks–peaked at #1), Country Juke Box chart (13 weeks–peaked at #1), Country Disc Jockey (12 weeks–peaked at #1), Rhythm & Blues (peaked at #5)
Sales: One million plus, plus, plus

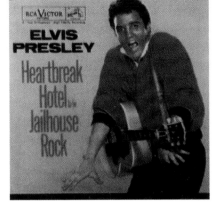

Singles: HEARTBREAK HOTEL/I Was the One, January 27,1956. Standard 78 RPM release, HEARTBREAK HOTEL/I Was the One, January 27,1956. Standard 45 RPM release, HEARTBREAK HOTEL/I Was the One, March 1959. Gold Standard Series reissue, HEARTBREAK HOTEL/I Was the One, October 1977. 15 Golden Records–30 Golden Hits, HEARTBREAK HOTEL/Jailhouse Rock, October 1984. Elvis' Greatest Hits—Golden Singles–Vol.2, HEARTBREAK HOTEL (by Elvis)/Heartbreak Hotel (by David Keith and Charlie Schlatter with Zulu Time), October 1988. From the movie *Heartbreak Hotel* (1988)
EPs: Heartbreak Hotel, The Sound of Leadership
LPs: Elvis—A Legendary Performer–Vol. 1, Elvis Aron Presley, Elvis as Recorded at Madison Square Garden, Elvis' Golden Records, The Elvis Medley, Elvis—TV Special, Elvis: Worldwide 50 Gold Award Hits–Vol. 1, A Golden Celebration, The Number One Hits, This Is Elvis (Stage Show; March 17, 1956), The Top Ten Hits

HELP ME
Written By: Larry Gatlin (1973)
Elvis Recorded: December 12, 1973–Stax Studios, Memphis
Since Recorded By: Ray Price
On The Charts: *Billboard's* Country Chart–15 Weeks (peaked at #6)
Flip Side: If You Talk in Your Sleep
Singles: If You Talk in Your Sleep/HELP ME, May 1974. Standard release, If You Talk in Your Sleep/HELP ME, May 1974. Disc jockey promotional release.
LPs: Elvis Recorded Live on Stage in Memphis, Promised Land

HELP ME MAKE IT THROUGH THE NIGHT
Written By: Kris Kristofferson, Fred Foster
Previously Recorded By: Sammi Smith, Joe Simon, O. C. Smith, Gladys Knight and The Pips
Elvis Recorded: May 17, 1971–RCA Nashville
LPs: Elvis Now, Welcome to My World

HERE COMES SANTA CLAUS (RIGHT DOWN SANTA CLAUS LANE)
Written By: Gene Autry, Oakley Haldeman (1947)
Elvis Recorded: September 6, 1957–Radio Recorders
EPs: Christmas with Elvis
LPs: Elvis' Christmas Album

HEY, HEY, HEY
Written By: Joy Byers
Elvis Recorded: February 21 or 22, 1967–RCA Nashville
Recorded For Film: *CLAMBAKE* (1967)
LP: Clambake

HEY JUDE
Written By: Paul McCartney
Previously Recorded By: The Beatles
Elvis Recorded: Winter 1969
LP: Elvis Aron Presley, Elvis Now

HEY, LITTLE GIRL
Written By: Joy Byers
Elvis Recorded: February 1965–RCA Nashville
Recorded For Film: *HARUM SCARUM* (1965)
LP: Harum Scarum

HIGH HEEL SNEAKERS
Written By: Robert Higginbotham
Previously Recorded By: Tommy Tucker (Robert Higginbotham), Jerry Lee Lewis, Stevie Wonder, Ramsey Lewis, Jose Feliciano
Elvis Recorded: September 11, 1967–RCA Nashville
Singles: Guitar Man/HIGH HEEL SNEAKERS, January 1968. Standard release, Guitar Man/HIGH HEEL SNEAKERS 1970. Gold Standard Series reissue.
LPs: Elvis Aron Presley, Reconsider Baby

HIS HAND IN MINE
Written By: Mosie Lister
Elvis Recorded: October 30, 1960–RCA Nashville
Singles: How Great Thou Art/HIS HAND IN MINE April 1969. Standard release, How Great Thou Art/HIS HAND IN MINE, December 1970. Gold Standard Series reissue, How Great Thou Art/HIS HAND IN MINE December 1986. Collectibles
LP: His Hand in Mine

(MARIE'S THE NAME) HIS LATEST FLAME
Written By: Doc Pomus, Mort Shuman
Elvis Recorded: June 26, 1961–RCA Nashville
On The Charts: *Billboard's* Hot 100 (11 weeks–peaked at #4), British (4 weeks–peaked at #1)
Sales: Over one million
Flip Side: Little Sister
Singles: Little Sister/(MARIE'S THE NAME) HIS LATEST FLAME, August 1961. Standard release, Little Sister/(MARIE'S THE NAME) HIS LATEST FLAME, August 1961. Compact 33 Single release, Little Sister/(MARIE'S THE NAME) HIS LATEST FLAME, November 1962. Gold Standard Series reissue, Little Sister/(MARIE'S THE NAME) HIS LATEST FLAME, October 1984. Elvis' Greatest Hits—Golden Singles–Vol. 2
EP: The EP Collection–Vol. 2
LPs: Elvis' Golden Records–Vol. 3, Elvis: The Other Sides–Worldwide Gold Award Hits–Vol. 2, Return of the Rocker, This Is Elvis, The Top Ten Hits

HOLLY LEAVES AND CHRISTMAS TREES
Written By: Red West, Glen Spreen
Elvis Recorded: May 15, 1971–RCA Nashville
LP: Elvis Sings the Wonderful World of Christmas

HOME IS WHERE THE HEART IS
Written By: Sherman Edwards, Hal David
Elvis Recorded: October 26, 1961–Radio Recorders
Recorded For Film: *KID GALAHAD* (1962)
Flip Side: King of the Whole Wide World
Singles: King of the Whole Wide World/HOME IS WHERE THE HEART IS, May 1962. Disc jockey promotional release.
EP: Kid Galahad
LP: I Got Lucky

HOT DOG
Written By: Jerry Leiber, Mike Stoller
Elvis Recorded: February 1957–Radio Recorders
Recorded For Film: *LOVING YOU* (1957)
EP: Loving You–Vol. 2
Lps: Elvis: The Other Sides—Worldwide Gold Award Hits–Vol. 2, Essential Elvis—The First Movies, Loving You

HOUND DOG
Written By: Jerry Leiber, Mike Stoller (1952)
Previously Recorded By: Willie Mae (Big Mama) Thornton (1953), Freddie Bell and The Bellboys (1955) (Elvis' Version)
Elvis Recorded: July 2, 1956–RCA New York City
On The Charts: *Billboard's* Top 100 (28 weeks–peaked at #2), Country Juke Box (3 weeks–peaked at #1), Rhythm & Blues–(3 weeks–peaked at #1), British (peaked at #2)
Flip Side: Don't Be Cruel

Sales: 6 million (1956), 9 million overall
Singles: **Don't Be Cruel/HOUND DOG,** July 1956. Standard 78 RPM release, **Don't Be Cruel/HOUND DOG,** July 1956. Standard 45 RPM release, **Don't Be Cruel/HOUND DOG,** March 1959. Gold Standard Series reissue, **Don't Be Cruel/HOUND DOG,** October 1977. 15 Golden Records–30 Golden Hits, **The Elvis Medley/Always on My Mind,** November 1982, **Hound Dog** is in a medley with **Jailhouse Rock, Teddy Bear, Don't Be Cruel, Burning Love,** and **Suspicious Minds, The Elvis Medley/The Elvis Medley** (short version) November 1982. Disc jockey promotional release, **HOUND DOG/Baby, Let's Play House,** August 1984. 50th anniversary of Elvis' birth, **HOUND DOG/Baby,Let's Play House,** August 1984. Disc jockey promotional release, **Don't Be Cruel/HOUND DOG,** October 1984. Elvis' Greatest Hits—Golden Singles–Vol. 1

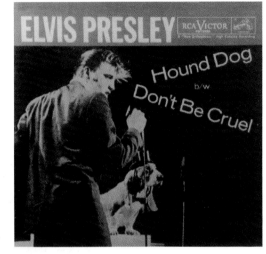

EPs: **Elvis Presley, The Real Elvis**
LPs: **Aloha from Hawaii via Satellite Elvis, Elvis—A Legendary Performer–Vol. 3, Elvis Aron Presley, Elvis as Recorded at Madison Square Garden, Elvis' Golden Records, Elvis in Concert, Elvis in Person, The Elvis Medley, Elvis Recorded Live on Stage in Memphis, Elvis: The First Live Recordings** (Louisiana Hayride; December 16,1956), **Elvis—TV Special, Elvis: Worldwide 50 Gold Award Hits–Vol. 1, From Memphis to Vegas/From Vegas to Memphis, A Golden Celebration, The Number One Hits, This Is Elvis, The Top Ten Hits**

HOUSE OF SAND
Written By: Bill Giant, Bernie Baum, Florence Kaye
Elvis Recorded: August 3, 1965–Radio Recorders
Recorded For Film: *PARADISE, HAWAIIAN STYLE* (1966)
LPs: **Paradise, Hawaiian Style**

A HOUSE THAT HAS EVERYTHING
Written By: Sid Tepper, Roy C. Bennet
Elvis Recorded: February 21, 1967–RCA Nashville
Film recorded for: *CLAMBAKE* (1967)
EP: **Clambake**
LP: **Clambake**

HOW CAN YOU LOSE WHAT YOU'VE NEVER HAD
Written By: Sid Wayne, Ben Weisman
Elvis Recorded: February 22, 1967
Recorded For Film: *CLAMBAKE* (1967) (cut)
LP: **Clambake**

HOW DO YOU THINK I FEEL
Written By: Wayne Walker, Webb Pierce (1954)
Previously Recorded By: Jimmie Rodgers Snow
Elvis Recorded: September 1, 1956–Radio Recorders
EP: **Strictly Elvis**
LP: **Elvis**

HOW GREAT THOU ART
Written By: Rev. Carl Boberg (1886)
Elvis Recorded: May 25, 1966–RCA Nashville
Singles: **HOW GREAT THOU ARE/So High,** April 1967 disc jockey promotional release, **HOW GREAT THOU ART/His Hand In Mine,** April 1969 Standard release, **HOW GREAT THOU ART/His Hand In Mine,** December 1970 Gold Standard Series reissue

LPs: **Elvis—A Legendary Performer, Elvis Aron Presley, Elvis In Concert, Elvis Recorded Live On Stage In Memphis, He Walks Beside Me, How Great Thou Art**

HOW THE WEB WAS WOVEN
Written By: Clive Westlake, David Most
Elvis Recorded: June 5, 1970–RCA Nashville
Recorded For Film: *Elvis–That's The Way It Is* (1970)
LP: **That's The Way It Is**

HOW WOULD YOU LIKE TO BE
Written By: Ben Raleigh, Mark Barkan
Elvis Recorded: September 1962–Radio Recorders
Recorded For Film: *IT HAPPENED AT THE WORLD'S FAIR* (1963)
Singles: **If Everyday Was Like Christmas/HOW WOULD YOU LIKE TO BE,** November 25, 1966 Standard release, **If Everyday Was Like Christmas/HOW WOULD YOU LIKE TO BE,** May 1972 Gold Standard Series reissue
LPs: **Elvis Sings For Children And Grownups Too!, Elvis Sings Hits From His Movies–Vol. 1, It Happened At The World's Fair**

HOW'S THE WORLD TREATING YOU
Written By: Chet Atkins, Boudleaux Bryant
Previously Recorded By: The Louvin Brothers
Elvis Recorded: September 1, 1956
LPs: **Strictly Elvis, Elvis**

HURT
Written By: Jimmie Craine, Al Jacobs
Previously Recorded By: Roy Hamilton (1954)
Elvis Recorded: February 5–6, 1971–Graceland
On The Charts: *Billboard*'s Hot 100–(11 weeks–peaked at #28), Country Best-Sellers (peaked at #6)
Flip Side: **For The Heart**
Sales: Over one million
Singles: **HURT/For The Heart,** March 1976 Standard release, **HURT/For The Heart,** March 1976 Gold Standard Series reissue
LPs: **Always On My Mind, Elvis In Concert** (Rapid City, SD–June 21, 1977), **From Elvis Presley Boulevard, Memphis, Tennessee**

I BEG OF YOU
Written By: Rose Marie McCoy, Kelly Owens
Elvis Recorded: February 23, 1957–Radio Recorders
Flip Side: **Don't**
On The Charts: *Billboard*'s Top 100 (12 weeks–peaked at #8), Country Disc Jockey (peaked at #5), Rhythm & Blues (peaked at #4)
Sales: One million plus
Singles: **Don't/I BEG OF YOU**, January 1958–Standard 78 RPM release, **Don't/I BEG OF YOU**, January 1958–Standard 45 RPM release, **Don't/I BEG OF YOU**, 1961–Gold Standard Series reissue
EP: **A Touch of Gold–Vol. 1**
LPs: **Elvis: Worldwide 50 Gold Award Hits–Vol. 1, Essential Elvis–Vol. 2, 50,000,000 Elvis Fans Can't Be Wrong—Elvis' Gold Records–Vol. 2, The Top Ten Hits**

I BELIEVE
Written By: Ervin Drake, Irvin Graham, Jimmy Shirl, Al Stillman
Previously Recorded By: Jane Froman, James Elmore, Frankie Lane, The Bachelors
Elvis Recorded: January 12, 1957–Radio Recorders
EP: **Peace in the Valley**
LP: **Elvis' Christmas Album**

I BELIEVE IN THE MAN IN THE SKY
Written By: Richard Howard
Elvis Recorded: October 30, 1960–RCA Nashville
Flip Side: **Crying in the Chapel**
Singles: **Crying in the Chapel/I BELIEVE IN THE MAN IN THE SKY**, April 1965–Gold Standard Series original release
LPs: **Elvis: The Other Sides—Worldwide Gold Award Hits–Vol. 2, His Hand In Mine, Known Only To Him**

I CAN HELP
Written By: Billy Swan (1974)
Previously Recorded By: Billy Swan
Elvis Recorded: March 11, 1975–RCA Hollywood
LPs: **Elvis Aron Presley—Forever–Elvis Today, Our Memories of Elvis–Vol. 2**

I CAN'T STOP LOVING YOU
Written By: Don Gibson (1957)
Previously Recorded By: Don Gibson, Ray Charles, Kitty Wells
Elvis Recorded: Live in Concert (Several Shows)
EP: **Aloha From Hawaii Via Satellite**
LPs: **Aloha From Hawaii Via Satellite, Elvis As Recorded At Madison Square Garden, Elvis In Person, Elvis Recorded Live On Stage In Memphis, From Memphis To Vegas/From Vegas To Memphis, Welcome To My World**

I DON'T CARE IF THE SUN DON'T SHINE
Written By: Mack David
Previously Recorded By: Patti Page, Dean Martin
Elvis Recorded: September 10, 1954–Sun Records
Flip Side: **Good Rockin' Tonight**
On The Charts: *Billboard*'s Top 100 (6 weeks–peaked at #74)
Singles: **Good Rockin' Tonight/ I DON'T CARE IF THE SUN DON'T SHINE** Sun Records–September, 1954, Standard 45 and 78 RPM releases, **Good Rockin' Tonight/ I DON'T CARE IF THE SUN DON'T SHINE**, RCA November 1955–78 RPM reissue, **Good Rockin' Tonight/ I DON'T CARE IF THE SUN DON'T SHINE**, RCA November 1955–45 RPM reissue, **Good Rockin' Tonight/ I DON'T CARE IF THE SUN DON'T SHINE**, RCA March 1959–Gold Standard Series reissue, **Good Rockin' Tonight/ I DON'T CARE IF THE SUN DON'T SHINE**, December 1986 Collectibles
EPs: **Any Way You Want Me, Good Rockin' Tonight**
LPs: **The Complete Sun Sessions, A Golden Celebration, The Sun Sessions**

I DON'T WANNA BE TIED
Written By: Bill Giant, Bernie Baum, Florence Kaye
Elvis Recorded: March, 1962–Radio Recorders
Recorded For Film: *GIRLS! GIRLS! GIRLS!* (1962)
LP: **Girls! Girls! Girls!**

I DON'T WANT TO
Written By: Janice Torre, Fred Spielman

Elvis Recorded: March 1962–Radio Recorders
Recorded for Film: *GIRLS! GIRLS! GIRLS!* (1962)
LP: **Girls! Girls! Girls!**

I FEEL SO BAD
Written By: Chuck Willis (1954)
Previously Recorded By: Chuck Willis, Ray Charles
Elvis Recorded: March 12, 1962–RCA Nashville
Flip Side: **Wild in the Country**
On the Charts: *Billboard*'s Hot 100 (9 weeks–peaked at #5), Rhythm & Blues (Peaked At #15)
Sales: One million plus
Singles: **I FEEL SO BAD/Wild in the Country**, May 1961–Standard release, **I FEEL SO BAD/Wild in the Country**, May 1961–Compact 33 release, **I FEEL SO BAD/Wild in the Country**, May 1961–Living Stereo release, **I FEEL SO BAD/Wild in the Country**, February 1962–Gold Standard Series reissue, **I FEEL SO BAD/Wild in the Country**, December 1986 Collectibles
LPs: **Elvis' Golden Records–Vol. 3, Elvis: Worldwide 50 Golden Award Hits–Vol. 1, Reconsider Baby, The Top Ten Hits**

I FEEL THAT I'VE KNOWN YOU FOREVER
Written By: Doc Pomus, Alan Jeffries
Elvis Recorded: March 19, 1962–RCA Nashville
Recorded For Film: *TICKLE ME*
EP: **Tickle Me**
LP: **Pot Luck**

I FORGOT TO REMEMBER TO FORGET
Written By: Stanly Kesler, Charlie Feathers (1955)
Elvis Recorded: July 1955–Sun Records
Flip Side: **Mystery Train**
On The Charts: Country Best-Seller (2 weeks–peaked at #1), Country Juke Box (5 weeks–peaked at #1), Total on charts: 39 weeks
Singles: **Mystery Train/I FORGOT TO REMEMBER TO FORGET**, August 1955 Sun Records–Standard 78 and 45 release, **Mystery Train/I FORGOT TO REMEMBER TO FORGET**, November 1955 RCA–78 RPM reissue, **Mystery Train/I FORGOT TO REMEMBER TO FORGET**, November 1955 RCA–45 RPM reissue, **Mystery Train/I FORGOT TO REMEMBER TO FORGET**, March 1959 RCA–Gold Standard Series reissue
EPs: **Heartbreak Hotel, SPD–15**
LPs: **The Complete Sun Sessions, A Date With Elvis, The Sun Sessions**

I GOT A FEELIN' IN MY BODY
Written By: Dennis Linde
Elvis Recorded: December 10, 1973–Stax Studios, Memphis
Flip Side: **There's a Honky Tonk Angel**
On The Charts: Country (13 weeks–peaked at #6)
Singles: **There's a Honky Tonk Angel/I GOT A FEELIN' IN MY BODY**, August 1979 Standard release, **There's a Honky Tonk Angel/I GOT A FEELIN' IN MY BODY**, August 1979 Disc jockey promotional release
LPs: **Good Times, Our Memories of Elvis–Vol. 2**

I GOT A WOMAN
Written By: Ray Charles
Previously Recorded By: Ray Charles, Ricky Nelson
Elvis Recorded: January 10, 1956–RCA Nashville
Flip Side: **I'm Counting on You**
Singles: **I GOT A WOMAN/ I'm Counting on You**, September 1956 Standard 78 RPM release, **I GOT A WOMAN/ I'm Counting on You**, September 1956 Standard 45 RPM release, **I GOT A WOMAN/ Money Honey**, September 1956 Disc jockey record prevue **I GOT A WOMAN/ I'm Counting on You**, March 1959 Gold Standard Series reissue, **I GOT A WOMAN/ I'm Counting on You**, December 1986 Collectibles
Eps: **Elvis Presley, Elvis Presley, Elvis Presley, Elvis Presley, Elvis Presley—The Most Talked About New Personality in the Past Ten Years of Recorded Music**
LPs: **Elvis Aron Presely, Elvis In Concert, Elvis In Nashville, Elvis Presley, Elvis Recorded Live On Stage In Memphis, Elvis: The Hillbilly Cat, A Golden Celebration, Pure Gold**

I GOT LUCKY
Written By: Dolores Fuller, Fred Wise, Ben Weisman
Elvis Recorded: October 27, 1961–Radio Recorders
Recorded For Film: *KID GALAHAD*
EP: Kid Galahad
LP: I Got Lucky

I GOT STUNG
Written By: Aaron Schroeder, David Hill
Elvis Recorded: June 11, 1958–RCA Nashville
Flip Side: **One Night**
On The Charts: *Billboard*'s Hot 100 (16 weeks–peaked at #8), British (3 weeks–peaked At #1)
Sales: One million plus
Singles: **I GOT STUNG/ One Night**, October 1958 Standard 78 RPM release, **I GOT STUNG/ One Night**, October 1958 Standard 45 RPM release, **I GOT STUNG/ One Night**, 1961 Gold Standard Series reissue, October 1977 **15 Golden Records–30 Golden Hits**
LPs: **Elvis, Elvis: Worldwide 50 Gold Award Hits–Vol. 1, 50,000,000 Elvis Fans Can't Be Wrong—Elvis' Gold Records–Vol. 2, The Top Ten Hits**

I GOTTA KNOW
Written By: Paul Evans, Matt Williams
Elvis Recorded: April 4, 1960–RCA Nashville
Flip Side: **Are You Lonesome Tonight?**
On the Charts: *Billboard*'s Hot 100 (11 weeks–peaked at #20)
Sales: One million plus
Singles: **Are You Lonesome Tonight?/ I GOTTA KNOW**, November 1960 Standard release, **Are You Lonesome Tonight?/ I GOTTA KNOW**, November 1960 Living Stereo release, **Are You Lonesome Tonight?/ I GOTTA KNOW**, February 1962 Gold Standard Series reissue, **Are You Lonesome Tonight?/ I GOTTA KNOW**, October 1977–15 Golden Records–30 Golden Hits
LPs: **Elvis' Golden Records–Vol. 3, Elvis: Worldwide 50 Gold Award Hits–Vol. 1**

I, JOHN
Written By: William Johnson, George McFadden, Ten Brooks
Elvis Recorded: June 9, 1971–RCA Nashville
LPs: **Elvis in Nashville, He Touched Me**

I JUST CAN'T HELP BELIEVIN'
Written By: Barry Mann, Cynthia Weil
Previously Recorded By: Barry Mann, B. J. Thomas, David Frizzel
Elvis Recorded: July 1970–MGM Hollywood
LP: **That's The Way It Is**

I ONLY LOVE ONE GIRL
Written By: Sid Tepper, Roy C. Bennet
Elvis Recorded: June 1966–Radio Recorders
Recorded For Film: *DOUBLE TROUBLE* (1967)
LPs: **Burning Love and Hits from His Movies–Vol. 2, Double Trouble**

I LOVE YOU BECAUSE
Written By: Leon Payne (1949)
Previously Recorded By: Leon Payne, Ernest Tubb, Jan Garner, Patti Page, Eddie Fisher, Johnny Cash, Al Martino, Jim Reeves
Elvis Recorded: July 5, 1954–Sun Records
Flip Side: **Tryin' To Get To You**
Singles: **Tryin' To Get To You/ I LOVE YOU BECAUSE**, September 1956 Standard 78 RPM release, **Tryin' To Get To You/ I LOVE YOU BECAUSE**, September 1956 Standard 45 RPM release, **Tryin' To Get To You/ I LOVE YOU BECAUSE**, March 1959 Gold Standard Series release, **Tryin' To Get To You/ I LOVE YOU BECAUSE**, December 1986 Collectibles
EPs: **Elvis Presley** (RCA EPA–830), **Elvis Presley–The Most Talked About New Personality in the Last Ten Years of Recorded Music**
LPs: **The Complete Sun Sessions, Elvis—A Legendary Performer–Vol. 1, Elvis Presley, The Sun Sessions**

I MET HER TODAY
Written By: Don Robertson, Hal Blair
Elvis Recorded: October 16, 1961–RCA Nashville
LPs: **Elvis For Everyone, Separate Ways**

I MISS YOU
Written By: Donnie Summer
Elvis Recorded: September 24, 1974–Palm Springs (Elvis' home)
LPs: **Always On My Mind, Raised on Rock/For Ol' Times Sake**

I NEED SOMEONE TO LEAN ON
Written By: Doc Pomus, Mort Shuman
Elvis Recorded: July 10, 1963–Radio Recorders
Recorded For Film: *VIVA LAS VEGAS*
EP: Viva Las Vegas
LPs: **I Got Lucky, A Valentine Gift For You**

I NEED YOU SO
Written By: Ivory Joe Hunter (1950)
Previously Recorded By: Ivory Joe Hunter
Elvis Recorded: February 23, 1957–Radio Recorders
Eps: **Just For You**
Lps: **Loving You**

I NEED YOUR LOVE TONIGHT
Written By: Sid Wayne, Bix Reichner
Elvis Recorded: June 10, 1958–RCA Nashville
Filp Side: **A Fool Such As I**
On the Charts: *Billboard*'s Hot 100 (13 weeks–peaked at #4)
Sales: One million plus
Singles: **A Fool Such As I/ I NEED YOUR LOVE TONIGHT** March 1959 Standard release, **A Fool Such As I/ I NEED YOUR LOVE TONIGHT**, 1961 Gold Standard Series reissue
LPs: **Elvis Aron Presley, Elvis: The Other Sides—Worldwide Gold Hits–Vol. 2, 50,000,000 Elvis Fans Can't Be Wrong—Elvis' Gold Award Records–Vol. 2, The Top Ten Hits, This Is Elvis**

I REALLY DON'T WANT TO KNOW
Written By: Don Robertson, Howard Barnes
Previously Recorded By: Eddy Arnold, Tommy Edwards, Solomon Burke, Little Esther Phillips, Ronnie Dove
Elvis Recorded: June 7, 1970–RCA Nashville
Flip Side: **There Goes My Everything**
On The Charts: *Billboard*'s Hot 100 (9 weeks–peaked at #21), Country (peaked at #9)
Singles: **I REALLY DON'T WANT TO KNOW/There Goes My Everything**, December 1970 Standard release, **I REALLY DON'T WANT TO KNOW/There Goes My Everything**, February 1972 Gold Standard Series reissue
LPs: **Elvis Country, Elvis in Concert, Elvis: The Other Sides—Worldwide Gold Award Hits–Vol. 2, Welcome To My World**

I SLIPPED, I STUMBLED, I FELL
Written By: Fred Wise, Ben Weisman
Elvis Recorded: November 8, 1960–Radio Recorders
Recorded For Film: *WILD IN THE COUNTRY* (1961)
LPs: **Separate Ways, Something For Everybody**

I THINK I'M GONNA LIKE IT HERE
Written By: Don Robertson, Hal Blair
Elvis Recorded: January 22, 1963–Radio Recorders
Recorded for Film: *FUN IN ACAPULCO* (1963)
LP: **Fun In Acapulco**

I WALK THE LINE
Written By: Johnny Cash (1956)
Previously Recorded By: Johnny Cash
Elvis Recorded: Live in concert (Las Vegas–LakeTahoe, 1969–70)
LPs: **The Entertainer, From Hollywood to Vegas, Long Lost Songs, To Know Him Is To Love Him**

I WANT TO BE FREE
Written By: Jerry Leiber, Mike Stoller (1957)
Elvis Recorded: April 30, 1957–Radio Recorders
Recorded For Film: *JAILHOUSE ROCK* (1957)
EP: Jailhouse Rock
LPs: A Date With Elvis, Elvis: The Other Sides—Worldwide Gold Award Hits–Vol. 2, Essential Elvis—The First Movies

I WANT YOU, I NEED YOU, I LOVE YOU
Written By: Maurice Mysels, Ira Kosoloff
Elvis Recorded: April 11, 1956–RCA Nashville
Flip Side: My Baby Left Me
On The Charts: *Billboard*'s Top 100 (24 weeks–peaked at #3), Country Best-Seller (2 weeks at #1), Country Juke Box (one week as #1), Rhythm & Blues (peaked at #10)
Sales: One million plus, plus
Singles: I WANT YOU, I NEED YOU, I LOVE YOU/My Baby Left Me, May 1956 Standard 78 RPM release, I WANT YOU, I NEED YOU, I LOVE YOU/My Baby Left Me, May 1956 Standard 45 RPM release, I WANT YOU, I NEED YOU, I LOVE YOU/My Baby Left Me, March 1959 Gold Standard Series reissue
EPs: Elvis Presley, The Real Elvis
LPs: Elvis, Elvis—A Legendary Performer–Vol. 2, Elvis' Golden Records, Elvis: Worldwide 50 Gold Award Hits–Vol. 1, A Golden Celebration, The Number One Hits, The Top Ten Hits

I WANT YOU WITH ME
Written By: Woody Harris
Elvis Recorded: March 12, 1961–RCA Nashville
LPs: Return Of The Rocker, Something For Everybody

I WAS THE ONE
Written By: Aaron Schroeder, Claude DeMetrius, Hal Blair, Bill Pepper
Elvis Recorded: January 11, 1956–RCA Nashville
Flip Side: Heartbreak Hotel
On The Charts: *Billboard*'s Top 100 (16 weeks–peaked at #23), Country (peaked at #11)
Sales: One million plus
Singles: Heartbreak Hotel/I WAS THE ONE, January 1956–Standard 78 RPM release, Heartbreak Hotel/I WAS THE ONE, January 1956–Standard 45 RPM release, March 1959–Gold Standard Series reissue, Heartbreak Hotel/I WAS THE ONE, October 1977–15 Golden Records–30 Golden Hits, I WAS THE ONE/Wear My Ring Around Your Neck, April 1983
EP: Heartbreak Hotel
LPs: Elvis: Worldwide 50 Gold Award Hits–Vol. 1, For LP Fans Only, A Golden Celebration, I Was The One, A Valentine Gift For You

I WASHED MY HANDS IN MUDDY WATER
Written By: Joe Babcock
Previously Recorded By: Stonewall Jackson, Charlie Rich, Johnny Rivers
Elvis Recorded: June 7, 1970–RCA Nashville
LP: Elvis Country

I WILL BE HOME AGAIN
Written By: Bennie Benjamin, Raymond Laveen, Lou Singer
Elvis Recorded: April 4, 1960–RCA Nashville
LP: Elvis Is Back

I WILL BE TRUE
Written By: Ivory Joe Hunter (1952)
Previously Recorded By: Ivory Joe Hunter
Elvis Recorded: May 19, 1971–RCA Nashville
LP: Elvis, Elvis Aron Presley

IF EVERY DAY WAS LIKE CHRISTMAS
Written By: Red West, Glen Spreen
Elvis Recorded: June 10, 1966
Flip Side: How Would You Like To Be
Singles: IF EVERY DAY WAS LIKE CHRISTMAS/How Would You Like To Be, November 1966 Standard release, IF EVERY DAY WAS LIKE CHRISTMAS/How Would You Like To Be, May 1972 Gold Standard Series reissue
LPs: Elvis' Christmas Album, Memories of Christmas

IF I CAN DREAM
Written By: W. Earl Brown
Elvis Recorded: June 29, 1968–NBC–TV (*Elvis*–TV Special)
Flip Side: Edge of Reality
On The Charts: *Billboard*'s Hot 100 (13 weeks–peaked at #12)
Sales: One million plus
Singles: IF I CAN DREAM/Edge of Reality, November 1968 Standard release, IF I CAN DREAM/Edge of Reality, December 1970 Gold Standard Series reissue
LPs: Elvis—A Legendary Performer–Vol. 2, Elvis' Gold Records–Vol. 2, Elvis—TV Special, Elvis: Worldwide 50 Gold Award Hits–Vol. 1, He Walks Beside Me

IF I GET HOME BY CHRISTMAS DAY
Written By: Tony Macaulay, John MacLeod
Elvis Recorded: May 15, 1971–RCA Nashville
LP: Elvis Sings The Wonderful World Of Christmas

IF I WERE YOU
Written By: Gerald Nelson
Elvis Recorded: June 8, 1970–RCA Nashville
LP: Love Letters From Elvis

IF I'M A FOOL (FOR LOVING YOU)
Written By: Stan Kesler
Previously Recorded By: Jimmy Clanton
Elvis Recorded: February 21, 1969–American Sound Studios, Memphis
LP: Let's Be Friends

IF THAT ISN'T LOVE
Written By: Dottie Rambo
Elvis Recorded: December 16, 1973–Stax Studios, Memphis
LP: Good Times

IF THE LORD WASN'T WALKING BY MY SIDE
Written By: Henry Slaughter
Elvis Recorded: May 28, 1966–RCA Nashville
LP: How Great Thou Art

IF WE NEVER MEET AGAIN
Written By: A. E. Burney
Elvis Recorded: October 31, 1960–RCA Nashville
LP: His Hand In Mine

IF YOU DON'T COME BACK
Written By: Jerry Leiber, Mike Stoller
Previously Recorded By: The Drifters
Elvis Recorded: July 21, 1973–Stax Studios, Memphis
LP: Raised On Rock and Roll/For Ol' Times Sake

IF YOU LOVE ME LET ME KNOW
Written By: John Rostill
Previously Recorded By: Olivia Newton–John
Elvis Recorded: Live in concert
LPs: Elvis Aron Presley, Elvis in Concert, Moody Blue

IF YOU TALK IN YOUR SLEEP
Written By: Red West, Johnny Christopher
Elvis Recorded: December 11, 1973–Stax Studios, Memphis
Flip Side: Help Me
On the Charts: *Billboard*'s Hot 100 (13 weeks–peaked at #17), Country (peaked at #6), Easy Listening (peaked at #6)
Singles: IF YOU TALK IN YOUR SLEEP/Help Me, May 1974 Standard release, IF YOU TALK IN YOUR SLEEP/Help Me, May 1974 Disc jockey promotional release, IF YOU TALK IN YOUR SLEEP/Raised On Rock, Gold Standard Series original
LPs: Elvis' Golden Records–Vol. 5, Promised Land

IF YOU THINK I DON'T NEED YOU
Written By: Red West, Joe Cooper
Elvis Recorded: July 9, 1963–Radio Recorders

Recorded For Film: *VIVA LAS VEGAS*
EP: Viva Las Vegas
LPs: Double Dynamite, I Got Lucky

I'LL BE BACK
Written By: Sid Wayne, Ben Weisman
Elvis Recorded: February 17, 1966–Radio Recorders
Recorded For Film: *SPINOUT*
LPs: Spinout

I'LL BE HOME FOR CHRISTMAS
Written By: Walter Kent, Kim Gannon, Buck Ram (1943)
Previously Recorded By: Bing Crosby and others
Elvis Recorded: September 7, 1957–Radio Recorders
EP: Elvis Sings Christmas Songs
LPs: Elvis' Christmas Album, Memories of Christmas

I'LL BE HOME ON CHRISTMAS DAY
Written By: Michael Jarrett
Elvis Recorded: May 16, 1971–RCA Nashville
LPs: Elvis Sings The Wonderful World Of Christmas, Memories Of Christmas

I'LL BE THERE
Written By: Bobby Darin (1960)
Previously Recorded By: Bobby Darin, Tony Orlando, Gerry and the Pacemakers
Elvis Recorded: January 23, 1969–American Sound Studios
LPs: Double Dynamite, Let's Be Friends

I'LL HOLD YOU IN MY HEART (TILL I CAN HOLD YOU IN MY ARMS)
Written By: Eddy Arnold, Hal Horton and Tommy Dilbeck
Previously Recorded By: Eddy Arnold
Elvis Recorded: January 23, 1969–American Sound Studios
LPs: From Elvis in Memphis, The Memphis Record

I'LL NEVER FALL IN LOVE AGAIN
Written By: Jim Currie, Lonnie Donegan
Previously Recorded By: Tom Jones
Elvis Recorded: February 5, 1976–Graceland
LPs: From Elvis Presley Boulevard, Memphis, Tennessee, Our Memories of Elvis

I'LL NEVER KNOW
Written By: Fred Karger, Ben Weisman, Sid Wayne
Elvis Recorded: June 5, 1970–RCA Nashville
LP: Love Letters From Elvis

I'LL NEVER LET YOU GO (LITTLE DARLIN')
Written By: Jimmy Wakely
Previously Recorded By: Jimmy Wakeley, Jimmy Liggins
Elvis Recorded: September 10, 1954–Sun Records
Flip Side: I'm Gonna Sit Right Down And Cry (Over You)
Singles: I'LL NEVER LET YOU GO (LITTLE DARLIN')/I'm Gonna Sit Right Down And Cry (Over You), September 1956 Standard 78 RPM release, I'LL NEVER LET YOU GO (LITTLE DARLIN')/I'm Gonna Sit Right Down And Cry (Over You), September 1956 Standard 45 RPM release, I'LL NEVER LET YOU GO (LITTLE DARLIN')/I'm Gonna Sit Right Down And Cry (Over You), March 1959 Gold Standard Series reissue, I'LL NEVER LET YOU GO (LITTLE DARLIN')/I'm Gonna Sit Right Down And Cry (Over You), December 1986 Collectibles
EPs: Elvis Presley, Elvis Presley—The Most Talked About New Personality in the Last Ten Years of Recorded Music
LPs: The Complete Sun Sessions, Elvis Presley, A Golden Celebration, The Sun Sessions

I'LL REMEMBER YOU
Written By: Kuiokalani Lee
Previously Recorded By: Kuiokalani Lee
Elvis Recorded: June 10, 1966–RCA Nashville
LPs: Elvis–A Legendary Performer–Vol. 4, Aloha From Hawaii via Satellite, The Alternate Aloha, Elvis Aron Presley, Spinout

I'LL TAKE LOVE
Written By: Dolores Fuller, Mark Barkan
Elvis Recorded: September 29, 1966–Radio Recorders
Recorded for Film: *EASY COME, EASY GO* (1966)
EP: Easy Come, Easy Go
LP: C'mon Everybody

I'LL TAKE YOU HOME AGAIN, KATHLEEN
Written By: Thomas Westendorf (1876)
Previously Recorded By: Slim Whitman
Elvis Recorded: May 19, 1971–RCA Nashville
LPs: Elvis, Elvis Aron Presley

I'M COMIN' HOME
Written By: Charlie Rich
Previously Recorded By: Carol Mann
Elvis Recorded: March 12, 1961–RCA Nashville
LPs: Return of the Rocker, Something For Everybody

I'M COUNTING ON YOU
Written By: Don Robertson
Elvis Recorded: January 11, 1956–RCA Nashville
Flip Side: I Got A Woman
Singles: I Got A Woman/I'M COUNTING ON YOU, September 1956 Standard 78 RPM release I Got A Woman/I'M COUNTING ON YOU, September 1956 Standard 45 RPM release Blue Suede Shoes/I'M COUNTING ON YOU, September 1956 Disc jockey prevue I Got A Woman/I'M COUNTING ON YOU, March 1959 Gold Standard Series reissue
I Got A Woman/I'M COUNTING ON YOU, December 1986 Collectibles
EPs: Elvis Presley, Elvis Presley—The Most Talked About New Personality in the Last Ten Years of Recorded Music
LP: Elvis Presley

I'M FALLING IN LOVE TONIGHT
Written By: Don Robertson
Elvis Recorded: September 22, 1962–Radio Recorders
Recorded For Film: *IT HAPPENED AT THE WORLD'S FAIR*
LPs: Elvis Aron Presley, It Happened At The World's Fair

I'M GONNA SIT RIGHT DOWN AND CRY (OVER YOU)
Written By: Joe Thomas, Howard Briggs
Previously Recorded By: Joe Thomas
Elvis Recorded: January 31, 1956–RCA New York City
Flip Side: I'll Never Let You Go (Little Darlin')
Singles: I'll Never Let You Go (Little Darlin')/I'M GONNA SIT RIGHT DOWN AND CRY (OVER YOU), September 1956 Standard 78 RPM release
I'll Never Let You Go (Little Darlin')/I'M GONNA SIT RIGHT DOWN AND CRY (OVER YOU), September 1956 Standard 45 RPM release
I'll Never Let You Go (Little Darlin')/I'M GONNA SIT RIGHT DOWN AND CRY (OVER YOU), March 1959 Gold Standard Series reissue
I'll Never Let You Go (Little Darlin')/I'M GONNA SIT RIGHT DOWN AND CRY (OVER YOU), December 1986 Collectibles
EPs: Elvis Presley, Elvis Presley—The Most Talked About New Personality in the Last Ten Years of Recorded Music, Save—On Records
LPs: Elvis Presley

I'M GONNA WALK DEM GOLDEN STAIRS
Written By: Cully Holt
Elvis Recorded: October 31, 1960–RCA Nashville
LPs: His Hand In Mine, Known Only To Him

I'M LEAVIN'
Elvis Recorded: May 20, 1971–RCA Nashville
Flip Side: Heart of Rome
On The Charts: *Billboard*'s Hot 100 (9 weeks–peaked at #36)
Easy-Listening (peaked at #2)
Singles: I'M LEAVING'/ Heart Of Rome, July 1971 Standard release
I'M LEAVIN'/ Heart of Rome, May 1972 Gold Standard Series reissue
LPs: Elvis Aron Presley

I'M LEFT, YOU'RE RIGHT, SHE'S GONE
Written By: Stanley Kesler, Bill Taylor
Elvis Recorded: December 18, 1954–Sun Records
Flip Side: Baby Let's Play House
Singles: Baby Let's Play House/I'M LEFT, YOU'RE RIGHT, SHE'S GONE, April 1955 Sun Standard 78–45 RPM release, Baby Let's Play House/I'M LEFT, YOU'RE RIGHT, SHE'S GONE, November 1955 RCA reissue Sun 78 RPM, Baby Let's Play House/I'M LEFT, YOU'RE RIGHT, SHE'S GONE, November 1955 RCA reissue Sun 45 RPM, Baby Let's Play House/I'M LEFT, YOU'RE RIGHT, SHE'S GONE, March 1959 Gold Standard Series reissue, Baby Let's Play House/I'M LEFT, YOU'RE RIGHT, SHE'S GONE, December 1986 Collectibles
EP: Any Way You Want Me
LPs: The Complete Sun Sessions, For LP Fans Only, A Golden Celebration, The Sun Sessions

I'M MOVIN' ON
Written By: Hank Snow (1945)
Previously Recorded By: Hank Snow, Ray Charles, Don Gibson
Elvis Recorded: January 15, 1969–American Sound Studios, Memphis
LPs: Elvis—A Canadian Tribute, From Elvis in Memphis, Guitar Man, The Memphis Record

I'M NOT THE MARRYING KIND
Written By: Mack David, Sherman Edwards
Elvis Recorded: July 5, 1961–RCA Nashville, Recorded For Film: FOLLOW THAT DREAM
EP: Follow That Dream
LP: C'mon Everybody

I'M SO LONESOME I COULD CRY
Written By: Hank Williams (1949)
Previously Recorded By: Hank Williams, B. J. Thomas, Leon Russell
Elvis Recorded: Live in concert
EPs: Aloha From Hawaii Via Satellite
LPs: Aloha From Hawaii Via Satellite, The Alternate Aloha, Welcome To My World

I'M YOURS
Written By: Don Robertson, Hal Blair
Elvis Recorded: June 26, 1961–RCA Nashville
Recorded For Film: TICKLE ME
Flip Side: (It's A) Long Lonely Highway
On The Charts: Billboard's Hot 100 (11 weeks–peaked at #11), Easy-Listening (3 weeks–peaked at #1)
Sales: One million plus
Singles: I'M YOURS/(It's A) Long Lonely Highway, August 1965 Standard release, I'M YOURS/(It's A) Long Lonely Highway, November 1966 Gold Standard Series reissue

THE IMPOSSIBLE DREAM
Written By: Joe Darion, Mitch Leigh (Man Of La Mancha)
Previously Recorded By: Richard Kiley, Jack Jones, The Hesitations
Elvis Recorded: Live in concert
Flip Side: An American Trilogy
Singles: THE IMPOSSIBLE DREAM/An American Trilogy, August 1982 Promotional copy only
LPs: Elvis As Recorded At Madison Square Garden, He Walks Beside Me

IN MY FATHER'S HOUSE
Written By: Aileene Hanks (1953)
Elvis Recorded: October 31, 1960–RCA Nashville
LPs: His Hand In Mine

IN MY WAY
Written By: Fred Wise, Ben Weisman
Elvis Recorded: November 7, 1960–Radio Recorders
Recorded For Film: WILD IN THE COUNTRY
LPs: Elvis For Everyone, Separate Ways

IN THE GARDEN
Written By: C. Austin Miles (1912)
Elvis Recorded: May 27, 1966–RCA Nashville
LPs: How Great Thou Art

IN THE GHETTO
Written By: Mac Davis
Elvis Recorded: January 21, 1969–American Sound Studios, Memphis
Flip Side: Any Day Now
On The Charts: Billboard's Hot 100 (13 weeks–peaked at #3), Country (peaked at #60), British (peaked at #2)
Singles: IN THE GHETTO/ Any Day Now, April 1969 Standard release IN THE GHETTO/ Any Day Now, December 1970 Gold Standard Series reissue, IN THE GHETTO/ Any Day Now, October 1977 15 Golden Records–30 Golden Hits, IN THE GHETTO/ If I Can Dream, October 1984 Elvis' Greatest Hits–Golden Singles–Vol. 1 (Boxed Set)
LPs: Elvis—A Legendary Performer–Vol. 3, Elvis Aron Presley, Elvis' Gold Records–Vol. 5, Elvis in Person, Elvis: Worldwide 50 Gold Award Hits–Vol. 1, From Elvis in Memphis, From Memphis to Vegas/From Vegas to Memphis, The Memphis Record, Pure Gold, The Top Ten Hits

IN YOUR ARMS
Written By: Aaron Schroeder, Wally Gold
Elvis Recorded: March 12, 1961–RCA Nashville
LP: Something For Everybody

INDESCRIBABLY BLUE
Written By: Darrell Glenn
Elvis Recorded: June 10, 1966–RCA Nashville
Flip Side: Fools Fall In Love
On The Charts: Billboard's Hot 100 (8 weeks–peaked at #33)
Singles: INDESCRIBABLY BLUE/Fools Fall In Love, January 1967 Standard release, INDESCRIBABLY BLUE/Fools Fall In Love, January 1967 Gold Standard reissue
LP: Elvis' Gold Records–Vol. 4

INHERIT THE WIND
Written By: Eddie Rabbitt
Elvis Recorded: January 16, 1969–American Sound Studios, Memphis
LPs: Back In Memphis, From Memphis To Vegas/From Vegas To Memphis, The Memphis Record

IS IT SO STRANGE
Written By: Faron Young
Previously Recorded By: Faron Young
Elvis Recorded: January 19, 1957–Radio Recorders
EP: Just For You
LPs: A Date With Elvis, Essential Elvis–Vol. 2, Separate Ways

ISLAND OF LOVE (KAUAI)
Written By: Sid Tepper, Roy C. Bennett
Elvis Recorded: March 22, 1961–Radio Recorders
Recorded For Film: BLUE HAWAII
LP: Blue Hawaii

IT AIN'T NO BIG THING (BUT IT'S GROWING)
Written By: Merritt, Joy Hall
Recorded: June 6, 1970–RCA Nashville
LP: Love Letters From Elvis

IT FEELS SO RIGHT
Written By: Fred Wise and Ben Weisman
Elvis Recorded: March 21, 1960
Recorded For Film: TICKLE ME (1965)
Flip Side: (Such An) Easy Question
On The Charts: Billboard's Hot 100 (6 weeks–peaked at #55)
Singles: (Such An) Easy Question/IT FEELS SO RIGHT, May 1965 Standard release, (Such An) Easy Question/IT FEELS SO RIGHT, November 1966 Gold Standard Series reissue
LPs: Elvis Is Back, A Valentine Gift For You

IT HURTS ME
Written By: Joy Byers, Charlie Daniels
Elvis Recorded: January 12, 1964–RCA Nashville
Flip Side: Kissin' Cousins

On The Charts: *Billboard*'s Hot 100 (7 weeks–peaked at #29)
Singles: **Kissin' Cousins/IT HURTS ME**, January 1964 Standard release, **Kissin' Cousins/IT HURTS ME**, May 1965 Gold Standard Series reissue
LPs: **Elvis—A Legendary Performer–Vol. 3, Elvis' Gold Records–Vol. 4, Elvis: The Other Sides—Worldwide Gold Award Hits–Vol. 2**

IT KEEPS RIGHT ON A-HURTIN'
Written By: Johnny Tillotson
Previously Recorded By: Johnny Tillotson, Margaret Whiting
Elvis Recorded: February 20, 1969–American Sound Studios, Memphis
LPs: **From Elvis in Memphis, The Memphis Record**

IT WON'T BE LONG
Written By: Sid Wayne, Ben Weisman
Elvis Recorded: June 1966–Radio Recorders
Recorded For Film: *DOUBLE TROUBLE* (1967)
LP: **Double Trouble**

IT WON'T SEEM LIKE CHRISTMAS (WITHOUT YOU)
Written By: J. A. Balthorp
Elvis Recorded: May 15, 1971–RCA Nashville
LP: **Elvis Sings The Wonderful World Of Christmas**

ITO EATS
Written By: Sid Tepper, Roy C. Bennett
Elvis Recorded: March 22, 1961–Radio Recorders
Recorded For Film: *BLUE HAWAII* (1961)
LP: **Blue Hawaii**

IT'S A MATTER OF TIME
Written By: Clive Westlake
Elvis Recorded: March 29, 1972–RCA Hollywood
Flip Side: **Burning Love**
On The Charts: *Billboard*'s Country (13 weeks–peaked at #36), Easy-Listening (peaked at #9)
Singles: **Burning Love/IT'S A MATTER OF TIME**
August 1972 Standard release
LPs: **Double Dynamite, Burning Love And Other Hits From His Movies–Vol. 2,**
IT'S A SIN
Written By: Zeb Turner, Fred Rose
Previously Recorded By: Eddy Arnold, Marty Robbins
Elvis Recorded: March 12, 1961–RCA Nashville
LP: **Something For Everybody**

IT'S A WONDERFUL WORLD
Written By: Sid Tepper, Roy C. Bennett
Elvis Recorded: March 1964–Radio Recorders
Recorded For Film: *ROUSTABOUT* (1964)
Lps: **Roustabout**

IT'S CARNIVAL TIME
Written By: Ben Weisman, Sid Wayne
Elvis Recorded: March 1964–Radio Recorders
Recorded For Film: *ROUSTABOUT* (1964)
LP: **Roustabout**

IT'S EASY FOR YOU
Written By: Andrew Lloyd Weber, Tim Rice
Elvis Recorded: October 30, 1976–Graceland
LP: **Moody Blue**

IT'S IMPOSSIBLE
Written By: Sid Wayne, Armando Manzanero
Previously Recorded By: Perry Como
Elvis Recorded: Live in concert (Several occasions in the 1970s)
LP: **Elvis, Pure Gold**

IT'S MIDNIGHT
Written By: Billy Edd Wheeler, Jerry Chestnut

Elvis Recorded: December 10, 1973–Stax Records
Flip Side: **Promised Land**
On The Charts: *Billboard*'s Country (14 weeks–peaked at #9), Easy-Listening (peaked at #8)
Singles: **Promised Land/IT'S MIDNIGHT**, October 1974 Standard release, **Promised Land/IT'S MIDNIGHT**, October 1974 Disc jockey promotional release, **Promised Land/IT'S MIDNIGHT**, February 1976 Gold Standard Series reissue
LPs: **Always On My Mind, Our Memories of Elvis, Promised Land**

IT'S NO SECRET (WHAT GOD CAN DO)
Written By: Stuart Hamblen
Previously Recorded By: Red Foley, The Andrews Sisters, Jo Stafford, Bill Kenny, The Song Spinners
Elvis Recorded: January 19, 1957–Radio Recorders
EP: **Peace In The Valley**
LPs: **Elvis' Christmas Album, Essential Elvis–Vol. 2, You'll Never Walk Alone**

IT'S NOW OR NEVER
Written By: Aaron Schroeder, Wally Gold
(Based on O Sole Mio by Capurro and di Capua, 1901)
Elvis Recorded: April 3, 1960–RCA Nashville
Flip Side: **A Mess of Blues**
On The Charts: *Billboard*'s Hot 100 (20 weeks–peaked at #1), Rhythm & Blues (peaked at #7), British (8 weeks–peaked at #1)
Sales: Over 22 Million Worldwide
Singles: **IT'S NOW OR NEVER/A Mess of Blues,** July 1960 Standard 45 RPM Release
IT'S NOW OR NEVER/A Mess of Blues, July 1960 Living Stereo release, **IT'S NOW OR NEVER/A Mess of Blues,** February 1962 Gold Standard Series reissue, **IT'S NOW OR NEVER/A Mess of Blues,** October 1977 15 Golden Records–30 Golden Hits, (Boxed Set), **IT'S NOW OR NEVER/Surrender,** October 1984 Elvis' Greatest Hits–Golden Singles–Vol. 1
EP: **Elvis By Request**
LPs: **Elvis, Elvis—A Legendary Performer–Vol. 2, Elvis Aron Presley, Elvis' Golden Records–Vol. 3, Elvis In Concert, Elvis: Worldwide 50 Gold Award Hits–Vol. 1, The Number One Hits, The Top Ten Hits**

IT'S ONLY LOVE
Written By: Mark James, Steve Tyrell
Previously Recorded By: B. J. Thomas
Elvis Recorded: May 21, 1971–RCA Nashville
Flip Side: **The Sound Of Your Cry**
On The Charts: *Billboard*'s Hot 100 (6 weeks–peaked at #51), Easy-Listening (peaked at #19)
Sales: One million plus
Singles: **IT'S ONLY LOVE/The Sound Of Your Cry,** September 1971 Standard release, **IT'S ONLY LOVE/The Sound Of Your Cry,** May 1972 Gold Standard Series reissue
LP: **Elvis Aron Presley**

IT'S OVER
Written By: Jimmie Rodgers
Previously Recorded By: Jimmie Rodgers, Eddy Arnold
Elvis Recorded: Live in concert (Mid 70s)
LPs: **Aloha From Hawaii Via Satellite, The Alternate Aloha**

IT'S STILL HERE
Written By: Ivory Joe Hunter
Elvis Recorded: May 19, 1971–RCA Nashville
LPs: **Elvis, Elvis Aron Presley, Elvis In Nashville**

IT'S YOUR BABY, YOU ROCK IT
Written By: Shirl Milete, Nora Fowler
Elvis Recorded: June 5, 1970–RCA Nashville
LPs: **Elvis Country, Elvis In Nashville**

I'VE GOT A THING ABOUT YOU BABY
Written By: Tony Joe White
Previously Recorded By: Billy Lee Riley
Elvis Recorded: July 22, 1973–Stax Studios, Memphis
Flip Side: **Take Good Care Of Her**

On The Charts: *Billboard*'s Hot 100 (12 weeks–peaked at #39), Country (peaked at #4), Easy-Listening (peaked at #27)
Singles: I'VE GOT A THING ABOUT YOU BABY/Take Good Care Of Her, January 1974 Standard release, I'VE GOT A THING ABOUT YOU BABY/Take Good Care Of Her, January 1974 Disc jockey promotional release, I'VE GOT A THING ABOUT YOU BABY/Take Good Care Of Her, March 1976 Gold Standard Series reissue
LPs: Good Times, This Is Elvis

I'VE GOT CONFIDENCE
Written By: Andrae Crouch
Elvis Recorded: May 18, 1971–RCA Nashville
LP: He Touched Me

I'VE GOT TO FIND MY BABY
Written By: Joy Byers
Elvis Recorded: June 1964–Radio Recorders
Recorded For Film: *GIRL HAPPY*
LP: Girl Happy

I'VE LOST YOU
Written By: Ken Howard, Alan Blaikley
Previously Recorded By: Matthew's Southern Comfort
Elvis Recorded: June 4, 1970–RCA Nashville
Flip Side: The Next Step Is Love
On The Charts: *Billboard*'s Hot 100 (9 weeks–peaked at #32), Country (peaked at #57), Easy-Listening (peaked at #5),
Sales: One million plus
Singles: I'VE LOST YOU/The Next Step Is Love, July 1970 Standard release, I'VE LOST YOU/The Next Step Is Love, August 1971 Gold Standard Series reissue
LPs: Always On My Mind, Elvis: The Other Sides—Worldwide Gold Award Hits–Vol. 2, That's The Way It Is

JAILHOUSE ROCK
Written By: Jerry Leiber, Mike Stoller
Elvis Recorded: April 30, 1957–Radio Recorders
Recorded For Film: *JAILHOUSE ROCK* (1957)
Flip Side: Treat Me Nice
On The Charts: *Billboard*'s Top 100 (27 weeks–7 weeks–#1), Country Best-Seller (peaked at #1), Rhythm & Blues (peaked at #1), British (entered at #1)
Sales: Many millions
Singles: JAILHOUSE ROCK/Treat Me Nice, September 1957 Standard 78 RPM release, JAILHOUSE ROCK/Treat Me Nice, September 1957 Standard 45 RPM release, JAIL-HOUSE ROCK/Treat Me Nice, 1961 Gold Standard Series release, The Elvis Medley/Always On My Mind, October 1982, Jailhouse Rock part of medley including Teddy Bear, Hound Dog, Don't Be Cruel, Burning Love and Suspicious Minds, The Elvis Medley/The Elvis Medley, October 1982 Disc jockey promotional release, Heartbreak Hotel/ JAILHOUSE ROCK, October 1984 15 Golden Records–30 Golden Hits JAILHOUSE ROCK/She's Not You, December 1986 Collectibles
EPs: Dealer's Prevue, Extended Play Sampler, Jailhouse Rock
LPs: Elvis, Elvis—A Canadian Tribute, Elvis–A Legendary Performer–Vol. 2, Elvis Aron Presley, Elvis' Golden Records, Elvis In Concert, Elvis In Hollywood, The Elvis Medley, Elvis Recorded Live In Memphis, Elvis–TV Special, Elvis: Worldwide 50 Gold Award Hits–Vol. 1, Essential Elvis—The First Movies, The Number One Hits, Pure Gold, This Is Elvis, The Top Ten Hits

JESUS KNOWS WHAT I NEED
(See: He Knows Just What I need)

JOHNNY B. GOODE
Written By: Chuck Berry
Previously Recorded By: Chuck Berry, Buck Owens, Johnny Winter
Elvis Recorded: Live in concert (1969–77)
LPs: Aloha From Hawaii Via Satellite, Elvis Aron Presley, Elvis In Concert, Elvis In Person, From Memphis to Vegas/From Vegas to Memphis

JOSHUA FIT THE BATTLE
Written By: (traditional spiritual)
Elvis Recorded: October 31, 1960
Flip Side: Known Only To Him

Singles: JOSHUA FIT THE BATTLE/ Known Only To Him, March 1966 Gold Standard Series Original
LPs: His Hand In Mine, Known Only To Him

JUDY
Written By: Teddy Redell
Previously Recorded By: Teddy Redell
Elvis Recorded: March 13, 1961–RCA Nashville
Flip Side: There's Always Me
Released: 1967
On The Charts: *Billboard*'s Hot 100 (5 weeks–peaked at #78)
Singles: There's Always Me/JUDY, August 1967 Standard release, There's Always Me/JUDY, September 1970 Gold Standard Series reissue
EP: The EP Collection–Vol. 2
LPs: Elvis In Nashville, Something For Everybody

JUST A LITTLE BIT
Written By: John Thornton, Piney Brown, Ralph Bass, Earl Washington
Previously Recorded By: Rosco Gordon
Elvis Recorded: July 22, 1973–Stax Studios, Memphis
LPs: Raised On Rock/For Ol' Times Sake

JUST BECAUSE
Written By: Bob Shelton, Joe Shelton, Sid Robin (1937)
Previously Recorded By: Dick Stabile
Elvis Recorded: September 10, 1954–Sun Records
Flip Side: Blue Moon
Singles: Blue Moon/JUST BECAUSE, September 1956 Standard 78 RPM release, Blue Moon/JUST BECAUSE, September 1956 Standard 45 RPM release, Blue Moon/JUST BECAUSE, March 1959 Gold Standard Series reissue
EPs: Elvis Presley, Elvis Presley—The Most Talked About New Personality In The Last Ten Years Of Recorded Music
LPs: The Complete Sun Sessions, Elvis Presley, The Sun Sessions

JUST CALL ME LONESOME
Written By: Rex Griffin
Previously Recorded By: Rex Griffin, Red Foley, Eddy Arnold
Elvis Recorded: September 11, 1967–RCA Nashville
LPs: Clambake, Elvis In Nashville, Guitar Man

JUST FOR OLD TIMES SAKE
Written By: Sid Tepper, Roy C. Bennett
Elvis Recorded: March 18, 1962–RCA Nashville
LP: Pot Luck

JUST PRETEND
Written By: Doug Flett, Guy Fletcher
Elvis Recorded: June 6, 1970–RCA Nashville
LP: That's The Way It Is

JUST TELL HER JIM SAID HELLO
Written By: Jerry Leiber, Mike Stoller
Elvis Recorded: March 19, 1962–RCA Nashville
Flip Side: She's Not You
On The Charts: *Billboard*'s Hot 100 (5 weeks–peaked at #55)
Singles: She's Not You/JUST TELL HER JIM SAID HELLO, July 1962 Standard release She's Not You/JUST TELL HER JIM SAID HELLO, June 1963 Gold Standard Series reissue
LPs: Elvis' Gold Records, Vol. 4, Elvis: The Other Sides–Worldwide Gold Award Hits–Vol. 2

KENTUCKY RAIN
Written By: Eddie Rabbit, Dick Heard
Elvis Recorded: February 19, 1969–American Sound Studios, Memphis
Flip Side: My Little Friend
On The Charts: *Billboard*'s Hot 100 (9 weeks–peaked at #16)
Country Best-Sellers (peaked at #31)
Sales: One million plus
Singles: KENTUCKY RAIN/My Little Friend, February 1971 Standard release, KEN-

TUCKY RAIN/My Little Friend, August 1971 Gold Standard Series reissue
LPs: Elvis Aron Presley, Elvis' Gold Records–Vol. 5, Elvis: Worldwide 50 Gold Award Hits–Vol. 1, The Memphis Record

KING CREOLE
Written By: Jerry Leiber, Mike Stoller
Elvis Recorded: January 23, 1958–Radio Recorders
Recorded For Film: *KING CREOLE* (1958)
EP: King Creole–Vol. 1
LPs: Elvis In Hollywood, Elvis: The Other Sides—Worldwide Gold Award Hits–Vol. 2, King Creole

KING OF THE WHOLE WIDE WORLD
Written By: Ruth Batchelor, Bob Roberts
Elvis Recorded: October 27, 1961–Radio Recorders
Recorded For Film: *KID GALAHAD* (1962)
Flip Side: Home Is Where The Heart Is
On The Charts: *Billboard*'s Hot 100 (7 weeks–peaked at #30)
Singles: KING OF THE WHOLE WIDE WORLD/Home Is Where The Heart Is, May 1962 Disc jockey promo (no general release)
EP: Kid Galahad
LPs: C'mon Everybody, Return Of The Rocker

KISMET
Written By: Sid Tepper, Roy C. Bennett
Elvis Recorded: February 24 1965–RCA Nashville
Recorded For Film: *HARUM SCARUM*
LP: Harum Scarum

KISS ME QUICK
Written By: Doc Pomus, Mort Shuman
Elvis Recorded: June 25, 1961–RCA Nashville
Flip Side: Suspicion
On The Charts: *Billboard*'s Hot 100 (6 weeks–peaked at #34)
Singles: KISS ME QUICK/Suspicion, April 1964 Gold Standard Original Series
LP: Pot Luck

KISSIN' COUSINS
Written By: Fred Wise, Randy Starr
Elvis Recorded: October 1963–RCA Nashville
Recorded For Film: *KISSIN' COUSINS*
Flip Side: It Hurts Me
On The Charts: *Billboard*'s Hot 100 (9 weeks–peaked at #12)
Sales: One million plus
Singles: KISSIN' COUSINS/It Hurts Me, January 1964 Standard release
KISSIN' COUSINS/It Hurts Me, May 1965 Gold Standard Series reissue
LPs: Elvis In Hollywood, Elvis: Worldwide 50 Gold Award Hits–Vol. 1, Kissin' Cousins

KNOWN ONLY TO HIM
Written By: Stuart Hamblen
Previously Recorded By: Stuart Hamblen, George Beverly Shea
Elvis Recorded: October 31, 1960–RCA Nashville
Flip Side: Joshua Fit The Battle

Singles: Joshua Fit The Battle/KNOWN ONLY TO HIM, March 1966 Gold Standard Series Original
LPs: He Walks Beside Me, His Hand In Mine, Known Only To Him

K–U–U–I–P–O (Sweetheart)
Written By: George Weiss, Hugo Peretti, Luigi Creatore
Elvis Recorded: March 21, 1961–Radio Recorders
Recorded For Film: *BLUE HAWAII* (1961)
LPs: Blue Hawaii, Mahalo From Elvis

THE LADY LOVES ME
Written By: Sid Tepper, Roy C. Bennett
Elvis Recorded: July 11, 1963–Radio Recorders
Recorded For Film: *VIVA LAS VEGAS* (1963) Not used
Released: 1983
LP: Elvis: A Legendary Performer–Vol. 4

THE LAST FAREWELL
Written By: Richard Whittaker, R.A. Webster
Elvis Recorded: February 3, 1976–Graceland
On The Charts: *Billboard*'s Hot 100 (peaked at#19)
LP: From Elvis Presley Boulevard, Memphis, Tennessee

LAWDY MISS CLAWDY
Written By: Lloyd Price
Previously Recorded By: Lloyd Price, Gary Stites, The Buckinghams
Elvis Recorded: February 3, 1956–RCA New York City
Flip Side: Shake, Rattle and Roll
Singles: Shake, Rattle and Roll/LAWDY MISS CLAWDY, September 1956 Standard 78 RPM release, Shake, Rattle and Roll/LAWDY MISS CLAWDY, September 1956 Standard 45 RPM release, Shake, Rattle and Roll/LAWDY MISS CLAWDY, March 1959 Gold Standard Series reissue
EP: Elvis Presley
LPs: Elvis Aron Presley, Elvis Recorded Live On Stage In Memphis, Elvis—TV Special, For Elvis Fans Only, A Golden Celebration

LEAD ME, GUIDE ME
Written By: Doris Akers
Previously Recorded By: Doris Akers, George Beverly Shea
Elvis Recorded: May 17, 1971–RCA Nashville
LPs: He Touched Me, Known Only To Him

LET IT BE ME
Written By: Pierre Delanoe and Gilbert Becaud (Translation by Mann Curtis)
Previously Recorded By: Jill Corey, The Everly Brothers, Glen Campbell, Bobbie Gentry, The Sweet Inspirations
Elvis Recorded: Live in concert (1970s)
LPs: Elvis—A Legendary Performer–Vol. 3, On Stage—February 1970

LET ME
Written By: Elvis Presley, Vera Matson, Ken Darby
Elvis Recorded: September 24, 1956–Radio Recorders
Recorded For Film: *LOVE ME TENDER* (1956)
EP: Love Me Tender
LPs: Elvis: The Other Sides—Worldwide Gold Award Hits–Vol. 2, Essential Elvis—The First Movies

LET ME BE THERE
Written by: John Rostill
Previously Recorded By: Olivia Newton–John
Elvis Recorded: Live in concert, (March 1974)
LPs: Elvis Aron Presley, Elvis Recorded Live On Stage In Memphis, Moody Blue

LET US PRAY
Written By: Ben Weisman, Buddy Kaye
Elvis Recorded: September 22, 1969–RCA Nashville
Recorded For Film: *CHANGE OF HABIT* (1969)
LP: You'll Never Walk Alone

LET YOURSELF GO
Written By: Joy Byers
Elvis Recorded: June 1967–MGM Culver City, California
Recorded For Film: *SPEEDWAY*
Flip Side: **Your Time Hasn't Come Yet, Baby**
On The Charts: *Billboard*'s Hot 100 (5 weeks–peaked at #71)
Sales: Almost one million
Singles: **Your Time Hasn't Come Yet, Baby/LET YOURSELF GO,** June 1968 Standard release, **Your Time Hasn't Come Yet, Baby/LET YOURSELF GO,** December 1970 Gold Standard Series reissue
LPs: **Elvis–A Legendary Performer–Vol. 3, Speedway**

LET'S BE FRIENDS
Written By: Chris Arnold, Geoffrey Morrow and David Martin
Elvis Recorded: March 5, 1969–Decca Recording Studios, Universal City, California
Recorded For Film: *CHANGE OF HABIT* (1969, Cut)
LP: **Let's Be Friends**

LET'S FORGET ABOUT THE STARS
Written By: Al Owens
Elvis Recorded: October 15, 1968–Samuel Goldwyn Studios, Los Angeles
Recorded For Film: *CHARRO!* (1968, Not Used)
LP: **Let's Be Friends**

LIFE
Written By: Shirl Milete
Elvis Recorded: June 6, 1970–RCA Nashville
Flip Side: **Only Believe**
On The Charts: *Billboard*'s Hot 100 (7 weeks–peaked at #53), Country (peaked at #34), Easy-Listening (peaked at #8)
Singles: **LIFE/Only Believe,** May 1971 Standard release, **LIFE/Only Believe,** May 1972 Gold Standard Series reissue
LP: **Love Letters From Elvis**

LIKE A BABY
Written By: Jesse Stone
Elvis Recorded: April 3, 1960–RCA Nashville
LPs: **Elvis Is Back, Return Of The Rocker**

A LITTLE BIT OF GREEN
Written By: Chris Arnold, Geoffrey Morrow, Davis Martin
Elvis Recorded: January 14, 1969–American Sound Studios, Memphis
LPs: **Back In Memphis, From Memphis To Vegas/From Vegas to Memphis**

LITTLE CABIN ON THE HILL
Written By: Bill Monroe, Lester Flatt (1948)
Previously Recorded By: Bill Monroe's Bluegrass Mountain Boys
Elvis Recorded: June 4, 1970–RCA Nashville
LPs: **Elvis Country, Elvis In Nashville**

LITTLE DARLIN'
Written By: Maurice Williams
Previously Recorded By: Maurice Williams,The Gladiolas, and The Diamonds
Elvis Recorded: Live in concert (Saginaw, Michigan–1977)
LPs: **Elvis—A Canadian Tribute, Elvis Aron Presley, Moody Blue**

LITTLE EGYPT
Written By: Jerry Leiber, Mike Stoller
Previously Recorded By: The Coasters
Elvis Recorded: March 1964–Radio Recorders
Recorded For Film: *ROUSTABOUT* (1964)
LPs: **Elvis—TV Special, Roustabout**

A LITTLE LESS CONVERSATION
Written By: Billy Strange, Mac Davis
Elvis Recorded: March 7, 1968–Western Recorders
Recorded For Film: *LIVE A LITTLE, LOVE A LITTLE*
Flip Side: **Almost In Love**
On The Charts: *Billboard*'s Hot 100 (4 weeks–peaked at #69)
Singles: **A LITTLE LESS CONVERSATION/Almost In Love,** September 1968 Standard release, **A LITTLE LESS CONVERSATION/Almost In Love,** December 1970 Gold Standard Series reissue
LP: **Almost In Love**

LITTLE SISTER
Written By: Doc Pomus, Mort Shuman
Elvis Recorded: June 26, 1961–RCA Nashville
Flip Side: **(Marie's The Name) His Latest Flame**
On The Charts: *Billboard*'s Hot 100 (13 weeks–peaked at #5), British (4 weeks–peaked at #1)
Sales: One million plus
Singles: **LITTLE SISTER/(Marie's The Name) His Latest Flame,** August 1961 Standard release, **LITTLE SISTER/(Marie's The Name) His Latest Flame,** August 1961 Compact 33 Single release, **LITTLE SISTER/(Marie's The Name) His Latest Flame,** November 1962 Gold Standard Series reissue, **LITTLE SISTER/Paralyzed,** June 1983 New release, **LITTLE SISTER/Paralyzed,** June 1983 Disc jockey promo, **LITTLE SISTER/Rip It Up,** June 1983 12" Single promo, **LITTLE SISTER/(Marie's The Name) His Latest Flame,** October 1984 **Elvis' Greatest Hits–Golden Singles**–Vol. 2
EP: **The EP Collection**–Vol. 2
LPs: **Elvis Aron Presley, Elvis' Golden Records, Vol. 3, Elvis In Concert, Elvis: Worldwide 50 Gold Award Hits–Vol. 1, I Was The One, Return Of The Rocker, The Top Ten Hits**

LONELY MAN
Written By: Bennie Benjamin and Sol Marcus
Elvis Recorded: November 7, 1960
Recorded For Film: *WILD IN THE COUNTRY* (1960)
Flip Side: **Surrender**
On The Charts: *Billboard*'s Hot 100 (5 weeks–peaked at #32)
Singles: **Surrender/LONELY MAN,** February 1961 Standard release, **Surrender/LONELY MAN,** February 1961 Living Stereo release, **Surrender/LONELY MAN,** February 1961 Compact 33 Single release, **Surrender/LONELY MAN,** February 1961 Living Stereo Compact 33 Single release, **Surrender/LONELY MAN,** Gold Standard Series reissue
LPs: **Elvis' Gold Records–Vol. 4, Elvis: The Other Sides—Worldwide Gold Award Hits–Vol. 2**

LONESOME COWBOY
Written By: Sid Tepper, Roy C. Bennett
Elvis Recorded: February 1957–Radio Recorders
Recorded For Film: *LOVING YOU* (1957)
EP: **Loving You**–Vol. 2
LPs: **Elvis: The Other Sides—Worldwide Gold Award Hits–Vol. 2, Essential Elvis—The First Movies, Loving You**

LONG BLACK LIMOUSINE
Written By: Bobby George, Vern Stovall
Previously Recorded By: Gordon Terry, Glen Campbell, Jody Miller
Elvis Recorded: January 13, 1969–American Sound Studios, Memphis
LPs: **From Elvis in Memphis, The Memphis Record**

LONG LEGGED GIRL (WITH THE SHORT DRESS ON)
Written By: J. Leslie McFarland, Winfield Scott
Elvis Recorded: June 1966–Radio Recorders
Recorded For Film: *DOUBLE TROUBLE* (1967)
Flip Side: **That's Someone You Never Forget**
On The Charts: *Billboard*'s Hot 100 (5 weeks–peaked at #63)
Single: **LONG LEGGED GIRL (WITH THE SHORT DRESS ON)/That's Someone You Never Forget,** May 1967 Standard release, **LONG LEGGED GIRL (WITH THE SHORT DRESS ON)/That's Someone You Never Forget,** 1970 Gold Standard Series reissue
LPs: **Almost In Love, Double Trouble, Elvis Sings From His Movies–Vol. 1**

LONG LIVE ROCK AND ROLL
(See: School Day)

LONG LONELY HIGHWAY, (IT'S A)
Written By: Doc Pomus, Mort Shuman
Elvis Recorded: May 27, 1963–RCA Nashville
Appeared In Film: *TICKLE ME* (1965)

Flip Side: I'm Yours
Singles: I'm Yours/(IT'S A) LONG LONELY HIGHWAY, August 1965 Standard release
I'm Yours/(IT'S A) LONG LONELY HIGHWAY, November 1966 Gold Standard Series reissue
LP: Kissin' Cousins

LONG TALL SALLY
Written By: Enotris Johnson, Bumps Blackwell, Richard Penniman (Little Richard)
Previously Recorded By: Little Richard, Pat Boone
Elvis Recorded: September 2, 1956–Radio Recorders
EP: Strictly Elvis
LPs: Aloha From Hawaii Via Satellite, Elvis, Elvis Aron Presley, Elvis Recorded Live On Stage In Memphis, A Golden Celebration

LOOK OUT, BROADWAY
Written By: Fred Wise, Randy Starr
Elvis Recorded: May 1965–Graceland
Recorded For Film: FRANKIE AND JOHNNY (1966)
LP: Frankie and Johnny

LOVE COMING DOWN
Written By: Jerry Chestnut
Elvis Recorded: February 7, 1976–Graceland
LP: From Elvis Presley Boulevard, Memphis, Tennessee

LOVE LETTERS
Written By: Edward Heyman, Victor Young
Previously Recorded By: The Paul Weston Orchestra, Kitty Lester
Elvis Recorded: May 26, 1966–RCA Nashville, Rerecorded: June 7, 1970–RCA Nashville
Flip Side: Come What May
On The Charts: Billboard's Hot 100 (7 weeks–peaked at #19,) Easy-Listening (peaked at #38)
Sales: One million plus
Singles: LOVE LETTERS/Come What May, June 1966 Standard release, LOVE LETTERS/Come What May, February 1968 Gold Standard Series reissue, Frankie and Johnny/LOVE LETTERS December 1986 Collectibles
LPs: Elvis' Gold Records–Vol. 4, Love Letters From Elvis (Recorded June 7, 1970), A Valentine Gift For You

THE LOVE MACHINE
Written By: Gerald Nelson, Fred Burch, Chick Taylor
Elvis Recorded: September 1966–Radio Recorders
Recorded For Film: EASY COME, EASY GO (1967)
EPs: Easy Come, Easy Go
LP: I Got Lucky

LOVE ME
Written By: Jerry Leiber, Mike Stoller
Previously Recorded By: Willie and Ruth, Georgia Gibbs
Elvis Recorded: September 1, 1956–Radio Recorders
On The Charts: Billboard's Top 100 (19 weeks–peaked at #6), Country Disc Jockey (peaked at #10), Country Juke Box (peaked at #10)
Singles: (Not released as single until 1986 Collectibles Series) Flaming Star/LOVE ME December 1986 Collectibles
EPs: Elvis–Vol. 1, Elvis/ Jaye P. Morgan, Perfect For Parties
LPs: Aloha From Hawaii Via Satellite, The Alternate Aloha, Elvis, Elvis, Elvis—A Legendary Performer–Vol. 2, Elvis Aron Presley, Elvis As Recorded at Madison Square Garden, Elvis' Golden Records, Elvis In Concert, Elvis Recorded Live On Stage in Memphis, Elvis: The Other Sides—Worldwide Gold Award Hits–Vol. 2, A Golden Celebration

LOVE ME, LOVE THE LIFE I LEAD
Written By: Tony Macaulay, Roger Greenway
Elvis Recorded: May 21, 1971–RCA Nashville

LP: Elvis

LOVE ME TENDER
Written By: Ken Darby (Based On: Aura Lee, 1861)
Elvis Recorded: August 2, 1956–Radio Recorders
Recorded For Film: LOVE ME TENDER (1956)
Flip Side: Any Way You Want Me
On The Charts: Billboard's Top 100 (9 weeks–peaked at #1), Country Best Seller (peaked at #3), Rhythm & Blues (peaked at #4)
Sales: One million plus, plus
Singles: LOVE ME TENDER/Any Way You Want Me October 1956 Standard 78 RPM release
LOVE ME TENDER/Any Way You Want Me, October 1956 Standard 45 RPM release, LOVE ME TEN-DER/Any Way You Want Me, March 1959 Gold Standard Series reissue, LOVE ME TEN-DER/Any Way You Want Me, October 1977 15 Golden Records–30 Golden Hits (Boxed Set), LOVE ME TENDER/Loving You, Elvis' Greatest Hits—Golden Singles–Vol. 2 (Boxed Set)
EPs: DJ–7, Great Country/Western Hits, Love Me Tender

LPs: Elvis, Elvis—A Legendary Performer–Vol.1, Elvis Aron Presley, Elvis As Recorded At Madison Square Garden, Elvis' Golden Records, Elvis—TV Special, Elvis: Worldwide 50 Gold Award Hits–Vol. 1, Essential Elvis—The First Movies, A Golden Celebration, The Number One Hits, Pure Gold, This Is Elvis, The Top Ten Hits

LOVE ME TONIGHT
Written By: Don Robertson
Elvis Recorded: May 26, 1963–RCA Nashville
LP: Fun In Acapulco

LOVE SONG OF THE YEAR
Written By: Chris Christian
Elvis Recorded: December 12, 1973–Stax Studios, Memphis
LP: Promised Land

LOVER DOLL
Written By: Sid Wayne, Abner Silver
Elvis Recorded: January 16, 1958–Radio Recorders
Recorded For Film: KING CREOLE (1958)
EP: King Creole, Vol. 1
LPs: Elvis: The Other Sides—Worldwide Gold Award Hits–Vol. 2, King Creole

LOVIN' ARMS
Written By: Tom Jans
Previously Recorded By: Dobie Gray, Kris Kristofferson and Rita Coolidge, Petula Clark
Elvis Recorded: December 13, 1973–Stax Studios, Memphis
Flip Side: My Boy
On The Charts: Billboard's Country (15 weeks–peaked at #8), (with new instrumental tracks recorded in 1980)
Singles: My Boy/ LOVIN' ARMS, 1974 Disc jockey promo, LOVIN' ARMS/ You Asked Me To, April 1981 Standard release, LOVIN' ARMS/ You Asked Me To, April 1981 Disc jockey promo
LPs: Good Times, Guitar Man (with new track)

LOVING YOU
Written By: Jerry Leiber, Mike Stoller
Elvis Recorded: February 24, 1957–Radio Recorders
Recorded For Film: *LOVING YOU* (1957)
Flip Side: Teddy Bear
On The Charts: *Billboard*'s Top 100 (22 weeks–peaked at #28), Country Disc Jockey (peaked at #15), Rhythm & Blues (peaked at #1)
Sales: One million plus, plus
Singles: Teddy Bear/LOVING YOU, June 1957 Standard 78 RPM release, Teddy Bear/LOV-ING YOU, June 1957 Standard 45 RPM release, Teddy Bear/LOVING YOU, 1961 Gold Standard Series reissue, Teddy Bear/LOVING YOU, October 1977 15 Golden Records–30 Golden Hits, (Boxed Set), Love Me Tender/LOVING YOU October 1984 Elvis' Greatest Hits–Golden Singles, Vol. 2 (Boxed Set)
EPs: Dealer's Prevue, Loving You–Vol. I
LPs: Elvis, Elvis—A Canadian Tribute, Elvis' Golden Records, Elvis: Worldwide 50 Gold Award Hits–Vol. I, Essential Elvis—The First Movies, Loving You, Pure Gold

MAKE ME KNOW IT
Written By: Otis Blackwell
Elvis Recorded: March 20, 1960–RCA Nashville
LPs: Elvis Is Back, Return Of The Rocker

MAKE THE WORLD GO AWAY
Written By: Hank Cochran,
Previously Recorded By: Ray Price, Timi Yuro, Eddy Arnold
Elvis Recorded: June 7, 1970–RCA Nashville
LPs: Elvis Country, Welcome To My World

MAMA
Written By: Charles O'Curran, Dudley Brooks
Elvis Recorded: March 1962–Radio Recorders
Recorded For Film: *GIRLS! GIRLS! GIRLS!* (1962)
LPs: Double Dynamite, Let's Be Friends

MAMA LIKED THE ROSES
Written By: Johnny Christopher
Elvis Recorded: January 16, 1969–American Sound Studios, Memphis
Flip Side: The Wonder Of You
Singles: The Wonder Of You/MAMA LIKED THE ROSES, May 1970 Standard release The Wonder Of You/MAMA LIKED THE ROSES, August 1971 Gold Standard Series reissue
LPs: Elvis' Christmas Album, The Memphis Record,

MANSION OVER THE HILLTOP
Written By: Ira Stanphill
Previously Recorded By: Red Foley
Elvis Recorded: October 30, 1960–RCA Nashville
LPs: His Hand In Mine

MARGUERITA
Written By: Don Robertson
Elvis Recorded: January 22, 1963–Radio Recorders
Recorded For Film: *FUN IN ACAPULCO*
LP: Fun In Acapulco

MARY IN THE MORNING
Written By: Johnny Cymbal, Michael Rashkow
Previously Recorded By: Al Martino, Tommy Hunter
Elvis Recorded: June 5, 1970–RCA Nashville
LP: That's The Way It Is

MAYBELLENE
Written By: Chuck Berry (based on Bob Wills' *Ida Red*)
Previously Recorded By: Chuck Berry

Elvis Recorded: Live in concert (*Louisiana Hayride* 1955–56)
LP: Elvis: The First Live Recordings

MEAN WOMAN BLUES
Written By: Claude DeMetrius
Elvis Recorded: January 13, 1957–Radio Recorders
Recorded For Film: *LOVING YOU* (1957)
Flip Side: Have I Told You Lately That I Love You
On The Charts: Country Disc Jockey (peaked at #11)
Singles: Have I Told You Lately That I Love You/MEAN WOMAN BLUES, 1957 Disc Jockey prevue
EP: Loving You–Vol. 2
LPs: Elvis Aron Presley—Forever, Elvis: The Other Sides—Worldwide Gold Award Hits–Vol. 2, Essential Elvis—The First Movies, Essential Elvis–Vol. 2, Loving You, This Is Elvis

THE MEANEST GIRL IN TOWN
Written By: Joy Byers
Elvis Recorded: June/July 1964–Radio Recorders
Recorded For Film: *GIRL HAPPY* (1965)
LP: Girl Happy

MEMORIES
Written By: Mac Davis, Billy Strange
Elvis Recorded: June 27, 1968–Western Recorders
Flip Side: Charro
On The Charts: *Billboard*'s Hot 100 (7 weeks–peaked at #35), Country (peaked at #56), Easy-Listening (peaked at #7)
Singles: MEMORIES/Charro, March 1969 Standard release, MEMORIES/Charro December 1970 Gold Standard Series reissue
LPs: Elvis–TV Special, This Is Elvis

MEMPHIS, TENNESSEE
Written By: Chuck Berry
Previously Recorded By: Chuck Berry, Johnny Rivers, Buck Owens
Elvis Recorded: January 12, 1964
EPs: See The USA, The Elvis Way
LP: Elvis For Everyone

MERRY CHRISTMAS, BABY
Written By: Lou Baxter, Johnny Moore
Previously Recorded By: Johnny Moore's Three Blazers, Chuck Berry
Elvis Recorded: May 15, 1971–RCA Nashville
Flip Side: O Come All Ye Faithful
Singles: MERRY CHRISTMAS, BABY/O Come All Ye Faithful, December 1971 Standard release, MERRY CHRISTMAS, BABY/Santa Claus Is Back In Town, November 1985 Standard release
LPs: Elvis Sings The Wonderful World Of Christmas, Memories of Elvis, Reconsider Baby, This Is Elvis

A MESS OF BLUES
Written By: Doc Pomus, Mort Shuman
Elvis Recorded: March 21, 1960–RCA Nashville
Flip Side: It's Now Or Never
On The Charts: *Billboard*'s Hot 100 (11 weeks–peaked at #32)
Sales: One million plus
Singles: It's Now Or Never/A MESS OF BLUES, July 1960 Standard release, It's Now Or Never/A MESS OF BLUES, July 1960 Living Stereo release, It's Now Or Never/A MESS OF BLUES, February 1962 Gold Standard Series reissue, It's Now Or Never/A MESS OF BLUES, October 1977 15 Golden Records–30 Golden Hits (Boxed Set)
LPs: Elvis' Gold Records–Vol. 4, Elvis: Worldwide 50 Gold Award Hits–Vol. I, Return Of The Rocker

MEXICO
Written By: Sid Tepper, Roy C. Bennett
Elvis Recorded: January 22, 1963–Radio Recorders (duet with Larry Domasin)
Recorded For Film: *FUN IN ACAPULCO* (1963)
LP: Fun In Acapulco

MILKCOW BLUES BOOGIE
Written By: James (Kokomo) Arnold as *Milk Cow Blues* (1935)
Previously Recorded By: Bob Crosby, Bob Wills, Ricky Nelson
Elvis Recorded: December 10, 1954–Sun Records
Flip Side: You're A Heartbreaker
Singles: MILKCOW BLUES BOOGIE/You're A Heartbreaker, January 1955 Sun Standard 78 & 45 RPM releases, MILKCOW BLUES BOOGIE/You're A Heartbreaker, November 1955 RCA Standard 78 RPM reissue, MILKCOW BLUES BOOGIE/You're A Heartbreaker, November 1955 RCA Standard 45 RPM reissue, MILKCOW BLUES BOOGIE/You're A Heartbreaker, March 1959 Gold Standard Series reissue, MILK-COW BLUES BOOGIE/You're A Heartbreaker, December 1986 Collectibles
EP: Great Country/Western Hits
LPs: The Complete Sun Sessions, A Date With Elvis, The Sun Sessions

MILKY WHITE WAY
Written By: (Traditional Gospel)
Elvis Recorded: October 30, 1960–RCA Nashville
Flip Side: Swing Down Sweet Chariot
Singles: MILKY WHITE WAY/Swing Down Sweet Chariot, March 1966 Gold Standard Series Original release
LP: His Hand In Mine

MINE
Written By: Sid Tepper, Roy C. Bennett
Elvis Recorded: September 11, 1967–RCA Nashville
LP: Speedway

MIRACLE OF THE ROSARY
Written By: Lee Denson
Elvis Recorded: May 19, 1971–RCA Nashville
LP: Elvis Now, He Walks Beside Me

MIRAGE
Written By: Bill Giant, Bernie Baum, Florence Kaye
Elvis Recorded: February 24, 1965–RCA Nashville
Recorded For Film: *HARUM SCARUM* (1965)
LP: Harum Scarum

MR. SONGMAN
Written By: Donnie Summer
Elvis Recorded: December 12, 1973–Stax Studios, Memphis
Flip Side: T–R–O–U–B–L–E
Singles: T–R–O–U–B–L–E/MR. SONGMAN, April 1975 Standard release, T–R–O–U–B–L–E/MR. SONGMAN, February 1976 Gold Standard Series reissue
LP: Promised Land

MONA LISA
Written By: Jay Livingston, Ray Evans
Previously Recorded By: Nat King Cole, Conway Twitty, Dennis Day
Elvis Recorded: Mid–60s–Graceland (found on tape recorder), Released: 1983
LP: Elvis—A Legendary Performer—Vol. 4

MONEY HONEY
Written By: Jesse Stone
Previously Recorded By: The Drifters
Elvis Recorded: January 10, 1956–RCA New York City
Flip Side: One–Sided Love Affair
On The Charts: *Billboard*'s Top 100 (EP: 5 weeks–peaked at #76)
Singles: MONEY HONEY/One–Sided Love Affair, September 1956 Standard 78 RPM release, MONEY HONEY/One–Sided Love Affair, September 1956 Standard 45 RPM release, MONEY HONEY/I Got A Woman, September 1956 Disc jockey prevue, MONEY HONEY/One–Sided Love Affair, March 1959 Gold Standard Series reissue, MONEY HONEY/One–Sided Love Affair, December 1986 Collectibles
EPs: Elvis Presley–The Most Talked About New Performer In The Last Ten Years Of Recorded Music, Heartbreak Hotel
LPs: Elvis Aron Presley, Elvis Presley, A Golden Celebration

MOODY BLUE
Written By: Mark James

Previously Recorded By: Mark James
Elvis Recorded: February 5, 1974–Graceland
Flip Side: She Still Thinks I Care
On The Charts: *Billboard*'s Hot 100 (13 weeks–peaked at #31), Country Best-Sellers (peaked at #1), Easy-Listening (peaked at #2)
Singles: MOODY BLUE/She Still Thinks I Care, December 1976 Standard release, MOODY BLUE/She Still Thinks I Care December 1976 Disc jockey promo, MOODY BLUE/For The Heart, August 1978 Gold Standard Series Original release
LPs: Elvis' Gold Record –Vol. 5, Moody Blue, This Is Elvis

MOONLIGHT SWIM
Written By: Sylvia Dee, Ben Weisman
Previously Recorded By: Nick Noble, Tony Perkins
Elvis Recorded: March 22, 1961–Radio Recorders
Recorded For Film: *BLUE HAWAII* (1961)
LP: Blue Hawaii

MY BABE
Written By: Willie Dixon, Charles Stone
Previously Recorded By: Little Walter Jacobs
Elvis Recorded: Live in concert (1969)
LPs: Elvis Aron Presley, Elvis In Person, From Memphis To Vegas/From Vegas To Memphis

MY BABY LEFT ME
Written By: Arthur Crudup
Previously Recorded By: Arthur Crupup
Elvis Recorded: January 30, 1956–RCA New York City
Flip Side: I Want You, I Need You, I Love You
On The Charts: *Billboard*'s Top 100 (14 weeks–peaked at #31), Country Best-Seller (peaked at #13)
Singles: I Want You, I Need You, I Love You/MY BABY LEFT ME, May 1956 Standard 78 RPM release, I Want You, I Need You, I Love You/MY BABY LEFT ME, May 1956 Standard 45 RPM release, I Want You, I Need You, I Love You/MY BABY LEFT ME, March 1959 Gold Standard Series reissue
EPs: Elvis Presley, The Real Elvis
LPs: Elvis Recorded Live On Stage In Memphis, Elvis: The Other Sides—Worldwide Gold Award Hits–Vol. 2, For LP Fans Only, I Was The One, Reconsider Baby, This Is Elvis

MY BABY'S GONE
(See: I'm Left, You're Right, She's Gone)

MY BOY
Written by: J. Claude Francois, Jean–Pierre Boutayre
(English Translation: Bill Martin, Phil Coulter)
Previously Recorded By: Richard Harris
Elvis Recorded: December 12, 1973–Stax Studios, Memphis
Flip Side: Thinking About You
On The Charts: *Billboard*'s Hot 100 (11 weeks–peaked at #20), Country Best-Sellers (peaked at #14)
Singles: MY BOY/Thinking About You, January 1975 Standard release, MY BOY/Thinking About You, January 1975 Disc jockey promo, MY BOY/Loving Arms, 1974 Disc jockey promo, MY BOY/Thinking About You, Gold Standard Series reissue, Always On My Mind/MY BOY, July 1985 Gold Standard Series reissue
LPs: Always On My Mind, Good Times, Our Memories

MY DESERT SERENADE
Written By: Stan Gelber
Elvis Recorded: February 24, 1965–RCA Nashville
Recorded For Film: *HARUM SCARUM* (1965)
LP: Harum Scarum

MY HEART CRIES FOR YOU
Written By: Carl Sigman, Percy Faith
Previously Recorded By: Vic Damone, Guy Mitchell, Dinah Shore
Elvis Recorded: Home Tape Recorder Mid 60s–Graceland
LP: A Golden Celebration

MY LITTLE FRIEND
Written By: Shirl Milete
Elvis Recorded: January 16, 1969–American Sound Studios, Memphis
Flip Side: Kentucky Rain
Singles: Kentucky Rain/MY LITTLE FRIEND, February 1970 Standard release, Kentucky Rain/MY LITTLE FRIEND, August 1971 Gold Standard Series reissue
LP: Almost In Love

MY WAY
Written By: Gilles Thibault, Claude Francois and Jacques Revaux
(English Lyrics By: Paul Anka)
Previously Recorded By: Frank Sinatra, Brook Benton
Elvis Recorded: Live in concert
Flip Side: America The Beautiful
On The Charts: Billboard's Hot 100 (12 weeks–peaked at #21), Easy-Listening (peaked at #6)
Sales: One million plus
Singles: MY WAY/America The Beautiful, November 1977 Standard release, MY WAY/America The Beautiful, November 1977 Disc jockey promo, Way Down/ MY WAY, May 1979 Gold Standard Series Original release
EP: Aloha From Hawaii
LPs: Aloha From Hawaii Via Satellite, The Alternate Aloha, Elvis—A Canadian Tribute, Elvis In Concert, This Is Elvis

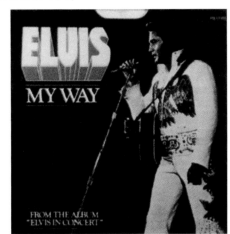

MY WISH CAME TRUE
Written By: Ivory Joe Hunter
Elvis Recorded: September 6, 1957–Radio Recorders
Flip Side: A Big Hunk O' Love
On The Charts: Billboard's Hot 100 (11 weeks–peaked at #12), Rhythm & Blues (peaked at #15)
Singles: A Big Hunk O' Love/MY WISH CAME TRUE, July 1959 Standard release, A Big Hunk O' Love/MY WISH CAME TRUE February 1962 Gold Standard Series reissue, A Big Hunk O' Love/MY WISH CAME TRUE December 1986 Collectibles
LPs: Elvis: The Other Sides—Worldwide Gold Award Hits—Vol. 2, 50,000,000 Elvis Fans Can't Be Wrong—Elvis Gold Records—Vol. 2

MYSTERY TRAIN
Written By: Herman (Little Junior) Parker, Sam Phillips
Previously Recorded By: "Little Junior" Parker
Elvis Recorded: July 11, 1955–Sun Records
Flip Side: I Forgot To Remember To Forget,
On The Charts: Billboard's Country Disc Jockey (peaked at #11),
Singles: MYSTERY TRAIN/I Forgot To Remember To Forget, August 1955 Sun Standard release 78 and 45 RPM release, MYSTERY TRAIN/I Forgot To Remember To Forget, November 1955 RCA Standard 78 RPM reissue, MYSTERY TRAIN/I Forgot To Remember To Forget, November 1955 RCA Standard 45 RPM reissue, MYSTERY TRAIN/I Forgot To Remember To Forget, March 1959 Gold Standard Series reissue
EPs: Any Way You Want Me, Great Country/Western Hits
LPs: The Complete Sun Sessions, Elvis Aron Presley, Elvis In Person, For LP Fans Only, From Memphis To Vegas/From Vegas To Memphis, The Sun Sessions

NEVER AGAIN
Written By: Billy Edd Wheeler, Jerry Chestnut
Elvis Recorded: February 7, 1976–Graceland
LPs: From Elvis Presley Boulevard, Memphis, Tennessee; Our Memories Of Elvis–Vol. 1

NEVER BEEN TO SPAIN
Written By: Hoyt Axton
Previously Recorded By: Three Dog Night
Elvis Recorded: Live in concert (June 10, 1972)
LP: Elvis As Recorded At Madison Square Garden

NEVER ENDING
Written By: Buddy Kaye, Phil Springer
Elvis Recorded: May 26, 1963–RCA Nashville
Flip Side: Such A Night
Singles: Such A Night/NEVER ENDING, July 1964 Standard release, Such A Night/NEVER ENDING, May 1965 Gold Standard Series reissue
LP: Double Trouble

NEVER SAY YES
Written By: Doc Pomus, Mort Shuman
Elvis Recorded: February 16, 1966–Radio Recorders
Recorded For Film: SPINOUT (1966)
LP: Spinout

NEW ORLEANS
Written By: Sid Tepper, Roy C. Bennett
Elvis Recorded: January 15, 1958–Radio Recorders
Recorded For Film: KING CREOLE (1958)
EPs: King Creole–Vol. 1, See The U.S.A. The Elvis Way
LPs: Elvis: The Other Sides–Worldwide Gold Award Hits–Vol. 2, King Creole

THE NEXT STEP IS LOVE
Written By: Paul Evans, Paul Parnes
Elvis Recorded: June 7, 1960–RCA Nashville
Filp Side: I've Lost You
On The Charts: Billboard's Hot 100 (9 weeks–peaked at #32), Easy-Listening (10 weeks–peaked at #5), Country Best-Sellers (6 weeks–peaked at #57)
Singles: I've Lost You/THE NEXT STEP IS LOVE, July 1970 Standard release, I've Lost You/THE NEXT STEP IS LOVE, August 1971 Gold Standard Series reissue
LPs: Elvis: The Other Sides—Worldwide Gold Award Hits–Vol. 2, That's The Way It Is

NIGHT LIFE
Written By: Bill Giant, Bernie Baum, Florence Kaye
Elvis Recorded: July 1963–Radio Recorders
Recorded For Film: VIVA LAS VEGAS (Not used)
Released: 1968
LPs: Elvis Sings Flaming Star, Singer Presents Elvis Singing Flaming Star And Others

NIGHT RIDER
Written By: Doc Pomus, Mort Shuman
Elvis Recorded: March 18, 1962–RCA Nashville
Used In Film: TICKLE ME (1965)
EP: Tickle Me
LPs: Elvis In Nashville, Pot Luck

NO MORE
Written By: Don Robertson, Hal Blair
Elvis Recorded: March 21, 1961–Radio Recorders
Recorded For Film: BLUE HAWAII (1961)
LPs: Blue Hawaii, Burning Love And Hits From His Movies–Vol. 2, Elvis Aron Presley–Forever, Mahalo From Elvis

(THERE'S) NO ROOM TO RHUMBA IN A SPORTS CAR
Written By: Fred Wise, Dick Manning
Elvis Recorded: January 23, 1963–Radio Recorders
Recorded For Film: FUN IN ACAPULCO (1963)
LP: Fun In Acapulco

NOTHINGVILLE
Written By: Billy Strange and Mac Davis
Elvis Recorded: June 21, 1968–Western Recorders

Recorded For: *ELVIS–TV SPECIAL* (1968)
LP: **Elvis–TV Special**

O COME ALL YE FAITHFUL (Adeste Fideles)
Written By: (Traditional Christmas Carol)
Elvis Recorded: May 16, 1971–Radio Recorders
Flip Side: **Merry Christmas, Baby**
Singles: **Merry Christmas, Baby/ O COME ALL YE FAITHFUL**, December 1971 Standard release
LPs: **Elvis Sings The Wonderful World Of Christmas, Memories Of Christmas**

OH LITTLE TOWN OF BETHLEHEM
Written By: Phillips Brooks, Lewis H. Redner (1868)
Elvis Recorded: September 7, 1957–Radio Recorders
LPs: **Christmas With Elvis, Elvis Christmas Album**

OLD MACDONALD
Written By: Traditional Children's Song
Elvis Recorded: June 1966–Radio Recorders
Recorded For Film: *DOUBLE TROUBLE* (1967)
LPs: **Double Trouble, Elvis Sings For Children and Grownups Too!, Elvis Sings From His Movies–Vol. 1**

OLD SHEP
Written By: Red Foley, Willis Arthur (1933)
Previously Recorded By: Red Foley
Elvis Recorded: September 2, 1956–Radio Recorders
(Elvis sang **OLD SHEP** in his first public appearance at the Mississippi–Alabama Fair And Dairy Show–1945)
Singles: **OLD SHEP/blank**, December 1956 Disc jockey promo, **OLD SHEP/You'll Never Walk Alone**, December 1986 Collectibles
EPs: **Elvis–Vol. 2**, Promotion Disc (RCA PRO–12
LPs: **Double Dynamite, Elvis, Elvis Sings For Children and Grownups Too!, Separate Ways**

ON A SNOWY CHRISTMAS NIGHT
Written By: Stanley A. Gelber
Elvis Recorded: May 16, 1971–RCA Nashville
LPs: **Elvis Sings The Wonderful World Of Christmas**

ONCE IS ENOUGH
Written By: Sid Tepper, Roy C. Bennett
Elvis Recorded: October 1963–RCA Nashville
Recorded For Film: *KISSIN' COUSINS* (1964)
LP: **Kissin' Cousins**

ONE BOY, TWO LITTLE GIRLS
Written By: Bill Giant, Bernie Baum and Florence Kaye
Elvis Recorded: October 1963–RCA Nashville
Recorded For Film: *KISSIN' COUSINS* (1964)
LP: **Kissin' Cousins**

ONE BROKEN HEART FOR SALE
Written By: Otis Blackwell, Winfield Scott
Elvis Recorded: September 1962–Radio Recorders
Recorded For Film: *IT HAPPENED AT THE WORLD'S FAIR* (1963)
Flip Side: **They Remind Me Too Much Of You**
On The Charts: *Billboard*'s Hot 100 (9 weeks–peaked at #11), Rhythm & Blues (peaked at #21)
Singles: **ONE BROKEN HEART FOR SALE/They Remind Me Too Much Of You**, February 1963 Standard release, **ONE BROKEN HEART FOR SALE/They Remind Me Too Much Of You**, August 1964 Gold Standard Series reissue, **ONE BROKEN HEART FOR SALE/You're The Devil In Disguise**, December 1986 Collectibles
LPs: **Elvis: Worldwide 50 Gold Award Hits, Vol. 1, It Happened At The World's Fair, Mahalo From Hawaii**

ONE NIGHT
Written By: Dave Bartholomew, Pearl King
Elvis Recorded: January 24, 1957–Radio Recorders

Flip Side: **I Got Stung**
On The Charts: *Billboard*'s Hot 100 (17 weeks–peaked at #4), Country Best-Sellers (peaked at #24), Rhythm & Blues (Peaked at #10), British (peaked at #1)
Sales: One million plus, plus, plus
Singles: **I Got Stung/ONE NIGHT**, October 1958 Standard 78 RPM release, **I Got Stung/ONE NIGHT**, October 1958 Standard 45 RPM release, **I Got Stung/ONE NIGHT** 1961 Gold Standard Series reissue, **I Got Stung/ONE NIGHT**, October 1977 **15 Golden Records–30 Golden Hits** (Boxed Set)
EPs: **A Touch Of Gold–Vol. 2**
LPs: **Elvis–A Legendary Performer–Vol. 4, Elvis Aron Presley, Elvis: The Other Sides–Worldwide Gold Award Hits–Vol. 2, Elvis–TV Special, 50,000,000 Elvis Fans Can't Be Wrong–Elvis' Gold, Records–Vol. 2, A Golden Celebration, Reconsider Baby, The Top Ten Hits**

ONE–SIDED LOVE AFFAIR
Written By: Bill Campbell
Elvis Recorded: January 30, 1956–RCA New York City
Flip Side: **Money Honey**
Singles: **Money Honey/ONE–SIDED LOVE AFFAIR**, September 1956 Standard 78 RPM release, **Money Honey/ONE–SIDED LOVE AFFAIR**, September 1956 Standard 45 RPM release, **Tutti Frutti/ONE–SIDED LOVE AFFAIR**, September 1956 Disc jockey promo, **Money Honey/ONE–SIDED LOVE AFFAIR**, March 1959 Gold Standard Series reissue, **Money Honey/ONE–SIDED LOVE AFFAIR**, December 1986 Collectibles
EPs: **Elvis Presley, Elvis Presley–The Most Talked About New Personality in the Last Ten Years of Recorded Music**
LPs: **Elvis Presley**

ONE–TRACK HEART
Written By: Bill Giant, Bernie Baum, Florence Kaye
Elvis Recorded: March 1964–Radio Recorders
Recorded For Film: *ROUSTABOUT* (1964)
Flip Side: **Roustabout**
Singles: **Roustabout/ONE–TRACK HEART**, November 1964 Disc jockey promo
LP: **Roustabout**

ONLY BELIEVE
Written By: Paul Rader
Elvis Recorded: June 8, 1970–RCA Nashville
Flip Side: **Life**
On The Charts: *Billboard*'s Hot 100 (2 weeks–peaked at #95)
Singles: **Life/ONLY BELIEVE**, May 1971 Standard release, **Life/ONLY BELIEVE**, May 1972 Gold Standard Series reissue
LPs: **Love Letters From Elvis**

ONLY THE STRONG SURVIVE
Written By: Jerry Butler, Kenny Gamble, Leon Huff
Previously Recorded By: Jerry Butler
Elvis Recorded: February 20, 1969–American Sound Studios, Memphis
LPs: **From Elvis In Memphis, The Memphis Record**

PADRE
Written By: Jacques Larue, Alain Romans
(English Lyrics By: Paul Francis Webster)
Previously Recorded By: Lola Dee, Toni Arden, Marty Robbins
Elvis Recorded: May 15, 1971–RCA Nashville
LPs: **Elvis, He Walks Beside Me**

PARADISE, HAWAIIAN STYLE
Written By: Bill Giant, Bernie Baum, Florence Kaye
Elvis Recorded: August 4, 1966–Radio Recorders
Recorded For Film: *PARADISE, HAWAIIAN STYLE* (1966)
LP: **Paradise, Hawaiian Style**

PARALYZED
Written By: Otis Blackwell
Elvis Recorded: September 2, 1956–Radio Recorders

Flip Side: **Little Sister**
On The Charts: *Billboard*'s Top 100 (7 weeks–peaked at #59), British (peaked at #8)
Singles: **Little Sister/PARALYZED**, June 1983 Standard Release, **Little Sister/PARA-LYZED**, June 1983 Disc jockey promo, **PARALYZED/Big Boss Man**, December 1986 Collectibles
EP: Elvis–Vol. 1, Elvis / Jaye P. Morgan
LPs: Elvis, Elvis: The Other Sides—Worldwide Gold Award Hits—Vol. 2, I Was The One

PARTY
Written By: Jessie Mae Robinson
Elvis Recorded: February 1957–Radio Recorders
Recorded For Film: *LOVING YOU* (1957)
On The Charts: *Billboard*'s Hot 100 (peaked at #37)
EPs: Loving You–Vol. 1
LPs: Essential Elvis—The First Movies, Loving You

PATCH IT UP
Written By: Eddie Rabbitt, Rory Bourke
Elvis Recorded: June 8, 1970–RCA Nashville
Flip Side: **You Don't Have To Say You Love Me**
On The Charts: *Billboard*'s Hot 100 (3 weeks–peaked at #90)
Sales: One million
Singles: **You Don't Have To Say You Love Me/PATCH IT UP**, October 1970 Standard release, **You Don't Have To Say You Love Me/PATCH IT UP**, February 1972 Gold Standard Series reissue
LPs: Elvis: The Other Sides—Worldwide Gold Award Hits–Vol. 2, Elvis—That's The Way It Is

PEACE IN THE VALLEY
Written By: Rev. Thomas A. Dorsey
Previously Recorded By: Red Foley, The Stamps Quartet
Elvis Recorded: January 13, 1957–Radio Recorders
On The Charts: *Billboard*'s Top 100 (10 weeks–peaked At #39)
EP: Peace In The Valley
LPs: Double Dynamite, Elvis—A Legendary Performer–Vol. 1, Elvis' Christmas Album, Essential Elvis–Vol. 2, A Golden Celebration, Known Only To Him, You'll Never Walk Alone

PETUNIA, THE GARDENER'S DAUGHTER
Written By: Sid Tepper, Roy C. Bennett
Elvis Recorded: May 1965–Radio Recorders
(Duet With: Donna Douglas)
Recorded For Film: *FRANKIE AND JOHNNY* (1966)
LP: Frankie And Johnny

PIECES OF MY LIFE
Written By: Troy Seals
Previously Recorded By: Charlie Rich
Elvis Recorded: March 13, 1975–RCA Hollywood
Flip Side: **Bringing It Back**
On The Charts: *Billboard*'s Country (10 weeks–peaked at #33)
Singles: **Bringing It Back/PIECES OF MY LIFE**, October 1975 Standard release, **Bringing It Back/PIECES OF MY LIFE**, October 1975 Disc jockey promo
LPs: Always On My Mind, Elvis Today, Elvis Aron Presley—Forever

PLANTATION ROCK
Written By: Bill Giant, Bernie Baum and Florence Kaye
Elvis Recorded: March 27, 1962–Radio Recorders
Recorded For Film: *GIRLS! GIRLS! GIRLS!* (1962)
LP: Elvis—A Legendary Performer—Vol. 4

PLAYING FOR KEEPS
Written By: Stanley A. Kesler
Elvis Recorded: September 1, 1956–Radio Recorders
Flip Side: **Too Much**
On The Charts: *Billboard*'s Top 100 (9 weeks–peaked at #34), Country Juke Box (peaked at #8)
Sales: One million

Singles: **Too Much/PLAYING FOR KEEPS**, January 1957 Standard 78 RPM release, **Too Much/PLAYING FOR KEEPS**, January 1957 Standard 45 RPM release, **Too Much/PLAYING FOR KEEPS**, March 1959 Gold Standard Series reissue, **Too Much/PLAYING FOR KEEPS**, December 1981 Collectibles
EP: DJ–56
LPs: Elvis: Worldwide 50 Gold Award Hits–Vol. 1, For LP Fans Only, A Valentine Gift For You

PLEASE DON'T DRAG THAT STRING AROUND
Written By: Otis Blackwell, Winfield Scott
Elvis Recorded: May 26, 1963–RCA Nashville
Flip Side: **(You're The) Devil In Disguise**
Singles: **(You're The) Devil In Disguise/PLEASE DON'T DRAG THAT STRING AROUND**, June 1963 Standard release, **(You're The) Devil In Disguise/PLEASE DON'T DRAG THAT STRING AROUND**, August 1964 Gold Standard Series reissue
LPs: Elvis' Golden Records–Vol. 4, Elvis: The Other Sides—Worldwide Gold Award Hits–Vol. 2

PLEASE DON'T STOP LOVING ME
Written By: Joy Byers
Elvis Recorded: May 1965–Radio Recorders
Recorded For Film: *FRANKIE AND JOHNNY* (1965)
Flip Side: **Frankie and Johnny**
On The Charts: *Billboard*'s Hot 100–(8 weeks–peaked at #45)
Singles: **Frankie and Johnny/PLEASE DON'T STOP LOVING ME**, March 1966 Standard release, **Frankie and Johnny/PLEASE DON'T STOP LOVING ME**, February 1968 Gold Standard Series reissue
LP: Frankie and Johnny

PLEDGING MY LOVE
Written By: Ferdinand Washington, Don Robey
Previously Recorded By: Johnny Ace, Teresa Brewer, Kitty Wells
Elvis Recorded: October 30, 1976–Graceland
Flip Side: **Way Down**
On The Charts: *Billboard*'s Country (17 weeks–peaked at #1)
Singles: **Way Down/PLEDGING MY LOVE**, July 1977 Standard release, **Way Down/PLEDGING MY LOVE**, July 1977 Disc jockey promo
LP: Moody Blue

POCKETFUL OF RAINBOWS
Written by: Fred Wise, Ben Weisman
Elvis Recorded: May 6, 1960–RCA Hollywood
Recorded For Film: *G.I. BLUES* (1960)
EP: The EP Collection–Vol. 2
LP: G.I. Blues

POISON IVY LEAGUE
Written By: Bill Giant, Bernie Baum and Florence Kaye
Elvis Recorded: March 1964–Radio Recorders
Recorded For Film: *ROUSTABOUT* (1964)
LP: Roustabout

POKE SALAD ANNIE
Written By: Tony Joe White
Previously Recorded By: Tony Joe White
Elvis Recorded: Live in concert (February 8, 1970–Las Vegas)
LP: Elvis Aron Presley, Elvis As Recorded At Madison Square Garden, On Stage—February, 1970

POOR BOY
Written by: Ken Darby (Credited to Elvis Presley and Vera Matson)
Elvis Recorded: September 24, 1956–Radio Recorders
Recorded For Film: *LOVE ME TENDER* (1956)
Flip Side: **An American Trilogy**
On The Charts: *Billboard*'s Top 100 (EP 11 weeks–peaked at #35)
Singles: **An American Trilogy/POOR BOY**, December 1986 Collectibles
EP: Love Me Tender
LPs: Elvis: The Other Sides—Worldwide Gold Award Hits–Vol. 2, Essential Elvis—The First Movies, For LP Fans Only

POWER OF MY LOVE
Written By: Bill Giant, Bernie Baum and Florence Kaye
Elvis Recorded: February 18, 1969–American Sound Studios, Memphis
LPs: From Elvis In Memphis, The Memphis Record

PROMISED LAND
Written By: Chuck Berry
Previously Recorded By: Chuck Berry, Freddie Weller, James Taylor
Elvis Recorded: December 15, 1973–Stax
Studios, Memphis
Flip Side: It's Midnight
On The Charts: *Billboard*'s Hot 100 (13
weeks–peaked at #14), Easy-Listening (8
weeks–peaked at #11)
Singles: PROMISED LAND/It's Midnight,
October 1974 Standard release, PROMISED
LAND/It's Midnight, October 1974 Disc
jockey promo, PROMISED LAND/It's
Midnight, February 1976 Gold Standard
Series reissue, Blue Suede Shoes/PROMISED
LAND, October 1984 Anniversary reissue
LPs: Promised Land, This Is Elvis

PROUD MARY
Written By: John Fogerty
Previously Recorded By: Creedence Clearwater Revival, Ike and Tina Turner
Elvis Recorded: Live in concert (February 17, 1970–Las Vegas)
LP: Elvis As Recorded At Madison Square Garden, On Stage–February 1970

PUPPET ON A STRING
Written By: Sid Tepper, Roy C. Bennett
Elvis Recorded: July 1964–Radio Recorders
Recorded For Film: *GIRL HAPPY* (1965)
Flip Side: Wooden Heart
On The Charts: *Billboard*'s Hot 100 (10 weeks–peaked at #14), Easy-Listening (peaked at #3)
Sales: One million plus
Singles: PUPPET ON A STRING/Wooden Heart, October 1965 Gold Standard Original release, Teddy Bear/PUPPET ON A STRING, August 1978 Special Issue, Teddy Bear/PUPPET ON A STRING, August 1978 Disc jockey promo
LPs: Elvis: The Other Sides—Worldwide Gold Award Hits—Vol. 2, Elvis Sings For Children And Grownups Too!, Girl Happy

PUT THE BLAME ON ME
Written By: Kay Twomey, Fred Wise and Norman Blagman
Elvis Recorded: March 13, 1961–RCA Nashville
Recorded For Film: *TICKLE ME* (1965)
EP: Tickle Me
LP: Something For Everybody

PUT YOUR HAND IN THE HAND
Written By: Gene MacLellan
Previously Recorded By: Beth Moore, Ocean
Elvis Recorded: June 8, 1971–RCA Nashville
LPs: Elvis—A Canadian Tribute, Elvis Now

QUEENIE WAHINE'S PAPAYA
Written By: Bill Giant, Bernie Baum and Florence Kaye
Elvis Recorded: July 27, 1965–Radio Recorders
Recorded For Film: *PARADISE, HAWAIIAN STYLE* (1966)
LP: Paradise, Hawaiian Style

RAGS TO RICHES
Written By: Richard Adler, Jerry Ross
Previously Recorded By: Tony Bennett
Elvis Recorded: September 22, 1970–RCA Hollywood
Flip Side: Where Did They Go, Lord
On The Charts: *Billboard*'s Hot 100 (5 weeks–peaked at #45)
Singles: RAGS TO RICHES/Where Did They Go, Lord, February 1971 Standard release,

RAGS TO RICHES/Where Did They Go, Lord, February 1972 Gold Standard Series reissue
LP: Elvis Aron Presley

RAISED ON ROCK
Written By: Mark James
Elvis Recorded: July 23, 1973–Stax Studios, Memphis
Flip Side: For Ol' Times Sake
On The Charts: *Billboard*'s Hot 100 (9 weeks–peaked at #41), Easy-Listening (7 weeks–peaked at #27)
Singles: RAISED ON ROCK/For Ol' Times Sake, September 1973 Standard release, RAISED ON ROCK/For Ol' Times Sake, September 1973 Disc jockey promo, If You Talk In Your Sleep/RAISED ON ROCK, March 1975 Gold Standard Series Original release
LP: Raised On Rock/For Ol' Times Sake

REACH OUT FOR JESUS
Written By: Ralph Carmichael
Elvis Recorded: June 8, 1971–RCA Nashville
LP: He Touched Me

READY TEDDY
Written By: John Marascalco, Bumps Blackwell
Previously Recorded By: Little Richard
Elvis Recorded: September 3, 1956–Radio Recorders
Singles: READY TEDDY/blank, October 1956 Disc jockey promo
EP: Elvis–Vol. 2
LPs: Elvis (RCA LPM–1382), A Golden Celebration, I Was The One

RECONSIDER BABY
Written By: Lowell Fulson
Previously Recorded By: Lowell Fulson
Elvis Recorded: April 4, 1960–RCA Nashville
Live in concert (Honolulu March 25, 1961)
LPs: Elvis Aron Presley, Elvis—A Legendary Performer–Vol. 4, Elvis Is Back, Reconsider Baby

RELAX
Written By: Sid Tepper and Roy C. Bennett
Elvis Recorded: September 1962–Radio Recorders
Recorded For Film: *IT HAPPENED AT THE WORLD'S FAIR* (1962)
LPs: It Happened At The World's Fair, Mahalo From Elvis

RELEASE ME
Written By: Eddie Miller and W.S. Stevenson
Previously Recorded By: Jimmy Heap, Ray Price, Kitty Wells, Engelbert Humperdinck
Elvis Recorded: Live in concert (February 18, 1970–Las Vegas)
LPs: On Stage–February, 1970, Welcome To My World

RETURN TO SENDER
Written By: Otis Blackwell and Winfield Scott
Elvis Recorded: March 1962–Radio Recorders
Featured In Film: *GIRLS! GIRLS! GIRLS!* (1962)
Flip Side: Where Do You Come From
On The Charts: Billboard's Hot 100 (16 weeks–peaked At #2), Rhythm & Blues (12 weeks–peaked At #5), British (3 weeks–peaked At #1)
Singles: RETURN TO SENDER/Where Do You Come From, October 1962 Standard Release, RETURN TO SENDER/Where Do You Come From, June 1963 Gold Standard Series reissue, RETURN TO SENDER/Where Do You Come From, October 1977, 15 Golden Records–30 Golden Hits (Boxed Set)
LPs: Elvis, Elvis: Worldwide 50 Gold Award Hits–Vol. 1, Girls! Girls! Girls!, Return Of The Rocker, The Top Ten Hits

RIDING THE RAINBOW
Written By: Fred Wise, Ben Weisman
Elvis Recorded: October 26, 1961–Radio Recorders
Recorded For Film: *KID GALAHAD* (1962)
EP: Kid Galahad
LP: I Got Lucky

RIP IT UP
Written By: John Marascalco, Bumps Blackwell
Previously Recorded By: Little Richard
Elvis Recorded: September 3, 1956–Radio Recorders
Flip Side: Little Sister
Singles: Little Sister/ RIP IT UP, June 1983 12" promo
EPs: Elvis, Vol. 1, Elvis/Jaye P. Morgan
LPs: Elvis, Elvis: The Other Sides—Worldwide Gold Award Hits–Vol. 2, I Was The One

ROCK–A–HULA BABY
Written By: Fred Wise, Ben Weisman and Florence Kaye
Elvis Recorded: March 23, 1961–Radio Recorders
Recorded For Film: *BLUE HAWAII* (1961)
Flip Side: Can't Help Falling In Love
On The Charts: *Billboard*'s Hot 100 (9 weeks–peaked at #23), British (4 weeks–peaked at #1)
Singles: Can't Help Falling In Love/ROCK–A–HULA BABY, December 1961 Standard release, Can't Help Falling In Love/ROCK–A–HULA BABY, December 1961 Compact 33, Can't Help Falling In Love/ROCK–A–HULA BABY, November 1962 Gold Standard Series reissue
LPs: Blue Hawaii, Elvis In Hawaii, Elvis: Worldwide 50 Gold Award Hits–Vol. 1

ROUSTABOUT
Written By: Bill Giant, Bernie Baum and Florence Kaye
Elvis Recorded: March 1964–Radio Recorders
Recorded For Film: *ROUSTABOUT* (1964)

Flip Side: One–Track Heart
Singles: ROUSTABOUT/One–Track Heart, November 1964 Disc jockey promo, ROUSTABOUT/ROUSTABOUT, November 1964 promo
LPs: Elvis In Hollywood, Roustabout

RUBBERNECKIN'
Written By: Dory Jones, Bunny Warren
Elvis Recorded: January 20, 1969–American Sound Studios, Memphis
Recorded For Film: *CHANGE OF HABIT* (1969)
Flip Side: Don't Cry Daddy
On The Charts: *Billboard*'s Hot 100 (5 weeks–peaked at #69)
Singles: Don't Cry Daddy/RUBBERNECKIN', November 1969 Standard release, Don't Cry Daddy/RUBBERNECKIN', December 1970 Gold Standard Series reissue
LPs: Almost In Love, Double Dynamite, The Memphis Record

RUN ON
Written By: (Traditional Gospel)
Elvis Recorded: May 25, 1966–RCA Nashville
LPs: How Great Thou Art, Known Only To Him

RUNAWAY
Written By: Del Shannon, Max T. Crook
Previously Recorded By: Del Shannon, Lawrence Welk
Elvis Recorded: Live in concert (August 22, 1969–Las Vegas)
LP: On Stage–February 1970

SAND CASTLES
Written By: Herb Goldberg, David Hess
Elvis Recorded: August 2, 1965–Radio Recorders
Recorded For Film: *PARADISE, HAWAIIAN STYLE* (1966) (Cut From Movie)
LP: Paradise, Hawaiian Style

SANTA, BRING MY BABY BACK (TO ME)
Written By: Aaron Schroeder, Claude DeMetrius
Elvis Recorded: September 7, 1957–Radio Recorders
EP: Elvis Sings Christmas Songs
LP: Elvis' Christmas Album

SANTA CLAUS IS BACK IN TOWN (CHRISTMAS BLUES)
Written By: Jerry Leiber, Mike Stoller.
Elvis Recorded: September 7, 1957–Radio Recorders.
Singles: Blue Christmas/SANTA CLAUS IS BACK IN TOWN, November 1965 Gold Standard Series Original release, Merry Christmas Baby/SANTA CLAUS IS BACK IN TOWN, November 1985 New release
EP: Elvis Sings Christmas Songs
LPs: Elvis' Christmas Album, Memories of Christmas

SANTA LUCIA
Written By: Teodoro Cottrau
Elvis Recorded: July 1963–Radio Recorders
Recorded For Film: *VIVA LAS VEGAS* (1964)
LPs: Burning Love and Hits from His Movies–Vol. 2, Elvis for Everyone

SAVED
Written By: Jerry Leiber, Mike Stoller
Elvis Recorded: June 21, 1968–Western Recorders, Hollywood.
LP: Elvis–TV Special

SCHOOL DAY
Written By: Chuck Berry
Previously Recorded By: Chuck Berry
Elvis Recorded: Live in concert (Dallas–June 6, 1975)
LP: Elvis Aron Presley

SCRATCH MY BACK (THEN I'LL SCRATCH YOURS)
Written By: Bill Giant, Bernie Baum and Florence Kaye
Elvis Recorded: August 3, 1965–Radio Recorders
Recorded For Film: *PARADISE, HAWAIIAN STYLE* (1966)
LP: Paradise, Hawaiian Style

SEE SEE RIDER
Written By: Big Bill Broonzy
Previously Recorded By: Big Bill Broonzy, Ma Rainey, Ray Charles
Elvis Recorded: Live in concert (April 9,1972–Hampton Roads, Virginia)
LPs: Aloha from Hawaii via Satellite, The Alternate Aloha, Elvis Aron Presley, Elvis in Concert, Elvis Recorded Live on Stage in Memphis, On Stage–February, 1970

SEEING IS BELIEVING
Written By: Red West, Glen Spreen
Elvis Recorded: May 19, 1971–RCA Nashville
LP: He Touched Me

SENTIMENTAL ME
Written By: Jimmy Cassin and Jim Morehead
Previously Recorded By: The Ames Brothers, Russ Morgan and Ray Anthony
Elvis Recorded: March 13,1961–RCA Nashville
LP: Double Dynamite

SEPARATE WAYS
Written By: Red West, Richard Mainegra
Elvis Recorded: March 27, 1972, RCA Hollywood
Filp Side: Always on My Mind
On The Charts: *Billboard*'s Hot 100 (12 weeks–peaked at #20), Country (peaked at #16), Easy-Listening (peaked at #3)

Sales: One million plus
Singles: **SEPARATE WAYS**/Always On My Mind, November 1972 Standard release, **SEPARATE WAYS**/Always on My Mind, February 1976 Gold Standard Series reissue
LPs: Always on My Mind, Double Dynamite, Separate Ways

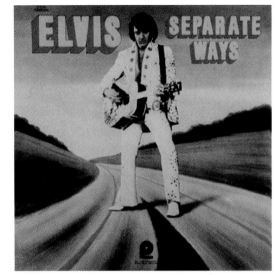

SHAKE A HAND
Written By: Joe Morris
Previously Recorded By: Faye Adams, Red Foley, Jackie Wilson
Elvis Recorded: March 12, 1975–RCA Hollywood
LPs: Elvis Aron Presley–Forever, Elvis Today

SHAKE, RATTLE AND ROLL
Written By: Charles E. Calhoun (Jesse Stone)
Previously Recorded By: Joe Turner, Bill Haley and His Comets
Elvis Recorded: February 3, 1956–RCA New York City
Flip Side: Lawdy Miss Clawdy
Singles: SHAKE, RATTLE AND ROLL/Lawdy Miss Clawdy, September 1956, Standard 78 RPM release, SHAKE, RATTLE AND ROLL/Lawdy Miss Clawdy, September 1956. Standard 45 RPM release, SHAKE, RATTLE AND ROLL/Lawdy Miss Clawdy, March 1959. Gold Standard Series reissue
EPs: Elvis Presley, Good Rockin' Tonight
LPs: For LP Fans Only, A Golden Celebration, This Is Elvis

SHAKE THAT TAMBOURINE
Written By: Bill Giant, Bernie Baum and Florence Kaye
Elvis Recorded: February 1965–RCA Nashville
LPs: Harum Scarum

SHE THINKS I STILL CARE
Written By: Dickie Lee
Previously Recorded By: George Jones, Connie Francis
Elvis Recorded: February 3, 1976–Graceland.
Flip Side: Moody Blue
On The Charts: Billboard's Hot 100 (13 weeks–peaked at #31), Country (peaked at #1).
Singles: Moody Blue/SHE THINKS I STILL CARE, December 1976. Standard release, Moody Blue/SHE THINKS I STILL CARE, December 1976, Disc jockey promo
LPs: Guitar Man, Moody Blue, Our Memories of Elvis

SHE WEARS MY RING
Written By: Boudleaux, Felice Bryant
Previously Recorded By: Roy Orbison
Elvis Recorded: December 16, 1973–Stax Studios, Memphis
LPs: Good Times, Our Memories of Elvis–Vol. 2

SHE'S A MACHINE
Written By: Joy Byers
Elvis Recorded: September 29, 1966–Radio Recorders
Recorded For Film: EASY COME, EASY GO (1967) (Not used)
LPs: Elvis Sings Flaming Star, Singer Presents Elvis Singing Flaming Star and Others

SHE'S NOT YOU
Written By: Jerry Leiber, Mike Stoller and Doc Pomus
Elvis Recorded: March 19, 1962–RCA Nashville
Flip Side: Just Tell Her Jim Said Hello
On The Charts: Billboard's Hot 100 (10 weeks–peaked at #5), Rhythm & Blues (peaked at #13), Easy-Listening (peaked at #2)
Sales: One million plus
Singles: SHE'S NOT YOU/Just Tell Her Jim Said Hello, July 1962, Standard release, SHE'S NOT YOU/Just Tell Her Jim Said Hello, June 1963, Gold Standard Series reissue, Jailhouse Rock/SHE'S NOT YOU December 1986. Collectibles Collectibles
LPs: Elvis' Golden Records–Vol. 3, Elvis: Worldwide 50 Gold Award Hits–Vol. 1, The Top Ten Hits

SHOPPIN' AROUND
Written By: Sid Tepper, Roy C. Bennett, Aaron Schroeder
Elvis Recorded: May 6, 1960–Radio Recorders
Recorded For Film: G. I. BLUES (1960) (Not used)
Released: 1980
LPs: Elvis Aron Presley, G. I. Blues

SHOUT IT OUT
Written By: Bill Giant, Bernie Baum, Florence Kaye
Elvis Recorded: May 1965–Radio Recorders
Recorded For Film: FRANKIE AND JOHNNY (1966)
LP: Frankie and Johnny

SILENT NIGHT
Written By: Father Joseph Mohr (1792–1848), Franz Gruber (1787–1863)
English Translation: Rev. John Freeman Young (1863)
Previously Recorded By: The Haydn Quartet (1905) Bing Crosby (30 Million Sold), Mahalia Jackson
Elvis Recorded: September 6, 1957–Radio Recorders.
EP: Christmas with Elvis
LPs: Elvis' Christmas Album, Memories of Christmas

SILVER BELLS
Written By: Jay Livingston, Ray Evans
Previously Recorded By: Bing Crosby, Carol Richards
Elvis Recorded: May 15, 1971–RCA Nashville
LPs: Elvis Sings the Wonderful World of Christmas, Memories of Christmas

SING, YOU CHILDREN
Written By: Gerald Nelson, Fred Burch
Elvis Recorded: September 28, 1966–Radio Recorders
Recorded For Film: EASY COME, EASY GO (1967)
EP: Easy Come, Easy Go
LP: You'll Never Walk Alone

SINGING TREE
Written By: A. Owens, A. Solberg
Elvis Recorded: September 12, 1967–RCA Nashville
LP: Clambake

SLICIN' SAND
Written By: Sid Tepper, Roy C. Bennett
Elvis Recorded: March 21, 1961–Radio Recorders
Recorded For Film: BLUE HAWAII (1961)
LP: Blue Hawaii

SLOWLY BUT SURELY
Written By: Sid Wayne, Ben Weisman
Elvis Recorded: May 27, 1963–RCA Nashville
Recorded For Film: TICKLE ME (1965)
EP: Tickle Me
LP: Fun in Acapulco

SMOKEY MOUNTAIN BOY
Written By: Lenore Rosenblatt, Victor Millrose
Elvis Recorded: October 1963–RCA Nashville
Recorded For Film: KISSIN' COUSINS (1964)
LP: Kissin' Cousins

SMORGASBORD
Written By: Sid Tepper, Roy C. Bennett

Elvis Recorded: February 17, 1966–Radio Recorders
Recorded For Film: *SPINOUT* (1966)
LP: **Spinout**

SNOWBIRD
Written By: Gene MacLellan
Previously Recorded By: Anne Murray, Chet Atkins
Elvis Recorded: September 22, 1970–RCA Nashville
LP: **Elvis Country**

SO CLOSE, YET SO FAR (FROM PARADISE)
Written By: Joy Byers
Elvis Recorded: February 24, 1965–RCA Nashville
Recorded For Film: *HARUM SCARUM* (1965)
LPs: **Harum Scarum, Mahalo from Elvis**

SO GLAD YOU'RE MINE
Written By: Arthur Crudup
Elvis Recorded: January 30, 1956–RCA New York City
EP: **Elvis–Vol. 2**
LPs: **Elvis, Reconsider Baby**

SO HIGH
Written By: (Traditional Gospel)
Previously Recorded By: LaVern Baker
Elvis Recorded: May 27, 1966–RCA Nashville studios
Flip Side: **How Great Thou Art**
Singles: **How Great Thou Art/SO HIGH**, March 1967, Disc jockey promo
LPs: **How Great Thou Art, Known Only to Him**

SOFTLY, AS I LEAVE YOU
Written By: G. Calabrese, A. DeVita and Hal Shaper
Previously Recorded By: Matt Monroe, Frank Sinatra, Eydie Gorme
Elvis Recorded: Live in concert, (December 13, 1975–Las Vegas Hilton)
Flip Side: **Unchained Melody**
On The Charts: *Billboard*'s Country (11 weeks–peaked at #6)
Singles: **Unchained Melody/SOFTLY, AS I LEAVE YOU**, March 1978, Standard release, **Unchained Melody/SOFTLY, AS I LEAVE YOU**, March 1978, Disc jockey promo
LP: **Elvis Aron Presley**

SOLDIER BOY
Written By: David Jones, Larry Banks
Previously Recorded By: The Four Fellows, Pat O'Day, Sunny Gale
Elvis Recorded: March 20, 1960–RCA Nashville (Elvis also taped in West Germany)
LPs: **Elvis Is Back, A Golden Celebration (West Germany: 1958–1960)**

SOLITAIRE
Written By: Neil Sedaka, Phil Cody
Previously Recorded By: Neil Sedaka, Andy Williams, The Carpenters
Elvis Recorded: February 3, 1976–Graceland
Flip Side: **Are You Sincere**
On The Charts: *Billboard*'s Country (12 weeks–peaked at #10)
Singles: **Are You Sincere/SOLITAIRE**, May 1979. Standard release, **Are You Sincere/SOLITAIRE**, May 1979, Disc jockey promo
LPs: **Always on My Mind, From Elvis Presley Boulevard, Memphis, Tennessee, Our Memories of Elvis**

SOMEBODY BIGGER THAN YOU AND I
Written By: Johnny Lange, Walter (Hy) Heath and Joseph Burke
Elvis Recorded: May 27, 1966–RCA Nashville
LP: **How Great Thou Art**

SOMETHING
Written By: George Harrison
Previously Recorded By: The Beatles, Shirley Bassey, Booker T and The M.G.s
Elvis Recorded: Live in concert (August 10, 1970–Las Vegas)
EP: **Aloha from Hawaii via Satellite**
LPs: **Aloha from Hawaii via Satellite, The Alternate Aloha**

SOMETHING BLUE
Written By: Paul Evans, Al Byron
Elvis Recorded: March 18, 1962–RCA Nashville
LPs: **Pot Luck**

SONG OF THE SHRIMP
Written By: Sid Tepper, Roy C. Bennett
Elvis Recorded: March 1962–Radio Recorders
Recorded For Film: *GIRLS! GIRLS! GIRLS!* (1962)
LP: **Girls! Girls! Girls!**

SOUND ADVICE
Written By: Bill Giant, Bernie Baum, and Florence Kaye
Elvis Recorded: July 5,1961–RCA Nashville
Recorded For Film: *FOLLOW THAT DREAM* (1962)
LP: **Elvis for Everyone**

THE SOUND OF YOUR CRY
Written By: Bill Giant, Bernie Baum and Florence Kaye
Elvis Recorded: June 4, 1970–RCA Nashville
Flip Side: **It's Only Love**
Singles: **It's Only Love/THE SOUND OF YOUR CRY**, September 1971 Standard release, **It's Only Love/THE SOUND OF YOUR CRY**, May 1972, Gold Standard Series reissue.
LP: **Greatest Hits–Vol. 1**

SPANISH EYES
(Moon Over Naples)
Written (As Instrumental) By: Bert Kaempfert
English Lyrics By: Charles Singleton, Eddy Snyder
Previously Recorded By: Bert Kaempfert, Al Martino
Elvis Recorded: December 16, 1973–Stax Studios, Memphis
LPs: **Good Times, Our Memories of Elvis** (without overdubbing)

SPEEDWAY
Written By: Mel Glazer, Stephen Schlaks
Elvis Recorded: June 21,1967–MGM Studios, Culver City, California
Recorded For Film: *SPEEDWAY* (1968)
LP: **Speedway**

SPINOUT
Written By: Sid Wayne, Ben Weisman and Dolores Fuller
Elvis Recorded: February 1966–Radio Recorders
Recorded For Film: *SPINOUT* (1966)
Flip Side: **All That I Am**
On The Charts: *Billboard*'s Hot 100 (7 weeks–peaked at #40)
Sales: One milllion plus
Singles: **SPINOUT/All That I Am**, September 1966, Standard release, **SPINOUT/All That I Am** February 1968, Gold Standard Series reissue.
LPs: **Elvis in Hollywood, Spinout**

SPRING FEVER
Written By: Bill Giant, Bernie Baum and Florence Kaye
Elvis Recorded: July 1964–Radio Recorders (Duet With Shelley Fabares)
Recorded For Film: *GIRL HAPPY* (1965)
LP: **Girl Happy**

STAND BY ME
Written By: Dr. C. H. Tindley
Elvis Recorded: May 26, 1966,–RCA Nashville

LPs: How Great Thou Art, Known Only to Him

STARTIN' TONIGHT
Written By: Lenore Rosenblatt, Victor Millrose
Elvis Recorded: July 1964–Radio Recorders
Recorded For Film: *GIRL HAPPY* (1965)
LP: Girl Happy

STARTING TODAY
Written By: Don Robertson
Elvis Recorded: March 13, 1961–RCA Nashville
LP: Something for Everybody

STAY AWAY
(Based On: Greensleeves)
Written By: Sid Tepper, Roy C. Bennett
Elvis Recorded: October 2, 1967–RCA Nashville
Recorded For Film: *STAY AWAY, JOE* (1968)
Flip Side: U.S. Male
On The Charts: *Billboard*'s Hot 100 (5 weeks–peaked at #67)
Sales: Over one million
Singles: U.S. Male/STAY AWAY, March 1968 Standard release, U.S. Male/STAY AWAY, 1970 Gold Standard Series reissue.
LP: Stay Away

STAY AWAY, JOE
Written By: Sid Wayne, Ben Weisman
Elvis Recorded: October 2,1967–RCA Nashville
Recorded For Film: *STAY AWAY, JOE* (1968)
LPs: Almost in Love, Let's Be Friends

STEADFAST, LOYAL, AND TRUE
Written By: Jerry Leiber, Mike Stoller
Elvis Recorded: January or February 1958–On The Set
Recorded For Film: *KING CREOLE* (1958)
LP: King Creole

STEAMROLLER BLUES
Written By: James Taylor
Previously Recorded By: James Taylor
Elvis Recorded: Live in concert (1973)
Flip Side: Fool
On The Charts: *Billboard*'s Hot 100 (12 weeks–peaked at #17), Country (peaked at #31)
Singles: STEAMROLLER BLUES/Fool, April 1973 Standard release, Burning Love/STEAMROLLER BLUES, March 1975 Gold Standard Series Original release
LPs: Aloha from Hawaii via Satellite, The Alternate Aloha, Greatest Hits–Vol. I

STEPPIN' OUT OF LINE
Written By: Fred Wise, Ben Weisman and Dolores Fuller
Elvis Recorded: March 22, 1961–Radio Recorders
Recorded For Film: *BLUE HAWAII* (1961)
LP: Pot Luck

STOP, LOOK AND LISTEN
Written By: Joy Byers
Elvis Recorded: February 15, 1966–Radio Recorders
Recorded For Film: *SPINOUT* (1966)
LP: Spinout

STOP WHERE YOU ARE
Written By: Bill Giant, Bernie Baum and Florence Kaye
Elvis Recorded: August 3, 1965–Radio Recorders
Recorded For Film: *PARADISE, HAWAIIAN STYLE* (1966)
LP: Paradise, Hawaiian Style

STRANGER IN MY OWN HOME TOWN
Written By: Percy Mayfield
Previously Recorded By: Percy Mayfield
Elvis Recorded: February 17, 1969–American Sound Studios

LPs: Back in Memphis, From Memphis to Vegas/From Vegas to Memphis, The Memphis Record, Reconsider Baby

STRANGER IN THE CROWD
Written By: Winfield Scott
Elvis Recorded: June 5,1970–RCA Nashville
LP: That's the Way It Is

STUCK ON YOU
Written By: Aaron Schroeder, J. Leslie McFarland
Elvis Recorded: March 21, 1960–RCA Nashville
Flip Side: Fame and Fortune
On The Charts: *Billboard*'s Hot 100 (16 weeks–peaked at #1), Country (peaked at #27), Rhythm & Blues (peaked at #6)
Sales: Two Million Plus
Singles: STUCK ON YOU/Fame and Fortune, March 1960 Standard release, STUCK ON YOU/Fame and Fortune, March 1960 Living Stereo release, STUCK ON YOU/Fame and Fortune, February 1962 Gold Standard Series reissue, STUCK ON YOU/Fame and Fortune, December 1986 Collectibles
LPs: Elvis, Elvis' Golden Records–Vol. 3, Elvis: Worldwide 50 Gold Award Hits–Vol. I, The Number One Hits, Return of the Rocker, The Top Ten Hits

SUCH A NIGHT
Written By: Lincoln Chase
Previously Recorded By: Clyde McPhatter and The Drifters, Johnnie Ray, Dinah Washington, Conway Twitty
Elvis Recorded: April 4, 1960–RCA Nashville
Flip Side: Never Ending
On The Charts: *Billboard*'s Hot 100 (8 weeks–peaked at #16)
Singles: SUCH A NIGHT/Never Ending, July 1964. Standard release, SUCH A NIGHT/Never Ending, May 1965 Gold Standard Series reissue, SUCH A NIGHT/SUCH A NIGHT, 1976 Rare disc jockey promo, Bossa Nova Baby/SUCH A NIGHT, December 1986 Collectibles
LPs: Elvis Aron Presley, Elvis Is Back

SUMMER KISSES, WINTER TEARS
Written By: Fred Wise, Ben Weisman and Jack Lloyd
Elvis Recorded: August 1960–Radio Recorders
Recorded For Film: *FLAMING STAR* (1960)(Cut From film)
EP: Elvis by Request
LP: Elvis for Everyone

SUPPOSE
Written By: Sylvia Dee, George Goehring
Elvis Recorded: June 21, 1967–MGM Culver City, California
Home Recording 1967–Graceland
Recorded For Film: *SPEEDWAY* (1968)(Not Used)
LPs: A Golden Celebration, Speedway

SURRENDER
Based On: Torna a Sorrento
Written By: G. D. de Curtis, Ernesto de Curtis (1911)
Previously Recorded By: Dean Martin, Toni Arden
English Lyrics By: Doc Pomus and Mort Shuman (1960)
Elvis Recorded: October 30, 1960–RCA Nashville
Flip Side: Lonely Man
On The Charts: *Billboard*'s Hot 100 (12 weeks–peaked at #1), British (peaked at #1)
Sales: Over five million
Singles: SURRENDER/Lonely Man, February 1961 Standard release, SURRENDER/Lonely Man, February 1961 Living Stereo release, SURRENDER/Lonely Man, February 1961 Compact 33 Single release, SURRENDER/Lonely Man, February 1961 Living Stereo Compact 33 Single release, SURRENDER/Lonely Man, February 1962 GoldStandard Series reissue., It's Now or Never/SURRENDER, October 1984 Elvis' Greatest Hits–Golden Singles–Vol. I (Boxed Set)
LPs: Elvis, Elvis–A Legendary Performer–Vol. 3, Elvis' Golden Records–Vol. 3, Elvis: Worldwide 50 Gold Award Hits–Vol. I, The Number One Hits, The Top Ten Hits

SUSAN WHEN SHE TRIED
Written By: Don Reid

Previously Recorded By: The Statler Brothers
Elvis Recorded: March 11, 1975–RCA Hollywood
LP: **Elvis Today**

SUSPICION
Written By: Doc Pomus and Mort Shuman
Elvis Recorded: March 19,1962–RCA Nashville
Flip Side: **Kiss Me Quick**
Singles: **Kiss Me Quick/SUSPICION**, April 1964 Gold Standard Series Original release
LP: **Pot Luck**

SUSPICIOUS MINDS
Written By: Mark James
Previously Recorded By: Mark James
Elvis Recorded: January 23, 1969–American Sound Studios
Flip Side: **You'll Think of Me**
On The Charts: *Billboard's* Hot 100 (15 weeks–peaked at #1)
Singles: **SUSPICIOUS MINDS/You'll Think of Me**, September 1969 Standard release, **SUSPICIOUS MINDS/You'll Think of Me**, December 1970 Gold Standard Series reissue, **SUSPICIOUS MINDS/You'll Think of Me**, October 1977 **15 Golden Records–30 Golden Hits** (Boxed Set), **THE ELVIS MEDLEY/Always on My Mind**, November 1982, **THE ELVIS MEDLEY/THE ELVIS MEDLEY**, November 1982 Disc jockey promo, **SUSPICIOUS MINDS/Burning Love**, October 1984, **Elvis' Greatest Hits—Golden Singles–Vol. 2** (Boxed Set)
LPs: **Aloha from Hawaii via Satellite, The Alternate Aloha, Elvis as Recorded at Madison Square Garden, Elvis' Gold Records–Vol. 5, Elvis in Person, The Elvis Medley, Elvis: Worldwide 50 Gold Award Hits–Vol. 1, From Memphis to Vegas/From Vegas to Memphis, Greatest Hits–Vol. 1, The Memphis Record, The Number One Hits, This Is Elvis, The Top Ten Hits**

SWEET ANGELINE
Written By: Chris Arnold, Geoffrey Morrow and David Martin
Elvis Recorded: September 24,1973–Palm Springs
LP: **Raised on Rock/For Ol' Times Sake**

SWEET CAROLINE
Written By: Neil Diamond
Previously Recorded By: Neil Diamond
Elvis Recorded: Live in concert (August 1970–Las Vegas)
LPs: **Elvis Aron Presley, On Stage – February, 1970**

SWING DOWN, SWEET CHARIOT
Based On: Swing Low, Sweet Chariot
Written By: (Tradtional Gospel)
Elvis Recorded: October 31, 1960–RCA Nashville
Recorded For Film: *THE TROUBLE WITH GIRLS* (1968)
Flip Side: **Milky White Way**
Singles: **Milky White Way/SWING DOWN, SWEET CHARIOT**, March 1966, Gold Standard Series Original release.
LPs: **Elvis Aron Presley, Elvis—A Legendary Performer–Vol. 4, His Hand in Mine, Known Only to Him**

SYLVIA
Written By: Geoff Stephens, Les Reed
Elvis Recorded: June 8,1970–RCA Nashville
LP: **Elvis Now**

TAKE GOOD CARE OF HER
Written By: Ed Warren, Arthur Kent
Previously Recorded By: Adam Wade, Johnny Mathis
Elvis Recorded: July 21, 1973–Stax Studios, Memphis
Flip Side: **I've Got a Thing About You, Baby**
On The Charts: *Billboard's* Hot 100 (7 weeks–peaked at #39), Country Best-Sellers (peaked at #4), Easy-Listening (peaked at #27)
Singles: **I've Got a Thing About You, Baby/TAKE GOOD CARE OF HER**, January 1974 Standard release, **I've Got a Thing About You, Baby/TAKE GOOD CARE OF HER**, January 1974 Disc jockey promo, **I've Got a Thing About You, Baby/TAKE GOOD CARE OF HER**, February 1976 Gold Standard Series reissue.
LPs: **Good Times, Our Memories of Elvis**

TAKE ME TO THE FAIR
Written By: Sid Tepper, Roy C. Bennett
Elvis Recorded: September 1962–Radio Recorders
Recorded For Film: *IT HAPPENED AT THE WORLD'S FAIR* (1963)
LP: **It Happened at the World's Fair**

TAKE MY HAND, PRECIOUS LORD
Written By: Thomas A. Dorsey (1939)
Elvis Recorded: January 13, 1957–Radio Recorders
EP: **Peace in the Valley**
LPs: **Elvis' Christmas Album, Essential Elvis–Vol. 2, Known Only to Him, You'll Never Walk Alone**

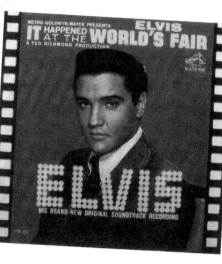

TALK ABOUT THE GOOD TIMES
Written By: Jerry Reed
Elvis Recorded: December 14, 1973–Stax Studios, Memphis
LP: **Good Times**

TEDDY BEAR (LET ME BE YOUR)
Written By: Kal Mann, Bernie Lowe
Elvis Recorded: January 24, 1957–Radio Recorders
Flip Side: **Loving You**
On The Charts: *Billboard's* Hot 100 (24 weeks–peaked at #1), Country Best-Seller (peaked at #1), Rhythm & Blues (peaked at #1)
Sales: One million plus
Singles: **TEDDY BEAR/Loving You**, June 1957 Standard 78 RPM release, **TEDDY BEAR/Loving You**, June 1957. Standard 45 RPM release, **TEDDY BEAR/Loving You**, March 1959 Gold Standard Series reissue, **TEDDY BEAR/Loving You**, October 1977, **15 Golden Records–30 Golden Hits** (Boxed Set), **TEDDY BEAR/Puppet on a String**, August 1978 New single release, **TEDDY BEAR/Loving You**, August 1978, Disc jockey promo, **The Elvis Medley/Always on My Mind**, November 1982, excerpts from Jailhouse Rock, Teddy Bear, Hound Dog, Don't Be Cruel, Burning Love, and Suspicious Minds, **THE ELVIS MEDLEY/THE ELVIS MEDLEY**, November 1982, Disc jockey promo **All Shook Up/TEDDY BEAR**, October 1984, **Elvis' Greatest Hits—Golden Singles–Vol. 1**
EPs: **Dealers' Prevue, Loving You–Vol. 1**
LPs: **Elvis, Elvis—A Canadian Tribute, Elvis Aron Presley, Elvis as Recorded at Madison Square Garden, Elvis' Golden Records, Elvis in Concert, The Elvis Medley, Elvis Sings for Children and Grownups Too!, Elvis: Worldwide 50 Gold Award Hits–Vol. 1, Loving You, The Number One Hits, This Is Elvis, The Top Ten Hits**

TELL ME WHY
Written By: Titus Turner
Previously Recorded By: Marie Knight, Gale Storm, Crew Cuts
Elvis Recorded: January 12,1957–Radio Recorders
Flip Side: **Blue River**
Released: 1965
On The Charts: *Billboard's* Hot 100 (7 weeks–peaked at #33)
Sales: One million plus
SIngles: **TELL ME WHY/Blue River**, December 1965 Standard release, **TELL ME WHY/Blue River**, February 1968 Gold Standard Series reissue.
LPs: **Elvis: The Other Sides—Worldwide Gold Award Hits–Vol. 2, Essential Elvis–Vol. 2, A Valentine Gift for You**

TENDER FEELING
Written By: Bill Giant, Bernie Baum and Florence Kaye
Elvis Recorded: October 1963–RCA Nashville
Recorded For Film: *KISSIN' COUSINS* (1964)
LPs: **Burning Love and Hits from His Movies–Vol. 2, Kissin' Cousins**

THANKS TO THE ROLLING SEA
Written By: Ruth Batchelor and Bob Roberts
Elvis Recorded: March 1962–Radio Recorders
Recorded For Film: *GIRLS! GIRLS! GIRLS!* (1962)
LPs: Elvis Aron Presley, Girls! Girls! Girls!

THAT'S ALL RIGHT (MAMA)
Written By: Arthur (Big Boy) Crudup
Previously Recorded By: Arthur (Big Boy) Crudup
Elvis Recorded: July 5, 1954–Sun Records
SIngles: THAT'S ALL RIGHT (MAMA)/Blue Moon of Kentucky, July 19, 1954 Standard Sun 78 and 45 RPM releases, THAT'S ALL RIGHT (MAMA)/Blue Moon of Kentucky, November 1955 RCA Standard 78 RPM reissue, THAT'S ALL RIGHT (MAMA)/Blue Moon of Kentucky, November 1955 RCA Standard 45 RPM reissue, THAT'S ALL RIGHT (MAMA)/Blue Moon of Kentucky, March 1959 Gold Standard Series reissue, THAT'S ALL RIGHT (MAMA)/Blue Moon of Kentucky, October 1984, Elvis' Greatest Hits—Golden Singles—Vol. 2 (Boxed Set)
EPs: SPD–15, A Touch of Gold–Vol. 2
LPs: The Complete Sun Sessions, Elvis–A Legendary Performer–Vol. 1, Elvis–A Legendary Performer–Vol. 4, Elvis Aron Presley, Elvis as Recorded Live at Madison Square Garden, Elvis in Concert, Elvis: The First Live Recordings, Elvis: The Hillbilly Cat, For LP Fans Only, The Sun Sessions, A Golden Celebration, This Is Elvis

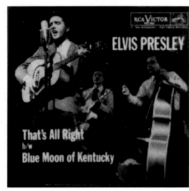

ELVIS PRESLEY
That's All Right
b/w
Blue Moon of Kentucky

THAT'S SOMEONE YOU NEVER FORGET
Written By: Red West
Elvis Recorded: June 25, 1961–RCA Nashville
Flip Side: Long Legged Girl (with the Short Dress On)
On The Charts: *Billboard*'s Hot 100 (1 week–peaked at #92)
Singles: Long Legged Girl (with the Short Dress On)/THAT'S SOMEONE YOU NEVER FORGET, May 1967 Standard Release, Long Legged Girl (with the Short Dress On)/THAT'S SOMEONE YOU NEVER FORGET, 1970 Gold Standard Series reissue
LP: POT LUCK

THAT'S WHEN YOUR HEARTACHES BEGIN
Written By: William J. Raskin, Billy Hill and Fred Fisher (1940)
Previously Recorded By: Ink Spots, Bob Lamb, Billy Bunn and His Buddies
Elvis Recorded: January 13, 1957–Radio Recorders
Flip Side: All Shook Up
On The Charts: *Billboard*'s Top 100 (7 weeks–peaked at #58)
SIngles: All Shook Up/THAT'S WHEN YOUR HEARTACHES BEGIN, March 1957 Standard 78 RPM release, All Shook Up/THAT'S WHEN YOUR HEARTACHES BEGIN March 1957 Standard 45 RPM release, All Shook Up/THAT'S WHEN YOUR HEARTACHES BEGIN, March 1959. Gold Standard Series reissue, All Shook Up/THAT'S WHEN YOUR HEARTACHES BEGIN, October 1977, 15 Golden Records–30 Golden Hits (Boxed Set)
LPs: Elvis' Golden Records, Elvis: Worldwide 50 Gold Award Hits–Vol. 1, Essential Elvis–Vol. 2

THERE AIN'T NOTHING LIKE A SONG
Written By: Joy Byers, William Johnston
Elvis Recorded: June 1967–MGM Culver City, California (Duet with Nancy Sinatra)
Recorded For Film: *SPEEDWAY* (1968)
LPs: Speedway

THERE GOES MY EVERYTHING
Written By: Dallas Frazier
Previously Recorded By: Jack Greene, Engelbert Humperdinck, Sue Raney
Elvis Recorded: June 8, 1970–RCA Nashville Flip Side
On The Charts: *Billboard*'s Hot 100 (9 weeks–peaked at #21)
Country Best-Seller (peaked at #9), Easy-Listening (peaked at #2)
Sales: One millon plus

Singles: I Really Don't Want to Know/THERE GOES MY EVERYTHING, December 1970 Standard release, I Really Don't Want to Know/THERE GOES MY EVERYTHING, February 1972 Gold Standard Series reissue, You'll Never Walk Alone/THERE GOES MY EVERYTHING, February 1982 New single release, You'll Never Walk Alone/THERE GOES MY EVERYTHING, February 1982 Disc jockey promo
LPs: Elvis Country, Elvis: The Other Sides—Worldwide Gold Award Hits–Vol. 2, Greatest Hits–Vol. I

THERE IS NO GOD BUT GOD
Written By: Bill Kenny
Elvis Recorded: June 9,1971–RCA Nashville
LP: He Touched Me

THERE IS SO MUCH WORLD TO SEE
Written By: Sid Tepper, Ben Weisman
Elvis Recorded: June 1966–Radio Recorders
Recorded For Film: *DOUBLE TROUBLE* (1967)
LP: Double Trouble

THERE'S A BRAND NEW DAY ON THE HORIZON
Written By: Joy Byers
Elvis Recorded: March 1964–Radio Recorders
Recorded For Film: *ROUSTABOUT* (1964)
LP: Roustabout

THERE'S A HONKY TONK ANGEL (WHO WILL TAKE ME BACK IN)
Written By: Troy Seals and Denny Rice
Previously Recorded By: Conway Twitty
Elvis Recorded: December 15, 1973–Stax Studios, Memphis
Flip Side: I've Got a Feelin' in My Body
On The Charts: *Billboard*'s Country (13 weeks–peaked at #6)
Singles: THERE'S A HONKY TONK ANGEL (WHO WILL TAKE ME BACK IN)/I've Got a Feelin' in My Body, August 1979 Standard release, THERE'S A HONKY TONK ANGEL (WHO WILL TAKE ME, BACK IN)/ I've Got a Feelin' in My Body, August 1979 Disc jockey promo.
LPs: Our Memories of Elvis–Vol. 2, Promised Land

Our Memories of ELVIS
THERE'S A HONKY TONK ANGEL
I'VE GOT A FEELIN' IN MY BODY

THERE'S ALWAYS ME
Written By: Don Robertson
Elvis Recorded: March 13, 1961–RCA Nashville studios.
Flip Side: Judy
On The Charts: *Billboard*'s Hot 100 (6 weeks–peaked At #56)
Singles: THERE'S ALWAYS ME/ Judy, August 1967 Standard release, THERE'S ALWAYS ME/Judy, 1970 Gold Standard Series reissue.
LP: Something for Everybody

THERE'S GOLD IN THE MOUNTAINS
Written By: Bill Giant, Bernie Baum and Florence Kaye
Elvis Recorded: October 1963–RCA Nashville
Recorded For Film: *KISSIN' COUSINS* (1964)
LP: Kissin' Cousins

THEY REMIND ME TOO MUCH OF YOU
Written By: Don Robertson
Elvis Recorded: September 22, 1962–Radio Recorders
Recorded For Film: *IT HAPPENED AT THE WORLD'S FAIR* (1963)
Flip Side: One Broken Heart for Sale
On The Charts: *Billboard*'s Hot 100 (4 weeks–peaked at #53)
SIngles: One Broken Heart for Sale/THEY REMIND ME TOO MUCH OF YOU, February 1963, Standard release, One Broken Heart for Sale/THEY REMIND ME TOO MUCH OF YOU, August 1984, Gold Standard Series reissue
LPs: Elvis Aron Presley, Elvis in Hollywood, Elvis Sings Hits from His Movies–Vol. I, Elvis: The Other Sides–Worldwide Gold Award Hits–Vol. 2, It Happened at the

World's Fair

A THING CALLED LOVE
Written By: Jerry Reed
Previously Recorded By: Jimmy Dean, Johnny Cash
Elvis Recorded: May 19, 1971–RCA Nashville
LP: He Touched Me

THINKING ABOUT YOU
Written By: Tim Baty
Elvis Recorded: December 12, 1973–Stax Studios, Memphis
Flip Side: My Boy
Singles: My Boy/THINKING ABOUT YOU, January 1975, Standard release, My Boy/THINKING ABOUT YOU, February 1976, Gold Standard Series reissue
LPs: Our Memories of Elvis–Vol. 2, Promised Land

THIS IS LIVING
Written By: Fred Wise, Ben Weisman
Elvis Recorded: October 27, 1961–Radio Recorders
Recorded For Film: KID GALAHAD (1962)
EP: Kid Galahad
LP: C'mon Everybody

THIS IS MY HEAVEN
Written By: Bill Giant, Bernie Baum and Florence Kaye
Elvis Recorded: August 2, 1965–Radio Recorders
Recorded For Film: PARADISE, HAWAIIAN STYLE (1965)
LP: Paradise, Hawaiian Style

THIS IS OUR DANCE
Written By: Les Reed and Geoff Stephens
Elvis Recorded: June 6,1970–RCA Nashville
LP: Love Letters from Elvis

THIS IS THE STORY
Written By: Chris Arnold, Geoffrey Morrow and David Martin
Elvis Recorded: January 13, 1969–American Sound Studios, Memphis
LP: Back in Memphis, From Memphis to Vegas/From Vegas to Memphis

THREE CORN PATCHES
Written By: Jerry Leiber, Mike Stoller
Previously Recorded By: T–Bone Walker
Elvis Recorded: July 21, 1973–Stax Studios, Memphis
LPs: Raised on Rock/For Ol' Times Sake

THRILL OF YOUR LOVE
Written By: Stan Kesler
Elvis Recorded: April 4, 1960–RCA Nashville
LP: Elvis Is Back

TIGER MAN
Written By: Joe Hill Louis, Sam Burns
Previously Recorded By: Rufus Thomas
Elvis Recorded: Live in concert (1968/69/70)
LPs: Elvis Aron Presley, Elvis in Person, Elvis Sings Flaming Star, From Memphis to Vegas/From Vegas to Memphis, A Golden Celebration, Singer Presents Flaming Star and Others

TODAY, TOMORROW AND FOREVER
(Based On: Liebestraum by Franz Liszt)
Written By: Bill Giant, Bernie Baum and Florence Kaye
Elvis Recorded: July 11, 1963–Radio Recorders
Recorded For Film: VIVA LAS VEGAS (1964)
EP: Viva Las Vegas
LP: C'mon Everybody

TOMORROW IS A LONG TIME
Written By: Bob Dylan
Elvis Recorded: May 26, 1966–RCA Nashville

LPs: Spinout, A Valentine Gift for You

TOMORROW NEVER COMES
Written By: Ernest Tubb, Johnny Bond
Previously Recorded By: Ernest Tubb, B. J. Thomas, Slim Whitman
Elvis Recorded: June 7, 1970–RCA Nashville
LP: Elvis Country

TOMORROW NIGHT
Written By: Sam Coslow, Will Gross
Previously Recorded By: Lonnie Johnson, LaVern Baker
Elvis Recorded: September 10, 1954–Sun Records
Released: 1965
LPs: The Complete Sun Sessions, Elvis for Everyone, Reconsider Baby

TONIGHT IS SO RIGHT FOR LOVE
(Based On: Barcarolle by Jacques Offenbach)
Written By: Sid Wayne, Abner Silver
Elvis Recorded: April 28, 1960–RCA Hollywood
Recorded For Film: G. I. BLUES (1960)
LPs: Burning Love and Hits from His Movies–Vol. 2, G. I. Blues

TONIGHT'S ALL RIGHT FOR LOVE
(Based On: Tales from the Vienna Woods by Johann Strauss)
Written By: Sid Wayne, Abner Silver and Joe Lilley
Elvis Recorded: May 6, 1960–Radio Recorders
Recorded For Film: G. I. BLUES (1960) European Versions
LPs: Elvis—A Legendary Performer–Vol. 1, Elvis Aron Presley

TOO MUCH
Written By: Lee Rosenberg, Bernard Weinman
Previously Recorded By: Bernard Hardison, Judy Trema, Frankie Castro
Elvis Recorded: September 2, 1956–Radio Recorders
Flip Side: Playing for Keeps
On The Charts: Billboard's Top 100 (17 weeks–peaked at #2), Country Juke Box (peaked at #3)
Sales: One million plus
Singles: TOO MUCH/Playing for Keeps, January 1957 Standard 78 RPM release, TOO MUCH/Playing for Keeps, January 1957 Standard 45 RPM release, TOO MUCH/Playing for Keeps, March 1959 Gold Standard Series reissue, TOO MUCH/Playing for Keeps, December 1986. Collectibles Collectibles
LPs: DJ–56, A Touch of Gold–Vol. 3, LPs: Elvis' Golden Records, Elvis: Worldwide 50 Gold Award Hits–Vol. 1, A Golden Celebration, The Number One Hits, The Top Ten Hits

TOO MUCH MONKEY BUSINESS
Written By: Chuck Berry
Previously Recorded By: Chuck Berry
Elvis Recorded: January 15, 1968–RCA Nashville
LPs: Elvis Sings Flaming Star, Guitar Man, Singer Presents Elvis Singing Flaming Star and Others, This Is Elvis

TREAT ME NICE
Written By: Jerry Leiber, Mike Stoller
Elvis Recorded: September 5 1957–Radio Recorders
Recorded For Film: JAILHOUSE ROCK (1957)
Flip Side: Jailhouse Rock
On The Charts: Billboard's Top 100 (10 weeks–peaked at #27), Country Disc Jockey (peaked at #11), Rhythm & Blues (peaked at #1)
Sales: One million plus
Singles: Jailhouse Rock/TREAT ME NICE, September 1957 Standard 78 RPM release October 10, Jailhouse Rock/TREAT ME NICE, September 1957 Standard 45 RPM release., Jailhouse Rock/TREAT ME NICE, 1961. Gold Standard Series reissue, Jailhouse Rock/TREAT ME NICE, October 1977, 15 GOLDEN RECORDS–30 GOLDEN HITS
LPs: Dealer's Prevue, A Touch of Gold–Vol. 2, Elvis' Golden Records, Elvis: Worldwide 50 Gold Award Hits–Vol. 1, Essential Elvis

T–R–O–U–B–L–E
Written By: Jerry Chesnut

Elvis Recorded: March 12, 1975–RCA Nashville
Flip Side: **Mr. Songman**
On The Charts: *Billboard*'s Hot 100 (9 weeks–peaked at #35), Country Best Sellers (peaked at #11)
Singles: **T–R–O–U–B–L–E/Mr. Songman**, April 1975 Standard release, **T–R–O–U–B–L–E/ T–R–O–U–B–L–E**, April 1975 Disc jockey promo, **T–R–O–U–B–L–E/Mr. Songman**, February 1976. Gold Standard Series reissue
LPs: **Elvis Aron Presley, Elvis Aron Presley–Forever, Elvis Today**

TROUBLE
Written By: Jerry Leiber, Mike Stoller
Elvis Recorded: January 15, 1958–Radio Recorders
Recorded For Film: *KING CREOLE* (1958)
EP: **King Creole–Vol. 2**
LPs: **Elvis: The Other Sides—Worldwide Gold Award Hits–Vol. 2, Elvis—TV Special, King Creole**

TRUE LOVE
Written By: Cole Porter
Previously Recorded By: Jane Powell, Bing Crosby, Grace Kelly
Elvis Recorded: February 23,1957–Radio Recorders
EP: **Loving You–Vol. 1**
LP: **Loving You**

TRUE LOVE TRAVELS ON A GRAVEL ROAD
Written By: Dallas Frazier, Al Owens
Previously Recorded By: Duane Dee
Elvis Recorded: February 17, 1969–American Sound Studios, Memphis
LPs: **From Elvis in Memphis, The Memphis Record**

TRYIN' TO GET TO YOU
Written By: Rose Marie McCoy, Margie Singleton
Elvis Recorded: July 11, 1955–Sun Records
Flip Side: **I Love You Because**, Singles: **TRYIN' TO GET TO YOU/I Love You Because**, September 1956 Standard 78 RPM release, **TRYIN' TO GET TO YOU/I Love You Because**, September 1956 Standard 45 RPM release, **TRYIN' TO GET TO YOU/I Love You Because**, March 1959 Gold Standard Series reissue, **TRYIN' TO GET TO YOU/I Love You Because**, December 1986, Collectibles
EPs: **Elvis Presley, Elvis Presley–The Most Talked About New Personality in the Last Ten Years of Recorded Music**
LPs: **The Complete Sun Sessions, Elvis–A Legendary Performer–Vol. 1, Elvis in Concert, Elvis Presley, Elvis Recorded Live on Stage in Memphis, A Golden Celebration, The Sun Sessions**

TUTTI FRUTTI
Written By: Dorothy LaBostrie
(Probably Based On Wop–Bop–a–Loo–Bop By: Little Richard)
Elvis Recorded: January 31, 1956–RCA's New York City
Flip Side: **Blue Suede Shoes**
Singles: **Blue Suede Shoes/TUTTI FRUTTI**, September 1956 Standard 78 RPM release, **Blue Suede Shoes/TUTTI FRUTTI**, September 1956, Standard 45 RPM release, **TUTTI FRUTTI/One–Sided Love Affair**, September 1956, Disc jockey record prevue, **Blue Suede Shoes/TUTTI FRUTTI**, March 1959, Gold Standard Series reissue, **Blue Suede Shoes/TUTTI FRUTTI**, October 1984, **ELVIS' GREATEST HITS—Golden Singles–Vol. 1** (Boxed Set)
EPs: **Elvis Presley, Elvis Presley** (RCA SPD–23), **Elvis Presley—The Most Talked About New Personality in the Last Ten Years of Recorded Music**
LPs: **Elvis Presley, A Golden Celebration**

TWEEDLEE DEE
Written By: Winfield Scott
Previously Recorded By: LaVern Baker, Vicki Young, Pee Wee King
Elvis Recorded: Live in concert (1955/56)
LPs: **Elvis: The First Live Recordings (Louisiana Hayride), The Rockin' Rebel–Vol. 2, Standing Room Only–Vol. 2**

TWENTY DAYS AND TWENTY NIGHTS
Written By: Ben Weisman, Clive Westlake
Elvis Recorded: June 4, 1970–RCA Nashville

LP: **That's the Way It Is**

UNCHAINED MELODY
Written By: Hy Zaret, Alex North
Previously Recorded By: Todd Duncan, Les Baxter, Al Hibbler, The Righteous Brothers
Elvis Recorded: Live in concert (June 21, 1977–Rapid City, South Dakota)
Flip Side: **Softly as I Leave You**
On The Charts: *Billboard*'s Country (11 weeks–peaked at #6)
Singles: **UNCHAINED MELODY/Softly as I Leave You**, March 1978, Standard release, **UNCHAINED MELODY/Softly as I Leave You**, March 1978, Disc jockey promo, **Are You Sincere/UNCHAINED MELODY**, May 1980 Gold Standard Series original release
LPs: **Always on My Mind, Elvis Aron Presley, Moody Blue**

UNTIL IT'S TIME FOR YOU TO GO
Written By: Buffy Sainte–Marie
Previously Recorded By: Buffy Sainte–Marie, Neil Diamond
Elvis Recorded: June 8, 1971–RCA Nashville
Flip Side: **We Can Make the Morning**
On The Charts: *Billboard*'s Hot 100 (9 weeks–peaked at #40), Country (peaked at #68), Easy-Listening (7 weeks–peaked at #9)
Singles: **UNTIL IT'S TIME FOR YOU TO GO/We Can Make the Morning**, January 1972 Standard release, **An American Trilogy/UNTIL IT'S TIME FOR YOU TO GO**, May 1973 Gold Standard Series original release, **UNTIL IT'S TIME FOR YOU TO GO/U.S. Male**, December 1986 Collectibles
LPs: **Elvis—A Canadian Tribute, Elvis Now**

UP ABOVE MY HEAD
Written By: Sister Rosetta Tharpe
Previously Recorded By: Al Hirt
Elvis Recorded: June 21, 1968–Western Recorders
LP: **Elvis—TV Special**

U.S. MALE
Written By: Jerry Reed
Previously Recorded By: Jerry Reed
Elvis Recorded: January 17, 1968–RCA Nashville
Flip Side: **Stay Away**
On The Charts: *Billboard*'s Hot 100 (9 weeks–peaked at #28), Country Best-Sellers (6 weeks–peaked at #55)
Singles: **U.S. MALE/Stay Away**, March 1968 Standard release, **U.S. MALE/Stay Away**, 1970. Gold Standard Series reissue, **Until It's Time for You to Go/U.S. MALE**, December 1986 Collectibles
EP: **Stay Away**
LPs: **Almost in Love, Double Dynamite**

VIENNA WOODS ROCK AND ROLL
(Original title for **TONIGHT'S ALL RIGHT FOR LOVE**
See: **TONIGHT'S ALL RIGHT FOR LOVE**)

VINO, DINERO Y AMOR
Written By: Sid Tepper and Roy C. Bennett
Elvis Recorded: January 22,1963–Radio Recorders
Recorded For Film: *FUN IN ACAPULCO* (1963)
LP: **Fun in Acapulco**

VIVA LAS VEGAS
Written By: Doc Pomus, Mort Shuman
Elvis Recorded: July 1963–Radio Recorders (One Take: Duet with Ann–Margret)
Recorded For Film: *VIVA LAS VEGAS* (1964)
Flip Side: **What'd I Say**

On The Charts: *Billboard*'s Hot 100 (7 weeks–peaked at #29)
Sales: One million
Singles: **VIVA LAS VEGAS/What'd I Say**, April 1964 Standard release, **VIVA LAS VEGAS/What'd I Say**, May 1965 Gold Standard Series reissue.
EPs: **See the U.S.A., the Elvis Way**
LPs: **Elvis in Hollywood, Elvis: Worldwide 50 Gold Award Hits–Vol. 1, This Is Elvis**

WALK A MILE IN MY SHOES
Written By: Joe South
Previously Recorded By: Joe South
Elvis Recorded: Live in concert (February 18, 1970–Las Vegas)
LP: **On Stage– February, 1970**

WALK THAT LONESOME VALLEY
(See: THAT LONESOME VALLEY)

THE WALLS HAVE EARS
Written By: Sid Tepper, Roy C. Bennett
Elvis Recorded: March 1962–Radio Recorders
Recorded For Film: *GIRLS! GIRLS! GIRLS!* (1962)
LP: **Girls! Girls! Girls!**

WAY DOWN
Written By: Layng Martine Jr.
Elvis Recorded: October 30, 1976–Graceland
Flip Side: **Pledging My Love**
On The Charts: *Billboard*'s Hot 100 (21 weeks–peaked at #18), Country Best-Sellers (17 weeks–peaked at #1), Easy-Listening (peaked at #14), British (peaked at #1)
Sales: One million plus
Singles: **WAY DOWN/Pledging My Love**, June 1977 Standard release, **WAY DOWN/Pledging My Love**, June 1977 Disc jockey promo, **WAY DOWN/Pledging My Love**, May 1979 Gold Standard Series reissue.
LPs: **Elvis' Gold Records–Vol. 5, Moody Blue, Our Memories of Elvis–Vol. 2**

WE CALL ON HIM
Written By: Fred Karger, Sid Wayne and Ben Weisman
Elvis Recorded: September 11, 1967–RCA Nashville
Flip Side: **You'll Never Walk Alone**
Singles: **You'll Never Walk Alone/WE CALL ON HIM**, April 1968 Standard release. **You'll Never Walk Alone/WE CALL ON HIM**, December 1970 Gold Standard Series reissue.
LPs: **Known Only to Him, You'll Never Walk Alone**

WE CAN MAKE THE MORNING
Written By: Jay Ramsey
Elvis Recorded: May 20,1971–RCA Nashville
Flip Side: **Until It's Time for You to Go**
On The Charts: *Billboard*'s Easy-Listening (7 weeks–peaked at #9)
Singles: **Until It's Time for You to Go/WE CAN MAKE THE MORNING**, January 1972 Standard release.
LP: **Elvis Now**

WEAR MY RING AROUND YOUR NECK
Written By: Bert Carroll, Russell Moody
Elvis Recorded: February 1, 1958–Radio Recorders
Flip Side: **Doncha' Think It's Time**
On The Charts: *Billboard*'s Top 100 (15 weeks–peaked at #3), Country Best-Seller (peaked at #3), Rhythm & Blues (peaked at #7)
Sales: One million plus
Singles: **WEAR MY RING AROUND YOUR NECK/Doncha' Think It's Time**, April 1958 Standard 78 RPM release, **WEAR MY RING AROUND YOUR NECK/Doncha' Think It's Time**, April 1958 Standard 45 RPM release, **WEAR MY RING AROUND**

YOUR NECK/Doncha' Think It's Time, 1961 Gold Standard Series reissue, Don't/**WEAR MY RING AROUND YOUR NECK**, January 1960 Disc jockey promo, **I Was the One/WEAR MY RING AROUND YOUR NECK**, April 1983. New single release, **I Was the One/WEAR MY RING AROUND YOUR NECK**, April 1983. Disc jockey promo
EP: **A Touch of Gold–Vol. 2**
LPs: **Elvis: Worldwide 50 Gold Award Hits–Vol. 1, 50,000,000 Elvis Fans Can't Be Wrong—Elvis' Gold Records–Vol. 2, I Was the One, The Top Ten Hits**

WEARIN' THAT LOVED ON LOOK
Written By: Dallas Frazier, Al Owens
Elvis Recorded: January 14, 1969–American Sound Studios, Memphis
LPs: **From Elvis in Memphis, The Memphis Record**

WELCOME TO MY WORLD
Written By: Ray Winkler, John Hathcock
Previously Recorded By: Jim Reeves Eddy Arnold
Elvis Recorded: Live in concert (January 14, 1973–Honolulu)
LPs: **Aloha from Hawaii via Satellite, The Alternate Aloha, Elvis Aron Presley Welcome to My World**

WE'LL BE TOGETHER
Written By: Charles O'Curran and Dudley Brooks
Elvis Recorded: March 1962–Radio Recorders
Recorded For Film: *GIRLS! GIRLS! GIRLS!* (1962)
Lps: **Burning Love and Hits from His Movies–Vol. 2, Girls! Girls! Girls!**

WE'RE COMING IN LOADED
Written By: Otis Blackwell, Winfield Scott
Elvis Recorded: March 1962–Radio Recorders
Recorded For Film: *GIRLS! GIRLS! GIRLS!* (1962)
LP: **Girls! Girls! Girls!**

WE'RE GONNA MOVE
Written By: Ken Darby
(Credited To: Elvis Presley and Vera Matson)
Elvis Recorded: August 2, 1956–Radio Recorders
Recorded For Film: *LOVE ME TENDER* (1956)
EP: **Love Me Tender**
LPs: **A Date With Elvis, Elvis: The Other Sides—Worldwide Gold Award Hits–Vol. 2, Essential Elvis—The First Movies**

WESTERN UNION
Written By: Sid Tepper and Roy C. Bennett
Elvis Recorded: May 27, 1963–RCA Nashville
LP: **Speedway**

WHAT A WONDERFUL LIFE
Written By: Sid Wayne and Jay Livingston
Elvis Recorded: July 5, 1961–RCA Nashville
Recorded For Film: *FOLLOW THAT DREAM* (1962)
EP: **Follow That Dream**
LP: **I Got Lucky**

WHAT EVERY WOMAN LIVES FOR
Written By: Doc Pomus, Mort Shuman
Elvis Recorded: May 1965–Radio Recorders
Recorded For Film: *FRANKIE AND JOHNNY* (1966)
LP: **Frankie and Johnny**

WHAT NOW, MY LOVE

Written By: P. Delanoe, Gilbert Becaud
English Lyrics By: Carl Sigman
Previously Recorded By: Herb Alpert, Sonny and Cher
Elvis Recorded: Live in concert (January 12, 1973–Honolulu)
EP: Aloha from Hawaii via Satellite
LPs: Aloha from Hawaii via Satellite, The Alternate Aloha

WHAT NOW, WHAT NEXT, WHERE TO
Written By: Don Robertson and Hal Blair
Elvis Recorded: May 26, 1963–RCA Nashville
LPs: Double Trouble, Separate Ways

WHAT'D I SAY
Written By: Ray Charles
Previously Recorded By: Ray Charles, Jerry Lee Lewis, Bobby Darin
Elvis Recorded: July 1964–Radio Recorders
Flip Side: Viva Las Vegas
On The Charts: Billboard's Hot 100 (6 weeks–peaked at #21)
Singles: Viva Las Vegas/WHAT'D I SAY, April 1964 Standard release, Viva Las Vegas/WHAT'D I SAY, May 1965 Gold Standard Series reissue
LPs: Elvis' Gold Records–Vol. 4, Elvis in Concert, Greatest Hits–Vol. 1

WHAT'S SHE REALLY LIKE
Written By: Sid Wayne, Abner Silver
Elvis Recorded: April 28,1960–RCA Hollywood
Recorded For Film: G. I. BLUES (1960)
EP: The EP Collection–Vol. 2
LP: G. I. Blues

WHEELS ON MY HEELS
Written By: Sid Tepper, Roy C. Bennett
Elvis Recorded: March 1964–Radio Recorders
Recorded For Film: ROUSTABOUT (1964)
LP: Roustabout

WHEN I'M OVER YOU
Written By: Shirl Milete
Elvis Recorded: June 7,1970–RCA Nashville
LP: Love Letters from Elvis

WHEN IT RAINS, IT REALLY POURS
Written By: William Robert Emerson
Previously Recorded By: William Robert Emerson
Elvis Recorded: February 24, 1957–Radio Recorders
LPs: The Complete Sun Sessions, Elvis—A Legendary Performer–Vol. 4, Elvis for Everyone, A Golden Celebration, Reconsider Baby

WHEN MY BLUE MOON TURNS TO GOLD AGAIN
Written By: Wiley Walker, Gene Sullivan
Previously Recorded By: Wiley Walker, Gene Sullivan, Tex Ritter
Elvis Recorded: September 2, 1956–Radio Recorders
On The Charts: Billboard's Top 100 (15 weeks–peaked at #27)
Singles: WHEN MY BLUE MOON TURNS TO GOLD AGAIN/Follow That Dream December 1986 Collectibles
EPs: Elvis, Vol. 1, Elvis/Jaye P. Morgan
LPs: Elvis, Elvis: The Other Sides–Worldwide Gold Award Hits–Vol. 2, A Golden Celebration

WHEN THE SAINTS GO MARCHING IN
(See DOWN BY THE RIVERSIDE/WHEN THE SAINTS GO MARCHING IN)

WHERE COULD I GO BUT TO THE LORD
Written By: James B. Coats
Previously Recorded By: Red Foley
Elvis Recorded: May 28,1966–RCA Nashville
LPs: Elvis–TV Special, How Great Thou Art, Known Only to Him

WHERE DID THEY GO, LORD
Written By: Dallas Frazier, Al Owens

Elvis Recorded: September 22,1970–RCA Hollywood
Flip Side: Rags to Riches
On The Charts: Billboard's Hot 100 (7 weeks–peaked at #33), Country (peaked at #55), Easy-Listening (peaked at #18)
Singles: Rags to Riches/WHERE DID THEY GO, LORD, February 1971 Standard release, Rags to Riches/WHERE DID THEY GO, LORD, February 1972. Gold Standard Series reissue
LP: He Walks Beside Me

WHERE DO I GO FROM HERE
Written By: Paul Williams
Previously Recorded By: Paul Williams
Elvis Recorded: March 27,1972–RCA Hollywood
LP: Elvis

WHERE DO YOU COME FROM
Written By: Ruth Batchelor and Bob Roberts
Elvis Recorded: March 1962 at Radio Recorders
Flip Side: Return to Sender
Recorded For Film: GIRLS! GIRLS! GIRLS! (1962)
On The Charts: Billboard's Hot 100 (1 week–peaked at #99)
Sales: One million
Singles: Return to Sender/WHERE DO YOU COME FROM, October 1962 Standard release, Return to Sender/WHERE DO YOU COME FROM, June 1963 Gold Standard Series reissue, Return to Sender/WHERE DO YOU COME FROM, October 1977 15 GOLDEN RECORDS—30 GOLDEN HITS (Boxed Set)
LPs: Elvis: Worldwide 50 Gold Award Hits–Vol. 1, Girls! Girls! Girls!

WHERE NO ONE STANDS ALONE
Written By: Moise Liste
Elvis Recorded: May 26, 1966–RCA Nashville
LPs: Elvis in Nashville, How Great Thou Art

WHISTLING TUNE, A
Written By: Sherman Edwards, Hal David
Elvis Recorded: October 26,1961–Radio Recorders
Recorded For Film: KID GALAHAD (1962)
EP: Kid Galahad
LP: C'mon Everybody

WHITE CHRISTMAS
Written By: Irving Berlin
Previously Recorded By: Bing Crosby
Elvis Recorded: September 6, 1957–Radio Recorders
EP: Christmas with Elvis
LP: Elvis' Christmas Album

WHO AM I
Written By: Charles (Rusty) Goodman
Elvis Recorded: February 22, 1969–American Sound Studios, Memphis
LPs: He Walks Beside Me, Known Only to Him, The Memphis Record, You'll Never Walk Alone

WHO ARE YOU (WHO AM I)
Written By: Sid Wayne, Ben Weisman
Elvis Recorded: June 1967–Radio Recorders
Recorded For Film: SPEEDWAY (1968)
LP: Speedway

WHO NEEDS MONEY
Written By: Randy Starr
Elvis Recorded: February 21,1967–RCA Nashville
Recorded For Film: CLAMBAKE (1967)
LPs: Clambake

WHOLE LOTTA SHAKIN' GOIN' ON
Written By: Dave (Curly) Williams, Roy Hall (1954)
Previously Recorded By: Big Maybelle, The Commodores, Jerry Lee Lewis
Elvis Finally Recorded: September 22,1970–RCA Nashville

LPs: Aloha from Hawaii via Satellite, Elvis Country, Elvis Recorded Live on Stage in Memphis

WHY ME LORD
Written By: Kris Kristofferson
Previously Recorded By: Kris Kristofferson
Elvis Recorded: Live in concert (March 20, 1974)
LPs: Elvis Aron Presley, Elvis Recorded Live on Stage in Memphis

WILD IN THE COUNTRY
Written By: Hugo Peretti, Luigi Creatore and George Weiss
Elvis Recorded: November 7,1960 - Radio Recorders
Recorded For Film: WILD IN THE COUNTRY (1961)
Flip Side: I Feel So Bad
On The Charts: Billboard's Hot 100 (5 weeks–peaked at #26)
Singles: I Feel So Bad/WILD IN THE COUNTRY, May 1961 Standard release, I Feel So Bad/WILD IN THE COUNTRY, May 1961 Compact 33 Single release, I Feel So Bad/WILD IN THE COUNTRY, May 1961 Living Stereo release, I Feel So Bad/WILD IN THE COUNTRY, February 1962 Gold Standard Series reissue, I Feel So Bad/WILD IN THE COUNTRY, December, 1986 Collectibles
LPs: Elvis Aron Presley, Elvis in Hollywood, Elvis: The Other Sides—Worldwide Gold Award Hits–Vol. 2

WINTER WONDERLAND
Written By: Dick Smith and Felix Bernard
Previously Recorded By: Guy Lombardo and His Royal Canadians, The Andrews Sisters, Perry Como
Elvis Recorded: May 16,1971–RCA Nashville
LPs: Elvis Sings the Wonderful World of Christmas

WISDOM OF THE AGES
Written By: Bill Giant, Bernie Baum and Florence Kaye
Elvis Recorded: February 24, 1965–RCA Nashville
Recorded For Film: HARUM SCARUM (1965) (Cut)
LP: Harum Scarum

WITCHCRAFT (Not Sinatra Hit)
Written By: Dave Bartholomew, Pearl King
Previously Recorded By: The Spiders
Elvis Recorded: May 26, 1963–RCA's Nashville
On The Charts: Billboard's Hot 100 (7 weeks–peaked At #32)
Sales: One million
Singles: Bossa Nova Baby/WITCHCRAFT, October 1963 Standard release, Bossa Nova Baby/WITCHCRAFT, August 1964. Gold Standard Series reissue.
LPs: Elvis' Gold Records–Vol. 4, Elvis: The Other Sides—Worldwide Gold Award Hits–Vol. 2, Return of the Rocker

WITHOUT HIM
Written By: Myron Lefevre
Elvis Recorded: May 27, 1966–RCA Nashville
LP: How Great Thou Art

WITHOUT LOVE (THERE IS NOTHING)
Written By: Danny Small
Previously Recorded By: Clyde McPhatter, Ray Charles, Oscar Toney Jr., Tom Jones
Elvis Recorded: January 23,1969–American Sound Studios, Memphis
LPs: Back in Memphis, From Memphis to Vegas/From Vegas to Memphis, The Memphis Record

WOLF CALL
Written By: Bill Giant, Bernie Baum and Florence Kaye
Elvis Recorded: July 1964–Radio Recorders
Recorded For Film: GIRL HAPPY (1965)
LP: Girl Happy

WOMAN WITHOUT LOVE
Written By: Jerry Chesnut
Previously Recorded By: Bob Luman, Johnny Darrell
Elvis Recorded: March 12,1975–RCA Nashville

LPs: Elvis Aron Presley–Forever, Elvis Today

WONDER OF YOU, THE
Written By: Baker Knight
Previously Recorded By: Ray Peterson
Elvis Recorded: Live in concert (February 19, 1970–LasVegas)
Flip Side: Mama Liked the Roses
On The Charts: Billboard's Hot 100 (12 weeks–peaked at #9), Country Best-Sellers (peaked at #37), British (peaked at #1)
Singles: THE WONDER OF YOU/Mama Liked the Roses, May 1970 Standard release, THE WONDER OF YOU/Mama Liked the Roses, August 1971 Gold Standard Series reissue.
LPs: Elvis Aron Presley, Elvis: The Other Sides—Worldwide Gold Award Hits–Vol. 2, Greatest Hits–Vol. 1, On Stage–February, 1970, The Top Ten Hits

WONDERFUL WORLD
Written By: Guy Fletcher, Doug Flett
Elvis Recorded: March 7, 1968–Radio Recorders
Recorded For Film: LIVE A LITTLE, LOVE A LITTLE (1968)
LPs: Elvis Sings Flaming Star, Singer Presents Elvis Singing Flaming Star and Others

THE WONDERFUL WORLD OF CHRISTMAS
Written By: Charles Tobias, Albert Frisch
Elvis Recorded: May 16,1971–RCA Nashville
LP: Elvis Sings the Wonderful World of Christmas

WOODEN HEART
(Based On: Muss I Denn Zum Stadtele Hinaus)
Written By: Bert Kaempfert, Kay Twomey, Fred Wise, Ben Weisman
Elvis Recorded: April 28, 1960–RCA Hollywood, Recorded For Film: G. I. BLUES (1960)
Flip Side: Blue Christmas
Sales: Well over one million
Singles: Blue Christmas/WOODEN HEART, November 1964 Gold Standard Series original, Puppet on a String/WOODEN HEART, October 1965 Gold Standard Series original
LPs: Elvis—A Legendary Performer–Vol. 4, Elvis Sings for Children and Grownups Too!, Elvis: Worldwide 50 Gold Award Hits–Vol. 1, G. I. Blues

WORDS
Written By: The Bee Gees
Elvis Recorded: Live in concert (August 22,1969–Las Vegas)
LPs: Elvis in Person, From Memphis to Vegas/From Vegas to Memphis

WORKING ON THE BUILDING
Written By: Hoyle, Bowles
Previously Recorded By: The Blackwood Brothers, The Jordanaires
Elvis Recorded: October 31,1960–RCA Nashville
LPs: Elvis in Nashville, His Hand in Mine

A WORLD OF OUR OWN
Written By: Bill Giant, Bernie Baum, Florence Kaye
Elvis Recorded: September 1962–Radio Recorders
Recorded For Film: IT HAPPENED AT THE WORLD'S FAIR (1963)
LP: It Happened at the World's Fair

WRITE TO ME FROM NAPLES
Written By: Alex Alstone and Jimmy Kennedy
Elvis Recorded: Home Taping Mid 60's–Graceland
LP: A Golden Celebration (Graceland; 1960s)

THE YELLOW ROSE OF TEXAS/THE EYES OF TEXAS
Written By: J. K. (1853) (Yellow Rose)
Written By: John L. Sinclair (1907) (Eyes Of Texas)
Previously Recorded By: Gene Autry, Mitch Miller, Johnny Desmond, Stan Freberg, Ernest Tubb
Elvis Recorded: July 1963 at Radio Recorders
Adapted By: Fred Wise, Ben Weisman
Recorded For Film: VIVA LAS VEGAS (1964)
LPs: Double Dynamite, Elvis Sings Flaming Star, Singer Presents Elvis Singing Flaming Star and Others

YESTERDAY
Written By: Lennon/McCartney
Previously Recorded By: The Beatles, Matt Monroe, Ray Charles (and 2,497 others including Elvis)
Elvis Recorded: Live in concert (August 25, 1969–Las Vegas)
LPs: **Elvis Aron Presley, On Stage–February, 1970**

YOGA IS AS YOGA DOES
Written By: Gerald Nelson and Fred Burch
Elvis Recorded: September 1966–Radio Recorders, (Duet With: Elsa Lanchester)
Recorded For Film: *EASY COME, EASY GO* (1967)
EP: **Easy Come, Easy Go**
LP: **I Got Lucky**

YOU ASKED ME TO
Written By: Billy Joe Shaver
Previously Recorded By: Waylon Jennings
Elvis Recorded: December 11, 1973–Stax Studios, Memphis
On The Charts: *Billboard*'s Country (15 weeks–peaked at #8)
Singles: **Lovin' Arms/YOU ASKED ME TO**, March 1981 Standard release, **Lovin' Arms/YOU ASKED ME TO**, March 1981. Disc jockey promo
LPs: **Guitar Man, Promised Land**

YOU CAN'T SAY NO IN ACAPULCO
Written By: Sid Feller, Dorothy Fuller, Lee Morris
Elvis Recorded: January 23, 1963–Radio Recorders
Recorded For Film: *FUN IN ACAPULCO* (1963)
LP: **Fun in Acapulco**

YOU DON'T HAVE TO SAY YOU LOVE ME
(Io Che Non Vivo [Senza Te])
Written By: V. Pallavicini and P. Donaggio
English Lyrics: Vicki Wickham and Simon Napier–Bell
Previously Recorded By: Dusty Springfield
Elvis Recorded: June 6, 1970–RCA Nashville
On The Charts: *Billboard*'s Hot 100 (10 weeks–peaked at #11), Easy-Listening (11 weeks–peaked at #1), Country Best-Sellers (peaked at #56)
Sales: One million plus
Singles: **YOU DON'T HAVE TO SAY YOU LOVE ME/Patch It Up**, October 1970 Standard release, **YOU DON'T HAVE TO SAY YOU LOVE ME/Patch It Up**, February 1972. Gold Standard Series reissue
LPs: **Elvis as Recorded at Madison Square Garden, Elvis: The Other Sides—Worldwide Gold Award Hits–Vol. 2, That's the Way It Is**

YOU DON'T KNOW ME
Written By: Eddy Arnold, Cindy Walker
Previously Recorded By: Jerry Vale, Ray Charles
Elvis Recorded: September 11, 1967–RCA Nashville
Recorded For Film: *CLAMBAKE* (1967)
On The Charts: *Billboard*'s Hot 100 (6 weeks–peaked at #34), Easy-Listening (peaked at #44)
Singles: **Big Boss Man/YOU DON'T KNOW ME**, September 1967. Standard release. **Big Boss Man/YOU DON'T KNOW ME**, 1970 Gold Standard Series reissue
EP: **Clambake**
LPs: **Clambake, Elvis Sings Hits from His Movies–Vol. 1**

YOU GAVE ME A MOUNTAIN
Written By: Marty Robbins
Previously Recorded By: Frankie Laine, Marty Robbins, Johnny Bush
Elvis Recorded: Live in concert (January 14,1973–Honolulu)
EP: **Aloha from Hawaii via Satellite**
LPs: **Always on My Mind, Aloha from Hawaii via Satellite, The Alternate Aloha, Elvis Aron Presley, Elvis in Concert**

YOU GOTTA STOP
Written By: Bill Giant, Bernie Baum, Florence Kaye
Elvis Recorded: September 29, 1966–Radio Recorders
Recorded For Film: *EASY COME, EASY GO* (1967)
EP: **Easy Come, Easy Go**

LP: **I Got Lucky**

YOU'LL BE GONE
Written By: Elvis Presley, Red West, Charlie Hodge
Elvis Recorded: March 18, 1962–RCA Nashville
Flip Side: **Do the Clam**
Singles: **Do the Clam/YOU'LL BE GONE**, February 1965 Standard release. **Do The Clam/YOU'LL BE GONE**, November 1965 Gold Standard Series reissue
LP: **Girl Happy**

YOU'LL NEVER WALK ALONE
Written By: Oscar Hammerstein II, Richard Rodgers (For: *Carousel*)
Previously Recorded By: Frank Sinatra, Judy Garland, Patti LaBelle
Elvis Recorded: September 11, 1967–RCA Nashville
Flip Side: **We Call on Him**
On The Charts: *Billboard*'s Hot 100 (2 weeks–peaked at #90)
Singles: **YOU'LL NEVER WALK ALONE/We Call on Him**, April 1968 Standard release, **YOU'LL NEVER WALK ALONE/We Call on Him**, December 1970 Gold Standard Series reissue, **YOU'LL NEVER WALK ALONE/There Goes My Everything**, February 1982 New release, **YOU'LL NEVER WALK ALONE/There Goes My Everything**, February 1982 Disc jockey promo, **Old Shep/YOU'LL NEVER WALK ALONE**, December 1986 Collectibles
LPs: **Double Dynamite, You'll Never Walk Alone**

YOU'LL THINK OF ME
Written By: Mort Shuman
Elvis Recorded: January 14,1969–American Sound Studios, Memphis
Flip Side: **Suspicious Minds**
Singles: **Suspicious Minds/YOU'LL THINK OF ME**, September 1969 Standard release, **Suspicious Minds/YOU'LL THINK OF ME**, December 1970 Gold Standard Series reissue, **Suspicious Minds/YOU'LL THINK OF ME**, October 1977, **15 GOLDEN RECORDS–30 GOLDEN HITS, Suspicious Minds/YOU'LL THINK OF ME** January 1983 Gold Standard Series reissue
LPs: **Back in Memphis, Elvis: The Other Sides—Worldwide Gold Award Hits–Vol. 2, From Memphis to Vegas/From Vegas to Memphis, The Memphis Record**

YOUNG AND BEAUTIFUL
Written By: Abner Silver, Aaron Schroeder
Elvis Recorded: April 30, 1957–Radio Recorders
Recorded For Film: *JAILHOUSE ROCK* (1957)
EP: **Jailhouse Rock**
LPs: **A Date with Elvis, Elvis: The Other Sides – Worldwide Gold Award Hits–Vol. 2, Essential Elvis–The First Movies, I Was the One, A Valentine Gift for You**

YOUNG DREAMS
Written By: Aaron Schroeder, Martin Kalmanoff
Elvis Recorded: January 23, 1958–Radio Recorders
Recorded For Film: *KING CREOLE* (1958)
EP: **King Creole–Vol. 2**
LPs: **Elvis: The Other Sides—Worldwide Gold Award Hits–Vol. 2, King Creole**

YOUR CHEATIN' HEART
Written By: Hank Williams
Previously Recorded By: Hank Williams, Joni James
Elvis Recorded: February 1, 1958–Radio Recorders
EP: **The EP Collection–Vol. 2**
LPs: **Elvis for Everyone, Welcome to My World**

YOUR LOVE'S BEEN A LONG TIME COMING
Written By: Rory Bourke
Elvis Recorded: December 15, 1973–Stax Studios, Memphis
LPs: **Our Memories of Elvis–Vol. 1, Promised Land**

YOUR MAMA DON'T DANCE
Written By: Kenny Loggins, Jim Messina

Elvis Recorded: Live in concert (March 20, 1974–Memphis)
LP: **Elvis Recorded Live on Stage in Memphis**

YOUR TIME HASN'T COME YET, BABY
Written By: Joel Hirschhorn, Al Kasha
Elvis Recorded: June 20, 1967–MGM Culver City, California
Recorded For Film: *SPEEDWAY* (1968)
Flip Side: **Let Yourself Go**
On The Charts: *Billboard*'s Hot 100 (7 weeks–peaked at #72), Country Best-Sellers (peaked at #50)
Singles: **YOUR TIME HASN'T COME YET, BABY/Let Yourself Go**, June 1968 Standard release, **YOUR TIME HASN'T COME YET, BABY/Let Yourself Go**, December 1970 Gold Standard Series reissue
LP: **Speedway**

YOU'RE A HEARTBREAKER
Written By: Charles (Jack) Alvin Sallee
Previously Recorded By: Jimmy Heap, Ray Anthony's Orchestra
Elvis Recorded: December 10, 1954–Sun Records
Flip Side: **Milkcow Blues Boogie**
Singles: **Milkcow Blues Boogie/YOU'RE A HEARTBREAKER**, January 8, 1955 Standard 78 & 45 RPM releases, **Milkcow Blues Boogie/YOU'RE A HEARTBREAKER**, November 1955 RCA Standard 78 RPM reissue (Sun), **Milkcow Blues Boogie/YOU'RE A HEART-BREAKER**, November 1955 RCA Standard 45 RPM reissue (Sun), **Milkcow Blues Boogie/YOU'RE A HEARTBREAKER**, March 1959 Gold Standard Series reissue, **Milkcow Blues Boogie/YOU'RE A HEARTBREAKER**, December 1986, Collectibles
LPs: **The Complete Sun Sessions, For LP Fans Only, The Sun Sessions**

YOU'RE RIGHT, I'M LEFT, SHE'S GONE
(See: **I'M LEFT, YOU'RE RIGHT, SHE'S GONE**)

YOU'VE LOST THAT LOVIN' FEELIN'
Written By: Barry Mann, Cynthia Weil
Previously Recorded By: The Righteous Brothers, Dionne Warwick
Elvis Recorded: Live in concert (August 14, 1970–Las Vegas)
LPs: **Elvis Aron Presley, Elvis as Recorded at Madison Square Garden, That's the Way It Is**

THE LONG PLAYING ALBUMS

•••

Standard Releases

Standard RCA, RCA Camden, Pickwick and Pairs Records
releases are included in this section.

•••

ALMOST IN LOVE
(RCA Camden CAS-2440) November 1970
Side 1: **Almost in Love, Long Legged Girl (with the Short Dress On), Edge of Reality, My Little Friend, A Little Less Conversation**
Side 2: **Rubberneckin', Clean Up Your Own Backyard, U.S. Male, Charro, Stay Away, Joe**

ALMOST IN LOVE
(Pickwick CAS-2440) December 1975
Reissue of the 1973 version of RCA Camden CAS-2440

ALOHA FROM HAWAII VIA SATELLITE
(RCA VPSX-6089) February 1973
Side 1: **Introduction, Also Sprach Zarathustra** (by Joe Guercio Orchestra), **See See Rider, Burning Love, Something, You Gave Me a Mountain, Steamroller Blues**
Side 2: **My Way, Love Me, Johnny B. Goode, It's Over, Blue Suede Shoes, I'm So Lonesome I Could Cry, I Can't Stop Loving You, Hound Dog**
Side 3: **What Now, My Love, Fever, Welcome To My World, Suspicious Minds, Introductions by Elvis**
Side 4: **I'll Remember You, Long Tall Sally/Whole Lotta Shakin 'Goin' On, An American Trilogy, A Big Hunk o' Love, Can't Help Falling in Love**

ALOHA FROM HAWAII VIA SATELLITE
(RCA CPD2-2642) 1977
New Number assigned to RCA VPSX-6089

THE ALTERNATE ALOHA
(RCA 6985-1-R) May 1988
Side 1: **Also Sprach Zarathustra** (Joe Guercio Orchestra), **See See Rider, Burning Love, Something, You Gave Me A Mountain, Steamroller Blues, My Way, Love Me, It's Over, Blue Suede Shoes, I'm So Lonesome I Could Cry**
Side 2: **What Now, My Love, Fever, Welcome To My World, Suspicious Minds, Introductions by Elvis, I'll Remember You, An American Trilogy, A Big Hunk O' Love, Can't Help Falling In Love, Blue Hawaii** (bonus)

ALWAYS ON MY MIND
(RCA AFL1-5430) May 1985
Side 1: **Separate Ways, Don't Cry Daddy, My Boy, Solitaire, Bigger They Are, Harder They Fall, Hurt, Pieces of My Life**
Side 2: **I Miss You, It's Midnight, I've Lost You, You Gave Me a Mountain, Unchained Melody, Always on My Mind**

BACK IN MEMPHIS
(RCA LSP-4429) November 1970
Side 1: **Inherit the Wind, This Is the Story, Stranger in My Own Home Town, A Little Bit of Green, And the Grass Won't Pay No Mind**
Side 2: **Do You Know Who I Am, From a Jack to a King, The Fair Is Moving On, You'll Think of Me, Without Love (There Is Nothing)**

BACK IN MEMPHIS
(RCA APLI-4429) 1977
Renumbering of RCA LSP-4429.

BLUE HAWAII
(RCA LPM-2426) October 1961
Soundtrack: *Blue Hawaii*
Side 1: Blue Hawaii, Almost Always True, Aloha Oe, No More, Can't Help Falling in Love, Rock-a-Hula Baby, Moonlight Swim
Side 2: Ku-u-i-po, Ito Eats, Slicin' Sand, Hawaiian Sunset, Beach Boy Blues, Island of Love (Kauai), Hawaiian Wedding Song

BLUE HAWAII
(RCA LSP-2426) October 1961
Stereo version of RCA LPM-2426

BLUE HAWAII
(RCA AFL1-2426) September 1977. Renumbering of RCA LSP2426

BLUE HAWAII
(RCA AYLI-3683) May 1980
Renumbering of RCA AFL1-2426

BURNING LOVE AND HITS FROM HIS MOVIES–VOL. 2
(RCA Camden CAS-2595) November 1972
Side 1: Burning Love, Tender Feeling, Am I Ready, Tonight Is So Right for Love, Guadalajara
Side 2: It's a Matter of Time, No More, Santa Lucia, We'll Be Together, I Love Only One Girl

BURNING LOVE AND HITS FROM HIS MOVIES–VOL. 2
(Pickwick CAS-2595) December 1975
Reissue of RCA Camden CAS-2595

CLAMBAKE
(RCA LPM-3893) November 19, 1967
Complete soundtrack with bonus cuts
Side 1: Guitar Man (bonus), Clambake, Who Needs Money, A House That Has Everything, Confidence, Hey, Hey, Hey
Side 2: You Don't Know Me, The Girl I Never Loved, How Can You Lose What You Never Had (bonus), Big Boss Man (bonus), Singing Tree (bonus), Just Call Me Lonesome (bonus)

CLAMBAKE
(RCA LSP-3893) November 19, 1967
Stereo release

CLAMBAKE
(RCA AFL1-2565) September 1977
New number assigned to RCA LSP-3893

C'MON EVERYBODY
(RCA Camden CAL-2518) 1971
Side 1: C'mon Everybody, Angel, Easy Come, Easy Go, A Whistling Tune, Follow That Dream
Side 2: King of the Whole Wide World, I'll Take Love, Today, Tomorrow and Forever, I'm Not the Marrying Kind, This Is Living

C'MON EVERYBODY
(Pickwick CAS-2518) December 1975
Reissue of RCA Camden CAL-2518

THE COMPLETE SUN SESSIONS
(RCA 6414-1-R) June 1987

All the master and many alternates and outtakes from Elvis' sessions at Sun with Sam Phillips. An important record.
Side A: THE MASTER TAKES
That's All Right (Mama), Blue Moon of Kentucky, Good Rockin' Tonight, I Don't Care If the Sun Don't Shine, Milkcow Blues Boogie, You're a Heartbreaker, Baby, Let's Play House, I'm Left, You're Right, She's Gone (My Baby's Gone)
Side B: THE MASTER TAKES
Mystery Train, I Forgot to Remember to Forget, I Love You Because, Blue Moon, Tomorrow Night, I'll Never Let You Go (Little Darlin'), Just Because, Tryin' to Get to You
Side C: THE OUTTAKES
Harbor Lights, I Love You Because (takes #1 and #2), That's All Right (Mama), Blue Moon of Kentucky, I Don't Care If the Sun Don't Shine, I'm Left, You're Right, She's Gone (My Baby's Gone), (take #9), I'll Never Let You Go (Little Darlin'), When It Rains, It Really Pours
Side D: THE ALTERNATE TAKES
I Love You Because (take #3), I Love You Because (take #4), I Love You Because (take #5), I'm Left, You're Right, She's Gone (My Baby's Gone, (take #7), I'm Left, You're Right, She's Gone (My Baby's Gone), (take #8), I'm Left, You're Right, She's Gone (My Baby's Gone) (take #10), I'm Left, You're Right, She's Gone (My Baby's Gone) (take #11), I'm Left, You're Right, She's Gone (My Baby's Gone) (take #13), I'm Left, You're Right, She's Gone (My Baby's Gone) (take #12)

A DATE WITH ELVIS
(RCA LPM-2011) September 1959.
Side 1: Blue Moon of Kentucky, Young and Beautiful, (You're So Square) Baby, I Don't Care, Milkcow Blues Boogie, Baby, Let's Play House
Side 2: Good Rockin' Tonight, Is It So Strange, We're Gonna Move, I Want to Be Free, I Forgot to Remember to Forget

A DATE WITH ELVIS
(RCA LSP-2011 [e]) January 1965
Reprocessed Stereo release

A DATE WITH ELVIS
(RCA AFL1-2011 [e]) 1977
Reissued with new number for RCA LSP-2011[e]

DOUBLE DYNAMITE
(Pickwick DL2-5001) December 1975
Side 1: Burning Love, I'll Be There, Fools Fall in Love, Follow That Dream, You'll Never Walk Alone
Side 2: Flaming Star, The Yellow Rose of Texas/The Eyes of Texas, Old Shep, Mama
Side 3: Rubberneckin', U.S. Male, Frankie and Johnny, If You Think I Don't Need You, Easy Come, Easy Go
Side 4: Separate Ways, Peace in the Valley, Big Boss Man, It's a Matter of Time

DOUBLE DYNAMITE
(RCA PDL2-1010) 1982
Reissue of Pickwick double LP DL2-5001 without You'll Never Walk Alone and If You Think I Don't Need You

DOUBLE TROUBLE
(RCA LPM-3787) June 1967
Complete soundtrack from *DOUBLE TROUBLE*
Side 1: Double Trouble, Baby If You'll Give Me All of Your Love, Could I Fall in Love, Long Legged Girl (with the Short Dress On), City by Night, Old MacDonald
Side 2: I Love Only One Girl, There Is So Much World to See, It Won't Be Long (bonus), Never Ending (bonus), Blue River (bonus), What Now, What Next, Where To (bonus)

DOUBLE TROUBLE
(RCA LSP-3787) June 1967
Stereo release

DOUBLE TROUBLE
(RCA AFL1-2564) September 1977
New number assigned to RCA LSP-3787

ELVIS
(RCA LPM-1382)
October 19, 1956
Side 1: Rip It Up,
Love Me, When My
Blue Moon Turns to
Gold Again, Long
Tall Sally, First in
Line, Paralyzed
Side 2: So Glad
You're Mine, Old
Shep, Ready Teddy,
Anyplace Is
Paradise, How's the
World Treating
You, How Do You
Think I Feel

ELVIS
(RCA LSP-1382 [e])
February 1962
Electronically
reprocessed stereo
release

ELVIS
(RCA AFL1-1382 [e]) 1977
New number assigned to RCA LSP-1382 (e)

ELVIS
(RCA AFM1-5199) 1985
For the 50th anniversary of Elvis' birth, Elvis
(RCA LPM-1382) was rereleased

ELVIS
(RCA APL1-0283) July 1973
Side 1: Fool, Where Do I Go from Here,
Love Me, Love the Life I Lead, It's Still Here,
It's Impossible
Side 2: For Lovin' Me, Padre, I'll Take You
Home Again, Kathleen, I Will Be True, Don't
Think Twice, It's All Right

ELVIS
(RCA DPL2-0056 [e]) August 1973
Though this double set of Elvis' biggest hits was
sold only on television, it was a tremendous
success, selling over 3 million copies Side 1:
Hound Dog, I Want You I Need You, I Love
You, All Shook Up, Don't, I Beg of You,
Side 2: A Big Hunk o' Love, Love Me, Stuck
on You, Good Luck Charm, Return to Sender
Side 3: Don't Be Cruel, Loving You, Jailhouse
Rock, Can't Help Falling in Love, I Got Stung
Side 4: Teddy Bear, Love Me Tender, Hard Headed Woman, It's Now or Never,
Surrender

ELVIS–A CANADIAN TRIBUTE
(RCA KKL1-7065) October 1978
Canadians are responsible for most of the tunes on the Tribute album.
Side 1: Introduction, Jailhouse Rock, Introduction, Teddy Bear, Loving You, Until It's
Time for You to Go, Early Morning Rain, Vancouver Press Conference (1957)
Side 2: I'm Movin' On, Snowbird, For Lovin' Me, Put Your Hand in the Hand, Little
Darlin', My Way

ELVIS–A LEGENDARY PERFORMER–VOL. I
(RCA CPL1-0341) January 1974
Side 1: That's All Right (Mama), I Love You Because, Heartbreak Hotel, Elvis Sails
interview (:34), Don't Be Cruel, Love Me, Trying to Get to You
Side 2: Love Me Tender, Peace in the Valley, Elvis Sails interview (2:14), A Fool Such as
I, Tonight's All Right for Love, Are You Lonesome Tonight?, Can't Help Falling in Love

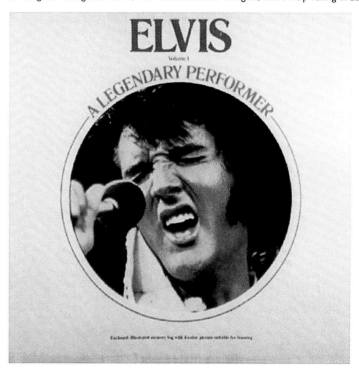

ELVIS—A LEGENDARY PERFORMER–VOL. 2
(RCA CPLI-1349) January 1976
Side 1: Harbor Lights, Jay Thompson Interviews Elvis, I Want You, I Need You, I Love
You, Blue Suede Shoes, Blue Christmas, Jailhouse Rock, It's Now or Never
Side 2: Cane and a High Starched Collar, Presentation of Awards to Elvis, Blue Hawaii,
Such a Night, Baby What You Want Me to Do, How Great Thou Art, If I Can Dream

ELVIS—A LEGENDARY PERFORMER–VOL. 3
(RCA CPL1-3082) December 1978
Side 1: Hound Dog, TV Guide Interview, Danny, Fame and Fortune, Frankfort Special,
Britches, Crying in the Chapel
Side 2: Surrender, Guadalajara, It Hurts Me, Let Yourself Go, In the Ghetto, Let It Be Me

ELVIS–A LEGENDARY PERFORMER–VOL. 3
(RCA CPLI-3078) December 1978
Limited edition, identical to RCA CPL1-3082

ELVIS–A LEGENDARY PERFORMER–VOL. 4
(RCA CPLI-4848) November 1983
The duet with Ann-Margret is included on this album for the first time since it was
recorded in 1963.
Side 1: When It Rains, It Really Pours, Interviews by Ray and Norma Pillow, One Night,
I'm Beginning to Forget You, Mona Lisa, Plantation Rock, Swing Down, Sweet Chariot
Side 2: The Lady Loves Me (Elvis and Ann-Margret from VIVA LAS VEGAS), Wooden Heart,
That's All Right (Mama), Are You Lonesome Tonight?, Reconsider Baby, I'll Remember You

ELVIS ARON PRESLEY
(RCA CPL8-3699) July 1980
Celebrating the 25th anniversary of Elvis' move from Sun Records to RCA, **ELVIS ARON
PRESLEY** is a boxed set of eight LPs that chart the course of Elvis' career.
Record 1: AN EARLY LIVE PERFORMANCE—Heartbreak Hotel, Long Tall Sally, Blue

Suede Shoes, Money Honey, An Elvis monologue
Record 2: AN EARLY BENEFIT PERFORMANCE—Heartbreak Hotel, All Shook Up, (Now and Then There's) a Fool Such as I, I Got a Woman, Love Me, Introductions, Such a Night, Reconsider Baby, I Need Your Love Tonight, That's All Right (Mama), Don't Be Cruel, One Night, Are You Lonesome Tonight?, It's Now or Never, Swing Down Sweet Chariot, Hound Dog
Record 3: COLLECTORS' GOLD FROM THE MOVIE YEARS:—They Remind Me Too Much of You, Tonight Is So Right for Love, Follow That Dream, Wild in the Country, Datin', Shoppin' Around, Can't Help Falling in Love, A Dog's Life, I'm Falling in Love Tonight, Thanks to the Rolling Sea
Record 4: THE TV SPECIALS–ELVIS: ALOHA FROM HAWAII; ELVIS IN CONCERT—Jailhouse Rock, Suspicious Minds, Lawdy Miss Clawdy/Baby What You Want Me to Do, Blue Christmas, You Gave Me a Mountain, Welcome to My World, Tryin' to Get to You, I'll Remember You, My Way
Record 5: THE LAS VEGAS YEARS—Polk Salad Annie, You've Lost That Lovin' Feelin', Sweet Caroline, Kentucky Rain, Are You Lonesome Tonight?, My Babe, In the Ghetto, An American Trilogy, Little Sister/Get Back, Yesterday
Record 6: LOST SINGLES—I'm Leavin, The First Time Ever I Saw Your Face, High Heel Sneakers, Softly As I Leave You, Unchained Melody, Fool, Rags to Riches, It's Only Love, America the Beautiful
Record 7: ELVIS AT THE PIANO—It's Still Here, I'll Take You Home Again Kathleen, Beyond the Reef, I Will Be True THE CONCERT YEARS PART 1—Also Sprach Zarathustra (Joe Guercio Orchestra), See See Rider, I Got a Woman/Amen/I Got a Woman, Love Me, If You Love Me (Let Me Know), Love Me Tender, All Shook Up, Teddy Bear/Don't Be Cruel
Record 8: THE CONCERT YEARS CONCLUDED–Hound Dog, The Wonder of You, Burning Love, Dialogue/Introductions/ Johnny B. Goode, Introductions/Long Live Rock and Roll, T-R-O-U-B-L-E, Why Me Lord, How Great Thou Art, Let Me Be There, An American Trilogy, Funny How Time Slips Away, Little Darlin', Mystery Train/Tiger Man, Can't Help Falling in Love

ELVIS ARON PRESLEY—FOREVER
(RCA PDL2-1185) March 1988
Side 1: Blue Hawaii, Hawaiian Wedding Song, No More, Early Morning Rain
Side 2: Pieces of My Life, I Can Help, Bringing It Back, Green, Green Grass of Home
Side 3: Mean Woman Blues, Loving You, Got a Lot o' Livin' to Do, Blueberry Hill
Side 4: T-R-O-U-B-L-E, And I Love You So, Woman Without Love, Shake a Hand

ELVIS AS RECORDED AT MADISON SQUARE GARDEN
(RCA LSP-4776) June 1972
All tracks on this album were recorded at Elvis' June 10, 1972, evening concert at Madison Square Garden.
Side 1: Also Sprach Zarathustra (Joe Guercio Orchestra), That's All Right (Mama), Proud Mary, Never Been to Spain, You Don't Have to Say You Love Me, You've Lost That Lovin' Feelin', Polk Salad Annie, Love Me, All Shook Up, Heartbreak Hotel, Teddy Bear/Don't Be Cruel, Love Me Tender
Side 2: The Impossible Dream, Introductions by Elvis, Hound Dog, Suspicious Minds, For the Good Times, An American Trilogy, Funny How Time Slips Away, I Can't Stop Loving You, Can't Help Falling in Love

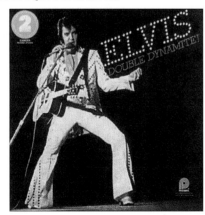

ELVIS AS RECORDED AT MADISON SQUARE GARDEN
(RCA AQLI-4776) 1979
New number assigned to RCA LSP-4776.

ELVIS' CHRISTMAS ALBUM
(RCA LOC-1035) November 1957
Side 1: Santa Claus Is Back in Town, White Christmas, Here Comes Santa Claus, I'll Be Home for Christmas, Blue Christmas, Santa, Bring My Baby Back (to Me)
Side 2: Oh Little Town of Bethlehem, Silent Night, Peace in the Valley, I Believe, Take My Hand, Precious Lord, It Is No Secret

ELVIS' CHRISTMAS ALBUM
(RCA LPM-1951) November 1958
New number assigned to RCA LOC-1035

ELVIS' CHRISTMAS ALBUM
(RCA LSP-1951 [e]) November 1964
Electronically reprocessed stereo reissue of RCA LPM- 1951

ELVIS' CHRISTMAS ALBUM
(RCA AFM1-5486) September 1985
Digitally remastered monaural reissue of RCA LPM-1951

ELVIS' CHRISTMAS ALBUM
(RCA Camden CAL-2428)
November 1970
Side 1: Blue Christmas, Silent Night, White Christmas, Santa Claus Is Back In Town, I'll Be Home For Christmas
Side2: If Every Day Was Like Christmas, Here Comes Santa Claus, Oh Little Town of Bethlehem, Santa, Bring My Baby Back (To Me), Mama Liked the Roses

ELVIS' CHRISTMAS ALBUM
(Pickwick CAS-2428) December 1975
Reissue of RCA Camden CAL-2428

ELVIS COUNTRY
(RCA LSP-4460) January 1971
Side 1: Snowbird, Tomorrow Never Comes, Little Cabin on the Hill, Whole Lotta Shakin' Goin' On, Funny How Time Slips Away, Really Don't Want to Know
Side 2: There Goes My Everything, It's Your Baby You Rock It, The Fool, Faded Love, I Washed My Hands in Muddy Water, Make the World Go Away

ELVIS COUNTRY
(RCA AFLI-4460) 1977
New number assigned to RCA LSP-4460.

ELVIS COUNTRY
(RCA AYMI-3956) May 1981
New number assigned to RCA AFLI-4460

ELVIS FOR EVERYONE
(RCA LPM-3450) July 1965
Side 1: Your Cheatin' Heart Summer Kisses, Winter Tears, Finders Keepers Losers Weepers, In My Way, Tomorrow Night, Memphis, Tennessee
Side 2: For the Millionth and Last Time Forget Me Never, Sound Advice, Santa Lucia, I Met Her Today, When It Rains, It Really Pours

ELVIS FOR EVERYONE
(RCA LSP-3450) July 1965
Stereo release.

ELVIS FOR EVERYONE
(RCA AFLI-3450) 1977
New number assigned to RCA LSP-3450

ELVIS FOR EVERYONE
(RCA AFLI-4332) February 1982
New number assigned to RCA AFLI-3450

ELVIS' GOLD RECORDS–VOL. 4

(RCA LPM-3921) February 1968
Side 1: Love Letters, Witchcraft, It Hurts Me, What'd I Say, Please Don't Drag That String Around, Indescribably Blue
Side 2: (You're the Devil) In Disguise, Lonely Man, A Mess of Blues, Ask Me, Ain't That Loving You, Baby, Just Tell Her Jim Said Hello

ELVIS' GOLD RECORDS–VOL. 4

(RCA LSP-3921) February 1968
Stereo release.

ELVIS' GOLD RECORDS–VOL. 4

(RCA AFL1-3921) 1977
New number assigned to RCA LSP-3921.

ELVIS' GOLD RECORDS–VOL. 5

(RCA AFL1-4941) March 1984
Side 1: Suspicious Minds, Kentucky Rain, In the Ghetto, Clean Up Your Own Back Yard, If I Can Dream
Side 2: Burning Love, If You Talk in Your Sleep, For the Heart, Moody Blue, Way Down

ELVIS' GOLDEN RECORDS

(RCA LPM-1707) April 1958
Side 1: Hound Dog, Loving You, All Shook Up, Heartbreak Hotel, Jailhouse Rock, Love Me, Too Much
Side 2: Don't Be Cruel, That's When Your Heartaches Begin, Teddy Bear, Love Me Tender, Treat Me Nice, Any Way You Want Me, I Want You, I Need You, I Love You

ELVIS' GOLDEN RECORDS

(RCA LSP-1707 [e]) February 1962
Electronically reprocessed stereo release

ELVIS' GOLDEN RECORDS

(RCA AFL1-1707 [e])
1977. New number assigned to RCA LSP-1707 (e)

ELVIS' GOLDEN RECORDS

(RCA AQL1-1707 [e]) 1979
New number assigned to RCA AFL1-1707(e)

ELVIS' GOLDEN RECORDS

(RCA AFM1-5196) 1985
Special release in which all tracks were digitally remastered and restored to monaural

ELVIS' GOLDEN RECORDS–VOL. 3

(RCA LPM-2765) September 1963
Side 1: It's Now or Never, Stuck on You,

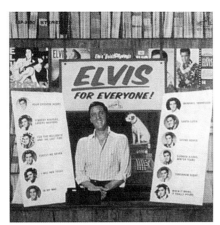

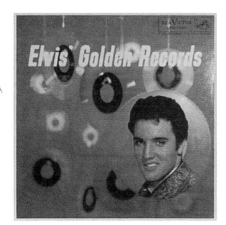

Fame and Fortune, I Gotta Know, Surrender, I Feel So Bad
Side 2: Are You Lonesome Tonight?, (Marie's the Name) His Latest Flame, Little Sister, Good Luck Charm, Anything That's Part of You, She's Not You

ELVIS' GOLDEN RECORDS–VOL. 3

(RCA LSP-2765) September 1963
Stereo release

ELVIS' GOLDEN RECORDS–VOL. 3

(RCA AFL1-2765) 1977
New number assigned to RCA LSP-2765

ELVIS IN CONCERT

(RCA APL2-2587) October 1977
Recorded live in Omaha, Nebraska (June 19, 1977), and Rapid City, South Dakota (June 21, 1977)
Side A: Elvis' Fans' Comments/Opening Riff, Also Sprach Zarathustra/Opening Riff (reprise), See See Rider, That's All Right(Mama), Are You Lonesome Tonight?, Teddy Bear/Don't Be Cruel, Elvis' Fans' Comments, You Gave Me a Mountain, Jailhouse Rock
Side B: Elvis' Fans' Comments, How Great Thou Art, Elvis' Fans' Comments, I Really Don't Want to Know, Elvis Introduces His Father, Hurt, Hound Dog, My Way, Can't Help Falling in Love, Closing Riff, Special Message from Elvis' Father, Vernon Presley
Side C: I Got a Woman/Amen, Elvis Talks, Love Me, O Sole Mio (Sherrill Nielsen)/It's Now or Never (Elvis), Tryin' to Get to You
Side D: Hawaiian Wedding Song, Fairytale, Little Sister, Early Morning Rain, What'd I Say, Johnny B. Goode, And I Love You So

ELVIS IN CONCERT

(RCA CPL2-2587) 1982
New number assigned to RCA APL2-2587

ELVIS IN HOLLYWOOD

(RCA DPL2-0168) January 1976
Sold only on television
Side 1: Jailhouse Rock, Rock-a-Hula Baby, G. I. Blues, Kissin' Cousins, Wild in the Country
Side 2: King Creole, Blue Hawaii, Fun in Acapulco, Follow That Dream, Girls! Girls! Girls!
Side 3: Viva Las Vegas, Bossa Nova Baby, Flaming Star, Girl Happy, Frankie and Johnny
Side 4: Roustabout, Spinout, Double Trouble, Charro, They Remind Me Too Much of You

ELVIS IN NASHVILLE

(RCA 8468-1-R) November 1988
Side 1: I Got a Woman, A Big Hunk o' Love, Working on the Building, Judy, Anything That's Part of You, Night Rider, Where No One Stands Alone
Side 2: Just Call Me Lonesome, Guitar Man, Little Cabin on the Hill, It's Your Baby, You Rock It, Early Mornin' Rain, It's Still Here, I, John

ELVIS IN PERSON AT THE INTERNATIONAL HOTEL, LAS VEGAS, NEVADA

RCA LSP-4428) November 1970
All songs on *Elvis in Person* were recorded live at the International Hotel from August 22 to 26, 1969
Side 1: Blue Suede Shoes, Johnny B. Goode, All Shook Up, Are You Lonesome Tonight? Hound Dog, I Can't Stop Loving You, My Babe
Side 2: Mystery Train/Tiger Man, Words, In the Ghetto, Suspicious Minds, Can't Help Falling in Love

ELVIS IN PERSON AT THE INTERNATIONAL HOTEL, LAS VEGAS, NEVADA

(RCA AFL1-4428) 1977
New number assigned to RCA LSP-4428

ELVIS IN PERSON AT THE INTERNATIONAL HOTEL, LAS VEGAS, NEVADA
(RCA AYL1-3892) February 1981
New number assigned to RCA AFL1-4428

ELVIS IS BACK
(RCA LPM-2231) April 1960
Elvis' return from the arm
Recorded in Nashville.
Side 1: Make Me Know It, Fever, The Girl of My Best Friend, I Will Be Home Again, Dirty, Dirty Feeling, Thrill of Your Love
Side 2: Soldier Boy, Such a Night, It Feels So Right, The Girl Next Door, Went a' Walking, Like a Baby, Reconsider Baby

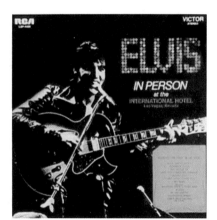

ELVIS IS BACK
(RCA LSP-2231) April 1960
Stereo release

ELVIS IS BACK
(RCA AFL1-2231) 1977
New number assigned to RCA LSP-2231

THE ELVIS MEDLEY
(RCA AHL1-4530) November 1982
This LP was based on the single release, The Elvis Medley.
Side 1: The Elvis Medley (Jailhouse Rock/Teddy Bear/HoundDog/Don't Be Cruel/Burning Love/Suspicious Minds), Jailhouse Rock, Teddy Bear, Hound Dog, Don't Be Cruel
Side 2: Burning Love, Suspicious Minds, Always on My Mind, Heartbreak Hotel, Hard Headed Woman

ELVIS NOW
(RCA LSP-4671) February 1972
Side 1: Help Me Make It Through the Night, Miracle of the Rosary, Hey Jude, Put Your Hand in the Hand, Until It's Time for You to Go
Side 2: We Can Make the Morning, Early Morning Rain, Sylvia, Fools Rush In, I Was Born About Ten Thousand Years Ago

ELVIS NOW
(RCA AFL1-4671) 1977
New number assigned to RCA LSP-4671

ELVIS PRESLEY
(RCA LPM-1254) March 13, 1956
The first album. Recorded in New York City and Nashville.
Side 1: Blue Suede Shoes, I'm Counting on You, I Got a Woman, One-Sided Love Affair, I Love You Because, Just Because
Side 2: Tutti Frutti, Tryin' to Get to You, I'm Gonna Sit Right Down and Cry (Over You), I'll Never Let You Go (Little Darlin'), Blue Moon, Money Honey

ELVIS PRESLEY
(RCA LSP-1254 [e]) February 1962
Electronically reprocessed stereo release

ELVIS PRESLEY
(RCA AFL1-1254 [e]) 1977
New number assigned to RCA LSP-1254 (e)

ELVIS PRESLEY
(RCA APM1-5198) 1985

A celebration of Elvis' 50th birthday

ELVIS RECORDED LIVE ON STAGE IN MEMPHIS
(RCA CPL1-0606) June 1974
Recorded in Memphis on March 20, 1974.
Side 1: See See Rider, I Got a Woman, Love Me, Tryin' to get to you, Long Tall Sally/Whole Lotta Shakin' Goin' On/Your Mama Don't Dance/Flip Flop and Fly, Jailhouse Rock/Hound Dog, Why Me Lord, How Great Thou Art
Side 2: Blueberry Hill/I Can't Stop Loving You, Help Me, An American Trilogy, Let Me Be There, My Baby Left Me, Lawdy Miss Clawdy, Can't Stop Loving You

ELVIS RECORDED LIVE ON STAGE IN MEMPHIS
(RCA APDI-0606) June 1974
Quadradisc release

ELVIS RECORDED LIVE ON STAGE IN MEMPHIS
(RCA AFL1-0606) 1977
New number assigned to RCA CPL1-0606

ELVIS RECORDED LIVE ON STAGE IN MEMPHIS
(RCA AQL1-4776) 1979
New number assigned to RCA AFL1-0606

ELVIS SINGS FLAMING STAR
(RCA Camden CAS 2304) April 1969
Side 1: Flaming Star, Wonderful World, Night Life, All I Needed Was the Rain, Too Much Monkey Business
Side 2: The Yellow Rose of Texas/The Eyes of Texas, She's a Machine, Do the Vega, Tiger Man

ELVIS SINGS FLAMING STAR
(Pickwick CAS-2304) December 1975
Pickwick reissue of RCA Camden CAS-2304

ELVIS SINGS FOR CHILDREN AND GROWNUPS TOO!
(RCA CPL1-2901) July 1978
Side 1: Teddy Bear, Wooden Heart, Five Sleepy Heads, Puppet on a String, Angel, Old MacDonald
Side 2: How Would You Like to Be, Cotton Candy Land, Old Shep, Big Boots, Have a Happy

ELVIS SINGS HITS FROM HIS MOVIES–VOL. I
(RCA Camden CAS-2567) June 1972
Side 1: Down by the Riverside/When the Saints Go Marching In, They Remind Me Too Much of You, Confidence, Frankie and Johnny, Guitar Man
Side 2: Long Legged Girl (with the Short Dress On), You Don't Know Me, How Would You Like to Be, Big Boss Man, Old MacDonald

ELVIS SINGS HITS FROM HIS MOVIES–VOL. I
(Pickwick CAS-2567) December 1975
Reissue of RCA Camden CAS-2567

ELVIS SINGS THE WONDERFUL WORLD OF CHRISTMAS
(RCA LSP-4579) October 1971
Side 1: O Come, All Ye Faithful, The First Noel, On a Snowy Christmas Night, Winter Wonderland, The Wonderful World of Christmas, It Won't Seem Like Christmas (Without You)
Side 2: I'll Be Home on Christmas Day, If I Get Home on Christmas Day, Holly Leaves and Christmas Trees, Merry Christmas, Baby, Silver Bells

ELVIS SINGS THE WONDERFUL WORLD OF CHRISTMAS
(RCA ANL1-1936) 1973
New number assigned to RCA LSP-4579 and released in the Pure Gold series. The album went Gold and then Platinum in December of 1973

ELVIS: THE FIRST LIVE RECORDINGS
(Music Works PB-3601) February 1984
Recordings from Elvis' appearances on *Louisiana Hayride*
Side 1: Introduction, Elvis with Horace Logan, Baby, Let's Play House, Maybellene, Tweedlee Dee
Side 2: That's All Right (Mama), Recollections by Frank Page, Hound Dog

ELVIS: THE HILLBILLY CAT
(Music Works PB-3602) July 1984
Elvis' first *Louisiana Hayride* appearance.
Side 1: Introduction, Elvis with Horace Logan, That's All Right (Mama), Elvis Talks with Horace Logan
Side 2: Blue Moon of Kentucky, Recollections by Frank Page, Good Rockin' Tonight, I Got a Woman

ELVIS: THE OTHER SIDE—WORLDWIDE GOLD AWARD HITS–VOL. 2
(RCA LPM-6402) August 1971
Side 1: Puppet on a String, Witchcraft, Trouble, Poor Boy, I Want to Be Free, Doncha' Think It's Time, Young Dreams
Side 2: The Next Step Is Love, You Don't Have to Say You Love Me, Paralyzed, My Wish Came True, When My Blue Moon Turns to Gold Again, Lonesome Cowboy
Side 3: My Baby Left Me, It Hurts Me, I Need Your Love Tonight, Tell Me Why, Please Don't Drag That String Around, Young and Beautiful
Side 4: Hot Dog, New Orleans, We're Gonna Move, Crawfish, King Creole, I Believe in the Man in the Sky, Dixieland Rock
Side 5: The Wonder of You, They Remind Me Too Much of You, Mean Woman Blues, Lonely Man, Any Day Now, Don't Ask Me Why
Side 6: (Marie's the Name) His Latest Flame, I Really Don't Want to Know, (You're So Square), Baby I Don't Care, I've Lost You, Let Me, Love Me
Side 7: Got a Lot o' Livin' to Do, Fame and Fortune, Rip It Up, There Goes My Everything, Lover Doll, One Night
Side 8: Just Tell Her Jim Said Hello, Ask Me, Patch It Up, As Long as I Have You, You'll Think of Me, Wild in the Country

ELVIS TODAY
(RCA APLI-1039) May 1975
Side 1: T-R-O-U-B-L-E, And I Love You So, Susan When She Tried, Woman Without Love, Shake a Hand
Side 2: Pieces of My Life, Fairytale, I Can Help, Bringing It Back, Green Green Grass of Home

ELVIS TODAY
(RCA APDI-1039) May 1975
Quadradisc release

ELVIS TODAY
(RCA AFL1-1039) 1977
New Number assigned to RCA APL1-1039

ELVIS–TV SPECIAL
(RCA LPM-4088) November 25, 1968
Side 1: Trouble/Guitar Man, Lawdy Miss Clawdy/Baby What You Want Me To Do, Dialogue, Heartbreak Hotel/Hound Dog/All Shook Up/Can't Help Falling in Love/Jailhouse Rock, Dialogue, Love Me Tender
Side 2: Dialogue, Where Could I Go but to the Lord/Up Above My Head/Saved, Dialogue, Blue Christmas, Dialogue, One Night, Memories, Nothingville/Dialogue/Big Boss Man/GuitarMan/Little Egypt/Trouble /Guitar Man, If I Can Dream

ELVIS–TV SPECIAL
(RCA AFM1-4088) 1977
New number assigned to RCA LPM-4088

ELVIS–TV SPECIAL
(RCA AYM1-3894) February 1981
New number assigned to RCA AFM1-4088

ELVIS: WORLDWIDE 50 GOLD AWARD HITS–VOL. 1
(RCA LPM-6401) August 1970
Side 1: Heartbreak Hotel, I Was the One, I Want You, I Need You, I Love You, Don't

Be Cruel, Hound Dog, Love Me Tender
Side 2: Any Way You Want Me, Too Much, Playing for Keeps, All Shook Up, That's When Your Heartaches Begin, Loving You
Side 3: Teddy Bear, Jailhouse Rock, Treat Me Nice, I Beg of You, Don't Wear My Ring Around Your Neck, Hard Headed Woman
Side 4: I Got Stung, (Now and Then There's) A Fool Such As I, A Big Hunk o' Love, Stuck on You, A Mess of Blues, It's Now or Never
Side 5: I Gotta Know, Are You Lonesome Tonight?, Surrender, I Feel So Bad, Little Sister, Can't Help Falling in Love
Side 6: Rock-a-Hula Baby, Anything That's Part of You, Good Luck Charm, She's Not You, Return to Sender, Where Do You Come From, One Broken Heart for Sale
Side 7: (You're the) Devil in Disguise, Bossa Nova Baby, Kissin' Cousins, Viva Las Vegas, Ain't That Loving You Baby, Wooden Heart
Side 8: Crying in the Chapel, If I Can Dream, In the Ghetto, Suspicious Minds, Don't Cry Daddy, Kentucky Rain, Excerpts from Elvis Sails

ESSENTIAL ELVIS–THE FIRST MOVIES
(RCA 6738-1-R) January 1988
All the songs from Elvis' first three films including 23 unreleased tracks
Side 1: Love Me Tender, Let Me, Poor Boy, We're Gonna Move, Loving You (unreleased slow version take #10), Party (unreleased version), Hot Dog, Teddy Bear, Loving You (unreleased fast version takes #20 and #21), Mean Woman Blues (alternate film version), Got a Lot o' Livin' to Do (unreleased version)
Side 2: Loving You (unreleased fast version take #1), Party, Lonesome Cowboy, Jailhouse Rock (unreleased with vocal overdub take #6), Treat Me Nice (unreleased version take #10, Young and Beautiful (unreleased version take #12), Don't Leave Me Now (original version take #12), I Want to Be Free (original version take #11), (You're So Square) Baby I Don't Care (original version take #16; vocal overdub take #6), Jailhouse Rock (unreleased version take #5), Got a Lot o' Livin' to Do, Love Me Tender (unreleased version)

ESSENTIAL ELVIS–VOL. 2
(RCA 9589-1-R) March 1989
Side 1: I Beg of You (take #1), Is It So Strange (take #1), Have I Told You Lately That I Love You (take #2), It Is No Secret (takes #1, #2 and #3), Blueberry Hill (take #2), Mean Woman Blues (take #4), Peace in the Valley (takes #2 and #3), Have I Told You Lately That I Love You (take #6)
Side 2: Blueberry Hill (take #7), That's When Your Heartaches Begin (takes #4, #5 and #6), Is It So Strange (takes #7 and #11), I Beg of You (takes #6 and #8), Peace in the Valley (take #7), Have I Told You Lately That I Love You (takes #12 and #13), I Beg of You (take #12)

50,000,000 ELVIS FANS CAN'T BE WRONG—ELVIS' GOLD RECORDS–VOL. 2
(RCA LPM-2075) December 1959
Side 1: I Need Your Love Tonight, Don't Wear My Ring Around Your Neck, My Wish Came True, I Got Stung
Side 2: One Night, A Big Hunk o' Love, I Beg of You, A Fool Such as I, Doncha' Think It's Time

50,000,000 ELVIS FANS CAN'T BE WRONG—ELVIS' GOLD RECORDS–VOL. 2
(RCA LSP-2075 [e])
February 1962
Electronically reprocessed stereo release

50,000,000 ELVIS FANS CAN'T BE WRONG—ELVIS' GOLD RECORDS–VOL. 2
(RCA AFL1-2075 [e])
1977
New number assigned to RCA LSP-2075 (e)

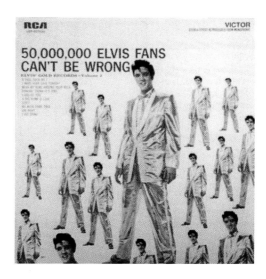

50,000,000 ELVIS FANS CAN'T BE WRONG—ELVIS' GOLD RECORDS–VOL. 2
(RCA AFMI-5197) 1985
Special digitally remastered release in original monaural

FOR LP FANS ONLY
(RCA LPM-1990) February 9, 1959
Side I: That's All Right (Mama), Lawdy Miss Clawdy, Mystery Train, Playing for Keeps, Poor Boy
Side 2: My Baby Left Me, I Was the One, Shake, Rattle and Roll, I'm Left, You're Right, She's Gone, You're a Heartbreaker

FOR LP FANS ONLY
(RCA LSP-1990 [e]) January 1965
Electronically reprocessed stereo release

FOR LP FANS ONLY
(RCA AFL1-1990 [e]) 1977
New number assigned to RCA LSP-1990 (e)

FRANKIE AND JOHNNY
(RCA LPM-3553) April 1966
Complete soundtrack album
Side I: Frankie and Johnny, Come Along, Petunia the Gardener's Daughter, Chesay, What Every Woman Lives For, Look Out Broadway
Side 2: Beginner's Luck, Down by the Riverside/When the Saints Go Marching In, Shout It Out, Hard Luck, Please Don't Stop Loving Me, Everybody Come Aboard

FRANKIE AND JOHNNY
(RCA LSP-3553) April 1966, Stereo release

FRANKIE AND JOHNNY
(RCA APLI-2559) September 1977
Reissue of RCA LSP-3553 after Elvis' death

FRANKIE & JOHNNY
(Pickwick ACL-7007) November 1976
Side I: Frankie and Johnny, Come Along, What Every Woman Lives For, Hard Luck, Please Don't Stop Loving Me
Side 2: Down by the Riverside/When the Saints Go Marching In, Petunia the Gardener's Daughter, Beginner's Luck, Shout It Out

FROM ELVIS IN MEMPHIS
(RCA LSP-4155) June 1969
Side I: Wearin' That Loved on Look, Only the Strong Survive, I'll Hold You in My Heart (Till I Can Hold You in My Arms), Long Black Limousine, It Keeps Right on a-Hurtin', I'm Movin' On
Side 2: Power of My Love, Gentle on My Mind, After Loving You, True Love Travels on a Gravel Road, Any Day Now, In the Ghetto

FROM ELVIS IN MEMPHIS
(RCA AFL1-4155) 1977
New number assigned to RCA LSP-4155

FROM ELVIS PRESLEY BOULEVARD, MEMPHIS, TENNESSEE
(RCA APLI-1506) May 1976
Side I: Hurt, Never Again, Blue Eyes Crying in the Rain, Danny Boy, The Last Farewell
Side 2: For the Heart, Bigger They Are, The Harder They Fall, Solitaire, Love Coming Down, I'll Never Fall in Love Again

FROM ELVIS PRESLEY BOULEVARD, MEMPHIS, TENNESSEE
(RCA APDI-1506) May 1976
Quadradisc release

FROM ELVIS PRESLEY BOULEVARD, MEMPHIS, TENNESSEE
(RCA AFL1-1506) 1977
New number assigned to RCA APL1-1506

FROM MEMPHIS TO VEGAS/FROM VEGAS TO MEMPHIS
(RCA LSP-6020) November 16, 1969
Elvis' first double LP
Side I: Blue Suede Shoes, Johnny B. Goode, All Shook Up, AreYou Lonesome Tonight?, Hound Dog, I Can't Stop Loving You, My Babe
Side 2: Mystery Train/Tiger Man, Words, In the Ghetto, Suspicious Minds, Can't Help Falling in Love
Side 3: Inherit the Wind, This Is the Story, Stranger in My Own Home Town, A Little Bit of Green, And the Grass Won't Pay No Mind
Side 4: Do You Know Who I Am, From a Jack to a King, The Fair Is Moving On, You'll Think of Me, Without Love (There Is Nothing)

FUN IN ACAPULCO
(RCA LPM-2576)
December 1963
Complete soundtrack
Side I: Fun in Acapulco, Vino, Dinero y Amor, Mexico, El Toro, Marguerita, The Lady was a Bullfighter, (There's) No Room to Rhumba in a Sports Car
Side 2: I Think I'm Gonna Like It Here, Bossa Nova Baby, You Can't Say No in Acapulco, Guadalajara, Love Me Tonight (bonus), Slowly but Surely (bonus)

FUN IN ACAPULCO
(RCA LSP-2756) December 1963
Stereo release

FUN IN ACAPULCO
(RCA AFL1-2756) 1977
New number assigned to RCA LSP-2756

G. I. BLUES
(RCA LPM-2256) October 1960
Complete soundtrack
Side I: Tonight Is So Right for Love, What's She Really Like, Frankfort Special, Wooden Heart, G. I. Blues
Side 2: Pocketful of Rainbows, Shoppin' Around, Big Boots, Didja' Ever, Blue Suede Shoes, Doin' the Best I Can

G. I. BLUES
(RCA LSP-2256) October 1960
Stereo release

G. I. BLUES
(RCA AFL1-2256) 1977
New number assigned to RCA LSP-2256

G. I. BLUES
(RCA AYL1-3735) 1980
New number assigned to RCA AFL1-2256

GIRL HAPPY
(RCA LPM-3338) April 1965
Complete soundtrack with bonus cuts
Side I: Girl Happy, Spring Fever, Fort Lauderdale Chamber of Commerce, Startin' Tonight, Wolf Call, Do Not Disturb
Side 2: Cross My Heart and Hope to Die, The Meanest Girl in Town, Do the Clam, Puppet on a String, I've Got to Find My Baby, You'll Be Gone (bonus)

GIRL HAPPY
(RCA LSP-3338) April 1965
Stereo release

GIRL HAPPY
(RCA AFL1-3338) 1977
New number assigned to RCA LSP-3338

GIRLS! GIRLS! GIRLS!
(RCA LPM-2621) November 1962
Complete soundtrack except for Dainty Little Moonbeams
Side 1: Girls! Girls! Girls!, I Don't Wanna Be Tied, Where Do You Come From, I Don't Want To, We'll Be Together, A Boy Like Me A Girl Like You, Earth Boy
Side 2: Return to Sender, Because of Love, Thanks to the Rolling Sea, Song of the Shrimp, The Walls Have Ears, We're Coming in Loaded

GIRLS! GIRLS! GIRLS!
(RCA LSP-2621) November 1962
Stereo release

GIRLS! GIRLS! GIRLS!
(RCA AFL1-2621) 1977
New number assigned to RCA LSP-2621

A GOLDEN CELEBRATION
(RCA CPM6-5172) October 1984
A six record birthday bash for Elvis' 50th
Side 1: THE SUN SESSIONS OUTTAKES—Harbor Lights, That's All Right (Mama), Blue Moon of Kentucky, I Don't Care If the Sun Don't Shine, I'm Left You're Right She's Gone (a.k.a. My Baby's Gone), I'll Never Let You Go (Little Darlin'), When It Rains It Really Pours
Side 2: THE DORSEY BROTHERS' STAGE SHOW—Shake Rattle and Roll/Flip Flop and Fly, I Got a Woman, Baby Let's Play House, Tutti Frutti, Blue Suede Shoes, Heartbreak Hotel
Side 3: THE DORSEY BROTHERS' STAGE SHOW (continued): Tutti Frutti, I Was the One, Blue Suede Shoes, Heartbreak Hotel, Money Honey, Heartbreak Hotel
Side 4 THE MILTON BERLE SHOW—Heartbreak Hotel, Blue Suede Shoes, Dialogue, Blue Suede Shoes, Hound Dog, Dialogue, I Want You, I Need You, I Love You, THE STEVE ALLEN SHOW: Dialogue, I Want You, I Need You, I Love You, Introduction, Hound Dog
Side 5: THE MISSISSIPPI-ALABAMA FAIR AND DAIRY SHOW—Heartbreak Hotel, Long Tall Sally, Introductions and Presentations, I Was the One, I Want You, I Need You, I Love You, I Got a Woman
Side 6: THE MISSISSIPPI-ALABAMA FAIR AND DAIRY SHOW—(continued): Don't Be Cruel, Ready Teddy, Love Me Tender, Hound Dog, Interviews (Vernon and Gladys Presley, Nick Adams, a Fan, and Elvis)
Side 7: THE MISSISSIPPI-ALABAMA FAIR AND DAIRY SHOW (continued)—Love Me Tender, I Was the One, I Got a Woman, Don't Be Cruel, Blue Suede Shoes, Baby, Let's Play House, Hound Dog, Announcements
Side 8: THE ED SULLIVAN SHOW—Don't Be Cruel, Love Me Tender, Ready Teddy, Hound Dog, Don't Be Cruel, Love Me Tender, Love Me, Hound Dog
Side 9: THE ED SULLIVAN SHOW (continued)—Hound Dog, Love Me Tender, Heartbreak Hotel, Don't Be Cruel, Too Much, When My Blue Moon Turns to Gold Again, Peace in the Valley
Side 10: ELVIS AT HOME— Danny Boy, Soldier Boy, The Fool, Earth Angel, He's Only a Prayer Away
Side 11: COLLECTORS' TREASURES—Excerpt from an Interview for *TV Guide*, My Heart Cries for You, Dark Moon, Write to Me from Naples, Suppose
Side 12: ELVIS—Blue Suede Shoes, Tiger Man, That's All Right (Mama), Lawdy Miss Clawdy, Baby What You Want Me to Do, Monologue, Love Me, Are You Lonesome Tonight?, Baby What You Want Me to Do, Monologue, Blue Christmas, Monologue, One Night, Trying to Get to You

GOOD TIMES
(RCA CPL1-0475) March 1974
Side 1: Take Good Care of Her, Lovin' Arms, I Got a Feelin' in My Body, If That Isn't Love, She Wears My Ring
Side 2: I've Got a Thing About You Baby, My Boy, Spanish Eyes, Talk About the Good Times, Good Time Charlie's Got the Blues

GOOD TIMES
(RCA AFL1-0475) 1977
New number assigned to RCA CPL1- 0475

GREATEST HITS—VOL. I
(RCA AHL1-2347) November 1981
Side 1: The Wonder of You, A Big Hunk o' Love, There Goes My Everything, Suspicious Minds, What'd I Say
Side 2: Don't Cry Daddy, Steamroller Blues, The Sound of Your Cry, Burning Love, You'll Never Walk Alone

GUITAR MAN
(RCA AAL1-3917) January 1981
Side 1: Guitar Man, After Loving You (alternate take), Too Much Monkey Business, Just Call Me Lonesome (alternate take), Lovin' Arms (alternate take)
Side 2: You Asked Me To, Clean Up Your Own Back Yard, She Thinks I Still Care (alternate take), Faded Love, I'm Movin' On (alternate take)

HARUM SCARUM
(RCA LPM-3468) October 1965, Complete soundtrack
Side 1: Harem Holiday, My Desert Serenade, Go East Young Man, Mirage, Kismet, Shake That Tambourine
Side 2: Hey Little Girl, Golden Coins, So Close Yet So Far (from Paradise), Animal Instinct (bonus), Wisdom of the Ages (bonus)

HARUM SCARUM
(RCA LSP-3468) October 1965
Stereo release

HARUM SCARUM
(RCA AFL1-2558) September 1977
New number assigned to RCA LSP-3468

HAVING FUN WITH ELVIS ON STAGE
(Boxcar Records) 1974
Candid commentary between numbers by Elvis during concert appearances. Col. Parker and Elvis formed Boxcar Records, compiled this album and sold it at concerts.
Elvis 1: Commentary
Elvis 2: Commentary

HAVING FUN WITH ELVIS ON STAGE
(RCA CPM1-0818) October 1974
RCA reissue of the Boxcar Records original

HAVING FUN WITH ELVIS ON STAGE
(RCA AFM1 -0818) 1977
New number assigned to RCA CPM1-0818

HE TOUCHED ME
(RCA LSP-4690) April 1972
Side 1: He Touched Me, I've Got Confidence, Amazing Grace, Seeing Is Believing, He Is My Everything, Bosom of Abraham
Side 2: An Evening Prayer, Lead Me, Guide Me, There Is No God But God, A Thing Called Love, I John, Reach Out to Jesus

HE TOUCHED ME
(RCA AFL1-4690) 1977
New number assigned to RCA LSP-4690

HE WALKS BESIDE ME
(RCA AFL1-2772) April 1978
Side 1: His Hand in Mine, I'm Gonna Walk Dem Golden Stairs, In My Father's House, Milky White Way, Known Only to Him, I Believe in the Man in the Sky
Side 2: Joshua Fit the Battle, He Knows Just What I Need, Swing Down Sweet Chariot, Mansion Over the Hilltop, If We Never Meet Again, Working on the Building

HIS HAND IN MINE
(RCA LSP-2328) December 1960
Living stereo release

HIS HAND IN MINE
(RCA ANL1-1319) March 1976
Pure Gold series reissue of RCA LSP-2328

HIS HAND IN MINE
(RCA AYM1-3935) May 1981
New number assigned to RCA ANL1-1319

HOW GREAT THOU ART
(RCA LPM-3758)March 81967
Side 1: How Great Thou Art, In the Garden, Somebody Bigger Than You and I,
Farther Along, Stand By Me, Without Him
Side 2: So High, Where Could I Go but to the Lord, By and By, If the Lord Wasn't
Walking by My Side, Run On, Where No One Stands Alone, Crying in the Chapel

HOW GREAT THOU ART
(RCA LSP-3758) March 1967
Stereo release

HOW GREAT THOU ART
(RCA AFL1-3758) 1977
New number assigned to RCA LSP-3758

HOW GREAT THOU ART
(RCA AQL1-3758) 1979
New number assigned to RCA AFL1-3758

I GOT LUCKY
(RCA Camden CAL-2533) October 1971
Side 1: I Got Lucky, What a Wonderful Life, I Need Somebody to Lean On, Yoga Is as
Yoga Does, Riding the Rainbow
Side 2: Fools Fall in Love, The Love Machine, Home Is Where the Heart Is, You Gotta
Stop, If You Think I Don't Need You

I GOT LUCKY
(Pickwick CAS-2533) December 1975
Pickwick reissue of RCA Camden CAL-2533

I WAS THE ONE
(RCA AHL1-4678) May 1983
Side 1: My Baby Left Me, (You're So Square) Baby I Don't Care, Little Sister, Don't
Wear My Ring Around Your Neck, Paralyzed
Side 2: Baby Let's Play House, I Was the One, Rip It Up, Young and Beautiful, Ready Teddy

IT HAPPENED AT THE WORLD'S FAIR
(RCA LPM-2697) April 1963
Complete soundtrack
Side 1: Beyond the Bend, Relax, Take Me to the Fair, They Remind Me Too Much of
You, One Broken Heart for Sale
Side 2: I'm Falling in Love Tonight, Cotton Candy Land, A World of Our Own, How
Would You Like to Be, Happy Ending

IT HAPPENED AT THE WORLD'S FAIR
(RCA LSP-2697) April 1963
Stereo release

IT HAPPENED AT THE WORLD'S FAIR
(RCA AFL1-2568) September 1977
New number assigned to RCA LSP-2697

KING CREOLE
(RCA LPM-1884) August 1958
Complete soundtrack
Side 1: King Creole, As Long as I Have You, Hard Headed Woman, Trouble, Dixieland Rock
Side 2: Don't Ask Me Why, Lover Doll, Crawfish, Young Dreams, Steadfast, Loyal and
True, New Orleans

KING CREOLE
(RCA LSP-1884 [e]) February 1982

Electronically reprocessed stereo release

KING CREOLE
(RCA AFL1-1884 [e]) 1977
New number assigned to RCA LSP-1884 (e)

KING CREOLE
(RCA AYL1-3733[e]) November 1980
New number assigned to RCA AFL1-1884 (e)

KISSIN' COUSINS
(RCA LPM-2894)March 1964
Complete soundtrack
Side 1: Kissin' Cousins (No. 2), Smokey Mountain Boy (bonus), There's Gold in the
Mountains, One Boy, Two Little Girls, Catchin' on Fast, Tender Feeling
Side 2: Anyone (Could Fall in Love with You), Barefoot Ballad, Once is Enough, Kissin'
Cousins, Echoes of Love (bonus), (It's a) Long Lonely Highway (bonus)

KISSIN' COUSINS
(RCA LSP-2894) March 1964
Stereo release

KISSIN' COUSINS
(RCA AFL1-2894) 1977
New number assigned to RCA LSP-2894

KISSIN' COUSINS
(RCA AYM1-4115) September 1981
New number assigned to RCA AFL1-2894

KNOWN ONLY TO HIM
(RCA 9586-1-R) May 1989
Side 1: Peace in the Valley, Take My Hand, Precious Lord, I'm Gonna Walk Dem
Golden Stairs, I Believe in the Man in the Sky, Joshua Fit the Battle, Swing Down,
Sweet Chariot, Stand By Me
Side 2: Run On, Where Could I Go but to the Lord, So High, We Call on Him, Who
Am I, Lead Me, Guide Me, Known Only to Him

LET'S BE FRIENDS
(RCA Camden CAS-2408) April 1970
Side 1: Stay Away Joe, If I'm a Fool (for Loving You), Let's Be Friends, Let's Forget
About the Stars, Mama
Side 2: I'll Be There, Almost, Change of Habit, Have a Happy

LET'S BE FRIENDS
(Pickwick CAS-2408) December 1975
Reissue of RCA Camden CAS-2408

LOVE LETTERS FROM ELVIS
(RCA LSP-4530) May 1971
Side 1: Love Letters, When I'm
Over You, If I Were You, Got
My Mojo Working, Heart of
Rome
Side 2: Only Believe, This Is
Our Dance, Cindy Cindy, I'll
Never Know It, Ain't No Big
Thing, Life

**LOVE LETTERS FROM
ELVIS**
(RCA AFL1-4530) 1977
New number assigned to RCA
LSP-4530

LOVING YOU
(RCA LPM-1515) July 1957
Complete soundtrack.
Side 1: Mean Woman Blues,

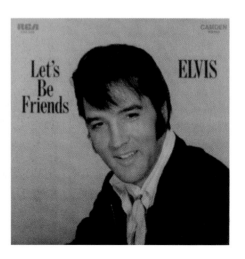

(Let Me Be Your) Teddy Bear, Loving You, Got a Lot o' Livin' to Do, Lonesome Cowboy, Hot Dog, Party
Side 2: Blueberry Hill, True Love, Don't Leave Me Now, Have I Told You Lately That I Love You, I Need You So

LOVING YOU
(RCA LSP-1515[e]) February 1962
Electronically reprocessed stereo release

LOVING YOU
(RCA AFL1-1515[e]) 1977
New number assigned to RCA LSP-1515(e)

MAHALO FROM ELVIS
(Pickwick ACL-7064) September 1978
Side 1: ELVIS: ALOHA FROM HAWAII TV SPECIAL, January 13, 1973
Blue Hawaii, Early Morning Rain, Hawaiian Wedding Song, Ku-u-i-po, No More
Side 2: VARIOUS SOUNDTRACKS
Relax Baby, If You'll Give Me All of Your Love, One Broken Heart for Sale, So Close Yet So Far (from Paradise), Happy Ending

MEMORIES OF CHRISTMAS
(RCA CPL1-4395) August 1982
Side 1: O Come All Ye Faithful, Silver Bells, I'll Be Home for Christmas, Blue Christmas
Side 2: Santa Claus Is Back in Town, Merry Christmass Baby, If Every Day Was Like Christmas, Silent Night

THE MEMPHIS RECORD
(RCA 6221-1-R) June 1987
Recorded: January and February 1969–American Sound Studios
Side A: Stranger in My Own Home Town, Power of My Love, Only the Strong Survive, Any Day Now, Suspicious Minds
Side B: Long Black Limousine, Wearin' That Loved on Look, I'll Hold You in My Heart, After Loving You, Rubberneckin', I'm Movin' On
Side C: Gentle on My Mind, True Love Travels on a Gravel Road, It Keeps Right on a-Hurtin', You'll Think of Me, Mama Liked the Roses, Don't Cry Daddy
Side D: In the Ghetto, The Fair is Moving On, Inherit the Wind, Kentucky Rain, Without Love, Who Am I

THE MILLION DOLLAR QUARTET
(RCA 2023-1-R) March 1990
December 4, 1956. Sun Records. Carl Perkins was doing a session with Jerry Lee Lewis sitting in and Johnny Cash was watching from the control booth. Elvis showed up fresh from Vegas and the four guys began to jam. The engineer put a fresh tape on the machine and the rest is history. The tape was archived and didn't surface until the early 70's. It took RCA almost 40 years to wade through the legal morass and do a commerical release. Several bootleg editions have hit the stands but this is the official RCA version of what happened that magic day.
Side 1: You Belong To Me, When God Dips His Love In My Heart, Just A Little Talk With Jesus, That Lonesome Valley, I Shall Not Be Moved, Peace In The Valley
Side 2: I'm With The Crowd (But Oh So Lonesome), Farther Along, Jesus Hold My Hand, On The Jericho Road, I Just Can't Make It By Myself, Little Cabin On The Hill, Summertime Has Passed and Gone, I Hear A Sweet Voice Calling, Sweetheart You Done Me Wrong, Keeper Of The Key, Crazy Arms, Don't Forbid Me, Brown-Eyed Handsome Man, Out Of Sight, Out Of Mind, Brown-Eyed Handsome Man
Side 3: Don't Be Cruel, Don't Be Cruel, Paralyzed, Don't Be Cruel, Home Sweet Home, When The Saints Go Marching In, Softly And Tenderly
Side 4: Is It So Strange, That's When Your Heartaches Begin, Brown-Eyed Handsome Man, Rip It Up, I'm Gonna Bid My Blues Goodby, Crazy Arms, That's My Desire, End Of The Road, Jerry's Boogie, You're The Only Star In My Blue Heaven, Elvis Farewell

MOODY BLUE
(RCA AFL1-2428) July 1977
Side 1: Unchained Melody, If You Love Me (Let Me Know), Little Darlin', He'll Have to Go, Let Me Be There
Side 2: Way Down Pledging My Love, Moody Blue, She Thinks I Still Care, It's Easy for You

MOODY BLUE
(RCA AQL1-2428) August 1977

New number assigned to RCA AFL1-2428.

THE NUMBER ONE HITS
(RCA 6382-1-R) June 1987
Side A: Heartbreak Hotel, I Want You I Need You I Love You, Hound Dog, Don't Be Cruel, Love Me Tender, Too Much, All Shook Up, Teddy Bear, Jailhouse Rock
Side B: Don't, Hard Headed Woman, A Big Hunk o' Love, Stuck on You, It's Now or Never, Are You Lonesome Tonight?, Surrender, Good Luck Charm, Suspicious Minds

ONSTAGE–FEBRUARY 1970
(RCA LSP-4362) June 1970
All songs on this album were recorded at the International Hotel in Las Vegas February 17-19, 1970 with the exception of **Runaway** and **Yesterday** which were recorded at the same hotel on August 22 and August 25, 1969, respectively.
Side 1: See See Rider, Release Me, Sweet Caroline, Runaway, The Wonder of You
Side 2: Polk Salad Annie, Yesterday, Proud Mary, Walk a Mile in My Shoes, Let It Be Me

ON STAGE–FEBRUARY 1970
(RCA AFL1-4362) 1977
New number assigned to RCA LSP-4362

ON STAGE–FEBRUARY 1970
(RCA AQL1-4362) February 1983
New number assigned to RCA AFL14362

OUR MEMORIES OF ELVIS
(RCA AQL1-3279) February 1979
Side 1: Are You Sincere, It's Midnight, My Boy, Girl of Mine, Take Good Care of Her, I'll Never Fall in Love Again
Side 2: Your Love's Been a Long Time Coming, Spanish Eyes, Never Again, She Thinks I Still Care, Solitaire

OUR MEMORIES OF ELVIS–VOL. 2
(RCA AQL1-3448) August 1979
Side 1: I Got A Feelin' In My Body, Green Green Grass of Home, For the Heart, She Wears My Ring, I Can Help
Side 2: Way Down, There's A Honky Tonk Angel (Who Will Take Me Back In), Find Out What's Happening, Thinking About You, Don't Think Twice It's All Right

PARADISE HAWAIIAN STYLE
(RCA LPM-3643) June 1966
Complete soundtrack plus bonus cuts
Side 1: Paradise Hawaiian Style, Queenie Wahine's Papaya, Scratch My Back (Then I'll Scratch Yours), Drums of the Islands, Datin'
Side 2: A Dog's Life, A House of Sand, Stop Where You Are, This Is My Heaven, Sand Castles (bonus)

PARADISE HAWAIIAN STYLE
(RCA LSP-3643) June 1966
Stereo release

PARADISE HAWAIIAN STYLE
(RCA AFL1-3643) 1977
New number assigned to RCA LSP-3643

PICKWICK PACK (Pickwick)
November 1978
Seven-LP boxed set for Christmas 1978
Albums: **Burning Love and Hits from His Movies–Vol. 2, Elvis' Christmas Album, Elvis Sings Hits from His Movies–Vol. 1, I Got Lucky, Mahalo from Elvis, Separate Ways, You 'Il Never Walk Alone**
February 1972: Elvis' Christmas Album replaced with **Frankie and Johnny**

POT LUCK

(RCA LPM-2523) June 1962
Side 1: Kiss Me Quick, Just for Old Time Sake, Gonna Get Back Home Somehow, (Such an) Easy Question, Steppin' Out of Line, I'm Yours
Side 2: Something Blue, Suspicion, I Feel That I've Known You Forever, Night Rider, Fountain of Love, That's Someone You Never Forget

POT LUCK

(RCA LSP-2523) June 1962
Stereo release
Side 1: Promised Land, There's a Honky Tonk Angel (Who Will Take Me Back In), Help Me, Mr. Songman, Love Song of the Year
Side 2: It's Midnight, Your Love's Been a Long Time Coming, If You Talk in Your Sleep, Thinking About You, You Asked Me To

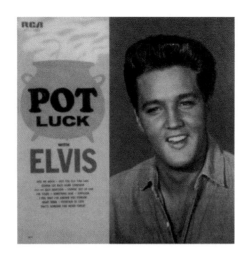

PROMISED LAND

(RCA APDI-0873) January 1975
Quadradisc release

PROMISED LAND

(RCA AFL1-0873) 1977
New number assigned to RCA APD1-0873

PURE GOLD

(RCA ANL1-0971[e]) June 1975
Side 1: Kentucky Rain, Fever, It's Impossible, Jailhouse Rock, Don't Be Cruel
Side 2: I Got a Woman, All Shook Up, Loving You, In the Ghetto, Love Me Tender

PURE GOLD

(RCA AYL1-3732) November 1980
New number assigned to RCA ANL1-0971[e]

RAISED ON ROCK/FOR OL' TIMES SAKE

(RCA APL1-0388) November 1973
Side 1: Raised on Rock, Are You Sincere, Find Out What's Happening, I Miss You, Girl of Mine
Side 2: For Ol' Times Sake, If You Don't Come Back, Just a Little Bit, Sweet Angeline, Three Corn Patches

RECONSIDER BABY

(RCA AFL1-5418) April 1985
Side 1: Reconsider Baby, Tomorrow Night, So Glad You're Mine, One Night, When It Rains It Really Pours, My Baby Left Me, Ain't That Loving You Baby
Side 2: I Feel So Bad, Down in the Alley, High Heel Sneakers, Stranger in My Own Home Town, Merry Christmas Baby

REMEMBERING ELVIS

(RCA PDL2-1037) 1983
Side 1: Blue Moon of Kentucky, Young and Beautiful, Milkcow Blues Boogie, Baby Let's Play House
Side 2: Good Rockin' Tonight, We're Gonna Move, I Want to Be Free, I Forgot to Remember to Forget
Side 3: Kiss Me Quick, Just for Old Time Sake, Gonna Get Back Somehow, (Such an) Easy Question
Side 4: Suspicion, I Feel That I've Known You Forever, Night Rider, Fountain of Love

RETURN OF THE ROCKER

(RCA 5600-1-R) 1986
Side 1: King of the Whole Wide World, (Marie's the Name) His Latest Flame, Little Sister, A Mess of Blues, Like a Baby, I Want You with Me
Side 2: Stuck on You, Return to Sender, Make Me Know It, Witchcraft, I'm Comin' Home, Follow That Dream

ROCKER

(RCA AFM1-5182) October 1984
Side 1: Jailhouse Rock, Blue Suede Shoes, Tutti Frutti, Lawdy Miss Clawdy, I Got a Woman, Money Honey
Side 2: Ready Teddy, Rip It Up, Shake Rattle and Roll, Long Tall Sally, (You're So Square) Baby I Don't Care, Hound Dog

ROUSTABOUT

(RCA LPM-2999) October 1964
Complete soundtrack
Side 1: Roustabout, Little Egypt, Poison Ivy League, Hard Knocks, It's A Wonderful World, Big Love, Big Heartache
Side 2: One Track Heart, It's Carnival Time, Carny Town, There's A Brand New Day On The Horizon, Wheels On My Heels

ROUSTABOUT

(RCA LSP-2999) October 1964
Stereo release

ROUSTABOUT

(RCA AFL1-2999) 1977
New number assigned to RCA LSP-2999

SEPARATE WAYS

(RCA Camden CAS 2611) January 1973
Side 1: Separate Ways, Sentimental Me, In My Way, I Met Her Today, What Now, What Next, Where To
Side 2: Always on My Mind, I Slipped I Stumbled I Fell, Is It So Strange, Forget Me Never, Old Shep

SEPARATE WAYS

(Pickwick CAS-2611) December 1975
Pickwick reissue of RCA Camden CAS-2611)

SINGER PRESENTS ELVIS SINGING FLAMING STAR AND OTHERS

(RCA PRS-279) November 1968
Available only at Singer Sewing Centers as part of the promotion for the 1968 NBC-TV special *ELVIS*
Side 1: Flaming Star, Wonderful World, Night Life, All I Needed Was the Rain, Too Much Monkey Business
Side 2: The Yellow Rose of Texas/The Eyes of Texas, She's a Machine, Do the Vega, Tiger Man

SOMETHING FOR EVERYBODY

(RCA LPM-2370) June 1961
Side 1: There's Always Me, Give Me the Right, It's a Sin, Sentimental Me, Starting Today, Gently
Side 2: I'm Comin' Home In Your Arms, Put the Blame on Me, Judy, I Want You with Me, I Slipped, I Stumbled, I Fell

SOMETHING FOR EVERYBODY
(RCA LSP-2370) July 1971
Stereo release

SOMETHING FOR EVERYBODY
(RCA AFL1-2370) 1977
New number assigned to RCA LSP-2370

SOMETHING FOR EVERYBODY
(RCA AYM1-4116) September 1981
New number assigned to RCA AFL1-2370

SPEEDWAY
(RCA LPM-3989) June 1968
Soundtrack plus bonus cuts
Side 1: Speedway, There Ain't Nothing Like a Song, Your Time Hasn't Come Yet, Baby Who Are You (Who Am I), He's Your Uncle Not Your Dad, Let Yourself Go
Side 2: Your Groovy Self (Nancy Sinatra solo), Five Sleepy Heads (bonus), Western Union (bonus), Mine (bonus), Goin' Home (bonus), Suppose (bonus)

SPEEDWAY
(RCA LSP-3989) June 1968
Stereo release

SPEEDWAY
(RCA AFL1-3989) 1977
New number assigned to RCA LSP-3989

SPINOUT
(RCA LPM-3702) October 1966
Side 1: Stop Look and Listen, Adam and Evil, All That I Am, Never Say Yes, Am I Ready, Beach Shack
Side 2: Spinout, Smorgasbord, I'll Be Back, Tomorrow Is a Long Time (bonus), Down in the Alley (bonus), I'll Remember You (bonus)

SPINOUT
(RCA LSP-3702) October 1966
Stereo release

SPINOUT
(RCA AFL1-2560) September 1977
New number assigned to RCA LSP-3702

SPINOUT
(RCA AYL1-3684) May 1980
New number assigned to RCA AFL1-2560

THE SUN SESSIONS
(RCA APM1-1675) March 1975
Side 1: That's All Right (Mama), Blue Moon of Kentucky, I Don't Care if the Sun Don't Shine, Good Rockin' Tonight, Milkcow Blues Boogie, You're a Heartbreaker, I'm Left, You're Right, She's Gone, Baby Let's Play House
Side 2: Mystery Train, I Forgot to Remember to Forget, I'll Never Let You Go (Little Darlin'), I Love You Because, Tryin' to Get to You, Blue Moon, Just Because, I Love You

Because (take #2)

THAT'S THE WAY IT IS
(RCA LSP-4445) December 1970
Side 1: I Just Can't Help Believin', Twenty Days and Twenty Nights, How the Web Was Woven, Patch It Up, Mary in the Morning, You Don't Have to Say You Love Me
Side 2: You've Lost That Lovin' Feelin', I've Lost You, Just Pretend, Stranger in the Crowd, The Next Step Is Love, Bridge Over Troubled Water

THAT'S THE WAY IT IS
(RCA AFL1-4445) 1977
New number assigned to RCA LSP-4445

THAT'S THE WAY IT IS
(RCA AYM1-4114) September 1981
New number assigned to RCA AFL1-4445

THIS IS ELVIS
(RCA CPL2-4031) March 1981
Complete soundtrack to the 1981 documentary
Side A: (Marie's the Name) His Latest Flame, Moody Blue, That's All Right (Mama), Shake Rattle and Roll/Flip Flop and Fly, Heartbreak Hotel, Hound Dog, Excerpt from Hy Gardner Interview, My Baby Left Me
Side B: Merry Christmas Baby, Mean Woman Blues, Don't Be Cruel, Teddy Bear, Jailhouse Rock, Army Swearing In, G. I. Blues, Excerpt from Departure for Germany Press Conference, Excerpt from Home from Germany Press Conference
Side C: Too Much Monkey Business, Love Me Tender, I've Got a Thing About You Baby, I Need Your Love Tonight, Blue Suede Shoes, Viva Las Vegas, Suspicious Minds
Side D: Excerpt from Jaycees' award to Elvis, Promised Land, Excerpt from Madison Square Garden Press Conference, Always on My Mind, Are You Lonesome Tonight?, My Way, An American Trilogy, Memories

THE TOP TEN HITS
(RCA 6383-1-R) June 1987
Side A: Heartbreak Hotel, I Want You I Need You I Love You, Hound Dog, Don't Be Cruel, Love Me Tender, Love Me Too Much, All Shook Up, Teddy Bear, Jailhouse Rock
Side B: Don't, I Beg of You, Wear My Ring Around Your Neck, Hard Headed Woman, One Night, I Got Stung, (Now and Then There's) A Fool Such As I, I Need Your Love Tonight, A Big Hunk o' Love
Side C: Stuck on You, It's Now or Never, Are You Lonesome Tonight?, Surrender, I Feel So Bad, Little Sister, (Marie's the Name) His Latest Flame, Can't Help Falling in Love, Good Luck Charm, She's Not You
Side D: Return to Sender, (You're the) Devil in Disguise, Bossa Nova Baby, Crying in the Chapel, In the Ghetto, Suspicious Minds, Don't Cry Daddy, The Wonder of You, Burning Love

A VALENTINE GIFT FOR YOU
(RCA APL1-5353) January 1985
Part of 50th anniversary of Elvis' birth
Side 1: Are You Lonesome Tonight?, I Need Somebody to Lean On, Young and Beautiful, Playing for Keeps, Tell Me Why, Give Me the Right, It Feels So Right
Side 2: I Was the One, Fever, Tomorrow Is a Long Time, Love Letters, Fame and Fortune, Can't Help Falling in Love

WELCOME TO MY WORLD
(RCA APL1-2274) March 1977
Side 1: Welcome to My World, Help Me Make It Through the Night, Release Me, I Really Don't Want to Know, For the Good Times
Side 2: Make the World Go Away, Gentle on My Mind, I'm So Lonesome I Could Cry, Your Cheatin' Heart, I Can't Stop Loving You

WELCOME TO MY WORLD
(RCA AFL1-2274) 1977
New number assigned to RCA APL1-2274

WELCOME TO MY WORLD
(RCA AQL1-2274) 1977
New number assigned to RCA AFL1-2274

YOU'LL NEVER WALK ALONE
(RCA Camden CALX-2472) March 5, 1971
Side 1: You'll Never Walk Alone, Who Am I, Let Us Pray, Peace in the Valley, We Call on Him
Side 2: I Believe, It Is No Secret, Sing You Children, Take My Hand, Precious Lord

YOU'LL NEVER WALK ALONE
(Pickwick CAS-2472) December 1975
Reissue of (RCA Camden CALX-2472)

THE EXTENDED PLAY ALBUMS

ALOHA FROM HAWAII VIA SATELLITE
Released: 1973
Side 1: You Gave Me a Mountain, I Can't Stop Loving You
Side 2: My Way, What Now My Love, I'm So Lonesome I Could Cry

ANY WAY YOU WANT ME
Released: 1956
Side 1: Any Way You Want Me, I'm Left, You're Right, She's Gone
Side 2: I Don't Care If the Sun Don't Shine, Mystery Train

CHRISTMAS WITH ELVIS
Released: 1958
Side 1: White Christmas, Here Comes Santa Claus
Side 2: Oh Little Town of Bethlehem, Silent Night

CLAMBAKE
Released: 1968
Side 1: Clambake, Hey, Hey, Hey
Side 2: You Don't Know Me, A House That Has Everything

DEALER'S PREVUE
Released: 1967
Side 1: Loving You, Teddy Bear, Now Stop (Martha Carson), Just Whistle or Call (Martha Carson)
Side 2: The Wife (Lou Monte), Musica Bella (Lou Monte), Mailman, Bring Me No More Blues (Herb Jeffries), So Shy (Herb Jeffries)

DEALER'S PREVUE
Released: 1957
Side 1: The Old Rugged Cross (Stuart Hamblen), Old Time Religion (Stuart Hamblen), Jailhouse Rock (Elvis Presley), Treat Me Nice (Elvis Presley), Till the Last Leaf Shall Fall (Statesmen Quartet), Every Hour and Every Day (Statesmen Quartet)
Side 2: A Slip of the Lip (Kathy Barr), Welcome Mat (Kathy Barr), Just Born (Perry Como), Ivy Rose (Perry Como), Sayonara (Eddie Fisher), That's the Way It Goes (Eddie Fisher)

EASY COME, EASY GO
Released: 1967
Side 1: Easy Come, Easy Go, The Love Machine, Yoga Is as Yoga Does
Side 2: You Gotta Stop, Sing You Children, I'll Take Love

ELVIS–VOL. 1
Released: 1956
Side 1: Rip It Up, Love Me
Side 2: When My Blue Moon Turns to Gold Again, Paralyzed

ELVIS–VOL. 2
Released: 1956
Side 1: So Glad You're Mine, Old Shep
Side 2: Ready Teddy, Any Place Is Paradise

ELVIS/JAYE P. MORGAN
Released: 1956
Dealer promo featuring Elvis–Vol. 1 and Jaye P. Morgan

ELVIS BY REQUEST
Released: 1961
Side 1: Flaming Star, Summer Kisses, Winter Tears
Side 2: Are You Lonesome Tonight?, It's Now or Never

ELVIS PRESLEY
Released: March 1956
Side 1: Blue Suede Shoes, Tutti Frutti
Side 2: I Got A Woman, Just Because

ELVIS PRESLEY
Released: September 1956
Side 1: Shake, Rattle and Roll, I Love You Because
Side 2: Blue Moon, Lawdy Miss Clawdy

ELVIS PRESLEY
Released: March 1956
Version #1
Side 1: Blue Suede Shoes, I'm Counting on You
Side 2: Tutti Frutti, Tryin' to Get to You
Side 3: I Got a Woman, One-Sided Love Affair
Side 4: I'm Gonna Sit Right Down and Cry (Over You), I'll Never Let You Go (Little Darlin')
Versions #2 and #3
Side 1: Blue Suede Shoes, I'm Counting on You
Side 2: I Got a Woman, One-Sided Love Affair
Side 3: Tutti Frutti, Trying to Get to You
Side 4: I'm Gonna Sit Right Down and Cry (Over You), I'll Never Let You Go (Little Darlin')

ELVIS PRESLEY
Released: October 1956
Not a general release, the EP came free with purchase of a 45 RPM portable record player autographed in gold by Elvis himself.
Side 1: Blue Suede Shoes, I'm Counting on You
Side 2: I Got a Woman, One-Sided Love Affair
Side 3: I'm Gonna Sit Right Down and Cry (Over You), I'll Never Let You Go (Little Darlin'
Side 4: Tutti Frutti, Tryin' to Get to You

ELVIS PRESLEY
Released: October 1956
Not a general release, the EP came free with purchase of a 45 RPM portable record player autographed in gold by Elvis himself.
Side 1: Blue Suede Shoes, I'm Counting on You

Side 2: I Got a Woman, One-Sided Love Affair
Side 3: I'm Gonna Sit Right Down and Cry (Over You), I'll Never Let You Go (Little Darlin')
Side 4: Tutti Frutti, Tryin' to Get to You
Side 5: Don't Be Cruel, I Want You, I Need You, I Love You
Side 6: Hound Dog, My Baby Left Me

ELVIS PRESLEY–The Most Talked About New Personality in the Last Ten Years of Recorded Music
Side 1: Blue Suede Shoes, I'm Counting on You, I Got a Woman
Side 2: One-Sided Love Affair, I Love You Because, Just Because
Side 3: Tutti Frutti, Tryin' to Get to You, I'm Gonna Sit Right Down and Cry (Over You)
Side 4: I'll Never Let You Go (Little Darlin'), Blue Moon, Money Honey

ELVIS SAILS
Released: 1958
Reissued: Gold Standard Series, 1965
Radio Interviews with Elvis before he left for Germany and the U.S. Army. Amazingly, this EP spent 12 weeks on Billboard's EP chart, peaking at #2.
Side 1: Press Interview with Elvis Presley
Side 2: Elvis Presley's Newsreel Interview. Pat Hernon Interviews Elvis in the Library of the USS *Randall* at Sailing

ELVIS SINGS CHRISTMAS SONGS
Released: 1957
Side 1: Santa, Bring My Baby Back (to Me), Blue Christmas
Side 2: Santa Claus Is Back in Town, I'll Be Home for Christmas

THE EP COLLECTION–VOL. 2
Released: 1982
Released only in England
(1) A Touch Of Gold–Vol. 2
Side 1: Wear My Ring Around Your Neck, One Night
Side 2: Your Cheatin' Heart, That's All Right (Mama)
(2) G. I. Blues–The Alternate Takes–Vol. 2
Side 1: What's She Really Like (alternate take), G.I. Blues (alternate take)
Side 2: Doin' the Best I Can (alternate take), Pocketful of Rainbows (alternate take)
(3) Collectors Gold
Side 1: (Marie's the Name) His Latest Flame (alternate take), Good Luck Charm (alternate take)
Side 2: Judy (alternate take), Little Sister (alternate take)

EXTENDED PLAY SAMPLER
Released: 1957
Samples of tunes by 12 artists including Elvis doing Jailhouse Rock.

FOLLOW THAT DREAM
Released: 1962
Soundtrack from the movie.
Side 1: Follow That Dream, Angel
Side 2: What a Wonderful Life, I'm Not the Marrying Kind

GOOD ROCKIN' TONIGHT
Released: 1956
Motion Picture "Service Hit" of the Month
Side 1: Good Rockin' Tonight, I Don't Care If the Sun Don't Shine
Side 2: Blue Moon of Kentucky, Shake, Rattle and Roll

GREAT COUNTRY/WESTERN HITS
Released: 1956
Side 1: Eddy Arnold
Bouquet of Roses, Molly Darling
Side 2: Chet Atkins
Alabama Jubilee, Unchained Melody
Side 3: Johnnie and Jack
The Banana Boat Song, Slow Poison
Side 4: Homer and Jethro
I'm My Own Grandpaw, Cigareetes and Whuskey and Wild, Wild Women

Side 5: Jim Ed and Maxine Brown
Looking Back to See, Draggin' Main Street
Side 6: Elvis Presley
Blue Moon of Kentucky, Love Me Tender
Side 7: Jim Reeves
According to My Heart, Am I Losing You
Side 8: Hank Snow
I Don't Hurt Anymore, I'm Movin' On
Side 9: Sons of the Pioneers
Cool Water, The Everlasting Hills of Oklahoma
Side 10: Porter Wagoner
Company's Coming, A Satisfied Mind
Side 11: Porter Wagoner
Seeing Her Only Reminded Me of You, Eat, Drink and Be Merry
Side 12: Sons of the Pioneers
I Wonder When We'll Ever Know, Red River Valley
Side 13: Hank Snow
Old Doc Brown, Grandfather's Clock
Side 14: Jim Reeve
Yonder Comes a Sucker, Waitin' for a Train
Side 15: Elvis Presley
Mystery Train, Milkcow Blues Boogie
Side 16: Del Wood
Down Yonder, Aloha Oe
Side 17: Homer and Jethro
Slow Poke, Over the Waves
Side 18: Johnnie and Jack
Love, Love, Love, We Live in Two Different Worlds
Side 19: Chet Atkins
San Antonio Rose, Arkansas Traveler
Side 20: Eddy Arnold
The Cattle Call, I Wouldn't Know Where to Begin

HEARTBREAK HOTEL
Released: 1956
Side 1: Heartbreak Hotel, I Was the One
Side 2: Money Honey, I Forgot to Remember to Forget

JAILHOUSE ROCK
Released: 1957
On The Charts: #1 for 28 Weeks–Total stay 49 Weeks
Side 1: Jailhouse Rock, Young and Beautiful
Side 2: I Want to Be Free, Don't Leave Me Now, (You're So Square) Baby, I Don't Care

JUST FOR YOU
Released: 1957
Side 1: I Need You So, Have I Told You Lately That I Love You
Side 2: Blueberry Hill, Is It So Strange

KID GALAHAD
Released: 1962
Side 1: King of the Whole Wide World, This is Living, Riding the Rainbow
Side 2: Home Is Where the Heart Is, I Got Lucky, A Whistling Tune

KING CREOLE
Released: 1958, Reissued: Gold Standard Series, 1959
Side 1: King Creole, New Orleans
Side 2: As Long as I Have You, Lover Doll

KING CREOLE–Vol. 2
Released: 1958
Side 1: Trouble, Young Dreams
Side 2: Crawfish, Dixieland Rock

LOVE ME TENDER
Released: 1956
Side 1: Love Me Tender, Let Me
Side 2: Poor Boy, We're Gonna Move

LOVING YOU–Vol. I
Released: 1957
Side I: Loving You, (Let's Have a) Party
Side 2: (Let Me Be Your) Teddy Bear, True Love

LOVING YOU–Vol. 2
Released: 1957
Side I: Lonesome Cowboy, Hot Dog
Side 2: Mean Woman Blues, Got a Lot o' Livin' to Do

PEACE IN THE VALLEY
Released: 1957
Reissued: Gold Standard Series, 1959
Side I: (There'll Be) Peace in the Valley (for Me), It Is No Secret (What God Can Do)
Side 2: I Believe, Take My Hand, Precious Lord

PERFECT FOR PARTIES
Released: 1956
Side I: Love Me (Elvis Presley), Anchors Aweigh (Tony Cabot and His Orchestra), That's a Puente (Tito Puente and His Orchestra)
Side 2: Rock Me but Don't Roll Me (Tony Scott and His Orchestra), Happy Face Baby (The Three Suns), Prom to Prom (Dave Peli Octet)

PROMOTION DISC
Released: 1956
Side I: Old Shep (Elvis Presley), I'm Movin' On (Hank Snow)
Side 2: The Cattle Call (Eddy Arnold with Hugo Winterhalter, Orchestra and Chorus), Four Walls (Jim Reeves)

RCA FAMILY RECORD CENTER
Released: 1962
Compact 33 1/3 promo for use only in record stores. None of the songs are complete takes.
Side I: Good Luck Charm (Elvis Presley), The Way You Look Tonight (Peter Nero), Younger Than Springtime (Paul Anka), Frenesi (Living Strings)
Side 2: Twistin' the Night Away (Sam Cooke), Easy Street (Al Hirt), Make Someone Happy (Perry Como), Moon River (Henry Mancini)

THE REAL ELVIS
Released: 1956
Reissued: Gold Standard Series, 1959
Side I: Don't Be Cruel, I Want You, I Need You, I Love You
Side 2: Hound Dog, My Baby Left Me

SAVE-ON RECORDS
Released: 1956
Sampler for club members who could use coupon books to discount record purchases.
Side I: Intermezzo (Frankie Carle), Moonlight Cocktail (Al Nevins), I'm Gonna Sit Right Down and Cry (Over You) (Elvis Presley), Adventure in Time (Sauter-Finegan Orchestra), Great Gettin' Up Morning (Harry Belafonte)
Side 2: Liebestraum (Artur Rubenstein), Voi Che Sapete (Rise Stevens), Beethoven: Symphony No. 9 (Arturo Toscanini), Jalousie (Arthur Fiedler and Boston Pops), Symphonie Fantastique (Boston Symphony Orchestra)

SEE THE USA, THE ELVIS WAY
Released: 1964
Released only in New Zealand
Side I: Memphis, Tennessee, Blue Moon of Kentucky
Side 2: New Orleans, Viva Las Vegas

THE SOUND OF LEADERSHIP
Released: 1956
Souvenir boxed set for RCA distributors
Side I: Vesti La Giubba (1907, Enrico Caruso), O Sole Mio (1916, Enrico Caruso)
Side 2: Ramona (1928, Gene Austin), Marie (1937, Tommy Dorsey)
Side 3: Boogie Woogie (1938, Tommy Dorsey), Jalousie (1938, Boston Pops Orchestra)
Side 4: Beer Barrel Polka (1938, Will Glahe), Begin the Beguine (1938, Artie Shaw)
Side 5: In the Mood (1939, Glenn Miller), Sunrise Serenade (1939, Glenn Miller)

Side 6: Blue Danube Waltz (1939, Leopold Stokowksi), Tuxedo Junction (1940, Glenn Miller)
Side 7: Stardust (1940, Artie Shaw), Tchaikovsky Piano Concerto (1941, Freddy Martin)
Side 8: Chattanooga Choo Choo (1941, Glenn Miller), Racing with the Moon (1941, Vaughn Monroe)
Side 9: Prisoner of Love (1946, Perry Como), Ballerina (1947, Vaughn Monroe)
Side 10: The Whiffenpoof Song (1947, Robert Merrill), Bouquet of Roses (1948, Eddy Arnold)
Side 11: Be My Love (1950, Mario Lanza), Anytime (1951, Eddie Fisher)
Side 12: The Loveliest Night of the Year (1951, Mario Lanza), Slow Poke (1951, Pee Wee King)
Side 13: Don't Let the Stars Get in Your Eyes (1952, Perry Como), You, You, You (1953, The Ames Brothers)
Side 14: I Need You Now (1954, Eddie Fisher), Cherry Pink and Apple Blossom White (1954, Perez Prado)
Side 15: Naughty Lady of Shady Lane (1954, The Ames Brothers), Rock and Roll Waltz (1955, Kay Starr)
Side 16: Hot Diggity (1956, Perry Como), Heartbreak Hotel (1956, Elvis Presley)

STAY AWAY
Released: 1968
Side I: Stay Away, U.S. Male
Side 2: Guitar Man, Big Boss Man

STRICTLY ELVIS
Released: 1957
Side I: Long Tall Sally, First in Line
Side 2: How Do You Think I Feel, How's the World Treating You

TICKLE ME
Released: 1965
Side I: I Feel That I've Known You Forever, Slowly but Surely
Side 2: Night Rider, Put the Blame on Me, Dirty, Dirty Feeling

A TOUCH OF GOLD–Vol. I
Released: 1959
Side I: Hard Headed Woman, Good Rockin' Tonight
Side 2: Don't, I Beg of You

A TOUCH OF GOLD–Vol. 2
Released: 1959
Side I: Wear My Ring Around Your Neck, Treat Me Nice
Side 2: One Night, That's All Right (Mama)

A TOUCH OF GOLD–Vol. 3
Released: 1960
Side I: All Shook Up, Don't Ask Me Why
Side 2: Too Much, Blue Moon of Kentucky

TUPPERWARE'S HIT PARADE
Released: 1973
A sample of All Shook Up was used on this promo for Tupperware.

VIVA LAS VEGAS
Released: 1964
Side I: If You Think I Don't Need You, I Need Somebody to Lean On
Side 2: C'mon Everybody, Today, Tomorrow and Forever

DJ PROMO
Released: 1956
Side I: Love Me Tender (Elvis Presley), Any Way You Want Me (Elvis Presley)
Side 2: Welcome to the Club (Jean Chapel), I Won't be Rockin' Tonight (Jean Chapel)

DJ PROMO
Released: 1957
Side I: Too Much (Elvis Presley), Playing for Keeps (Elvis Presley)
Side 2: Chantez Chantez (Dinah Shore), Honky Tonk Heart (Dinah Shore)

GENERAL PROMO
Released: 1956
10-EP boxed-set general promo including Elvis'
Side 7: That's All Right (Mama), Baby, Let's Play House
Side 14: I Forgot to Remember to Forget, Mystery Train

THE CASSETTES AND COMPACT DISCS

The days of putting a stack of 45s on the Victrola and dancing a Saturday night away are gone forever. For better or worse, advances in technology have made 45s and LPs a thing of the past. These days vinyl is used for the floor, not for listening. The world rocks now to cassettes and compact discs. Almost all of Elvis' songs and many of his records are available on cassette and CD. Some are exact duplicates of the old LPs and some are new configurations with previously unreleased material, but the King still comes through loud and clear.

THE ALTERNATE ALOHA
Cassette: RCA G 6985-4-R
Compact Disc: RCA CD-O 6985-2-R
Same selections as RCA 6985-1-R plus three bonus tracks that were recorded after the audience left: Blue Hawaii, Hawaiian Wedding Song, Ku-u-i-po

ALWAYS ON MY MIND
Cassette: RCA AFK1-5430
Compact Disc: RCA PCD1-5430
Same selections as RCA AFL1-5430

BLUE CHRISTMAS
Cassette: RCA A2 9800-4-R
Compact Disc: RCA CD-T1 59800-2
Contents: O Come All Ye Faithful, The First Noel, Winter Wonderland, Silver Bells, Blue Christmas, Silent Night, White Christmas, I'll Be Home For Christmas

BLUE HAWAII
Cassette: RCA E AYK1-3683
Compact Disc: RCA CD-A 3683-2-R
Same selections as RCA LSP-2426

BURNING LOVE And Hits From His Movies–Vol. 2
Compact Disc: RCA Camden CAD1-2595
Same selections as RCA Camden CAS-2595

CHRISTMAS CLASSICS
Cassette: RCA E 9801-4-R
Compact Disc: RCA CD-A 9801-2RL
Contents: A combination of two issues of the same LP.
RCA Camden CAL-2428
Blue Christmas, White Christmas, I'll Be Home for Christmas, Oh Little Town of Bethlehem, Silent Night
RCA LSP-4579
O Come All Ye Faithful, The First Noel, Winter Wonderland, Silver Bells

COLLECTOR'S GOLD
Cassette: RCA Q7 3114-4-R (set of 3)
Compact Disc: RCA CD-S 3114-2-R (set of 3)
Cassette/Disc #1:
G.I. Blues, Pocketful Of Rainbows, Big Boots, Black Star, Summer Kisses, Winter Tears, I Slipped, I Stumbled, I Fell, Lonely Man, What A Wonderful Life, A Whistling Tune, One Broken Heart For Sale, You're The Boss, Roustabout, Girl Happy, So Close Yet So Far, Stop Look And Listen, Am I Ready, How Can You Lose What

You've Never Had
Cassette/Disc #2:
Like A Baby, There's Always Me, I Want You With Me, Gently, Give Me The Right, I Met Her Today, Night Rider, Just Tell Her Jim Said Hello, Ask Me, Memphis, Tennessee, Witchcraft, Come What May (You Are Mine), Love Letters, Going Home
Cassette/Disc #3:
Blue Suede Shoes, I Got A Woman, Heartbreak Hotel, Love Me Tender, Baby What Do You Want Me To Do, Runaway, Surrender, Are You Lonesome Tonight?, Rubberneckin', Memories, Introductions By Elvis, Jailhouse Rock, Don't Be Cruel, Inherit The Wind, This Is The Story

THE COMPLETE SUN SESSIONS
Cassette: RCA E 6414-4-R
Compact Disc: RCA CD-A 6414-2-R
Same selections as RCA 6414-1-R with six tracks deleted:
I Love You Because (takes # 1 & 4), I'm Left, You're Right, She's Gone (My Baby's Gone) (takes #8, #10, #11 and #12)

A DATE WITH ELVIS
Cassette: RCA A2 2011-4-R
Compact Disc: RCA CD-T1 2011-2-R
Same selections as RCA LPM-2011

DON'T BE CRUEL
Compact Disc: RCA 62404 (new release)
Contents:
Don't Be Cruel, Ain't That Lovin' You Baby, Blue Christmas, Love Me Tender, Heartbreak Hotel

DOUBLE DYNAMITE
Compact Disc: RCA PCD2-1010
Same selections as the double-LP set released by Pair
Records (RCA PDL2-1010)

ELVIS
Cassette: RCA E AFK1-5199
Compact Disc: RCA CD-A PCD1-5199
Same selections as RCA LPM-1382

ELVIS–ALOHA FROM HAWAII VIA SATELLITE
Cassette: RCA E 2765-4-R
Compact Disc: RCA CD-A 2765-2-R
Same selections as RCA VPSX-6089

ELVIS AS RECORDED LIVE AT MADISON SQUARE GARDEN
Cassette: RCA E AQK1-4776
Compact Disc: RCA CD-A 4395-2-R
All selections are the same as RCA LSP 4776

ELVIS–A LEGENDARY PERFORMER–Vol. 1
Compact Disc: (RCA CAD1-2705)
Same selections as RCA CPL1-0341 without:
I Love You Because, A Fool Such as I, Are You Lonesome Tonight?, Love Me

ELVIS–A LEGENDARY PERFORMER–Vol. 2
Compact Disc: RCA CAD1-2706
Same selections as RCA CPL1-1349 without:
Blue Christmas, Cane and a High Starched Collar, Jay Thompson Interviews Elvis, Presentation of Awards to Elvis

ELVIS ARON PRESLEY–FOREVER
Compact Disc: RCA PCD2-1185
Same selections as the double-LP set released by Pair
Records (PDL2-1185)

ELVIS–BACK IN MEMPHIS
Cassette: RCA E 61081-4
Compact Disc: RCA CD-A 61081-2
Same selections as RCA LSP-4429

ELVIS' CHRISTMAS ALBUM
Cassette: RCA E AFKI-5486
Compact Disc: RCA CD-A PCDI-5486
Same selections as RCA LPM-1951

ELVIS COUNTRY
Cassette: RCA A 6330-4-R
Compact Disc: RCA CD-TI 6330-2-R
Based on Elvis Country (1971, RCA LSP-4460)
Contents: Whole Lotta Shakin' Goin' On, Funny How Time Slips Away, Baby, Let's Play House, Rip It Up, Lovin' Arms, You Asked Me To, She Thinks I Still Care, Paralyzed

ELVIS COUNTRY–I'M 10,000 YEARS OLD
Cassette: RCA E 66278-4
Compact Disc: RCA CD-A 66278-2
Contents: Snowbird, Tomorrow Never Comes, Little Cabin On The Hill, Whole Lot Of Shakin' Goin' On, Funny How Time Slips Away, I Really Don't Want To Know, It's You Baby, You Rock It, The Fool, Faded Love, I Washed My Hands In Muddy Water, Make The World Go Away

AN ELVIS DOUBLE FEATURE
Compact Disc: RCA PDC2-1250
Songs from Clambake (RCA LSP-3893) and Speedway (RCA LSP-3989)
Contents: Clambake: A House That Has Everything , Hey Hey Hey The Girl, I Never Loved, How Can You Lose What You Never Had, Guitar Man, Big Boss Man, Just Call Me Lonesome
Speedway: Speedway, There Ain't Nothing Like a Song, Who Are You (Who Am I), Let Yourself Go, Your Groovy Self (sung by Nancy Sinatra), Western Union, Goin' Home, Suppose

ELVIS' GOLD RECORDS–Vol. 2
50 Million Elvis Fans Can't Be Wrong
Cassette: RCA E AFKI-5197
Compact Disc: RCA CD-A PCDI-5197
Same selections as RCA LPM-2075

ELVIS' GOLD RECORDS–Vol. 4
Cassette: RCA E PK-1297
Compact Disc: RCA CD-A 1297-2-R
Same selections as RCA LSP-3921

ELVIS' GOLD RECORDS–Vol. 5
Cassette: RCA AFKI-4941
Compact Disc: RCA CD-A PCDI-4941
Same selections as RCA AFLI-4941

ELVIS' GOLDEN RECORDS
Cassette: RCA E AFKI-5196
Compact Disc: RCA CD-A PCDI-5196
Same selections as RCA LPM-1707

ELVIS' GOLDEN RECORDS, Vol. 3
Cassette: RCA E 2765-4-R
Compact Disc: RCA CD-A 2765-2-R
Same selections as RCA LSP-2765

ELVIS GOSPEL 1957–1971: KNOWN ONLY TO HIM
Cassette: RCA G 9586-4-R
Compact Disc: RCA CD-O 9586-2-R
Contents: Peace In The Valley, Take My Hand Precious Lord, I'm Gonna Walk Dem Golden Stairs, I Believe In The Man In The Sky, Joshua Fit The Battle, Swing Down, Sweet Chariot, Stand By Me, Run On, Where Could I Go But To The Lord, So High, We Call On Him, Who Am I?

ELVIS IN CONCERT
Cassette: RCA K CPK2-2587
Compact Disc: RCA CD-N 52587-2
Same selections as RCA APL2-2587

ELVIS IN PERSON AT THE INTERNATIONAL HOTEL, LAS VEGAS, NEVADA
Cassette: RCA E AYKI-3892
Compact Disc: RCA CD-A 53892-2
Same selections as RCA LSP-4428

ELVIS IS BACK
Cassette: not released at this time
Compact Disc: RCA CD-A 2231-2-R
Same selections as RCA LSP-2231

ELVIS NOW
Cassette: RCA E 54671-4
Compact Disc: RCA CD-A 54671-2
Same selections as RCA LSP-4671

ELVIS PRESLEY
Cassette: RCA E AFKI-5198
Compact Disc: RCA CD-A PCDI-5198
Same selections as RCA LPM-1254, digitally remastered and restored to monaural sound

ELVIS RECORDED LIVE ON STAGE IN MEMPHIS
Cassette: RCA E CPKI-0606
Compact Disc: not released at this time
Same selections as RCA CPLI-0606

ELVIS SINGS LEIBER & STOLLER
Cassette: RCA E 3026-4-R
Compact Disc: RCA CD-A 3026-2-R
Contents: Hound Dog, Love Me, Loving You, Hot Dog, I Want To Be Free, Jailhouse Rock, Treat Me Nice, (You're So Square), Baby I Don't Care, Santa Claus Is Back In Town, Don't, Trouble, King Creole, Steadfast, Loyal And True, Dirty, Dirty Feeling, Just Tell Her Jim Said Hello, Girls! Girls! Girls!, Bossa Nova Baby, You're The Boss, Little Egypt, Fools Fall In Love, Saved

ELVIS SINGS "THE WONDER-FUL WORLD OF CHRISTMAS"
Cassette: RCA E ANKI-1936
Compact Disc: RCA CD-A 4579-2-R
Same selections as RCA LSP-4579
along with Blue Christmas

ELVIS–TV SPECIAL
Cassette: RCA E AYKI-3894
Compact Disc: not released at this time
Same selections as RCA AFMI-4088

ELVIS' WORLDWIDE 50 GOLD AWARD HITS
Vol. 1, Parts 1 & 2
Cassette: not released at this time
Compact Disc: (RCA CD-AI 6041-2-R)
Contents: Sides 1, 2, 3 and 4 of the boxed set RCA LPM-6401

ELVIS–A LEGENDARY PERFORMER–Vol. 1
Cassette: RCA E CPKI-0341
Compact Disc: not released at this time
Same selections as RCA CPLI-1349

ESSENTIAL ELVIS: THE FIRST MOVIES
Cassette: RCA E 6738-4-R
Compact Disc: RCA CD-A6738-2-R
Same selections as RCA 6738-1-R) plus four tracks:

Mean Woman Blues, Loving You (unreleased fast version, take #8), Treat Me Nice, Love Me Tender (unreleased version)

ESSENTIAL ELVIS–VOL. 3–HITS LIKE NEVER BEFORE
Compact Disc: RCA 2229
Contents: King Creole (take #18), I Got Stung (take #1), A Fool Such As I (take #3), Wear My Ring Around My Neck (take #22), Your Cheatin' Heart (take #9), Ain't That Lovin' You Baby (take #1), Doncha' Think It's Time (take #40), I Need Your Love Tonight (takes #2 & #10) Lover Doll (take #7), As Long As I Have You (take #8), Danny (take #8), King Creole (take #3), Crawfish (take #7), Big Hunk O' Love (take #1), Ain't That Lovin' You Baby (takes #5 & #11), I Got Stung (takes #13 & 14), You're Cheatin' Heart (take #10), Wear My Ring Around Your Neck (take #22), Steadfast, Loyal And True (take #6), I Need Your Love Tonight (take #5), Doncha' Think It's Time (take #12), I Got Stung (take #12), King Creole (take #8), As Long As I Have You (take #4)

FOR LP FANS ONLY
Cassette: RCA A2 1990-4-R
Compact Disc: RCA CD-T1 1990-2-R
Same selections as RCA LPM-1990 restored to original monaural sound

FRANKIE AND JOHNNY/PARADISE, HAWAIIAN STYLE
Cassette: RCA E 3553-4-R
Compact Disc: RCA CD 3553-2-R
Same selections as 1966 Frankie And Johnny (RCA LPM-3553) and Paradise, Hawaiian Style (RCA LPM-3643)

FROM ELVIS IN MEMPHIS
Cassette: RCA A2 PK-1456
Compact Disc: RCA CD-T1 51456-2
Same selections as RCA LSP-4155

FROM ELVIS PRESLEY BOULEVARD, MEMPHIS, TENNESSEE
Cassette: RCA E APK1-1506
Compact Disc: RCA CD- A 1506-2-R
Same selections as RCA APL1-1506

FROM NASHVILLE TO MEMPHIS–THE BOX
Compact Disc: RCA 66160, on five discs
Contents: Stuck On You, It's Now Or Never, Are You Lonesome Tonight?, Surrender, Good Luck Charm, Suspicious Minds, I Feel So Bad, (Marie's The Name) His Latest Flame, Little Sister, She's Not You, (You're The) Devil In Disguise, In The Ghetto, Don't Cry Daddy, Beyond The Reef (previously unreleased), Come What May (previously unreleased), I'll Remember You (previously unreleased), Suppose (previously unreleased)
Medley A: Man (previously unreleased), What'd I Say (previously unreleased), High-Heeled Sneakers (previously unreleased)
Medley B: This Time (previously unreleased), I Can't Stop Loving You (previously unreleased), In The Ghetto (previously unreleased), Suspicious Minds (previously unreleased), Kentucky Rain (previously unreleased), Big Boss Man (previously unreleased), Down In The Valley (previously unreleased), Memphis, Tennessee (previously unreleased), I'm Yours (previously unreleased), (Marie's The Name) His Latest Flame (previously unreleased), That's Someone You Never Forget (previously unreleased), Surrender (previously unreleased), It's Now Or Never (previously unreleased)
Medley C: Love Me Tender–with Frank Sinatra (previously unreleased), Witchcraft–with Frank Sinatra (previously unreleased)

G. I. BLUES
Cassette: RCA A2 AYK1-3735
Compact Disc: RCA CD-T1 3735-2-R
Same selections as RCA LSP-2256 plus one bonus track:
Tonight's All Right for Love

GIRL HAPPY
Original Soundtrack
Cassette: RCA A2 PK-1018
Compact Disc: not released at this time
Same selections as RCA LPM-3338

GIRLS! GIRLS! GIRLS!/KID GALAHAD
Cassette: RCA G 66130-4
Compact Disc: RCA CD-C 66130-2
Same selections as RCA LPM-2621 and RCA EP-4371

GREAT PERFORMANCES
Cassette: RCA G 2227-4-R
Compact Disc: RCA CD-C 2227-2-R
This compact disc was released by Pair Records
Contents: That's All Right (Mama), Tryin' To Get To You, Heartbreak Hotel, Don't Be Cruel, I Want You, I Need You, I Love You, Love Me Tender, Peace In The Valley, Jailhouse Rock, It's Now Or Never, Such A Night (with false starts), Tonight's All Right For Love, Can't Help Falling In Love, Blue Suede Shoes, Baby, What Do You Want Me To Do, If I Can Dream, Blue Hawaii

HARUM SCARUM/GIRL HAPPY
Cassette: RCA G 66128-4
Compact Disc: RCA CD-C 66128-2
Same selections as RCA LPM-3338 and RCA LPM-3468

HE TOUCHED ME
Cassette: RCA E 9K-1923
Compact Disc: RCA CD-A 51923-2
Same selections as RCA LSP-4690

HE WALKS BESIDE ME:
Favorite Songs of Faith and Inspiration
Cassette: RCA E AFK1-2772
Compact Disc: not released at this time
Same selections as RCA AFL1-2772

HEARTBREAK HOTEL, HOUND DOG And Other Top Ten Hits
Cassette: RCA A2 2079-4-R
Compact Disc: RCA CD-T1 2079-2-R
Contents: Heartbreak Hotel, Hound Dog, Don't Be Cruel, Love Me Tender, Jailhouse Rock, Anyway You Want Me (That's How I Will Be), That's When Your Heartaches Begin, Teddy Bear (Let Me Be)

HIS HAND IN MINE
Cassette: RCA E AYK1-3935
Compact Disc: RCA CD-A 1319-2-R
Same selections as RCA ANL1-1319 plus three bonus songs:
It Is No Secret, You'll Never Walk Alone, Who Am I?

HITS LIKE NEVER BEFORE
Essential Elvis,–Vol. 4
Cassette: RCA E 2229-4-R
Compact Disc: RCA CD-A 2229-2-R

HOW GREAT THOU ART
Cassette: RCA E AQK1-3758
Compact Disc: RCA CD-A 3758-2-R
Same selections as RCA LSP-3758 with the addition of Peace in the Valley

IT HAPPENED AT THE WORLD'S FAIR/FUN IN ACAPULCO
Cassette: RCA G 66131-4
Compact Disc: RCA CD-C 66131-2
Same selections as RCA LPM-2697 and RCA LPM-2576

KING CREOLE
Cassette: RCA E AYK1-3733
Compact Disc: RCA CD-A 3733-2-R
Same selections as RCA LPM-1884, digitally remastered and restored to monaural sound

THE KING OF ROCK 'N' ROLL: The Complete Fifties Masters
Cassette: RCA L2 66050-4 (set of 5)
Compact Disc: RCA CD-W 66050-2 (set of 5)
To be released in 1994 along with: The King of Rock 'n' Roll: The Complete Sixties Masters

THE LOST ALBUM
Cassette: RCA G 61024-4
Compact Disc: RCA CD-O 61024-2
Contents: Long Lonely Highway, Western Union, Witchcraft, Love Me Tonight, What Now, What Next, Where To, Please Don't Drag That String Around, Blue River, Never Ending, Devil In Disguise (You're The), Finders Weepers, Losers Keepers, Echoes Of Love, Slowly But Surely, It Hurt Me, Memphis, Tennessee, Ask Me

LOVE LETTERS FROM ELVIS
Cassette: RCA E 54350-4
Compact Disc: RCA CD-A 54350-2
Same selections as RCA LSP-4530

LOVING YOU
Original Soundtrack
Cassette: RCA A2 1515-4-R
Compact Disc: RCA CD-T1 1515-2-R
Same selections as RCA LPM-1515, digitally remastered and restored to monaural sound

MEMORIES OF CHRISTMAS
Cassette: RCA E CPK1-4395
Compact Disc: RCA CD-A 4395-2-R
Same selections as RCA CPL1-4395

THE MEMPHIS RECORD
Cassette: RCA E 6221-4-R
Compact Disc: RCA CD-A 6221-2-R
Same selections as RCA 6221-1-R

THE MILLION DOLLAR QUARTET
Cassette: RCA E 2023-4-R
Compact Disc: RCA CD-A2023-2-R
Same selections as RCA 20231-R

MOODY BLUE
Cassette: RCA E AQK1-2428
Compact Disc: RCA CD-A 2428-2-R
Same selections as RCA AFL1-2428

MERRY CHRISTMAS
New Release
Compact Disc: RCA PCDI-5301
Contents: I'll Be Home For Christmas, White Christmas, Blue Christmas, Santa Claus Is Back In Town, Merry Christmas Baby, O Come, All Ye Faithful, The First Noel, Oh Little Town Of Bethlehem, Silent Night, Peace In The Valley

NBC–TV SPECIAL
Cassette: RCA E 61021-4
Compact Disc: RCA CD-A 61021-2
Contents: Guitar Man, Lawdy, Miss Clawdy, Baby What Do You Want Me To Do
Medley A: Heartbreak Hotel, Hound Dog, All Shook Up, Can't Help Falling In Love, Jailhouse Rock, Don't Be Cruel, Blue Suede Shoes, Love Me Tender, Where Could I Go But To The Lord Up Above My Head, Saved, Baby, What Do You Want Me To Do, That's All Right, Blue Christmas One Night, Tiger Man, Trying To Get To You, Memories
Medley B: Nothingville, Big Boss Man, Let Yourself Go, It Hurts Me, Guitar Man, Little Egypt, Trouble, Guitar Man, If I Can Dream

THE NUMBER ONE HITS
Cassette: RCA G 6382-4-R
Compact Disc: RCA CD-O 6382-2-R
Same selections as RCA AFL1-2428

ON STAGE–February 1970
Cassette: RCA E AQK1-4362
Compact Disc: RCA CD-A 54362-2
Same selections as RCA LSP-4362

POT LUCK WITH ELVIS
Cassette: RCA A2 2523-4-R
Compact Disc: RCA CD-T1 2523-2-R
Same selections as RCA LSP-2523

PROMISED LAND
Cassette: RCA E APK1-0873
Compact Disc: RCA CD-A 0873-2-R
Same selections as RCA APL1-2523

PURE GOLD
Cassette: RCA E AYN1-3732
Compact Disc: RCA CD-A 3733-2-R
Same selections as RCA ANL1-0971[e]

RECONSIDER BABY
Cassette: RCA A2 AFK1-5418
Compact Disc: RCA CD-T1 PCD-5418
Same selections as RCA AFL1-5418

ROCKER
Cassette: RCA E AFK1-5182
Compact Disc: RCA CD-A PCD1-5182
Same selections as RCA AFM1-5182

ROUSTABOUT/ VIVA LAS VEGAS
Cassette: RCA G 66129-4
Compact Disc: RCA CD-C 66129-2
Same selections as RCA LPM-2999 and RCA EPA-4382

SOMETHING FOR EVERYBODY
Cassette: RCA A 2370-4-R
Compact Disc: RCA CD-T1 2370-2-R
Same selections as RCA LPM-2370

STEREO '57–Essential Elvis–Vol. 2
Cassette: RCA E 9589-4-R
Compact Disc: RCA CD-A 9589-2-R
Same selections as RCA 9589-1-R plus five bonus takes:
I Believe (take #4), Tell Me Why (take #5), Got A Lot Of Livin' To Do (take #9), All Shook Up (take #10), Take My Hand Precious Lord (take #14)

THAT'S THE WAY IT IS
Cassette: RCA A2 AYK1-4114
Compact Disc: RCA CD-A 54114-2
Same selections as RCA LSP-4445

THIS IS ELVIS
(Selections From The Original Motion Picture Soundtrack)
Cassette: RCA K CPK2-4031
Compact Disc: not released at this time
Same selections as RCA CPL2-4031

TODAY
New Release
Cassette: RCA E 51039-4
Compact Disc: RCA CD-A 51039-2
Contents: Trouble, And I Love You So, Woman Without Love, Shake A Hand, Pieces Of My Life, Fairytale, I Can Help Bringing It Back, Green Green Grass Of Home

THE TOP TEN HITS
Cassette: RCA K 6383-4-R
Compact Disc: RCA CD-A1 6383-2-R

Same selections as the two-LP set
RCA 6383-1-R

A VALENTINE GIFT FOR YOU
Cassette: RCA E AFK1-5353
Compact Disc: RCA CD-A PCD1-5353
Same selections as RCA AFL1-5353

WELCOME TO MY WORLD
Cassette: RCA E AQK1-2274
Compact Disc: RCA CD-A 52274-2
Same selections as RCA APL1-2274

THE ELVIS RECORD BOOK

ELVIS' NUMBER-ONE RECORDS

ALBUMS
Elvis' 18 number-one hits rank second on the all-time list.
#1 Hits
1. The Beatles 20
2. Elvis Presley 18
3. The Supremes 12
4. Michael Jackson 11
5. Stevie Wonder 10

But he spent far more weeks occupying number one than any other artist or group of all time:
Weeks at #1
1. Elvis Presley 80
2. The Beatles 59
3. Paul McCartney/Wings 30
4. Michael Jackson 29
5. The Bee Gees 27

TOP TEN
1. Blue Hawaii (#1–20 Weeks)
2. Elvis Presley (#1–10 Weeks)
3. Loving You (#1–10 Weeks)
4. G. I. Blues (#1–10 Weeks)

COUNTRY
1. Heartbreak Hotel (17 Weeks)
2. Don't Be Cruel (7 Weeks)
3. I Forgot To Remember To Forget (5 Weeks)
4. Hound Dog (3 Weeks)
5. I Want You, I Need You, I Love You (2 Weeks)
6. All Shook Up (1 Week)
7. Teddy Bear (1 Week)
8. Jailhouse Rock (1 Week)
9. Moody Blue/She Still Thinks I Care (1 Week)
10. Way Down/ Pledging My Love (1 Week)
11. Guitar Man (1 Week)

RHYTHM & BLUES
1. Jailhouse Rock (5 Weeks)
2. Treat Me Nice (5 Weeks)
3. All Shook Up (4 Weeks)

4. Don't Be Cruel (1 Week)
5. Hound Dog (1 Week)
6. Teddy Bear (1 Week)
7. Loving You (1 Week)

EASY LISTENING
1. Crying In The Chapel (7 Weeks)
2. Can't Help Falling In Love With You (6 Weeks)
3. I'm Yours (3 Weeks)
4. (Such An) Easy Question (2 Weeks)
5. The Wonder Of You (1 Week)
6. You Don't Have To Say You Love Me (1 Week)
7. My Boy (1 Week)

BRITISH
1. It's Now Or Never (8 Weeks)
2. All Shook Up (7 Weeks)
3. Wooden Heart (6 Weeks)
4. The Wonder Of You (6 Weeks)
5. A Fool Such As I (5 Weeks)
6. I Need Your Love Tonight (5 Weeks)
7. Good Luck Charm (5 Weeks)
8. Way Down (5 Weeks)
9. Are You Lonesome Tonight? (4 Weeks)
10. Surrender (4 Weeks)
11. (Marie's The Name) His Latest Flame (4 Weeks)
12. Little Sister (4 Weeks)
13. Can't Help Falling In Love (4 Weeks)
14. Rock-A-Hula Baby (4 Weeks)
15. Jailhouse Rock (3 Weeks)
16. One Night (3 Weeks)
17. I Got Stung (3 Weeks)
18. She's Not You (3 Weeks)
19. Return To Sender (3 Weeks)
20. Crying In The Chapel (2 Weeks)
21. (You're The) Devil In Disguise (1 Week)

ON THE CHARTS FOUR MONTHS OR MORE

TOP/HOT 100
1. All Shook Up (30 Weeks)
2. Hound Dog (28 Weeks)

3. Don't Be Cruel (27 Weeks)
4. Heartbreak Hotel (27 Weeks)
5. Jailhouse Rock (27 Weeks)
6. Teddy Bear (25 Weeks)
7. I Want You, I Need You, I Love You (24 Weeks)
8. Love Me Tender (23 Weeks)
9. Loving You (22 Weeks)
10. Way Down (21 Weeks)
11. Don't (20 Weeks)
12. It's Now Or Never (20 Weeks)

COUNTRY
1. I Forgot To Remember To Forget (39 weeks)

RHYTHM & BLUES
1. Don't Be Cruel (18 weeks)
2. Hound Dog (18 weeks)

GOLD RECORDS

1956
SINGLES
Heartbreak Hotel, I Was The One, I Want You, I Need You, I Love You, Don't Be Cruel, Hound Dog, Love Me Tender, Any Way You Want Me
LPs
Elvis Presley, Elvis

1957
SINGLES
Too Much, Playing For Keeps, All Shook Up, That's When Your Heartaches Begin, Teddy Bear, Loving You, Jailhouse Rock, Treat Me Nice, Don't, I Beg Of You
EPs
Peace In The Valley, Jailhouse Rock
LPs
Loving You, Elvis' Christmas Album

1958
SINGLES
Wear My Ring Around Your Neck, Hard Headed Woman, I Got Stung, One Night

EP
King Creole–Vol. I
LPs
Elvis, Golden Records, King Creole

1959
SINGLES
(Now And Then There's) A Fool Such As I, I Need Your Love Tonight, A Big Hunk O' Love
LPs
50 Million Elvis Fans Can't Be Wrong: Elvis' Gold Records–Vol. 2

1960
SINGLES
Stuck On You, It's Now Or Never, A Mess Of Blues, Are You Lonesome Tonight?, I Gotta Know, Wooden Heart (Europe)
LPs
Elvis Is Back, G. I. Blues, His Hand In Mine

1961
SINGLES
Surrender, I Feel So Bad, Little Sister, (Marie's The Name) His Latest Flame, Can't Help Falling In Love, Rock-A-Hula Baby
EP
Elvis By Request
LPs
Something For Everybody, Blue Hawaii

1962
SINGLES
Good Luck Charm, Anything That's A Part Of You, She's Not You, Return To Sender, Where Do You Come From
EP
Follow That Dream
LPs
Pot Luck, Girls! Girls! Girls!

1963
SINGLES
One Broken Heart For Sale, (You're The) Devil In Disguise, Bossa Nova Baby
LPs
Elvis' Golden Records–Vol. 3, Fun In Acapulco, It Happened At The World's Fair

1964
SINGLES
Kissin' Cousins, Viva Las Vegas, Ain't That Loving You Baby, Blue Christmas
LP
Kissin' Cousins

1965
SINGLES
Crying In The Chapel, I'm Yours, Puppet On A String
LPs
Girl Happy, Elvis For Everyone, Harum Scarum

1966
SINGLES
Tell Me Why, Frankie And Johnny, Love Letters, Spinout, All That I Am, If Every Day Was Like Christmas
LP
Paradise, Hawaiian Style

1967
SINGLES
Indescribably Beautiful, Big Boss Man

LP
How Great Thou Art

1968
SINGLES
Guitar Man, Stay Away, We Call On Him, Let Yourself Go, Almost In Love, If I Can Dream
LP
Elvis–TV Special

1969
SINGLES
Charro, His Hand In Mine, In The Ghetto, Clean Up Your Own Back Yard, Suspicious Minds, Don't Cry, Daddy
LPs
Elvis Sings Flaming Star, From Elvis In Memphis, From Memphis To Vegas/From Vegas To Memphis

1970
SINGLES
Kentucky Rain, The Wonder Of You, Mama Liked The Roses, I've Lost You, You Don't Have To Say You Love Me, Patch It Up, I Really Don't Want To Know
LPs
On Stage–February 1970, Elvis: Worldwide 50 Golden Award Hits–Vol. I, That's The Way It Is

1971
SINGLES
Where Did They Go, Lord, Only Believe, I'm Leavin', It's Only Love
LPs
Elvis Country, Elvis Sings The Wonderful World Of Christmas

1972
SINGLES
An American Trilogy, Burning Love, Separate Ways
LPs
Elvis As Recorded At Madison Square Garden

1973
SINGLE
Raised On Rock
LPs
Aloha From Hawaii Via Satellite, Elvis

1974
SINGLES
Take Good Care Of Her, It's Midnight
LP
Elvis—A Legendary Performer–Vol. I

1975
SINGLES
My Boy, T-R-O-U-B-L-E
LPs
Promised Land, Pure Gold

1976
SINGLE
Hurt
LPs
Elvis—A Legendary Performer–Vol. 2, From Elvis Presley Boulevard, Memphis, Tennessee

1977
SINGLES
Way Down, My Way

LPs
Welcome To My World, Moody Blue, Elvis In Concert

1978
LP
Elvis—A Legendary Performer–Vol. 3

ELVIS AND THE GRAMMYS: 14 NOMINATIONS, 3 VICTORIES

1959
1. Nominated for Record of the Year:
A Fool Such As I, Lost to Mack The Knife (Bobby Darin)
2. Nominated for Best Performance by a "Top 40" Artist:
A Big Hunk o' Love, Lost to Nat King Cole (Midnight Flyer)
3. Nominated for Best Rhythm & Blues Performance:
A Big Hunk o' Love, Lost to Dinah Washington (What A Difference A Day Makes)

1960
4. Nominated for Record of the Year:
Are You Lonesome Tonight?, Lost to theme from 'A Summer Place' (Percy Faith)
5. Nominated for Best Vocal Performance, Male:
Are You Lonesome Tonight? Lost to Ray Charles (Georgia On My Mind)
6. Nominated for Best Performance by a Pop Singles Artist: **Are You Lonesome Tonight?,** Lost to Ray Charles (Georgia On My Mind)
7. Nominated for Best Vocal Performance, Male, Album:
G. I. Blues, Lost to Ray Charles (Genius of Ray Charles)
8. Nominated for Best Soundtrack Album or Recording of Original Cast from a Motion Picture or Television:
G .I. Blues, Lost to *Can-Can*

1961
9. Nominated for Best Soundtrack Album or Recording of Original Cast from a Motion Picture or Television:
Blue Hawaii, Lost to *West Side Story*

1967
10. Nominated for Best Sacred Performance:
How Great Thou Art (Album), WON

1968
11. Nominated for Best Sacred Performance:
You'll Never Walk Alone (Album), Lost to *Beautiful Isle of Somewhere* (Jake Hess)

1972
12. Nominated for Best Inspirational Performance:
He Touched Me (Album), WON

1974
13. Nominated for Best Inspirational Performance:
How Great Thou Art (from Elvis Recorded Live On Stage in Memphis), WON

1978
14. Best Country Vocal Performance, Male:
Softly As I Leave You, Lost to *Georgia On My Mind* (Willie Nelson)

THE COMPLETE LIST OF ELVIS' TOP 40 HITS

Title	Debut Date	Highest Rank	Weeks On Top Forty				
				Kentucky Rain	2/21/70	8	16
				King of the Whole Wide World	10/06/62	4	30
A Big Hunk O' Love	7/13/59	10	1	Kiss Me Quick	5/23/64	2	34
A Fool Such As I	3/30/59	11	2	Kissin' Cousins	3/07/64	7	121
A Mess of Blues	8/01/60	23	2	Little Sister	8/25/61	10	5
Ain't That Loving You Baby	10/24/64	8	16	Lonely Man	3/13/61	2	32
All Shook Up	4/06/57	22	1	Love Letters	7/09/66	5	19
Anything That's Part of You	4/07/62	5	31	Love Me	11/24/56	14	2
Anyway You Want Me	11/10/56	4	20	Love Me Tender	10/20/56	19	1
Are You Lonesome Tonight?	11/14/60	14	1	Loving You	7/08/57	13	20
Ask Me	10/24/64	8	12	Memories	4/12/69	2	38
Big Boss Man	11/04/67	2	38	Moody Blue	2/05/77	5	31
Blue Suede Shoes	4/28/56	5	20	My Baby Left Me	6/09/56	3	31
Bossa Nova Baby	11/02/63	7	8	My Boy	2/15/75	6	20
Burning Love	9/09/72	12	2	My Way	12/03/77	7	22
Can't Help Falling in Love	12/18/61	12	2	My Wish Came True	7/13/59	10	12
Clean Up Your Own Back Yard	8/02/69	4	35	One Broken Heart for Sale	2/23/63	7	11
Crying in the Chapel	5/08/65	11	3	One Night	11/10/58	14	4
Devil In Disguise	7/13/63	8	3	Peace in the Valley	4/29/57	1	29
Do the Clam	3/13/65	6	21	Playing For Keeps	2/09/57	4	21
Don't	1/27/58	16	1	Poor Boy	1/05/57	3	24
Don't Be Cruel	8/04/56	24	1	Promised Land	11/09/74	9	14
Don't Cry Daddy	12/13/69	11	6	Puppet On a String	12/04/65	6	14
Doncha' Think It's Time	5/05/58	2	15	Rags to Riches	3/27/71	4	33
Easy Question	7/03/65	6	11	Return to Sender	10/27/62	14	2
Fame and Fortune	4/25/60	7	17	Rock-A-Hula Baby	12/18/61	5	23
Flaming Star	4/26/61	3	14	Separate Ways	12/23/72	8	20
Follow That Dream	5/19/62	7	15	She's Not You	8/11/62	9	5
Frankie and Johnny	4/09/66	5	8	Spinout	11/05/66	2	40
Good Luck Charm	3/24/62	11	1	Steamroller Blues	5/05/73	7	17
Guitar Man	2/28/81	3	28	Stuck On You	4/11/60	13	1
Hard Headed Woman	6/30/58	14	1	Such A Night	8/08/64	6	16
Heartbreak Hotel	3/10/56	22	1	Surrender	2/20/61	11	1
His Latest Flame	9/04/61	7	4	Suspicious Minds	9/20/69	13	1
Hound Dog	8/04/56	23	1	T-R-O-U-B-L-E	6/02/75	3	35
Hurt	5/01/76	5	28	Teddy Bear	6/24/57	18	1
I Beg Of You	2/03/58	7	8	Tell Me Why	1/22/66	3	23
I Feel So Bad	5/22/61	7	5	The Next Step is Love	8/22/70	3	32
I Gotta Know	11/28/60	8	20	The Wonder of You	5/23/70	11	9
I Need Your Love Tonight	3/30/59	10	4	There Goes My Everything	1/20/72	8	21
I Really Don't Want to Know	1/20/72	8	23	Too Much	1/26/57	14	1
I Want You, I Need You,				Treat Me Nice	10/21/57	6	18
I Love You	6/02/56	10	1	U.S. Male	4/20/68	4	28
I Was the One	3/17/56	10	19	Until It's Time For You To Go	3/11/72	1	40
I'm Leavin'	8/14/71	2	36	Viva Las Vegas	5/30/64	4	29
I'm Yours	9/18/65	7	11	Way Down	7/16/77	12	18
I've Got A Thing About You,				Wear My Ring Around Your			
Baby	3/23/74	2	39	Neck	4/21/58	13	2
I've Lost You	8/22/70	3	32	What'd I Say	5/30/64	5	21
If I Can Dream	12/14/68	11	12	When My Blue Moon Turns			
If You Talk in Your Sleep	6/29/74	7	17	to Gold Again	12/29/56	4	19
In the Ghetto	5/17/69	11	3	Where Did They Go, Lord	3/27/71	4	33
Indescribably Blue	2/15/67	4	33	Wild in the Country	6/19/61	2	26
It Hurts Me	3/14/64	4	29	Witchcraft	11/09/63	3	32
It's Now Or Never	7/25/60	16	1	You Don't Have to Say You			
Jailhouse Rock	10/14/57	19	1	Love Me	11/07/70	8	11

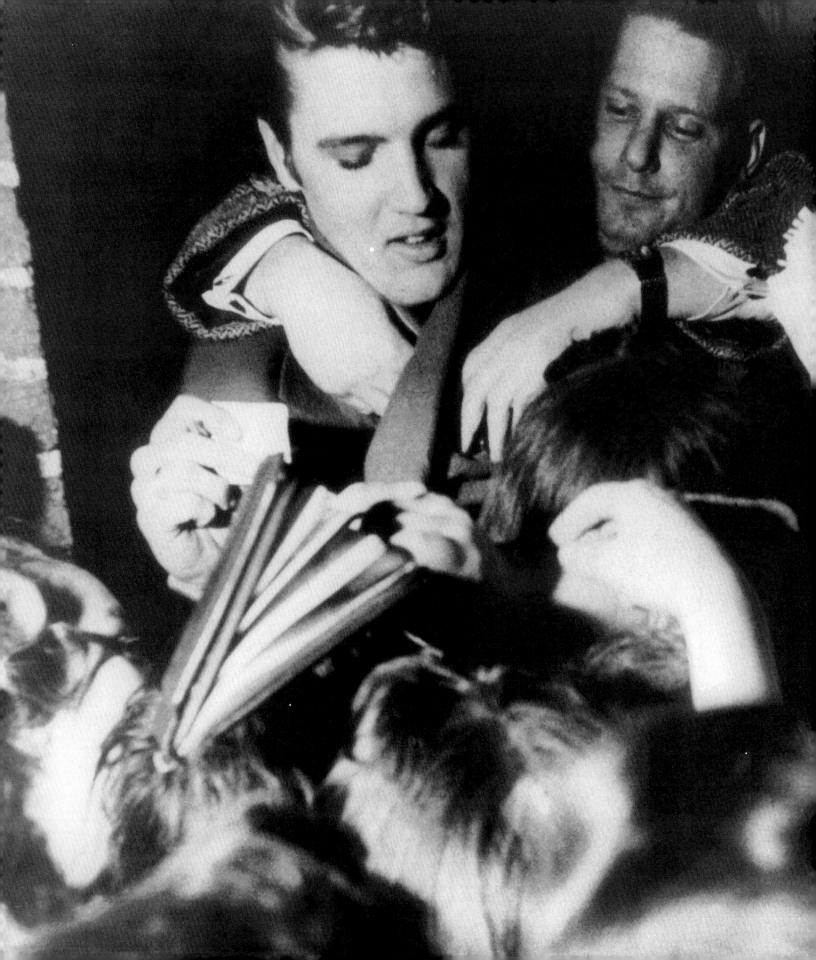

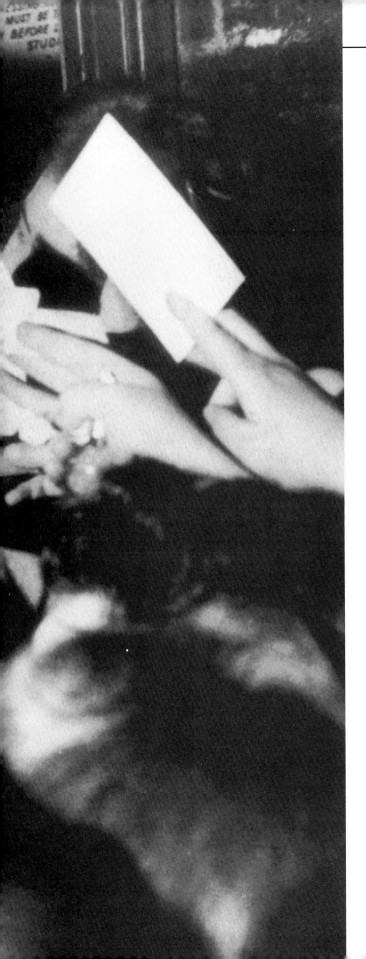

ELVIS TRIVIA

*"The only time I can be me is when
I walk through the door and lock it from the inside..."*

—ELVIS

THE KING'S VITAL STATISTICS
Born: January 8, 1935. Tupelo, Mississippi
Died: August 16, 1977. Memphis, Tennessee
Blood Type: O Positive
Height: 6'0"
Weight: 168 to 250 (his weight increased after 1975)
Neck: 15 1/2 - 16
Waist: 30 - 42
Chest: 39"
Eyes: Blue
Hair: Dishwater Blond (Dyed Black)
Shoe Size: 11D
Favorite Drink: Pepsi Cola
Favorite Cigar: Roi-Tan Blunts
Favorite Foods: Peanut Butter, Mashed Potatoes, Sauerkraut, Cheeseburgers,
       Porkchops, Burnt Bacon, Grape Jelly
Favorite Toothpaste: Colgate
Favorite Soap: Neutrogena
Favorite Aftershave: Brut

ELVIS' FAVORITE CO-STARS
1. Ann-Margret
2. Nancy Sinatra
3. Mary Ann Mobley
4. Juliet Prowse
5. Shelley Fabares

ELVIS' LEAST FAVORITE CO-STARS
1. Stella Stevens
2. Barbara McNair
3. Mary Tyler Moore
4. Carolyn Jones

ELVIS' 10 FAVORITE FILMS
1. Patton
2. Dr. Strangelove
3. Monty Python and the Holy Grail
4. The Party
5. The Pink Panther
6. The Dirty Harry films
7. The Wild Bunch
8. Across 110th Street
9. One Flew Over the Cuckoo's Nest
10. A Streetcar Named Desire

ELVIS' FAVORITE BOOKS
1. The Bible
2. The Face of Jesus
3. The Impersonal Life
4. The Prophet
5. The Shroud of Turin

Last Words: "OK, I won't." (To Ginger Alden)

Elvis' television network debut was on *The Milton Berle Show* on April 3, 1956. The first song he sang was *Heartbreak Hotel*.

By 1956, Elvis was a millionaire.

The first time Elvis wore his famous Gold Lamé suit was at a concert at the International Amphitheater in Chicago in 1957.

Elvis loved the movie *Patton* so much, he could quote much of the dialogue verbatim.

As a teenager, Elvis had a severe case of acne.

Elvis' favorite board game was Monopoly.

Elvis' private dream was to be an actor of the stature of James Dean.

The first house Elvis bought was for his parents. It was located at 1034 Audubon Drive in Memphis and cost $40,000.

Elvis collected badges from police departments the way other people collect stamps. Almost every city he played in made him an honorary officer of some kind. The biggest coup was getting a Federal Narcotics Badge from then President, Richard M. Nixon.

Elvis made one TV commercial in 1954. It was for Southern Made Doughnuts and his line of copy was, "You get 'em piping hot after 4 A.M."

Elvis never played football for the L. C. Humes High School Tigers. He became friends with local football star Red West when West defended his right to dress like he wanted.

The Eagle's Nest in Memphis was the first nightclub Elvis ever played. He was paid $25.

Elvis carried an array of weapons from a .45 caliber army-issue sidearm to a two-shot derringer almost everywhere he went. He was very safe and had a very thorough knowledge of firearms.

Elvis left an estate valued at more that $15 million dollars.

In a May 1994 auction, Elvis' American Express Card sold for $36,000 and a pair of designer sunglasses for $23,000.

Elvis and Priscilla divorced on August 18, 1972. Priscilla got custody of Lisa Marie and moved to Los Angeles with Mike Stone.

Lamar Fike noticed early that Elvis had his own style of dressing and he asked him where he got his clothes. Elvis told him it was Lansky's Clothing Emporium on Beale Street in Memphis. Lansky's was frequented by black musicians who liked to dress in style. Elvis shopped at Lansky's for years.

Elvis is from a Norse word meaning "all wise."

The first song Elvis recorded professionally was *Harbor Lights* at Sun Studios in Memphis on July 5, 1954.

Elvis believed that he could speak to his twin brother Jesse, who died at birth.

Gladys Love Presley was born on April 25, 1912 and died on August 14, 1958. She was 46 years old.

Lisa Marie Presley was born on February 1, 1968. She weighed 6 lbs. and 15 ounces.

Vernon Presley was born on April 19, 1916 and died of a heart attack in Memphis on June 26, 1979.

Elvis' 33 films grossed $150,000,000 dollars.

The name of Elvis' favorite horse was Rising Sun.

Elvis dyed his hair jet black after meeting Roy Orbison at Sun Studios in Memphis. He had to have it dyed two to three times each month to keep it black. His sideburns were starting to show gray towards the end of his life.

The Shroud of Turin was the book Elvis was reading when he died.

Elvis was named one of the Ten Most Outstanding Young Men of America by the Jaycees on June 16, 1971.

SOME NICKNAMES FOR ELVIS
Big E
E
El
E.P.
Elvis the Pelvis
The Boss
Bunting
Crazy (on his personal ID bracelet)
and The King

Elvis' favorite car for sentimental reasons was undoubtedly the 1957 Pink Cadillac he gave to Gladys that year. His favorite car to drive was his black 1971 Dino Ferrari.

Elvis liked and copied the way Tony Curtis combed his hair.

Elvis said he wore his sideburns "truckdriver style."

According to the IRS, at one time Elvis was the largest single taxpayer in the United States.

Elvis' second choice of a career would have been in law enforcement.

Elvis' favorite singer was Tom Jones. They hung out together in Vegas. Elvis always thought Tom was a better singer than he was.

Elvis' high school sweetheart was Dixie Locke. They dated from 1953 to 1955. He took her to her prom in 1954.

Elvis graduated from L.C. Humes High School in June of 1953.

NAMES OF SOME PRESLEY DOGS
Boy
Duke
Getlo
Foxhugh
Sweetpea

Elvis had a chimp named Scatter that lived at Graceland and traveled with him to Los Angeles. Scatter had a taste for Scotch and Bourbon whiskey.

Elvis' horse ranch in Mississippi was called the Circle G Ranch.

Colonel Parker and Elvis formed Boxcar Enterprises in 1974 to handle Elvis-related merchandise.

The call signs for Elvis' personal jets were the *Lisa Marie* and *Hound Dog One*.

For her high school graduation on June 14, 1963, Priscilla received a brand-new Corvair from Elvis.

The first job Elvis had after graduation from High School was as a shopman for Crown Electric Company in Memphis. He soon was promoted to delivery driver.

Elvis weighed 5 lbs. at birth. He was never circumcised.

Elvis said his favorite sport was football and favorite pro team was the Cleveland Browns.

TCB means "Taking Care Of Business" and was Elvis' motto. The lighting bolt meant do it in a flash. The symbol appeared on a special necklace that Elvis had designed and given to the Memphis Mafia as gifts. It also appeared on some of his personal items such as the side of his sunglasses, personal stationery and the tail of the *Lisa Marie*.

Elvis' favorite actors were James Dean, Marlon Brando and George C. Scott.

The motto of Elvis' division in the army was Spearhead, Third Armor Division.

ELVIS' DUETS WITH LEADING LADIES
1. "Crawfish"
   Kitty White, *King Creole*
2. "Datin'"
   Donna Butterworth, *Paradise, Hawaiian Style*
3. "Earth Boy"
   Ginny & Elizabeth Tiu, *Girls! Girls! Girls!*
4. "Happy Ending"
   Joan O'Brien, *It Happened At The World's Fair*
5. "How Would You Like To Be"
   Vicki Tiu, *It Happened At The World's Fair*
6. "Husky Dusky Day"
   Hope Lange, *Wild In The Country*
7. "Petunia, The Gardener's Daughter"
   Donna Douglas, *Frankie and Johnny*
8. "Queenie Wahine's Papaya"
   Donna Butterworth, *Paradise, Hawaiian Style*
9. "Scratch My Back (Then I'll Scratch Yours)"
   Marianna Hill, *Paradise, Hawaiian Style*
10. "Signs Of The Zodiac"
    Marilyn Mason, *The Trouble With Girls*
11. "The Lady Loves Me"
    Ann-Margret, *Viva Las Vegas*
12. "There Ain't Nothing Like A Song"
    Nancy Sinatra, *Speedway*
13. "Yoga Is As Yoga Does"
    Elsa Lanchester, *Easy Come, Easy Go*

ELVIS' DUETS WITH LEADING MEN
1. "Mexico"
   Larry Domasin, *Fun In Acapulco*
2. "Who Needs Money"
   Will Hutchins, *Clambake*

ELVIS' BACKUP GROUPS (1955-1977)
1. The Amigos
2. The Anita Kerr Singers
3. The Blossoms
4. The Carole Lombard Quartet
5. The Carole Lombard Trio
6. The Imperials
7. J.D. Sumner And The Stamps Quartet
8. The Jordanaires
9. The Jubilee Four
10. The Ken Darby Trio
11. Lea Jane Berineti Singers
12. The Mello Men
13. The Nashville Edition
14. The Surfers
15. The Sweet Inspirations
16. Voice

A GALLERY OF ELVIS' ADDRESSES
The Presley's lived in a lot of places over the years—sometimes on the wrong side of the tracks, finally on the right one. One thing's for sure, the Presleys kept moving. Following is a Presley Address Book listing some of the places the family hung their hats after Elvis was born:

Old Saltillo Road - Tupelo, Mississippi (Elvis' birthplace, 1935)
510 1/2 Maple Street - Tupelo, Mississippi
1010 North Green Street - Tupelo, Mississippi
572 Poplar Avenue - Memphis, Tennessee
185 Winchester Street - Memphis, Tennessee
698 Saffarans Street - Memphis, Tennessee
462 Alabama Street - Memphis, Tennessee
2414 Lamar Avenue - Memphis, Tennessee
1414 Getwell Street - Memphis, Tennessee
1034 Audubon Drive - Memphis, Tennessee (The first house Elvis bought and he bought it for Gladys.)
3764 Elvis Presley Boulevard - Memphis, Tennessee (Graceland - The King's Castle)
565 Perugia Way (Bel Air) - Los Angeles, California
1059 Bellagio Road (Bel Air) - Los Angeles, California
10550 Rocco Place (Bel Air) - Los Angeles, California
1174 Hillcrest - Los Angeles, California
144 Monovale (Holmby Hills) - Los Angeles, California
845 Chino Canyon Road - Los Angeles, California
1350 Leadera Circle - Los Angeles, California

Elvis' final resting place is alongside his mother, father, grandmother and brother, Jesse Garon, in the Meditation Gardens located on the grounds of Graceland.

TOURING GRACELAND

Address: 3764 Elvis Presley Boulevard, Memphis, Tennessee 38116
Open: 7 days a week, March – October
Closed Tuesdays, November – February
Closed Thanksgiving Day, Christmas, New Year's Day
Hours: 8 a.m. to 6 p.m. during the summer; 9 a.m. to 5 p.m. the rest of the year
Cost: 90-minute guided house tour is $7.95 for adults and $4.75 for children ages 4-11.
Guided house tour plus two Elvis airplanes, the "Sincerely Elvis" museum, and Elvis car collection is $15.95 for adults and $10.95 for children 4-11.
Parking: $5.00. Reservations suggested. Call: (800) 238-2000

HOW FAR IS IT TO GRACELAND FROM...?

Atlanta	371
Boston	1296
Chicago	530
Cleveland	712
Denver	1040
Detroit	713
Houston	516
Kansas City	451
Los Angeles	1817
Miami	1018
Minneapolis-St. Paul	826
Montreal	1332
New Orleans	390
New York	1100
Philadelphia	1000
St. Louis	285
San Francisco	2125
Seattle	2290
Washington, DC	975

THE ELVIS TRIVIA QUIZ

1. What were the three shortest Elvis songs to make *Billboard*'s Hot 100?

2. What was Elvis' shortest single to reach #1?

3. What was Elvis' longest single to reach #1?

4. What did Elvis sing for his screentest at Paramount in April of 1956?

5. What was Elvis' first #1 song after The Beatles' "British Invasion?"

6. What three Elvis singles reached #1 on the three major charts at the same time: Country Best Sellers, Country Juke Box and Rhythm & Blues?

7. What was Elvis' first stereo release?

8. Between 1961 and 1969, Elvis didn't have a #1 single. What 1961 million seller was his last to top the charts?

9. What was Elvis' first gold record?

10. What was the first Elvis record played in England on BBC Radio One?

11. What was the first black group to perform an Elvis song, and what was the song?

12. In what film did Elvis sing a duet with himself? And what was the song?

13. Where does the name Elvis come from, and what does it mean?

14. What is Elvis' middle name, and how is it spelled?

15. Who wrote the most songs for Elvis, and how many did they write?

16. When did Elvis get his first guitar, who bought it for him, and how much did it cost?

17. What kind of books did Elvis like to read?

18. What was Elvis' favorite movie?

19. What was the song that made Priscilla Beaulieu fall for Elvis?

20. What type of clothing did Elvis hate and never wear because they reminded him of the darkest days of his youth when his Daddy was in jail and his Momma toiled in the cotton fields?

21. Who was the man with whom Priscilla had the affair that precipitated her breakup with Elvis?

22. What was the name of Elvis' cattle ranch in Mississippi?

23. Who made Tom Parker a Colonel?

24. What movie did Colonel Parker make Elvis turn down, and why?

25. What was the name of Elvis' mother's poodle?

26. Elvis had the first single in recording history to achieve advance sales of over one million copies. What was it, when was it recorded, and what was on the flip side?

27. What was Elvis' favorite football team?

28. What was the name of Elvis' own touch football team in Memphis?

29. What was the only Elvis tune ever considered for an Oscar nomination?

30. What Elvis single sold the most copies?

31. What was Elvis' first LP, on what label, and when was it released?

32. What was the first song Elvis recorded when he returned from the army, and when did he record it?

33. Elvis blew his chance to record Roy Orbison's *Only The Lonely*. What happened?

34. What was the favorite song of Anita Wood and Elvis while they were dating?

35. What's the theme song of the International Elvis Presley Fan Club?

36. Elvis sold over 1,250,000 advance copies of what 1960 single that was also #1 before it was released?

37. What was the last Elvis single to reach #1 on *Billboard*'s Hot 100?

38. Elvis was one of 2500 artists to perform the most recorded tune in rock history. Which song?

39. What was the first Elvis tune that was released as sheet music?

40. Elvis made three movies in black and white. What were they?

41. How many films did Elvis make, and how much did they gross in all at the box office?

42. Colonel Tom Parker, as most Elvis fans know, was listed in the credits of all but nine of Elvis' films. In what capacity?

43. In two films, Elvis' female costar lost her bikini while swimming in the ocean. What were the films, and who were the actresses?

44. Hawaii was the setting for which three Elvis films?

45. Where did Elvis rank among the Top Ten "Stars of Tomorrow" in 1957, and with whom did he share the list?

46. What actor performed in more Elvis films than any other, and in how many films did he appear?

47. Elvis' papa, Vernon Presley, appeared in two of his son's films, and his mother, Gladys, appeared with Vernon in one of those two. Which ones?

48. Was Elvis a hit in his Las Vegas debut at the Frontier Hotel in 1956?

49. Elvis emerged from the movie lot and the recording studio after a ten-year absence from the stage for a triumphant return to live performance in a single show that launched him back onto the road and into Las Vegas superstardom. When and where was this historic public appearance?

50. How old was Elvis when he died, and when did it happen?

ANSWERS TO THE ELVIS TRIVIA QUIZ

1. *Long Legged Girl (With the Short Dress On)*–1:26
   One Broken Heart For Sale–1:34
   Follow That Dream–1:34

2. *Teddy Bear*–1:43

3. *Suspicious Minds*–4:22

4. *Blue Suede Shoes*

5. *Crying In The Chapel* (Recorded in 1960 – Released in 1965)

6. *Don't Be Cruel, Teddy Bear, Jailhouse Rock*

7. *Fame and Fortune* (1960)

8. *Good Luck Charm*

9. *Hard Headed Woman* (August 11, 1958)

10. *Hard Headed Woman* (1958)

11. The Cadets: *Heartbreak Hotel* in 1956

12. *Kissin' Cousins* (1964), the title song, sung by "twins" Josh Morgan and Jodie Tatum, both played by Elvis.

13. From the Norwegian name Alviss, which means "all wise"

14. Aron—misspelled Aaron by father Vernon on the birth certificate

15. The team of Sid Tepper and Roy C. Bennett: 43

16. For his twelfth birthday in 1946, instead of the .22 caliber rifle he asked for, from his mother Gladys, for $7.75.

17. Texts that leaned toward the spiritual and the occult, such as the *Bible* and *Autobiography of a Yogi*. He used to take more than 250 such books on tour with him in two trunks.

18. *Patton*

19. *Love Me Tender*

20. Blue jeans

21. Karate teacher Mike Stone

22. The Circle G Ranch

23. Parker gave himself that designation, but Governor Frank Clement of Tennessee made it official with an honorary title in 1953.

24. *The Defiant Ones* (1958) with Sidney Poitier, because there was no singing. The role went to Tony Curtis.

25. Duke, after John Wayne

26. *Love Me Tender* (1956) and on the flip side: *Any Way You Want Me*

27. The Cleveland Browns

28. E.P. Enterprises

29. *It's A Wonderful World* (by Tepper and Bennett) in the movie *Roustabout* (1964)

30. *It's Now or Never* (1960)—over 22 million worldwide

31. *Elvis Presley* – RCA, March 1956

32. *Make Me Know It* (March 20, 1960)

33. Orbison stopped by Graceland to offer him the song, but Elvis was taking a nap.

34. *Soldier Boy* (recorded by Elvis in 1960)

35. *Steadfast, Loyal and True* (1958)

36. *Stuck On You*

37. *Suspicious Minds* (1969)

38. *Yesterday* (by Paul McCartney)

39. *You're a Heartbreaker* (1954)

40. *Love Me Tender, Jailhouse Rock* and *King Creole*

41. 33, including two concert films, earning $150 million in all

42. Technical Advisor

43. *Blue Hawaii* (Joan Blackman) and *Clambake* (Shelley Fabares)

44. *Blue Hawaii, Girls! Girls! Girls!* and *Paradise, Hawaiian Style*

45.   1. Anthony Perkins
       2. Sophia Loren
       3. Jayne Mansfield
       4. Don Murray
       5. Carroll Baker
       6. Martha Hyer
       7. **Elvis Presley**
       8. Anita Ekberg
       9. Paul Newman
       10. John Kerr

46. Boyhood friend and Memphis Mafia bodyguard Red West, with bit parts in fourteen films.

47. Vernon did a walk-on in *Live a Little, Love a Little,* and with his wife in *Loving You.*

48. Far from it. His Vegas debut at the Frontier Hotel in 1956 was a disaster and closed before the end of its run, and he didn't return to Vegas until 1969 at the International Hotel, where he soon became the biggest nightclub draw in history.

49. Elvis returned to live performance on an hour-long NBC television special that was aired on December 3, 1968 to huge ratings and rave reviews.

50. He was 42 when he died on August 16, 1977.

INDEX

A

Adams, Frank, 149
Adams, Julie, 186
Adams, Nick, 35, 36, 45, 48, 85
Alden, Ginger, 142, 143, 145, 146, 149, 154
Alden, Terry, 145
American Bandstand, 51, 71
Andress, Ursula, 65, 181
Ann-Margret, 65, 66, 67, 71, 85, 103, 157, 183
Arnold, Eddy, 28
Arthur Godfrey's Talent Scouts, 27
Astrodome, Houston, 95
Atkins, Chet, 30

B

Balin, Ina, 197
Beale Street, 20
Beatles, 35, 68, 69, 71, 73, 74, 90
Beaulieu, Donald, 103
Beaulieu, Michele, 82
Berle, Milton, 32
Berlin, Irving, 104
Berner, Joseph, 132
Bible, 132, 146
Bing Crosby Award, 104
Birth Certificate, Elvis, 18
Black, Bill, 22, 23, 24, 26, 30, 32, 34, 38, 41, 42
Blackman, Joan, 176
Blondell, Joan, 83
Blue Hawaii, 60, 61, 176
Blue Moon Boys, 26, 27
Book Of Numbers, 132
Boyd, Pat, 61
Bradley, C.W., 151
Bullock, Bill, 29

C

Campbell, Glen, 108, 110
Carey, Michele, 85, 196
Cash, Johnny, 28, 37
Change Of Habit, 90, 92, 93, 100, 199
Charro, 87, 92, 197
Cheiro, 132
Circle G Ranch (aka Flying Circle G), 76, 78, 79, 82, 92, 111
Clambake, 78, 79, 82, 83, 193
Clark, Dick, 51
Coca, Imogene, 33
Cocke, Marion, 135
Cowboy Songs, 27
Cramer, Floyd, 30
Crosby, Bing, 104

Crown Electric, 21, 24
Crudup, Arthur, 23
Curry, Grant, 52
Curtiz, Michael, 45

D

Davis, Richard, 110, 154
Davis, Jr., Sammy, 103
Day, Annette, 192
Dean, James, 84
Dean, Jimmy, 27
Double Trouble, 76, 192
Douglas, Donna, 188

E

Eagle's Nest, 24
Easy Come, Easy Go, 76, 77, 79, 191
Ed Sullivan Show, 34, 35, 36, 38, 68
Eden, Barbara, 174
Egan, Richard, 169
Ellington, Buford, 60
Ellington, Duke, 104
Ellis Auditorium, 33
Elvis (Comeback TV Special 1968), 2-3, 86, 87, 89, 92, 93
Elvis: Aloha From Hawaii Via Satellite, 116, 117, 118
Elvis In Concert, 148
Elvis On Tour, 109, 110, 111, 114, 201
Elvis Presley Boulevard, 104, 151
Elvis Presley Center Courts, Inc., 138
Elvis Presley Enterprises (football team), 66, 67
Elvis Presley Fan Club of Great Britain, 70
Elvis Presley Jamboree Tour, 28, 29
Elvis Presley Museum, 22
Elvis Presley Music, Inc., 29
Elvis—That's The Way It Is, 96, 99, 200
Elvis Trivia, (Trivia Chapter), 270-282
Elvis: What Happened?, 141, 148
Esposito, Joan, 82
Esposito, Joe, 79, 82, 85, 97, 110, 129, 131, 135, 138, 149, 150, 151, 154
Evans, Marilyn, 37
Fabares, Shelley, 70, 75, 185, 190, 193
Face Of Jesus, 149
Fadal, Eddie, 46
Fike, Lamar, foreword 11-12, sidebar "On Meeting Elvis" 23, sidebar "Overnight Success" 26, sidebar "On Disc Jockeys" 29, sidebar "On The Screen Test" 32, sidebar "Hound Dog" 33, sidebar "On Gladys

Presley" 34, sidebar "On Elvis And Destiny" 34, sidebar "On Joining Elvis" 39, sidebar "On Elvis' Expectations For Himself" 41, sidebar "On Elvis And The Draft" 42, 45, sidebar on "On Elvis Going Into The Army" 45, 47, sidebar "On Gladys' Death" 47, sidebar "On Red West And Elvis" 47, 48, sidebar "On Elvis On Guard Duty" 48, sidebar "On The Apartment In Germany" 49, sidebar "On Elvis As A Gunner" 49, 51, 55, 56, sidebar "On PR Subterfuge" 58, sidebar "On His Friendship With Elvis" 58, 60, sidebar "On Elvis And Flying" 62, 67, sidebar "On Elvis Not Listening To Other Music" 79, sidebar "On Bobby Darin" 93, 97, 98, sidebar "On The Colonel" 109, 110, 120, sidebar "On Elvis And Drugs" 121, sidebar "On Elvis' Generosity" 123, sidebar "On Elvis' Iron Constitution" 125, 142, sidebar "On Elvis The Gunslinger" 144, 151, 154-155, 162

F

Finlater, John, 100
Fisher, Eddie, 29, 33
Fitzgerald, Ella, 104
Flaming Star, 58, 59, 174
Follow That Dream, 61, 62, 177
Fontana, D.J., 26, 30, 32, 34, 38, 41, 42
Forrest, Steve, 174
Fortas, Alan, 48, 155
Francisco, Dr. Jerry T., 150
Frank Sinatra Timex Show, 56
Frankie and Johnny, 72, 74, 75, 188
Fun In Acapulco, 64, 181

G

Gamble, Gee Gee, 93, 110
Gamble, Patsy, 93
Geller, Celeste, 155
Geller, Larry, 155
Gentry, Bobby, 103
Getlo, 130, 134
Ghanem, Dr. Elias, 135
G.I. Blues, 51, 56, 61, 173
Gibran, Kahlil, 132
Girl Happy, 70, 72, 185
Girls! Girls! Girls!, 62, 63, 179
Gleaves, Cliff, 41, 155
Gold Lamé Suit, 39
Graceland, 20, 23, 38, 39, 41, 43, 45, 47, 55, 62, 63, 67, 68, 74, 75, 77, 83, 88; Christmas

at, 89, 92, 93, 127; 107, 114, 120, 137, 138, 145, 148, 149, 151
Grammy, 130
Grand Old Opry, 24
Grant, Currie, 155
Greene, Shecky, 32
Grimes, J.C., 19
Grob, Dick, 110, 155

H

Haley, Bill, 49
Harmony, Dottie, 37
Hart, Dolores, 39, 170
Harum Scarum, 72, 74, 187
Hawaii, Satellite Concert 1973, 117
Hawkins, Hawkshaw, 43
Hearst, Patty, 124
Hebler, David, 140, 143, 148
Hepburn, Katharine, 32
Hill And Range Publishing Company, 29
His Inner Circle (Biographies Chapter), 152-165
His Life (Chronology Chapter), 16-151
His Movies (Filmography Chapter), 166-201
His Music (Discography Chapter), 202-269
Hodge, Charlie, 48, 51, 56, 85, 97, 110, 139, 146, 150, 155-156, 156
Hodge, Rex, 51
Holiday Hop, 37
Holly, Buddy, 29
Hookstratten, Ed, 138
Hoover, J. Edgar, 100
Humbard, Rex, 151
Husky, Ferlin, 43

I

Impersonal Life, 132
It Happened At The World's Fair, 63, 65, 180

J

J.D. Sumner And The Stamps Quartet, 105, 109, 132, 151
Jackie Gleason's Stage Show, 29, 30, 31
Jagger, Mick, 141
Jailhouse Rock, 38, 39, 41, 42, 43, 55, 171
Jarvis, Felton, 75, 90, 120, 145, 156
Jaycees, 102
Jenkins, Mary, 156, 157
John, Elton, 139
Jones, Carolyn, 172
Jones, Tom, 85, 87, 92, 96, 103, 126
Jordanaires, 35, 38, 156
Jumpsuits, 136

K

Kahane, Jackie, 109, 151

Keisker, Marion, 21, 22, 24, 156
Kid Galahad, 61, 178
King, B.B., 20
King Creole, 39, 43, 45, 47, 172
Kissin' Cousins, 67, 69, 77, 182
Klein, George, 77, 97, 112, 157

L

L.C. Humes High School, 20; Elvis' Diploma 20, 21; Band Annual Minstrel Show 21; 24
Lacker, Marty, 21, 61, 79, 97, 157
Lancaster, Burt, 32
Lange, Hope, 175
Lansbury, Angela, 176
Las Vegas, 1956, 32; comeback in 1969, 91, 90-93; 94—95, 96
Lawhon School, 19
Led Zeppelin, 123
Leech, David, 137
Leigh, Suzanna, 189
Lennon, John, 98, 100, 111, 141
Lewis, Jerry Lee, 37, 142
Liberace, 36, 37
Life, 32
Lime, Yvonne, 38
Lisa Marie (Elvis' jet), 128-129, 131, 132, 135, 145
Live A Little, Love A Little, 85, 87, 89, 196
Locke, Dixie, 22, 157
Loew's State Theater, 20, 76
Louisiana Hayride, 24, 26, 27, 28, 29, 31, 32, 37
Love Me Tender, 33, 34, 35, 36, 39, 51, 168, 169
Loving You, 39, 41, 170

M

Madison Square Garden, 111
Marl Metal, 21
Marshall, Dodie, 191
Martin, Tony, 29
Martindale, Wink, 37
Mason, Marilyn, 198
Matthau, Walter, 172
McCann, Betty, 19
McCartney, Paul, 111
McCalla, Irish, 33
Memphis Auditorium, 20
Memphis Recording Service, 21, 22
Meredith, Burgess, 194
Milam Junior High School, 19
Million Dollar Quartet, 37
Milton Berle Show, 32, 33
Mississippi-Alabama Fair And Dairy Show, 19, 35
Mobley, Mary Ann, 187

Moore, Mary Tyler, 199
Moore, Scotty, 22, 23, 24, 26, 30, 34, 37, 35, 38, 41, 42, 158
Morgan, Judy, 100
Morris, Bill, 71, 97, 100
Murphy, George, 100

N

Neal, Bob, 26, 27, 28, 29, 158
Newman, Dr. Thomas, 135
Nichopoulos, Dr. Constantine "Dr. Nick," 97, 128, 132, 135, 138, 145, 146, 150, 158
Nichopoulos, Dean, 131
Nixon, Richard, 98, 100, 101, 159
Nixon, Roy, 97
Nudie, 39

O

O'Brien, Joan, 180
O'Connell, Arthur, 177, 181
O'Grady, John, 98, 133, 138, 141, 149
Old Barn Dance, 24

P

Paget, Debra, 169
Paradise, Hawaiian Style, 73, 74, 76, 189
Paramount, 31, Signing With, 32
Parker, Ed, 125, 132, 159
Parker, Thomas "The Colonel," 27, 28, 29, 31, 32, 33, 34, 37, 39, 41, 45, 46, 49, 51, 52, 53, 54, 55, 56, 62, 67, 69, 74, 75, 77, 78, 79, 83, 84, 90, 93, 95, 96, 106, 109, 111, 113, 114, 118, 120, 123, 130, 132, 145, 147, 159, 159-160, 168
Parker Machinists Shop, 21
Parker, Patricia, Paternity Suit, 96, 99, 102, 107
Payne, Angela, 107
Pepper, Gary, 75, 77
Perkins, Carl, 37, 160
Perry, Patti, 160
Person, Minnie, 134
Peters, Gerald, 143
Phillips, Dewey, 23, 29, 89, 160
Phillips, Sam, 21, 22, 23, 24, 29, 37, 89, 90, 160
Pink Cadillac, 24, 34
Plant, Robert, 123
Precision Tool Company, 19, 20, 21, 89
Presley, Dee Stanley, 53, sidebar "On Meeting Vernon" 53, 63, 76, 77, 79, 82, 90, 93, 95, 121, 147, 163
Presley, Gladys, 18, 20, 21, 24, 27, 32, 34, 35, 39, 41, 45, 46, 47, 106, 121, 160
Presley, Jesse Garon, 18, 161
Presley, Jesse "Grandpa," 37

Presley, Johnny, 21
Presley, Lisa Marie, 85, 88, 89, 90, 92, 97, 102,
   106, 109, 111, 112, 114, 117, 118, 120, 124,
   125, 127, 139, 141, 143, 146, 148, 149, 161
Presley, Minnie "Grandma," 20, 47, 48, 76, 82
Presley, Priscilla Ann Beaulieu, 52, 53, 59, 63,
   64, 65, 67, 74, 77, 78, 79; wedding with
   Elvis, 79-82, 80-81; 82, 83, 85, 87, 89, 90,
   92, 93, 95, 96, 97, 99, 102, 103, 106, 107,
   109, 111, 112, 114, 118, 120, 121, 125, 127,
   141, 143, 146, 161
Presley, Travis, 21, 76
Presley, Vernon, 18, 19, 20, 24, 27, 32, 35, 39,
   41, 42, 45, 46, 47, 48, 53, 63, 76, 77, 79, 82,
   89, 90, 93, 95, 97, 103, 106, 107, 110, 111,
   121, 126, 127, 128, 139, 140, 143, 146, 147,
   148, 149, 162
Presley, Vester, 19, 45, 128
Prophet, 132
Prowse, Juliet, 56, 173

R
RCA, Signing With, 29
Rebel Without A Cause, 75
Rivera, Geraldo, 149
ROTC, Humes High, 20
Rainbow Rollerdome, 22
Rainmaker, 31, 33
Robbins, Marty, 24
Roustabout, 68, 71, 184
Ryan, Sheila, 126

S
Schilling, Jerry, 79, 97, 100, 110, 132, 151, 163
Scott, Lizabeth, 170
Scrivener, Mildred, 163
Shapiro, Dr. Max, 135, 145
Shepherd, Cybill, 112
Sholes, Steve, 29, 30
Shotgun House, 19
Sinatra, Frank, 32, 56, 104, 122
Sinatra, Nancy, 55, 82, 93, 113, 195
Slim Whitman Show, 23
Smith, Billy, 97, 149, 150, 163
Smith, Gene, 20, 21, 48, 163
Smith, Johnny, 89
Smith, Roger, 103
Smith, Steve, 131
Snow, Hank, 24, 26, 27, 28, 68
Speedway, 82, 87, 195
Spinout, 75, 76, 77, 190
Spreckles, Judy, 45, 163
Stanley, David, introduction 9-10, 57, 58, side-
   bar "On Priscilla As Big Sister" 63, 76, side-
   bar "On Elvis The Rancher" 79, 81, sidebar
   "On Elvis' Entourage" 85, sidebar "On Elvis'

Show Business Friends" 85, sidebar "On
Christmas At Graceland" 89, sidebar "On
Elvis Getting Ready For His Vegas
Comeback" 90, sidebar "On Elvis And
Barbra Streisand" 90, sidebar "On Elvis
Singing 'Hey Jude'" 90, sidebar "On
Watching Elvis' Opening Show" 92, sidebar
"On Elvis As Number One" 92, sidebar "On
The Manson Scare" 92, 95, sidebar "On
Elvis As A Narc" 98, sidebar "On Elvis'
Politics" 100, sidebar "On Elvis On Stage"
99, sidebar "On Elvis' Bodyguards" 104,
sidebar "On Elvis' Stamina" 106, sidebar
"On Elvis And Fireworks" 107, 111, sidebar
"On Elvis And George Harrison" 111, side-
bar "On Elvis' Relationship With Priscilla"
113, sidebar "On Seeing Priscilla" 113, side-
bar "On Elvis' Biggest Concert Ever" 117,
sidebar "On Elvis' Rage Over Mike Stone"
118, 119, sidebar "On Elvis' Drug Abuse"
119, sidebar "On Elvis' Choice Of Music"
120, sidebar "On Elvis Locking Himself Up"
121, 122, sidebar "On Elvis Meeting Led
Zeppelin" 123, sidebar "On The Tahoe
Fight" 124, sidebar "On Elvis' Iron
Constitution" 125, sidebar "On Elvis'
Restlessness" 125, sidebar "On A Surprise
Present For Elvis" 128, 128, sidebar "On
Elvis In The Hospital" 130, sidebar "On Elvis
And Eric Clapton" 130, 131, 132, sidebar
"On Two Death Threats" 133, sidebar "On
An Aborted 'Intervention'" 138, sidebar
"On The Firing Of Red And Sonny" 140,
140, sidebar "On Red And Sonny's Book"
141, sidebar "On Linda's Leaving" 142, side-
bar "On Elvis The Seeker" 142, sidebar "On
Graceland's Drugstore" 145, sidebar "On
Ginger Alden" 145, sidebar "On Cancelling
The Last Show Of The Tour" 146, sidebar
"On Elvis And Drugs" 146, 148, 149, side-
bar "On Finding Elvis' Body" 149, sidebar
"On The Vigil At Baptist Hospital" 150,
sidebar "On A Strange Accusation" 151,
sidebar "On Seeing Elvis For The Last Time"
151, sidebar "On The Day The Music Died"
151, 156, 162, 163
Stanley, Richard "Ricky," 57, 58, 81, 95, 98,
   110, 111, 131, 132, 134, 156, 163-164
Stanley, William "Bill," 53, 57
Stanley, William "Billy," 57, 58, 76, 81, 95, 98,
   107, 162, 164
Stanwyck, Barbara, 184
Star, Ben, 51
Star Is Born, 130
Stay Away, Joe, 83, 85, 184
Stefaniak, Elizabeth, 51

Steve Allen Show, 33
Stevens, Stella, 179
Stoller, Mike, 41
Stone, Mike, 87, 113, 114, 118, 141
Strada, Al, 131, 132, 149, 150
Streisand, Barbra, 90, 92, 130
Sullivan, Ed, 33, 34, 36, 46
Sumner, J.D., 20, 105, 133, 142
Sun Records, 22, 23, 24, 26, 27, 29, 37
Sweet Inspirations, 133
Symbionese Liberation Army, 124

T
Taking Care Of Business, 103
Taurog, Norman, 164
Thomas, Danny, 68
Thompson, Linda, 112, 114, 117, 121, 124,
   127, 128, 129, 134, 135, 137, 138, 139, 140,
   142, 164
Thompson, Sam, 164
Tickle Me, 71, 73, 74, 186
Trouble With Girls, 89, 93, 198
Tschechowa, Vera, 51
Tyler, Judy, 171
Typical Tour Day For Elvis, 132

V
Vanderhoot, Bruce, 35
Velvet, Jimmy, 22
Vesco, Robert, 128, 129
Viva Las Vegas, 65, 66-67, 70, 85, 183

W
Wallis, Hal B., 31, 32, 39, 45, 60, 74
Weld, Tuesday, 175
West, Pat, 137
West, Red, 20, 21, 23, 26, 37, 47, 48, 49, 51,
   60, 61, 66, 67, 76, 81, 82, 97, 110, 118, 124,
   125, 129, 132, 139, 140, 141, 143, 145, 148,
   165
West, Sonny, 97, 100, 102, 110, 118, 124,
   129, 132, 139, 140, 141, 143, 145, 148, 164
Wild In The Country, 59, 61, 175
Wood, Anita, 41, 45, 46, 47, 48, 52, 55, 56,
   61, 63, 64, 165
Wood, Natalie, 36, 165

Y
Yarbrough, Aurelia, 132
Young, Faron, 43
Young, Gig, 178

Z
Zancan, Sandra, 112

PHOTO CREDITS